Book Wars

Book Wars

The Digital Revolution in Publishing

John B. Thompson

polity

First published in 2021 by Polity Press

Polity Press
65 Bridge Street
Cambridge CB2 1UR, UK

Polity Press
101 Station Landing
Suite 300
Medford, MA 02155, USA

ISBN-13: 978-1-5095-4678-7

A catalogue record for this book is available from the British Library.

Typeset in 10.5 on 12 pt Sabon
by Fakenham Prepress Solutions, Fakenham, Norfolk NR21 8NL
Printed and bound in Great Britain by TJ Books Limited

The publisher has used its best endeavours to ensure that the URLs for external websites referred to in this book are correct and active at the time of going to press. However, the publisher has no responsibility for the websites and can make no guarantee that a site will remain live or that the content is or will remain appropriate.

Every effort has been made to trace all copyright holders, but if any have been overlooked the publisher will be pleased to include any necessary credits in any subsequent reprint or edition.

For further information on Polity, visit our website:
politybooks.com

CONTENTS

Preface   vi

Introduction   1

1   The Faltering Rise of the Ebook   20

2   Re-inventing the Book   68

3   The Backlist Wars   103

4   Google Trouble   122

5   Amazon's Ascent   141

6   Struggles for Visibility   172

7   The Self-publishing Explosion   216

8   Crowdfunding Books   283

9   Bookflix   319

10 The New Orality   349

11 Storytelling in Social Media   393

12 Old Media, New Media   414

Conclusion: Worlds in Flux   474

Appendix 1: Sales Data from a Large US Trade Publisher   485

Appendix 2: Note on Research Methods   488

Index   498

PREFACE

During the last few decades, we have been living through a technological revolution that is as radical and far-reaching as any that
came before in the long history of the human species. Among other
things, this new revolution is transforming our information and
communication environment and disrupting many of the industries
that played a central role in shaping this environment for most of
the twentieth century and before. The traditional media industries –
newspapers, radio, television, music, cinema – have all been hurled
into a whirlpool of change as old analogue technologies were pushed
aside by new technologies based on the digital codification and
transmission of symbolic content. Many of the media institutions
that were key players in the analogue age have found themselves
threatened by the digital transition, their revenues collapsing and
their once-dominant positions undermined, while powerful new
players have emerged and begun to reshape the contours of our information space. Today we live in a world which, in terms of the forms
and channels of information and communication, is fundamentally
different from the world that existed just half a century ago.

The book publishing industry is no exception – it too has been
caught up in the turmoil brought about by the digital revolution.
And, in some ways, there is more at stake here than with other media
industries: not only is the book publishing industry the oldest of the
media industries, it is also an industry that has played a pivotal role
in the shaping of modern culture, from the scientific revolution in
early modern Europe to the profusion of literatures and forms of
knowledge that have become such an important part of our lives and
societies today. So what happens when the oldest of our media industries collides with the great technological revolution of our time?

What happens when a media industry that has been with us for more than 500 years and is deeply embedded in our history and culture finds itself confronted by, and threatened by, a new set of technologies that are radically different from those that have underpinned its practices and business models for centuries? If you were working in the book publishing industry during the first decade of the twenty-first century, you wouldn't have had to look far to find reasons to feel anxious about your future: the music industry was in freefall, the newspaper industry was experiencing a sharp decline in revenue and some of the big tech companies were becoming seriously interested in the digitization of books. Why wouldn't the book industry be swept up in the maelstrom unleashed by the digital revolution? No hard-headed manager or disinterested analyst would have been sanguine about the chances of the book publishing industry surviving its encounter with the digital revolution unscathed.

But what form would the digital disruption of the book publishing industry assume, exactly? Would the industry undergo a root-and-branch transformation like the music industry, where physical formats morphed into digital downloads and the major record labels that had controlled the production and distribution of music experienced a dramatic collapse in revenues? Would ebooks take off and become the new medium of choice for readers, consigning the print-on-paper book to the dustbin of history? Would bookshops disappear and publishers be disintermediated by a technological revolution that would enable readers and writers to communicate directly via the internet, unhindered by the traditional gatekeepers of the book publishing industry? In the early 2000s, all of these possibilities – and more – were being seriously contemplated, both by senior managers within the industry and by the many commentators and consultants who were happy to offer their views on the future of an industry that seemed to be on the cusp of disruption.

As the years went by, this remarkable encounter between the oldest of our media industries and the great technological revolution of our time gradually took shape, producing outcomes that very few commentators had anticipated. It is not simply that the commentators were wrong – though, in many cases, they were, and wildly so. It is that their ways of thinking about what happens when technologies disrupt established industries were based far too much on the analysis of the technologies themselves and on a belief – usually implicit, rarely examined – that new technologies, by virtue of their intrinsic and advantageous features, would prevail eventually. What seldom featured in these accounts was any real awareness of how the development of new technologies, and their adoption or non-adoption as the case may be, are always embedded in an array of pre-existing social institutions, practices and preferences, and are always part of a dynamic social process in which individuals and organizations are pursuing their own interests and aims, seeking to improve their own positions and out-manoeuvre others in a competitive, and at times ruthless, struggle. In short, what most commentators lacked was any real understanding of the forces that were shaping the particular social space or 'field' within which these technologies were being developed and deployed. They focused on the technologies themselves, as if technologies were a *deus ex machina* that would sweep all before it, without taking account of the complex social processes in which these technologies were embedded and of which they were part. Of course, this abstraction from social processes made the commentators' task a whole lot easier: the social world is a messy place and it's much easier to predict the future if you ignore the messiness of the present. But it doesn't make your predictions more accurate, and you don't improve our understanding of technological change by discounting the social, economic and political factors that shape the contexts within which technologies exist.

This book is based on the assumption that we can understand the impact of the digital revolution on an industry like book publishing – and indeed any industry, media or otherwise – only by immersing ourselves in the messiness of the social world and understanding how technologies are developed and deployed, how they are taken up or passed over, by individuals and organizations who are situated in certain contexts, guided by certain preferences and pursuing certain ends. Technologies never produce effects *ex nihilo*, but always in relation to the individuals and organizations who decide to invest time and energy and resources in them as a way of pursuing their interests and aims (whatever they might be). The messiness of the social world is not a distraction from technology's path but is the path itself, for it is the interaction between the affordances of new technologies – that is, what these technologies enable or make possible – and the messiness of the social world that determines what impact new technologies will have and the extent to which, if at all, they will disrupt existing institutions and practices.

My immersion in the messy world of the publishing industry began two decades ago, when I set out to study the structure and transformation of the modern book publishing industry. I spent five years studying the world of academic publishing in the US and the UK, followed by another five years of deep immersion in the world of Anglo-American trade publishing, and I wrote two books about these worlds, *Books in the Digital Age* (about academic publishing) and *Merchants of Culture* (about trade publishing). In both of these books, I devoted a lot of attention to the impact of the digital revolution on these two very different sectors of the book publishing industry – this was a key issue in both sectors of this industry from the mid-1990s on, so no serious study of the publishing industry at this time could ignore it. But understanding the impact of the digital revolution was not my sole or even my primary concern in these earlier studies: my primary concern was to understand the key structural characteristics of these sectors – or 'fields' as I called them – and to analyse the dynamics that shaped the evolution of these fields over time. When the digital revolution began to make its presence felt in the world of book publishing, it did so by building upon, and in some cases disrupting, a set of institutions, practices and social relations that already existed and were structured in certain ways. Digital technologies and innovations enabled established organizations to do old things in new ways and to do some new things – to improve the efficiency of their organizations; offer better services to authors, readers and clients; repackage their content; develop new products; and, in a myriad of different ways, develop and strengthen their position in the field. But they also enabled new players to enter the field and challenge incumbent stakeholders by offering new products and services. The proliferation of new players and possibilities created a mixture of excitement, alarm and trepidation in the field and generated a profusion of new initiatives, developments and conflicts, as new entrants sought to gain a foothold in a field that had been dominated hitherto by the established players of the publishing industry. Of course, there was nothing new about conflict and change in the publishing industry – the industry had experienced many periods of turbulence and upheaval in the past. But the turbulence generated by the unfolding of the digital revolution in publishing was unprecedented, both in terms of its specific characteristics and in terms of the scale of the challenges it posed. Suddenly, the very foundations of an industry that had existed for more than 500 years were being called into question as never before. The old industry of book publishing was thrust into the limelight as bitter conflicts erupted between publishers and new entrants, including powerful new tech companies who saw the world in very different ways. Skirmishes turned into battles that were fought out in full public view, in some cases ending up in the courts. The book wars had begun.

Books are part of culture and book wars could be seen as culture wars, but they are not the kind of culture war that is normally referred to by this term. The term 'culture war' is commonly used to refer to social and political conflicts based on diverging and deeply held values and beliefs, such as those concerning abortion, affirmative action, sexual orientation, religion, morality and family life. These are conflicts rooted in values and value systems to which many people are deeply attached. They tap into identities as well as interests, into different senses of who we are as individuals and collectivities and of what does and should matter to us – hence the passion with which these culture wars have so often been fought in the public domain. The book wars are a very different kind of conflict. They don't arouse the passions as the culture wars do, no one has marched in the streets or burned books in protest. By the standards of the culture wars, the book wars are distinctly low-key. Indeed, 'book wars' might seem like a rather dramatic term for a state of affairs that involves no overt displays of violence, no demonstrations and no shouting in the streets. But the absence of overt displays of violence should not mislead us into thinking that the conflicts are not real or that they don't really matter. On the contrary, the struggles that have broken out over the last couple of decades in the normally placid world of publishing are very real; they have been fought with a determination and conviction that attests to the fact that, for those involved, these are hugely important struggles that touch on vital interests and in which matters of principle are at stake. At the same time, they are symptoms of the fact that the book industry is undergoing a profound transformation which is disrupting the field, calling into question accepted ways of doing things and thrusting established players into conflict both with new entrants and with old hands who have spotted new opportunities opened up by technological change and seized them, sometimes at the expense of others.

My aim in this book is to examine what actually happened, and what continues to happen, when the digital revolution takes hold in the world of book publishing. Not surprisingly, this is a complicated story with many different players and developments, as established organizations sought to defend and advance their positions while many new players sought to enter the field, or to experiment with new ways of creating and disseminating what we have come to think of as 'the book'. Given that the world of book publishing is itself immensely complex, consisting of many different worlds with their own players and practices, I have not tried to be comprehensive: I have reduced the complexity and narrowed the scope by focusing on the world of Anglo-American trade publishing – the same world that was the focus of *Merchants of Culture*. By 'trade publishing', I mean that sector of the industry that publishes books, both fiction and nonfiction, that are aimed at general readers and sold through bookstores like Barnes & Noble, Waterstones and other retail outlets, including online booksellers like Amazon. By 'Anglo-American' trade publishing, I mean English-language trade publishing that is based in the US and the UK, and for various historical reasons the publishing industries based in the US and the UK have long had a dominant role in the international field of English-language trade publishing. To understand the impact of the digital revolution on other sectors of publishing, such as academic publishing or reference publishing, or on publishing industries operating in other languages and other countries, would require different studies, as the processes and players would not be the same. While my focus here is on the world of Anglo-American trade publishing, I have not restricted myself to the traditional players in this field. The traditional players are important – no question about it. But a key part of the disruption caused by the digital revolution is that it is a shake-up that opens the door for other players to enter the field. These include some of the large tech companies with their own agendas and their own battles to fight, equipped with resources on a scale that dwarfs even the largest of the traditional publishers. But they also include a myriad of small players and enterprising individuals who are located on the margins of the field or in separate spaces altogether, in some cases impinging directly on the publishing field and in other cases subsisting in a parallel universe that connects only indirectly, if at all, with what we might think of as the world of the book.

While some of these new players and their initiatives gain real traction and develop into substantial undertakings, others fizzle out and die – the history of technology is littered with inventions that fail. But when historians come to write the history of technologies and of the companies that develop them, they tend to focus on the successful ones, on the technologies and organizations that, in some sense or some respect, change the world. We read history backwards through the lens of the inventions and companies that succeed. We are fascinated by the Googles and Apples and Facebooks and Amazons of this world – those exceptional 'unicorns' that have become so large so quickly that they have assumed an almost mythical status. What gets filtered out of this process are all of those inventions, initiatives and new ideas that seemed like good ideas at the time, maybe even great ideas in which some people passionately believed, but that, for one reason or another, didn't make it – all those small histories of the great ideas that failed. Maybe the time wasn't right, maybe the money ran out, maybe it wasn't such a good idea after all – whatever the reason, the vast majority of new ventures fail. But the history of the new ventures that failed is often just as revealing as the history of those that succeeded. The failures and false starts tell us a lot about the conditions of success precisely because they underscore what happens when those conditions, or some of those conditions, are absent. And if the vast majority of new ventures end in failure, then an account that focused only on the successes would be very partial at best. Writing the history of technologies by focusing only on the successes would be as one-sided and misleading as writing the history of wars from the perspective of the victors.

Of course, it would be much easier to write the history of the digital revolution in publishing if we had all the advantages of hindsight, if we could transport ourselves forward to the year 2030 or 2040 or 2050, look back at the publishing industry and ask ourselves how it had been changed by the digital revolution. We would have lots of historical data to scrutinize and some of the people who had lived through the transformation would still be around to talk about it. It is much more difficult to write this history when you're in the middle of it. What can you say about a technological revolution that is still so young, still just beginning to disrupt the traditional practices of an old and well-established industry when, undoubtedly, there is still so much more to come? How can you speak and write with any confidence about a world that is still in the throes of change, where so much is still unsettled and where everyone in the industry is still struggling to make sense of what is happening around them? How, in other words, do you recount a revolution *in medias res*?

To this question, there is no easy answer, and any account we give will have to be hedged with conditions and qualifications. But at least it is easier to try to give an account of this kind from the vantage point of 2020 than it would have been in 2010 or 2012 or 2015. By 2020, we have had more than a decade of serious ebook sales, so the patterns have had longer to establish themselves and will have achieved a degree of clarity they didn't have when ebooks were just beginning to take off. Some of the early experiments and more radical projects in digital publishing will have been tried and tested, some will have succeeded and many will have failed, and both the successes and the failures will tell us something about what is viable in this domain and what is not. Moreover, after ten years, the novelty factor will have worn off to some extent and early developments that may have been affected by the attractions of the new may have given way to patterns that reflect more enduring preferences and tastes. All of these are reasons (albeit small) to think that, while a time machine would have made our task much easier, it may not be impossible to say something worthwhile about a transformation that is still under way.

Not only is it difficult to discern what is most important when writing about a process that is still under way, it is also impossible to provide an account that is fully up to date. What I have tried to provide here is not so much a snapshot in time but rather a dynamic portrait of a field in motion, as individuals and organizations within the field struggle to make sense of, adapt to and take advantage of the changes that are taking place around them. To do this properly, you have to home in on some of these individuals and organizations and follow them as they seek to forge a path in the midst of uncertainty, reconstruct the options they faced, the choices they made and the developments that affected them at different points in time. But you can only follow them so far: at some point the story must be cut off and drawn to a close. History is frozen in the act of writing it, and the account you offer will always necessarily refer to a time that precedes the moment when your account is read. As soon as you finish a text, the world moves on and the portrait you have painted is outdated: instant obsolescence is the fate that awaits every chronicler of the present. There is no alternative but to embrace this fate and hope that readers will have a capacious understanding of timeliness.

Most of the research on which this book is based took place between 2013 and 2019, during which time I did more than 180 interviews with senior executives and other staff in a variety of organizations in the US and the UK, mainly in New York, London and Silicon Valley – organizations ranging from the large trade publishers to numerous start-ups, self-publishing organizations and innovative publishing ventures. (A detailed account of my research methods and sources can be found in appendix 2.) When it was helpful and relevant to do so, I also drew on some of the 280 interviews that I had conducted previously for *Merchants of Culture*. I am very grateful to the Andrew W. Mellon Foundation in New York, which funded the research from 2013 to 2019 (Grant 11300709) and enabled me to spend extended periods of time in the field, and grateful to the Economic and Social Research Council in the UK, which funded the earlier research (RES-000-22-1292). I am also very grateful to the many organizations which opened their doors to me, gave me access to their staff and, in some cases, their data;

most sources of data are acknowledged in the text, although there are instances where data were provided on condition that the source remains anonymous and, where this is the case, I have scrupulously honoured this commitment. Above all, I am deeply grateful to the many individuals who gave very generously of their time, allowing me to interview them, sometimes repeatedly over several years: I simply could not have written this book without their help. I have quoted directly from only a small proportion of these interviews, and only a fraction of the organizations I studied are used as case studies in the book, but every interview was invaluable in terms of deepening my understanding of a world in flux and the many players who are active, or were active, in it. Most of the individuals I interviewed remain anonymous and I often use pseudonyms when referring both to individuals and to companies. But there are occasions when the real names of interviewees and their companies are used, always with their consent, simply because their stories are so unique that it would be impossible to write about them with any degree of rigour and preserve anonymity. When the real name of an individual is used, the full name is given – first name plus surname – on the first occasion of use. When I use a pseudonym, by contrast, I use an invented first name only – Tom, Sarah, etc. – on the first and subsequent occasions. When I use a pseudonym for a company, I put the pseudonym in inverted commas on the first occasion of use – 'Everest', 'Olympic', etc. (Again, these conventions and the rationale are explained more fully in appendix 2.)

On those occasions where I quoted from interviews with individuals who are given their real names in the text, I subsequently wrote to these individuals, sent them the text I had written about them and/ or their organization, and gave them the opportunity to comment on it: many did so, sometimes in considerable detail, and I took account of their comments in the final version of the text. I am very grateful to these individuals for their willingness to read these texts and provide me with feedback. I am also very grateful to Michael Cader, Angus Phillips and Michael Schudson who read the entire text, and to Jane Friedman and Michele Cobbs who read the chapters dealing with their areas of expertise (self-publishing and audiobooks, respectively): they provided me with many helpful comments and suggestions and saved me from numerous errors and oversights. Any errors that remain are, of course, my own. I am grateful to Leigh Mueller for her meticulous copyediting and to the many people at Polity – including Neil de Cort, Rachel Moore, Evie Deavall, Julia Davies, Clare Ansell, Sue Pope, Sarah Dobson, Breffni O'Connor,

Adrienn Jelinek, Clara Ross, Madeline Sharaga, Emma Longstaff, Lydia Davis and Lucas Jones – who steered this book through the publication process. My thanks, finally, to Mirca and Alex, who displayed uncommon patience and understanding over the years when this book was in gestation and who endured a very cold winter in New York while some of the research was being done: this book is for them, small recompense for the many sacrifices they made while it was being written.

J. B. T., Cambridge

INTRODUCTION

Andy Weir couldn't believe his luck. He always wanted to be a writer and he started writing fanfiction when he was 9. But, being a sensible young man, he doubted he could make a living as a writer, so he trained to be a software engineer and became a computer programmer instead. As a resident of Silicon Valley, this turned out to be a wise decision, and he had a successful career as a programmer for twenty-five years. But he never gave up his dream of being a writer and he continued to write stories in his spare time. He even had a go in the late 1980s at writing a book and trying to get it published, but no one was interested: 'It was the standard struggling author's story, couldn't get any interest – publishers weren't interested, no agent wanted to represent me, it just wasn't meant to be.' Undeterred, Andy continued to write in his spare time – writing was his hobby. As the internet became more prevalent in the late 1990s and early 2000s, he set up a website and began posting his stories online. He had a mailing list that people could sign up to, and he sent them an email whenever he posted a new story. Over a period of ten years, he gradually built up a list of some 3,000 email addresses. Then he started writing serial fiction, posting a chapter at a time on his website and letting his readers know. One of these stories was about a manned space mission to Mars. Being a software engineer, Andy was interested in problem-solving, and he began to think, 'OK, what if something goes wrong, how do we make sure the crew survives? What if two things go wrong, what do we do then? And suddenly I realized I had a story.' He wrote in the evenings and at weekends, whenever he had spare time and felt the urge, and when he finished a chapter he posted it on his website. His readers became very engaged in the story and picked him up on some of the technical details about

1

the physics or the chemistry or the maths of a manned mission to Mars, and he would go back and fix it. This active engagement with his readers spurred him on. Chapter by chapter, the story unfolded of an unfortunate astronaut, Mark Watney, who had been knocked unconscious by a violent dust storm shortly after arriving on Mars and woke up to discover that his crewmates had taken him for dead and made an emergency escape without him, leaving Mark alone to survive indefinitely on a remote planet with limited supplies of food and water and no way to communicate with Earth.

After the last chapter of *The Martian* had been posted on his website, Andy was ready to move on to another project, but he started getting emails from some of his readers saying, 'Hey, I really love *The Martian* but I hate reading it in a web browser. Can you make an e-reader version?' So Andy figured out how to do that – it wasn't too hard for a software engineer – and he posted an ePub and a Mobi file on his website so that people could download it for free. Then he started getting emails from people saying, 'Thanks, I really appreciate that you put up e-reader formats, but I'm not very technically savvy and I don't know how to download a file from the internet and put it on my e-reader. Can you just put it up as a Kindle?' So Andy did that too – filled in the form on Amazon, uploaded the file and, presto, there it was on the Amazon site, now available as a Kindle ebook. Andy wanted to give it away for free but Amazon require you to put a price on your ebook, so he chose the lowest price that Amazon allowed, 99¢. He sent an email out to his readers and said, 'There you are everybody, you can read it for free on my website, you can download the free ePub or Mobi version from my website or you can pay Amazon a buck to put it on your Kindle for you', and to his surprise more people bought it from Amazon than downloaded it for free. The ebook swiftly moved up Amazon's bestseller list, reaching number one in the sci-fi category and staying there for quite some time. Pretty soon the book was selling about 300 copies a day, but, having never published a book before, Andy had no idea whether this was good, bad or indifferent. He was just pleased that it was getting good customer reviews and lingering in the number one spot for sci-fi on Kindle.

Then something happened that he never expected. One day he got an email from an agent who said, 'I think we could get your book into print and if you don't have an agent, I'd like to represent you.' Andy couldn't believe it. Some years earlier, he had written to agents all over the country, begging them to represent him, and no one wanted to know. Now he gets an email out of the blue from an agent who is offering to represent him, and he didn't even have to ask. 'I'm like, wow.'

What Andy didn't know at the time is that, 3,000 miles away in New York, a science-fiction editor at Crown, an imprint of Random House, had been browsing around some of his favourite internet sci-fi sites, as he did from time to time when things were a little slow, and he had come across several mentions of *The Martian*, so he decided to check it out. He noticed it was number one on the Kindle sci-fi bestseller list and it had lots of good customer reviews, so he bought a copy, dipped into it and liked what he read, though he wasn't sure what to make of all the hard science. He had a phone call lined up with an agent friend of his and, in the course of the conversation, he mentioned the book to him, told him he'd been tracking it on Amazon and suggested he take a look and let him know what he thought. He did, loved it ('I was just blown away by it' – the hard science appealed to his geeky nature), got in touch with Andy and signed him up. This was an agent who was accustomed to finding new authors online, sometimes by reading an interesting article on the internet and getting in touch with the author, sometimes by coming across a self-published book on Amazon that looked interesting, so he knew how to navigate this terrain. Out of courtesy to the editor who had called this book to his attention, the agent got back in touch with him and gave him a little time to consider it as an exclusive. The editor sent it around to a few of his colleagues at Crown and asked them to look at it over the weekend; they liked it too, and on Monday they made a generous offer to pre-empt the book and take it off the table. Andy was thrilled and the deal was done. 'It was a no-brainer', said Andy; 'it was more money than I make in a year in my current job, and that was just the advance.'

At around the same time, a small film production company had also spotted *The Martian* on the Kindle bestseller list and got in touch with Andy, who put them in touch with his new agent. The agent contacted his film co-agent and they used the interest of the small production company to pique the interest of Fox, who snapped up the film rights and announced that the movie would be directed by Ridley Scott with Matt Damon in the lead. With publishing rights now sold to Random House and a Hollywood blockbuster in the works, the scouts began to work their magic with foreign publishers. The buzz machine was spinning and it ramped up quickly. Before long, rights were sold in thirty-one international territories and Andy's substantial advance was earned out before the book was even published.

To Andy, who was oblivious to these distant conversations, the sudden interest in his book seemed somewhat unreal. He was at work the week that the deals with Random House and Fox were done, in his programming cubicle as usual, and he had to go to a conference room to take a call about the movie deal. 'It's like, hey, out of nowhere, all of your dreams are going to come true. It was so unbelievable that I literally didn't believe it. I hadn't actually met any of these people, it was all just emails and phone calls, and in the back of my mind I kept thinking, "This might just be a scam."' It only hit home when the contract finally arrived and the return address was Random House, 1745 Broadway, New York, NY, and then the cheque for the advance arrived. 'I thought, "If this is a scam, they're very bad at it."'

Once the deal with Random House was done, Andy was asked to take down the Kindle edition, which he did. The text was lightly edited and then sent out to various prominent authors for pre-publication blurbs – the responses were amazing. An array of well-known sci-fi authors raved about this new addition to their genre. All of this helped the editor to get people talking about the book, generate excitement inside the house and encourage the sales reps to get behind the book and push it when they met with the buyers at the major retail outlets – critical factors in the attempt to make a book stand out from the thousands of new titles that are published every week. The Random House edition of *The Martian* was eventually published as a hardcover and ebook in February 2014 and went straight onto the *New York Times* bestseller list, where it remained for six weeks. A glowing review in the *Wall Street Journal* described it as 'utterly compelling ... This is techno sci-fi at a level even Arthur Clarke never achieved.' The paperback edition was released in October 2014 and again went quickly onto the *New York Times* bestseller list, reaching the number one spot and remaining on the list well into 2015.

There was something remarkable and unprecedented about Andy's success: through a series of metamorphoses, a text that started life as a blog on someone's personal website ended up as an international bestseller and a blockbuster film and, with it, a life and a career were transformed. A generation earlier, none of this would have been possible and a talent like Andy's might well have gone undiscovered. That was one of the many upsides of the digital revolution in publishing: thanks to the internet, talent could be discovered in new ways and a writer who had been beavering away in relative obscurity could suddenly be catapulted into international stardom. Everyone gains – writer, publisher, millions of readers all over the world. But, remarkable though Andy's success was, this was only one side of the story. The very changes that had enabled Andy to realize his childhood dream were wreaking havoc in an industry that had operated in pretty much the same way for as long as anyone could remember. The industry by which Andy was so pleased to be embraced had, largely unbeknown to Andy, become a battleground where powerful new players were disrupting traditional practices and challenging accepted ways of doing things, all facilitated by a techno-logical revolution that was as profound as anything the industry had experienced in the five centuries since Gutenberg. The astonishing success of *The Martian* – from blog to bestseller – epitomizes the paradox of the digital revolution in publishing: unprecedented new opportunities are opened up, both for individuals and for organiza-tions, while beneath the surface the tectonic plates of the industry are shifting. Understanding how these two movements can happen simultaneously, and why they take the form that they do, is the key to understanding the digital revolution in publishing.

The digital revolution first began to make itself felt in the book publishing industry in the 1980s. At this time, the world of Anglo-American trade publishing was dominated by three sets of players that had become increasingly powerful in the period since the 1960s: the retail chains, the literary agents and the publishing corporations.[1] The rise of the retail chains began in the US in the late 1960s with the emergence of B. Dalton Booksellers and Waldenbooks, two bookselling chains that took root in the suburban shopping malls that were becoming increasingly prevalent at that time, as the middle classes moved out of city centres into the expanding suburbs. In the course of the 1970s and 1980s, these mall-based bookstores were eclipsed and eventually absorbed by the so-called book superstore chains, especially Barnes & Noble and Borders, which competed ferociously with one another throughout the 1980s and 1990s as they rolled out their superstores across America. Unlike the mall-based bookstores, these book superstore chains located their stores in prime city locations with large floor areas to maximize stock-holding capacity. The stores were designed as attractive retail spaces that would be welcoming and unthreatening to individuals who were not accustomed to going into a traditional bookstore – clean,

---

[1] The rise of these three sets of players and their impact on the world of Anglo-American trade publishing are analysed in more detail in John B. Thompson, *Merchants of Culture: The Publishing Business in the Twenty-First Century*, Second Edition (Cambridge: Polity; New York: Penguin, 2012).

spacious, well-lit spaces with sofas and coffee shops, areas to relax and read and no need to check in bags as you entered or left the store. Similar developments occurred in the UK with the rise of Dillons and Waterstones, two book retail chains that competed with one another and with WH Smith, the general high-street newsagent and stationer, in the 1980s and 1990s, until Dillons was eventually absorbed into Waterstones.

The result of these and similar developments (such as the increasing role of mass merchandisers and supermarkets as retail outlets for books) was that, by the late 1980s and early 1990s, a substantial proportion of books published by trade publishers were being sold through retail chains that, between them, controlled a large and growing share of the market. The market share of the retail chains put them in a very strong position when it came to negotiating terms with publishers, as the scale of their commitment to a book, and whether they were willing to feature it in front-of-store displays and at what cost, could make a big difference to the visibility and success of a title. The independent bookstores, by contrast, experienced a steep decline. Hundreds were forced into bankruptcy during the 1990s, unable to compete with the extensive stock range and aggressive discounting of the large retail chains. That was the retail setting of the book trade when a small internet start-up called Amazon opened for business from a suburban garage in Seattle in July 1995.

The second key development that shaped the field of Anglo-American trade publishing in the late twentieth century was the growing power of literary agents. Of course, literary agents were not new – they had been around since the late nineteenth century. But for much of the first century of their existence, literary agents had understood their role as intermediaries who were bringing together authors and publishers and negotiating deals that both parties would regard as fair and reasonable. This self-conception of the literary agent began to change in the 1970s and early 1980s as a new breed of agent – what I call the super-agent – began to appear in the publishing field. Unlike most agents, many of whom had previously worked in publishing houses, the new super-agents were outsiders in the world of publishing and were not attached to the traditional practices of literary agents. They understood the role of the agent in a more legalistic way, not so much as intermediaries but rather as advocates of their clients' – the authors' – interests. They were prepared to fight, and to fight hard, to maximize the returns to the authors they represented. They didn't care whether they ruffled the feathers of the big publishers: good public relations were not part of the role of an agent as they understood it. They knew that there was plenty of money to be made in the publishing business, especially with the massive expansion of bookselling capacity that was being created by the rise of the retail chains, and they believed that authors should get their fair share. They also knew that publishers would not hand out large advances and give better terms to authors unless someone was prepared to fight for them.

The more aggressive, combative style of the super-agents was not shared by all agents – indeed, some abhorred the practices of these new kids on the block. But slowly, almost imperceptibly, the culture of agenting began to change. Agenting became less and less about striking deals that kept everyone happy, and more and more about getting the best deal you could for your authors, even if it meant, on occasion, upsetting a publisher or editor with whom you had a long and amicable relationship. This didn't mean that the size of the advance became the only basis for deciding which publisher to go with – there were always going to be other considerations, such as the nature of the publishing house, the relationship with the editor, the commitment in terms of marketing, etc. But money up front did matter, and increasingly so. Not only was it a means of livelihood for authors, many of whom wanted to live by their writing if they could, but it was also taken as a sign of the publisher's commitment: the bigger the advance, the more the publisher would be willing to put behind the book in terms of the size of the print run, the marketing budget, the sales effort and so on. In a market where agents controlled access to the most prized new content, the size of the publisher's advance became an increasingly important factor in deciding who would acquire the rights to a book. Advances escalated, auctions became more common, and eventually it was only the publishers with access to the deepest pockets – and increasingly that meant the pockets of large corporations – who were able to compete for the most sought-after works.

The third key development that shaped the field of Anglo-American trade publishing was the growth of the publishing corporations. From the early 1960s on, several waves of mergers and acquisitions swept through the world of Anglo-American trade publishing, and many formerly independent publishing houses – Simon & Schuster, Scribner, Harper, Random House, Alfred Knopf, Farrar, Straus & Giroux, Jonathan Cape, William Heinemann, Secker & Warburg, Weidenfeld & Nicolson, to name just a few – were transformed into imprints within large corporations. The reasons for these mergers and acquisitions were complex and they varied from case to case, depending on the circumstances of the houses that were being acquired and the strategies of the acquiring firms; but the overall result was that, by the late 1990s, the landscape of Anglo-American trade publishing had been dramatically reconfigured. In a field where there had once been dozens of independent publishing houses, each reflecting the idiosyncratic tastes and styles of their owners and editors, there were now just five or six large publishing corporations, each acting as an umbrella organization for numerous imprints and each owned, in turn, by a much larger multimedia conglomerate that stood behind it and to which the publishing corporation reported. Most of these conglomerates were large, diversified, transnational businesses with interests in many different industries and countries. Some, such as the German groups Bertelsmann and Holtzbrink, remained private and family-owned, while others, like Pearson, NewsCorp, Viacom and Lagardère, were publicly traded companies. In most cases, these conglomerates acquired trade publishing assets both in the US and in the UK, assembling them under a corporate umbrella that carried the same name – Penguin, Random House (now Penguin Random House following their merger in 2013), Simon & Schuster, HarperCollins, Hachette or Macmillan – even if in practice the operations in the US and in the UK operated largely independently of one another and reported directly to the parent company.

The large publishing corporations became major players in the field of Anglo-American trade publishing, together accounting for around half of total retail sales in the US and the UK by the early 2000s. In a field characterized by large retail chains and powerful agents who controlled access to customers and content respectively, there were clear advantages to being big. Scale gave them leverage in their negotiations with the large retail chains, where terms of trade could make a real difference to the profitability of the publisher. It also gave them access to the deep pockets of the large conglomerates, which greatly strengthened their hand when it came to competing for the most sought-after content, where, thanks in part to the growing power of agents, the size of the advance was often the decisive consideration. Smaller and medium-sized publishers simply couldn't compete with the financial clout wielded by the new publishing corporations, and many eventually hauled up the white flag and joined one of the groups.

In broad terms, these were the three developments that shaped the field of Anglo-American trade publishing during the last four decades of the twentieth century, from roughly 1960 to the early 2000s. Of course, there were many other factors that were important in shaping this field, and many other organizations that were active and significant players in the world of trade publishing during this time: this is a world of bewildering complexity, full of arcane practices, highly ramified supply chains and countless organizations doing a myriad of different things. But if we wanted to understand why the world of Anglo-American trade publishing in the 1980s, 1990s and early 2000s was so different from the world of trade publishing that existed in the 1950s and before, and if we wanted to understand the most significant practices that had become prevalent and taken-for-granted in the industry by the early 2000s – including auctions for new books, mouth-wateringly high advances, stack-'em-high book displays in the major retail outlets, bestsellers on a scale and with a frequency that was unprecedented, high discounts and high returns – then the three developments outlined above would give us the keys.

It was in the context of an industry structured in this way that, from the early 1980s on, the digital revolution began to make its presence felt. Initially, this was a low-key affair, invisible to the outsider. Like so many other sectors of industry, the early impact of the digital revolution was in the area of logistics, supply-chain management and the gradual transformation of back-office systems. For an industry like book publishing, where thousands of new products – that is, books – are published every week, each bearing a unique numerical identifier or ISBN, the potential for achieving greater efficiencies in supply-chain management through the use of IT was enormous. Huge investments were made throughout the 1980s and 1990s to create more efficient systems for managing all aspects of the publishing supply chain, from production, rights and royalties to ordering, warehouse management, sales and fulfilment. Improved IT systems enabled publishers to manage the publishing process more efficiently, enabled wholesalers to offer much better services to retailers, and enabled retailers to monitor their stock levels and re-order on a daily basis in the light of computerized point-of-sale data. Behind the scenes, the entire book supply chain was being quietly but radically transformed. These were not the kinds of developments that would get blood racing through the veins, but it would be hard to overstate their significance for the day-to-day operations of the publishing industry.

Yet the digital revolution in publishing was never going to be only about the logistics of supply-chain management and the improvement of back-office systems, however important these things are in the day-to-day running of businesses. For the digital revolution had the potential to be far more disruptive than this. Why? What was it about the digital revolution that made it so much more disruptive, indeed threatening, than the many other technological innovations that had impinged on the publishing industry often enough in the course of its 500-year history?

What made the digital revolution unique is that it offered the possibility of a completely different way of handling the content that was at the heart of the publishing business. For, at the end of the day, publishing, like other sectors of the media and creative industries, is about symbolic content – that is, about a particular kind of information that takes the form of stories or other kinds of extended text. What the digital revolution made possible was the transformation of this information or symbolic content – indeed, *any* information or symbolic content – into sequences of digits (or streams of bits) that can be processed, stored and transmitted as data. Once information takes the form of digitized data, it can be easily manipulated, stored, combined with other data and transmitted using networks of various kinds. Now we're in a new world, very different from the world of physical objects like cars, refrigerators and print-on-paper books. It is a world of weightless data that can be subjected to a whole new set of processes and transmitted via networks that have their own distinctive properties. And the more that publishing is drawn into this new world, the further it moves away from the old world of physical objects which had been its home since the time of Gutenberg. In short, the symbolic content of the book is no longer tied to the physical print-on-paper object in which it was traditionally embedded.

This, in essence, is why the digital revolution has such far-reaching consequences for the publishing industry and for other sectors of the media and creative industries: digitization enables symbolic *content* to be transformed into data and separated from the material *medium* or substratum in which it has been embedded hitherto. In this respect, publishing is very different from, say, the car industry: while the car industry can be (and has been) transformed in many ways by the application of digital technologies, the car itself will always be a physical object with an engine, wheels, doors, windows, etc., even if it no longer has a driver. Not so the book. The fact that, for more than 500 years, we have come to associate the book with a physical object made with ink, paper and glue is, in itself, a historical contingency, not a necessary feature of the book as such. The print-on-paper book is a material medium in which a specific kind of symbolic content – a story, for example – can be realized or embedded. But there were other media in the past (such as clay tablets and papyrus) and there could be other media in the future. And if the content can be codified digitally, then the need to embed that content in a particular material substratum like print-on-paper, in order to record, manipulate and transmit it, disappears. The content exists virtually as a code, a particular sequence of 0s and 1s.

But the digital revolution did much more than this: it transformed the whole information and communication environment of contemporary societies. By bringing together information technology, computers and telecommunications, the digital revolution enabled ever-increasing quantities of digitized information to be transmitted at enormous speeds, thereby creating new networks of communication and information flow on a scale that was unprecedented. The informational life-worlds of ordinary people were changing as never before. Soon they would be carrying around in their pocket or bag a small device that would function simultaneously as a phone, a map and a computer, enabling them to stay permanently connected to others, to pinpoint their location and get directions, and to access vast quantities of information at the touch of a screen. Traditional creative industries like publishing found themselves caught up in a vortex of change that deeply affected their businesses, but over which they had little or no control. This was a process that was being driven by others – by large technology companies based primarily on the West Coast of the US, far away from the traditional heartlands of Anglo-American trade publishing. These companies were governed by different principles and animated by an ethos that was alien to the traditional world of publishing, and yet their activities were creating a new kind of information environment to which the old world of publishing would have to adapt.

The area of book publishing where the disruptive impact of the digital revolution was first experienced was not in the sphere of consumption, however: it was in the sphere of production. The traditional methods of the publishing industry, whereby a manuscript was received from an author, usually in the form of a typescript, and then edited, copyedited and marked up for the typesetter, were swept aside as the entire production process was turned, step by step, into a digital workflow. Indeed, as more and more authors began to compose their texts by typing on the keys of a computer rather than using a pen and paper or a typewriter, the text became a digital file from the moment of creation – it was born digital, existing only as a sequence of 0s and 1s stored on a disc or in the memory of a

11

computer. The material forms of writing were changing,[2] and, from that point on, the transformation of the text that leads to the creation of the object that we call 'the book' could, at least in principle, be done entirely in digital form: it could be edited on screen, revised and corrected on screen, marked up for the typesetter on screen, designed and typeset on screen. From the viewpoint of the production process, the book was reconstituted as a digital file, a database. To a production manager in a publishing house, that's all the book now is: a file of information that has been manipulated, coded and tagged in certain ways. The reconstitution of the book as a digital file is a crucial part of what I call 'the hidden revolution'.[3] By that, I mean a revolution not in the *product* but rather in the *process*: even if the final product looks the same as it always did, a physical book with ink printed on paper, the process by which this book is produced is now completely different.

While all these steps in the production process could in principle be done digitally, it was never so easy in practice. Digitization did not always simplify things – on the contrary, it often made them more complex. The digital world, with its plethora of file types and formats, programming languages, hardwares, softwares and constant upgrades, is in many ways more complicated than the old analogue world of print. A central part of the history of the publishing industry since the early 1980s has been the progressive application of the digital revolution to the various stages of book production. Typesetting was one of the first areas to be affected. The old linotype machines, which were the standard means of typesetting in the 1970s and before, were replaced in the 1980s by big IBM mainframe typesetting machines and then, in the 1990s, by desktop publishing. Typesetting costs plummeted: whereas, in the 1970s, it typically cost $10 a page to get a book typeset from manuscript, by 2000 it was costing between $4 and $5 a page, despite the decrease in the value of the dollar produced by two decades of inflation. While the shift was decisive and dramatic, it was a confusing time for those who lived through the changes and found themselves having to adapt to new ways of doing things. The job of the typesetter was redefined

---

[2] On the history of how, from the 1960s on, literary writers shifted increasingly to the use of word-processing technologies, see Matthew G. Kirschenbaum, *Track Changes: A Literary History of Word Processing* (Cambridge, Mass.: Harvard University Press, 2016).

[3] See John B. Thompson, *Books in the Digital Age: The Transformation of Academic and Higher Education Publishing in Britain and the United States* (Cambridge: Polity, 2005), ch. 15.

and lines of responsibility were blurred. Some of the tasks formerly carried out by typesetters were eliminated and others were thrown back on in-house production staff, who suddenly found themselves on the front line of the digital revolution in publishing, obliged to use new technologies and learn new programmes that were themselves constantly changing.

By the mid-1990s, many of the technical aspects of book production, including typesetting and page design, had been thoroughly transformed by the application of digital technologies. Progress was more erratic in other areas, such as editing and printing: here too there were aspects of the workflow that became increasingly digital in character, though in ways that were more complex than a one-way shift from analogue to digital. While many authors were composing texts on computers and hence creating digital files, their files were often too full of errors for publishers to use. It was often easier and cheaper for the publisher to print out the text, edit and mark-up the printed page, and then send the edited and marked-up manuscript to a compositor in Asia who would re-key the text and add the tags for the page layout. So while in principle the author's keystrokes were the point at which the digital workflow could begin, in practice – at least in trade publishing – the digital workflow typically began at a later point, when the edited and marked-up manuscript was re-keyed by the compositor, who supplied the publisher with a file that included additional functionality.

Printing is another area where digitization had a huge impact, though again in ways that were more complex than a simple one-way shift from analogue to digital. Until the late 1990s, most publishers used traditional offset printing for all of their books. Offset has many advantages: print quality is high, illustrations can be reproduced to a high standard and there are significant economies of scale – the more you print, the lower the unit cost. But there are disadvantages too: most notably, there are significant set-up costs, so it is uneconomic to print small quantities. So backlist titles that were selling a few hundred copies or less per year were commonly put out of print by many publishers, and the large trade houses often drew the line much higher. It simply wasn't economic for them to keep these books in print, taking up space in the warehouse and reprinting in small quantities if and when the stock ran out.

The advent of digital printing changed all that. The basic technology for digital printing had existed since the late 1970s, but it wasn't until the 1990s that the technology was developed in ways that would enable it to become a serious alternative to the traditional offset

13

presses. As reproduction quality improved and costs came down, a variety of new players entered the field, offering a range of digital printing services to publishers. It was now possible to keep a backlist title in print by sending the file to a digital printer who could reprint small quantities – 10, 20, 100 or 200 copies, far fewer than would have been possible using traditional offset methods. The unit costs were higher than they were with traditional offset printing but still manageable for the publisher, especially if they were willing to raise the retail price. It was even possible to turn the traditional publishing fulfilment model on its head: rather than printing a fixed quantity of books and putting them in a warehouse to wait for them to be ordered and sold, the publisher could give the file to a print-on-demand supplier like Lightning Source, who would hold the file on its server and print a copy of the book only when it received an order for it. In this way, the publisher could keep the book permanently available without having to hold stock in a warehouse: physical stock was replaced by a 'virtual warehouse'.

By the early 2000s, many publishers in the English-speaking world were using some version of digital printing for their slower-moving backlist titles, whether short-run digital printing or true print-on-demand. Those in the fields of academic and professional publishing were among the first to take advantage of these new opportunities: many of their books were specialized works that sold in small quantities at high prices, and were therefore well suited to digital printing. Many trade publishers were accustomed to dealing in the larger print quantities for which offset printing is ideal, but they too came to realize – in some cases spurred on by the long-tail thesis first put forward by Chris Anderson in 2004[4] – that there was value locked up in some older backlist titles that could be captured by using digital print technology. Publishers – academic, professional and trade – began to mine their backlists, looking for older titles for which they still held the copyright, scanning them, turning them into PDFs and re-releasing them as digitally printed books. Titles that had been put out of print many years ago found themselves being brought back to life. Thanks to digital printing, publishers no longer had to put books out of print at all: they could simply reprint in small quantities or put the file in a print-on-demand programme, thereby keeping the title available in perpetuity. This was one of the first great ironies of the digital revolution in publishing: far from killing

---

[4] See Chris Anderson, *The Long Tail: Why the Future of Business is Selling Less of More* (New York: Hyperion, 2006).

14

off the printed book, the digital revolution gave it a new lease of life, enabling it to live well beyond the age at which it would have died in the pre-digital world. From now on, many books would never go out of print.

These developments in print technology, together with the substantial reduction in costs associated with the digitization of typesetting and book design, also greatly lowered the barriers to entry and opened the way for new start-ups to enter the publishing field. It was now easier than ever to set up a publishing company, typeset and design a book using desktop publishing software on a PC or a Mac, and print in small quantities – or even one at a time – using a digital printer or print-on-demand service. The digital revolution spawned a proliferation of small publishing operations. It also opened the way for an explosion in self-publishing – a process that began in earnest in the late 1990s and early 2000s with the appearance of a variety of organizations using print-on-demand technology, but took on a new character from around 2010, when a plethora of new players entered the self-publishing field.

While these developments were dramatic in their own way, they were only the first stages in a process of transformation that would soon prove to be far more challenging for the established structures and players of Anglo-American trade publishing. With the rise of the internet in the 1990s, the weaving together of information and communication technologies and the growing availability of personal computers and mobile devices with high-speed internet connections, it became possible not just to transform supply chains, back-office systems and production processes, but also to revolutionize the ways in which customers, i.e. readers, acquire books, the form in which they acquire them and, indeed, the ways in which the readers of books relate to those who write them. The traditional print-on-paper book, and the industry that had grown up over a period of some 500 years to produce this object and distribute it to readers through a network of retail outlets, constituted, in effect, a channel of communication that put one set of individuals (writers) in communication with another set of individuals (readers) through a particular medium (the book) and a ramified network of organizations and intermediaries (publishers, printers, wholesalers, retailers, libraries, etc.) which made this communication process possible. The great challenge posed by the digital revolution to creative industries like publishing is that it opened up the possibility of creating entirely new channels of communication between creators and consumers that would bypass the intermediaries that had hitherto enabled this process to take place. Traditional players could be 'disintermediated' – that is, cut out of the supply chain altogether.

Perhaps the most dramatic demonstration of the disruptive potential of this aspect of the digital revolution was provided by the music industry. For decades, the music industry, dominated by a small number of major record labels, had been based on an economic model in which recorded music was inscribed in a physical medium, traditionally the vinyl LP, and sold through a network of retail outlets. The first major impact of the digital revolution on the music industry – the development of the CD in the 1980s – did not fundamentally disrupt this model: on the contrary, it simply substituted one physical medium for another and resulted in a surge in sales as consumers replaced their LPs and cassette tapes with CDs. But the development of the MP3 format in 1996, and the coming together in the late 1990s and early 2000s of personal computers and the internet, resulted in a sudden and dramatic change in the way that music was acquired, shared and consumed. Very quickly, the world of recorded music changed from one in which consumers bought albums in bricks-and-mortar stores, occasionally sharing them with friends, to a world in which music could be downloaded, uploaded and shared online, potentially with anyone who had access to the internet.

The explosive implications of this transformation were highlighted most vividly by Napster, the peer-to-peer (P2P) file-sharing service that was launched in 1999. The site catalogued the music files of millions of users so you could see who had what, and then enabled you to download a file from a remote PC, seamlessly and with no money changing hands. Napster grew exponentially – at its peak, it had 80 million registered users worldwide. As music sales began to decline, the music companies and the Recording Industry Association of America (RIAA) sued Napster for infringement of copyright, succeeding in closing it down in 2001. But the genie was out of the bottle and the short life of Napster brought home to everyone the massive disruptive potential of online distribution. A plethora of P2P file-sharing services flourished in the wake of Napster's demise, many using the BitTorrent protocol that gathers bits of a file from a variety of hosts rather than downloading a file from a single server, making it much harder to shut down.

Quite apart from P2P file sharing, legitimate channels for the online distribution of music grew rapidly in the early 2000s. Apple, the most significant of these, launched the iTunes music player in 2001, the same year that it released the iPod MP3 player, and added the iTunes

16

music store in 2003. Now it was possible for customers to download songs, perfectly legally, for 99¢ a track. By 2008, Apple had become the number one music retailer in the US, outstripping Walmart, Best Buy and Target. During the same period, the sales of CDs in the US collapsed, from 938 million units in 1999 to 296 million in 2009, less than a third of what they had been a decade earlier.[5] Total revenues from US recorded music sales also plummeted, falling from $14.6 billion in 1999 to $7.8 billion in 2009.[6] The collapse of revenues was cataclysmic, as can be seen in figure 0.1.

Consumers who were still buying music were paying much less for it than they had paid in the late 1990s, when CDs were the overwhelmingly dominant format. In 1999, 938 million CD sales generated revenue of $12.8 billion, or $13.66 per CD; there were no download sales at that time. By 2009, CD sales had fallen to 296 million units; these were still generating revenue of $14.58 per CD but, because the units sold were less than a third of what they had been a decade earlier, the total revenue generated from CD sales had fallen to $4.3 billion. By contrast, music downloads had grown dramatically since 2004, and by 2009 there were 1,124 million single downloads and 74 million album downloads; taken together, however, these downloads generated only another $1.9 billion, and therefore came nowhere near to making up for the loss of $8.5 billion of revenue on CD sales.[7] Moreover, while many people were paying for downloads through legitimate channels like iTunes, a very large but unknowable number of others were downloading music for free – according to one estimate by the online download tracker BigChampagne, the volume of unauthorized downloads still represented around 90 per cent of the music market in 2010.[8]

There were many in the book publishing industry who were looking over their shoulders at the tumultuous developments in the music industry and wondering anxiously if music was the future of books foretold. What would the book publishing industry look like if piracy became rife and total book revenues were cut in half? What kind of revenue models would replace the tried-and-tested model on which the industry had been based for more than 500 years, and how robust

---

[5] RIAA, US Sales Database, at www.riaa.com/u-s-sales-database.
[6] Ibid.
[7] RIAA. There were additional sources of revenue during this period, such as vinyl and music videos and, from 2005 on, ringtones and ringbacks, subscriptions, etc., but they don't alter materially the overall pattern of revenue decline.
[8] David Goldman, 'Music's lost decade: Sales cut in half', *CNN Money* (3 February 2010), at http://money.cnn.com/2010/02/02/news/companies/napster_music_industry.

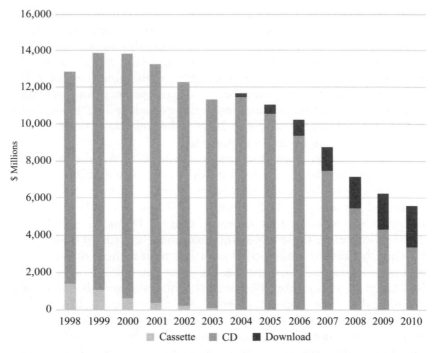

Figure 0.1   US recorded music revenues by format, 1998–2010
Note: revenues are for cassettes, CDs and downloads (singles and albums) only.
Source: The Recording Industry Association of America (RIAA)

would these new models be? How could the book industry protect itself from the rampant file sharing that had become commonplace in the world of music? What would happen to bookstores if more and more books were downloaded as files, or even ordered online rather than bought in bricks-and-mortar bookstores – how could physical bookstores survive? And if they disappeared, or even declined significantly, how would readers discover new books? It didn't take too much imagination to see that the book publishing industry could be hit just as hard by the tsunami that swept through the music industry in the late 1990s and early 2000s. Senior managers looking out of the windows of their high-rise office blocks in Manhattan might well be wondering whether the days of their panoramic views were numbered.

And yet, during the first few years of the new millennium, the signs of what would actually happen in the book publishing industry were anything but clear. There was no shortage of speculation in the late

1990s and early 2000s about the impending ebook revolution – one much-cited report by PricewaterhouseCoopers in 2000 forecast an explosion of consumer spending on electronic books, estimating that by 2004 consumer spending on electronic books would reach $5.4 billion and would comprise 17 per cent of the market. Expectations were also raised by the startling success of one of Stephen King's early experiments with digital publishing. In March 2000, he published his 66-page novella *Riding the Bullet* electronically, available only as a digital file that could be downloaded for $2.50; there was an overwhelming response, resulting in around 400,000 downloads in the first twenty-four hours, and 600,000 in the first two weeks. But, notwithstanding Stephen King's good fortune, the predictions made by PricewaterhouseCoopers and others turned out to be wildly optimistic, at least in terms of the timescale. Those publishers who were actively experimenting with ebooks in the early 2000s invariably found that the levels of uptake were extremely low, indeed negligible: sales of individual ebooks numbered in the tens, in some cases, the hundreds, but were nowhere near the hundreds of thousands, let alone millions, of units that many had expected. Whatever was happening here, it didn't seem to bear much resemblance to the sudden and dramatic transformation of the music industry – or at least not yet.

The story of the ebook's rise turned out to be much more compli-cated than most commentators had thought, and as this story unfolded through the first decade of the twenty-first century and into the second, countless predictions, uttered a few years earlier with great conviction, turned out to be wide of the mark. Very few people accurately anticipated what actually happened, and, at every stage in this unfolding story, future developments were always unclear. The truth is that no one really knew what would happen, and for years everyone in the publishing industry was living in a state of deep uncertainty, as if they were moving towards a cliff but never knew whether they would ever reach the edge and what would happen if they did. For some within the publishing industry and many on the fringes of it, ebooks were a revolutionary new technology that would finally drag the publishing world, with its arcane practices and ineffi-cient systems, into the twenty-first century. For others, they were the harbinger of doom, the death-knell of an industry that had flourished for half a millennium and contributed more to our culture than any other. In practice, they were neither, and champions and critics alike would be dumbfounded by the curious course of the ebook.

— Chapter 1 —

THE FALTERING RISE OF THE EBOOK

Any attempt to recount the history of ebooks presupposes some understanding of what an ebook is. As noted earlier, our understanding of what constitutes a book has been shaped for centuries by the particular form that the book has assumed since Gutenberg – ink printed on sheets of paper that are bound together (glued, sometimes also sewn) along one edge, so that they can be read sequentially and turned over one page at a time, similar to the traditional codex but transformed by the use of paper, ink and the printing press. This form places certain limits on what can and cannot be treated as a book. It would be hard to treat a 20-word text as a book, for instance, as there simply wouldn't be enough text to fill more than a page (unless this were a very unusual design with 1 or 2 words on a page). Similarly, the text cannot go on indefinitely, or even into millions of words, and still be produced as 'a book' in any straightforward sense (though it could be produced as a series of books). In other words, the welding together of content and form in the traditional print-on-paper book places certain contingent limits on what can and cannot be treated as a book. But separate the content from the form and suddenly it is no longer so clear what exactly a book is. Could a 20-word text be a book if there were no pages to turn and the text told a story from beginning to end with splendid conciseness? For the purposes of gathering statistics on book production by country, UNESCO famously defined a book as 'a non-periodic publication of at least 49 pages exclusive of the cover pages, published in the country and made available to the public'.[1] It is understandable that UNESCO wanted to come up with

---

[1] UNESCO, 'Recommendation Concerning the International Standardization of Statistics Relating to Book Production and Periodicals' (19 November 1964), at

a clear criterion that would enable it to gather cross-national statistics on a comparable basis, but as a way of conceptualizing the book this is clearly an arbitrary number. Why 49 pages? Why not 48, or 45, or 35, or even 10 – why would a text of 45 pages not count as a book if a text of 49 pages would? On the other hand, could a text of several million words be a book if there were no need to print pages, and the form placed no limits on the extent? Once content and form are no longer tied together in the print-on-paper book, it becomes less clear what a book is, and hence what distinguishes, if anything does, a text from a book. Is an ebook simply an electronic text, or is an ebook a species of electronic text that has certain distinguishing properties – and, if so, what are those properties?

These are all perfectly legitimate questions that have exercised commentators, innovators and scholars since the beginnings of the digital revolution, and we will return to them in a later chapter. But for now, I will take a more pragmatic, historical approach: when did the term 'ebook' and its cognates enter our vocabulary, who used these terms, and what did they use them to refer to?

The origins and rise of the ebook

The terms 'electronic book', 'e-book' and 'ebook' came into general circulation in the 1980s. The American computer scientist and specialist in computer graphics Andries van Dam is usually credited with coining the term 'electronic book', though related work on the characteristics of electronic document systems was being done as early as the 1960s by Theodore Nelson, Douglas Engelbart and others.[2] The creation of the first actual ebook is usually attributed to a chance event in July 1971. Michael Hart, a freshman at the University of Illinois, decided to spend the night at the Xerox Sigma V mainframe at the University's Materials Research Lab rather than walk home and then have to return the next day.[3] On the way to the

---

http://portal.unesco.org/en/ev.php-URL_ID=13068&URL_DO=DO_TOPIC&URL_SECTION=201.html.

[2] Nicole Yankelovich, Norman Meyrowitz and Andries van Dam, 'Reading and Writing the Electronic Book', *Computer*, 18, 10 (October 1985), 15–30.

[3] See Michael Hart, 'The History and Philosophy of Project Gutenberg', at www.gutenberg.org/wiki/Gutenberg:The_History_and_Philosophy_of_Project_Gutenberg_by_Michael_Hart; Marie Lebert, *A Short History of eBooks* (NEF (Net des études françaises / Net of French Studies), University of Toronto, 2009), pp. 5ff., at www.etudes-francaises.net/dossiers/ebookEN.pdf.

21

Lab, he stopped at a shop to pick up some groceries for the night ahead, and when they packed the groceries they put in the bag a faux parchment copy of the US Declaration of Independence. That night at the Lab, Michael was fortuitously given a computer operator's account with a virtually unlimited amount of computer time – 100 million dollars' worth – credited to it. As he unpacked his groceries, thinking about what to do with all that computer time, the faux parchment copy of the Declaration of Independence fell out of the bag, and that gave him an idea: why not type in the Declaration of Independence and make it as widely available as possible? That was the beginning of Project Gutenberg. The plan was to find books and documents in the public domain that would be of general interest, key them into the computer and make them available in the simplest electronic form possible – 'Plain Vanilla ASCII' – so that they could be easily shared. A book would be turned into a continuous text file instead of a set of pages, with capital letters used where italics, bold or underlined text appeared in the printed text. After typing in the Declaration of Independence, Michael typed in the Bill of Rights and a volunteer keyed in the US Constitution, followed by the Bible and Shakespeare, one play at a time. And so the process continued, text by text, and eventually, by August 1997, Project Gutenberg had created 1,000 ebooks, ranging from the King James Bible and *Alice's Adventures in Wonderland* to *La Divina Commedia*, in Italian.

Project Gutenberg was, and remains, an open archive of ebooks that can be downloaded for free, but, in the course of the 1990s, many publishers also began to explore the possibility of making some of their books available as ebooks. The main difference between initiatives like Project Gutenberg and the first forays of publishers into the emerging world of ebooks was that publishers were dealing for the most part with material that was under copyright, rather than public-domain documents, and hence publishers had to ensure that they had the right to release their titles in an electronic format before they actually did so. This was not a straightforward matter since, prior to around 1994, most publishers' contracts did not include any mention of ebooks, electronic formats or digital editions – this simply wasn't envisaged as a format that publishers might want to exploit at some point, so no explicit provision for this format was made in the contracts that publishers negotiated and signed with authors and agents. This changed around 1994: from this point on, many publishers did add to their contracts an explicit provision for electronic formats or digital editions. The specific wording of the clauses, the ways in which revenues would be split and the timing of these contractual changes varied from publisher to publisher, and, even at the same publisher, varied over time – Random House introduced the first changes to their contracts in 1994, others followed suit later. However, for all those books for which contracts had been signed prior to 1994, publishers who wished to release electronic editions had to go back to authors, agents and estates and seek to negotiate an addendum to the original contract that would give them the explicit right to release an electronic edition of the work. Even when authors were amenable, this was a time-consuming and laborious process. Moreover, given the uncertainties surrounding the digital revolution and its potential impact on the publishing industry, it was also a contentious and conflict-ridden process in some cases, as the various parties tried to use whatever leverage they had to negotiate new and better terms in a context where previous norms for print editions could not necessarily be construed as a reliable guide.

And then there was the non-trivial issue of how a book released in an electronic format would actually be read. Texts could, of course, be read on desktops and laptops, and various dedicated reading applications were available for these devices; but desktops and laptops lacked the convenience and portability that many readers had come to associate with the print-on-paper book. A variety of portable, hand-held devices and PDAs (Personal Digital Assistants) appeared in the 1980s and 1990s, and software was made available for reading ebooks on these devices, but the screen sizes were typically small and the resolutions were relatively poor. In 1998, the first two dedicated ebook readers were released in Silicon Valley: the Rocket eBook, a paperback-size device that held 10 books, weighed a pound and cost $270, was released by Nuvomedia in Palo Alto; and the SoftBook, which held 250 books, weighed 3 pounds and cost around $600, was released by SoftBook Press in Menlo Park. While the devices were innovative and attracted a lot of attention, they sold poorly (less than 50,000 units between them). In 2000, both Nuvomedia and SoftBook Press were acquired by Gemstar, a large technology company that developed interactive programme guide technology for cable and satellite television providers. The Rocket eBook and the SoftBook were phased out and replaced in November 2000 by two versions of the new Gemstar eBook, one with a black and white screen and the other with colour, manufactured by RCA under licence to Gemstar. But, again, sales were disappointing, and in 2003 Gemstar stopped selling ebook readers and ebooks.

Numerous other reading devices appeared and disappeared in the late 1990s and early 2000s – enough to fill a small museum of now-defunct consumer technology. But the first real breakthrough came in April 2004 when Sony launched the Librié 1000-EP in Japan, which was the first reading device to use e-ink technology. Unlike backlit screens, e-ink uses reflected light to simulate the appearance of a printed page. The screen is filled with tiny capsules containing charged pigment; when the electrical charge applied to each capsule is adjusted, its appearance changes, thereby altering the display and producing a page of text. The screen holds that display until the charge is adjusted again to produce a new page of text. E-ink is much gentler on the eye than backlit screens and is easy to read in direct sunlight; it is also very economical in terms of battery use, since electricity is used only when the page is changed. The Sony Reader was launched in the US in October 2006, selling at around $350 and capable of holding 160 books, and ebooks could be purchased from Sony's own ebook library which offered up to 10,000 titles.

The Sony Reader was a major advance, but it was the Amazon Kindle, released a year later in November 2007, that was the real game-changer. Like the Sony Reader, the Kindle used e-ink technology rather than backlit screens; but, unlike Sony, Amazon used wireless 3G connectivity, free for the user, to enable readers to download ebooks directly from Amazon's Kindle Store. Readers could now buy ebooks directly from their reading device, without having to use their computer to go online to download the ebook and then transfer it to their reading device via a USB cable. Now, buying ebooks was as easy as a single click. The first Kindle retailed at $399 and was capable of holding 200 books, and the Kindle Store claimed to stock 90,000 titles, including most of the books on the *New York Times* bestseller list. When the Kindle was released on 19 November 2007, it sold out in five and a half hours and remained out of stock for five months – though what exactly that meant in terms of actual sales remains a mystery because Amazon never disclosed how many they produced. In 2009, Amazon released the Kindle 2, a slimmer version with much more internal memory, capable of holding around 1,500 books, and it reduced the price to under $300. (The development of the Kindle is examined in more detail in chapter 5 below.)

By late 2009, Amazon faced new competition from Barnes & Noble, which launched its own ebook reader, the Nook, in November 2009. Barnes & Noble had been an early entrant in the online marketplace for books, having created an online bookstore, barnesandnoble.com, in 1997, two years after Amazon went live, but barnesandnoble.com struggled to compete with its more creative and efficient rival; the launch of the Nook was Barnes & Noble's attempt to gain a foothold in the emerging ebook market and to compete head-to-head with the Kindle. Like the Kindle, the Nook used e-ink technology and wireless 3G connectivity to enable readers to buy ebooks directly from the Barnes & Noble store. The Nook retailed at $259 – the same price to which Amazon had reduced the Kindle 2 in October 2009. A year later, Barnes & Noble released the Nook Color, equipped with a 7-inch full-colour LCD touchscreen and priced at $249. Although Barnes & Noble was a relatively late entrant in the e-reader market-place, it had one important advantage that it exploited to the full: the company had over 700 retail bookstores across the US and it devoted prime space in many of these stores to exhibit, demo and hand-sell the Nook. And, like Amazon, Barnes & Noble already had a large and established customer base of readers who were accustomed to buying books from its stores.

When Apple finally entered the ebook market with the launch of the first iPad in April 2010, they were entering a market in which the two largest book retailers in the US, Amazon and Barnes & Noble, already had major stakes. What Apple did, however, was to integrate the ebook reading experience into the environment of an ultra-stylish, state-of-the-art, multi-purpose tablet computer with a high-resolution LCD touchscreen. Unlike the Kindle and the Nook, the iPad was not a dedicated reading device, but it offered users the option of reading ebooks by downloading an iBook app from the App Store, which displays ebooks and other content that can be purchased from Apple's iBookstore. The iPad proved hugely successful: 3 million devices were sold in the first eighty days, and by the time the iPad 2 was launched in March 2011, more than 15 million iPads had been sold worldwide. The iPad was much more expensive than the Kindle or the Nook (the initial models were selling for between $499 and $829, depending on the capacity and functionality), but this was much more than a reading device: with the iPad, books entered a new world in which reading was just one of the many things you can do on a small, portable computer, and where the potential for creating new kinds of content, capable of being read and consumed in new kinds of ways, far exceeded anything that had been possible on the Kindle, the Nook and other dedicated reading devices.

The appearance of a new generation of reading devices that were much more stylish and user-friendly than the ebook readers of the early 2000s, coupled with the aggressive promotion of ebooks by major booksellers with large and established clienteles, were the critical factors that underpinned the dramatic upsurge in ebook sales from 2008 on. This remarkable pattern of growth can be seen in table

Table 1.1   US ebook revenue for trade books, $ millions, 2008–2012

2008	69.1
2009	187.9
2010	502.7
2011	1095.1
2012	1543.6

Source: Association of American Publishers

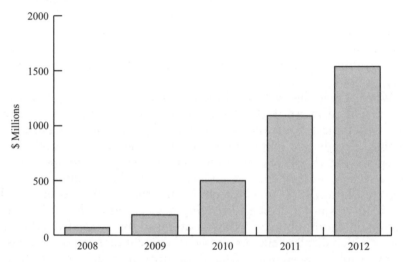

Figure 1.1   US ebook revenue for trade books, 2008–2012
Source: Association of American Publishers

1.1 and figure 1.1, which show overall ebook sales for trade books in the US between 2008 and 2012.[4] In the period up to 2006, ebook sales had remained very low and largely static – probably under $10 million. This was a tiny proportion, a small fraction of 1 per cent, of a sector in which total annual sales were around $18 billion. Ebook sales showed some growth in 2006 and 2007, thanks in part to the Sony Reader, but by the end of 2007 ebook sales were still well under $50 million. But from 2008 on, ebook sales began to increase dramatically, reaching $69 million in 2008 – the first full year of the Kindle – and jumping to $188 million in 2009, an increase of nearly 3-fold

[4] The data from the Association of American Publishers are based on primary data for around 1,200 publishers from 2011 onwards; data for 2008 to 2010 were adjusted to account for participant and definitional changes.

26

in one year. By 2012, ebook sales had reached over $1.5 billion, a 22-fold increase in just four years. This was dizzying growth.

For the large trade publishers in the US, the surge in ebook sales meant that a growing proportion of their revenue was being accounted for by ebooks rather than traditional print books, whether hardcover or paperback. Although the precise figures varied from house to house, the overall pattern of growth of ebook sales as a percentage of overall revenue during the period from 2006 to 2012 looked roughly like figure 1.2. For many large US trade publishers, ebooks accounted for around 0.1% of overall revenue in 2006 and 0.5% in 2007; in 2008, this grew to around 1%; in 2009, this was up to about 3%; by 2010, it had risen to around 8%; by 2011, it was around 17%; and by 2012, it had risen to between 20 and 25%, depending on the publisher and the nature of their list. It was no longer a negligible figure – far from it.

The steep rise in ebook sales in the four years from 2008 to 2012 was dramatic and unsettling for many in the industry: after several years during which the much-heralded ebook revolution seemed like a false dawn, suddenly it was an uncontestable reality. Moreover, given the staggering rate of growth, there was no telling where this would end. It's not hard to see that, if you were a publisher watching this take place around you in 2010, 2011 and 2012, you really would be wondering what was going to happen to your industry. You might even be panicking. You would almost certainly be wondering if publishing was going to go the same way as the music industry. Would ebook sales keep growing at this dramatic rate and become 40 or 50 per cent of your business, maybe even 80 or 90 per cent, in a few years' time? Were books heading in the same direction as CDs and vinyl LPs – on a precipitous downward slope and likely to be eclipsed by digital downloads? Was this the beginning of the end of the physical book? These were the questions in the minds of most people in the industry at the time – they were seriously worried, and understandably so.

But then something equally dramatic happened: the growth suddenly stopped. It levelled off in 2013 and 2014 and then began to decline. No one at the time had expected this – even the most unswayable sceptics were surprised by this sudden reversal of fortune. In 2013, ebook sales did not continue their meteoric rise but actually fell slightly – from $1,543 million in 2012 to $1,510 million in 2013, a decline of 2.1%, as shown in table 1.3 and figure 1.3. Ebooks showed a small increase in 2014 and then fell more sharply in 2015, down to $1,360 million, a decline of 15%, which was matched

Table 1.2   Ebook sales as a percentage of total revenues of major US trade publishers, 2006–2012

2006	0.1
2007	0.5
2008	1.1
2009	2.9
2010	7.6
2011	17.3
2012	23.2

Source: Association of American Publishers

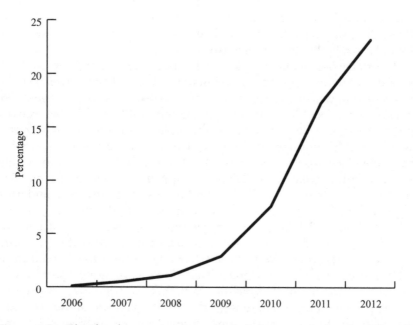

Figure 1.2   Ebook sales as a percentage of total revenues of major US trade publishers, 2006–2012
Source: Association of American Publishers

by a similar decline in the following year. Figure 1.3 also shows the rate of growth from one year to the next. It shows that the rate of growth was extremely high in 2009 and 2010, around 170% each year, but then the rate of growth began a steep decline until it reached a number just below zero in 2013. After a small increase in 2014, the rate of growth remained negative from 2015 to 2018.

Table 1.3   US ebook revenue for trade books and rate of growth of ebook sales, 2008–2018

	Revenue ($ millions)	Rate of growth (%)
2008	69.1	
2009	187.9	171.9
2010	502.7	167.5
2011	1095.1	117.8
2012	1543.6	41
2013	1510.9	−2.1
2014	1601.1	6
2015	1360.5	−15
2016	1157.7	−15
2017	1054.3	−8.9
2018	1016.1	−3.6

Source: Association of American Publishers

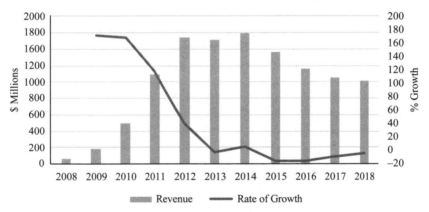

Figure 1.3   US ebook revenue for trade books and rate of growth of ebook sales, 2008–2018
Source: Association of American Publishers

If we then look at print books and ebooks as percentages of total sales (table 1.4 and figure 1.4), we can see that ebooks level off at 23–24% in 2012, 2013 and 2014 and then begin to decline, falling to around 15% in 2017 and 2018. Print books, on the other hand, continue to account for the lion's share of sales, falling to around 75% of total sales in 2012, 2013 and 2014 but then rebounding, rising to between 80 and 85% from 2015 to 2018.

Table 1.4   Print books and ebooks as percentages of total US trade sales

	Print books	Ebooks
2008	98.9	1.1
2009	97.1	2.9
2010	92.4	7.6
2011	82.7	17.3
2012	76.8	23.2
2013	76.6	23.4
2014	75.9	24.1
2015	79.3	20.7
2016	83.2	16.8
2017	84.3	15.7
2018	85.3	14.7

Source: Association of American Publishers

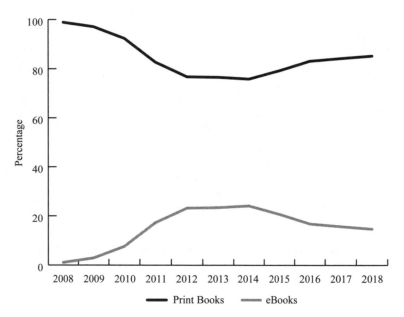

Figure 1.4   Print books and ebooks as percentages of total US trade sales
Source: Association of American Publishers

And if we then extract the ebook percentages and reformat the vertical scale of this graph (figure 1.5), we can see that the growth of ebooks during this period displays the pattern of the classic technology S-curve: adoption is slow at the beginning, it then takes

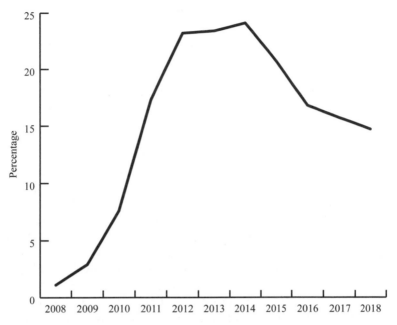

Figure 1.5   Ebooks as percentage of total US trade sales, 2008–2018
Source: Association of American Publishers

off and grows rapidly when there is a breakthrough of some kind, and then levels off when the market has been saturated or the limits of performance have been reached. In some cases, the S-curve may decline after this point as the technology no longer improves, alternative technologies appear that steal market share, novelty fades or demand wanes for other reasons. In the case of ebooks, the take-off occurred in 2008–9, following the introduction of the Kindle, and sales rose steeply until 2012 when they levelled off and then fell back.

Of course, this does not mean that ebook sales in US trade publishing will remain at around 15 per cent in the future, or will continue to decline, or will never rise above this level – we simply don't know what will happen in the future. But, with the benefit of hindsight, we can now see that the dramatic growth that followed the introduction of the Kindle in November 2007 was short-lived, and it came to an abrupt halt in 2012. While the future is unpredictable, it would be a bold soul who, knowing what we now know, suggested that mainstream trade publishers were likely to experience a strong resurgence of ebook sales in the near future – the numbers could fluctuate from year to year, affected by various factors, but, given the evidence to date, a strong and sustained resurgence seems unlikely.

The differentiated pattern of ebook sales: delving beneath the surface

The issues are more complicated than they appear at first sight, however. While the S-curve gives a neat picture of the overall trend, it is misleading because it collapses all the different kinds of books into one average number. We shouldn't assume that different kinds of books perform in the same way – they don't. The extent to which books have migrated from print to digital formats has varied enormously from one kind of book to another. We can see this by looking at some sales data from a large US trade publisher that I'll call 'Olympic'. Table 1.5 and figures 1.6a and 1.6b give a breakdown of ebook sales as a percentage of total sales at Olympic from 2006 to 2016. All data are based on net units and net sales – that is, sales net of any returns. We should not assume that these data are represent-ative of the industry as a whole, or that the experiences of all trade publishers will have been identical to this one – the data from each publishing house will be unique and will reflect to some extent the specific titles they've published. But Olympic is a mainstream trade publisher with a large and varied list, and the occasional truly excep-tional title has been stripped out of the data to minimize the distorting

Table 1.5 Ebooks as a percentage of total sales at Olympic, units and dollars

	Ebooks units	Ebooks $
2006	0.1	0.1
2007	0.1	0.1
2008	0.5	0.5
2009	1.9	2.6
2010	6.2	8.6
2011	16.4	19.5
2012	22.2	25.9
2013	20.7	23.8
2014	19.8	23.7
2015	19.7	22.6
2016	16.4	17.1

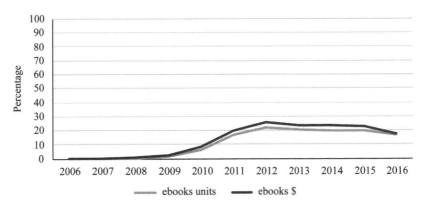

Figure 1.6a   Ebooks as a percentage of total sales at Olympic, units and dollars

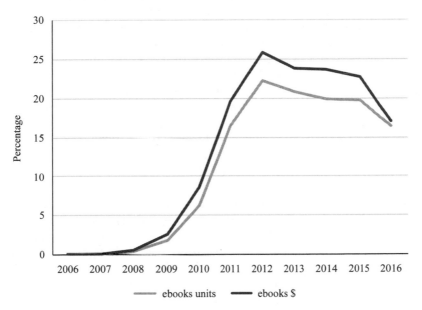

Figure 1.6b   Ebooks as a percentage of total sales at Olympic, units and dollars

effect of outliers. So while the experiences of each publisher will be unique, it is unlikely that the sales patterns of other major trade houses will differ radically from the patterns experienced by Olympic.

There is another important qualification to make about these data: they are for the period 2006–16 only and we cannot extrapolate, on the basis of these data, to the sales patterns for 2017 and subsequent years. Future patterns could change. I'll return to this issue below. But, for now, let's focus on what actually happened in the crucial decade from 2006 to 2016.

Table 1.5 and figure 1.6a show all ebooks as a percentage of Olympic's total sales by both units and revenue. We see that Olympic's ebook sales were negligible in 2006 and 2007 but they began to grow rapidly from 2008 on, reaching a peak in 2012, when ebook sales accounted for just under 26% of Olympic's total revenue. From that point on, ebook sales began to decline as a proportion of total sales, falling to below 23% in 2015 and then down to 17% in 2016. The pattern is very similar for both units and revenue, as one would expect. The levelling off in ebook sales is more vividly displayed when we change the scale of the y-axis on the graph, as in figure 1.6b: here, again, we see that the pattern of ebook sales at Olympic displays the classic technology S-curve.

However, looking at all ebooks as a percentage of total sales gives us a very partial view of what has happened because it masks the variations between different categories of books. In the early 2000s, before ebooks began to take off, many commentators assumed that when the ebook revolution began, it would be driven primarily by businessmen who wanted to carry business books with them on their business trips, reading at airports and on planes: it was adult nonfiction, and especially business books and 'big idea' books, that would, they thought, spearhead the ebook revolution. Were they right? Is that what actually happened?

Table 1.6 and figure 1.7 break down ebooks into three broad categories: adult fiction, adult nonfiction and juvenile (where juvenile includes all children's books as well as young adult). The figure shows ebooks as a percentage of Olympic's total sales, by both revenue and units, in each of these broad categories. (As with figure 1.6b, the y-axis has been adjusted to display the S-curve.) It is immediately clear that the category where the biggest change has occurred is not nonfiction but, rather, adult fiction: in terms of revenue, ebooks as a percentage of total revenue in adult fiction increased from 1.0% in 2008 to 43.4% in 2014, before falling back to 37.4% in 2015 and then rebounding slightly to 38.9% in 2016. This contrasts sharply with adult nonfiction, where ebooks as a percentage of total revenue rose from 0.4% in 2008 to 16.6% in 2015, before falling back to 13.2% in 2016 – remaining well below 20% throughout this period. Juvenile lagged even further behind: here ebooks as a percentage of total revenue increased from 0.1% in 2008 to 12.2% in 2014, before

Table 1.6   Ebooks as a percentage of total sales by broad category at Olympic, units and dollars

	Adult Fiction units	Adult Fiction $	Adult NF units	Adult NF $	Juv units	Juv $
2006	0.2	0.1	0.1	0.1	0	0
2007	0.2	0.2	0.1	0.1	0	0
2008	0.9	1	0.4	0.4	0.1	0.1
2009	4	4.7	1.5	1.8	0.2	0.4
2010	12.6	14.3	4.4	4.9	0.9	1.4
2011	29.1	30.4	12.2	12.6	3.5	5.3
2012	37.2	38.2	15.9	15	5	8.4
2013	40.9	40.2	16	15.3	5.9	9.2
2014	42.6	43.4	16.6	15.8	7.5	12.2
2015	40.6	37.4	18.2	16.6	4	7.4
2016	35	38.9	16.4	13.2	6	6

falling back to 7.4% in 2015 and 6% in 2016.[5] Each broad category displays an S-curve but the shape of the curve is different in each case. Adult fiction nearly reaches 45% before it levels off and starts to decline, adult nonfiction levels off at around 15% and, in the case of juvenile, the ebooks peak at around 12% and then fall off. Both adult fiction and juvenile show a sharp downturn in 2015, while adult nonfiction continues to grow very modestly before falling off in 2016.

---

[5] In juvenile and some categories of adult books such as mystery and science fiction, there is a significant gap between the percentages for revenue and for units, where ebook sales in dollars account for a higher percentage of total sales than ebook sales in units. This might seem counter-intuitive, in so far as ebooks are generally priced lower than print books, and hence one might expect that percentages for net dollars would, if anything, be lower than percentages for net units. So what explains this seemingly counter-intuitive discrepancy? The explanation lies in the technical details of the settlement agreement imposed on publishers by the Department of Justice in the wake of the price-fixing suit (see chapter 5). The settlement banned the publishers concerned from using the agency model for two years, but allowed them to use a pricing model – dubbed 'Agency Lite' – which is similar to agency but which allows the retailer to discount titles, provided that the total amount of discount is not less than their cost for the publisher's entire catalogue over a one-year period. What this meant in practice is that retailers could discount specific titles, and they did so very heavily in some cases, e.g. selling ebooks for certain bestselling titles as low as $2.99. At various peak times – holiday seasons, the release of a new movie, etc. – one retailer might fund a special promotion by dropping the price and other retailers would follow. This was particularly common in certain categories of books, such as juvenile, mystery and sci-fi. Millions of ebooks were sold at very low prices, but under the terms of Agency Lite, the publisher was paid on full list price. Hence, Agency Lite tended to inflate the dollar percentages of ebook sales.

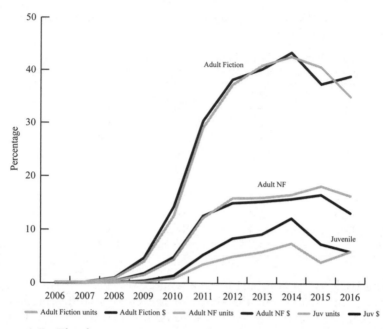

Figure 1.7 Ebooks as a percentage of total sales by broad category at Olympic, units and dollars

We are still working with very broad categories, however. Let's drill down a little further and examine the patterns for different categories of books, using a selected number of standard BISAC subject headings.[6] Figures 1.8 and 1.9 break down ebooks as a percentage of total sales by subject at Olympic (for the data on which these figures are based, see appendix 1). Figure 1.8 is net dollars and Figure 1.9 is net units. (Again, the y-axis has been adjusted to display the S-curves.) These graphs vividly display the enormous variation in the uptake of ebooks across different categories of books, and underscore how misleading it is to collapse all of these categories into the single category of 'ebook'. We see the huge spectrum of trajectories here, with each category of book displaying its own distinctive S-curve. Each S-curve rises in its own unique way and begins to level off at a point and in a manner that is specific to that category. In some cases,

---

[6] BISAC subject headings, also known as BISAC subject codes, are produced by BISG, the Book Industry Study Group, and used by many companies in the book supply chain to categorize books based on their subject matter. The full list of subject headings can be found at www.bisg.org/bisac-subject-codes.

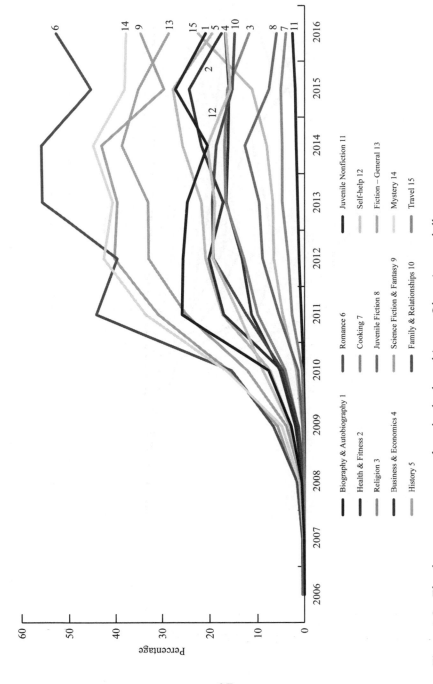

Figure 1.8   Ebooks as a percentage of total sales by subject at Olympic, net dollars

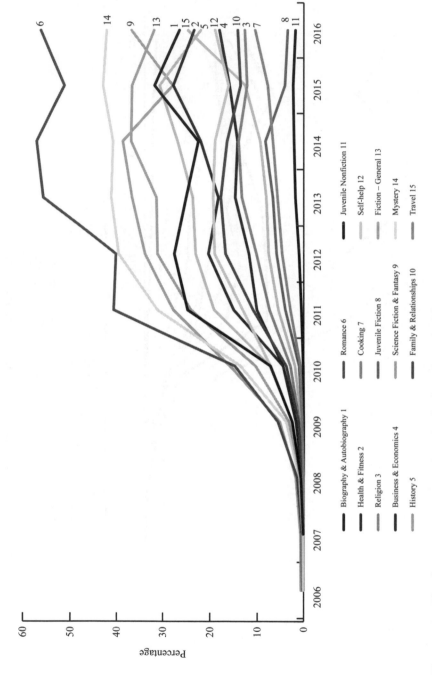

Figure 1.9 Ebooks as a percentage of total sales by subject at Olympic, net units

Biography & Autobiography 1
Health & Fitness 2
Religion 3
Business & Economics 4
History 5

Romance 6
Cooking 7
Juvenile Fiction 8
Science Fiction & Fantasy 9
Family & Relationships 10

Juvenile Nonfiction 11
Self-help 12
Fiction – General 13
Mystery 14
Travel 15

38

the growth plateaus and then stabilizes more or less at that level; in some cases, it plateaus and then begins to decline; in some cases, the growth levels off and declines and then shoots back up; and in other cases, the growth never takes off at all. We also see a lot of movement up and down – the lines jump about, dips are followed by rises and rises are followed by dips as the numbers for each category fluctuate from one year to the next. There's nothing too surprising about that: these graphs are based on sales figures from one large trade house which has a limited number of books in any one category in any one year, so one or two books selling strongly as ebooks (or other special circumstances, like the disposal or acquisition of an imprint) can produce an ebook spike or dip in that category. The sales figures from one publisher – even a large publisher like Olympic – will display idiosyncrasies of this kind and therefore cannot be taken as a proxy for the industry as a whole. But by focusing on the broad patterns and trends rather than the fluctuations from one year to the next, we can get a good sense of how different categories of books have performed over time.

As these data make clear, the top-performing category in terms of ebook uptake is not business books after all, it is romance fiction – this outperforms every other category by a significant margin. Here we see steep growth from 2008 to 2011, by which time ebooks were accounting for 44.2% of all Olympic's sales of romance books. Ebook sales dipped the following year but then rose again, accounting for around 55% of all romance sales in 2013 and 2014. In 2015 they fell back to 45% but then rebounded in 2016, when they once again amounted to around 53% of all Olympic's sales of romance books. Of all the different categories of books published by Olympic, romance is the one where ebooks have accounted for the highest proportion of overall sales – more than half – and it's a category where ebook sales remain high despite the downturn in other categories.

At the other end of the scale, juvenile nonfiction has seen very low levels of ebook uptake. The line for this category is flat and hardly rises off the floor of the graph – ebooks accounted for only 2% of Olympic's revenue in the category of juvenile nonfiction in 2015, rising slightly to 2.6% in 2016. Here we don't see an S-curve because there has not yet been any perceptible take off in terms of ebook sales in this category of books: 97% of the revenue in 2016 was still being generated by printed books.

Between romance at the top and juvenile nonfiction at the bottom there is a huge range and variation in terms of ebook uptake – each category leaves its own distinctive footprint. But while the trajectories are all unique, the lines band together in certain groups. The top four lines all represent categories of fiction, and the top three lines are all genre fiction categories – romance at the top, followed by mystery and detective fiction, and then sci-fi and fantasy. General fiction is among this set of categories in which ebooks perform strongly, although the line for general fiction is below the genre fiction lines.[7] Ebook sales in all four categories show a steep rise between 2008 and 2012, reaching levels that are much higher than with other categories of books. While romance plateaus at around 55% and then fluctuates after that, the other three fiction categories plateau at between 30 and 40%. Most of these categories display some modest decline after the peak period of 2012–14, though ebook sales of romance titles at Olympic experienced a new upsurge in 2016.

The next band of lines in the middle of the graphs all represent nonfiction categories – biography and autobiography, history, business and economics, family and relationships, health and fitness, religion, self-help. Once again, all of these lines rise steeply in the period between 2008 and 2011 and then begin to level off, though at lower levels than the fiction categories. Biography and autobiography and history continued to edge upwards after 2011, reaching 27% in 2015, and then fell sharply after that. Health and fitness reached 24% in 2015 and then began to fall. Other nonfiction categories like business and economics, family and relationships, religion and self-help reached plateaus of between 15 and 20%, and either stabilized at that level or began to fall off. So, between 2011 and 2015, all of these nonfiction categories appear to have plateaued somewhere between 16 and 27% – or, to put it more roughly, between 15 and 25%, with biography and autobiography and history at the top of this band.

At the bottom of the graphs is another set of categories where ebooks have so far failed to take off in any significant way and, by 2016, they still accounted for only a small proportion of overall revenue. Here we find cooking, where ebooks never rose above 5% of sales, juvenile nonfiction, where ebook sales never rose above 3% of sales, and juvenile fiction, where ebooks rose to 12.7% in

---

[7] Here, 'general fiction' includes all the categories of fiction *except* mystery, romance, sci-fi and fantasy, which are broken out separately. So 'general fiction' includes the BISAC categories Literary Fiction, General Fiction, Historical Fiction, etc. – there are dozens of categories; the only categories it doesn't include are Mystery, Romance, Science Fiction and Fantasy.

2014 and then fell back to 6% in 2016.[8] Travel also belongs in this band: ebook sales in travel never took off at Olympic, generally remaining below 12% of total sales, and the spike in 2016 was an anomaly accounted for by particular circumstances at the time. Given that ebooks have not taken off in any significant way in these categories (excluding young adult), the growth lines since 2008 don't display the pattern of the classic S-curve: they look more like flat lines with gentle inclines that tilt upwards (and occasionally downwards).

Explaining the variations

The data from Olympic make it very clear that there are enormous variations in the uptake of ebooks across different categories of books, and data from other large trade houses would almost certainly display similar patterns – they would not be identical, but the overall patterns would be broadly similar. How can we explain these differences? Why do some categories display much higher percentages of ebook sales relative to total sales, and higher e/p ratios (that is, ebook sales relative to print sales), than other categories?

We can't explain the differences in terms of the factors that are commonly associated with ebooks – namely, the convenience of being able to purchase ebooks quickly, easily, any time and any place; the convenience of being able to carry multiple ebooks with you wherever you go – indeed, to carry a small library that has no more weight and bulk than a small paperback; the convenience of being able to vary the size of the typeface; and, of course, the price – the fact that ebooks are generally cheaper than print books (though how much cheaper depends on many factors, as we shall see in a later chapter). These factors don't explain the differences because they are common to all ebooks – a travel book or cookbook is just as easy to purchase and just as lightweight in ebook format as a romance or a thriller. So the explanation must lie elsewhere.

---

[8] With juvenile fiction, it is important to note that this category includes both children's books and young adult fiction, and these two sub-categories display very different patterns. If you separated juvenile fiction into young adult and non-young-adult, non-young-adult would be much lower – under 5% – while young adult would be somewhere in the 20s. Young adult fiction behaves a bit more like general fiction for adults – indeed, some books that are categorized as young adult, such as Stephanie Meyer's 'Twilight' series and the *Hunger Games* trilogy, are likely to be read by readers of different ages, including many adults.

The most striking difference between the categories that sell well as ebooks and those that don't is that the former consist of narrative linear text and the latter do not. A romance or a thriller is straight narrative text: you generally start reading on p. 1 and read continuously until you reach the end (or until you give up). The text is structured as a story with a plot that unfolds sequentially, one step at a time, and the reader follows the sequence. By contrast, a cookbook or a travel book or a practical how-to book is not a book that is generally read from beginning to end. It is more like a reference work that is used for particular purposes – to get a particular recipe, to find information about a city or a country you are planning to visit, to accomplish some practical task. These are very different kinds of books that are read, used and/or consulted in very different ways.

We can understand why this matters in terms of the level of ebook uptake by linking it to the user experience. From the viewpoint of the user, reading narrative linear text on an e-reading device like a Kindle is generally a good experience: you can move easily and swiftly from one page to the next, the text flows smoothly and you, the reader, flow with it from beginning to end. This works particularly well for genre fiction: it's a fast, immersive read and there is nothing in the device itself, and in the way that the text is presented on the screen, that would obstruct you or slow you down as you follow the plot and move towards the denouement. As those in the business say, the 'form factor' is good, where 'form factor' refers here to the quality of the experience of reading a particular book on a particular device. The experience of reading genre fiction on an e-reading device like a Kindle is probably as good as – maybe even better than, given the ability to change the type size, etc. – the experience of reading the same text on paper.

However, with non-linear texts that may be more practical in character and/or heavily illustrated, the form factor is nowhere near as good. These non-linear texts are not necessarily meant to be read from beginning to end. They may not tell a story that the reader follows, page by page, in a sequential fashion. A non-linear text like a cookbook or a travel book or a practical how-to book may require the reader or user to jump back and forth, getting the information they need and then perhaps dipping in at another point in the text. They might be used more as a reference work that the reader returns to time and again, possibly to the same place or to another part of the text. For non-linear texts of this kind, the experience of reading or using them on an e-reading device like a Kindle is much less appealing than it is with straight linear texts. And if you then add illustrations, the appeal is likely to diminish still further, especially for readers who have e-reading devices that use black and white e-ink technology, like the Kindle.

To say that the form factor for non-linear texts is nowhere near as good as it is for linear texts is not to say that it never will be as good. Someday it might be – indeed, it might be already with some devices and some forms of content. For example, using a custom-built app developed for the iPad can be an exemplary user experience for certain kinds of content. The app format allows for a navigation experience that is non-linear in character: you can dip in and move around using a customized user interface. It also allows for high-resolution colour illustrations, high-quality sound and a much higher level of interactivity – it can be an altogether different kind of user experience from the reading of straight linear text. But creating content of this kind involves challenges and problems of its own and it is by no means clear at this stage whether, and to what extent, it is a viable undertaking. These are issues to which we shall return in the next chapter.

Another factor that is important for explaining the different levels of ebook uptake is what I'll call the 'possession value' of the content. What I mean by this is that some books are the kinds of books that a reader wants to have in order to consume the content, and once the content has been consumed the book itself is redundant: the reader has no particular desire to hold on to the book for the sake of it. Jane, a senior trade publisher, described this as 'disposable fiction' – the kind of book that 'you don't need to put on your shelf'. On the other hand, there are some books that readers want to own, keep, put on their shelf, return to at a later date, perhaps even display in their living room as a signifier, a symbolic token of who they are and the kinds of books they like and value (or would like others to think that they like and value). These books have a much higher possession value for the reader. For books with a low possession value, the ebook is ideal: once the content has been consumed, the ebook can be deleted – or simply kept in a digital collection where it takes up no physical space, only a small amount of memory. For books with a high possession value, however, the printed book is much more attractive. Printed books have a kind of permanence that digital files lack: file formats and reading devices change with time, but a printed book can be read again at a future date regardless of whether technologies change; printed books can be shared, lent or given to others without restrictions; they can be displayed on a table or a shelf for others to see and pick up and admire; and they have a set of aesthetic traits – a beautiful cover, a well-designed interior, a sensuous materiality – that constitute the printed book as something more than simply a conveyor of content, that constitute it as an aesthetic object that is valued both for its content and for the material form in which that content is conveyed. 'So the real question is going to be: which books do you need to *own* and which ones can you simply *delete*', continued Jane; 'and the real trick is going to be figuring out the distinction between the disposable books and the ones you want to keep on your shelf.' Each reader will figure this out in his or her own way depending on a variety of factors that will affect individuals in different ways, from the extent to which they value certain books as signifiers to the amount of shelf space they have in their office, study or home.

Technology is also an important factor in explaining the different levels of ebook uptake. The categories of books that have high e/p ratios are categories where it is easy and relatively cheap to produce digital files for different devices and upload them into the relevant vendor systems. Older backlist titles can be converted relatively easily and cheaply by sending a hard copy to a third party who will scan the text and turn it into an XML file using OCR (Optical Character Recognition) software – the whole process would cost under $200 for a book of 300 pages or less. In the case of new titles, most publishing houses now have a digital workflow that generates multiple file formats as standard outputs of the production process: ebooks are just another set of files that are stored alongside the PDFs and other files that are held by publishers and used by printers to print physical books. Once the systems are in place, it is very inexpensive to produce the ebook files as additional outputs of the production process. In the case of some non-linear and heavily illustrated books, however, it may be much more complicated and costly to produce the kind of digital version that makes for a positive user experience. It may be necessary to go back to the drawing board and recreate the book as a different kind of digital experience – for example, as an app that is organized in an altogether different way. This is not easy to do and success is by no means guaranteed, and this by itself has impeded the process of making available certain categories of books in suitable digital formats.

Figure 1.10 summarizes the main features of what we could call 'the ebook uptake model'. According to this model, there are four key factors that explain the variations in the uptake of ebooks across different categories of books: textual character, user experience (or form factor), possession value and technology. Taken together, these

Feature	High e/p ratio	Low e/p ratio
Textual character	Narrative linear text	Non-linear Heavy illustrated
User experience ('form factor')	Fast read Continuous read Immersive reading experience	Slow read Discontinous read Reference use
Possession value	High turnover Disposable	Low turnover Keep, reuse/reread, display
Technology	Easy and relatively cheap to produce digital files in suitable formats and upload to vendor systems	More complicated and costly to produce; may require specialist production teams and processes

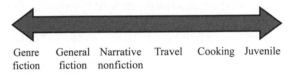

| Genre
fiction | General
fiction | Narrative
nonfiction | Travel | Cooking | Juvenile |

Figure 1.10   The ebook uptake model

four factors generate a spectrum of possibilities. At one end of the spectrum is fiction – both genre fiction (romance, mystery, sci-fi, etc.) and general fiction. Genre fiction displayed the most rapid and dramatic shift to digital. Books in these categories are characterized by narrative linear text; they are read quickly and continuously in an immersive reading experience where the e-reading form factor is good; there is a high turnover or consumption rate and the books are often not kept after they are read (or not kept as physical copies); and the digital files are easy and cheap to produce. These are the categories of books where ebooks as a percentage of total sales reached the highest levels at Olympic – between 40 and 60 per cent by 2014, although most have levelled off at between 30 and 40 per cent, with the exception of romance, which remains significantly higher, in the 50–60 per cent range.

In the case of general fiction, the switch to digital was not quite so rapid and dramatic as it was with genre fiction, but it wasn't far behind, and by 2014 the ebook percentage for general fiction at Olympic was very similar to that for sci-fi and fantasy and mystery, although still well below romance. The kinds of books that are included in the category of general fiction share many of the properties of genre fiction. As narrative linear text that is read continuously in an immersive reading experience, these books are easy to read on e-reading devices like the Kindle – the form factor is good. The digital files are also easy and cheap to produce. The one thing that might differentiate some forms of general fiction, like literary fiction, from genre fiction is their possession value. For some readers, literary fiction, and certain books and authors, may have more possession value than genre fiction has – that is, they may be more inclined to want to own these books, and to own books by these authors, and to keep them on their shelves, partly as a way of signalling who they are and of displaying their cultural tastes. They may also be more inclined to give these books as gifts, which is another way of showing their possession value, since a gift is an object that you think someone else might wish to possess, and a physical book functions as a gift in a way that an ebook does not – ebooks make terrible gifts. These factors help to explain why general fiction, which includes literary fiction, is a category where the shift to ebooks has been a little slower than it has been for genre fiction and where the percentage reached in 2015 – 38.7 per cent – was still well below romance.

At the other end of the spectrum are travel books, cookbooks and juvenile books. Books in these categories tend to be non-linear and/or heavily illustrated. They are commonly read more slowly and often discontinuously – in many cases, they are not read in a linear fashion, from beginning to end, but are used more like a reference book that you return to time and again. Turnover is low and the book may be re-used, re-read or consulted again at a later date. In the case of some heavily illustrated books, it may also be displayed on a shelf or a coffee table. Unlike straight narrative text, it is often more difficult and more costly to make the content of these books available in digital formats that are attractive and easy to use. These are the categories of books where ebooks as a percentage of total sales remain at the lowest levels – below 12 per cent for Olympic (excluding the anomalous figures for travel books in 2016).

Between these two extremes are the categories of narrative nonfiction. The label 'narrative nonfiction' is a loose notion that includes a diverse range of BISAC nonfiction subject headings, from history, biography and autobiography to health and fitness, religion and self-help. We should not expect all of these categories to display the same ebook pattern, and they don't. Those categories that are made up of books that are mainly narrative linear text, like biographies, autobiographies and works of narrative history, would be expected to display a higher level of ebook uptake, and this is indeed the case – the speed of ebook uptake was slower for narrative nonfiction than it was for fiction, but by 2015 the percentages for biography/autobiography and history at Olympic were only 5–10 per cent below the percentages for some categories of fiction, including general fiction and sci-fi. It is likely that 'big ideas' books, like the books of Malcolm Gladwell or Jaron Lanier, will also display a relatively high level of ebook uptake since they consist mainly of straight narrative text, although they don't fit neatly into the BISAC categories analysed above. On the other hand, books that are more like reference works that might be read discontinuously and consulted from time to time, such as self-help and family and relationships books, would be expected to display a lower level of ebook uptake – and, again, this is what we find. In most cases, however, narrative nonfiction books display lower levels of ebook uptake than narrative fiction – both genre fiction and general fiction. This can be explained by the fact that the categories of genre fiction and general fiction will contain a higher proportion of books that are: (a) likely to display the character of pure narrative text, without illustrations; (b) likely to be read quickly and continuously in an immersive reading experience; and (c) likely to be turned over quickly as the reader moves on to a new reading experience. The categories of narrative nonfiction, by comparison, will contain a higher proportion of books that are likely to contain illustrations, to be read more slowly and discontinuously as the reader moves back and forth in the text, and to have a lower turnover rate, since the reader may want to hold on to the book with a view to returning to it at some later point in time.

It is worth dwelling for a moment on business and economic books in relation to other categories. As I noted earlier, many commentators in the early 2000s predicted that, when the ebook revolution came, it would be driven primarily by businessmen reading business books on their digital devices – the tech-savvy international jet-setters using spare moments at airports to keep up with the latest literature on business trends. In practice, business and economics books have performed very modestly when it comes to ebook uptake – relatively slow to take off, rising to 20 per cent by 2014 and then falling back to 15 per cent in 2015. This is well below the levels reached by fiction and other categories of narrative nonfiction, like biography/autobiography and history – the commentators in the early 2000s were wide of the mark. When ebooks did eventually take off, the dramatic growth was driven less by businessmen reading business books in airport lounges and more by women reading romance novels on their Kindles (most romance readers are women). Viewed through the lens of the model developed here, the relatively low ebook uptake of business books is not surprising. Many business and economics books are not the kind of books that you would typically read quickly and continuously in an immersive reading experience: they are more likely to be books that you would read more slowly and even discontinuously, where you may want to move back and forth in the text in order to remind yourself of information provided or points made earlier in the text. They are also books that you may want to come back to at a later point, consult again and use more like a reference work than a book that could be quickly read and then discarded. These features would suggest that business and economics books would perform more like self-help books and family and relationship books than fiction, and this is indeed what has happened.

Form vs format

What, if anything, does the experience of ebook sales since 2008 tell us about the likely impact of the digital revolution on the *form* of the book? Does it suggest that the digital revolution, by separating the symbolic content of the book from the print-on-paper medium in which it was traditionally embedded, has liberated the book from the constraints that were imposed on it by the medium of print and paved the way for a thorough re-invention of the book as a textual entity that displays very different characteristics from the entity we have come to know as 'the book'? In the late 1990s and early 2000s, there were many who speculated that the book would be re-invented in this way, that the very form of the book – that is, the way in which the text was organized, typically as a work of a certain length arranged as a sequence of chapters, etc. – could be and would be radically reworked in the digital age when the constraints imposed by the medium of print would fall away. One well-known example of this kind of thinking is Robert Darnton's pyramid model of the scholarly book: a book no longer written as a straight linear text but constructed in multiple layers where the linear text is merely the top layer of a complex digital architecture that contains many more layers, enabling the reader to tack back and forth between a summary account on the surface and rich layers of documentation and illustrative material in the layers below.[9] There are many examples in the world of trade publishing too: the digital book conceived of no longer as a capsule of content that can be embedded in a physical form of 200 or 300 pages of printed text, but rather as a book that exists entirely and exclusively in the digital medium, a book that is born digital and exists digitally *sui generis*. It may never have a physical equivalent, or, if it does, the physical book may be but a partial and subsequent realization, in print-on-paper, of content that was conceived of in relation to, and created for, a digital medium.

In the next chapter, we'll look in detail at some of the attempts that have been made in the world of trade publishing to re-invent the book as a digital entity and examine what came of them, but here I want to reflect on what we can learn from the pattern of ebook sales at mainstream trade publishers from 2008 to the present: does this pattern suggest that the *form* of the book is being re-invented in the digital medium? Or does it suggest that the digital medium has provided publishers with just another *format* in which the book, which remains largely unchanged in terms of its organizational features, can be packaged and made available to readers?

My view is that what we have witnessed so far is not so much the invention of a new form of the book, as some of the more radical proponents of the ebook revolution promised, but rather the creation of a new format for the book, which, in terms of its basic organizational features, has remained largely unchanged by the digital revolution. The creation of a new format is certainly not insignificant and it has major implications for the book publishing industry and the many players within it. But it is nowhere near as disruptive as it might have been – or could conceivably still be – if the very form of the book were being re-invented. Let's explore this distinction a little further.

By the 'form' of the book, I mean the way that the symbolic content that makes up the book is structured – e.g., as a sequence of chapters organized in a certain way, extended in length, etc. The 'format' of the book is the way that the book is packaged and presented to readers; the same book, structured in the same way, can be packaged and presented in multiple different formats

---

[9] Robert Darnton, 'A Historian of Books, Lost and Found in Cyberspace', *Chronicle of Higher Education*, 12 March 1999; Robert Darnton, 'The New Age of the Book', *New York Review of Books*, 18 March 1999. Both are reprinted in Robert Darnton, *The Case for Books: Past, Present, and Future* (New York: Public Affairs, 2009).

without altering its form. (I elaborate this distinction in more detail in chapter 12.) To say that the digital revolution so far has created a new format for the book but has not changed its form is to say that, for the most part, books remain structured in the same way as they were prior to the digital revolution, but that they are now being packaged and presented to readers in new ways: that is, in a new format – the ebook.

The history of book publishing has been characterized repeatedly by the invention of new formats (or the relaunching of formats previously invented). The classic example of this was Allen Lane's launching of a new series of cheap sixpenny paperbacks in the 1930s. These were books previously published by other publishers as hardbacks – typically at 7s 6d for a novel, and 12s 6d for a biography or history book – licensed by Allen Lane and reissued in a cheap paperback edition, priced at a mere sixpence, as part of a new series with a distinctive and recognizable brand: Penguin. The paperback itself, as a physical object, was not invented by Lane – paperback books had existed in the late nineteenth century and before, though they were generally regarded as 'a lower form of life'.[10] Part of Lane's genius was to rebrand the paperback as a stylish new format that occupied a legitimate and valued position in the marketplace and in the life-cycle of the book. 'We aimed at making something pretty smart, a product clean and as bright as two pins, modern enough not to offend the fastidious high-brow, and yet straightforward and unpretentious', reflected Lane.[11] He had sensed an emerging market – an expanding middle class with a degree of disposable income and an interest in reading good books if they were priced affordably – and he created a new and effective way of repackaging books to serve this market.

Not that it was all plain sailing. Lane faced much resistance at the time, especially from publishers and booksellers who felt that pricing books so cheaply would only result in people spending less money on books. 'Nobody can live off sixpenny books', remarked Charles Evans of Heinemann. 'Nobody makes any money out of them except the Penguin publishers and possibly their printers.'[12] Evans refused to license Enid Bagnold's bestselling novel *National Velvet* to Penguin, despite repeated pleas by the author. But over time the inexpensive

---

[10] Jeremy Lewis, *Penguin Special: The Life and Times of Allen Lane* (London: Penguin, 2005), p. 74.
[11] Quoted in ibid., p. 96.
[12] Quoted in ibid., p. 94.

paperback edition championed by Allen Lane and epitomized by Penguin would establish itself as a legitimate format – that is, as another way in which the same content can be repackaged, re-priced and delivered to the consumer.

The paperback format subsequently morphed into three separate formats with different dimensions and properties. The A format, 110 mm × 178 mm, commonly called the mass-market paperback, is typically used for books aimed at a wide readership; they are printed on cheap paper, sold at low prices and distributed through a wide range of retail outlets, including supermarkets and drug stores as well as bookstores. The B format, slightly larger in size at 130 mm × 198 mm, is used for more literary authors, while the C format, at 135 mm × 216 mm, is the same size as many hardbacks. Both B- and C-format paperbacks are typically printed on a higher-quality paper and sold at higher price points than the mass-market paperbacks; both are commonly referred to as trade paperbacks, to distinguish them from the mass-market paperbacks in the A format.

When there is more than one format available for delivering the same content to consumers and the pricing of the formats varies significantly, then the timing or phasing of the formats becomes important – in the business, this is known as 'windowing'. In Anglo-American trade publishing, a book could potentially move through three phases or windows: it would typically start life as a trade hardback, with a list price in the region of $25–$35, depending on the size and the kind of book it is. Around 12–18 months later, it might be released as a trade paperback in a B or C format, depending again on the type of book, and priced in the region of $14–$17. And then, depending again on what kind of book it is, it could subsequently be released as a mass-market paperback in A format and priced under $10. But not all books follow this pattern: a book could go from a trade hardback to trade paperback and never be released as a mass-market paperback; or it could go from trade hardback directly into mass-market paperback; or it could be published initially as a trade paperback (a 'paperback original', as it's sometimes called), without being published in hardback at all – there are many possible permutations. The publisher can use these different formats to maximize revenues and margins, target the book at different readerships and prolong the selling life of the book.

In the period from 2008 to 2012, when ebooks were taking off in Anglo-American trade publishing, it wasn't clear whether ebooks would eclipse print books altogether, at least in some categories, and, if they did, what implications that would have for the form of the book – whether it would open the way for books to be reconfigured in some fundamental way. As it turned out, however, ebooks remained tied to print books – ebook files were just another output of the production process, along with the print-ready files that were produced for the printer. The content was essentially the same; what differed was the packaging, the delivery mechanism and the price. Many publishers experimented with creating ebooks in which the content was modified in some way – we'll examine some of these experiments in the next chapter – but for the most part these experiments proved unsuccessful and the kind of ebook that came to prevail was the ebook that replicated the content of the print book but made it available as a digital file to be read on a screen, rather than as a print-on-paper book. In other words, the ebook became another format.

If indeed it is the case that ebooks are another format rather than a new form of the book, then the implications of this for the publishing industry are significant. Publishers know how to work with formats: there is nothing new, as we have seen, about the invention of new formats, and, despite initial resistance and anxieties that may run high, they are generally adept at integrating new formats into the array of options that are available to them to package and deliver their content to consumers. Ebooks simply become another revenue stream into which publishers can tap, in precisely the same way that, in previous decades, they tapped into the new revenue streams created by cheap paperback editions, whether these were mass-market paperbacks or trade paperbacks.

But if ebooks are best understood as another format, as I believe they are, then it is also important to see that this is a new format that comes with an array of special features, some of which have real advantages for publishers. First and foremost, the cost of sales is much lower than for printed books because nothing has to be printed and stored in a warehouse and there are no shipping costs (although there are real distribution costs, a fact often overlooked by those outside the industry). Just as importantly, there are no returns – that wasteful aspect of the traditional trade publishing supply chain simply doesn't exist in the ebook world. Prices are typically lower and royalties are typically higher on ebooks, but the savings more than compensate for the lower prices and higher royalties, with the result that publishers' profitability improves. Moreover, the shopping experience is now 24/7 and readers can get books virtually instantaneously if they're happy to read them on a screen – no need to wait for a bookstore to open or wait for a book to be delivered by post.

We find some support for the idea that ebooks are a new format (rather than a new form) if we look at the sales patterns of ebooks in relation to print formats at Olympic. Table 1.7 and figures 1.11a and 1.11b show sales by book format at Olympic in the period between 2006 and 2016, first by units and then by dollars, as a percentage of total sales. What these figures show is that the steep rise of ebooks in the period between 2008 and 2012 was accompanied by a substantial decline in the sales of mass-market paperbacks, both by units and by dollars: mass-market paperbacks declined from 24% of units and 15% of revenue in 2006 and 2007 to a mere 10% of units and 6% of revenue in 2016. By contrast, neither the hardback nor the trade paperback formats experienced such severe decline. Hardcover units remained fairly stable at around 25%; they dipped in 2012 to as low as 18% but then recovered, returning to 25% in 2015 and rising to 32% in 2016 – higher than it had been at any time in the previous decade. Hardcover revenue was accounting for 40% of overall revenue in 2006; this fell to 25% in 2012 but then rebounded to 32% in 2015 and 43% in 2016 – again, higher than it had been at any time in the previous decade. Trade paperback unit sales declined from 40% in 2008 to 33% in 2013 but then rebounded, climbing back up to 38% by 2016. Similarly, trade paperback dollar sales declined from 37% in 2008 to 27% in 2013, rising back to 31% in 2016.

The data from Olympic show pretty clearly that the rise of ebooks has eroded the markets for paperbacks, both trade and mass market, but that it has hit mass-market paperbacks particularly hard: in the decade when ebooks rose from virtually nothing to 20% of Olympic's revenue, the share of Olympic's revenue accounted for by mass-market paperback's fell from 15% to 6%. The decline of the mass-market paperback is not a new phenomenon: mass-market paperback sales have been falling since the 1980s, their market undermined by various factors, including the heavy discounting of hardcover editions by the book superstore chains and the mass merchandisers. Why wait a year for the mass-market paperback of a new novel by James Patterson or Nora Roberts if you could buy the hardcover as soon as it's published for less than $20? But the rise of ebooks has driven a few more nails into the coffin of the mass-market paperback.

To understand why ebooks have had a differential impact on print formats and have hit mass-market paperbacks particularly hard, we have to return to the point about windowing. In the world of print,

Table 1.7 Sales in percentages by format, units and dollars at Olympic, 2006–2016

	Ebooks units	Ebooks $	Hardcover units	Hardcover $	Trade paperback units	Trade paperback $	Mass market units	Mass market $
2006	0	0	24	40	38	35	24	15
2007	0	0	23	36	38	37	24	15
2008	0	1	24	38	40	37	23	15
2009	2	3	26	41	39	35	20	13
2010	6	9	23	36	40	35	18	12
2011	16	19	22	33	36	30	14	9
2012	22	26	18	25	39	35	10	6
2013	21	24	23	32	33	27	11	7
2014	20	24	22	29	36	30	10	7
2015	20	23	25	32	33	28	9	6
2016	20	20	32	43	38	31	10	6

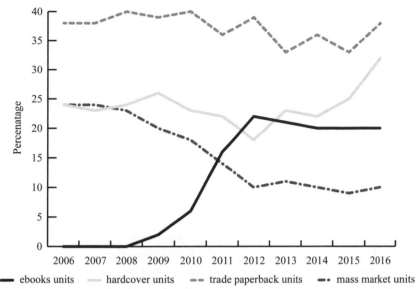

Figure 1.11a Sales in percentages by format and units at Olympic, 2006–2016

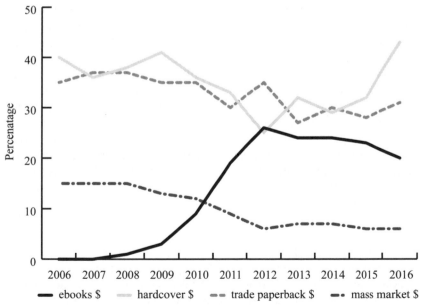

Figure 1.11b Sales in percentages by format and dollars at Olympic, 2006–2016

the different formats of trade publishing are typically windowed: books are first published as hardcover at relatively high price points, and then brought out a year or so later as a paperback, either trade or mass market, at significantly lower price points. Windowing segments consumers into those who are willing to pay a higher price to get a new book quickly, on the one hand, and those who are willing to wait a year or more to get the book at a significantly lower price. But ebooks are typically not windowed: they are usually published at the same time as the first print edition, though typically at a lower price than the print edition. Some attempts were made by publishers to window ebooks in the early stages of the ebook take-off, in 2009 and 2010, partly as a way of trying to minimize the cannibalization of hardcover sales, but these attempts didn't last long – publishers came under enormous pressure from ebook retailers, including Amazon and Apple, to abandon ebook windowing, and all of the major publishers soon did. But the fact that ebooks were now available at the same time as the first print edition was published, and generally priced below the print edition, meant that the windowing rationale for the remaining print editions was now significantly weakened. Why wait a year or more for a cheaper paperback edition if a cheaper edition was available at the same time as the hardcover edition, albeit in a digital format? In format terms, it was the cheaper paperback editions, released at later dates and lower price points, that were hardest hit by the non-windowed ebook upstart.

So ebooks may turn out to be no different from the trade or mass-market paperback: a new format, hugely significant as such, but not a new form. And if that is how it turns out, then it is likely to be far less disruptive for the publishing industry than many commentators thought and many insiders feared. Despite initial anxieties that ebooks might be the harbinger of a much more radical disruption in the publishing industry, many in the industry have now come to the view that ebooks are just another format in the sense that I've described here, albeit one that comes with an array of special features. This is how the CEO of one large trade house put it in 2017:

> Fifty years after Allen Lane's invention of the paperback we received the gift of a new format and, with it, we received the gift that people could, all of a sudden, read everywhere without having the book at hand because they had their reading device. And the gift was also that someone had developed an ecosystem that was so compelling that people were willing to actually pay for that experience – it was

not something that started free like music and the Napster experience. So we had a paid ecosystem that was extremely compelling and convinced people that it made sense given the convenience not to steal books but actually to pay for them in a digital format.

This publisher has always been of the view that ebooks were more of a gain for the industry than a threat: publishers were lucky because others went to the expense of creating an ecosystem in which it was attractive for readers to purchase books in a digital format, thereby opening up a new revenue stream for publishers while obviating the need for consumers to acquire digital content illegally.

But will it turn out like that in the end – a revolution in format but not in form? There are two reasons why we can't yet give a firm answer to this question, and one reason why the picture we've painted so far is incomplete at best. The first reason is that the stability of the current sales patterns, and in particular the levelling off of ebook sales relative to print sales, is dependent on the continuation of the current retail environment, which, despite the bankruptcy of Borders in 2011 and the closing of many Barnes & Noble stores, is still characterized by the existence of many bricks-and-mortar bookstores, both chain and independent. While Amazon has become the single largest customer for many trade publishers, the continued existence of a multiplicity of bookstores provides a vital shop window for publishers' books – and that means, of course, their print books, which continue to get retail exposure thanks to the display space and shelf space of bookstores. Were this retail environment to change significantly in the coming years – were, for example, Barnes & Noble or Waterstones to scale back dramatically or even close down, or were bookstores forced to close for other reasons – then this could have a significant impact on the sales of physical books. We simply don't know what would happen in that case to the relation between physical book sales and ebook sales, and how the different categories of book would be affected by this change. The second reason why we can't give a firm answer to this question is that we simply don't know what the future holds in store. On the basis of the evidence so far, there is a good prima facie case for saying that ebooks are best understood as another format rather than a new form of book, but only the future will tell whether this judgement holds in the long run.

The picture we've painted so far is, however, incomplete in one very important way: we've been relying on data from one large trade publisher, and, given the centrality of this publisher and the nature of their list, it is reasonable to assume that their experience will be similar to that of other large trade publishers. But the book market is populated not just with the output of large trade publishers: it is also populated with the output of many small and medium-sized publishers and, crucially, with the output of many self-publishers and many authors using self-publishing platforms of various kinds, from Amazon's Kindle Direct Publishing (KDP) to a plethora of other platforms (we'll examine these in more detail in chapter 7). The experiences of many small and medium-sized publishers may not differ greatly from the experience of large trade publishers like Olympic, but the world of self-publishing is another matter entirely. Many of the self-publishing platforms, including Kindle Direct, are publishing in ebook only,[13] and some self-published ebooks have become bestsellers.[14] So the patterns in the world of self-publishing are likely to look quite different from the patterns of the large trade publishers who are publishing in print and ebook formats, and for whom print remains a key revenue stream. They are also likely to differ from the patterns that appear in the data supplied by professional organizations like the Association of American Publishers (AAP), since these data are drawn from traditional publishers and therefore don't take account of self-publishing. So there is likely to be a substantial body of material, a high proportion of which is being published as ebooks, that is not being factored into these calculations about the patterns of ebook sales. How big a body of material? Nobody knows. We can try to estimate its size – we'll return to this in chapter 7 – but any estimate is going to be a very rough guess. What we can say with some confidence is that it's not small. Self-publishing is the submerged continent that could, if we were ever to know its true extent, put all of our calculations so far in a very different light.

There is one other reason why this point is important: in the wake of the Department of Justice case against Apple and five of the large trade publishers in 2012 (see chapter 5 below), these publishers were obliged to adopt for two years a modified version of the agency agreement that allowed retailers to discount ebooks to some extent. When this requirement expired in 2014, all the large trade publishers moved to full agency agreements, which meant that they set the prices of ebooks within agreed bands and retailers were no longer

---

[13] Amazon developed a parallel self-publishing platform for print, called CreateSpace, but many authors publishing through Kindle Direct do not release print editions – more on this in chapter 7 below.
[14] Again, more on this in chapter 7 below.

allowed to discount. This meant that new ebooks from the large trade publishers were – especially from 2014 on – typically selling at much higher prices than self-published ebooks. The difference might be as much as $13–$14 for the ebook of a newly released title from a large trade house compared to $3.99, $2.99 or less for a new ebook from a self-published author. And when you take account of the fact that a large proportion of books self-published on Kindle can be accessed for no charge by joining Kindle Unlimited for $9.99 per month (with a 30-day free trial), the cost per unit read of books self-published on Kindle becomes a small fraction of the cost per read of ebooks published by traditional publishers. Of course, there is the question of whether you want to read that material, however inexpensive it may be. But the fact that the price differential is now so great is likely to have the effect of driving down ebook sales from traditional publishers while self-published ebooks take a larger and larger share of the ebook cake, however large (or small) that cake may be.

We simply don't know at this stage how the overall picture of ebook sales relative to total book sales, in both units and dollars, would change if we were able to take account of all books published and sold in the US in any particular year, including self-published books, and how the picture would vary by category of book. We might still see a plateau effect, though the levels at which ebooks begin to plateau might be quite a lot higher, especially in certain book categories, such as romance and mystery, which are popular in the world of self-publishing. Indeed, it could be that some of the decline we see in traditional publishers' ebook sales in certain categories, like romance and mystery, attests not to an overall decline in ebook sales but rather to a revenue flight from traditional publishers to self-publishers, as readers migrate from higher-priced ebooks published by traditional publishers to much cheaper ebooks self-published through Kindle and through other self-publishing platforms. We'll return to these questions in due course.

Beyond the US

So far we've been looking at the patterns of ebook sales for trade publishing in the US, but the US case is somewhat exceptional: the uptake of ebook sales to date has been much stronger there than elsewhere. Among the markets outside of North America, the ebook sales patterns for the UK bear the closest resemblance to the US. This is not altogether surprising: the UK and US book markets share many similarities, the big trade publishers in both markets belong to the same large conglomerates, and Amazon is a major retailer in both the UK and the US. There was a time lag, however: ebook sales were minimal in the UK prior to 2010, and they only began to increase significantly from 2011 on. This delay can be partly explained by the fact that Amazon did not launch the Kindle in the UK until August 2010, almost three years after it had been released in the US. Both the Sony Reader and the iPad were already available in the UK by that time (the Sony Reader was launched in the UK in September 2008 and the iPad in May 2010), but the surge in ebook sales in the UK occurred only after the Kindle had been introduced.

So does this mean that the UK pattern of ebook sales is simply lagging behind the US pattern by a year or two and will eventually catch up? There were many who thought this, but the evidence doesn't entirely support this thesis. Table 1.8 and figures 1.12a, 1.12b and 1.12c, based on data from Nielsen and the Publishers Association, show ebook sales as a percentage of total consumer book sales in the UK from 2008 to 2018.[15] These figures show that the ebook surge in the UK followed a pattern that was very similar to the US: ebook sales rose quickly following the introduction of the Kindle in August 2010, jumping from £22 million in 2010 to £106 million in 2011 and £250 million in 2012, a growth rate of around 375% in 2011 and around 135% in 2012. Growth then quickly slowed down and ebook sales peaked at £312 million in 2014, after which they fell back, declining by 4% in 2015 and 7% in 2016 and 2017. As a percentage of total consumer book sales, ebooks accounted for 6.3% of total sales in the UK in 2011; this jumped to 13.5% in 2012 and then continued to rise until it reached 18.3% in 2014, after which it fell back to around 13% in 2017 and 2018. So, while the pattern is broadly similar to the US – an initial surge leading to a plateau and then a modest decline – there are two significant differences. First, there is the time lag: the take-off and plateauing in the UK were a year or two behind the US. In the US, ebooks took off in 2009–10 and

---

[15] Relevant data can be found in the *PA Statistics Yearbook 2015* (London: The Publishers Association, 2016) and the *PA Statistics Yearbook 2018* (London: The Publishers Association, 2019). However, in the *PA Statistics Yearbook*, 'digital sales' include more than ebooks: it includes ebooks, audiobook downloads, downloads of all/part of books, subscriptions/access to online book publications, and any other wholly digital material delivered online or via CD-Rom (*PA Statistics Yearbook 2018*, Technical Appendix A, p. 83). My figures are based on supplementary data provided by Nielsen and the Publishers Association, which separate out consumer ebook sales from the broader category of 'digital sales'.

Table 1.8   UK ebook revenue for trade books, 2008–2018

	Consumer total (£ millions)	Consumer ebook (£ millions)	Ebook %	Rate of growth
2008	1717	0.7	0	
2009	1684	3.1	0	342.9
2010	1727	22.5	1.3	625.8
2011	1700	106.7	6.3	374.2
2012	1847	250	13.5	134.3
2013	1766	296	16.8	18.4
2014	1709	312	18.3	5.4
2015	1751	299	17.1	–4.2
2016	1872	276	14.7	–7.7
2017	1912	256	13.4	–7.2
2018	1910	251	13.1	–2

Source: Publishers Association

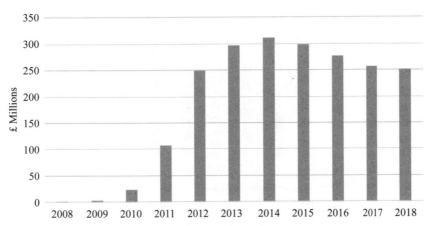

Figure 1.12a   UK ebook revenue for trade books, 2008–2018

reached their peak in 2012, where they remained until 2014, after which they began to decline; in the UK, ebooks took off in 2010–11 and peaked in 2014, after which they began to decline. The second difference is that, when ebook sales began to plateau, they did so at a lower level in the UK – they never reached the same high points that you see in the US. The UK figure plateaued at 18.3% in 2014 and then fell back to around 13% in 2017–18: this is well below the high point reached in the US, where ebook sales plateaued at 24.1% in 2014 before falling back to around 15% in 2017 and 2018.

61

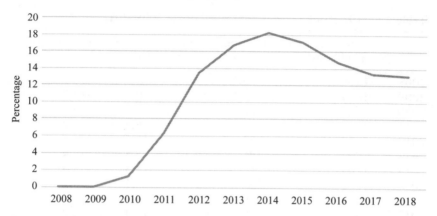

Figure 1.12b   Ebook revenue as a percentage of total trade sales in the UK

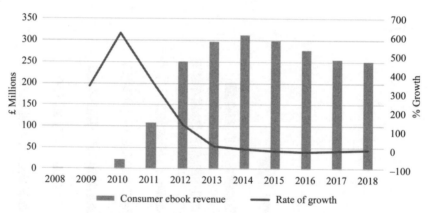

Figure 1.12c   Ebook revenue and rate of growth of ebook sales in the UK

The PA data breaks out ebook sales by broad categories of books – for our purposes here, the relevant categories are fiction, nonfiction/ reference and children's books. Table 1.9 and Figure 1.13 show ebook sales as a proportion of total book sales, print plus digital, in each of these three categories. We see that the ebook surge went much further in the area of fiction: here, ebook sales account for just over 40% of total fiction sales in 2014 and 2015 before levelling off. In the nonfiction/reference category, ebook sales rose to 8.4% of total sales in 2014 and then fell back slightly after that. The lowest levels of ebook uptake are in the children's category, where ebook sales

Table 1.9 UK ebook sales by category, 2008–2018

	Fiction £m	Non-fiction/reference £m	Children's £m	TOTAL FICTION PRINT+ DIGITAL £m	TOTAL NF/REF PRINT+ DIGITAL £m	TOTAL CHILDREN'S PRINT+ DIGITAL £m	Fiction e/total %	NF/Ref e/total %	Children's e/total %
2008	2.8	1.6	0.1	524.8	868.9	323.0	0.6	0.2	0.0
2009	7.6	1.8	0.5	568.9	781.7	333.7	1.3	0.2	0.1
2010	22.0	8.0	1.8	570.5	823.6	332.8	3.9	1.0	0.5
2011	85.0	25.0	9.0	576.7	807.6	315.9	14.7	3.1	2.8
2012	205.0	47.0	14.4	710.1	814.2	324.0	28.9	5.8	4.4
2013	233.0	64.0	18.5	632.7	817.0	316.3	36.8	7.8	5.8
2014	248.0	63.0	25.0	611.5	745.6	353.0	40.6	8.4	7.1
2015	249.0	63.0	19.0	616.1	817.9	317.8	40.4	7.7	6.0
2016	234.0	65.0	18.0	593.7	908.3	370.0	39.4	7.2	5.0
2017	220.0	69.0	18.0	605.9	946.7	358.7	36.3	7.3	5.0
2018	229.0	75.0	17.0	588.0	953.8	368.4	38.9	7.9	4.6

Source: Publishers Association

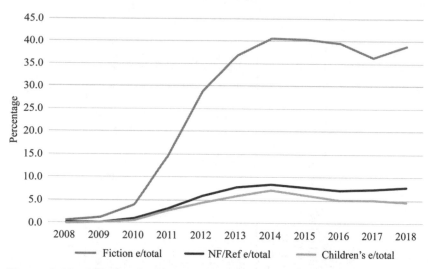

Figure 1.13   UK ebook sales as a percentage of total sales by category, 2008–2018

accounted for 7.1% of total sales in 2014 and then fell back to 5% or less from 2016 on. In each of these broad categories, we see the classic S-curve, represented most clearly by fiction, as ebook sales rise rapidly between 2011 and 2013, peak in 2014 and then begin to level off from 2015 on. The pattern is very similar to the US, though time-shifted to around a year later and plateauing at levels that are lower than those achieved in the US.

Beyond the US and the UK, the take-up of ebooks has been much more modest to date. It is difficult to gather accurate data which are strictly comparable to the data for the US and the UK, as the methods used for gathering data vary from one country to another. Rüdiger Wischenbart and his colleagues have produced what is probably the most thorough comparative analysis of ebook market trends, and their analysis is regularly updated in their annual Global eBook report.[16] Table 1.10 summarizes some of their findings, showing ebooks as a percentage of the total trade market in five European countries. The findings of Wischenbart and his colleagues suggest that ebooks account for around 5% of trade sales in many European countries, although overall percentages of this kind conceal a great

---

[16] Rüdiger Wischenbart, together with Carlo Carrenho, Javier Celaya, Yanhong Kong and Miha Kovac, *Global eBook 2017: A Report on Market Trends and Developments*, at www.global-ebook.com.

Table 1.10   Estimated ebook share of total trade revenue in selected European markets, 2016

	% of total trade market
Germany	4.6
France	3.1
Italy	4
Spain	6
Netherlands	6.6

Source: *Global eBook 2017*

deal of variation between different kinds of books and between different publishing houses. As in the US and the UK, the highest percentages for ebook sales are found in general fiction and in genre fiction, such as romance, mystery, sci-fi and fantasy.

There is also some evidence to suggest that ebook growth is slowing down in some non-English markets and may be plateauing, though at significantly lower levels than in the US and the UK. Figure 1.14 shows ebooks as a percentage of total sales in the trade market in Germany between 2010 and 2016.[17] This shows that ebooks took off in Germany after 2011, rising from less than 1% in 2011 to around 4% in 2013; ebooks then levelled off, rising to only 4.6% by 2016. Some publishers surveyed in 2013 by the German book trade association, the Börsenverein des Deutschen Buchhandels, reported higher ebook sales, closer to 10% of overall revenue, but in any case the figure remained well below the percentage reached in the US and the UK before ebook sales began to level off.[18] By the end of 2015, all German trade publishers had found that ebook sales were largely flat.

Patterns in other parts of the world are difficult to compare, partly because the bases on which data is gathered may be different and partly because the infrastructures and markets are often very different. In Brazil, for example, digital sales probably accounted for around 3% of trade publishers' revenue in 2016.[19] For other large markets, such as India and China, it's hard to get reliable and comparable data. Wischenbart and his colleagues estimate that ebook sales in India were less than 1% of total sales in 2015,[20] and estimate that

---

[17] Börsenverein, reproduced in ibid., p. 65.
[18] Ibid.
[19] Wischenbart et al., *Global eBook 2017*, p. 100.
[20] Rüdiger Wischenbart, together with Carlo Carrenho, Dayou Chen, Javier Celaya,

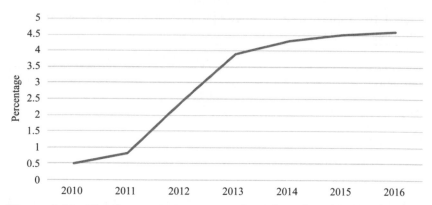

Figure 1.14   Ebooks as a percentage of total trade sales in Germany, 2010–2016
Source: Börsenverein

ebook sales for trade books in China were around 1% in 2014,[21] though it's impossible to know how accurate these estimates are. The most common reading devices in China are smartphones rather than dedicated reading devices, and China Mobile, one of two major telecom providers in China, owns the largest online mobile reading platform. With over 700 million smartphone users in China by 2018 and with the second-largest book market in the world after the US, the potential for the growth of digital reading in China is considerable, even if ebook sales to date have been modest.

This cursory glance at patterns in Europe and elsewhere highlights the enormous variability in the ways in which the digital revolution has affected the book publishing industry in different countries and regions of the world, and underscores the fact that one cannot generalize from the US experience. Indeed, so far from being the harbinger of future developments globally, the US experience may turn out to be the exception – we simply don't know. For the extent to which ebooks replace traditional print-on-paper books depends not only on the type of book, but also on a host of factors such as the role of large corporations like Amazon and the extent to which they have invested, or might be willing to invest, in creating platforms

---

Yanhong Kong, Miha Kovac and Vinutha Mallya, *Global eBook 2016: A Report on Market Trends and Developments,* pp. 107, 110, at www.global-ebook.com.
[21] Rüdiger Wischenbart, together with Carlo Carrenho, Javier Celaya, Miha Kovac and Vinutha Mallya, *Global eBook 2015: A Report on Market Trends and Developments,* p. 118, at www.global-ebook.com.

and distribution systems; the availability of reading devices that are attractive and affordable for local populations; the availability of desirable content in appropriate languages and formats; the different pricing and taxation regimes that apply and, in particular, whether there is a fixed price regime that forbids or limits the discounting of books – this factor alone can make a huge difference to the attractiveness or otherwise of ebooks; and the role that govern- ments, legislators and judicial authorities might play in regulating practices and adjudicating disputes – not to mention the cultural tastes, preferences and practices of readers, all of which may vary considerably from one country, region, culture and linguistic regime to another. There is no reason to assume that the digital revolution will disrupt the publishing industry in the same way everywhere, sweeping through it like a technological tsunami, and the evidence to date suggests that this is not what is happening. Rather than a single consistent pattern, we see enormous variability in levels of digital uptake in trade publishing, with the US and, to a lesser extent, the UK standing out as the two countries where ebooks have become a major revenue stream, but where the surge has now subsided, at least for the time being.

— Chapter 2 —

RE-INVENTING THE BOOK

In the previous chapter, I argued that ebooks are best seen as another format rather than a new form of the book, but I put to one side the more radical possibility that the digital revolution might enable us to re-invent what 'the book' is. The ebook is commonly understood as a book that is delivered to the reader as a digital file rather than as a physical object, and read on a screen rather than by turning the physical pages of a print-on-paper book. An ebook in this sense is derivative from, and limited by, the physical properties of the print-on-paper book, for the ebook is based on the same content and the same core file as the printed book and is simply converted to the file requirements of the relevant ebook vendors and reading devices – the ebook, in this sense, is a replica of the printed text, what Angus Phillips calls the 'vanilla ebook'.[1] The ebook as replica is not necessarily identical to the printed text in every respect. Some details may differ – the cover, pagination and typography, for example, as well as other paratextual features such as the style and positioning of dedications, epigraphs, illustrations, chapter headings and notes. While some of these variations may be significant to literary and bibliographical scholars, they don't alter the fact that the ebook as replica remains tied to the textual content of the printed book. But books constructed, delivered and read in an electronic form do not *have* to be derivative from the physical properties and textual content of the print-on-paper book. They can be created in different ways and endowed with different sets of properties. There are lots of ways that this could be done – some already tried, some yet to be invented. One

[1] Angus Phillips, *Turning the Page: The Evolution of the Book* (Abingdon: Routledge, 2014).

straightforward way of creating a new kind of book is to develop an ebook as a linear text but in digital form only – digital *sui generis* – and to experiment with the properties of the text. For example, you could experiment with the properties by keeping the text very short, perhaps as short as 10,000 words, and sell it as an ebook at a low price – a type of ebook that has been dubbed 'the digital short' or 'e-single'.

Another way of creating a new kind of book would be to start with an existing book, fiction or nonfiction, and enrich the ebook version by adding multimedia features of various kinds, like audio clips, video clips, pop-up graphics and animation – in the business, these are commonly referred to as 'enhanced ebooks'. With the widespread adoption of iPads and colour tablets such as the Kindle Fire, Nook Tablet and Google Nexus, which can play multimedia features, enhanced ebooks seemed to many publishers like a promising avenue to pursue, and indeed a good deal of experimentation of this kind took place from 2011 on.

A third way of re-inventing the book would be more radical. It would start with a clean slate and ask: how do we create a book that uses the full range of functions and possibilities afforded by the digital medium and the existing range of operating systems and reading devices? It wouldn't start with an existing print book and seek to enhance it for the digital reading experience; rather, it would start with the digital reading experience and seek to create a book for it. Here the book would begin life not as a text envisaged for the medium of print, but as something quite different – e.g., as an app, a text that is part of a reading and user experience that exists only in the digital medium and only on screen, and that has no direct print-on-paper equivalent.

Between the two extremes of ebook-as-replica and book-as-app, there are numerous variations and permutations: we have, in practice, a whole spectrum of possibilities here, ranging from the ebook as a straight reproduction of the printed text at one end to the fully re-invented book at the other end, with digital shorts, enhanced ebooks and other experimental forms occupying the intermediate ground, as illustrated in figure 2.1.

In this chapter, I want to explore some of these new experimental forms of the book – not the vanilla ebook but the strawberry ebook, the lemon-sorbet ebook, the cherry-and-dark-chocolate ebook. I'll look at some of the initiatives that have been undertaken by mainstream publishers – and mainstream publishers have been much more proactive about experimenting with new forms than many

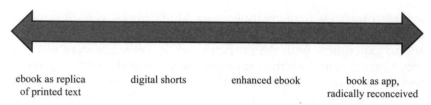

| ebook as replica of printed text | digital shorts | enhanced ebook | book as app, radically reconceived |

Figure 2.1   Some experimental forms of the book

people outside the industry might think. But I also want to look at some of the many start-ups that were launched with the aim of trying to create a new kind of book that would be tailored to, and would take advantage of, the distinctive features and affordances of the digital medium. In some respects, the new start-ups were less constrained than mainstream publishers, simply because they had no investment in traditional print technology and were therefore free to experiment with a clean slate; but, unlike mainstream publishers, the start-ups had no print business to fall back on if the new venture didn't pan out, and therefore their financial position was more precarious. In exploring these experimental forms, I will of course attend to the distinctive features of the forms themselves, but I don't want to restrict our attention to the properties of these forms as if this were a purely textual exercise, nor do I want to speculate abstractly on what might be possible on the basis of technological affordances: decontextualized analyses of this kind are common but they are of limited value for understanding what has actually happened in this domain, and what is likely to happen in the foreseeable future. My approach is different: I go inside the organizations that are (or were) seeking to develop these innovative new forms of the book, talk to the individuals involved in developing them, find out what they were trying to achieve, why they were trying to do it, how they were trying to do it, whether they succeeded and, if not, why not. Only in this way will we understand whether the book really is being re-invented in the digital age, whether the form of the book is being redesigned for the digital medium rather than retaining the form it has in the medium of print, and whether any new form that might be invented in the digital age has any chance of surviving beyond a brief experimental phase. It is one thing to have great ideas and to dream up new literary forms that could be created using new digital technologies; it is quite another to come up with a viable product that embodies this form, establish a stable organizational structure to produce it and find a revenue stream of sufficient magnitude to enable this form to become a sustainable cultural output. Great ideas are one thing; making them work in practice is quite another.

The life and times of the digital short

Tom is a digital publisher at 'Mansion House', a large trade publisher in the UK. He joined the company in 2011, having worked previously at a small avant-garde independent where he pioneered their digital strategy and earned a reputation in the industry as an innovator and cutting-edge thinker about the digital future. Brought in as the digital publisher at a much larger house, Tom was now responsible for thinking creatively about new digital initiatives in order to keep Mansion House at the forefront of new developments. One of the first things he did was to commission a series of short books, 10,000 words each, that would be published as ebooks only – 'long-form journalism, which I saw as an opportunity area', explained Tom. These were nonfiction books, mostly dealing with current affairs, that could be published very quickly and priced cheaply – £2.99 at the time, or under $5. They did moderately well – most sold a couple of thousand copies; one, by a well-known author, sold over 5,000. Tom then began to expand the series by finding stuff in the archives of Mansion House, mostly by well-known authors, that could be repackaged as digital shorts, paying a small refresher advance and putting it out as an ebook. Some of these did even better – one sold over 10,000 copies. For nonfiction digital shorts, that was the range in Tom's experience: a couple of thousand copies at the lower end, 10,000 copies at the upper end. It was viable, provided the advances and refreshers were low, but overall sales were limited and revenues were modest, especially given the low prices.

With fiction, however, it was a different matter. At the same time as Tom was developing his series in long-form journalism, colleagues in one of the commercial divisions of Mansion House were developing plans to release short stories as digital-only ebooks by some of their brand-name fiction writers. The idea was to go to their brand authors whose books sell hundreds of thousands of copies – crime thriller authors, for example – and ask them to write a short story, between 7,500 and 10,000 words, preferably a kind of prequel or spin-off that touches on the theme of their forthcoming book; they would add a preview of the new book that would link to a pre-order. The story would be released a few months before the publication of the new novel and sold at a low price, between 99p and £1.99, marketed to the fans and used as a way to stimulate interest in the forthcoming book. 'As a type of monetized marketing, it's an extremely effective strategy', said Tom. 'You'll sell over 100,000 of these stories and you get the pre-order. You see the pre-order numbers triple.' It's a win-win situation: you're generating a significant new revenue stream that wouldn't have existed in the world of print and, at the same time, you're priming the pump for the new novel, generating pre-orders that will eventually translate into increased sales of the book.

Other publishing houses carried out similar experiments with digital shorts in the early 2010s, with roughly similar results. Clearly, there was a market for short books published as ebooks only and priced very cheaply – books that, in most cases, simply would not have existed in the world of print, since, at 7,500–10,000 words, they were too short to be published as a printed book in English.[2] Might this be the basis for a new kind of publishing – a new publishing venture that could be built on the digital short?

This is an idea that had been gestating in the mind of John Tayman since late 2006 and early 2007. John was a writer, not a publisher, and he was frustrated by the fact that a conventional nonfiction book typically took several years to research and write. He had been a magazine editor at an earlier stage of his career, so he was accustomed to keeping a folder of interesting ideas that could be developed, but most of these ideas fell into a kind of literary no man's land: they were too complicated for a short magazine article but they didn't merit the time, commitment or extent of a full-length book. John was also a heavy reader, but many of the books he bought and stacked up on his nightstand were books that he never read: reading a book was a seven- or eight- or ten-day commitment, and he simply didn't have the time to read them all. He began to think: 'I would like a story that I could digest more quickly than that. I would like a reading experience that maps to the experience that I have when I go to the movies. I want to consume a story – start, middle, finish – in one sitting. That's when the germ of Byliner started coming up.'

It was too early, however: this was late 2006, early 2007, the Kindle hadn't been launched and the iPad was still three years off. There was no way of getting short stories of this kind in front of readers – the discovery and distribution systems just didn't exist. So John put the idea on the back burner while he worked on other

---

[2] Very short books, of 10,000 words or less, are more common in other languages such as French or Spanish. In English-language trade publishing, however, it is rare for texts of 10,000 words or less to be published as printed books.

things. In November 2007, the Kindle came out, but the Kindle was a closed loop and that didn't seem like the best way to go. When the first versions of the iPad appeared in early 2010, John decided that the timing was right and he began putting together a prototype. He started talking to authors, friends and investors, secured seed funding and then several phases of additional funding – he brought in almost $11 million of venture capital (VC) funding in total. One of the writers he was talking to said he had a project that was not well served by his book publisher or his magazine publisher and was actually perfect for this thing that lives in between the two. So they put that together and published this title as their first book, before the whole platform had been established. This was Jon Krakauer's *Three Cups of Deceit* – a hard-hitting, 22,000-word exposé of the misrepresentations and literary fabrications that pervade Greg Mortenson's account of self-transformation and philanthropy in his bestselling memoir *Three Cups of Tea*. The timing couldn't have been better: the ebook was published a day after a *60 Minutes* documentary on Mortenson aired on CBS on 17 April 2011, and it was made available as a free download for 72 hours. In those first 3 days, 75,000 copies were downloaded. This was far in excess of what John had allowed himself to hope for and it augured well for the future of Byliner. With this auspicious start, Byliner was looking like a project that could turn out to be a great success.

For the next year, John and his colleagues worked hard to ramp up Byliner's output and make sure their books were available through the major ebook retailers, especially Amazon, Apple, Barnes & Noble and Kobo, all of whom opened special sections of their bookstores dedicated to short ebooks that could be read in a single sitting. Byliner pioneered the space of what John preferred to call 'e-singles' – short books, between 5,000 and 30,000 words, that could be written quickly and read quickly, published as ebooks only. That was the original concept of the e-single, as John explained: 'We wanted to allow authors to publish a book that could be on and off their desks as writers in a month or two rather than a year or two, and as a reader, it could be on and off my nightstand in an evening or an afternoon.' John used the VC funds to take on staff – three people to begin with, two in editorial and operations and one in technology, and then, as they published more books, built out the platform and began to do marketing and other things, the team grew to around twenty people in total. They aimed to publish one book a week, though that proved to be a little too ambitious and they eventually settled into a pattern of one book every ten days to two weeks. Authors were given a straight 50:50 split on net receipts – that is, after 30 per cent of the sale price had been taken by the vendor. They also paid authors an 'assignment fee' (a term they preferred to 'advance' – 'we tried not to use traditional publishing nomenclature') that ranged from 0 to $3–5,000; the highest they ever paid was $20,000, though that was exceptional. 'We did an extraordinarily good job of acquiring the very best authors and of publishing great books', said John; 'I think we had 32 bestsellers in our first year.' Their authors included many established writers, such as Margaret Atwood, Nick Hornby, Ann Patchett, Jodi Picoult, Chuck Palahniuk, Richard Russo and Amy Tan. They eventually shifted 160,000 copies of *Three Cups of Deceit*, and they had several titles that outsold this.

In 2011, this innovative new venture in digital publishing seemed to have a bright future with everything going for it. E-singles 'are the format of our time', purred technology reporter Laura Owen; they 'fit perfectly with the curl-up-with-your-iPad phenomenon. They're long enough that you don't blow through them in ten minutes, but most can be read in under an hour.'[3] But three years after it launched with its stunning debut success, Byliner was in trouble. Sales were static, margins were being squeezed and managers were looking for ways to cut costs. The dream was over. What went wrong?

There were two main factors, in John's view, that undermined Byliner. On the one hand, the marketplace became flooded with e-singles. A form that Byliner had pioneered was quickly taken up by others and the quantity of e-singles increased exponentially, but much of this escalating output was of rather uneven quality. 'The signal-to-noise ratio moved in the wrong direction', and consumers stopped going to those sections of the ebook retailers that were dedicated to e-singles. On the other hand, prices plummeted. Byliner had been pricing their ebooks between $2.99 and $4.99, but there was tremendous pressure in the marketplace, and especially from Amazon, to drive the price of e-singles down to 99¢. 'When Amazon came out they set hard limits on what you could price at', explained John. 'It had to fall between 99¢ and $4.99. We always wanted to price towards the higher end, in part to signal quality and also because we thought our authors didn't want their work associated with 99¢. We were in continual fights with Amazon about that.' But it was difficult to resist the downward pressure on prices when so much of

---

[3] Laura Hazard Owen, 'Why 2012 Was the Year of the E-Single', Gigaom (24 December 2012), at https://gigaom.com/2012/12/24/why-2012-was-the-year-of-the-e-single.

what was being published in the e-singles category was priced at 99¢. With the flooding of the market, the decline of consumer activity in the e-singles stores and the intense downward pressure on prices, the numbers just stopped working: 'You had to move so many units at 99¢ and then, once you'd carved out 30 per cent for the vendors, it just didn't work.'

It quickly became clear that Byliner needed to find another revenue model – individual transactions at 99¢ with a 30 per cent fee to the vendors simply wasn't going to generate enough revenue to make this a viable business. So they began experimenting with a subscription model that would give readers access to all its content through its website and mobile apps for a monthly subscription of $5.99. But they didn't get enough subscribers to make this work. Perhaps it was too early for a subscription model, maybe consumers were not yet accustomed to paying for reading material in this way – 'I'm still not convinced that there is a viable business model for subscription at that level', reflected John, 'but if there is, it's still two, three, four years away. And so we just sort of flat-lined.'

Byliner's trajectory was not uncommon for a VC-funded start-up in Silicon Valley. Like most start-ups of this kind, they were going for growth so that they could 'own' the category. Profitability was not the key concern in the early stages, either for the senior managers of Byliner or for their financial backers. 'We were what they call out here "pre-revenue"', said John, a little facetiously. 'There wasn't a tremendous amount of pressure to get to profitability as long as we were showing growth. So as long as the numbers are going up, you just lean into that growth.' Venture capitalists typically want to see a growth trajectory that suggests either you will hit profitability eventually or you will get acquired. They keep an eye on 'the burn' – 'you know, how much your monthly expenses are, what you've got coming in.' Byliner was generating a seven-digit revenue, 'but for a VC-funded company those numbers aren't interesting'. So the VCs were hoping that Byliner would be acquired. 'And you take VC money, you're assuming that your exit is going to have a multiple', continued John. For technology investors in Silicon Valley, the multiples can be as high as 20, 50 or 100 times what they're putting in, though multiples of that kind are rare. Investors recognize that most of their investments will fail; they're looking for a return on one in ten investments, and one has to hit at a multiple that will compensate for the losses accrued by the other nine. The VCs who had invested in Byliner soon realized that they weren't going to be able to exit with a serious multiple, but they hoped nonetheless that they would be able to exit with something – what's euphemistically described in VC jargon as a soft landing.

In early 2014, Byliner was at a critical juncture. They weren't generating enough revenue to sustain a viable business at their current level of staffing, and they were unlikely to be able to raise further venture capital given their trajectory of growth. Could they have scaled back, reduced their staff and overheads and restructured the business as a small, boutique publishing operation specializing in e-singles? Possibly. That might have been an option. But scaling back and turning yourself into a boutique business is not part of the script for a VC-funded company – it's not an option that would be of any interest to their investors. Nor did this option appeal to its founder. He had already devoted four years of his life to pursuing this particular dream and given it everything, so the idea of managing the decline of the business was hardly an attractive prospect. Moreover, he was finding it difficult to hold on to his staff, especially the software engineers. 'This is such a super-heated growth environment that for anyone who's on the technology side, there are many better opportunities than trying to eke out a nice little nifty publishing play. It's hard to get and retain staff, and be honest with staff, because they're going to lunch with people whose company trajectories are from launch product to hundred-million-dollar acquisition in months, much less years.' Staff began to leave, and John himself got tired. 'I'm a writer, and I hadn't written anything for four years. I found myself running a company and going into the office every day and not being excited about the growth.' He took a back seat, brought in someone else to run the company and started doing other things. In September 2014, it was announced that Byliner had been sold to Vook, a New York-based company that offers digital publishing services to authors and organizations.[4] It's not exactly the exit John would have liked – 'I would have loved for the team to have a giant exit', he confessed. But there's no shame in a soft landing either.

The three-year story of the rise and fall of Byliner suggests that, while there may well be a market for short books published as ebooks only, this market is probably not sufficiently robust to support a standalone publishing operation. The flooding of the market with content and the downward pressure on prices, creating a category where 99¢ has become the norm, have meant that it's difficult to generate revenue growth and achieve profitability on the

---

[4] Vook was subsequently rebranded as Pronoun in May 2015, and Pronoun was acquired by Macmillan US in May 2016.

basis of publishing e-singles only. Byliner was able to pioneer the development of e-singles with the help of venture capital funding but it never achieved the kind of growth or scale that was meaningful in the VC world of Silicon Valley, and never achieved the kind of profitability that might have enabled it to float off as a boutique indie publisher, even if that option had been open to it. It published some remarkable and successful books in its short life, but the model was unsustainable in the long run.

But maybe Byliner had been too conservative. Maybe you needed to be more radical in the way you were thinking about digital publishing – not just doing ebooks that were shorter than traditional print books, but experimenting in more fundamental ways with the very form of the book, creating ebooks that incorporate the multimedia features that are possible in the digital medium. Maybe another venture with a more radical agenda would stand a greater chance of success – would it?

A radical experiment

In 2012, the media businessman Barry Diller and film producer Scott Rudin approached the former Vintage and Picador publisher Frances Coady with the idea of starting a new kind of publishing company. Barry was Chairman of IAC/InterActiveCorp, a large digital media company headquartered in the Frank Gehry-designed building in the Chelsea district of New York; they owned a range of internet-based businesses, including *The Daily Beast* and match.com, the online dating service, and they were looking for new ideas to expand their digital holdings. Why not try to invent a new kind of publishing for the digital age? Start afresh, find someone very clever who knows a lot about publishing, invest a substantial amount of money – say $20 million – and see what happens. Try to imagine what the book is going to look like in ten, twenty, thirty years' time and create it now. Experiment with the future. This was 2012 and the digital revolution was in full swing. Ebooks were soaring and the future was digital, surely. Here was a well-funded opportunity to marry the old world of publishing with the new world of hi-tech. For someone with a love of books and a taste for adventure, the opportunity was irresistible – Frances couldn't say no. She suggested to Barry and Scott that they should consider collaborating with The Atavist Magazine, a Brooklyn-based internet start-up that had built a platform to exper- iment with new kinds of storytelling in an online environment. It was a great platform, visually beautiful, and it enabled people to engage with stories in innovative ways. They would be the perfect partner: Frances and her colleagues could use their platform and benefit from their technical skills, and The Atavist Magazine, as a hard-pressed start-up, would welcome a cash injection. And so, in September 2012, Atavist Books was born.

Given a free hand, Frances's plan was to experiment as radically as she could with digital publishing – 'I want to make, first and foremost, beautiful ebooks.' The Atavist Magazine had demonstrated the aesthetic potential of the digital medium and she wanted to do something similar for ebooks – turn them into something beautiful. Don't just take an existing ebook and 'enhance' it by adding a few bells and whistles – rather, think of the ebook as a digital project and create something entirely new, an ebook with sound and movement, something which barely existed at the time. It seemed pretty clear to Frances that these digital books, or projects, should be short – partly because, at that time, Byliner was already up and running and their style of e-singles seemed to be gaining some traction, and partly because The Atavist Magazine was working with a similar form, though in their case they thought of their stories as 'long-form journalism'. But, apart from being short, there were no constraints: invent a new form – whether we still want to call it a book is neither here nor there.

Frances didn't just want to do beautiful ebooks, however: she also wanted to do print and to experiment with the relation between print and digital – experiment with pricing, with timing, with how the print book relates to the ebook, and with the very format of print itself. Rather than printing a hardcover edition, for example, try printing an expensive paperback with flaps and see how that goes. This part of the plan quickly ran into difficulties, however. Frances wanted to sign up excellent authors and, as a former publisher, she knew this meant that she had to talk to agents and persuade them to go with her plan. So she made presentations to agents. They loved the fact that she was going to pay competitive advances – that was music to the ears of an agent. They loved the ebook royalties, which were considerably higher than the 25 per cent of net receipts that was being paid by most traditional publishers. They loved the involvement of Barry Diller and Scott Rudin and the substantial financial backing of IAC. But when she said that she wanted to publish digital first, print later, there were gasps of astonishment. They wanted the windowing reversed – print first, digital later. Frances reminded them that this had been tried and it didn't work, but there was a lot of resistance nonetheless, so she had to drop that idea straightaway ('that whole brilliant idea was going down the tubes'). Acquiring the print rights was far from straightforward – they managed it with some authors, but for some of the more well-known authors, the agents held on to the rights for print editions and sold them to their traditional publishers.

Atavist Books published its first title in March 2014 – a 110-page digital-only novella by Karen Russell called *Sleep Donation*. Russell was a well-known writer whose debut novel, *Swamplandia!*, had been published by Knopf in 2011 and had been long-listed for the Orange Prize. In *Sleep Donation*, she recounts the story of an epidemic of insomnia that sweeps across America and that can be treated only by collecting 'sleep donations' from healthy volunteers; the donations are stored in a sleep bank and given as transfusions to insomniacs who are in danger of dying from sleeplessness. The book, which had a striking cover designed by Chip Kidd with sound and moving parts, was very well received, with glowing reviews in the *New York Times*, the *Los Angeles Times* and elsewhere, and it did very well, selling more than 20,000 copies. While the success of its first book augured well for the new venture, it wasn't long before problems began to mount.

Sleep Donation was a critical and commercial success but it was also a very straightforward ebook – this was straight text that could be bought from Amazon at $3.99 and read on a Kindle. Apart from the interactive cover, there was nothing technically compli-cated, or indeed experimental, about the ebook as such. As soon as Atavist Books tried to do something more complicated, they ran into problems. In May 2014, they published Hari Kunzru's *Twice Upon a Time: Listening to New York*, described as 'a unique, multi-layered digital experience combining a beautiful prose essay on the sounds of New York with the extraordinary music of Moondog and binaural recordings of the city itself'. After moving from London to New York's East Village in 2008, the British novelist had found the street noise oppressive. It kept him awake at night. Rather than trying to block it out, he decided to listen to it. He wandered through the streets with binaural microphones that amplified sounds as he recorded them. He also rediscovered the music of the street performer Moondog, aka Louis Hardin – a blind percussionist who dressed as a Viking and played on the corner of Sixth Avenue and 53rd or 54th Street from the late 1940s until 1972 – and wove his music together with the binaural recordings of street sounds to produce a rich collage of an ebook in which the soundtrack was synched to the reading experience. This was experimental, no doubt about it, but the problem now was distribution: how would readers read this multimedia ebook? Neither Amazon nor Apple would host a multimedia ebook of this kind, so they decided to use the Atavist app to make it available. If you wanted to read the ebook you had to download the Atavist app first, then you had to sign in, and then you could buy the ebook and read it in the app. It was a solution, but it was cumbersome. It was just too many steps, too many hurdles, and people didn't want to do it – 'if it's not one click away, then, frankly, forget it'. So the more technically sophisticated the projects became, the more difficult it was to make them work. Distribution was overly complicated and the market just wasn't there.

Then they faced another problem: creating awareness of the ebooks. *Sleep Donation* had not been a problem in this regard: it got lots of review coverage – partly because the author was so well known, partly because of the novelty of being the first ebook by a new, high-profile digital publishing venture and partly because Atavist Books had spent heavily on promotion, since it was an opportunity to promote the new venture as well as the new book. But *Sleep Donation* turned out to be the exception, not the rule; from that point on, it was much more difficult. With no print edition, review editors just didn't want to know. It was only when a print edition was released by an established publisher like Farrar, Straus and Giroux that the book got serious review coverage: 'When the book came out as a print book, which we edited and worked on, it got rave reviews. When it came out as digital, either people were completely traumatized by it, or confused by it, or it didn't get reviewed at all because nobody knew what it was.' Moreover, with no print edition in the bookstores, it was hard to get people to realize that the book even existed. Atavist did a lot of marketing for these books – 'we did a huge amount of outreach, we did everything you can imagine, Facebook, this, that and the other', explained Frances. 'But I think the combination of it's not in the bookstore, I'm not hearing about it from the sources I rely on, I can't see it anywhere and now I've got to go to an app – are you kidding? Am I going to do all that for something when I don't even know what it is?'

By September 2014, it was becoming clear to Frances that this wonderful venture in digital publishing was rapidly going nowhere. The splendid idea of producing beautiful ebooks that were not just replicas of printed text but digital projects *sui generis* was running up against the rocky shores of no review coverage and overly complicated delivery systems. How could the shipwreck be avoided? Two possibilities suggested themselves. One was to give up on the idea of doing multimedia ebooks with lots of audio-visual material and do straightforward e-singles that could be bought on Amazon and read on a Kindle, like *Sleep Donation*. But this was hardly consistent with the original idea behind Atavist Books, which was to experiment more radically and creatively with digital publishing. Moreover, by this time, Byliner was in trouble and the e-single model they had pioneered 'was becoming slightly less fabulous'. Quite apart from Byliner's fate, Frances had come to the view independently that e-singles, which had at first seemed like a good way forward, were not going to generate enough revenue to enable you to pay writers and create growth: 'I looked really hard at the e-single thing and as a business model, it doesn't work. It's really hard to grow. You're doing these little books and people think they shouldn't be paying anything for them.'

The other possibility was to ramp up the print side of the business. At least with print, you knew that you could get review coverage and good distribution, and you had a tried and tested revenue model that would enable you to establish the company while you tried to figure out how to make the digital experiments work. By this stage, they had quite a few print books under contract and they could add more. That might have been a sensible way forward if you weren't in business with IAC. IAC was a digital company, they owned *The Daily Beast* and a host of other internet-based companies: why would they want to tie up resources in warehousing and inventory? It's not a business strategy that would've made sense for IAC, nor would it have furthered in any obvious way the original aim of the investment in Atavist Books, which was to experiment with digital publishing.

So six months after the first book was published, it was clear that Atavist Books had reached a dead end. Digitally elaborate ebooks were not going to work anytime soon, e-singles were not going to generate enough revenue to be viable on their own, and ramping up the print side of the business wouldn't make sense for IAC. It was time to throw in the towel. In October 2014, Atavist Books announced that it would close at the end of the year. Authors whose books had not yet been published were found homes with other publishers. In total, Atavist published half a dozen ebooks, including some that were very creative and beautiful, but this bold new experiment in digital publishing was over shortly after it had begun.

The failures of Byliner and Atavist Books demonstrate how difficult it is to create something new in the publishing spaces opened up by the digital revolution. The digital medium makes possible new ways of creating texts and engaging with them, new ways of creating 'books' whatever they might be, and both Byliner and Atavist Books were bold attempts to experiment in this space. But their short lives attest to the difficulty of creating something that is both new and sustainable – that is, that has sufficient support, institutional as well as financial, to enable it to survive beyond the initial fanfare of excitement that greets the invention of the new. They created new forms but they were unsustainable – forms without a viable business model and without a large enough audience to make them work.

Of course, this does not mean that the new forms with which Byliner and Atavist Books experimented are of no enduring value and have no role to play in a diversified publishing programme and a mixed ecology of digital and print. On the contrary, as the experience of Tom at Mansion House showed, digital-only shorts can work well for different purposes – for example, as a kind of 'monetized marketing' for new books by brand authors. But in this case, digital shorts are parasitic on pre-existing structures and formats of the publishing world: they are a new and innovative publishing format that existing publishers can use to generate supplementary revenue streams and to build demand for new books by their bestselling authors. Understood in this way, digital shorts are not so much a radical re-invention of what 'the book' is but rather a format that supports and feeds into more traditional formats, serving as a kind of prequel that appeals to existing fans and primes the pump for a forthcoming book. Similarly, the experience of Atavist Books showed how difficult it is – at least in the current environment – to make innovative ebooks work in the absence of print, and Atavist Books was not the only new publishing venture to discover the need to re-invent the wheel and build a print business if they wanted to sustain their digital publishing programme.[5]

---

[5] Another example is the Brooklyn-based Restless Books. Established in 2013 by Ilan Stavans, a professor of humanities and Latin American culture at Amherst College, Restless Books set out to translate books from Mexico and elsewhere and publish them as ebooks in English; it was initially funded by a sympathetic benefactor but its ambition was to become a self-supporting, going concern. Being an ebook-only publisher seemed like a good idea at the time – 'it's cheap and easy. You don't have to have a printer, you don't have to have a distributor, you can just start publishing ebooks', explained one employee. But they quickly discovered that it was very hard to be an ebook-only publisher. They started with five or six books in October 2013, but the books went nowhere – no one knew about them, they were not in bookstores and they got no review coverage. Sales were pitifully low – in the dozens of units, not the hundreds, let alone the thousands: 'The books were essentially disappearing into the ether.' Six months after they published their first books, they realized they

One could perhaps say, however, that Atavist Books suffered from a particular technical problem: it was creating digitally elaborate ebooks that required the reader to download and sign in to another application – the Atavist app – in order to buy and read the ebook, and this multi-step structure was just too complicated and off-putting for users. In the age of the iPad, why not just create the book itself as an app that can be purchased and downloaded directly from the App Store – that would be much simpler, surely. Wouldn't that stand a better chance of success?

Ebooks as apps

Tom at Mansion House experimented a lot with app development, both at Mansion House and at the small, cutting-edge indie for which he previously worked. The procedure he followed at both houses was pretty much the same: come up with an idea for an app, either on his own or in discussion with one of the in-house editors, scope out the project and then put it out to tender either to an agency or to an app developer. Tom developed a good relationship with a small developer, 'BirchTree', to whom he gave a lot of his app development work. BirchTree is a small operation, two guys in their early thirties, self-taught programmers who worked briefly for a games company, became disillusioned, left, set up on their own and now work from home. One day, one of them got a phone call out of the blue from someone at a publishing company asking him if they'd be interested in developing an app with a scientist. That was 2010, shortly after the iPad had been launched. They'd done lots of iOS stuff, so they knew they could build an app – yes, they were interested. 'He asked me how much it was going to cost and I was like, hmmm, I just picked a number out of the air, I said £20,000. And he said, yeah, that sounds fine, that sounds about right.' So the deal was done. The publisher, Tom, was then working for a small indie, and the app was for a digital-only publication by a young American scientist about the future of the internet. The text didn't exist in advance – he wrote the text as the app was being developed. It took the two guys at

had to change course and print physical books. 'We made ebooks the initial mission of Restless, to be innovative, to be new and fresh and think of ways of transmitting information digitally as a way to cross borders and boundaries, and that is still true. But funnily enough, in order to be innovative, we had to go way old-school. We had to become a print publisher.' Unlike Atavist Books, Restless survived and, by 2015, around 90 per cent of its sales was accounted for by print.

BirchTree about two months to produce the app. They built a unique non-linear navigational interface and enhanced the author's text with interactive 3D models, video, images and other content pulled from the internet. It was available from the App Store for £4.99. Tom was happy with the way the app came out and had nothing but praise for the two guys at BirchTree ('they're fucking brilliant') but he had to confess that sales were disappointing – 'you get to 1,000 copies and that's about it.' With development costs of £20,000 and revenue after Apple's commission of less than £4,000, that's a serious loss – and that's without taking account of any fees or royalties paid to the author.

It isn't always like that, however. Tom described another app he did, this time for one of the commercial imprints of Mansion House. The author was a well-known scientist who had written many books of popular science. His new book was a lavishly illustrated book aimed at showing young people how science can explain natural phenomena. Tom and his publishing colleagues at Mansion House came up with the idea of doing an app that could be released at the same time as the book was published. They put the project out to tender at various agencies and developers, and those who were interested pitched their ideas to them. Tom and his colleagues decided to go with an agency, 'Phantom', that worked across different platforms and industries and had an in-house team of app developers. They told Phantom that they had a fixed amount of money for the project, £40,000, and they needed the app ready to be released by the publication date of the book. This sum was considerably less than Phantom would have needed to develop the kind of app they had in mind – they would normally have wanted at least twice that amount. But they liked the project and could see benefits in developing their collaboration with publishers, so they were willing to be flexible on the terms. They agreed a deal where the publisher put up £40,000 to cover the production costs, and the agency took a share of the revenues. Phantom had three months to deliver. They put five people full-time on the project and brought in specialists and freelancers when they needed them. They used the text from the book and supplemented it with specially created illustrations, animations, audio and video clips of the author and a variety of interactive activities and games. The main technical challenge for Phantom was to find a way to link large amounts of text to a single image – they were using the entire text of the book in the app, not an abbreviated version. In a large-format book, you can fit a lot of text around a single illustration, but you can't do this on a tablet screen in landscape mode. Phantom's solution was to develop different layers of content so that images and text would move at different speeds as you swiped the screen. It was a technique they borrowed from game design, where it's used to create the illusion of depth – for example, clouds in the background move slowly while things in the foreground move quickly, giving the illusion of depth. But none of their developers had done this before, so they had to invent processes on the fly and then go back and fix the things that didn't work. Despite these challenges, they delivered on time and the app was released a week after the hardcover edition was published in September 2011, available from the App Store at £9.99 and $13.99.

This one worked. 'It followed a very traditional kind of app sales curve', explained Steve, the project manager at Phantom. 'Huge initial spike and then a long tail of ongoing sales. So we sold 15,000, 20,000 in the first couple of months, and then a similar amount again over the next couple of years.' In total, the app sold around 35,000 copies, about half of which were in North America, a quarter in the UK and a quarter in the rest of the world. 'Everyone involved made money, which was a huge surprise', added Steve. It's easy to see why Steve said that – the maths are simple. Once you've taken off Apple's 30 per cent commission, the net revenue is around £230,000, or $360,000. With production costs pegged at £40,000, this app was a resounding commercial success. What explains its success?

Steve's answer is that of a software engineer who was focused on the user experience:

> A lot of apps at the time did things because you could, not because you should. The process of picking up a book and getting lost in it was missing from them. They had lots of 'look at me moments' – press this, hit that. One of our guiding principles was that when you pick up a book and start to read, the interface disappears – you're just lost in the content. So we wanted to apply that to the digital book, and I think we did that in a smart way. I felt like we managed to blend light-touch animation and textual content and make a serious scientific work that was still a book reading experience. It wasn't a game, it wasn't really an app, it was a book.

While there is undoubtedly some truth in Steve's explanation, the stylish technical design and smooth interface of the app are only part of the story. A good part of the app's success can almost certainly be attributed to factors that are linked more directly to traditional aspects of trade publishing: release of the app to coincide with the publication of the print edition of the book; a large marketing budget for the book and the app together, and an intensive promotion campaign by the publisher; and an author with a high international profile and a strong track record of successful trade books. While the app was a very innovative product that built upon but went well beyond the printed book, its success was attributable in part to the traditional structures and processes of the publishing industry – take away those structures and processes, release this as a standalone app without a simultaneous book publication and the marketing budget and promotion campaign that went with it, and it might well have performed less impressively.

As these two examples show, much of the activity in this area is what we could describe as hybrid publishing – that is, a traditional trade publisher, whether a small cutting-edge indie or a large corporate house or something in between, experimenting with innovative forms of publishing by commissioning the development of an app, to be released either as a standalone product or as an ebook in which text taken from a printed book is reworked, enhanced and/or supplemented in various ways. In hybrid publishing of this kind, innovation is heavily dependent on traditional book publishers who are seeking to experiment with digital publishing forms, explore new possibilities and test the market to see if there is sufficient uptake to justify further investment. The app developers can play a crucial role in conceptualizing the way that the app is built – they know what can be done from a technical point of view, and they will often pitch their ideas to the publisher. But, ultimately, the initiative in these cases is being taken by the publisher, which is funding the development and paying the developers either a fixed fee or a share of the revenue (or, in some cases, a mixture of the two). Without the initiative from the publisher and its willingness to invest in experimental forms of this kind, these hybrid forms of publishing would not exist.

So is it worth it from the publisher's point of view? From a strictly financial point of view, the experience of most publishers has been decidedly mixed. There have been some notable successes, like the one described above – and some apps have done even better than this, selling 100,000, 200,000 copies or more. But for every success of this kind, there are many apps where the sales have been disappointingly low. Sales in the hundreds or low thousands are not uncommon. In the light of low sales and downward pressure on prices, there were many within publishing houses who questioned the wisdom of developing apps and enhanced ebooks of this kind, especially when it was a matter of taking a pre-existing narrative text and adding digital supplements of various kinds. Evan Schnittman, then Sales Director at Bloomsbury, summed up the reservations of many when he said, at the London Book Fair Digital Conference in 2011, 'The idea of innovating on the immersive narrative reading process is just a nonstarter.'[6] Schnittman may well have been right about that when it comes to straight narrative text: in many cases, it's not clear that there is much to be gained by taking a pre-existing text, adding audio-digital supplements of various kinds and seeking to turn it into something else in a digital medium. But there are other categories of book, such as cookbooks, travel books and children's books, where there may be opportunities of a different kind for digital innovation. And there is no need to take a pre-existing narrative text as a starting point. Why not set aside our preconceptions about what a book is, start with a clean slate and see what happens?

Re-inventing the book as app

Touch Press was housed in a small, two-storey building in Warple Mews, a quiet cul-de-sac on an old industrial estate in west London. The factories are now silent and many of the buildings have been converted into office spaces for small businesses and start-ups of various kinds. Touch Press had two units in Warple Mews – they owned one and rented the other, and they'd knocked a hole through the wall so that the units interconnected. It was a compact space for thirty employees. Mostly open plan, there were rows of desks with programmers working on Macs, and at the far end of one room there was a meeting space with a large oval table and a generous skylight, closed off from the rest of the room by a glass screen and door. Touch Press earned a reputation as a high-end app developer – the Rolls-Royce of the app world. But they didn't think of themselves as an app developer: they thought of themselves as a publisher, and they thought of what they made as books. 'If you say "app developer" to someone, they think of a purely technical company that is brought in by a publisher to turn a book into an app, and we're clearly not in that business', explained Max Whitby, one of the founders of the company. He continued:

---

[6] Evan Schnittman, London Book Fair 2011 Digital Conference, at www.youtube.com/watch?v=fiUapEUGRhY.

We're trying to create something which is a thing in itself. I also think that a lot of what is associated with thinking of oneself as a book publisher is critical to the success of what we make. So you want an author with a voice, and we give them a medium in which to express themselves, you care about good typography and things being spelt correctly and being grammatical, and you curate the information – and that's what a publisher does. And you're a filter – you select, you decide, you're in the swim of the culture and help to choose the things that will make a difference.

Like many start-ups, Touch Press emerged from a fortuitous convergence of circumstances. Max Whitby, a former television producer for the BBC, and Theo Gray, a software engineer and author with a background in chemistry who lives two hours south of Chicago, happened to share a hobbyist's interest in the Periodic Table. They found themselves bidding for the same samples of elements on ebay and losing to one another, and decided it was time to meet, which they did in 2002. They struck up a friendship and, indeed, a collaboration, building a small business around their shared interest in the elements – 'a kind of empire of the Periodic Table'. It just so happened that Theo was working at the time for a software company that was commissioned by Apple to supply some of the software for the iPad. Although the iPad was still in development, Theo and Max immediately saw an opportunity to do something new with the enormous amount of material they'd gathered on the Periodic Table. In the course of preparing for a book he wanted to publish on the elements, Theo had photographed each element on a turntable to get a set of 360-degree images. It suddenly dawned on him that he could use the software they were supplying for the iPad – a technical programme called Mathematica that Theo had helped to create – to combine these photos in a way that would enable you to 'spin' the object with a flick of your finger on the iPad. It's a unique experience. It's hard to imagine what it's like until you actually do it, and the first time you flick your finger and make an object spin 360 degrees, it's captivating. Flick it faster and it spins faster, touch it and it stops in its tracks. You would never have imagined that a flat screen could produce such a compelling and dynamic 3D effect.

Now they had a serious challenge: could they build an app of the elements in just sixty days, so it was ready to launch at the same time as the first iPad was released in April 2010? Using Mathematica, they would need to come up with an algorithm that would tell the program how to integrate and resize the photographs to produce the spin effect, how to position the rotating objects on the page and how to combine the objects with the text and labels. They also needed to persuade Apple that what they were producing was something new, not just a static piece of text on a screen. They knew that one of the questions that would be asked about the iPad was: how does this compare with the Kindle? If the iPad was thought of as an ebook reader, then it wouldn't compare very favourably: it would have a battery life measured in hours rather than weeks, you couldn't read in sunlight and it would cost a lot more. If your definition of ebooks is static pieces of text that you read on a screen, then the Kindle is going to be a better ebook reader than the iPad. So their pitch to Apple was to seize this opportunity to think differently about what an ebook is. 'Suppose you change the conversation about what the future of ebooks is – that's a conversation you can win', they said. 'Suppose you can convince people that, sure, the Kindle has a million books, but who cares – they're a million old books. Look at this amazing thing – this is what ebooks are going to be. And there are half a dozen reasons why it can't run on a Kindle – the screen is crap, the processor is nothing like what it needs to be, there's not enough memory and so on. There's lots of reasons why the future of ebooks cannot exist on a Kindle. Never mind the present, look at the shining future.' Apple was convinced. The Elements was finished on time and the app was one of a couple of dozen apps that were installed on the small batch of embargoed iPads that were sent out to journalists a few days before the public launch of the iPad. The response from reviewers was euphoric. Stephen Fry tweeted 'Best App of all ... Everything is animated and gorgeous. Alone worth iPad.'

The publicity was exceptional and the app took off – they sold 3,600 copies on the first day, priced at $13.99 and £9.99. It went on to sell over a million copies and came out in fourteen different versions, including Japanese, French and German, generating over $3 million in net revenue. Theo had actually published a book called *The Elements* in September 2009 with Black Dog & Leventhal, a small New York trade house. It had been translated into several languages and had sold about 70,000 copies in all languages before the app came out. When the app was released, sales of the print book went through the roof. By 2012, more than 580,000 copies of the print edition had been sold in all languages. It was a stunning success, both as an app and as a book.

The success of The Elements was the basis on which Touch Press was founded. The company was incorporated in summer 2010, a few months after The Elements had been released, and they raised about half a million dollars, partly from two angel investors, to get the company off the ground. They saw themselves as pioneering a new kind of publishing: the book-as-app. As they saw it, there were three kinds of companies that were experimenting with this medium: traditional book publishing companies, traditional media companies with expertise in video and TV, and video game companies. Each had something important to contribute but they understood only part of what was essential for this new medium to work. Traditional book companies understood the importance of storytelling and of authors, but they lacked the expertise in video and the technical skills to develop the book-as-app – hence they generally had to outsource this development to specialist firms. Film and television companies understood talent, storytelling and visual media, but they too lacked the software skills to develop good apps. Game companies, on the other hand, have the technical skills to produce good interactive video game experience, but they don't understand storytelling and the value of authors. So that's what Touch Press set out to do: bring together these three sets of skills in a way that none of the other kinds of companies had managed to do.

A key part of this was to see that the software engineer must be on the same level as the other parties involved in developing the app: 'You don't bring an engineer in once you've decided what you're going to do: the engineer is part of the process of deciding what you do.' The senior management team included an engineer, John Cromie, who joined the team in 2010 to help build The Elements in sixty days and became the CTO; John managed the technical team and was part of all the key decisions about which new projects to take on. Once the management team had decided to embark on a new project, the planning and development of the book-as-app took place in development meetings at which the CTO and some of the programmers were present. There was a large screen on the wall and the engineers around the table plugged in their laptops so they could manipulate images and text on the screen as they talked about what to do. Sample pages were displayed, options were explored, technical limitations were discussed, costs were considered, decisions about what can and cannot be done were taken. This was a creative process in which the technical input of software engineers was factored in as the book was being written, shaping the way that the text was developed and how it was combined with the visual and audio elements of the app.

While Touch Press was strong on technical skills and audio-visual expertise (given Max's background in television), they were less experienced on the publishing side. None of the principals had a background in book publishing, and, while Theo was a successful author, his knowledge of the publishing process was based on his arm's-length dealings with a small New York trade house. The publishing perspective was the weakest part of their skill set. Moreover, apart from The Elements, they lacked the kind of intellectual property that an established publisher would have, and lacked the experience of dealing with authors and agents. So it is not surprising that they soon found themselves collaborating with publishers and other creative organizations as a way of developing new projects. Sometimes, publishers came to them; in other cases, Touch Press came up with ideas and sought out organizations with which they could partner. 'Almost every project we've done since The Elements has been in partnership with a carefully selected owner of IP, owner of expertise, often owner of brands with a marketing department', observed Max; 'we see partnerships as a 21st-century way of publishing.' Their partners included traditional publishers, such as Faber, HarperCollins, Egmont, Barefoot Books and the University of Chicago Press; TV production companies, such as Wide-Eyed Entertainment, the team behind the BBC's *Walking with Dinosaurs* TV series; classical music organizations, including the Philharmonia – the London-based orchestra – and Deutsche Grammophon; and large media corporations, notably the Walt Disney Animation Studios. In each case, a profit share was worked out that involved dividing the net revenue (after Apple's 30% commission and sales tax are deducted) between Touch Press as the app developer, the publisher or other partner who typically controlled the IP, the author, and the party (or parties) that invested the capital to produce the app. So, for example, a typical split might be: 50% of net receipts to Touch Press, the partner and the author, and 50% to the investors; and, between Touch Press, the partner and the author, it might be 50% to Touch Press and 50% to the partner and author; or 50% to Touch Press, 30% to the partner and 20% to the author. If Touch Press or the partner put in all or some of the investment capital, then their percentage of the net receipts would be increased proportionately.

Among the publishers, Touch Press's partnership with Faber proved to be particularly fruitful, leading to a series of books-as-apps that attracted a great deal of attention, starting with Solar System, released in December 2010, followed by T. S. Eliot's The Waste Land, released in June 2011, and Shakespeare's Sonnets, released in June 2012. The Waste Land took Eliot's iconic poem – the crown jewel of Faber's list – and brought it to life in ways that are simply not possible in the medium of print, allowing the reader to read it but also to *hear* the poem being read (in no less than seven readings, two by Eliot himself) and to *watch* it being read in a remarkable, captivating performance by Fiona Shaw that was filmed specifically for the app. The extensive apparatus of notes that weighed down the printed version of the poem are conveniently relegated to a side panel that can be turned on or off with a simple touch of the screen, while the reader can listen to and watch various individuals, from poets to pop singers, talk about *The Waste Land* and what it meant to them. The result is that a poem that had existed for ninety years as print on paper was now recast in a new medium, enabling the reader to experience the poem in a unique and unprecedented way, combining the reading of text with listening to and watching the poem being read and discussed. The app was a surprising success: it went to the number one position among worldwide bestselling book apps, and sold around 20,000 units in the first year. It was also a critical success and the reviews were glowing. 'When I began to use the *Waste Land* app', extolled one professor of literature, 'I immediately understood why so many people were buying it. While it presented the same poem, it presented it in a very different light … . The *Waste Land* app's marvelous feat, as I have come to understand it, is to have rescued a vibrant and dynamic poem from a print medium that had entombed and shrouded it, for nearly a century.'[7]

While The Waste Land involved recasting in a digital medium a poem that had previously existed in print, many of the apps produced by Touch Press are digital creations *sui generis* – that is, they had no previous existence in print but were created specifically for the iPad. Their music apps are good examples of this. The Orchestra, produced in collaboration with the London-based Philharmonia Orchestra and The Music Sales Group, was released in December 2012; it was followed by Beethoven's 9th Symphony, released in May 2013; The Liszt Sonata in B Minor with Stephen Hough, released in July 2013; and Vivaldi's *Four Seasons* with Max Richter, released in May 2014. The first of these apps, The Orchestra, enables you to watch and listen to eight orchestral pieces, composed over a period of 250 years, from Haydn's Symphony No.

---

[7] Adam Hammond, 'How Faber's App Rescues Eliot's Masterpiece from the Waste Land of Print', *The Toronto Review of Books*, 17 April 2012, at www.torontoreviewofbooks.com/2012/04/how-faber-and-fabers-ipad-app-rescues-t-s-eliots-masterpiece-from-the-waste-land-of-print.

6 and Beethoven's Symphony No. 5 to Salonen's Violin Concerto. The music is reproduced in high fidelity, and the video of the orchestra offers close-up images of individual musicians playing their instruments. You can also choose to watch a 'beat map' that represents each musician in the orchestra with a coloured dot that flashes when they are playing, so that you can see how the music correlates with the activity of different sections and instruments. A full or curated score – again, you can choose which you want to see – scrolls across the lower half of the screen as you listen to the music and watch the video or the beat map. The app also provides an encyclopedic guide to the sections and instruments of the orchestra; touch on any one of them and you're given an account of how the instrument works, narrated by the musician himself or herself, who speaks to you directly and shows you what the instrument can do; touch the instrument and it enlarges and leaps into the foreground, flick it with your finger and it spins 360 degrees, just like the objects in The Elements. Touch the conductor, Esa-Pekka Salonen, and he'll give you a personal account of the art of conducting. There is text too, including a short, illustrated history of the orchestra and a guide to listening to orchestral music and reading a score, written by *LA Times* music critic Mark Swed. The Orchestra and its successor apps, with their fluent blending together of music, voice, video, image and text, are works that could only exist in the kind of digital medium offered by an app.

It would be difficult to deny that the apps produced by Touch Press were a creative success. They exploited the new medium of the app to its full, using it to breathe a new kind of life into texts that had previously existed only on the printed page and to create entirely new works in which text is woven together with audio-visual materials to produce a kind of user experience that is simply not possible in the medium of print. Of course, Touch Press were not alone in doing this. There were, and are, many other players in this space, ranging from one or two individuals working from home to much larger organizations, including the large publishing corporations, who have been actively experimenting with apps. But Touch Press stood out as one of the most accomplished of them all. They established a position as a leader in the market of what one could call 'the premium app' – that is, the app that was developed as a high-end product, beautifully crafted, making full use of the high resolution and functionality of the iPad. Their apps were regularly selected as App of the Week and Editor's Choice in the App Store, and they were given rapturous reviews in the press. The *Sunday Times* devoted the front page of its Culture Section to The Waste Land,[8] and The Orchestra was described in the *Guardian* as 'an instant classic ... one of the most impressive bits of app-ology I've ever seen.'[9] Few app developers have enjoyed such consistently laudatory critical acclaim.

There can be little doubt that Touch Press was producing apps of the highest quality, but had they built a creative organization that was sustainable in the medium to long term? That was a question that preoccupied everyone at Touch Press too: they wanted to know more than anyone whether they had a viable business because their livelihoods depended on it. Some of their apps had been not just critical successes but commercial successes too – The Elements, of course, but also Solar System, The Waste Land, The Orchestra and others. They had earned back their costs and become profitable titles. But for every successful app of this kind, there were others that flopped – sometimes dismally so, selling 1,000 copies or less. Given the time and expense that goes into developing a premium app of this kind, that is a serious loss for a small business. To make this work, you need to be able to count on a regular flow of successful apps. You can take risks on some projects, but you have to be able to count on others to deliver high enough sales to cover their costs and be sufficiently profitable to keep the business going. Could it be done?

In 2012, Touch Press had reached a point where they needed to answer this question – not least because their investment capital was drying up and they needed to know if they had a viable business. Apart from the initial half a million dollars they had raised in 2010 to get the company off the ground, they had secured another £2 million of investment capital which had kept them going and enabled them to build the business, but by late 2012 their funds were running low. They were fortunate that, at just this time, a terrific opportunity came their way that would enable them to test their business model: some senior figures at Disney had seen The Waste Land and been impressed by it, and they approached Touch Press to see if they would be interested in partnering with them to do an app on the history of animation. It was a great project in itself: what could be more amenable to the medium of the app than a richly illustrated account of the history of animation? And who could be a better partner in a project of this kind than Disney, with their pivotal role in the history of animation and their incomparably rich archive of iconic characters and copyrighted material dating back to the 1920s?

---

[8] *The Sunday Times*, 26 June 2011.
[9] *The Guardian*, 7 December 2012.

If you were setting out to find a partner for a book-as-app on the history of animation, Disney would be top of your list – and now they were saving you the trouble since they were knocking at your door. Moreover, with Disney's powerful marketing machine behind you, this app would have everything going for it. If you couldn't make this app work in financial terms, then what would your chances be with others?

Touch Press worked out a deal with Walt Disney Animation Studios in autumn 2012 and began working on the app in earnest in December, though much of the preparatory work had been done before then. A substantial part of Touch Press's staff was assigned to this app – about ten people in total from the Press's side, plus those on Disney's side who also contributed to the project – and it required a good eight months of intensive work. The budget was substantial – around £400,000. Theo took on the role of author, and he wrote the text as the app was being developed. The app recounts the history of animation at Disney in a way that is thematically structured, with chapters or sections covering plot, character, the art of animation, visual effects, sound, etc. The text is interwoven throughout with a rich array of visual material that comes to life at the touch of a finger – the interweaving of text and image is so integral to the design that when you touch on a character to bring it to life, the text itself breaks up and reforms on the page to make way for the character, which now assumes centre stage. There are clips from Disney cartoons, starting with 'Steamboat Willie', the first Mickey Mouse cartoon that was released in 1928, and from all of the great Disney animated films – *Snow White and the Seven Dwarfs, Bambi, The Lion King, Winnie the Pooh, Frozen*, etc. Interactive tools are used to explain the principles of animation and enable younger users to have a go at producing simple animation effects, like adding and removing layers and creating movements. The app was released on 8 August 2013 at $13.99 and was immediately selected by Apple as Editor's Choice, which ensured that it was featured on the front page of the App Store.

The release of the app was timed to coincide with the D23 Expo, the biennial exposition of the official Disney fan club which took place in Anaheim, California, on 9–11 August. This helped to give the app visibility in the community of Disney fans and contributed to a steep spike of sales during the first couple of weeks after its release. Sales then followed the normal pattern of app sales, falling off quite quickly and ticking over at modest levels – until, that is, Disney Animated was selected by Apple as iPad App of the Year for

2013. When this was announced on 16 December, it was followed by another steep spike in sales that lasted until the end of December, during which they sold another 20,000 or so. In January, Disney Animated won yet another accolade: it was named Best App in the Academic/Reference category of the 2014 Digital Book Awards, prizes that are handed out annually as part of the Digital Book World conference. It also won a Children's BAFTA in the Interactive: Adapted category, and the Best Adult Digital Book in the *Bookseller*'s FutureBook Innovation Awards. In terms of critical recognition and awards, Disney Animated could hardly have achieved more: this is about as close as you can get to a clean sweep in the world of the book-as-app.

And yet, despite all this, Disney Animated was not an unqualified success in commercial terms. Given the costs involved in developing the app, the number of staff that was involved over a period of more than eight months, the extra effort and expense that was put into marketing, and the distribution of revenues between the partners, Touch Press needed to sell 100,000 copies to recoup their costs, and needed to sell considerably more than this – 300,000, maybe even 500,000 – to make a real financial contribution to the company. The app did well, but not as well as it needed to do to demonstrate that the business of developing premium apps of this kind is viable and sustainable in the medium to long term. 'Disney Animated was a critical litmus test for us because it was a beautifully produced app into which we poured our soul, people worked nights and weekends and we couldn't have made it better. It's also on a popular subject that has deep roots in popular culture – the history of animated film is a subject that should interest lots of people. And, by God, it had Disney behind it – a bigger marketing machine it would be hard to find. And yet it ended up selling 70,000 units in the first five or six months. What this tells us is that our business model doesn't work', reflected Max. 'We built this company and secured investment on the assumption that we could repeat The Elements. You make a beautiful title, very difficult to make, you sell large numbers and that's a profitable, exciting business. You rinse and repeat, you scale up and you have a company that's worth a lot. No.' The sense of disappointment, conveyed by the hard reality of the 'No', was palpable. Max and his colleagues had spent four years embarked on an ambitious project committed to the invention of a new kind of digital book, building a team of around thirty talented staff who were able to exploit to the full the new media of the app and the iPad, and now they were faced with the stark realization that it could all be in vain. Nice idea, but it just doesn't work.

Why not? 'It's partly because the ground has been moving under our feet as we've been working', explained Max. 'When The Elements came out, it was one of the very few games in town. And if you really wanted to see what your iPad could do, that's what you got. Now there are over a million apps in the App Store and most of them are free.' The number of apps was increasing and the average price was getting lower over time. The numbers bear him out. In January 2015, Apple reported that there were more than 1.4 million apps available in the App Store, and more than 725,000 of these were made for the iPad. Around 40,000–50,000 new apps were being added every month. Most analyses show that the vast majority of apps in the App Store – over two-thirds – are free. Many free apps contain In-App Advertising and offer In-App Purchases of various kinds – what's commonly referred to as the 'freemium' model – but they are free at the point of download. After free apps, the most common price point is the cheapest one, 99¢ – they account for just under 50% of all paid apps. Apps priced at $1.99 are the next most popular tranche, and they comprise nearly 20% of all paid apps. Apps priced at $1.99 or less account for 89% of all apps available in the App Store, and they account for 66% – two-thirds – of all paid apps.[10] From the consumer's point of view, buying an app is a risk: if you pay $10 for an app and don't like it, in all likelihood that's $10 down the drain. 'Because of that', explained one app developer, 'apps tend to be either lower priced and you try to sell more units or tend to be free and use In-App Purchase as the way to get money from people.'

For publishers like Touch Press, these developments posed two big problems. First is the problem of visibility – or 'discoverability', to use the term that is often used in publishing circles. How do you get your apps noticed in a world where there is only one store which is filled with over a million apps, and to which 40,000–50,000 new apps are being added every month? Book publishers often complain about how the dwindling number of bricks-and-mortar bookstores, with the loss of shop windows, display tables and front-of-store browsing space, is making it harder and harder for their books to get discovered, but compared to the challenges facing app developers, the retail environment of book publishers looks like an embarrassment of riches. App developers are launching their app in a world where

---

[10] See Thomas Sommer, 'App Store Stats Bonanza' (7 August 2014), at www.applift. com/blog/app-store-stats-bonanza.html.

there is only one store with only one storefront controlled by one player that selects and features a few apps each week entirely at its discretion, and tens of thousands of new apps are being added every month to this store which already holds over a million apps. You have to hope and pray that your app will get featured in that store-front and, better still, get selected as Editor's Choice because without that, you're screwed – a tiny speck lost in an ocean of content. Sure, there are some places where you can get reviews of a new app that will help to get it noticed, but these are nowhere near as numerous and varied as the review spaces still available to book publishers. And then there's the problem of price: with two-thirds of all apps downloadable for free, and nearly 90 per cent of all apps priced at $1.99 or less, how do you persuade consumers to spend $13.99 on one app? In a world where information goods are increasingly free or very cheap, how do you overcome the risk factor and get consumers to pay for quality?

These two problems – visibility (or rather invisibility) and price (or rather the downward pressure on price) – worked against a publisher like Touch Press, which positioned itself at the quality end of the app marketplace. Touch Press was committed to developing premium apps, which require a great deal of time, expertise and expense to produce – in the case of Disney Animated, around ten people worked on this app pretty much full-time over a period of eight months, with a development budget of £400,000. They had to be able to sell this app in a quantity that numbered in the hundreds of thousands, and at a price that was well above the very low prices at which most apps are sold. They had everything going for them on this occasion, and they simply couldn't generate enough revenue to cover their costs and provide the additional funds you need to make a business work: 'We tested the model exquisitely well and it doesn't work.'

So where could they go from here? What were their options? One was to scale back, let some staff go, produce apps of much lower quality, charge a lot less for them and hope you can make the business work on a smaller budget. But to Max and Theo, that felt like an admission of failure. They started this business in the belief that they could create something genuinely new, help to invent a new kind of publishing and a new kind of book – the book-as-app – that would bring important works to life on a digital device as a rich audio, visual and textual experience. To scale back now would almost certainly mean that their ability to produce apps of this kind and quality would be seriously compromised. They might be able to make small savings here and there and produce their apps for less – maybe 10 or 20 per cent less – but they couldn't cut more than that and still produce apps of the kind of quality that was their trademark. Producing cheap apps that got the job done but had no real aesthetic value was not the kind of business they wanted to be in. They would also risk losing their best staff, who may not want to stay at a company that was downsizing and couldn't afford to pay top rates.

Another option was to try to re-orient the business – to 'pivot', as they say in the world of start-ups. They could move more into agency work, for example, selling services to other businesses rather than, or in addition to, developing apps for individual consumers. They'd developed a set of technical skills that could be used to develop apps for companies and other organizations that were seeking to promote a product or build their brand. This had the potential to generate significant revenue and produce good margins, provided that your negotiating position was strong enough to enable you to charge a fee based on a substantial mark-up of 50 per cent or more from your actual costs. They could build on the reputation they'd established as a high-end app developer – 'cash in' their accumulated symbolic capital – to try to turn the company into a profitable business. The potential gains would be financial: it might enable them to generate sufficient revenue at a sufficient margin to turn the organization into a profitable business. The downside would be the loss of creative control. 'I know that once you take on one of those commissions you find that you have absolutely no freedom of choice but to deliver the project to the highest possible quality on time, and you have to put your best people on to it to do that', reflected Max. 'And ultimately, if the client wants something, that's what the client gets. So there's much less room to do the new, totally different kind of work that we've tried to do. I just couldn't see something like The Waste Land ever coming out of that kind of work.'

In the course of 2014, it became increasingly clear that the company would need to do something. They couldn't continue to produce these big, beautiful apps, put their heart and soul into them, and hope for success: they would simply run out of cash. The Board brought in a new CEO who had a background in business development, and her remit was to cut the losses and make the business profitable. The company moved premises to a stylish suite of offices in central London, subtly altered its name from Touch Press to touchpress and tried to build up the agency side of the business. Relations between the principals of the old Touch Press and the new management cooled, Max stepped down from the Board and he and Theo began to put their energies into other things. The agency business didn't pan out for the rebranded touchpress, and by early 2016 the company was in serious trouble. The new CEO was fired and the company sold its portfolio of science and literature apps to a new, venture capital-backed publisher in the educational content market, Touch Press Inc., that was formed through the collaboration of the Irish digital publisher StoryToys and the educational games specialist Amplify Games. Rebranded as Amphio, it was announced that the new venture would focus on developing interactive tools and content for educational and cultural institutions. The bold attempt to create a new kind of publishing by building beautiful apps for the general consumer that made full use of the technical possibilities opened up by the iPad was effectively at an end.

For Max and Theo, the two creative driving forces behind Touch Press, it was a disappointing realization. They'd set out six years earlier with the aim of creating a completely new kind of ebook, a book-as-app that worked in ways that were completely different from the printed book and that engaged the reader/user in a rich, multi-layered, multimedia experience, and with the aim of building a business that would enable them to sustain this creative activity. They succeeded in the former but not in the latter. 'I think we've shown that the medium is capable of creating a really strong engagement between the subject and the reader', reflected Max; 'I think we've shown that the material has a way of inspiring somebody who has an interest in a subject and giving them the best possible way of exploring it.' But he had to accept that the model didn't work in the end. There was a brief moment in the two to three years after the iPad had been introduced when it was possible to produce a beautiful app and get people to pay $10 or $15 for it, and you could build a publishing venture around it. But that moment is now over. 'It was a brief moment that opened and closed and I'm delighted it happened because it allowed us to take some steps forward in the long-term development of interactive media. But as a business venture it just didn't work.'[11]

---

[11] Others came to a similar conclusion. Dave Addey founded Agant, an app development agency, in 2002, and had great success with the National Rail Enquiries app for the iPhone that was launched in 2009. He went on to build numerous apps for publishers, among others, including several apps for Faber – one of which, Malcolm Tucker: The Missing iPhone, an app version of the book *The Thick of It: The Missing DoSAC Files*, was nominated for a BAFTA in 2011. He had enough projects under way to move into a suite of offices in Leamington Spa and take on several additional members of staff. But he found that the same pincer movement of pressures that had undermined Touch Press – the difficulty of achieving visibility in the App Store and

False dawn

The period from 2010 to 2015 witnessed a flurry of ambitious new publishing ventures that were riding the wave of the digital revolution, seeking in different ways to re-invent the book for the digital age – Touch Press was one of the most original and ambitious of these but they were just one of many. What 're-inventing the book' meant varied greatly from one venture to the next – it was the sheer openness of what it *could* mean that was part of the excitement of the time. For some, it was a matter of experimenting with the length of what was normally regarded as 'a book': liberated from the need to produce texts of a certain extent to be long enough for the purposes of producing a conventional physical book, it now seemed possible to re-invent the book as something much shorter, something that could be written quickly and read in a single sitting, something much closer to a short story or a long article – the e-single or digital short. For others, re-inventing the book meant something more radical: it meant thinking of 'digital books' as something other than digital replicas of print books, something other than digital images of static text that can be read on a screen rather than on paper, something other than 'vanilla ebooks'. Rather, it meant experimenting not just with the length of the text but with its very form: use the digital medium and all the technical possibilities afforded by it to think in new ways about what 'a book' is. Don't take for granted the form that has been bequeathed to us by 500 years of print-on-paper, as if the only thing that the digital revolution could do for the book was to make the same text available on screen, rather than as a physical object. Take the opportunity afforded by the digital revolution to create something entirely new where text is interwoven with music, spoken words, images and video, where text is no longer static but fluid, where readers become part of the very story they are reading and where the story comes alive in ways that were just not possible in the old static world of printed text. Such was the promise of the digital revolution: the dawn of a new age in the long history of the book when the very form of the book, and the very nature of what 'a book' is, could be re-invented from scratch.

---

the downward pressure on prices – was also making life very difficult for Agant. In the end, he threw in the towel and closed down the business in 2013: 'I don't see the creation of apps as products being worth the risk, especially when I am the person taking the risk.'

The first few steps into this brave new world have turned out to be much more difficult than anyone thought. Not that it's difficult to *imagine* new possibilities, or even that difficult to *create* them – this can all be done, and the period from 2010 to 2015 was full of new experiments and ventures that did exactly this. We were showered with the bounties of digital creativity. What is much more difficult is to come up with an organizational structure and a business model that will enable these new digital outputs to be produced in an ongoing, sustainable way. Wonderful new digital objects have been created, one might even call them new forms of the book that stretch our understanding of what 'a book' is and can be, but the processes that led to their creation were, for the most part, unsustainable – most of the organizations in which these processes were embedded failed. For one reason or another, they just couldn't generate sufficient revenue to continue their creative activities. They may have had one or two or even several great successes but, as markets changed and windows of opportunity closed, their ability to secure a viable revenue stream declined. Success turned into failure, excitement and hope turned into disappointment, and the idea that the digital revolution might lead to the invention of a new *form* of the book, as distinct from a new *format*, began to look less likely. This was turning out to be a false dawn.

We are still in the early stages of the digital age, of course, and it would be unwise to jump to conclusions about future developments on the basis of what has happened so far. The experiments that took place in the period from 2010 to 2015 were conditioned by the technologies and delivery systems available at the time, as well as by the broader features of an information environment in flux, and it could well be that, as this environment continues to evolve and as new technologies and delivery systems emerge, new opportunities for the re-invention of the book will arise. But then, as before, the same question of sustainability will arise, and new forms will endure only if the processes and organizations that bring them into being are able to survive and maintain these forms beyond the initial start-up phase.

— Chapter 3 —

THE BACKLIST WARS

While new books are the glamorous side of publishing, the backlist is in many ways the financial heart of the business. Once a book moves off the frontlist and on to the backlist, it will get much less media attention and much less marketing effort, but if it continues to sell, it will be much more profitable for the publisher – by this stage, production costs are likely to have been covered, the advance will either be recouped or written off and marketing costs will be much lower, so the net receipts from sales will make a much bigger contribution to the publisher's bottom line. Publishers with a large backlist are therefore in a much stronger position in the market-place. If 50 per cent of their revenue is accounted for by backlist sales, then they're already halfway up the mountain at the start of each new financial year and they only have to climb the second half with their list of new titles – still challenging, but much less onerous than starting again from the bottom of the mountain (or the low foothills) at the beginning of each financial year. But the problem is that backlists take a long time to build. Year after year, last year's frontlist becomes this year's backlist, slowly expanding its size. This partly explains why, for forty years, from 1960 to the end of the millennium, the large publishing corporations were so eager to acquire other publishing houses: this was the best shortcut there was to building the backlist – the only way you could short-circuit the long and arduous process of building a backlist. It also explains why publishers were so incensed when the digital revolution opened up a space for a handful of start-ups who saw the opportunity to snap up the digital rights on backlist titles and release them as ebooks, eating into the backlist of the established publishers and launching the backlist wars.

There are two dates that made the backlist wars possible: 1923 and 1994. The year 1994 is important because that is the year when many publishers first began to realize that they needed to add a clause to their standard author contracts that dealt with ebooks and expressly assigned ebook rights to the publisher. Prior to that, most author contracts didn't explicitly mention ebooks, or even digital rights. Some contracts might have included a clause that covered uses 'in storage and retrieval systems', and might even have referred to storage and retrieval 'through computer, mechanical or other electronic means now known or hereafter invented' or some such phrase; but with no explicit mention of ebooks, it wasn't clear whether generic clauses of this kind would cover the sale of the work as an ebook. From 1994 on, however, most publishers twigged that there was a potentially dangerous loophole here and they took steps to close it by adding a clause to their author contracts that expressly assigned ebook rights to the publisher, with an agreed royalty payable on net receipts of all ebooks sold.

The year 1923 is important because all books published before 1923 are in the public domain. Books published from 1923 on may or may not be in the public domain, depending on various considerations. The general rule in US copyright law is that books remain in copyright for seventy years after the death of the author, though there are various conditions that can affect the application of this rule.[1] So books published in the seventy years from 1923 to 1993 formed a vast ocean of backlist content where ebook rights were still potentially available. The right to exploit this content in ebook form, as distinct from the printed book, might still rest with the author or the author's estate and could, at least in theory, be assigned to some party other than the publisher of the printed book. 'Might' because many publishers, seeing the risk, took action pre-emptively to close the loophole by writing to authors, agents and estates and agreeing addenda to their pre-1994 contracts that expressly assigned ebook rights to the publisher. 'In theory' because,

---

[1] For example, a work that was granted copyright before 1978 had to have its copyright renewed in the work's twenty-eighth year in order to extend its term of protection. The need to renew copyrights was eliminated by the Copyright Renewal Act of 1992, but works that had entered the public domain through non-renewal were not granted copyright protection again. So works published before 1964 that were not renewed are in the public domain. For a useful summary of the various conditions that affect term of copyright, see Peter B. Hirtle, 'Copyright Term and the Public Domain in the United States' (1 January 2015), at https://copyright.cornell.edu/resources/publicdomain.cfm.

until the famous RosettaBooks case of 2001, no one had tested this in the courts.

Opening salvo

RosettaBooks was the brainchild of Arthur Klebanoff, an agent-turned-publisher who founded the company with a couple of colleagues in 2000.[2] As a literary agent with a training in law, Arthur had been convinced for some time that authors owned the electronic rights to any title where the publishing contract was silent on electronic rights, so he decided to set up an electronic publishing company that would focus on acquiring exclusive electronic rights to selected backlist titles. This was the late 1990s and he was well aware that many publishers were actively seeking to tie down electronic rights for their key backlist titles and authors, but he thought that, as a small, independent electronic-only publisher, he might have certain advantages. He knew that most backlist titles were no longer actively promoted by their publishers and that many authors and agents resented this. He knew that many publishers were concerned not to price ebooks too cheaply, for fear of under-mining the sales of their print editions and eroding their revenues; as an electronic publisher acquiring electronic rights on backlist titles, he would have more flexibility on pricing. He also knew that most publishers were not paying advances for electronic rights and were expecting to be granted these rights for life of copyright. So the offer of a modest advance, coupled with a short-term licence of five – or even three – years, could amount to a compelling argument.

Encouraged by Steve Riggio at Barnes & Noble, who was eager to have a portfolio of ebooks that might help him to position B&N at the forefront of what was then a largely non-existent ebook marketplace, Arthur and his colleagues set out to acquire electronic rights for a range of prominent backlist titles. Taking advantage of the contacts he had established as an agent and as a rights manager for Easton Press, a leather-bound publisher in the US, Arthur and his colleagues acquired electronic rights from the estate of Aldous Huxley for *Brave New World* and *Brave New World Revisited*;

---

[2] Arthur Klebanoff gives his own illuminating account of the founding of RosettaBooks in his memoir, *The Agent: Personalities, Politics, and Publishing* (New York: Texere, 2001), pp. 1–29.

they acquired electronic rights for Kurt Vonnegut's *Slaughterhouse Five* and four other Vonnegut titles; for Pat Conroy's *The Prince of Tides* and three other titles; for Agatha Christie's *And Then There Were None* and two other titles; for Theodore Dreiser's *An American Tragedy*; for George Orwell's *1984*; and for the six volumes of Winston Churchill's *The Second World War*. Many others followed – soon they had acquired electronic rights on nearly a hundred titles in fiction, science fiction, mystery and serious nonfiction.

RosettaBooks was launched on 26 February 2001. The very same morning, they received a hand-delivered letter from Random House's lawyers demanding that they immediately take down eight books by Kurt Vonnegut, William Styron and Robert Parker – three authors published by Random House. Random House made it clear that they would sue if they didn't comply. Arthur and his colleagues were caught off guard – they knew publishers wouldn't like what they were doing but they didn't expect to be sued, certainly not on day one. They had to make a quick decision: do they fight or do they fold? They decided to fight the case. Random House argued that the basic publishing right covered by their contracts – namely, 'the right to print, publish, and sell works in book form' – included electronic books, and they asked a federal district court in New York to grant an injunction. In July 2001, Judge Sidney Stein rejected Random House's request for a preliminary injunction and concluded that Random House's right, as stated in the contract, 'to print, publish and sell the work in book form', did not include the format 'that has come to be known as the e-book'. Random House appealed to the Second Circuit, and in March 2002 the Second Circuit unanimously upheld Stein's opinion. The parties decided not to pursue the matter further in the courts and they reached a settlement in December 2002 that enabled Rosetta to continue publishing electronically the eight titles that had triggered the lawsuit and to release electronic editions of a few dozen other Random House titles that were formally licensed to Rosetta. The case never went to trial and Random House continued to maintain that their contracts gave it ebook rights, but a precedent was set. Publishers now knew that they had to be very careful. They could not assume that 'the right to print, publish, and sell works in book form' automatically included the right to publish the book in an electronic format. They would need to contact authors, agents and estates, if they hadn't done so already, and work out special ebook agreements if they wanted to be confident that they had these rights.

106

Arthur and his colleagues at Rosetta felt vindicated by the judges' decisions. 'The judge's fundamental ruling', said Arthur, 'was that absent the specific grant of digital rights to the publisher, the digital rights were retained by the author' – this had always been Arthur's view and now it seemed to have judicial support. He and his colleagues pressed ahead with their project of licensing backlist titles and publishing them as ebooks, expanding their list of available titles. New acquisitions were going well; the only problem was that no one was buying the ebooks. They were at least five years ahead of the market. The business went nowhere – until, that is, Amazon launched the Kindle in November 2007.

Once the Kindle had been launched, Amazon wanted more strong-selling titles available as ebooks – the more they could get, the better, from their point of view. But publishers were still in the process of contacting authors and estates to tie down ebook rights – this was slow work and Amazon was in a hurry. So in 2009, the content team at Kindle contacted Arthur to let him know that they were keen to have strong backlist titles from Rosetta. Moreover, if Amazon were given an exclusive on the title for a year, they would make certain commitments in terms of site merchandising that might be attractive to authors and agents. With this in mind, Arthur acquired the electronic rights for two of Stephen Covey's books, *The 7 Habits of Highly Effective People* and *Principle-Centered Leadership*, as Kindle exclusives. *The 7 Habits* was a huge bestseller. Originally published by Simon & Schuster in 1989, it had sold more than 15 million copies and was still the number one nonfiction title of Simon & Schuster's backlist. 'Simon & Schuster went beserk', recalled Arthur. 'They threatened to sue but didn't. Barnes & Noble went beserk, threatened all kinds of things, didn't do anything.' The ebook was published by Rosetta in December 2009 and went quickly to number one in the Kindle store. It generated very substantial royalties for the author, since in this case Rosetta was paying a royalty of more than 50 per cent of net receipts.

With the surge in ebook sales that followed the introduction of the Kindle, Rosetta's revenues suddenly took off. They went from nothing to $4 million in a few years – their time had come. From 2013 on, sales levelled off, reflecting the broader trends in the ebook marketplace, but by then they had established what appeared to be a viable business. By taking on Random House and getting two judicial rulings in his favour, Arthur had also helped to open the door for others who saw the backlist as a large, unruly continent that could be mined for ebook rights.

Bringing the greats back to life

Jane Friedman was one such person. Jane had been a vice-president of Random House and Knopf and publisher of Vintage before becoming CEO of HarperCollins, so she knew the world of trade publishing extremely well. After her departure from HarperCollins in 2008, she started Open Road Integrated Media with VC funding. Like Rosetta, Open Road was premised on the assumption that the ebook rights on most books published prior to 1994 were unassigned unless the publishers of the print editions had contacted the authors, agents or estates and entered into separate agreements for ebook rights. Jane was well aware that most publishers' contracts prior to 1994 didn't deal explicitly with ebook rights because she was working at Random House at that time and she knew what their contracts said. She also knew, like everyone else, that Judge Stein had refused to grant Random House's request for a preliminary injunction against RosettaBooks in 2001 and that the case had been settled out of court. Like Klebanoff, she had no truck with the idea that e-rights were implicitly granted to publishers by generic clauses about 'the right to print, publish, and sell works in book form', or by generic clauses about 'storage and retrieval by electronic means', or by non-competition clauses. If the contract did not specifically mention e-rights, then they were, in Jane's view, unassigned and could legitimately be acquired by Open Road if they had not already been sewn up by the original publisher of the print edition or by some other party. But every contract needed to be scrutinized and every word needed to be carefully weighed. If the contract was ambiguous and her lawyers were not convinced that the ebook rights were free, they would simply pass.

By the time Open Road was founded in 2008, the Kindle had been launched and ebooks were beginning to take off in the US. There was widespread recognition of the fact that ebook rights were a valued asset and that if publishers had not already agreed an explicit contract or addendum with the author, agent or estate, then they'd better move quickly. So Jane was entering a field where another player, Rosetta, was already active and where established publishers had a practical (if not a clear legal) advantage, having published the print edition of the book. So what could Open Road offer that the original publishers could not, or might not be willing to, offer?

Four things, reckoned Jane. First, lots of enthusiasm. Jane knew the value of backlist, and many of the titles she was pursuing had languished for years, decades even, at publishing houses that had lost interest in them long ago. Her message was simple: 'We want to bring the greats back to life.' She could go to authors or their estates and tell them that their books were the ones she really cared about, and that she and her company could breathe new life into them by republishing them as ebooks and promoting them in energetic and innovative ways. If there were several books that made up a corpus of an author's work, even better: the corpus could be repackaged and promoted as a whole. In a world that had become overly preoccupied with frontlist bestsellers, this was a powerful message.

Second, Jane could offer an attractive royalty split. By 2008–9, it had become conventional in trade publishing for publishers to pay a royalty of 25 per cent of net receipts on all ebook sales. This was not uncontested – many agents believed it should be more, especially on backlist titles, and in some cases sliding scales were agreed, starting at 25 per cent of net and rising to higher percentages after certain thresholds were passed. But 25 per cent of net receipts had settled into a kind of industry norm, at least for the time being, enabling the different parties to get on with the business of ebook publishing and to see how things panned out. Jane took a different view. She offered a straight 50:50 split on net receipts once the cost of digitization had been taken off. 'It's a very clean model: you give us the content, we give you the marketing. Everything is 50:50.' The cost of digitization for a typical book is pretty modest – usually no more than $400 – and this is recouped pretty quickly. 'The author is in the money at about 60 downloads', explained Jane.

Third, she offered to acquire ebook rights for limited time periods. Initially, she negotiated five-year licences – 'I felt it would be easier for us to get books for five years', said Jane. This contrasted sharply with the practice of most mainstream publishers, who were generally seeking to ensure that their ebook rights were aligned with their print rights, which meant in most cases that ebook rights would be granted for the full term of copyright. For an author, agent or estate, granting ebook rights for five years is going to look a lot more attractive than granting them for the full term of copyright, especially given the uncertainty at the time about where ebook sales would end up. Jane later acknowledged, however, that longer licences would have been better for Open Road.

Fourth, and most importantly in Jane's view, they could offer a concerted marketing campaign. In Jane's conception, Open Road was designed to be a marketing operation above all else – it's 'a great marketing machine'. The entire organization was built around marketing. It didn't look like a traditional publisher with a marketing department: it looked more like a marketing company with a publisher attached. Most of the staff were involved in marketing: in 2012, there were around forty people working in the open-plan office in the SoHo district of Manhattan where they were then based, most of them under 30, and 80 per cent were marketers. Most of the editorial work was outsourced. There was one publisher and one person who worked on backlist acquisition, but the vast majority of the staff were working in marketing. 'We build bibles of information about the author', explained Jane, 'and the authors say they've never been treated like this in their lives. Our whole premise is that we market 365 days a year throughout the term of license.' Most authors feel that their backlist books are neglected by publishers. They feel that traditional book publishers are only interested in marketing new books, and they think that, if older books are not marketed, they'll be forgotten. They're largely right. So the idea of rescuing books that were published decades ago, repackaging them and giving them a serious and innovative marketing boost, is a pretty compelling proposition to many authors, agents and estates. Who doesn't want their book returned to the limelight once again?

What Jane didn't offer – unlike Rosetta – is advances. In her view, advances were part of an old model of publishing that is pretty much broken, and she didn't want to carry it over into this new digital domain. She wanted a new model, a partnership, where net receipts would be shared 50:50 once the cost of digitization had been taken out. It's simple, easy to understand, and compelling in its own way.

Armed with these arguments and backed by several million dollars of VC funding, Jane set out to build a list – fast. Speed was essential, partly because she needed critical mass and partly because, with VC backing, she needed to show revenue growth quickly. The main objective was to identify 'brand authors' and acquire their catalogues – not just one isolated title but the whole corpus of their backlist. In May 2010, Open Road released its first ebook: *Sophie's Choice* by William Styron. Other Styron titles soon followed, including *The Confessions of Nat Turner*, *Lie Down in Darkness* and *Darkness Visible*. Random House had published Styron in print but they accepted that they could not prevent the Styron family from negotiating a separate deal with Open Road for these and other titles, all of which had been originally contracted by Random House before the contracts included a clause dealing with electronic rights. Rose Styron, William Styron's widow, said the family was attracted by the marketing plan and the 50:50 profit share – 'My children and I felt

110

it would be a fine way to get him back into the public eye', she said in an interview with the *New York Times*.[3] Many other authors and books followed – soon Open Road was releasing ebook editions of titles by Pat Conroy, Alice Walker, James Jones, Pearl S. Buck and many others. By August 2011, they had published 780 titles, and by August 2012 – just over two years after they launched – they had published nearly 3,000.

While Random House and most publishers stood back and watched as Open Road released a growing number of backlist titles as ebooks – concerned, but generally resigned to the fact that the contractual status was sufficiently unclear to make a legal challenge risky – the company of which Jane was formerly the CEO, HarperCollins, took a less benevolent view. On 23 December 2011, HarperCollins filed a copyright infringement lawsuit against Open Road over publication of the ebook edition of Jean Craighead George's bestselling children's book *Julie of the Wolves*. HarperCollins claimed that its contract with George, signed in 1971, gave it the right to be the exclusive publisher of *Julie of the Wolves* 'in book form', including via 'computer, computer-stored, mechanical or other electronic means now known or hereafter invented', and that the ebook edition released by Open Road, who had signed an agreement with the author for ebook rights, was in violation of HarperCollins's contractual rights. In March 2014, US District Court Judge Naomi Reice Buchwald ruled in favour of HarperCollins. Unlike the Rosetta case, the George contract included an unusual combination of clauses that enabled HarperCollins to argue that the contract granted them the exclusive right to license an electronic edition of the book, albeit with the permission of the author. Moreover, unlike the Rosetta case, where the contract made no mention of electronic exploitation, Paragraph 20 of the George contract specifically referred to future computer-based technologies, 'now known or hereafter invented'. 'This language, encompassing as it does the forward-looking reference to technologies "now known or hereafter invented", is sufficiently broad to draw within its ambit e-book publication', said Judge Buchwald, who viewed this as consistent with 'new use' precedent – that is, previous cases in related industries that established a procedure for evaluating whether a contract covers later-invented technology. 'Although no commercial market for e-books existed at the time of its drafting, e-book

---

[3] Motoko Rich, 'Random House Cedes Some Digital Rights to Styron Heirs', *The New York Times*, 25 April 2010, at www.nytimes.com/2010/04/26/books/26random. html?_r=0.

technology comprises a later-invented version of the very "computer, computer-stored, mechanical or other electronic means" provided by Paragraph 20.'[4] This was not a judgment with which Jane and her colleagues at Open Road agreed. In their view, the phrase 'computer, computer-stored, mechanical or other electronic means now known or hereafter invented' referred to electronic databases, not ebooks. Based on new use precedent, Judge Buchwald took a more expansive view. But, in any case, the language was specific to this contract, and indeed it had been inserted into this contract by the agent, not by the publisher, so it was unlikely to appear in many other contracts. Open Road lost the case, but their aggressive acquisitions strategy continued more or less undeterred. From that point on, they would avoid contracts that included phrases like 'electronic storage and retrieval', not because they believed that this meant 'ebooks' – in their view, 'electronic storage and retrieval' meant 'database' – but simply because it wasn't worth taking the risk that another decision of this kind might go against them.

Alongside their aggressive acquisitions strategy, Open Road built a formidable marketing machine. The idea was simple enough: build a massive database and fill it with content about your brand authors and books. Tag everything so that it can be searched and accessed easily. And then create stories that you can push out to the relevant social communities at the right time – 'what I call the passion communities', explained Jane: 'We push these stories out to websites, we push these stories out to blogs, we push these stories out on video channels and we push these stories out through all the marketing channels of all the e-tailers. So the whole notion is that we reach the consumer where the consumer is living, online, with these stories we have created. And these stories lead them to a video that is one click away from the sale of the book.' For example, for Father's Day, they write a story about a letter that one of their authors wrote to his father, talking about the book he'd just written, and they make this the centrepiece of their Father's Day promotion, which they send out with a video link to lots of websites and blogs, and it gets picked up by Motherlode and the *New York Times* and viewed by millions. Similarly with National Depression Awareness Month, Black History Month, Women's History Month, National Teacher's Day, National Bullying Prevention Month, National Take-Your-Child-to-Work Day,

---

[4] Naomi Reice Buchwald, *HarperCollins Publishers LLC* v. *Open Road Integrated Media, LLP*, United States District Court, S. D. New York, 7 F. Supp. 3d 363 (SDNY 2014), p. 7, at https://casetext.com/case/harpercollins-publishers-llc-v-open-rd-integrated-media.

etc. – all are opportunities to create stories from the database that are rich and interesting in themselves and push them out to all the relevant passion communities you can find, thereby raising awareness of your authors and books and giving readers an easy way of buying them.

Crucial to the marketing machine was the ability to create their own high-quality video content – 'video is part of our secret sauce', said Jane. They had an in-house video production team and they put a great deal of time, effort and thought into shooting videos with their authors. While many publishers have produced short book trailers for the books they were publishing, that was not Open Road's approach. They wanted to produce something much richer and more innovative that was focused on the author. 'The author is always the brand', explained Luke, a former movie maker who headed up Open Road's video production team. Their aim was to create a setting that enabled the author to talk naturally about some aspect of their life, in a context where they felt entirely comfortable. The video production team did a great deal of research about the life of an author before they began, and they then sent a small production team to the author's home turf for the shoot. They gathered lots of content on each shoot – six to seven hours, maybe more. Three to four hours of this was interview material with the author, the rest was 'B-roll' – that is, shots of the house, the gardens, local landscapes, etc. – that could be used in making a video. The vast majority of this material went into the archive as tagged content. A small amount was used to make a short video that could be posted on Open Road's website and pushed out to other sites – and 'short' means very short, 1 minute 49 seconds to be precise. That was their understanding of the attention span for viewing videos online: given the distractions of the internet, you're doing well if you can hold people's attention for that long. So that's the challenge: to tell an engaging story with a three-act structure in 1 minute 49 seconds. 'We break everything down into three acts', explained Luke, 'that's the age-old way of constructing a movie. So, in essence, establishing, developing, resolving within 1 minute 49 seconds.' Translated into this context, the three-act structure turns into this: 'introduce the author, tell the audience something about the author that they didn't know or that we think is appealing, and finish up with something that leaves you wanting more of the author.' Music is then woven in to help create mood and flow. The results were compelling. Each video was a carefully crafted audio-visual experience that engaged the viewer, enabled them to connect briefly with an author and told them something about this author that they probably didn't know. And the large amount of video material that didn't get used in this short video became part of the content database, where it was coded and organized so that it could be pulled out at any time and used for the mashups that they were constantly putting together and pushing out to websites, blogs and passion communities of various kinds.

Like Rosetta, Open Road had shown that it was possible to build a new publishing business by acquiring unassigned ebook rights for backlist titles. They married this with an innovative marketing operation that took advantage of the new information environments that were being created by the internet – a combination that delivered impressive growth: by 2014, a mere four years after publishing their first ebook, they had a list of around 9,000 titles, they were employing around fifty people and they had revenues of around $15 million. Like Rosetta, they faced the occasional legal challenge; but authors' contracts that were devised in the pre-digital era were, for the most part, either silent on electronic publishing or sufficiently ambiguous to make a legal challenge risky, and hence the universe of books published between 1923 and 1994 was likely to contain a large number of titles for which ebook rights remained unassigned. The real challenge for a publishing venture like Open Road was less likely to be legal than economic: it was the old-fashioned challenge of turning a growing business with significant revenues into a profitable one. 'It's hard to make a profit', conceded Jane. The problem was two-fold: on the one hand, high overheads, and on the other, downward pressure on prices. The overheads were high because Open Road had expanded its staff aggressively, especially on the marketing side. Jane had taken the view that intensive marketing was essential for the company's success, and the kind of marketing model she developed, which included the shooting of original video on-site, didn't come cheap. 'Our overheads are high and they have to be', she averred, 'because if we don't deliver on what we promised then we're not going to have the authors and then we're not going to have the revenue.' On the other hand, the downward pressure on prices in the world of ebooks is intense. 'Making money in the digital world is the most difficult part of it', continued Jane, 'and the very fast declension of price is what is troubling me as a business because my business model was based on a certain sale price.' She had assumed that they were going to sell their ebooks at around $14[5] and they were going

---

[5] This was the 'digital list price' – that is, the price that the publisher gave to the ebook. But since ebooks were supplied to retailers like Amazon using a wholesale

to receive $7, half of which they would pass on to the author, so their revenue per sale would be $3.50. But in practice it didn't work out like that. The prices have gone much, much lower, and 'the prices have gone so low because this is a promotional business. This is the mass market of this generation. People want deals.' Amazon's Daily Deals are particularly popular, where prices are dropped to $1.99 for a limited time period. Special promotions of this kind do generate a spike in sales, but the revenue per sale is much lower. So, rather than earning $3.50 per sale, they might be earning 50¢ or less. Promotions like the Daily Deal show that there is some elasticity in the ebook marketplace: if you drop the price significantly, you are likely to sell more copies. But the experience of publishers like Open Road is that the increase in unit sales does not compensate for the decline in revenue per unit.

The limits of backlist-only ebook publishing

So is there a way forward here? Can a viable publishing business be built on the basis of acquiring ebook rights for backlist titles, as both Rosetta and Open Road sought to do? Of course, these are two very different organizations with different philosophies and strategies: Rosetta, with no external investment, built a small, curated list of around 700 titles and had a staff of only eight people and revenue of around $4 million in 2015, whereas Open Road used VC funding to expand its list and organization aggressively, so that by 2015 it had around 10,000 titles, more than fifty members of staff and revenues of around $15 million. In their differing ways, they both sought to build viable businesses by acquiring ebook rights for backlist titles, and in so doing they have shown three things. First, they have shown that there is a large body of material that is still under copyright (that is, published after 1923) and that is not yet available in electronic formats, and that the legal status of the electronic rights for many of these books is sufficiently unclear to enable organizations like Rosetta and Open Road to acquire these rights in direct negotiations with authors, agents and estates. Most contracts between publishers and authors prior to 1994 did not countenance the possibility of publishing the book in electronic formats and did not explicitly

---

model and a trade discount of around 50 per cent, Amazon and other retailers would commonly pass on some of the discount to consumers and sell the ebook for, say, $9.99. On a $14 book, the publisher would still receive $14 less 50 per cent, or $7.

address this issue. There were many variations in the language used in earlier contracts and some publishers or agents did introduce words, phrases or clauses that tried to anticipate possible future developments, thus creating a rather messy contractual landscape. But in those cases where contracts are completely silent on electronic, digital or ebook rights, then a strong case can be made that these rights remain with the author and can be assigned by the author, or by his or her estate, either to the publisher of the original print book or to another party, on terms to be agreed. Both Rosetta and Open Road built their businesses on the assumption that unassigned ebook rights on backlist titles remain with the author unless there is some special language in the contract that would lead one to assume otherwise, and so far this assumption has not been overturned in the courts.

Second, they have shown that there is still a great deal of untapped value in the backlist and that some of this value can be realized by making backlist titles available again as ebooks. The revenue growth that these companies achieved in the period from 2010 to 2014 was impressive by any reckoning. True, they were starting from a low base (zero in the case of Open Road), but they quickly rose to a position where they were generating revenues that exceeded those of many small publishers of a more traditional kind. They were greatly assisted in this regard by the broader surge in ebook sales that characterized the period from 2008 to 2014: in some ways, they were riding the wave of ebook growth, there at just the right time to take advantage of a broader shift that was occurring around them. But this also means that the slow-down and levelling off of this growth since 2014 has been, and may continue to be, a downward pressure on their revenue stream (a point to which we'll return).

Third, they have both shown, in their own ways, the value of innovative marketing that takes advantage of the opportunities afforded by the online environment. Open Road was particularly imaginative in this regard and found new ways to raise the profile of authors and books that had slipped long ago into the backwaters of contemporary culture – to make them visible again, bring them back to life and inject them into contemporary discussions and debates, many of which now take place online. Rosetta, too, emphasized innovative online marketing; it worked closely with BookBub, the subscription-based service that offers readers special deals on ebooks (more on this later), and built various tools that enabled it to connect with potential readers online and send out e-cards and e-codes to deliver ebooks, although Rosetta's investment in marketing was nowhere near as substantial as Open Road's. Both companies also put a great deal of thought and creativity into the repackaging of backlist titles for an electronic format – for example, completely redesigning covers so that they work well on a screen rather than a physical book, creating consistent covers across the whole corpus of an author's backlist, and so on.

But is this kind of publishing viable in the medium to long term? There were several factors working against these organizations – let me mention five. First, there is the levelling off of ebook sales: as the growth in ebook sales slowed down and began to flatten, they could no longer count on a rising tide that lifts all boats. The rapid growth of these organizations, which was underpinned by the ebook surge in the period from 2008 to 2012, would be difficult to sustain in an environment where ebook sales are largely static or even declining; and, unlike a traditional publisher, for whom ebooks are just one format among others, they would not find it easy to offset this decline by relying on print sales. With ebook rights as their only asset, they were particularly vulnerable to any downturn in the ebook marketplace. Second, the downward pressure on ebook prices, and the emphasis on special promotions like the Daily Deal and BookBub, meant that revenue per unit sale was likely to decline, and, while there is clearly some elasticity in the ebook marketplace, it is unlikely that the fall off in revenue per title would be wholly made up for in terms of increasing unit sales. Third, these factors combined were likely to place growing pressure on both revenues and profitability. Organizations that were modestly staffed, like Rosetta, were in a stronger position to cope with pressure on profitability. Larger organizations with many more staff, like Open Road, were likely to find themselves facing growing pressure to reduce overheads by freezing or cutting staff levels. Fourth, the main assets of these companies – the contracts that grant them ebook rights – are time-limited and need to be renewed or renegotiated after five or seven years, thus leading to new potential costs (in the form of refresher advances), revised terms that may be less favourable to the licensee and/or the risk of losing the most valuable titles. Fifth, the pool of valuable in-copyright backlist titles with unassigned ebook rights is finite and diminishing, as more and more of these rights are either tied down by the original print publisher or assigned to an ebook backlist publisher like Rosetta or Open Road. Hence, the capacity to grow by acquiring highly valued backlist titles with unassigned ebook rights is likely to decline with time. This is not a consideration that overly troubled Jane at Open Road – 'it's an infinite space', said Jane. Not only are there still thousands of backlist titles and authors still to be rediscovered and acquired, but there are also time-limited licences held by other publishers that could be moved over to Open Road when they expire. She was never worried about the drying up of the pool. Others are less sanguine – 'the pool has shrunk quite a lot', observed Arthur at Rosetta. If your aim is to publish not just any backlist titles and authors but, rather, works of quality that will be valued by readers – 'to bring the greats back to life' to use Jane's words – then it's not so clear that the pool of available acquisitions is of unfathomable depth.

Faced with these pressures, it's not surprising that organizations that built their businesses on acquiring ebook rights for backlist titles were soon looking for ways to diversify their revenue streams. For Rosetta, this search evolved into a two-pronged strategy. On the one hand, they set out to complement their backlist publishing programme by building a frontlist and offering authors a full range of publishing services, print as well as ebook – 'full service publishing', as Arthur put it. But, to do this, Rosetta would now have to compete directly with mainstream publishers – they would no longer be drinking from a different pool but would have to try to persuade authors to assign all publishing rights, not just ebook rights, to Rosetta. Of course, Rosetta couldn't compete with the large publishers in terms of advances, but they could offer attractive terms in other ways. They presented ebook royalties to authors as a 50:50 joint venture: once production costs had been covered, the author would receive 50 per cent of all revenue. This is much higher than the 25 per cent royalty on ebooks that is standard among traditional publishers. They could also offer authors a great deal of enthusiasm and a high level of control. Each book they publish will be treated as a priority, they said: it won't be lost in the bottom third of a large publisher's list of new titles. And authors would be given maximum editorial autonomy – 'we're saying to the author, we will give you our opinion on what we think you might do to make this the best book it can be but ultimately it's your decision. We will publish it – we will see that there is no filter between you and the audience.' Their ambitions were modest: if they could sign fifteen to eighteen new titles a year, that would be fine. It would create a new revenue stream that would offset some of their overhead costs and that could, if a book took off, make a real difference to both their revenue and their profitability. The second prong of Rosetta's strategy was to expand its collaboration with corporations and institutions. They developed a series of more than twenty books with the Mayo Clinic, for example, on topics ranging from diet and family health to Alzheimer's Disease, which have done very well.

Given Open Road's staffing levels and overheads, the task of developing an effective response to the pressures they faced was always going to be more challenging. In fact, the original business model of Open Road was based on the assumption that the company would have three revenue streams. One would come from publishing backlist titles as ebooks; a second would come from partnerships with other publishers, where Open Road would provide ebook publishing services to a publisher whose books were only available in print; and a third would come from publishing a small number of ebook originals, intended to be short books of 20,000 words or less, published as ebooks only – in other words, digital shorts. The split between these three strands was intended to be 45:45:10, though in practice it shifted over time to something more like 60:35:5, partly because, as other publishers found, the market for digital shorts turned out to be weak. With renewed pressure on revenue, Open Road moved further away from the original plan of publishing some original books and placed even more emphasis on building its marketing capacity in innovative ways, launching a series of community sites or 'verticals' which aimed to market directly to consumers. The prototype was a site aimed at true-crime and horror fans, called The Lineup: it would offer a steady stream of original content tailored to the interests of true-crime and mystery fans and showcase relevant ebooks, published both by Open Road and by other publishers. The aim was to roll out similar sites in other areas, mystery and thriller, sci-fi and fantasy, romance, etc., expanding Open Road's ability to reach consumers directly. A new senior manager was brought in, charged in part with the task of closing the gap between expenditure and revenue and putting the company on a pathway towards profitability. Some staff were laid off, others were appointed in different roles and new title acquisition ground to a halt. Jane took a back seat and eventually stepped down as Chairman and executive publisher of the company. She felt she had achieved her main goal – 'we had acquired 10,000 books, re-energized them and brought them back to life' – but the company was now moving in a different direction. The original idea of creating a profitable and growing business that would be based primarily on the acquisition of digital rights for backlist titles and the publication of an expanding list of ebooks had succeeded only in part: they had indeed acquired a substantial number of titles and built an innovative marketing machine that enabled them to re-promote backlist books in a new digital environment, but they were never able to achieve profitability on that basis. In the search for profitability, Open Road morphed from being a digital publishing company that was using innovative marketing methods to bring the greats back to life into what was becoming a digital marketing company that was providing a suite of marketing tools to other publishers.

RosettaBooks and Open Road Media were not the only start-ups that sought to build a new business by acquiring ebook rights for backlist titles, but they were the most prominent and they demonstrated very effectively that the digital revolution can revitalize the backlist, enabling new value to be extracted from titles that in many cases had long ceased to be regarded as valuable assets.[6] Books and authors that had largely been forgotten have been recovered, repackaged, re-promoted and injected back into the circuits of contemporary culture in ways that simply would not have happened in the pre-digital age, and even books and authors that had not been entirely forgotten have been made available in new ways, presented to new audiences and given a new lease on life. That this occasionally led to conflicts and legal battles with those publishers who had originally published the books in print is not surprising given that most contracts prior to 1994 had not envisaged the possibility of ebooks, and some contractually savvy entrepreneurs were bound to challenge the rights that some traditional publishers assumed were theirs; today, with the benefit of hindsight, it is also unsurprising that the urgency and intensity of these conflicts should have relented with time as the pool of available content began to dry up and the ebook surge began to subside. The backlist wars were a product of their time – a set of disputes that arose at a particular moment when the digital revolution was opening up new possibilities that could be seized upon by entrepreneurial individuals and start-ups and when

---

[6] Other start-ups that were based on the idea of acquiring ebook rights for backlist titles include E-Reads and Start Publishing. E-Reads was founded by Richard Curtis in 1999; its list of more than 1,200 ebooks was acquired by Open Road in 2014. Start Publishing was founded in 2012 as a spin-off of Start Media; they began by acquiring a large public-domain library, and then grew rapidly by acquiring the ebook assets of various companies, including Night Shade Books, Salvo Press, Cleis Press and Viva Editions; by 2017, they had sixteen different imprints and a list of some 7,300 titles, mostly in particular genres and niches like sci-fi, thriller, historical fiction, Christian fiction, etc. Unlike Rosetta and Open Road, Start Publishing's model is based on acquiring titles for term-of-copyright, not time-limited, licences. Also unlike Rosetta and Open Road, they steered clear of anything that might land them in legal conflicts with other parties; as one of their principals said, 'if someone claims they have the rights to something, then you should always err on the side of caution.'

the legal apparatus of the publishing industry had not yet caught up with the emerging technological capabilities. These were disputes that thrust some start-ups into conflict with mainstream publishers, new entrants into conflict with established incumbents of the field and, in some cases, erstwhile collaborators into conflict with one another.[7] But, however fraught they were at the time, these were skirmishes in comparison to some of the conflicts that were emerging elsewhere.

While the backlist wars underscored the importance of the backlist and the ways in which it could be revitalized in the digital age, it seems unlikely that a publishing programme based primarily or exclusively on the republishing in electronic formats of books originally published some years ago could ever be more than a niche operation in the ecology of publishing. A vibrant publishing ecology needs the constant creation of the new as well as the repackaging of the old. It needs publishers who are willing to take risks with the new, and who have to be able to offset the risks involved in publishing the new by relying on backlist sales to make up a substantial part of their revenue. A publisher focused largely or exclusively on acquiring the ebook rights for backlist titles can certainly enrich our contemporary culture of the written word by injecting new life into older works, but it will not stretch this culture by adding work that had never existed before. It is, by definition, a renovator of the old, not a creator of the new.

---

[7] A prominent example of conflict among erstwhile collaborators was the launching of Odyssey Editions by the agent Andrew Wylie in 2010. Frustrated by the unwillingness of mainstream publishers to pay higher royalties on the ebook sales of backlist titles, Wylie set up his own publishing venture to release ebook editions of backlist titles by some of his clients, including Saul Bellow, John Updike and Philip Roth. Intended as a way of putting pressure on publishers to pay higher royalties on ebook backlist sales, this initiative was met with outrage by the publishers themselves, and, shortly after Odyssey was launched, Random House announced that it would no longer do business with the Wylie agency. The normally canny Wylie was caught off guard by this abrupt counter-move by the largest of the trade publishers. After a series of meetings between Wylie and the CEO of Random House, a satisfactory agreement was reached and the Random House titles were removed from the Odyssey list. The launching of Odyssey was not so much the creation of a new publishing venture as, rather, a new move in an old game that was played by well-entrenched players in the publishing field, though a game in which something new – the royalties paid on ebook sales of backlist titles – was now at stake.

— Chapter 4 —

GOOGLE TROUBLE

It was undoubtedly very irritating for Random House, and a source of real concern to them and other publishers, when, in February 2001, a small New York start-up published ebook versions of a handful of books for which they believed they held the rights. But it was altogether more alarming when, in December 2004, Google – one of the largest and most powerful of the new tech giants emerging in Silicon Valley – announced that it had partnered with the university libraries of Harvard, Stanford, Michigan and Oxford, and with the New York Public Library, to scan and digitize millions of books that they held in their vaults. And so began a saga that would drag on for twelve long years, pitching the old world of East-coast publishing against the new West-coast world of high tech, move in and out of courtrooms and conference rooms and rack up millions of dollars in legal fees.

The dream of gathering together all the books of the world into a universal library has long been a feature of the human imagination, from the Library of Alexandria to Borge's Library of Babel. But with the enormous increase in the number of books published in the world, this dream seemed destined to recede further and further from reality. In the digital age, however, this old dream suddenly began to appear in a new light. Might it not be possible to digitize and deposit a substantial proportion of the world's books, if not all of them, in a database that would take up a tiny fraction of the space of a physical library and that could be accessed virtually and remotely – potentially by anyone in the world? Might it not be possible to build a universal library after all, a Library of Alexandria for the digital age? This lofty idea has fuelled the imagination of many. Michael Hart, who launched Project Gutenberg on a summer night in 1971, and Brewster

Kahle, a computer scientist who created the Internet Archive in 1996 and sought to expand it into an internet library that would be free to all, were but two of many who nourished the hope that the digital revolution would at long last make it possible to realize the dream of a universal library freely accessible to all. But, in fact, the origins of the Google Library Project were altogether more mundane.

The search engine wars

In the early 2000s, Google was a new entrant in the field of search engines, having launched a few years before as a classic Silicon Valley start-up. Larry Page and Sergey Brin had met in 1995 as graduate students at Stanford, where they had worked together to develop a search algorithm they called PageRank.[1] The distinctive feature of PageRank is that it used information about links – about the number and importance of the links that were pointing to a site – to rank the site. So if a very popular site A, like the Yahoo! homepage, linked to another site B, then B instantly became more important and was ranked higher in search results. By quantifying the number and importance of links pointing to a site, they could generate a mathematically rigorous way of ranking pages. This basic insight was then refined in innumerable ways, combining information about words and links with many other variables, to produce better and better search results. In 1998, Page and Brin persuaded an angel investor that the PageRank system for ranking search results was worth developing as a business, and with $100,000 in their pockets they took leave from Stanford and set up shop in a friend's garage in Menlo Park. A year later, they had secured $25 million in VC funding from Kleiner Perkins and Sequoia Capital. The company grew quickly and, by March 2001, Google had 12 per cent of the search engine market share in the US. But it was still overshadowed by Yahoo!, the dominant player by far with 36.5 per cent of the search engine market, and by Microsoft's MSN, which had 15 per cent.[2] The question of how to grow Google and overtake its main competitors – and especially its arch-rival Microsoft – was the question that

---

[1] On the origins of Google, see David A. Vise with Mark Malseed, *The Google Story* (New York: Bantam Dell, 2005).
[2] 'Search Engine Market Shares', Frictionless Data, at http://data.okfn.org/data/rgrp/search-engine-market-shares#readme.

preoccupied Page and Brin. What could Google do that would give it the edge in the increasingly heated search engine wars?

Search engines work by using automated bots – or spiders – to crawl the web and gather information which is then indexed and deposited in large databases that are used as the basis for responding to search queries. The search engine's algorithm displays what it regards as the most relevant documents that match a user's query. It follows that the quality of the search results depends both on the sophistication of the algorithm and on the quality of the material that has been deposited in the database, and you can improve results both by improving the algorithm and by improving the quality of the material in the database. The PageRank algorithm had proven to be very effective as a way of ordering search results by taking account of links and weighing their relative importance, so that users were more likely to find what they were looking for without having to scroll through pages and pages of results. But how could you improve the quality of material in the database? If the information in the database is simply the information gathered by crawling the web, then the quality is dependent on the quality of the material that was being made available by the millions of users and organizations that were populating the web with content. This material is going to be very uneven – some of it will be good but a lot will be pretty poor. But what if you didn't just rely on what was out there on the web? Why not look for other content – content that was more likely to be consistently of high quality that could be digitized and added to your database? This was the line of thinking that led Page and Brin to the idea that one very good way of increasing the quality of the material in Google's database, and thereby improving its search results, would be to digitize the content of books and add this content to its data repository. 'The first, second and third reason why we invested in digitizing books has everything to do with increasing our search quality', explained one senior manager at Google. 'Books are highly authoritative, there are millions of them and they're mostly invisible to end users using the web, so we're looking to make better matches for people using Google. The idea that you could search all the world's books in all languages is obviously a huge competitive advantage for a search engine, since the search engine is only as good as what it crawls.' If a person searching for information about, say, cervical cancer were able to retrieve information not just from websites but also from the best scientific and medical books on the topic, then the quality of information they got would be greatly improved. As a repository of knowledge and high-quality content, books are hard to beat. The Google principals may well have harboured their own dreams of creating a universal library that would make all knowledge available online (Page had worked on a Digital Libraries Project as a graduate student at Stanford)[3], but the motivation for digitizing book content was rooted firmly in Google's determination to strengthen its competitive advantage vis-à-vis Yahoo! and Microsoft in the search engine wars.

To pursue this strategy, Google launched two ambitious book digitization programmes in 2004, the Partner Program and the Library Project. The two programmes were developed separately with different sets of clients, but together they comprised the Google Books program, sometimes referred to as 'Google Books'. The Partner Program, formally announced as 'Google Print' at the Frankfurt Book Fair in October 2004, involved collaborating with publishers and persuading them to give Google permission to scan their books and deposit the scanned text in their database. In response to a search query, a user would get a link to a relevant text and, by clicking on the link, would be able to see the full page containing the search term as well as a few pages before and after that page. The benefit to the publisher was that the book would be called to the attention of the user, who would be able to browse a few pages in Book Search and click on a link to Amazon, to the publisher's website or to another retailer to buy the book – it was, in effect, a free form of online marketing. Since the publisher had a contract with Google that regulated the conditions under which the text could be viewed and enabled the publisher to remove any title at any time, most publishers felt comfortable with this programme. There were some who declined to participate, in part because they preferred to retain control of how their books were browsed online, and in part because they were nervous about handing over their most valuable asset – their book content – to a large and powerful corporation whose motives, while not perhaps entirely clear to outsiders, seemed unlikely to spring from a desire to enhance the long-term wellbeing of the book publishing industry. While many publishers were suspicious of large tech companies who had suddenly found a reason to like books, most were willing to participate in a programme that was regulated by a contract between the publisher and the tech

---

[3] Vise with Malseed, *The Google Story*, pp. 36, 230. 'Even before we started Google, we dreamed of making the incredible breadth of information that librarians so lovingly organize searchable online', recalled Page (quoted in Vise with Malseed, p. 230).

company, that gave publishers some control over the amount of content that was made available for free browsing and that held out the possibility of generating more visibility, and possibly more sales, for their books in a world that was rapidly migrating online.

The Library Project was another matter entirely. At the same time as Google was working with publishers and seeking to persuade them to participate in the Partner Program, they were conducting separate conversations, unbeknown to publishers, with the librarians of a number of research libraries. They had started with Page's alma mater, the University of Michigan, where Page met with the librarian on a visit to the University sometime between 2002 and 2004 and offered to digitize their entire collection.[4] At around the same time, they made a similar offer to the librarian of Stanford University, where Page and Brin had been graduate students. Both Michigan and Stanford responded positively: 'Larry said he wanted to digitize all books in the world. He asked if Stanford would like to do that. I said yes',[5] recalled Michael Keller, the librarian at Stanford. The offer to digitize the university library's entire collection, at no cost to the university, was one that seemed too good to refuse. Having secured the cooperation of Michigan and Stanford, Google proceeded to get several other libraries on board. On 14 December 2004, Google announced that it had entered into agreements with five libraries – the University of Michigan, Stanford, Harvard, the Bodleian at Oxford, and New York Public Library – to scan books from their collections and add them to their database. The details of the agreements varied from library to library.[6] Michigan was the only library that committed itself at the outset to digitizing its entire collection of 7 million books. Stanford started off with a more modest commitment that would involve digitizing 2 million books in the first instance, with the aim of expanding the programme to include its entire collection of 8 million volumes. Harvard's initial commitment was for a much smaller collection of 40,000 public-domain volumes to be digitized in the first instance. Oxford was proposing to allow Google to digitize only nineteenth-century materials, and the New York Public Library was proposing to make available only out-of-copyright material. Google would set up scanners inside the libraries, scan the books, index them and add the digitized content to its

---

[4] Deanna Marcum and Roger C. Schonfeld, *Along Came Google: The Brief, Eventful History of Library Digitization* (Princeton University Press, 2021).
[5] Michael Keller, quoted in ibid.
[6] Marcum and Schonfeld, *Along Came Google*.

database. A user carrying out a search on Google would then see in their search results links to books that were relevant to their query. Clicking on the link would deliver a Google Print page where users could see the full text of public-domain works and brief excerpts – a few sentences around the search term, what Google called a 'snippet' – from books still under copyright. Each library would receive in return a digital copy of the scanned books in its collection. 'Google's mission is to organize the world's information', said Page in typically immodest Googlespeak when he announced the Library Project, 'and we're excited to be working with libraries to help make this mission a reality.'[7]

Many publishers and authors saw the matter differently. To them, this looked like a systematic infringement of copyright on a massive and unprecedented scale. Since the discussions with librarians had been conducted in secret, most publishers and authors were unaware that these plans were afoot and they were taken by surprise when the Library Project was announced. The Association of American University Presses wrote to Google in May 2005, objecting to the programme and requesting further clarification about how Google planned to protect copyrights. The Association of American Publishers wrote to Google in June asking them to suspend the book digitization project for six months to allow more time to consider the copyright issues. On 20 September 2005, the Authors Guild – a New York-based organization that represents 8,000 authors in the US – filed a class action lawsuit against Google for copyright infringement. A month later, on 19 October, the Association of American Publishers (AAP) filed suit against Google on behalf of five publishers – McGraw-Hill, Pearson Education, Penguin, Simon & Schuster and John Wiley & Sons – after lengthy discussions had broken down. The AAP suit sought a court declaration that Google commits infringement when it scans entire books covered by copyright, and a court order preventing Google from doing so without permission from copyright owners. The suit against Rosetta Books may have been a minor skirmish, but now the books wars had well and truly begun.[8]

---

[7] 'Google Checks Out Library Books', *News from Google*, 14 December 2004, at http://googlepress.blogspot.co.uk/2004/12/google-checks-out-library-books.html.
[8] For a detailed account of the Google Library Project and the legal issues raised by it, see the excellent series of papers by Jonathan Band: 'The Google Library Project: The Copyright Debate' (American Library Association, Office for Information Technology Policy, January 2006), at www.policybandwidth.com/doc/googlepaper.pdf; 'The Google Library Project: Both Sides of the Story' (University of Michigan

Google always took the view that the Library Project was not an infringement of copyright because the displaying of snippets was, in their view, consistent with fair use doctrine under US copyright law. In response to criticism from the AAP and the Authors Guild, however, Google announced an opt-out policy in August 2005 that would enable copyright holders to opt out of the Library Project by providing Google with a list of titles they wished to exclude. They also said that they would temporarily suspend the scanning programme until 1 November, to give copyright holders the opportunity to decide whether they wished to exclude books from the project. For many copyright holders, however, Google's opt-out was turning the basic principle of copyright on its head. Rather than requiring a user to seek and be granted permission to use copyrighted material (an opt-in system), Google was requiring the copyright holder to inform Google if it didn't want its copyrighted material to be used (the opt-out). This placed the burden of responsibility on copyright holders to act, rather than on Google to seek permission. In the eyes of publishers and authors, Google's opt-out policy was getting things back to front.

Settlements come and go

Representatives of the plaintiffs and Google entered into a process of discussion and, after many months of negotiations, they announced a

Library, 2006), at http://quod.lib.umich.edu/p/plag/5240451.0001.002/--google-library-project-both-sides-of-the-story?rgn=main;view=fulltext; 'A Guide for the Perplexed: Libraries and the Google Library Project Settlement' (American Library Association and Association of Research Libraries, 13 November 2008), at www.arl.org/storage/documents/publications/google-settlement-13nov08.pdf; 'A Guide for the Perplexed Part II: The Amended Google–Michigan Agreement' (American Library Association and Association of Research Libraries, 12 June 2009), at www.arl.org/storage/documents/publications/google-michigan-12jun09.pdf; 'A Guide for the Perplexed Part III: The Amended Settlement Agreement' (American Library Association and Association of Research Libraries, 23 November 2009), at www.arl.org/storage/documents/publications/guide-for-perplexed-part3-nov09.pdf; 'A Guide For the Perplexed Part IV: The Rejection of the Google Books Settlement' (American Library Association and Association of Research Libraries, 31 March 2011), at www.arl.org/storage/documents/publications/guide-for-perplexed-part4-apr11.pdf. See also Jonathan Band, 'The Long and Winding Road to the Google Books Settlement', *The John Marshall Review of Intellectual Property Law*, 9, 2 (2009), 227–329, at https://repository.jmls.edu/ripl/vol9/iss2/2. There are also many other useful publications listed on the Google Books page of the Association of Research Libraries website: www.arl.org/component/taxonomy/term/summary/75/135#.V6im28_rvmH.

settlement on 28 October 2008.[9] The settlement proposed to create a new mechanism – the Books Rights Registry, or BRR – that would enable Google to pay rights holders for the right to display books. Google would pay out $125 million, some of which would go to the rights holders of the books they scanned without permission and some of which would fund the BRR, and Google would cover the plaintiffs' court costs. Google would also be able to generate revenue by selling the ability to see full text and to print out books, at prices that could be set by the rights holder (failing which, Google would set the price using a pricing algorithm); any revenues generated in this way would be split 37:63 between Google and the BRR, which would distribute its share among the rights holders. The settlement distinguished between three categories of books – in-copyright and commercially available (meaning, roughly, in print or available through print on demand), in-copyright and not commercially available, and public domain – and it established default rules for what Google could do with the two categories of in-copyright books. Since the rights holders could remove specific books from Google's database, vary the default rules or opt out altogether, the category that would probably be most affected by the settlement's default rules was that of in-copyright books that are no longer commercially available (Google estimated that around 70 per cent of all published works fell into this category, while 20 per cent were in the public domain and 10 per cent were in copyright and commercially available).

The proposed settlement provided an ingenious way out of the legal log-jam that would have enabled the Library Project to proceed while addressing many of the concerns of copyright holders – to many participants and observers, it seemed like a good, or at least a satisfactory, outcome. But the settlement came in for a great deal of criticism, both from within the US and from abroad, and it had a rough ride in the US justice system. In September 2009, the US Department of Justice raised objections to the settlement, prompting the parties to withdraw the original agreement and submit a revised version, which they did on 13 November 2009. The revisions dealt primarily with the mechanisms for handling orphan works – that is, works that are still in copyright but where the copyright owner cannot be identified – and with the restriction of the settlement to books published in the US, UK, Australia or Canada. The latter

---

[9] The full text of the settlement can be found at www.googlebooksettlement.com/agreement.html. For a helpful summary, see Band, 'A Guide for the Perplexed: Libraries and the Google Library Project Settlement'.

restriction was intended to meet objections from the French and German governments, which argued that the settlement did not abide by copyright laws in their countries; since a large proportion of the books in the libraries partnering with Google are not in English (perhaps as much as 50 per cent), this represented a significant reduction in the scope of the settlement.[10] Since it was a settlement of class litigation, the revised settlement was subject to approval by the US District Court for the Southern District of New York, and, on 22 March 2011, US Circuit Judge Denny Chin announced that he was rejecting the settlement on the grounds that it 'is not fair, adequate or reasonable'. By placing the onus on copyright owners to come forward to protect their rights, the settlement was, argued Chin, inconsistent with the basic principles of copyright law – and in this respect he was affirming what many publishers had always thought. Chin also contended that the settlement would give Google 'a de facto monopoly over unclaimed works', rewarding it for engaging in the unauthorized copying of books and giving it a significant advantage over any potential competitor. While Chin's judgment was undoubtedly a serious blow to those who had worked out the settlement, he did leave the door ajar, noting that some of the objections could be met if the settlement were converted from an opt-out to an opt-in agreement. In Chin's view, the status of orphan works should be dealt with separately, by congressional legislation rather than by an agreement among private, self-interested parties.[11]

Following Judge Chin's rejection of the revised settlement, Google and the AAP, acting on behalf of the five publishers, reconvened their negotiations and, on 4 October 2012, they announced that they had settled their seven-year legal dispute. This was a private settlement between the parties to the litigation, so it didn't require the Court's approval, and the terms remained confidential. The press release confirmed that publishers can choose to make available or remove their books and journals from any material digitized by Google for its Library Project.[12] The settlement also provided a new route for

---

[10] For a more detailed account of the main changes in the amended settlement agreement, see Band, 'A Guide for the Perplexed Part III: The Amended Settlement Agreement'.

[11] The full judgment can be found at: *The Authors Guild et al. v. Google Inc.*, 05 Civ. 8136 (2011), at www.nysd.uscourts.gov/cases/show.php?db=special&id=115. For a more detailed account of the rejection, see Band, 'A Guide For the Perplexed Part IV: The Rejection of the Google Books Settlement'.

[12] 'Publishers and Google Reach Agreement', at http://googlepress.blogspot.co.uk/2012/10/publishers-and-google-reach-agreement.html.

books that are part of the Library Project to be sold by Google: books scanned by Google in the Library Project could be included by publishers within Google Books, which allows users to browse up to 20 per cent of books, and users could then purchase a digital copy through Google Play, the digital distribution service and media store that was launched by Google in March 2012. But, unlike the earlier settlement, there is no indication that Google had agreed to pay out compensation to rights holders.

The private settlement between Google and the AAP meant that other parties that had rights over books scanned by Google, including authors and foreign publishers, would have to pursue action separately. Notwithstanding the settlement with the AAP, the Authors Guild pressed ahead with its class action lawsuit. On 14 November 2013, Judge Chin ruled in favour of Google, arguing that Google's use of the copyrighted works was 'fair use' under US copyright law.[13] In coming to this judgment, Chin drew heavily on Pierre Leval's influential interpretation of fair use doctrine.[14] The fair use doctrine was designed as a way of limiting the scope of the monopoly rights granted to the creators of intellectual property by copyright law so that other forms of creativity, such as criticism and research, are not stifled. There is no simple criterion of fair use – each case has to be considered on its merits. But §107 of the US Copyright Act specifies four factors to be considered in determining whether the use made of a work in any particular case is a fair use:

1. the purpose and character of the use, including whether such use is of a commercial nature or is for nonprofit educational purposes;
2. the nature of the copyrighted work;
3. the amount and substantiality of the portion used in relation to the copyrighted work as a whole;
4. the effect of the use upon the potential market for or value of the copyrighted work.

In his account of fair use doctrine, Leval placed particular emphasis on the first of these factors as decisive in determining whether a secondary user's fair use defence is justified: 'I believe the answer to the question of justification turns primarily on whether, and to

---

[13] *The Authors Guild et al. v. Google, Inc.*, 05 Civ. 8136 (2013), at www.nysd.uscourts.gov/cases/show.php?db=special&id=355.
[14] Pierre N. Leval, 'Toward a Fair Use Standard', *Harvard Law Review*, 103 (March 1990), 1105, at www.yalelawtech.org/wp-content/uploads/leval.pdf.

what extent, the challenged use is transformative. The use must be productive and must employ the quoted matter in a different manner or for a different purpose from the original.'[15] Chin argued that Google's use of the copyrighted material is 'transformative' in precisely this sense: it doesn't merely reproduce the original material but uses words for a different purpose – namely, to facilitate search. Google's use is also transformative in the sense that it transforms book text into data for the purposes of substantive research, including data mining, thereby opening up new fields of research. 'Google Books does not supersede or supplant books because it is not a tool to be used to read books. Instead, it "adds value to the original" and allows for "the creation of new information, new aesthetics, new insights and understandings"', argued Chin, quoting Leval. 'Hence, the use is transformative.'[16] Moreover, there is no evidence that Google's scans are having a negative impact on the market for books – 'To the contrary', remarked Chin, 'a reasonable factfinder could only find that Google Books enhances the sales of books to the benefit of copyright holders.'[17] In the view of the Authors Guild, this was a questionable expansion of fair use doctrine and a misunderstanding of the real harm that could be caused to authors. The Authors Guild appealed the ruling to the US Second Circuit but, in October 2015, the Second Circuit unanimously affirmed the judgment in Google's favour. Undeterred, the Authors Guild petitioned for the Supreme Court to review the decision of the Second Circuit, and in April 2016 the Supreme Court denied the petition.

In a parallel series of developments, the Authors Guild became involved in a separate but related dispute involving the HathiTrust. The HathiTrust is a digital depository for academic library content. The name was inspired by the Hindu word for elephant, *hathi* – an animal reputed never to forget. The origins of the HathiTrust go back to 2008, when some of the libraries participating in the Google Library Project decided to create a repository to store, manage and preserve the millions of files of scanned books that were being generated by their participation in the Library Project. As part of the Project, Google provided a digital copy of each scanned work to the library which held the work; the libraries would then deposit the digital copy in the HathiTrust Digital Library, a shared digital repository that would be searchable. The search capabilities would

---

[15] Ibid., p. 4.
[16] *The Authors Guild et al.* v. *Google, Inc.*, p. 21.
[17] Ibid., p. 25.

allow users to carry out a full-text search for a particular term across all the works in the repository, but for works that are not in the public domain or for which a copyright owner has not granted permission, the full-text search would indicate only the page numbers on which a particular term is found and the number of times the term appears on each page. Led by the University of Michigan, one of the participants in the Library Project, the initiative was joined at the outset by the University of California library system and the libraries of the twelve members of the Committee on Institutional Cooperation, a consortium of the Big Ten universities plus the University of Chicago. Other institutions soon joined, including Cornell, Dartmouth, Princeton and Yale. By 2011, it had more than 7.6 million volumes in its repository. The core of this repository was made up of the material being scanned in the Google Library Project, but the database included other material too. In September 2011, the Authors Guild and other writers' associations and writers sued the HathiTrust and the participating libraries for infringement of copyright.

On 10 October 2012, US District Court Judge Harold Baer, Jr., ruled in favour of the HathiTrust.[18] As Judge Chin would later argue in the *Authors Guild* v. *Google* case, Judge Baer contended that the HathiTrust's uses of digitized content were transformative, and therefore justified under fair use doctrine. The digitized content allows libraries to create a searchable inventory of their works and preserve their collections against the risk of natural disasters and other catastrophes, allows scholars to search large quantities of material and identify relevant works without revealing in-copyright material, and allows print-disabled individuals to gain access to library collections on an equal footing with sighted individuals – all of these factors leaned in favour of the fair use defence in Baer's view. He also dismissed the plaintiffs' argument that the HathiTrust's uses would cause market harm by leading to lost sales. This argument ignores the fact that purchasing an additional copy would not have allowed either full-text searches or access for print-disabled individuals, two transformative uses that were central to the Mass Digitization Project (MDP), the term used by Baer to refer to the large-scale scanning of books involved in the Google Library Project. Baer's conclusion was unequivocal: 'I cannot imagine a definition of

---

[18] *The Authors Guild et al.* v. *HathiTrust et al.*, 11 CV 6351 (HB), at http://cases. justia.com/federal/district-courts/new-york/nysdce/1:2011cv06351/384619/156/0. pdf?ts=1428708650.

fair use that would not encompass the transformative uses made by Defendants' MDP and would require that I terminate this invaluable contribution to the progress of science and cultivation of the arts that at the same time effectuates the ideals espoused by the ADA [Americans With Disabilities Act].'[19] The Authors Guild appealed to the Second Circuit Court of Appeals and, on 10 June 2014, the Second Circuit also ruled in favour of the HathiTrust, upholding its right to maintain a full-text searchable database of copyrighted works and to make those works available in accessible formats to print-disabled individuals.[20]

The HathiTrust decisions were important because they confirmed the right of libraries to digitize their book collections – in the case of the HathiTrust, largely facilitated by the Google Library Project – and to make the content searchable, although they addressed the issue of full-text access only in the context of the print-disabled. This left open the question of whether full-text access to individuals other than the print-disabled could be justified under fair use doctrine – a question which will no doubt become a focus of attention, and perhaps contestation, at some point.[21]

It was not only writers and publishers and their professional associations that took action against Google, however: in April 2010, a group of photographers, graphic artists and their professional associations – including the American Society of Media Photographers (ASMP), the Professional Photographers of America (PPA) and the Graphic Artists Guild (GAG) – filed their own class action lawsuit against Google. The plaintiffs had initially filed a motion in November 2009 seeking to join the negotiations in what became the ill-fated settlement between Google and the AAP, but they had been advised by Judge Chin at that time to file a separate action. Discussions between Google and the photographers, graphic artists and professional associations continued for several years and, in September 2014, they announced that they had reached a private settlement, the terms of which remain undisclosed.

Given the twists and turns of this long legal saga, one could be forgiven for losing track of who was suing whom and who had settled and who hadn't – for those who are finding that the details are

---

[19] Ibid., p. 22.

[20] *Authors Guild* v. *HathiTrust*, 121-4547-cv, at http://law.justia.com/cases/federal/appellate-courts/ca2/12-4547/12-4547-2014-06-10.html#.

[21] See Jonathan Band, 'What Does the HathiTrust Decision Mean for Libraries?' 7 July 2014, at www.librarycopyrightalliance.org/storage/documents/article-hathitrust-analysis-7jul2014.pdf.

already beginning to slip away, figure 4.1, based on Jonathan Band's helpful 'litigation family tree', may be a useful reminder.[22]

How big is a snippet?

With the Supreme Court decision in April 2016, this prolonged and multi-stranded conflict was finally brought to a close. By this stage, Google had scanned more than 20 million books in the Library Project, some 4 million of which were still in copyright, depositing digital copies in their database to enrich their search results. Google appeared to have emerged victorious after a decade of complex legal battles. Their view had always been that the Library Project was not an infringement of copyright because the displaying of snippets was consistent with fair use doctrine, and Judge Chin's ruling, together with the Supreme Court decision, seemed to vindicate their view. But in truth this was almost certainly a Pyrrhic victory, as the time and cost involved in achieving this outcome almost certainly exceeded the gains. Google had already surpassed Yahoo! and MSN as the leading search engine by 2003, a year before the Library Project was launched, and by 2005 they were in a commanding position with 65 per cent of the market, compared to 15 per cent for Yahoo! and 10 per cent for MSN:[23] Google had won the search engine war without the help of the extra artillery that would be provided by digitizing millions of books. And the search impact of having all those snippets available might not be so great after all.

As for the publishers, this saga might seem to have turned out badly in the end. It was a long slog that absorbed a great deal of time and money, and the hard-won settlement that would have seen a substantial payout by Google was rejected by the court. But many publishers don't see it this way. Although the terms of the private settlement reached between the publishers and Google in 2012 remain confidential, there are some on the publishers' side who see this as a victory of sorts. 'We ring-fenced Google and, more importantly, we ring-fenced the libraries', said Tom, a senior publisher at a large house. 'To me, the danger wasn't actually Google. I never thought Google ever wanted to do more than copy the books in

---

[22] Adapted from Jonathan Band, 'Google Books Litigation Family Tree', 16 October 2015, at www.librarycopyrightalliance.org/storage/documents/google-books-litigation-tree-16oct2015.pdf.
[23] 'Search Engine Market Shares'.

Google Library Project Litigation

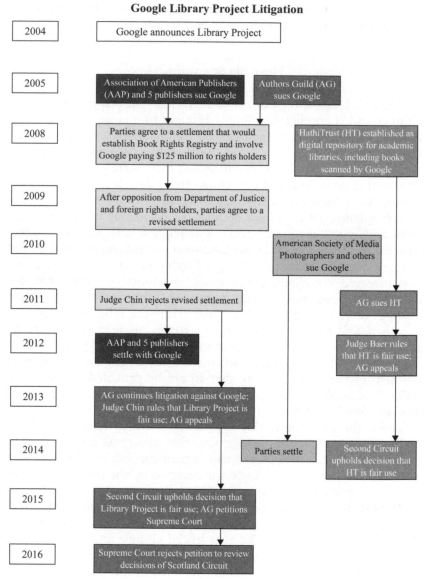

Figure 4.1   Google Library Project litigation

order to use them in search. What scared me was that they were giving digital copies back to the libraries, and the library mandate is to get as much material free to as many patrons as possible. So the danger to me was always that Google was the intermediary: the

136

libraries were the danger.' This danger was exacerbated by the fact that state university libraries are part of states and the Supreme Court has interpreted the 11th Amendment to the Constitution as granting states sovereign immunity from lawsuits seeking money damages – what is commonly referred to as the US doctrine of state sovereign immunity.[24] This may have emboldened officials at the University of Michigan and other state universities to do ambitious deals with Google in the first place, knowing that they would not be sued for copyright infringement if the fair use defence failed (the participation of private universities like Harvard and Stanford was more limited),[25] and it meant that suing Google was the only legal step that publishers could take to try to limit what state university libraries could do with the files. Moreover, just having all that digital content out there, and people beginning to think that every book in every language should be available for free online, would be a dangerous precedent not only for publishers but for writers too. So there was a lot at stake. The agreement that was struck between the publishers and Google placed limits on what Google could do going forward, and limits on what the libraries could do with the digital copies they received from Google. And now, after all that happened with the Google Library Project, anyone tempted to embark on a similar project is going to think twice. 'Before you were going to drop, say, $10 billion into a project of scanning all the books in the world again, you would look at what happened last time and what you discover is not a lot', said Tom. You'd have seven years of haggling with angry publishers to look forward to, you'd be taking on a huge risk because if you're sued and you lose you could be penalized for each book you copied and the gain at the end of the day wouldn't be very clear. So by standing up to Google, the publishers created a powerful disincentive for others to follow suit. 'It was a moment in time and by establishing what we did at that moment in time, I think we actually took that one off the table. I don't think anyone's coming back to try it again.'

But didn't the fair use decision in favour of Google and against the Authors Guild weigh against publishers too? To some extent it did, and there are some in the publishing community who find it difficult to understand why the Authors Guild persisted with their litigation when a private agreement with Google was at hand. 'The publishers settled, the Authors Guild kept going. Why, I have no idea', said

---

[24] Pamela Samuelson, 'The Google Book Settlement as Copyright Reform', *Wisconsin Law Review*, 479 (2011), 479–562.
[25] Ibid., pp. 485–6.

Tom. 'I said to them, what are you doing? We have what we need, the publishers and authors together, why are you going to keep going? And they kept going, they never settled. They kept going and they lost.' The publishers still have their deal with Google – that remains intact despite the ruling against the Authors Guild on fair use. But the legal situation is now less favourable from the publishers' point of view. 'We have some difficult law now in place that says as long as you want to make a snippet, you can copy a book. I don't think that hurts us, really; I don't think that copying a book to deliver a snippet undermines our business', said Tom. 'But the question will be, how big is a snippet? And they'll start to push against that.' If a snippet is a sentence, that may not be a problem in most cases, but what if a snippet becomes a page? Or two pages? Or three? A snippet is not a clearly defined concept in copyright law and it could be stretched by players who want to make more rather than less text available. And what about works that contain information that is primarily factual and referential in character, like dictionaries, encyclopedias and other reference works? Google decided not to display snippets for certain reference works, such as dictionaries, because it recognized that even snippets could harm the market for these works. But why should others follow Google in this regard? And what about books that are less easy to categorize as straightforward reference works but which are nonetheless valued for the information they contain, like cook books, handbooks and almanacs? If the information can be made freely available in snippet form, then it's going to be difficult to maintain the value of these books.

Whither Google Books?

These issues, opened up by Judge Chin's 2014 ruling in favour of Google, will no doubt preoccupy legal scholars, and possibly the courts, in the years to come. The Google Books controversy has been settled but, by the time it was finally over, the issues seemed less urgent to many. In part, this was because some of the parties had already settled out of court by the time Chin delivered his final verdict, and in part it was because the digital revolution in publishing had moved on. Many of the anxieties that had fuelled the concern of publishers and authors in 2004, when Google announced the Library Project, had faded into the background and other issues had become more pressing. By 2010, there were many publishers who were looking to Google and wishing, a little ironically perhaps, that they would take ebooks more seriously and become a more aggressive player in the retail space, in the hope that they, along with Apple, might have the scale and the clout to counter the power of what many publishers now saw as the new 500-pound Gorilla in their midst – Amazon. But Google's interest in books was never primarily to sell them – why would you want to go into the book retail business, with its wafer-thin margins, when your primary business is search and you can make a fortune from advertising? Google entered the book market in service of another goal – to use book text as a way of augmenting the value of their search results. They were never a book retailer, and adding the ability to purchase ebooks was just an extension of a project that was motivated by other concerns. By the time Google had rolled out Google Play and integrated its eBookstore into a multimedia digital distribution service, the ebook marketplace was so dominated by Amazon that it would be difficult for a new entrant to take a significant market share, especially if its ability to discount were curtailed by agency agreements (more on this in chapter 5) and if its primary concerns, strategic and financial, lay elsewhere. Of course, Google could become a serious retail competitor if it really wanted to – it certainly has the resources to do so and it is far more profitable than Amazon. But why would it wish to move in this direction when its principal focus has always been on other things, and when its principal mechanism of revenue generation has always been advertising rather than retail? One Google insider who had a ring-side seat in the decade-long controversy about books put it like this:

> The irony of all this is that we're now in this box and it's very difficult to see how we're going to go forward. Which might lead us to exit the business and give it over to Amazon or enter and compete against them. Because what the hell do we care? We make plenty of money elsewhere. Do we really need this as a business? And if it's this difficult, at some point you say 'screw it'. Or we enter into the market and become that big player that the publishers all dreamed we would become years ago. It's very much the toss of a coin at this point [2016]. But I know that the path we're currently on is not going to work long-term for this company.

Google entered the world of books in 2004 to find new content that would strengthen its position in the search engine war – a war that was won, to all intents and purposes, by 2005, without the help of this content. And once the search engine war was won, the arguments in favour of scanning more and more books in the face of dogged opposition from copyright holders, and of investing heavily in a book retail operation that was never likely to make more than a very minor financial contribution to the company, looked less and less compelling. There was a time when Page and Brin might have fancied the idea that Google could take the physical contents of libraries and turn them into a universal library accessible to all, but that was never their primary motivation for launching the Library Project and the idea fell by the wayside once their position as the overwhelmingly dominant search engine had been established.

— Chapter 5 —

AMAZON'S ASCENT

'The power of Amazon is the single biggest issue in publishing.'
CEO of a large US trade publisher

If we had to pinpoint one thing brought into being by the digital revolution that has done more than any other to disrupt the traditional structures of the book publishing industry, it would not be ebooks: it would be Amazon. From its humble origins in a suburban garage in Seattle in July 1995 to its position today as the single most important retailer of books – both physical books and ebooks – and the world's largest retailer, Amazon has seared itself into the consciousness of every player in the publishing world. Given Amazon's overwhelming market dominance, it is very difficult for publishers to do without it – for many publishers, Amazon has become their single most important account. And yet the more dominant Amazon becomes, the more challenging it is to do business with them, as it uses its continuously growing market share as a tool to extract better terms from publishers in negotiations that are sometimes fraught and have on occasion become the focus of public controversy. This has overshadowed to some extent the extraordinary transformation that Amazon has brought about in the nature of bookselling. Amazon's website has become the de facto catalogue of record for available books. It has given readers access to a range of books – backlist as well as frontlist – that far exceeds anything that existed in the pre-Amazon world and provided them with a level of customer service that other retailers find hard to match. Today, with the benefit of hindsight, we can see that the emergence of Amazon was something of a watershed in the history of the modern publishing industry, and that the book world before Amazon was a different kind of place from the world that we now know. The retail transformation brought about by Amazon was made possible by the digital revolution – Amazon wouldn't exist without it. And this is a transformation that began well before the Kindle: Kindle was an important part of Amazon's transformative impact on the publishing industry but the transformation was much broader and more fundamental than this, embracing print books as well as ebooks and feeding into many other aspects of the digital revolution in publishing. For many readers and publishers in the English-speaking world today, it is almost hard to remember or imagine what book buying and bookselling were like before Amazon, so central has this organization now become to the world of the book.

In some ways, the retail revolution brought about by Amazon is only the latest in a series of developments that have transformed the landscape of bookselling since the 1950s, though its long-term consequences are likely to be more profound and far-reaching than previous developments. The traditional ways of selling books in the Anglo-American world – namely, through a plethora of small independent bookstores, on the one hand, and a variety of non-book retailers like drugstores, department stores and newsagents, on the other – were first disrupted in the US by the rise of the mall bookstore chains, B. Dalton and Waldenbooks, which opened bookstores in the suburban shopping malls across America in the 1960s.[1] The mall-based bookstores were then eclipsed by the rise of the book superstore chains in the 1980s and 1990s, especially Barnes & Noble and Borders. The 1990s were the heyday of the book superstore chains and, as they rolled out their chains across America, opening more and more superstores in major metropolitan areas and vying for dominance, the small independent bookstores and smaller chains were increasingly forced out of business. A very similar development occurred in the UK, with Waterstones and Dillons competing with one another in the 1980s and 1990s, until both were acquired by the HMI Media Group and merged under the Waterstones brand. The bookselling landscape in the 1990s was dominated by a small number of book superstore chains – Barnes & Noble and Borders in the US, Waterstones and Dillons in the UK – and by the mass merchandisers in the US (Walmart, Kmart, Target and the wholesale clubs like Price Club, Sam's and BJ's) and the supermarkets in the UK

---

[1] For an excellent account of the development of bookselling in America, see Laura J. Miller, *Reluctant Capitalists: Bookselling and the Culture of Consumption* (University of Chicago Press, 2006), ch. 2.

(Tesco, Asda and Sainsbury's), which became increasingly important channels for books aimed at a general readership.

The rise of Amazon

It was in this landscape that Amazon took its first tentative steps into bookselling in the summer of 1995. In the early 1990s, Jeff Bezos was working for a New York hedge fund called D. E. Shaw, and it was there in 1994 that he came up with the idea of 'the everything store' – an internet-based company that would be an intermediary between customers and manufacturers and sell nearly every kind of product all over the world.[2] These were the early days of the internet and Bezos and his colleagues were casting around for ideas about new business ventures that would take advantage of the internet's rapid growth. Bezos knew that he couldn't start with everything, so he made a list of twenty product categories, from computer software to apparel and music, and decided to plump for books as the starting point. Books were an ideal starting point for an internet store aspiring to be comprehensive for three reasons. First, they were 'pure commodities', in the sense that a copy of a book was the same as another copy of the same book regardless of where you bought it; second, there were two main wholesalers of books in the US, so there would be no need to deal with the many different publishers – most books could be sourced from the wholesalers; and third, there were 3 million books in print, which was far more than any bricks-and-mortar bookstore could ever stock. The huge number of books in print meant that you could offer something in an online bookstore that no physical bookstore could ever provide – namely, exhaustive selection.[3] So, books it would be. In opting for books as the starting point, Bezos was not seeking to fulfil a deep-seated desire to participate in and contribute to the culture of the book: he was first and foremost an entrepreneur with an eye on the future, and in opting for books he was making a business decision about how to maximize the chances of growth and success for a retail organization in the internet age. Such was the beginning of Amazon.

---

[2] Brad Stone, *The Everything Store: Jeff Bezos and the Age of Amazon* (New York: Little, Brown, 2014), p. 24. I draw on Brad Stone's excellent account of Amazon throughout this chapter. See also Robert Spector, *Amazon.com: Get Big Fast* (London: Random House, 2000).
[3] Stone, *The Everything Store*, p. 26.

Bezos moved to Seattle, raised some money, set up shop in a converted garage, employed some programmers and began to build a website that eventually went live on 16 July 1995. At that stage, the company held no physical stock. When a customer bought a book, Amazon would place an order with one of the wholesalers, and when the book arrived it would be packed in the basement (by then, they had moved to premises in downtown Seattle) and shipped to the customer – the whole process would take at least a week, maybe two or more for rarer titles. The first week after the launch, they took $12,438 in orders and shipped $846 worth of books[4] – a small beginning but growth would come quickly. By early 1996, Bezos and his colleagues were in discussions with some of the venture capitalists who were funding tech start-ups in Silicon Valley, and they were beginning to take on board the principle that underpinned – and continues to underpin – the entrepreneurial culture of Silicon Valley: get big fast. The idea was simple: the internet was opening up a new space of opportunities that will eventually deliver big rewards to the players who are able to establish a dominant market position, and to establish a dominant position you need to move fast so that others don't get there before you. Don't worry now about profitability: growth is the key. Marc Andreessen – the co-founder of Netscape and Silicon Valley guru who went on to co-found the influential venture capital firm Andreessen Horowitz – put it like this: 'One of the fundamental lessons is that market share now equals revenue later, and if you don't have market share now, you are not going to have revenue later. Another fundamental lesson is that whoever gets the volume does win in the end. Just plain wins.'[5] It was the 'Microsoft lesson', said Andreesen: 'If you get ubiquity, you have a lot of options, a lot of ways to benefit from that.' In spring 1996, Bezos and his colleagues secured $8 million in financing from Kleiner Perkins Caufield and Byers, the leading VC firm in Silicon Valley, and set about the task of growing the company as fast as they could. Speed was of the essence: if they could establish a dominant position before others – 'ubiquity' in Andreesen's terms – then they could use their dominance to secure better prices from suppliers, provide a better service to customers and build a business that would eventually be profitable.

Amazon's sales grew at a phenomenal rate throughout the late 1990s, increasing from $15.75 million in 1996 to $2.76 billion in

---

[4] Ibid., p. 39; Spector, *Amazon.com*, p. 93.
[5] Marc Andreessen, quoted in Robert H. Reid, *Architects of the Web: 1,000 Days that Built the Future of Business* (New York: John Wiley & Sons, 1997), p. 31.

2000. By 2000, internet bookselling was accounting for just under 10 per cent of adult trade book sales in the US, and Amazon was the largest of the online booksellers.[6] The large chains, and especially Barnes & Noble and Borders, were still the dominant book retailers in 2000, accounting for just under 30 per cent of adult trade book sales,[7] but this was soon to change. Amazon's sales continued to grow while sales at Barnes & Noble stagnated; Borders went bankrupt in 2011, having piled up too much debt that it could no longer service with its declining sales, and by September of that year it had closed all its stores. By 2010, Amazon was in a dominant market position. Amazon's North American media sales (which include books, music, movies, TV shows, video games, software and digital downloads – Amazon's accounts don't separate out book sales) had reached $6.88 billion and were growing steeply (up 15 per cent on the previous year), while Barnes & Noble's store sales were under $4.5 billion and falling. Moreover, with the successful launch of the Kindle in November 2007, the rapid growth in ebook sales after 2008 and Amazon's overwhelming dominance in the ebook marketplace, Amazon was well placed to strengthen its position further.

The origins of the Kindle date back to 2004, to the period just after Apple had launched the iTunes music store. Apple had stunned Bezos and many others in the high-tech world by the speed with which they were able to grow their music business and overtake Amazon and other music retailers. Given that the sales of books, music and movies accounted for 74 per cent of Amazon's annual revenue at the time, Bezos knew they were vulnerable if Apple or some other competitor were to come up with an effective digital distribution system like iTunes in Amazon's core business of books. To protect their core business in a world where media were increasingly shifting to digital formats, Amazon needed to control the ebook business in the way that Apple controlled the music business – that is the lesson Bezos drew from the phenomenal success of iTunes.[8] Just as Apple had done for music, Amazon needed to create an integrated consumer experience that combined stylish hardware with a digital bookstore that was easy to use and comprehensive in its coverage. Amazon would have to become the iTunes of the book world.

---

[6] Stephanie Oda and Glenn Sanislo, *The Subtext 2002–2003 Perspective on Book Publishing: Numbers, Issues and Trends* (Darien, Conn.: Open Book Publishing, 2003), p. 80.
[7] Ibid.
[8] Stone, *The Everything Store*, p. 231.

Like many in the business world, Bezos and his fellow managers had read Clayton Christensen's *The Innovator's Dilemma* and had been impressed by the idea that one of the great dangers for companies was their reluctance to embrace disruptive change and open up new markets for fear of undermining their traditional businesses.[9] They had ingested Christensen's observation that the companies that were most likely to avoid this danger were those that had set up autonomous organizations that were completely independent from the core business and given them a free hand to build new ventures around disruptive technologies, unconstrained by any worries about whether these new ventures would undermine existing businesses. So Bezos decided that this is exactly what Amazon should do. They set up a secret research group in Silicon Valley called Lab126 and charged it with the task of producing an iTunes solution for books that would include the development of a new reading device.[10] And they would need to act quickly: Bezos was convinced that if Amazon didn't take the lead and develop a compelling ebook solution, with a reading device that was much more stylish and user-friendly than the rather clunky e-readers that were on the market at the time, then Apple or Google would beat them to it.

After three years of intensive development, the Kindle was finally released on 19 November 2007. Publishers had been persuaded and cajoled into making many of their titles available as Mobi files, which was the proprietary file format supported by the Kindle. By the time of the launch, Amazon had more than 90,000 titles in the Kindle store, including many frontlist bestsellers. However, the price at which Amazon would be selling ebooks had been kept a closely guarded secret. It was only on the day of the launch that Bezos announced, 17 minutes into his product spiel at the W Hotel in lower Manhattan, that *New York Times* bestsellers and many new releases would be sold on the Kindle at $9.99. Many publishers were aghast: they simply had no idea that this was coming. Bezos had settled on this price some while ago, modelling his strategy on Apple's price of 99¢ for a single in iTunes, but had decided not to tell publishers until the launch. The $9.99 price tag meant that Amazon was selling many of their ebooks at a loss. They were buying from publishers on the standard wholesale model, getting a discount of around 50 per cent off the list price, which was typically pegged by the publishers

---

[9] Clayton M. Christensen, *The Innovator's Dilemma: When New Technologies Cause Great Firms to Fail* (Boston, Mass.: Harvard Business Review Press, 1997).
[10] Stone, *The Everything Store*, pp. 234–9.

146

to the prevailing print edition. So, for each ebook sold of a frontlist hardcover book with a $26 list price, Amazon was losing just over $3. (This assumes that the publisher was pegging the ebook to the list price of the hardcover, which wasn't always the case – sometimes publishers fixed the 'digital list price' at 20 per cent below the print list price, which would reduce Amazon's loss in this example to 41¢.)

What worried publishers was not that Amazon was losing money on the ebooks they sold – that was Amazon's problem. Publishers were worried for two other reasons. First, they were worried that Amazon's bold pricing move would set an expectation in the minds of consumers that an ebook was 'worth' $9.99, just as Apple had created the expectation that a song was 'worth' 99¢. But this number was arbitrary: it was an artefact of a marketing strategy. It bore little relation to the costs actually incurred anywhere along the value chain. Bezos wanted to fix the price of bestsellers and new releases below the symbolic threshold of $10 because he knew it would draw consumers to the Kindle, and he was prepared to accept the losses for the time being. But if this threshold became established as a norm in the marketplace, shaping the expectations of consumers, then prices across the industry would, publishers feared, be pulled down inexorably as they gravitated to the new norm. Publishers' revenues would be subjected to intense downward pressure, their slim margins would be squeezed further and their write-offs of unearned advances would increase. Publishers also feared that, if the new price caught on and Amazon captured a dominant market share in ebooks, becoming a de facto monopoly, then Amazon would use its market strength to put intense pressure on publishers to lower their prices on ebooks and give them better terms so that Amazon could continue to sell at $9.99 (or less) without a loss, thereby squeezing publishers' margins still further. Their fears were not entirely misplaced, as we shall see.

That the Kindle turned out to be such a success was a surprise to many. They had seen e-readers come and go, none making much of an impression on the reading public, which seemed to prefer to read books on the printed page. But the Kindle was different. Why did Amazon succeed where so many others had failed?

The Kindle had half a dozen things going for it. First, Amazon got the technology more or less right. The Kindle was compact, light and easy to use. It wasn't as stylish as an Apple product, but it was a good deal more stylish than many of the e-readers that had been developed previously. Like the Sony e-reader, the Kindle used e-ink technology, which was easy on the eyes, eliminated glare, enabled you to read in direct sunlight and gave a long battery life – anything from several days to a week. Second, the Kindle store had good content and lots of it. Bezos knew that previous ebook readers had been undermined by the pitifully small list of desirable titles that were available to be read on them, and a great deal of effort was therefore invested in ensuring that the Kindle store was well stocked with desirable books by the time the Kindle launched. This included 101 of 112 current *New York Times* bestsellers and new releases. Third, the prices were attractive, at least on the most visible titles: the eye-catching $9.99 for *New York Times* bestsellers and many new releases was an effective marketing strategy and created the impression that ebook prices were low, even if many other ebooks were selling at higher prices on Amazon. The initial outlay for a Kindle was substantial – the first Kindles were retailing for $399 – but with lower prices for many books you could recoup at least some of the initial outlay, if not all of it, over time. Fourth, the Kindle came pre-connected to a wireless network, Amazon Whispernet, that enabled you to find and buy ebooks directly from the Kindle store. There was no need to have a wi-fi connection or to connect the Kindle to a computer and no need to pay a wireless network fee – the cost of the network was included in the cost of the book. This greatly simplified the purchasing process: wherever you were – at home, on the train, in the office, away for the weekend – you could buy an ebook and have it on your Kindle in less than a minute.

The fifth thing that the Kindle had going for it is that it was released into a pre-existing web of social relationships characterized by high levels of trust that had been built up over time – this was crucial. For many readers, Amazon was a known quantity: they had been buying books from Amazon for years, had given their credit card details to them and had grown to trust them as a reliable supplier of books. Buying an e-reading device was an act of trust – indeed, it involved a great deal of trust. You had to assume not only that the device would work and be easy to use, but also that you would be able to get the books you wanted to read, buy them electronically without fear of your credit card details being stolen or mis-used and, crucially, not have to worry about whether the device and the books on it would become obsolete and unusable in a year or two. That's a lot to assume. If you're going to place all this trust in someone, who better to choose than an organization that had demonstrated its commitment to books and had already earned your trust as a reliable bookseller?

Sixth, and finally, Amazon was able to promote the Kindle aggressively on its website and directly to readers through the data it held on millions of customers and their previous purchases. No technology company could match Amazon's ability to market directly to that particular segment of the population that would be interested in a state-of-the-art reading device – namely, consumers who bought books.

The growth of ebook sales and the success of the Kindle were inextricably intertwined. By the time Barnes & Noble entered the e-reader marketplace with the launch of the Nook in November 2009, Amazon had been selling the Kindle for a full two years and had built up what seemed like an impregnable lead. Although the ebook market was still tiny, accounting for less than 3 per cent of trade book sales, Amazon's market share was commonly estimated to be around 90 per cent at the time. Publishers feared that, if the ebook market continued to grow and Amazon maintained its overwhelming market share, it would use its market dominance to exact lower prices and better terms. They could find themselves in a situation where ebooks were becoming more and more important, increasingly displacing print sales, and the vast majority of ebook sales were going through one retailer who was determined to drive down prices – it was an alarming prospect. Publishers were keen to see a more diversified market, with more players and more devices that could compete seriously with Amazon. They therefore welcomed Barnes & Noble's belated entry into the e-reader marketplace, and welcomed the fact that Apple was, in late 2009, at last approaching publishers with a view to acquiring content for the new device, still shrouded in secrecy at the time, that it was planning to launch in spring 2010 – the iPad.

When the iPad was finally unveiled in San Francisco on 27 January 2010, Apple had signed agreements with five of the six big publishers to sell ebooks in the iBookstore, which was to be launched at the same time as the iPad was released, on 3 April 2010. Unlike Amazon, Apple used an agency model, according to which the publisher could set the price (although it had to be within certain pre-established price tiers that were fixed largely by Apple) and Apple would then take a 30 per cent commission as the selling agent – the same model that Apple used in the App store. All the publishers had signed contracts with Apple that included a controversial price-matching provision – the so-called Most Favoured Nation clause, or MFN – which stipulated that, if a competitor was selling an ebook for less, then the publisher would have to offer the same lower price in the iBookstore. This clause meant, in effect, that publishers would have a strong incentive to move other retailers over to the agency model so that they could not discount ebook prices and force publishers to match the lower prices in the iBookstore, where they would receive only 70 per cent of the lower price. Publishers also had other reasons to prefer the agency model to the traditional wholesale model for the sale of ebooks, but the MFN clause strengthened the case. And so began a series of fraught negotiations between five of the six largest publishing houses, on the one hand, and Amazon, on the other, starting with the now-legendary trip of John Sargent, CEO of Macmillan, the US group owned by Holzbrinck, who flew out to Seattle on 28 January 2010 to propose new terms of trade to Amazon, based on the agency model. The discussion did not go well. Amazon rejected the proposal and ushered Sargent unceremoniously to the door. By the time he had arrived back in New York on the Friday evening, Amazon had removed the buy buttons from all of Macmillan's books, both print and Kindle editions, on the Amazon site – exactly the kind of aggressive action by Amazon that publishers had long feared.

Over a long weekend at the end of January 2010, many in the publishing industry were riveted to their computer screens, watching in astonishment as a conflict that had been simmering beneath the surface for months suddenly burst into open warfare. Position statements were issued by both parties while authors, readers and bloggers weighed in on different sides. Two days later, Amazon decided to change course. They realized that they were going to face similar demands imminently for a move to agency from another four of the Big Six publishers and they couldn't refuse to sell books from all five. On Sunday, 31 January 2010, Amazon posted a message on its website conceding defeat: 'We have expressed our strong disagreement and the seriousness of our disagreement by temporarily ceasing the sale of all Macmillan titles', announced Amazon. 'We want you to know that ultimately, however, we will have to capitulate and accept Macmillan's terms because Macmillan has a monopoly over their own titles, and we will want to offer them to you even at prices we believe are needlessly high for e-books.'[11] Sargent had won the opening battle in the new price war around ebooks, but the war was only just beginning.

[11] www.amazon.com/tag/kindle/forum/ref=cm_cd_et_md_pl?_encoding=UTF8&cd Forum=Fx1D7SY3BVSESG&cdMsgNo=1&cdPage=1&cdSort=oldest&cdThread= Tx2MEGQWTNGIMHV&displayType=tagsDetail&cdMsgID=Mx5Z9849POTZ4P #Mx5Z9849POTZ4P.

The DOJ weighs in

This was the background to what was to become one of the most acrimonious episodes in the modern history of book publishing: the US Department of Justice's antitrust lawsuit against Apple and five of the big trade publishers over ebook pricing. Shortly after the stand-off with Macmillan, Amazon wrote to the Federal Trade Commission, setting out the chain of events and expressing its concern that the publishers and Apple were engaged in an illegal conspiracy to fix ebook prices. The Department of Justice (DOJ) took up the case. Two years later, on 11 April 2012, the DOJ filed a civil antitrust lawsuit against Apple and the five publishers, alleging that they conspired to raise ebook prices and limit competition in the sale of ebooks, in violation of Section 1 of the Sherman Antitrust Act.[12] The DOJ marshalled evidence to suggest that the publishers communicated with one another – in emails, over the telephone and in person, including meetings 'in private dining rooms of upscale Manhattan restaurants' – to discuss and agree on a common strategy to adopt the agency model and force Amazon to raise ebook prices, thus engaging, the suit alleged, in a horizontal conspiracy. The suit alleged that Apple had seized the opportunity to give the publishers what they wanted – namely, higher prices for ebooks – while shielding itself from retail price competition by proposing the agency model, adding the 'Most Favoured Nation' clause to its contracts and informing each publisher of the status of its negotiations with other publishers, thus orchestrating the collective action of the alleged conspirators and acting as 'a critical conspiracy participant'. This kind of arrangement, where one party controls and orchestrates the actions of numerous co-conspirators, is referred to in antitrust law as a 'hub-and-spoke' conspiracy. A conspiracy among competitors to fix the retail price of their products is a *per se* violation of Section 1 of the Sherman Antitrust Act, and Apple, as a vertical enabler of a horizontal price conspiracy, was also, the suit alleged, in breach of the Act.

Faced with this legal challenge and the prospects of lengthy and costly litigation if they contested the suit in court and lost, three of the five publishers quickly settled with the DOJ and agreed to terminate

---

[12] www.justice.gov/file/486986/download. For a detailed account of the legal issues involved in this case, see Chris Sagers, *United States v. Apple: Competition in America* (Cambridge, Mass.: Harvard University Press, 2019).

existing agency arrangements, including the controversial 'Most Favoured Nation' clause which, in the DOJ's view, was the clause that effectively forced the publishers to impose the agency model on all retailers, including Amazon, and eliminate price competition. They could continue to use the agency model – the agency model *per se* was not regarded by the DOJ as illegal; but for a period of two years they would have to allow retailers to discount ebook prices to some extent (retailers would be allowed to discount but not more than the value of the commission earned from the sale of the publisher's entire catalogue over a one-year period – in other words, the commission could be used as a discount pool but they couldn't discount more than that, an arrangement that was aptly dubbed 'Agency Lite'[13]). They also agreed to a $69 million settlement fund that would be used to compensate readers who bought ebooks between 1 April 2010 and 21 May 2012. Apple and two other publishers held out, though in December 2012 Penguin announced that it had settled with the DOJ, in advance of its merger with Random House, and in February 2013 Macmillan announced that it too had settled. As each publisher settled, the costs faced by the remaining defendants in the event of an unfavourable outcome grew, increasing the pressure to settle, regardless of whether they agreed with the allegations. 'A few weeks ago I got an estimate of the maximum possible damage figure. I cannot share the breathtaking amount with you, but it was much more than the entire equity of our company', said Macmillan's CEO John Sargent in a letter posted online.[14] Sargent continued to deny categorically that he and Macmillan had been involved in a conspiracy to raise prices, but the risks involved in continuing to fight the case were simply too high.

Apple alone decided to fight the case, which proceeded to trial in the US District Court in Manhattan in June 2013. In her opinion, Judge Denise Cote ruled against Apple, finding that Apple played a central role in facilitating and executing a conspiracy to eliminate retail price competition and raise ebook prices. 'Apple seized the moment and brilliantly played its hand', said Cote. 'It provided the Publisher Defendants with the vision, the format, the timetable, and the coordination that they needed to raise e-book prices.'[15] Apple

---

[13] Michael Cader, 'Hurry Up, Wait, and What the … !? Life Under Agency Lite', *PublishersLunch*, 7 September 2012, at http://lunch.publishersmarketplace.com/2012/09/hurry-up-wait-and-what-the-life-under-agency-lite.

[14] www.cnet.com/news/macmillan-reaches-e-book-pricing-settlement-with-doj.

[15] *United States* v. *Apple*, 12 Civ. 2826 (SDNY 2013), p. 11, at www.nysd.uscourts.gov/cases/show.php?db=special&id=306.

appealed, and in June 2015 the Second US Circuit Court of Appeals upheld the 2013 judgment, with two of the three judges endorsing the 2013 judgment while a third judge, Dennis Jacobs, dissented.[16]

In Judge Jacobs's dissenting opinion, both the District Court and his colleagues in the Court of Appeals misconstrued Apple's position. The Courts did not sufficiently recognize, in Jacobs's view, that Apple was operating in a different competitive space. It was competing in a 'distinct horizontal plane of retailers' and it was proposing to enter a market where another player, Amazon, had an effective monopoly, with around 90 per cent of the ebook market. Viewed in this way, Apple's conduct was not anti-competitive, in Jacobs's view. On the contrary, it was 'unambiguously and overwhelmingly pro-competitive. Apple was a major potential competitor in a market dominated by a 90 per cent monopoly, and was justifiably unwilling to enter a market on terms that would assure a loss on sales or exact a toll on its reputation.' Apple's actions broke Amazon's monopoly, concluded Jacobs, leading to a de-concentration of the ebook market, where Amazon's market share fell (at least temporarily) from around 90 per cent to around 60 per cent, and removing barriers to entry for others.

Jacobs's dissent was a minority opinion, vigorously rejected by Circuit Judge Debra Ann Livingston, who, writing for the majority, argued that 'the dissent's theory – that the presence of a strong competitor justifies a horizontal price-fixing conspiracy – endorses a concept of marketplace vigilantism that is wholly foreign to the antitrust laws.' She continued:

> By organizing a price-fixing conspiracy, Apple found an easy path to opening its iBookstore, but it did so by ensuring that market-wide ebook prices would rise to a level that it, and the Publisher Defendants, had jointly agreed upon. Plainly, competition is not served by permitting a market entrant to *eliminate price competition* as a condition of entry, and it is cold comfort to consumers that they gained a new ebook retailer at the expense of passing control over all ebook prices to a cartel of book publishers – publishers who, with Apple's help, collectively agreed on a new pricing model precisely to *raise* the price of ebooks and thus protect their profit margins and their very existence in the marketplace in the face of the admittedly strong headwinds created by the new technology.[17]

---

[16] *United States* v. *Apple, Inc.*, 13-3741-cv (L), at www.justice.gov/file/628971/download.
[17] Ibid., pp. 9–10.

Livingston took the view that Apple, by participating in a conspiracy that eliminated price competition and resulted in higher prices to consumers, violated the Sherman Antitrust Act. Jacobs argued that the market conditions were a material consideration and that, in a market where there was an incumbent player with a de facto monopoly of 90 per cent, Apple acted in the only way it reasonably could to break the monopoly and open the market to competitors. The decision went 2–1 in Livingston's favour and Apple was obliged to pay out $450 million, most of it to ebook buyers, as part of the settlement. Apple appealed to the Supreme Court, but on 7 March 2016 the Supreme Court announced that it would not hear the appeal, thereby upholding the previous court decision. The case was finally closed.

While this long unsavoury affair worked its way through the courts, Amazon enjoyed an unexpected boon. The settlement decree imposed by Judge Cote required the publishers to terminate their existing agency agreements and allow ebooks to be discounted again, which suited Amazon nicely. Apple's share of the ebook market did not grow as rapidly as many had expected, and the third major player in the ebook market, Barnes & Noble with its Nook, found itself losing market share after early gains. Google, which entered the ebook market in a serious way rather late in the game with the launch of Google Play in March 2012, had yet to make serious inroads. By early 2014, Amazon's market share in ebooks was increasing again, largely at Barnes & Noble's expense, while Apple's share remained modest, in the region of 15–20 per cent. Moreover, Amazon continued to strengthen its position in print as well as digital sales. For many publishers, Amazon had become their single most important customer, both for the sale of print books and for the sale of ebooks. One study found that, in March 2014, Amazon accounted for 41% of all new book unit sales in the US, print and digital combined, and that it had a 67% share of the ebook market.[18] Amazon also accounted for 65% of all new book units sold online, print and digital, and online outlets accounted for 41% of book purchases by 2013, compared to 22% accounted for by bookstore chains.[19] Other estimates suggested that, by 2016, Amazon

---

[18] Research conducted by the Codex Group, reported in Jim Milliot, 'BEA 2014: Can Anyone Compete with Amazon?' *Publishers Weekly* (28 May 2014), at www.publishersweekly.com/pw/by-topic/industry-news/bea/article/62520-bea-2014-can-anyone-compete-with-amazon.html.
[19] Ibid.

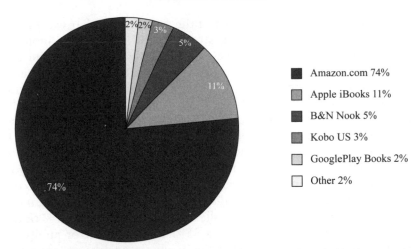

Amazon.com 74%

Apple iBooks 11%

B&N Nook 5%

Kobo US 3%

GooglePlay Books 2%

Other 2%

Figure 5.1   Estimated market shares of US retailers of paid ebook unit sales, 2016
Source: Author Earnings

accounted for 74% of paid ebook unit sales in the US, compared to 11% for Apple iBooks, 5% for Barnes & Noble's Nook, 3% for Kobo, 2% for GooglePlay Books and 2% for various others – see figure 5.1. Even this under-represented Amazon's actual share of the ebook market because it didn't take account of ebooks accessed and read in Amazon's ebook subscription service, Kindle Unlimited (more on this in chapter 9).[20] No other retailer came anywhere near Amazon's market share in ebooks, and for many publishers Amazon had become the largest retailer for their print books as well. For an organization that had not even existed twenty years earlier, this was an extraordinary transformation of the retail landscape.

---

[20] According to Paul Abbassi, who produced the 2016 estimate of market shares for Author Earnings, Amazon's market share in ebooks has continued to increase since 2016, as the Barnes & Noble Nook market share has continued to decline (to around 3% today) with the lost market share migrating to Amazon. Moreover, the expansion of Amazon's Kindle Unlimited programme has increased still further Amazon's market share: Abbassi calculates that Amazon accounted for 91% of the 540 million ebook unit sales in 2019, including KU full reads. For most traditional publishers, however, Amazon would account for around 75% of their ebook unit sales in 2019, since most traditional publishers don't participate in KU. Amazon's market share of unit sales is significantly higher than its share of dollar sales due to KU and to Amazon's dominance of sales of lower-priced ebooks (personal communication). For further discussion of Amazon's market shares in print books and ebooks, see chapter 12, pp. 430–44.

But that wasn't all. In the midst of the controversy that was raging around Amazon's ebook pricing strategy, and at the very moment when publishers were in the process of switching to the agency model, Amazon announced, on 20 January 2010, that they would offer a new 70% royalty option for authors who published directly with Amazon on the Kindle Digital Text Platform (DTP). DTP was the self-publishing tool that enabled anyone, authors or publishers, to upload their texts directly to Amazon and sell them in the Kindle Store. It was launched at the same time as the Kindle in November 2007 and it enabled anyone to self-publish with a minimum of fuss – all you needed was a title, an author's name and a text. The author selected a price – anything between 99¢ and $200 – and the text appeared, more or less instantaneously, in the Kindle Store. Amazon kept 65% of the receipts from any sales, and passed 35% to the author or publisher. But, in January 2010, aware that the agency model being offered to publishers by Apple was based on a 70:30 split in which Apple kept a 30% commission on sales and passed 70% to the publisher, Amazon announced that they would now offer a new 70% royalty rate on books published on DTP, provided they met certain conditions.[21] The author would have to choose a list price between $2.99 and $9.99 and ensure that this price was at least 20% below the lowest list price for any print edition of the book, but if these and a few other conditions were met, then authors would receive 70% of the list price net of delivery costs – the same percentage that publishers received from Apple on the agency model. Had Amazon been trying to stoke the anxieties of publishers, they could hardly have chosen a better time to make this announcement. Already worried that Amazon's aggressive ebook pricing strategy would undermine their revenue and have long-term deleterious consequences for the industry, publishers now had new grounds to fear that Amazon would seek to publish more and more authors directly, offering them a royalty that was much higher than the ebook royalty they would receive if they published with a traditional publisher (commonly 25% of net receipts) and thereby bypassing the publisher completely. Introducing the new 70% royalty rate at this point in time was a bold and aggressive counter-move by Amazon in the war it was waging with publishers over ebook pricing, and it also had the effect of acting as a massive shot in the arm for the self-publishing movement, which was well under way by this time.[22]

---

[21] http://phx.corporate-ir.net/phoenix.zhtml?ID=1376977&c=176060&p=irol-newsArticle.
[22] See chapter 7.

156

And there was more: Kindle Digital Text Platform (DTP), subsequently renamed Kindle Direct Publishing (or KDP), was just one strand of Amazon's own multi-faceted publishing programme that was now taking shape. In May 2009, Amazon launched AmazonEncore, a publishing programme aimed at identifying books and authors that had been overlooked, re-publishing them and selling them both through Amazon (the Book Store and the Kindle Store) and through other retail outlets. A year later, they announced AmazonCrossing, a new imprint that extended their publishing programme to translations. Then, in May 2011, Amazon launched two genre imprints, Montlake Romance and Thomas & Mercer, an imprint focused on mystery; and in October, it launched 47North, an imprint for fantasy, science fiction and horror. In May 2011, it was also announced that the literary agent Larry Kirshbaum – formerly the CEO of the Time Warner Book Group and a well-known figure in the publishing world – would be heading up Amazon Publishing's New York office with a remit to develop a general list in literary and commercial fiction, young-adult titles, business and general nonfiction. Now it really did seem like Amazon had ambitions to compete directly with traditional publishers, signing up authors and offering them a comprehensive and fully integrated publishing service, from editorial through marketing, sales and distribution. What were publishers to think when their most important retail customer, accounting for more than 60% of their ebook sales and a large and growing proportion of their print sales, was now competing directly with them through an expanding publishing programme of its own? You didn't have to be a conspiracy theorist to think that Amazon might be planning to eat your lunch.

Stand-off with Hachette

It was against the backcloth of these increasingly fraught relations between Amazon – now the dominant book retailer in the US – and the publishers who supplied it with books, themselves bruised by the punishing terms of the settlement decree, that the public relations disaster of the Amazon–Hachette dispute unfolded. Many of the post-settlement agreements between the major publishers and Amazon had run through 2013 and were due to expire in the course of 2014. New contracts had to be negotiated, and Hachette was the first up – their contract with Amazon was coming to an end in March 2014. In January 2014, Amazon called on Hachette's offices in New York and proposed terms that were substantially different from the terms that had been agreed previously. Senior managers at Hachette were taken aback by the scale of Amazon's ask. Their response was not to respond. The contract automatically renewed itself every thirty days until a new contract was in place, so they decided to play for time. The end of March came and went. Discussions took place but the parties were so far apart that it wasn't clear when a new agreement would be reached, or whether it could be reached at all. Amazon began to intensify the pressure on Hachette, using various tools at its disposal, such as not accepting pre-orders for forthcoming books, delaying shipping and reducing discounting, to discourage customers from buying Hachette's books.[23] Working relationships deteriorated and Hachette's sales began to suffer. As the dispute dragged on into the summer, authors became increasingly vocal in expressing their concerns. An open letter written by David Preston and signed by more than 900 authors, including many well-known writers like John Grisham, Stephen King, Paul Auster and Donna Tartt, appeared as a full two-page ad in a Sunday edition of the *New York Times* in August, calling on Amazon to stop using sanctions against Hachette's books and denouncing it for inflicting 'harm on some of the very authors who helped it become one of the largest retailers in the world'.[24] Other authors, mobilized by prominent figures in the world of self-publishing like Hugh Howey and Barry Eisler, issued a petition of their own that was strongly supportive of Amazon and highly critical of Hachette.[25] The dispute had now become very public and very ugly.

After several more weeks of negotiations, Hachette and Amazon eventually reached an agreement that was announced in November. Hachette had succeeded in maintaining the agency model for ebook sales, which enabled it to set the prices of its ebooks, but it had to pay more in terms of fees to Amazon. Negotiating this agreement had taken nearly a year and had resulted in a great deal of bad publicity, especially for Amazon. In the eyes of many, Amazon's reputation had been tarnished by this unseemly display of corporate power. So why were they willing to risk so much bad press on a negotiation over terms of trade with one supplier? And,

---

[23] David Streitfeld, 'Writers Feel an Amazon–Hachette Spat', *The New York Times*, 9 May 2014, at www.nytimes.com/2014/05/10/technology/writers-feel-an-amazon-hachette-spat.html; David Streitfeld and Melissa Eddy, 'As Publishers Fight Amazon, Books Vanish', *The New York Times*, 23 May 2014, at http://bits.blogs.nytimes.com/2014/05/23/amazon-escalates-its-battle-against-hachette.
[24] http://authorsunited.net.
[25] www.change.org/p/hachette-stop-fighting-low-prices-and-fair-wages.

more generally, why had relations become so fraught between America's largest book retailer, on the one hand, and its largest trade publishers, on the other?

Amazon has built its entire business around the idea of being customer-focused, of offering the best service it could to customers, including the lowest prices. Competing on price is crucial for Amazon because it is a vital way of delivering good value to customers and, at the same time, undercutting its competitors. What made the agency model so unattractive to Amazon is that it removes one of the key tools they have used systematically – even ruthlessly, at times – to compete with other retailers and build their market share. While the special conditions imposed on publishers in the aftermath of the DOJ price-fixing lawsuit allowed retailers to discount ebooks for a limited time period under certain conditions (Agency Lite), any discounting that a retailer did during this period was at the retailer's expense, since it was eating into the commission they received for selling the ebooks. Amazon's margins were therefore under a great deal of pressure, and the only way they could improve their margins without giving up on discounting and asking customers to pay more was to squeeze their suppliers. They could ask for a higher commission and they could ask for co-op[26] for ebook sales – these (and other things) would improve their margins and enable them to continue discounting ebooks while they were still able to do so. The publisher, on the other hand, would be squeezed. The sheer magnitude of Amazon's ask, together with the reluctance of Hachette's management to enter into negotiations when the gulf to be bridged was so great, goes a long way to explaining why this confrontation became so protracted and so bitter.

Market power

Beyond the specific circumstances of this dispute, there were larger issues at stake. There is considerable disquiet among many in the industry about the sheer magnitude of the market power that

---

[26] Co-op, short for 'co-operative advertising', is a financial arrangement between a manufacturer or supplier and a retailer, whereby the supplier pays for part of the retailer's promotion costs. Co-op arrangements are common in the publishing industry for the promotion of print books: co-op funds are typically used to pay for in-store book displays in windows and on front-of-store tables, for example. Amazon also wanted co-op for ebook sales, on the grounds that the promotions on their website and via email to their customer base were growing sales of both print books and ebooks.

Amazon now wields as a key retailer for both print books and ebooks, and concern in some quarters that Amazon may be a monopsony that is abusing its market power. In economic terms, monopsony is the mirror image of monopoly. Whereas a monopoly is a single (or overwhelmingly dominant) *seller* who, by virtue of its market dominance, is able to use its power to increase the prices it charges consumers, a monopsony is a single (or overwhelmingly dominant) *buyer* who, by virtue of its market dominance, is able to use its power to drive down the prices it pays its suppliers. The classic example of monopsony would be an agricultural market in which there was only one buyer – say one large poultry processor who was buying chickens from small farmers, so that farmers had no alternative but to sell to this buyer, enabling the buyer to drive down the price it pays farmers for their chickens. There could also be cases of collusive monopsony where several buyers collude to drive down the prices paid to suppliers. To the extent that a monopsony amounts to an abuse of power, it would fall within the scope of antitrust law, and there are cases where firms and organizations have been prosecuted for monopsony under antitrust legislation.[27] Is Amazon a monopsony in this sense? And if it is, does it abuse its power in ways that could be a violation of antitrust law?

There are some who think so. 'Amazon.com, the giant online retailer, has too much power, and it uses that power in ways that hurt America', asserted Paul Krugman at the height of the Amazon–Hachette stand-off.[28] Of course, Amazon does not dominate online retail, let alone retailing as a whole, and it probably never will. But when it comes to books, says Krugman, Amazon does have the robber-baron-type of market power that Standard Oil once had in the oil business before it was broken up: 'Amazon overwhelmingly dominates online book sales, with a market share comparable to Standard Oil's share of the refined oil market when it was broken up in 1911. Even if you look at total book sales, Amazon is by far the largest player.'[29] Krugman acknowledges that Amazon has not tried to exploit its dominant market position by raising prices to consumers – on the contrary, it has made a point of keeping its

---

[27] For a good overview of the issues involved, see Roger D. Blair and Jeffrey L. Harrison, *Monopsony in Law and Economics* (New York: Cambridge University Press, 2010).

[28] Paul Krugman, 'Amazon's Monopsony is not O.K.', *The New York Times*, 19 October 2014, at www.nytimes.com/2014/10/20/opinion/paul-krugman-amazons-monopsony-is-not-ok.html?_r=0.

[29] Ibid.

prices to consumers low, often undercutting other retailers. 'What it has done, instead, is use its market power to put a squeeze on publishers, in effect driving down the prices it pays for books.' The question is whether this constitutes an abuse of power that could be actionable under antitrust law, or just normal business practice. The argument that this is something *more* than normal business practice, that Amazon is acting as a monopsony and abusing its market power, might go something like this. Given that Amazon accounts for over 40 per cent of all new book sales and 70 per cent or more of the ebook market, it is in an immensely strong negotiating position vis-à-vis its suppliers, able to cut off around half of a publisher's revenue stream if terms can't be agreed. This would have crippling consequences for a publisher and for the authors published by them, simply because the other retail outlets could not come anywhere near to making up the shortfall in sales that would result if their books were no longer available through Amazon. Moreover, if Amazon then uses the means at its disposal to apply pressure on a publisher by discouraging customers from buying the publisher's books or making it difficult for them to do so, this might well begin to look like an abuse of market power. Krugman, for his part, has no doubts: 'Don't tell me that Amazon is giving consumers what they want, or that it has earned its position. What matters is whether it has too much power, and is abusing that power. Well, it does, and it is.'[30] Others may be less sure. But the stand-off with Hachette put the issue of Amazon's market power on the table in a way that is now much harder to ignore.

So why does Amazon not appear to have been subjected to the same kind of antitrust scrutiny by the Department of Justice as Apple and the large trade publishers were in 2010–12? There are several reasons that may help to explain this. In the first place, US antitrust law distinguishes between unilateral and multilateral action on the part of firms, and it is much more concerned about the latter than the former.[31] US courts have taken the view that it would be harder for one firm acting on its own to harm anyone, whereas several firms acting in concert or collusion are likely to represent a much more serious threat. Moreover, horizontal price-fixing agreements are unlawful under Section 1 of the Sherman Act, and in 1940 the US Supreme Court established the *per se* rule against horizontal

---

[30] Ibid.

[31] I am indebted, here and elsewhere in this section, to conversations with Chris Sagers, who generously shared his knowledge of US antitrust law with me.

price fixing, which means that the court will assume that any such agreement is illegal *per se* and will not hear arguments to the contrary.[32] So if the Department of Justice suspects that several firms may be acting in collusion to fix prices, it is very likely to investigate: this is low-hanging fruit in antitrust terms[33] and the DOJ knows that it can bring a case and stand a good chance of success. Hence what appeared to be collusive action on the part of Apple and the large publishers to fix ebook prices was bound to catch the attention of antitrust authorities, whereas one retailer acting on its own, selling ebooks at lower prices than its competitors, was less suspect in prima facie terms.

A second reason, related to this, is that the main focus of US antitrust law has been on sellers rather than buyers.[34] There are occasions when antitrust authorities have taken action against large buyers – the Federal Trade Commission's case against Toys "R" Us is a good example.[35] But, in recent US antitrust enforcement, cases against buyers have been much less common than cases against sellers. This doesn't mean that the lack of attention given to buyer power is justified – this may well be a serious shortcoming of antitrust law that should be addressed. But it helps to explain why antitrust authorities have been reluctant so far to take action against large buyers like Amazon.

A third reason is that what exactly constitutes 'monopsony power' is not easy to establish in practice, nor is it easy to establish what exactly would constitute an abuse of this power. The antitrust literature often distinguishes between 'monopsony power' and 'countervailing power', and antitrust policy has traditionally placed much more emphasis on monopsony power than on counter-vailing power, though countervailing power is much more common.[36] Roughly speaking, monopsony power is restricted to cases where two conditions apply: (1) the buyer purchases from an array of sellers who lack significant market power and face rising supply costs; and (2) the buyer has sufficient power over these suppliers to force them

---

[32] *United States* v. *Socony-Vacuum Oil Co., Inc.*, 310 US 150 (1940), at https://supreme.justia.com/cases/federal/us/310/150/case.html.
[33] Sagers, *United States* v. *Apple*, p. 13.
[34] See John B. Kirkwood, 'Powerful Buyers and Merger Enforcement', *Boston University Law Review*, 92 (2012), 1488.
[35] *Toys "R" Us, Inc.* v. *FTC*, 221 F.3d 928 (2000), at http://scholar.google.co.uk/scholar_case?case=11480829751523506812.
[36] Kirkwood, 'Powerful Buyers and Merger Enforcement', p. 1490.

to supply their output at prices below the competitive level.[37] These two conditions are said to distinguish monopsony power from the more common case of countervailing power, where suppliers have significant market power and the buyer negotiates prices that are closer to the competitive level. Using these definitions, Amazon's power might well look like a case of countervailing power rather than monopsony power, and this is indeed the position taken by some legal scholars.[38] But the distinction between these two forms of power is less clear than it might seem at first sight. How much power does a seller need for their power to be regarded as 'significant'? Even if some sellers had 'significant' power, what if there were many smaller sellers who did not and who were obliged to accept the buyer's terms or go out of business? How, moreover, would you determine whether the prices demanded by the powerful buyer were at or above 'the competitive level' or below it? And if, in the messy reality of actual markets and the fraught negotiations between buyers and sellers, the distinction between monopsony power and countervailing power may be hard to draw, should not competition authorities be more willing to investigate the power of large buyers, regardless of whether it appears to fit the textbook definition of monopsony?[39]

The fourth reason that might help to explain why action against powerful buyers is rare is the difficulty of building a compelling case about harm. Who exactly is harmed by the tough negotiating tactics of a powerful buyer, especially if the buyer passes on some of the benefits of lower costs to customers in the form of lower prices? It could be argued that the actions of a powerful buyer harm upstream suppliers by reducing their revenues and squeezing their margins – and could even put them out of business if they refused to agree to the buyer's terms. This in turn could potentially harm downstream customers by reducing the resources available to suppliers to innovate and invest in new product development – or, in the case of books, to invest in the development of new content, including the payment of advances and royalties to authors at a level that would enable them to write new books, etc. But while the welfare of suppliers may be harmed, it is much harder, in the case of Amazon and books, to demonstrate

---

[37] Ibid., p. 1496
[38] See John B. Kirkwood, 'Collusion to Control a Powerful Customer: Amazon, E-Books, and Antitrust Policy', *University of Miami Law Review*, 69, 1 (2014), 1–63.
[39] This is indeed Kirkwood's position: while he is of the view that the DoJ was right to prosecute Apple and the large trade publishers for conspiring to fix ebook prices, he also believes that there are cases – albeit rare – when collusion to control a powerful buyer, possessing either monopsony or countervailing power, would be justified.

convincingly that the welfare of consumers is being harmed by tough negotiations with suppliers – especially when Amazon uses its power, almost as an article of faith, to deliver lower prices to customers. If consumer welfare is treated as the issue of paramount importance, then the cries of suppliers who are being squeezed ever harder by a large and powerful buyer are unlikely to be heard above the happy chatter of consumers who are enjoying the low-price feast.

A final reason is that, in current US antitrust policy, the fact that Amazon is a large corporation is not, in and by itself, a reason for taking action against it. This reflects a broad shift in US antitrust policy that began in the 1970s.[40] Prior to that, US antitrust policy was more concerned about the size of corporations, both because large corporations could harm consumers and small businesses and because they represented undesirable concentrations of economic and social power. From around 1970 on, however, a growing group of legal scholars, including Robert Bork and Richard Posner, as well as Chicago School economists like George Stigler, began developing a new approach to antitrust law that was rooted in neoclassical economics. Traditional antitrust concerns about concentration and the size of large corporations were being eclipsed by a growing emphasis on consumer welfare, free competition and deregulated markets. To the extent that a large corporation abused its market power to raise prices or reduce output, or conspired with other corporations to raise prices or reduce output, then that could well be viewed as detrimental to consumer welfare and subjected to antitrust action. But 'bigness' as such was not a problem for the Chicago-school thinkers. Big corporations might be more efficient and deliver lower prices to consumers. In Bork's view, many antitrust policies at the time helped to protect some inefficient businesses from competition, enabling them to keep prices high without producing any other goods – what he referred to as 'the antitrust paradox'.[41] For Bork, antitrust law should be minimized and focused primarily on a limited range of overtly anticompetitive actions, including horizontal price-fixing agreements, horizontal mergers that create monopolies or duopolies, and a limited set of exclusionary behaviours. This agenda resonated with the political agenda of neoliberalism and deregulation

---

[40] This shift is well documented in Rudolph J. R. Peritz, *Competition Policy in America, 1988–1992: History, Rhetoric, Law* (New York: Oxford University Press, 1996), chs. 5–6, and in Jonathan B. Baker, *The Antitrust Paradigm: Restoring a Competitive Economy* (Cambridge, Mass.: Harvard University Press, 2019), ch. 2.
[41] Robert Bork, *The Antitrust Paradox* (New York: Free Press, 1978).

that characterized the Reagan era, and many of the ideas of Bork and his colleagues were incorporated into the practices of the Department of Justice and the Federal Trade Commission and into the decisions of the courts. In this new climate, protecting small businesses from larger and more powerful corporations – which, partly because of their size, might be more efficient and able to deliver lower prices to consumers – is not something with which antitrust authorities are going to be greatly concerned. When antitrust policy is focused more on consumer welfare than corporate power, then large corporations that are committed to driving down prices are less likely to be of interest to antitrust regulators, even if these corporations may be squeezing suppliers in order to deliver lower prices.

These various reasons help explain why the Department of Justice took action against Apple and the large trade publishers but has not – or at least not yet – taken action against Amazon. Multiple sellers who appear to be engaging in collusive action to raise prices are always going to ring alarm bells more loudly in the offices of US competition authorities than the actions of a single buyer negotiating hard with its suppliers. What is puzzling about the case against Apple and the publishers is not that the DOJ chose to investigate this matter, given that price-fixing agreements are a *per se* violation of antitrust law; the puzzle is why so many large corporations, with their legions of well-paid corporate lawyers, could have allowed their CEOs and senior managers to have walked so seemingly unaware into this trap. Why were they not advised in more forceful terms that it would be sensible to avoid conversations, communications and dinners among the CEOs of competing firms at such a sensitive time in the fraught discussions with Amazon over ebook pricing and pricing models – or, if they were so advised, why did they choose to ignore it? It's true that New York publishing is a small world, more like a private members' club than an intensely competitive field, where CEOs and other senior managers from different companies know one another on a first-name basis and often chat informally about any number of issues, from authors they share in common to the quality of local schools. But, regardless of what they actually talked about in those conversations and dinners, the mere fact that they took place at a critical time in the unfolding of a fraught series of negotiations with the most important retailer in the industry was bound to raise suspicions in the minds of investigators who were inclined to believe the worst. It just didn't look good. Apple and the publishers may or may not have been involved in a conspiracy: without knowing the actual content of the conversations that took place, much of the evidence is circumstantial. But in conspiracy cases of this kind, where courts know that co-conspirators may have gone to some lengths to conceal or destroy any evidence of a conspiracy, circumstantial evidence, or limited direct evidence, is often regarded as sufficient to establish culpability, and the DOJ had plenty of evidence of this kind.[42] Given the circumstances, it was undoubtedly unwise, to put it mildly, for the CEOs and senior managers of large competing corporations to engage in direct communication with one another when each was also engaged in tense negotiations with one of its most important customers.

Standing back from the details of this case, one may wonder, nonetheless, whether the DOJ got the right target in its sights. Conspiracy among suppliers to fix prices was an obvious target but was it the right one? If Amazon had 90 per cent of the ebook market before publishers moved over to the agency model, and their market share fell to 60–65 per cent after agency was adopted, then maybe the publishers' actions were justified after all. Maybe, by acting in concert, they were able to break Amazon's apparent stranglehold on the ebook market and open up the space for other retailers, including Apple, to enter the field, thereby creating a more diverse ebook marketplace – might that be possible? It could well be, and there were many observers and commentators who sympathized with this view and saw Amazon as the real threat. But Judge Cote had no truck with this line of argument: the view that a particular state of affairs is undesirable for the industry, or that the practices of a powerful retailer are harmful or unfair, is not, in itself, an acceptable justification for collusion among competitors to end that state of affairs. 'The remedy for illegal conduct is a complaint lodged with

---

[42] See Sagers, *United States* v. *Apple*, pp. 193–7. Sagers is in no doubt that, by the standards of proof normally required in conspiracy cases, the government's case was strong: 'the evidence of both conspiracies the government alleged was explicit and overwhelming. For whatever reason, these particular defendants, despite some evidence that they knew their conduct was illegal, made relatively little effort to keep it secret' (p. 194). Not everyone shares Sager's view, however. Shortly after Judge Cote ruled against Apple in 2013, Ankur Kapoor, a partner at the law firm Constantine Cannon who specializes in antitrust cases, expressed his strong disagreement with the ruling: 'I think the decision is completely wrong', said Kapoor. 'I didn't see anything that tied Apple to the conspiracy among the publishers.' In Kapoor's view, the government did not provide sufficient evidence to prove that Apple acted as a go-between in the alleged conspiracy among publishers: 'getting the publishers to move to a different model of distribution is not in itself an agreement on what pricing should be' (Ankur Kapoor quoted in Jeff Bercovici, 'Apple Conspired on E-Book Pricing, Judge Rules. But Did It?' *Forbes*, 10 July 2013, at www.forbes.com/sites/jeffbercovici/2013/07/10/apple-conspired-on-e-book-pricing-judge-rules-but-did-it/#351a56433f88).

the proper law enforcement offices or a civil suit or both', commented Cote. 'Another company's alleged violation of antitrust laws is not an excuse for engaging in your own violations of law.'[43]

Judge Cote's response is perfectly reasonable: two wrongs don't make a right. But we're still left with a problem with which the antitrust authorities, the courts and the existing interpretations of antitrust law have difficulty coming to terms: a single powerful retailer, commanding a large share of the market, can have effects in a field or market that can be just as pernicious as the effects of collusion among suppliers. One powerful buyer with a dominant market share can distort market processes and reduce competition just as effectively as several smaller suppliers acting in concert. Moreover, in the digital age, when a powerful player like Amazon is acting not just as a retailer but also as a platform, and, as such, can exercise new forms of exclusion by virtue of its position as the dominant platform, there is an urgent need to look again at some of the basic assumptions of antitrust law and enforcement. Norms that were established for an earlier era may need to be revised to take account of the new forms of power wielded by corporations who are able to benefit from network effects and from their proprietary control of large quantities of customer data, conditions that simply did not exist in the pre-digital age. There is a growing recognition in some quarters that the time has come to revisit some of these norms and to sharpen the antitrust scrutiny of large tech companies which, thanks to network effects and their role as platforms or operating systems, have become de facto monopolies that can have anti-competitive and harmful consequences.[44] Of course, whether this is likely to happen anytime soon, given the current composition of the Supremc Court and the current leadership of the antitrust authorities in the US, which largely still adhere to the Chicago approach, is another matter. But the intellectual case for reform is strong. We'll return to these issues later.

An uneasy truce

To many outside observers it may seem strange that, once the temporary agreements imposed by the settlement decree had run

---

[43] *United States* v. *Apple*, 12 Civ. 2826 (SDNY 2013), p. 157, at www.nysd.uscourts.gov/cases/show.php?db=special&id=306.
[44] See, especially, Baker's excellent account of how new technologies have presented new challenges to antitrust thinking and policy in *The Antitrust Paradigm*.

their course and new ebook agreements had been negotiated between Amazon and the publishers involved in the dispute, all of these new agreements were based on the agency model. Why would Amazon be willing to accept the agency model now, post-settlement decree, when they had fought against it so fiercely four years earlier? Maybe their market power was not so great after all?

To understand this strange turn of events, we have to see that, by 2014, the market situation had changed in ways that made agency agreements look attractive not just to publishers but to Amazon too. There were at least five reasons why agency now suited Amazon, in a way that it hadn't a few years before. In the first place, by 2014, Kindle sales were no longer growing in the way that they were in 2008, 2009 and 2010. In 2008–10, drawing customers into Kindle was a great way to draw them into the Amazon ecosystem. If you can get a new customer by taking a book that cost you $13 and selling it at $9.99, then it cost you $3 to get that new customer – that's very cheap if you think about the lifetime value of a customer. Kindle was a very cost-effective way of acquiring new customers, and, once they were in the Amazon ecosystem, had registered and supplied their credit card and other details, they were locked in and could become lifetime customers not just for ebooks but for other things too. So there was tremendous value in getting them in the door, and it was in Amazon's interests to maximize their market share. Agency was a serious obstacle at that stage because it impeded Amazon's ability to attract new customers by offering discounted ebooks – hence their opposition. But when ebook sales levelled off, Kindle sales levelled off too. People who were reading ebooks on Kindle would have their Kindles already, so there was no longer the same new-customer effect. You don't need to lose $3 on each ebook sale to try to acquire new customers because there are now relatively few new customers to acquire. As Kindle sales declined, agency was no longer the obstacle it once was.

Second, by 2014 the ebook market had matured and Amazon was in a dominant position with around 67 per cent of the market. To all intents and purposes, the war had been won and, with ebook sales levelling off and the competition floundering, there was no need to keep firing the artillery. Gaining another 2 or 3 per cent of market share was not a big deal for Amazon now, so why sell books at a loss? Better to call a truce and enjoy the benefits that would come from quietly transitioning to agency. This connects with a third point: Amazon was facing growing pressure from investors to be profitable. They also needed to invest in new things, so they needed to make money on their mature businesses. Books were one of their mature businesses – indeed, books are where they started. So it was time to stop treating books as a loss leader and actually make some money on them. And if you want to make money on books as a retailer, then agency is great: it guarantees you a margin of 30 per cent, at whatever price the book is sold. Perfect: let's go agency now. We're the dominant retailer, the market isn't growing significantly anymore and this will ensure that our ebook business is profitable.

Fourth, by 2014, Amazon had a whole other ebook business that was growing fast and where they had much more control over all aspects of the business, including prices and margins: self-publishing through Kindle Direct (more on this later). If the mainstream trade publishers want to keep their ebook prices at $12.99, that's absolutely fine with Amazon – in fact, it now suits them very well, since it means that their Kindle Direct self-publishing business and their Kindle Unlimited subscription business are going to appear much cheaper to the reader: $1.99 or $2.99, maybe less, compared to $12.99 for a new ebook from a mainstream house, or $9.99 per month for subscription access to Kindle Unlimited. And the margin Amazon earns on self-published books and Kindle Unlimited is entirely within Amazon's control. No need for prolonged and difficult negotiations with awkward New York publishers.

Fifth, going along with agency now means that no competitors or new entrants are going to be able to steal market share from you by discounting heavily and undercutting your price. The ability to discount was crucial for Amazon when the market was expanding rapidly, because that was the time when you needed to win over new customers and lock them into your ebook ecosystem. But when the market is no longer expanding and there are relatively few new customers to win over, you don't want any of your competitors, actual or potential, to be given the discount weapon to use against you. Agency is the perfect bulwark against this: the publisher sets the price and no retailer can discount it. What was once the bane of Amazon has now become an effective means of defending its market dominance against competitors and new entrants.

Viewed in this way, it's not surprising that some have begun to wonder whether agency is such a good thing after all. 'The publishers did a great service for Amazon', said one senior manager in a large tech company that has the scale and clout to compete with Amazon but now doubts whether it will. 'They gave them margin for Wall Street, which is what they wanted, and they killed their competitors, which was great for them. They found this détente because Amazon needed margin. It was a perfect storm of bad ideas.' The return to agency worked for Amazon in 2014 but, in a mature market where Amazon was now dominant, it also created a formidable barrier to entry for any new player who might want to try to gain market share by competing with Amazon on price.

That may well be true, although it's also true that other ebook retailers found it difficult to compete effectively against Amazon and take significant market share from them when ebooks were being sold on a wholesale rather than an agency basis. Why would they stand a better chance now? Moreover, the agency model does have real advantages for publishers – first, it ends ebook discounting and creates a level playing field for ebook retailers who can no longer undercut others by offering discounted prices; second, it protects the print edition of the book, and therefore also supports bricks-and-mortar bookstores, by not allowing the print edition to be undermined by much lower ebook prices; and third, it protects the value of the intellectual property by allowing publishers to fix the price at a level that ensures there is enough money for authors and publishers. That, in essence, is why the large trade publishers have opted for the agency model for ebooks and why, despite reservations in some quarters, they are likely to stand by it, at least for the foreseeable future.

While the Department of Justice case against Apple and the five publishers is now history and a détente has emerged between Amazon and the big trade houses on agency, the issues around the pricing and discounting of ebooks are unlikely to go away, for they press to the heart of what is at stake in the digital revolution. A key feature of information is that, while it may be costly to produce it in the first place, the marginal cost of reproduction is close to zero. And since information is very cheap to reproduce, it can be used by large tech companies and retailers as a way to increase market share and become dominant in their domains – in other words, information becomes cannon fodder in struggles between players who are pursuing their own aims. So there is intense downward pressure on the prices of information and symbolic content online: information and symbolic content are used as a way to achieve scale, gain market share and gather more and more user-data, and the cheaper this information is, the more effective it is for achieving these goals. This produces a deep structural conflict between information and content producers, on the one hand, and network players, on the other. For network players, information and symbolic content are a means to an end, which is to get big fast and to become a dominant player in the field – or at least sufficiently dominant to command a significant degree of attention. But for information and content producers, information and symbolic content are not means to an end but ends in themselves, something that takes time, effort and creativity to produce and is to be valued in and for itself. For the network players, driving down the price of information and symbolic content makes sense, because the marginal cost of reproduction is close to zero and lower prices will strengthen your competitive edge and enable you to pursue your aims more effectively. But for information and content producers, the downward pressure on prices is damaging to their vital interests because it sucks value out of the content creation process, leaving less and less resource available for those individuals and organizations – including authors and publishers – who must set aside the time and invest the effort and imagination to create the content in the first place. The agency model enables publishers to retain control over the pricing of digital content, and thereby to set prices that work in concert with print prices and that, taken together, might enable sufficient revenue to be generated to sustain the creative process. Abandoning the agency model would allow retailers to discount and might enable other players to challenge the dominance of Amazon, but it would carry the risk – by no means hypothetical, as the music industry shows – of a haemorrhaging of value out of the industry, making it harder and harder to sustain an industry that is able to produce work of quality over time.

— Chapter 6 —

STRUGGLES FOR VISIBILITY

Amazon's power in the field of publishing stems not just from its large and growing market share as a retailer, formidable though that is. It also stems from the rich data it has gathered – and continues to gather with every search and every purchase – on the more than 300 million active customers who use its site.[1] This enables Amazon to tap into a source of power that has become increasingly important in the digital age but that has been largely unavailable to the publishers who supply it with books – namely, user data, which is a specific form of what I'm going to call 'information capital'. I'll discuss information capital in more detail in chapter 12 but let me give a brief definition here: by 'information capital', I mean a particular kind of resource that consists of bits of information that can be gathered, stored, processed and combined with other bits of information and used as a source of power to pursue specific aims. Of course, there is nothing new about information as an organizational resource: organizations have always sought to gather information about their customers, competitors, citizens, enemies and others, and to use this information for their own purposes, whether that is to improve products and services, gain advantages, counter threats or defeat enemies. But in the digital age, the capacity to gather and store information, the kinds of information that can be gathered and the uses to which it can be put have changed in fundamental ways. Whenever

---

[1] As of the first quarter of 2016, Amazon had 310 million active customer accounts worldwide (see www.statista.com/statistics/476196/number-of-active-amazon-customer-accounts-quarter). At the end of 2019, Amazon reported 150 million paid Prime members worldwide, up from 100 million paid Prime members around the world at the end of the first quarter of 2018 (see www.statista.com/statistics/829113/number-of-paying-amazon-prime-members).

an individual uses a network, they leave a trace, a digital footprint, that can be recorded, processed and used by an organization for its own ends. One way that it can be used is to be fed into algorithms that will enable the organization to refine and improve the services it provides – this is what Google does when it uses the results of every search to improve the effectiveness of the search engine and the accuracy with which it can identify relevant pages for future searches. The data generated by users are fed recursively into the algorithm, and the more data there are, the more effective this recursive process of refinement is. User data become the foundation of the organization's success.

The same principle lies behind the recommendation algorithms that are a crucial part of many online organizations, including Amazon. Here the data generated by users' profiles and their network behaviour, including their page views, selections and purchases, are used to generate recommendations for new purchases, and these recommendations are constantly refined by incorporating new user data over time: with each new purchase, the recommendations are further refined, altering and personalizing the browsing experience for each individual customer. As a marketing mechanism, this is immensely powerful, as the recommendations are closely tailored to the actual and potential purchases of individual users. At the same time, this is a mechanism that is controlled by the online retailer who owns the data that populate and drive the algorithms. Both the data and the recommendation algorithms that are constructed with them are closely guarded secrets: they are the keys to the retailer's success and its ability to put more relevant products in front of its customers and entice them to buy. But neither the data nor the details of the recommendation algorithms are available to the retailer's suppliers, including the publishers whose books are being sold with their help.

In this respect, the digital revolution has built on a feature that was always characteristic of the book supply chain but, given the characteristics of the digital environment and the power associated with recommendation algorithms based on network behaviour, it has raised this feature to an altogether different level of significance. It was always part of the book supply chain because publishers rarely sold their books directly to the ultimate customers – that is, the readers. Publishers' main customers were always intermediaries – namely, bookstores and wholesalers. But in the world of bricks-and-mortar bookstores, retailers generally had much less information about their customers and their browsing and purchasing behaviour than Amazon and other tech companies have in the digital age, when so much browsing and purchasing behaviour takes place online and when every move in the network can be captured, stored and used by the company once you are on its platform. In this new world, the asymmetry between what the retailer knows about the customer and what the publisher knows is much greater than it was in the pre-digital age, simply because the online retailer now knows so much more than retailers ever knew in the past. And this further increases the dependency of publishers on this powerful new retail intermediary, Amazon, who now not only accounts for a large proportion of their sales but also owns the data on their customers and uses this data to construct a powerful new marketing machine that is controlled entirely by the retailer, not by the publisher. This is a kind of dependency that simply did not exist in the pre-digital age.

The creation of this new marketing machine based on user data is symptomatic not only of a shift in the balance of power towards the retailers who control this data: it is also symptomatic of the new forms of visibility and discoverability that become increasingly important in the digital age. The book business is a business of abundance: a huge number of new titles is published every year in all major book markets. Moreover, with the new forms of publishing that are made possible by digital technology, the traditional industry calculations of the number of new books published each year, which were based on ISBNs issued in each calendar year, are even less reliable than they were.[2] This problem is exacerbated by the fact that many self-published books have no ISBN at all. So we really have no accurate account of how many 'new books' are being published each year in markets like the US and the UK, or, indeed, of what should be counted as a 'new book' for these purposes, though we know that the number is very large – in the hundreds of thousands at the very least and quite possibly in the millions.[3] With an avalanche of new

---

[2] They were never terribly reliable anyway, as a single book published in more than one format (e.g. hardback, trade paperback, mass-market paperback, etc.) would have several ISBNs. This problem has only been exacerbated by the digital revolution, since each different ebook format may be assigned a different ISBN. For a more detailed discussion of the issues surrounding title output and the difficulty of measuring it accurately, see Thompson, *Merchants of Culture*, pp. 239–43.

[3] According to Bowker, the leading provider of bibliographic information and official ISBN agency for the US, 'traditional publishers' produced 309,957 titles in 2012. However, in the same year, the 'non-traditional publishing sector' produced 2,042,840 titles according to Bowker; the 'non-traditional sector' includes reprint houses specializing in public-domain works, self-publishers and presses producing 'micro-niche' publications. However, these numbers appear to fluctuate greatly from one year to the next, so it is hard to know how stable and reliable they are. In 2013,

content appearing every week, readers would be overwhelmed if they were left to trawl through new titles on their own and would quickly give up. They need ways to reduce complexity and shorten the time needed to find what might interest them. They already have their ways of reducing complexity, of course – tried-and-tested methods like relying on the recommendations of trusted friends, reading reviews and sticking with authors they've read already and know they like. Reader loyalty based on familiarity with an author's style and engagement with their characters is the basis of brand authors' success. But this doesn't mean that readers would not be open to other methods of reducing complexity if they were available. Similarly, publishers need to find ways to get their books noticed among the confusion of content, picked out by readers as sufficiently worthy of their time and attention to be bought and possibly read by them. How would readers know about their new books, find or 'discover' them amid the avalanche of new content, unless publishers could find effective ways to put their books in front of them, directly or indirectly, physically or virtually, so that they were visible and discoverable? Although publishers, for the most part, are not selling directly to consumers but are selling to the intermediaries (i.e., to the retailers and wholesalers), nevertheless they need to have ways of bringing their books to the attention of readers and encouraging them to buy – otherwise, the books that the publishers are selling to the intermediaries will come back to the publishers as returns. Without sell-through, a publisher's sales to retailers and wholesalers are little more than the movement of stock from one warehouse to another, sales on consignment, and ultimately the cost of unsold stock will be borne by the publisher. In the traditional world of publishing, the strategies used by publishers to achieve sell-through were a combination of marketing, publicity and in-store placement – placement, that is, in the high-visibility physical spaces of the bookstore chains and other retail outlets, like mass merchandisers and supermarkets. In the online world, however, visibility assumes a very different form.

---

for example, Bowker reported a 2 per cent decline in output by traditional publishers and a 46 per cent decline in output from the non-traditional sector ('Traditional Print Book Production Dipped Slightly in 2013', at www.bowker.com/news/2014/ Traditional-Print-Book-Production-Dipped-Slightly-in-2013.html). Moreover, since Bowker's figures are based on ISBN registrations, they don't include books that are produced without an ISBN, including many of the books self-published through Kindle Direct Publishing – the largest self-publishing channel. They also double-count or triple-count – or more – those titles that have different ISBNs assigned to different formats.

Visibility in the bricks-and-mortar world

Prior to the digital revolution, publishers had to rely on a mixture of mediated visibility and physical or 'situated visibility' in order to get their books noticed by readers.[4] Publishers typically used a variety of media strategies to achieve visibility for their books, from advertising to review coverage in traditional print media like newspapers, magazines and specialist review media. But a large part of the marketing budget of many trade publishers was devoted to achieving physical or situated visibility in the high-churn spaces of the bookstore chains and other key retail outlets – this is where the real battle for eyeballs took place. Like the wars of old, it was a battle that took place on a battlefield – a physical place, situated in time and space. The main battlefield was the front-of-store space where half a dozen or so tables were strategically situated to obstruct the progress of unwitting customers as they walked through the doors, slowing them down so that they noticed the face-out books that were displayed on the tables before them, encouraging them to pick up books and browse through the pages, to move from one title to another and one table to another – New Fiction, New Nonfiction, Bestsellers, etc. – and, while they were still captive customers in this space, inviting them to cast their eyes around and notice the stepladder stands overflowing with books and the wall shelves lined with yet more brightly covered books on display, typically ranked in terms of their bestsellerdom. This physical space was – and, indeed, remains – a crucial site in the struggle to get books noticed and bought by readers.

Not surprisingly, given its importance, this front-of-store space is not free – on the contrary, it is an intensively commodified space. The main mechanism used to commodify this space is the fee euphemistically called 'co-op'.[5] Essentially, co-op is a financial contribution that the publisher makes to pay for part of the retailer's promotion costs. Each publisher will have its own co-op policy. Most trade publishers calculate what they are prepared to make available to a particular account as a percentage of that account's net sales in the previous year. The amount can vary from 2 to 4 per cent, depending on the publisher. So if a publisher's terms are 4 per cent of prior year's

---

[4] For an extended discussion of the concept of visibility, see John B. Thompson, 'The New Visibility', *Theory, Culture and Society*, 22, 6 (December 2005), 31–51.
[5] See chapter 5, note 26.

sales, then a retailer who sold $100,000 of this publisher's books in the previous year would be entitled to $4,000 of co-op to spend in the current year. This money goes into a pool which can be used by that account to promote the publisher's books in their bookstore or on their website, in ways that are agreed on a book-by-book basis between the publisher's sales rep or account manager and the buyer. Sometimes incremental supplements are made to the pool in order to include specific titles in special bookstore promotions, like a 'buy one get one free' or '3 for 2' promotion on paperbacks. For the large trade houses, the total amount spent on co-op grew enormously in the late 1990s and early 2000s, so that, by 2010, it accounted for half or more of the total marketing spend of many houses, compared to 30–35 per cent in the 1980s.

To get a book in a front-of-store display in a major retail chain like Barnes & Noble is not entirely within the publisher's control. What typically happens is that the sales managers for the national accounts will present the new titles to the central buyers at the retail chains and let them know what their expectations are for key books – how big a book it is for them, how many copies they'd like the retailer to take, etc. The buyers decide which titles they want to buy in what quantities based on their own assessment of the book, the sales histories of the author's previous books, the cover and various other factors, and they often tie co-op money into the buy. There's a to-and-fro between the sales rep and the buyer to determine how many copies they're going to take and how much the publisher is going to spend to support the buy. The sales managers and buyers then negotiate what kind of in-store promotion would be appropriate – placement on a front-of-store table, a middle-of-store section, an endcap or a stepladder, how many stores for how many weeks, etc. The rates vary depending on the type of placement, the type of book (cloth, trade paperback, mass market), the buy size, the number of stores, the number of weeks and the time of year. The most expensive table is right at the front, and the farther back you go the less expensive it becomes. Typically, placement on a central front-of-store table in a major US retail chain like Barnes & Noble for two weeks would cost the publisher $10,000 for all stores, perhaps half that for stores in the major markets (about a third of the number of stores), and less again for so-called A-Stores (perhaps 10–15 per cent of the number of stores). For a table in a back section, you might pay $3,500. And a stepladder could cost $25,000 for a week. These placements will be linked to the quantity of the buy. As a rough rule of thumb, in-store placement works out at around a dollar a book for a new hardcover.

177

Given the cost of putting a book in a front-of-store display in a major retail chain, it's crucial that the book performs – crucial not just for the publisher, who is paying a premium to put the book there, but also for the retailer, who is tying up valuable real estate. It is therefore not surprising that publishers tend to monitor the sales of new books very closely in the first few days and weeks after publication. The major trade publishers get daily sales feeds from the big retail chains which enable them to see on a day-to-day basis just how quickly their top-selling books, including those with in-store promotions, are moving. If the books are moving fast, they put more resources behind them, ramping up the promotional activity – the large publishing houses are very quick to respond to the first signs of success, and very good at pouring more fuel on the flames. On the other hand, if the books with in-store promotions are not selling, it's hard to justify the expense of keeping them there. The first few weeks are a crucial make-or-break time for key trade titles and if the books aren't moving, they're pulled out of expensive in-store promotions pretty quickly. The physical spaces at the front of bookstores and in other key retail outlets can generate high visibility and high sales, but the price paid to occupy this space is also high. In practice, very few books are afforded the luxury of appearing in these high-value, high-visibility spaces, and, for those that are, the time spent there can be vanishingly short.

The morphing of mediated visibility

Given the cost of in-store promotion and the scarcity of the real estate, using a variety of media to try to achieve some degree of visibility for their books was always going to be a more compelling option for most publishers and most books. There are many tried-and-tested methods for achieving this kind of mediated visibility and all publishers will have their specialist staff – marketers, publicists, product managers, etc. – whose job it is to work with media of various kinds to get their books and authors seen, noticed, heard, talked about and reviewed in the media, all with the aim of driving sell-through. But, thanks to the digital revolution, this media space is changing in fundamental ways, and mediated visibility is morphing in the process. The broad contours of this change are easy enough to discern: the traditional so-called mass media are declining in significance, and online media, including social media, are becoming more and more important. But, like so many generalizations in this domain, the broad contours conceal a multitude of complexities that belie any simple suggestion of a one-way flow.

Part of the reason why traditional 'mass' media are declining in significance as a platform for achieving visibility for books is that these media face new pressures of their own and they are less inclined to devote scarce space to books. 'Mass media' was always a misleading term – it conjures up the image of a vast audience comprising millions of readers or viewers, although in practice the audiences for many media products are much smaller than this. The important contrast here is between those media that developed prior to the digital revolution – including newspapers, magazines, radio and television, all of which were oriented towards the dissemination of content to a relatively large number of recipients – and those newer media that have emerged in the wake of the digital revolution, and especially those media that are intrinsically linked to the internet and to the distinctive forms of content creation, dissemination and interaction that have been made possible by it. Newspapers – one of the most important of the traditional media when it comes to creating visibility for books – have been in decline for some time. They are shrinking in number and circulation, and the space available for book reviews is declining or disappearing altogether. Many stand-alone book review supplements have either been closed down or reduced in size. In 2001, the *Boston Globe* merged its book review and commentary pages; in 2007, the *San Diego Union-Tribune* closed down its book review section; and in 2008, the *Los Angeles Times* killed its stand-alone 'Sunday Book Review' section and merged it into another section in the Saturday edition of the paper, reducing the amount of space devoted to books. Even the *New York Times*, which is one of the few metropolitan newspapers in the US to have retained a stand-alone book review section, has shrunk the size of its 'Book Review' supplement by nearly half, from the 44 pages it averaged in the mid-1980s to the 24 to 28 pages it typically has today.[6] It is much the same with mainstream television. *The Today Show*, *Good Morning America* and *The Early Show* all used to have book producers and give a lot of space to books, but books have become less of a priority for them. Even Oprah's Book Club, which for fifteen years was able to give visibility to books and drive sales like no other media channel, came to an end in May 2011; it was relaunched as Oprah's Bookclub 2.0 on The Oprah Winfrey Network

---

[6] Steve Wasserman, 'Goodbye to All That', *Columbia Journalism Review*, September/October 2007.

and various social media, though it no longer had the audience reach that Oprah's Book Club had in its heyday. A similar fate befell the Richard & Judy Book Club in the UK, which had been part of *The Richard & Judy Show* on Channel 4 in the early 2000s and played a hugely important role in generating visibility for books and driving book sales: in August 2008, the show was axed and, after a short run on a UK digital network, the Book Club was turned into a website run in conjunction with the stationer and bookseller WH Smith.

In the late 1990s and early 2000s, it was clear to most marketing managers that the traditional media on which they had relied to achieve visibility for their books were a declining asset and that they would need to find other ways, or at least additional ways, to bring their books to the attention of readers. Throughout the early 2000s, there was a systematic shift away from a heavy reliance on traditional media towards more diversified marketing strategies that combined traditional media and new media in differing ways, depending on the book, the author, the likely audiences and the publisher's resources and know-how. The information environment was changing rapidly – online sites were proliferating and, with the development of Web 2.0 in the early 2000s, blogs and social media platforms were taking off; publishers – like those in many other industries – were trying to figure out how to navigate this brave new world and how to adapt their marketing strategies to it. How could books be made visible in the online world? What tools were available to you to bring books to the attention of readers in the virtual spaces of the internet? And how does this new kind of marketing activity – in a world that is changing rapidly and that most publishers are struggling to understand – relate to the traditional practices of marketing staff?

In many publishing houses, there will be a meeting about a year before a book is published when marketing managers will set the marketing budget for the book and draw up a marketing campaign. The budget is typically set as a percentage of the expected revenue based on the book's P&L – for example, 6.5 per cent of total revenue. 'So at the lower end, maybe that budget is $5,000, maybe it's $3,500. At the upper end, maybe that budget is $500,000. Most books fall in the middle, if not closer to $5,000', explained the marketing manager at one of the imprints of a large trade house. 'And what we do is we say, "OK, we have this much money to spend, $5,000 or $500,000. What is it we need to do to reach the reader? Who are the readers? Where are they? How are we going to reach them?" That's a conversation that includes, in our company, the publisher, the editor, the publicist, a sales representative and the marketing team.' The challenge is to figure out what you can do with a given amount of money to try to reach what you think is the main audience for the book.

Some elements of the traditional book marketing campaign, like print advertising and author tours, have become less important and fewer resources are devoted to them by most publishers. Instead, most marketing managers focus their efforts more and more on trying to identify specific, fine-grained ways of reaching the people who comprise what they see as the readership for the book, using an array of different channels, which, in addition to traditional print and electronic media, include a variety of new media, from email lists to blogs, websites, online news sites and social media. They try to identify the groups, communities and sets of individuals who they think might be interested in this book and try to figure out how best to reach out to them, whether by a targeted email campaign or by going to a conference or convention or by posting or advertising on social media or by sending copies of the book to well-placed individuals who might be willing to write or talk about the book, to generate chatter and word of mouth in any medium available to them, whether this is face-to-face, through blogs and social media or in the traditional print and electronic media. No one minds how the chatter spreads, so long as it does.

For most marketing managers at mainstream trade houses, the growing emphasis on new media is pursued not in isolation from marketing efforts aimed at securing publicity and review coverage in traditional media, but rather in conjunction with them. In this noisy, hybrid world of multiple media channels, the challenge for marketing managers is to get their books noticed, seen, discussed and talked about, wherever this noticing and seeing and talking might occur, and an excellent way to get them noticed and seen and talked about online is to get them noticed and seen and talked about offline, in traditional print and electronic media, and vice versa: these are not mutually exclusive but potentially complementary channels, and if all goes well they can support and reinforce one another, creating a kind of virtuous circle of chatter amplification. And, given that most traditional print and electronic media are now hybrid media themselves, with their online content reflecting, reproducing and in some cases greatly exceeding their offline content, it is easier than ever for online media to link to traditional media, and vice versa. The media have always been self-referential, constantly reporting and commenting on what is reported and commented on in the media. The advent of

181

the digital age does not change this fundamental characteristic of the media but only raises it by an order of magnitude.

Let us consider the example of *The Martian* – the book by Andy Weir that began life as a blog and became a *New York Times* bestseller when it was published by Crown in 2014. In this case, an in-house publicist was responsible for dealing with the traditional media while the online media campaign was outsourced to Andrea, a freelance publicist with special expertise in online media. Just as the publicist working with traditional media has to know the different editors and producers at different newspapers, magazines, TV and radio programmes, has to build relationships of trust with them and get to know what interests them, so too the publicist working with online media has to understand the cartography of the online space, get to know who the key players are and build relationships with them, and has to know where the people who might be interested in the books they are seeking to promote might be hanging out online. Andrea has her own elaborate cognitive map of the online space and of who the key players are for the kinds of publicity she is trying to achieve – 'the key influencers', as she calls them, because 'they have huge traffic and people pick them up. People know that they are conversation starters.' Part of Andrea's value as an online publicist, and one of the reasons why publishers want to employ her, is that she knows who these key influencers are and she has formed relationships with them, so that when she has a book that she knows might interest them, she can reach out to them and talk to them about it – and she knows precisely who to reach out to for each of the books she is handling. This is what she did with *The Martian*: she reached out to Mark Frauenfelder, one of the founders and co-editors of Boing Boing, a site/blog that describes itself as 'a directory of mostly wonderful things'. She knew that, if Mark liked the book, he could do something on Boing Boing, but he could also do other things for the book because he is an exceptionally well-networked person who is often invited to appear on shows and comment on the latest trends in popular culture. And that's exactly what happened. Mark loved the book, decided to interview the author for his weekly Boing Boing podcast, and that got picked up and cross-linked on lots of other sites. Then she asked Mark to do a Reddit chat and that went to the front page of Reddit. Then, on 4 February 2014, Mark was a guest of Jesse Thorn on Bullseye, a public radio programme on popular culture that is distributed by National Public Radio (NPR), and Mark used this opportunity to rave about *The Martian*, describing it as 'Robinson Crusoe on Mars' and lauding it as 'a fantastic book, I loved it and tore through it'. Mark's enthusiastic comments were immediately picked up by social media, tweeted on Twitter and posted on Facebook, and quickly spread through social media like a contagion. Then, on 7 February, Tom Shippey's glowing review in the *Wall Street Journal* ('utterly compelling') appeared and got picked up and tweeted/posted on social media, contributing to a growing crescendo of online and offline media coverage, all playing into and reinforcing one another. At this point in our conversation, Andrea opens a folder and pulls out a large sheet of paper on which she had tracked the ways in which each of these key media events was picked up and retransmitted by other media, both online and offline – a veritable map of the linking together of all these discrete media events that, in the inextricably interconnected world of online and offline media, were picked up, retransmitted, amplified and diffused very quickly, spreading out to ever wider networks of individuals, like a form of instantaneous syndication that was helped along where possible by Andrea but not controlled or orchestrated by her. 'Everything you're trying to do is to get as many people to see, hear and just be overwhelmed by it. What is this Martian? It's everywhere, it's everywhere.'

So in this new hybrid world of online–offline media, neither online nor offline is the key, but rather the reciprocal and concerted inter-action between them – an interaction which, if all goes well, can create a virtuous circle of chatter amplification. This is how one experienced marketing manager put it:

> At the end of the day, you can't say online media are more effective than offline because that's just not true. What's really effective is to have everything working in concert. So we definitely have seen that NPR moves books, it just does. It depends on the content but generally speaking, when someone gets a big feature on NPR we see a spike. So that's just an awesome channel for us, we absolutely want to be there. But what makes it even more effective is if we also have some echoing of that content online. So somebody hears the thing, they do a search and oh my god they see an ad for that exact title because they're looking for so and so and there it is. Then you go onto Apple and you get distracted by something else and then you see on iTunes – hey look, there's so and so merchandised on the feature titles section. Each of those events alone would be kind of interesting, but all three together can result in much more effective sales. And so the trick for us is really figuring out how to make all these programs work together, to just amplify the sound so you get that reiteration in the market place. We look at them in concert.

The triumph of the algorithm

The growing role of online retailers – and especially Amazon – transforms the visibility of books in another way: it gives rise to an entirely new set of tools for putting books in front of consumers and calling their attention to them. There are plenty of ways of making books visible in the bricks-and-mortar bookstore – the front-of-store display tables and stepladders are only the most obvious but there are many others, ranging from staff recommendations to displaying books with covers facing out in the more specialized sections of the bookstore. There are two features of this kind of visibility that are worth highlighting: first, the visibility is standardized – that is, the same books are visible to anyone who enters the store; and, second, the visibility is spatial – that is, the customer actually has to enter the store in order to see the books. Standardized spatial visibility: that is what you can achieve in a bricks-and-mortar bookstore. It can be powerful and can work extremely well – you can sell an awful lot of books from a front table or a stepladder in Barnes & Noble or Waterstones. But the physical properties of the bookstore prevent you from doing much more than this.

In the online environment, however, a whole range of new opportunities for achieving visibility are opened up. Suppose the bookstore you enter can be customized in such a way that every book you see has in some way been selected for you: it's a personalized bookstore in which the books shown to you are books that are selected because they seem to match the kind of books that interest you. So you won't be shown the latest thriller by John Grisham if you've never bought a thriller before or shown any interest in buying one. What's the point? Making that John Grisham book visible to you is a waste of your scarce time and attention. If, on the other hand, the books you generally buy or browse are political biographies and historical books about the First World War, then the bookstore can show you a selection of new political biographies and new books about the First World War – it would be like walking into a bookstore designed for you. Visibility is customized, personalized, tailored to the interests, tastes and preferences of each individual visitor. And there isn't even any need to leave your home or desk and walk into a physical store: personalized virtual visibility is delivered to your screen wherever you are.

The idea of personalizing a version of the website for each user, based on his or her previous purchases, was part of Bezos's original vision for Amazon and, shortly after the site had launched in 1995, Bezos and his staff set about turning this vision into a reality. This required them to construct an algorithm that enabled recommendations to be generated by computer based on some previous set of data. So what data were they going to use and how could the algorithm be constructed?

In their first attempt to personalize the website, Amazon relied on a software program called Bookmatch that was developed by a third party, a firm called Firefly Network.[7] Customers were asked to rate a number of books and the program would then generate recommendations based on their ratings. But the system didn't work very well, and many customers were reluctant to go to the effort of rating books in order to provide data for the program to generate recommendations. So Amazon developed their own algorithm, which generated recommendations based on books that customers had actually bought. The first version of this recommendation algorithm, called Similarities, grouped together customers with similar purchasing histories and then found books that appealed to the people in each group.[8] It resulted in an immediate increase in sales. Similarities replaced Bookmatch and evolved into Amazon's personalization machine.

Amazon's initial attempt to crack the recommendation algorithm was based on the use of 'cluster models' – that is, the customer base is divided into segments and the algorithm assigns each user to the segment containing the most similar customers; the purchases and ratings of the customers in the segment are then used to generate recommendations. But cluster models tend to generate relatively low-quality recommendations because the customers in the segment may be quite diverse. Amazon therefore changed to an algorithm which it calls 'item-to-item collaborative filtering'.[9] Whereas cluster models match the user to similar *customers*, item-to-item collaborative filtering matches the user's purchased and rated items to similar *items*. The algorithm first builds a similar-items table by finding items that customers tend to purchase together and computing the similarity between the items in terms of the frequency with which they are bought together. Once the similarity between each pair

---

[7] Stone, *The Everything Store*, p. 51.
[8] Ibid.
[9] Greg Linden, Brent Smith and Jeremy York, 'Amazon.com Recommendations: Item-to-Item Collaborative Filtering', *IEEE Internet Computing* (January–February 2003), p. 77.

of items has been determined and given a numerical value, the algorithm generates recommendations based on the most highly correlated items. The creation of the similar-items table, which is very demanding in computational terms, can be done offline, which enables the algorithm to be scalable over very large catalogues and customer bases. The algorithm's online component involves looking up similar items for the user's purchases and ratings, and this can be done relatively easily. Hence the algorithm is very fast and it can respond immediately to changes in a user's data, as when he or she makes a new purchase. The recommendations tend to be highly relevant because the algorithm recommends highly correlated similar items. The algorithm also performs well with very limited user data.[10]

Amazon rolled out its recommendation algorithm across many different areas of its customer interface – on the home page recommendations, on the personalized 'your Amazon' page, the shopping cart recommendations ('similar to the impulse items in a supermarket checkout line, but our impulse items are targeted to each customer'[11]) and in the many email campaigns that Amazon regularly targets to its customers. With purchasing and browsing data on more than 300 million customers worldwide and the capacity to market and sell directly to them, this gives Amazon a huge competitive advantage as a retailer. It is able to tap into a wealth of user data that is unprecedented both in terms of quantity and in terms of detail – every purchase, every page browsed, every click – and use this data to tailor its marketing efforts as effectively as possible.

Visibility could not be more different in the two worlds, old and new. In the old world of the bricks-and-mortar bookstore, visibility is standardized and spatialized and restricted to a small number of titles: there are only so many titles that can be displayed on the front tables and in the windows of bookstores and other retail outlets. Even if every bookstore displayed different books (and they don't – far from it), the total number of titles displayed would be a tiny fraction of the number of books published. By contrast, in the world of the online bookseller, visibility is personalized and virtual or de-spatialized and the number of titles that can be made visible in this de-spatialized space is potentially unlimited, since each user can be presented with a selection of titles that is tailored to his or her interests and tastes.

Not only are the forms of visibility very different: the drivers of visibility are different too. In the world of the bricks-and-mortar

---

[10] Ibid., p. 79.
[11] Ibid., p. 78.

bookstore, achieving visibility in the high-visibility spaces at the front of a bookstore is the outcome of a social process of negotiation in which the sales reps from publishing houses and the buyers from booksellers or bookselling chains propose or suggest titles for display and, in some cases, negotiate an appropriate financial contribution from the publisher in the form of co-op to support the display. This is a social process, conducted face-to-face or via phone or email, in which individuals representing two key organizations in the book supply chain – publishers and booksellers – reach an agreement on a small number of titles, selected from a large number of potential candidates, that will be made visible in the high-visibility spaces at the front of stores, and on the terms and conditions of this visibility. In the world of the online bookseller, by contrast, the selection process is driven primarily by algorithms. Of course, humans are involved in this process because they write the algorithms and decide how much weight to give to different factors. But the selection of which title is made visible to which user is based primarily on the automated analysis of user data – on which books he or she bought or browsed previously and which books are similar to them. This is not a negotiated agreement between publishers and the bookseller but rather an automated process in which the bookseller uses its proprietary user data to generate recommendations based on the online behaviour of its customers. This process is controlled entirely by the online bookseller, and publishers are excluded from it. Of course, publishers can participate in this process – at a price. Like traditional booksellers, online booksellers can also negotiate extra payments from publishers in return for online placement and personalized recommendations. In the case of Amazon, these payments can be in the form of increased 'co-op' fees or payments linked to pay-per-click (PPC) advertising campaigns on Amazon, which enable publishers to place ads for their books on Amazon search results pages and on the pages of competing books. But the primary driver of visibility in the online space is not title-by-title placement backed up by co-op or PPC, it is the use of algorithms based on user data.

Table 6.1 summarizes some of the differences between these two forms of visibility. Bricks-and-mortar bookstores use standardized spatial visibility to bring books to the attention of consumers: a small selection of books are displayed in the high-visibility spaces at the front of the store, on the tables and shelves in the entrance area and in the front-of-store windows, and the same books will be visible to everyone who enters these spaces. The selection of titles is made by the bookseller and, in some cases, is conditional on agreements

Table 6.1 Forms of visibility

	Standardized spatial visibility	Personalized virtual visibility
Retailer	Bricks-and-mortar bookstore	Online bookseller
Selection	Standardized	Personalized
Display	Spatialized	Virtual
Range	Restricted	Unlimited
Driver	Deals between publishers and bookstores	Algorithms based on user-data; fees paid by publishers

reached between the bookseller and the publisher to fund the display through co-op. Online booksellers like Amazon use personalized virtual visibility to bring books to the attention of consumers: for each consumer, a personalized selection of titles is presented to them either in regular email alerts or on the constantly updated home page and shopping cart recommendations. The recommendations are generated by algorithms based on each consumer's previous browsing and buying behaviour. In some cases, this personalized virtual visibility is paid for by publishers in the form of co-op fees or PPC advertising.

In general terms, the emergence of a new form of visibility for books in the online space can only be a good thing for books, as the more ways there are for making books visible to potential readers, the better it is for books, authors and publishers. But at the same time there are dangers associated with this development – let me focus here on two.

The first danger is linked to the fact that, with the growth of Amazon and the decline of physical retail space for books, the kind of visibility that can be achieved for books has shifted from the physical, front-of-store visibility to visibility in the online space. Viewed from a long-term perspective, this shift has already occurred in a substantial way. In 2006, Barnes & Noble, then the largest bookseller in the US, was operating 723 bookstores across the United States, which included 695 superstores and 98 mall stores operating under the B. Dalton brand; the Borders Group was operating around 1,063 bookstores in the US at that time, including 499 superstores and 564 mall-based Waldenbooks stores. Ten years later, in 2016, Barnes & Noble was still operating 640 stores but it had closed all the B. Dalton stores; Borders had gone bankrupt in 2011 and nearly all of its stores had been liquidated. These two developments alone represented a dramatic decline in physical retail space in the US – the number of stores accounted for by these two chains had been more than halved in a decade.[12] This matters not only because it means that there is less space to make books visible, but also because the kind of visibility that is being lost is a kind that facilitates the discovery of the new. Let us explore this point a little further.

Anyone walking into a bookstore encounters a range of books that is much greater than what they encounter in the personalized recommendations they receive from Amazon, precisely because the books that are displayed at the front of bookstores are not tailored to the personal interests and tastes of particular users. This has its drawbacks, to be sure – you may have no interest at all in commercial thrillers, and yet there in front of you as you walk into the store is the latest book by James Patterson. But it also encourages diversity and discoverability in the marketplace. Diversity because it means that individuals are exposed to a wide range of books regardless of whether they match previous buying or browsing behaviour – provided, of course, that they walk into a bookstore in the first place, which is not a minor qualification. Discoverability because it means that individuals who walk into a bookstore are likely to discover books that they did not intend to look for when they went in. The problem with the online environment is that, because the recommendations are algorithm-driven, the range is narrowed to a set of titles that are similar to those you've bought or browsed before. It's as if you were dropped in the middle of an enormous library, larger than any that had ever existed before, it was pitch black and all you had was a pen light: you switch on the pen light and you can see only what's immediately in front of you, while the millions of other books that fill this vast library are plunged into darkness. The algorithm is the pen light, though the reality is worse than the metaphor because in the real world of algorithm-driven recommendations, it is Amazon, not you, that controls the pen light, decides when to turn it on and where to point it and when to turn it off again. Diversity and discoverability are sacrificed to similarity and predictability as the

---

[12] When Barnes & Noble was sold to a hedge fund, Elliott Management Corporation, in 2019, it was operating 627 stores; whether store closures will continue under the management of the new CEO James Daunt remains to be seen. It should also be noted that, quite apart from Barnes & Noble, independent bookstores have staged something of a comeback in recent years, after the closures of the 1990s and early 2000s. According to the American Booksellers Association, between 2009 and 2015 there was a 35 per cent growth in the number of independent booksellers, from 1,651 to 2,227 stores. However, this trend could be reversed if the coronavirus lockdowns of 2020 result in some permanent bookstore closures.

range of titles promoted to particular individuals is narrowed down in order to maximize the likelihood of sales.

This is a serious issue for publishers and one of the reasons why it is so important for them – and for the culture of the book more generally – to ensure that physical bookstores do not disappear. Bookstores are not only the shop windows for publishers and their books: they are also spaces where the experience of browsing is not pre-determined by the prior browsing and shopping patterns of the individual. The experience of browsing in a bookstore is not completely random, of course, as the front-of-store space is a commodified space in which the titles displayed are based on deals that are struck between publishers and bookstores underpinned by co-op money, as we noted earlier. But browsing in this space is still a very different experience from browsing the titles recommended to you by an algorithm based on your previous browsing and purchasing history. It is not personalized, and for that very reason it is more varied, more open and more likely to surprise the individual browser by confronting him or her with the unexpected.

The second danger stems from the fact that there is one corporation that plays a preponderant role in shaping the online visibility that exists today in the world of books – Amazon. With the decline of physical retail space and the shift over time from physical visibility to online visibility, this means that the most powerful retailer is increasingly in control of determining which books get made visible to individuals in the course of their day-to-day lives as they receive their daily email alerts from Amazon ('Hot new releases in ...', 'Hello Jane Dancy, Amazon has new recommendations for you', 'Hello Tim Blake, Based on your recent activity, we thought you might be interested in this', and so on). The more that this becomes the principal way in which individuals encounter new books, the more power this gives to Amazon to determine which books they see. If Amazon has a dispute with a publisher, they could not only decline to sell their books, they could decline to recommend them, thereby depriving them of the exposure they get through Amazon's personalized recommendations. In the space of online visibility, publishers are more and more at Amazon's mercy.

What can publishers do to counter Amazon's seemingly unassailable domination of the space of online visibility for books? What can they do, if anything, to wrest back some control? Three of the large trade houses – Hachette, Simon & Schuster and Penguin – tried to join forces and create a book recommendation and retail site that would provide an alternative to Amazon, called Bookish, but it got off to a slow start, launching after some delay in February 2013, and struggled to make an impact; it was sold less than a year later to Zola Books, a start-up ebook retailer. So must publishers simply give up, admit that Amazon has effectively conquered the space of online visibility and hope that it will exercise its formidable marketing power in an even-handed and benevolent way? Or are there concrete things they can do, and other channels they can open up, to try to achieve more control of the online visibility for their books?

We'll return to these important questions in a moment, but, before we do, let's consider another intriguing twist to this story. In November 2015, Amazon opened its first physical bookstore in Seattle and, by October 2018, it was operating a total of seventeen stores in various cities across the US, from New York to LA, with several more planned. In some ways, this might seem a puzzling development: why would a company that has built its business as an online retailer, that has ridden the wave of the digital revolution so effectively and seen its fortunes rise exponentially while those of its bricks-and-mortar competitors have declined, now decide to move into the business of running physical bookstores, with all the problems that this involves – renting expensive real estate in city centres, holding stock, dealing with returns, wafer-thin margins, etc.? No doubt this is intended in part to be a way to market and sell non-book products, especially technology products like Echo and Fire TV, enabling consumers to see and experiment with new devices before they buy them, in much the way that an Apple store does. But it can't all be about using books as a pretence for selling technology – Amazon's bookstores really are filled with shelves of books. So why open physical bookstores when you already have an immensely effective bookselling operation online, with over 40 per cent of all new book unit sales in the US, print and digital combined? Why does Amazon think they can run physical bookstores any more successfully than the many booksellers who have tried, and all too often failed, before them, and what will they gain?

By opening physical bookstores, Amazon is experimenting with and, indeed, inventing a new kind of browsing experience – not the personalized kind of browsing that is part of Amazon's online offering, nor the kind of generic browsing that is characteristic of other physical bookstores, but rather something in between that blends aspects of both models. To walk into an Amazon bookstore is to enter a bookselling space unlike any other you've ever encountered. In the first place, it is surprisingly small: for a bookseller that built its reputation on the claim to offer its customers over a million titles to choose from ('Earth's Biggest Bookstore'), the smallness of Amazon's physical bookstores, and the small number of titles on display, is immediately striking. Equally striking is the fact that every book in the bookstore is displayed face-out. The shelves are not packed with countless titles displaying only their spines: instead the consumer sees an array of books with their front covers fully displayed, concealed lights shining on each cover to highlight them and make the most of the cover artwork. Look a little closer and you see that beneath each book is a stylish card discreetly displayed, white text on a black background, with a quote from an Amazon customer review and a ranking from Amazon's online customer reviews – '"'Manhattan Beach' is a feast. How often can you crack open a novel that is beautifully written, well plotted, reflective of a certain historical era and 'tone', with characters that are a perfect balance of revealed and mysterious … " – Mary Lins. 3.8 stars – 840 reviews as of 5/4/2018'. Keep browsing and you'll come to a section called 'Fiction Top Sellers in New York' (if you happen to be in one of Amazon's New York bookstores), and another called 'Nonfiction Top Sellers in New York'. Walk around the corner and you'll find a section called 'If you like …' where there is one book displayed face-out on the left and four displayed face-out on the right, separated by a simple sign: 'If You Like [arrow pointing left] You'll Love [arrow pointing right]', 'If You Like *Crazy Rich Asians*, You'll Love *Erotic Stories for Punjabi Widows*', etc.

The more you browse, the more you realize that this small selection of face-out titles is in no way haphazard but is carefully curated, and the more you examine the book displays, the more you realize that the curation is based on information that is specific to Amazon – including their data on sales and pre-orders, customer ratings and reviews on Amazon's online site and popularity on Goodreads, the social media site for readers that was acquired by Amazon in 2013,[13]

---

[13] Goodreads is a social media platform focused on reading and reviewing books. Founded in 2006 by Otis Chandler and Elizabeth Khuri Chandler, the aim was to create a social network where people could show others the books they liked, discuss books with them and discover books through their online interactions with others – the online equivalent of walking into someone's home, browsing their bookshelves and talking with them about books. It also provides an alternative review space for books where readers can rate and review the books they've read and can discover – both through other readers' ratings and reviews and through recommendations generated by Goodreads' algorithm – other books they might want to read. By 2012, Goodreads had 10 million members and 20 million monthly visits, and 330 million books had been rated on the site. In 2013, Amazon acquired Goodreads for an

and the data Amazon holds on customers, including their addresses and zip codes and their online book-buying and book-browsing histories. The impression is confirmed by Alice, a young shop assistant in her twenties with pink-tinted hair and a nose stud who is eager to assist any customer browsing the shelves. She explained that the books are chosen by the curation team at Amazon based on Amazon and Goodreads reviews and customer ratings and on what they know about the interests and tastes of people in the local area – 'what people in New York are interested in will be different from what people in Chicago or LA are interested in', she said. They get a refresher list once a week from the curation team and they change some titles on a weekly basis. 'Why the face-out display?', I ask. 'It's all about discovery', continued Alice. 'It's much easier to browse and discover books when you're looking at the covers and not bending your head sideways to try to read the spine.'

After responding to a few more questions from me, Alice had a question of her own: 'Do you have the Amazon app?' I didn't. 'No problem, we have free wifi – here, I'll show you.' Effortlessly, Alice takes control of my iPhone and within seconds she has installed the Amazon app. Noticing a bar code reader on my iPhone, she explains that I won't be needing that anymore because I could now use the bar code reader that was built into the Amazon app – it was much better, she assured me, and with a couple more swift finger movements the old bar code reader was gone and replaced by the Amazon app (I never used that bar code reader anyway). Alice demonstrated how to scan the cover of a book to get the price and pointed out the advantages of being an Amazon Prime member: if you're a Prime member, she explained, then you pay the same price as you would on Amazon.com, where books are often sold at a big discount like 33 per cent, and if you're not a Prime member, then the books in the store are sold at list price. 'Here's Dave Egger's *The Lifters*', she said, scanning the face-out cover: 'if you're a Prime member, you'll pay $12.03; if you're not a Prime member, the price is $17.99. You can become a Prime member now if you want.' I politely declined the invitation. Friendly, engaging, savvy, persuasive, Alice is the public face of the new Amazon bookstore who, like the bookstore itself, moves seamlessly between the attractive displays of books in the physical bookstore and the online world of Amazon.com, inviting you almost irresistibly into the all-embracing online–offline ecosystem of Amazon.

---

undisclosed sum, thereby integrating a leading social media platform for readers and reading into Amazon's ecosystem.

Amazon's physical bookstores are experiments in a new kind of visibility, a customized, data-driven spatial visibility that is different both from the standardized spatial visibility of a traditional bookstore and from the personalized virtual visibility of Amazon's online operation. Like the latter, Amazon's physical bookstores use Amazon's proprietary data to determine which books to display in which stores, customizing the selection to the geographical locale. By displaying all books face-out, they maximize their visibility in the physical space of the bookstore, creating a browsing experience that is visually rich and unlike that of any other bricks-and-mortar bookstore. Data-driven selection is more important than the sheer quantity of titles stocked: the contrast with the Barnes & Noble superstores – those great cathedrals of books which were designed to maximize stock-holding, with their countless shelves of books, mostly spine-out and tightly packed, spread across several floors – could not be more striking. As an invitation into the Amazon ecosystem, books and the latest technology products on full display and the attractions of Prime membership highlighted at every turn, the Amazon bookstores are an enticing proposition. How this experiment in customized, data-driven visibility will turn out remains to be seen but you cannot but be impressed by the boldness of the plan.

Reaching out to readers

As we noted earlier, Amazon, with over 70 per cent of the ebook market and over 40 per cent of all new book unit sales, print and digital, in the US, has exclusive proprietary information on the browsing and purchasing practices of a large proportion of book buyers, far more than any retail organization ever had before. It's hard to overestimate the historical significance of this. Even in its heyday, Barnes & Noble probably had no more than 25 per cent of retail book sales in the US.[14] Moreover, since many books bought in physical stores are bought at the till rather than on a customer account and the browsing practices of individuals in a physical store are not tracked and recorded, the amount of information that Barnes

---

[14] In 2006, for example, superstores and mall chains accounted for about 45 per cent of the approximately $12.4 billion book retail market in the US, and Barnes & Noble was the largest of the three chains (which included Borders and Books-A-Million) with just over half of total chain sales. See Stephanie Oda and Glenn Sanislo, *The Subtext Perspective on Book Publishing 2007–2008: Numbers, Issues & Trends* (Darien, Conn.: Open Book Publishing, 2007), pp. 64–6.

& Noble would have been able to capture and store on its customers was much less than Amazon, for whom every online customer is by definition a registered user whose browsing behaviour, as well as purchasing history, is tracked, recorded and stored. The quantity and detail of the customer information now held by one retailer is historically unprecedented and this produces a structural asymmetry between publishers and Amazon that is far greater than anything that existed previously in the retail space for books. It is for this reason, as well as their dominant and growing market share, that many in the publishing world worry about Amazon's power: the CEO quoted at the beginning of the previous chapter was by no means a lone voice.

So is there anything that publishers can do to try to counter-balance this structural asymmetry? Why, in this new digital age, should publishers stick with old practices that effectively cut them off from any access to, and contact with, the individuals who are the ultimate consumers and readers of their books? Why should they allow one retailer to monopolize information about book buyers, turn this information into a proprietary asset and then use this asset as a means to strengthen their own position in the field, sometimes at the expense of the very publishers who supply them with books?

These are questions that have preoccupied many publishers as they have watched the power of Amazon grow. The irony of a situation in which the popularity of their own books becomes an asset that can be used against them is not lost on the managers of publishing houses. But what, in practice, can they do? They could bypass Amazon and work with other retailers instead, or sell their books direct to customers – a bold step taken by one small, radical indie publisher, OR Books, which sells most of its books directly to customers, a practice that has the double advantage of giving them a better margin on each sale (since there is no discount to a retailer) and of giving them the customers' details (since they must register with OR in order to buy direct). But for most established publishers, cutting out Amazon would be a hard move to make, given that Amazon is their largest single customer, in many cases accounting for 40 per cent or more of their sales. And, while many publishers have had the capacity to sell directly to consumers from their website for some time, this has been of limited success for most: why would consumers buy directly from publishers when they can buy books from an efficient, well-organized, customer-friendly online retailer like Amazon, which is a one-stop-shop with an unrivalled range of books from all publishers and where the prices are probably the same (if not less, when you take account of Amazon's discounts and free delivery service)? No need to give your credit card details to lots of different publishers you don't know and don't have any reason to trust. This doesn't mean that direct sales are a non-starter – there might well be more effective ways to do it than simply creating a shopping basket on the publisher's website. Nor does it mean that there aren't other things publishers could do to reach out directly to the people who are interested in, and read, their books.

So if they're not going to take the radical step of bypassing Amazon, what can publishers do? This is the question that lies behind some of the new initiatives being undertaken by senior managers at publishing houses in recent years, including Melissa. Melissa heads up a unit concerned with developing new kinds of consumer outreach at 'Titan', a large US trade house with a full range of general-interest books. 'My job is to figure out how to build a relationship with readers', she explained. 'So understanding who readers are, how to reach them, how to influence them, how to get them to take some action.' This has become a key concern for Titan and for many other publishers – large, medium-sized and small: trying to build direct relationships with readers is the new holy grail of trade publishers. 'It's sort of natural when you start to think about the way the marketplace is shifting', said Melissa. Of course, the big shift is the growth of Amazon at the expense of the superstore chains, but the dynamics on Amazon are also changing. It used to be a lot easier for Titan to influence the kind of placement and marketing it was getting on Amazon – they could secure spots on the home page, purchase spots in certain merchandising areas, influence which emails were going out and so on. 'We had a lot of leverage on the platform to be able to drive sales to our titles there.' They would pay for it, of course – it might be co-op, it might be pay-per-click advertising, it might be something else. It wasn't cheap, but at least they got exposure on Amazon's platform. But now things are different, explained Melissa. Amazon is bigger, they have other priorities and, in the area of books, self-publishing is a much more important part of their business, so Titan could no longer rely on Amazon to drive sales:

> They're stronger, they're driving people to their self-published authors, they're driving people to things that they want to build. So it behoves us to figure out ways to drive sales on their platform because they're still a great fulfilment account. And when they get behind a book it still works. But we have a broad list and they're creating a retail universe that is bigger and more diverse, and so in order to get the

signal through the noise we want to be able to drive that ourselves. So rather than depending on their email list, we should be building our own.

Melissa had to persuade her colleagues that it would be a good use of resources to divert some away from marketing specific titles in order to build a proprietary database of email addresses. This is easier said than done because marketers, editors and others in a publishing organization are understandably concerned about the books that are being published next week and next month – they need to get attention for these books and move the units because that's how they're going to be assessed at the end of the year. The fiscal demands and incentives of publishing organizations favour short-termism. You have to persuade colleagues to set aside the short-termism and see that there could be immense long-term value in building a database that would be a renewable asset, one that could be used again and again to reach out directly to consumers. 'So instead of spending x thousand on new online ad spend for every single book, what if we just had a million people on file that we could reach out to directly. Yes, we have to pay the costs of the email service provider and the deployment on top of that but it's still much cheaper on a cost-per-thousand basis – and, by the way, much more engaged, because they've given us permission to reach out to them, than just doing search marketing through Google and Facebook.'

This strategy is premised on the view that email is a lot more valuable as an online marketing tool than many were inclined to think. 'There was a long time in the mid-2000s when email was perceived as sort of old-school, not as sexy or interesting as social media', continued Melissa. 'Everyone was spending money and time on getting Facebook likes so that you could reach out to everybody through Facebook, which is still valuable. But it turns out that social media platforms are very fickle. Facebook changes its algorithm all the time, they have different relationships with brands depending on who you are, and it's also something that you can't really control. Whereas with email you have tremendous control.' You can decide when and how often you want to reach out to people, exactly what you want to share with them, you can segment your audience in lots of different ways, and so on. The relative effectiveness of email has become common knowledge among marketers across different industries – Melissa mentioned a McKinsey study that suggested that email is nearly 40 times more effective than Facebook and Twitter combined as a way of acquiring customers.[15] That's general retail, but for books the effectiveness of email might even be greater, explained Melissa, because people are more likely to open emails that are linked to specific author brands and specific genres. 'The benchmark is 20 per cent', said Melissa, 'but if you look at the open rates for real brands, like a Danielle Steele, they're like 60 per cent, which is unbelievable. So the engagement you get through email is staggering.' This is not really surprising when you think about it. Many people have an emotional connection with authors whose books they love and they want to know more about them and about any new book they've just finished or published. 'People want to connect with these incredibly creative people. And so we have this advantage and we need to make the most of it, and actually email is a really solid way to do it.'

So that's the theory, but how do you actually do it in practice? What kind of system do you build and how do you get people to give you their email addresses? Melissa has thought a lot about the structure – she pulls out a large piece of drawing paper, sketches a handful of boxes and arrows and quickly writes in some labels (see figure 6.1). The core is the consumer database – the structured database of all the email addresses and other information on customers, including their interests. On top of this is a layer of technology services that define how you interact with the data. There's also a layer that deals with reporting and data analytics. 'And all of this basically supports the different channel programs', said Melissa, pointing to a row of boxes across the top of the drawing. First there's email, where they use an email service provider, or ESP, to deploy to readers. This can be segmented, it can be personalized, it can be dynamic pricing recommendations. It can be an author newsletter, it can be a series newsletter, it can be a completely hand-drawn, hand-signed, 'you know, old-school communication letter'. They can happen at lots of different levels – corporate level, category level, author level, book level. It's very flexible – every email or newsletter can be customized and carefully targeted.

The next channel is the web, which includes Titan's core dotcom as well as the sites for its various imprints, many of which have their own branded website. But, crucially, it also includes a range of

---

[15] Nora Aufreiter, Julien Boudet and Vivian Weng, 'Why Marketers Should Keep Sending You E-mails', McKinsey & Company (January 2014), at www.mckinsey.com/business-functions/marketing-and-sales/our-insights/why-marketers-should-keep-sending-you-emails.

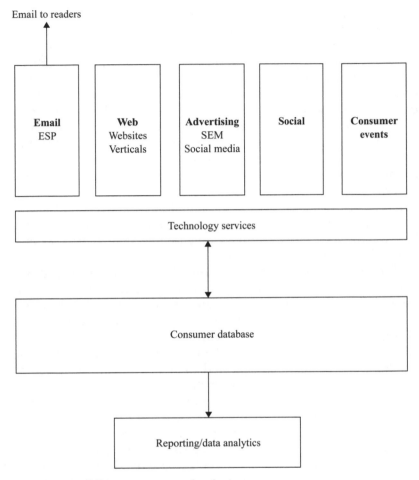

Figure 6.1   Building a consumer database

verticals that Titan has built, and others that it is building, which are consumer facing – more on these in a minute. The email channel and the web channel, and especially the verticals, are the most important channels for the initiative that Melissa is spearheading, because these are the channels where they have a great deal of control and where they are reaching out directly to readers and gathering data about them.

The next channel is advertising, which includes search engine marketing (SEM), like Google AdWords, as well as social media advertising on Facebook and other social media. By building a consumer database, Melissa can target her advertising much more precisely. She can pre-select the set of people she wants to target with the ad. Say, for example, you're publishing a new book aimed at moms and you're having a special launch in LA: you can take your email list, select all moms in LA from your database, load those email addresses directly into your social media ad platforms and directly target people who you know are moms in LA and interested in books. Social media are good at targeting but they don't necessarily filter for interest in books. 'So our spend becomes much more effective', explained Melissa, 'because we can use the data we have already in our universe to inform where we're spending out in the general universe.' Then there are also the many other ways of using social media, like creating pages and building followers on Facebook and Twitter and other platforms, and consumer events of various kinds – 'there's a gazillion things down here', said Melissa, pointing to the final two boxes in her row.

Having worked out the structure, the big challenge is then to populate the database with email addresses and relevant customer information – to build it as fast as you can and with as much accurate and relevant customer data as you can get. In a big company like Titan, there's a lot they can do with the customer data they already have – though harvesting this data and integrating it into a new database can be more complicated than it might seem. In the first place, there are rules that govern what you can do with this data: the customers may have given their permission to use it for some purposes but not for others, and if you want to use it for other purposes then you have to get in touch with them and ask their permission. The key goal here is to get the broadest possible permission, so that you have maximum latitude in what you can use the data to do. Some of the data may also be old, some email addresses may be abandoned, and some customers may no longer be interested; the information may be poorly organized, or just differently organized – cleaning up historical customer data can be a big task in itself. By the time you've been through a list of this kind and weeded out non-responsive emails, duplications, and customers who choose to unsubscribe, the number might be halved. So that's a start. But how do you then build the list with new subscribers? You can have a sign-up form on the website, 'sign up to our mailing list if you'd like to hear more' – 'that's the traditional way of doing things and it's OK', explained Melissa: you will get some new email addresses that way, but it's not enough. It's too passive. You have to be much more proactive about customer acquisition. That's where the verticals come in.

A lot of Melissa's time is now involved in developing a new site – let's call it GoodFood.com. 'Although it's a website, the primary thinking behind GoodFood.com is that it's actually an email program', said Melissa. 'It's an email sign-up primarily for women. It doesn't look that way on the site just because we don't want to alienate dads.' They chose to focus on women for several reasons: women are heavy readers and book buyers, they buy across channels in lots of different categories and they are very active on social media, so they share and chat about recommendations more than any other segment. Melissa set herself an ambitious goal: try to get half a million women signed on with an open rate of over 30 per cent in twelve months' time. They used a variety of methods to drive women to the site and get them to subscribe – paid ads, partnerships with food companies and super-markets, sweepstakes to win a Nook or an iPad or gift vouchers for books, and so on. The sweepstakes work particularly well, explained Melissa. 'We basically said, we're going to give away 25 books of your choice, something like that. And the reason we did it that way, "of your choice", is because we also wanted to gather preferences. Because you don't just want names: you also want people to tell you what they like. You do an ad on Facebook and then people click through to GoodFood.com and say, yes, sign me up. They give us their address and they put in preferences, which was fantastic and a very cost-effective way to do it.' Some of these people are only interested in the sweepstakes but a substantial proportion – over half – opt in to receive news and information from GoodFood, and half of those again opt in to receive information from Titan. Then, once someone has signed up, the key is to personalize the communication with them through targeted emails. You want to know what people like and what they want to hear about. So this is Amanda, a working mom with two kids who doesn't have time to cook elaborate meals but wants her kids to eat well, so you want to target your emails to Amanda with that in mind. Amanda doesn't want to know about cordon bleu cuisine but if you can recommend books about quick and healthy food and make her laugh, then she'll open your emails every time.

Melissa and her team did actually achieve their goal of getting half a million email addresses in the first year: 'We have 500,000 people who have signed up to receive information. Of that, I think half, or more than half, are actively engaged.' Having these email addresses and customer information in their own database is much more effective than relying on social media. 'It used to be that you would start your Facebook account and you would do daily posts

201

and everyone who wanted to get those posts would receive the posts and get that news', explained Melissa. 'But what we've seen is that there's been a dramatic drop in exposure on people's newsfeeds. So you may have 100,000 followers for a particular Facebook page but when you post, you only reach really 1 per cent of that group because of the way the algorithm at Facebook is now constructed.' Facebook remains very important as a way of getting access to customers, where an ad for a sweepstake can produce a very good response. But the key thing from Melissa's point of view is to migrate as many of these customers as possible into Titan's own database, which gives them much more control.

Melissa and her team produce a lot of content for the site – by the end of the first year, over 500 pieces of content had been produced. Most of the content – 'I would say 90, 95 per cent' – is 'inspirational', explained Melissa, by which she meant short articles about which recipes work best for which purposes, how best to deal with certain practical problems, and so on – 'people are looking for guidance, so that is really the bread and butter of what we do, as opposed to "buy this book now". This is not the hard sell. This is information, inspiration, almost lifestyle.' But Melissa is confident, nonetheless, that it does sell books: 'I know it's selling books because we track everything we do. It's a super-light sell. Some of our articles don't even have a click through. I would say that 30 per cent of our articles actually have buy links and it's very subtle – there's a buy-it button and you press on it and it drives you into retail. We're seeing conversions from retail at a higher rate than some of the other programs that we're running – even those programs that are much more focused on selling.'

Having created this successful prototype, Melissa's goal is now to roll out this model across the company and build a limited number of other topic-focused sites. By developing GoodFood.com, they've created a set of tools, templates and methodologies that can be used by other groups and divisions in the company to build dedicated customer databases that will enable them to reach out directly and effectively to the kinds of readers who might be interested in their books. These initiatives are part and parcel of a broader plan to grow substantially Titan's database of customer information. Melisa is nothing if not ambitious. 'This is the way I think about it: we have a population of 380 million in the United States; 25 per cent of that population is actually really dedicated readers. Those are our best readers. They read several books a month, they're high value, core. That's the population we should be targeting. I think, realistically, a little less than half would probably be a good number to target

– I'd say 30 million people.' She admits it's an ambitious target – it might seem wildly over-optimistic. On the other hand, Titan already has 7 million customers in its database and it added a million in the previous year without trying too hard. So 30 million is not an impossible goal. But the number itself is not the key thing. What's important is that people across the company are now focused on the importance of building a customer database, and thinking hard about how to use the information in this database to reach out to readers in ways that are carefully tailored to their interests.

As Melissa sees it, building the customer database has become a critical part of what a publisher is – and what it needs to be – in a world where people are increasingly learning about things, and buying things, online. People are not walking into bookstores as much as they used to, and not seeing physical displays of books: book marketing is becoming more personalized and is increasingly happening online. But publishers can't assume that the big retailers like Amazon will do this marketing for them. 'I can't trust that they will do this on our behalf – in fact, I'm increasingly worried about getting shut out. Amazon used to do a snip for every single book release; they're not doing that anymore. They're migrating a lot of their email strategy towards more profitable products. So for us, it's not about whether they're doing it right or properly. It's are they doing it at all.' Given these fundamental shifts, publishers must do what they can, in Melissa's view, to develop the capacity to engage directly with the people who are, or could be, interested in the books they're publishing. This is how Melissa put it:

> I think at this point the critical piece for us is we aim to provide the best possible service to our authors, and, increasingly, the best possible service to our authors is connecting them with as many readers and engaging them with as many readers as we possibly can. And so this is just one of the critical pieces of that puzzle. Traditionally, that has been about getting books most efficiently through the supply chain to the point of purchase and supporting our retailers. At this point, we have to continue to do that but then we also have to find ways that we can reach and influence readers so that our authors are front and center, easily findable. That is the scale game at this point, I think, for the whole industry.

Titan is not alone in pursuing this strategy. Many publishers are developing their own customer databases, and many have launched sites similar to GoodFood.com – there is Brightly.com, a site run by

Penguin Random House aimed at mothers with young children; Epic Reads, a site run by HarperCollins aimed at teens and young adults; Tor.com, a site run by Macmillan aimed at readers of science fiction and fantasy; Work in Progress, a site and newsletter run by FSG aimed at readers of literary fiction; and many more. Most of these work on a similar model: a publisher creates the site, populates it with content that is often linked to authors and books (some of which will be the publisher's own books, though they may also feature and recommend authors and books published by others), and uses a variety of methods to encourage people to sign up, adding their email addresses and perhaps other information to the publisher's customer database. While the model is similar, there are many variations and permutations. One variation on this theme that is particularly interesting is the Literary Hub.

Literature's Switzerland

Literary Hub is the brainchild of Morgan Entrekin, the President and publisher of Grove Atlantic and a well-known figure in the world of literary publishing. What Morgan set out to do was to create a literary website that was not tied to a particular publisher but genuinely open to all. The aim was simple: 'Discoverability. There's a huge amount of literary content being produced but it's scattered so widely that 90 per cent of it goes unseen', said Morgan. His thinking was that, for most people who are interested in reading high-quality literature, what matters are the authors and the books, not the publishers – most readers don't really care who the publisher is, they just want to know about the books. So rather than trying to persuade readers to visit a publisher's site, why not create a site that is just focused on good authors and good books, regardless of who publishes them – a site that is a co-operative venture by many different publishers rather than a proprietary product of any one of them? Try to create a single resource that combines the efforts of many different publishers and becomes the go-to site for anyone interested in quality literature. No single publisher, on its own, is ever going to become the go-to site – even the largest publisher, Penguin Random House, would still be limited, since it wouldn't have the books published by FSG, Scribner, Ecco, Little, Brown, Norton and many others. But, by pooling their efforts and their books, publishers together could create something that no single publisher on its own could ever do.

However, to create a shared resource like this is not easy, especially in a field like publishing where competitive rivalries between publishers are as strong as – if not stronger than – any spirit of fraternal collaboration. To pull it off would require someone who was uniquely positioned in the field and willing to put in a lot of time, effort and money. Grove could do it, in Morgan's view, because they weren't one of the Big Five, but they weren't a small indie press either. Had any of the Big Five tried to do it, the other big houses would have been wary, and no small indie publisher would have the resources you need to make this happen. But Grove, as one of the few remaining medium-sized publishers in the field of American trade publishing, would be seen as sufficiently neutral to allay the competitive anxieties of other houses. 'Grove is the kind of Switzerland of the literary community', ventured Morgan, 'so it can do it and host it. And we've bent over backwards to make sure that it's not privileging Grove stuff. In fact, I think it's un-privileging Grove stuff.'

The model for the site was to 'crowdsource by invitation' – that is, invite other publishers and content creators to participate in the site as partners who would contribute an agreed number of pieces per year – say, 14 to 16. If you had 100 or 150 partners, including literary magazines as well as publishers, each committed to contributing a certain number of pieces per year that feature authors or books or something about the literary world, then this would give you a steady flow of new content – enough to ensure that you could change the site every day by adding new features and excerpts. So Morgan set out to persuade other publishers to come on board; as it turned out, it wasn't so hard: 'I've gone around town talking to people about it and every single person that I've asked has said yes.' The fact that Morgan was prepared to fund the site for three years, with no expectation of financial returns, undoubtedly helped. 'I was asked by one publisher, "So, what's your revenue model?" I said, "Well, it's brilliant. There is no revenue model. Zero revenue. First year, zero revenue. Second year, zero revenue. Third year, zero revenue. So if we have any revenue at all, we're way ahead of budget.' Morgan didn't want to raise external funding because the financial expectations of investors would tie him down, nor did he want to try to persuade other publishers to put money into a speculative venture of this kind. It would be cleaner and simpler to fund it himself, using the resources of Grove Atlantic. If Lit Hub turned out to be a success – if, in other words, a large number of people were visiting the site regularly and signing up for the newsletter – then he could invite publishers to buy ad space on the site and use this revenue to help finance it. But that would come later. First, he had to see if the idea would work.

But why would it work? Hadn't publishers tried to do something similar with Bookish a few years earlier, and hadn't that experiment ended in failure? That's true, but Morgan had something different in mind. 'I think the reason Bookish failed is because it went for too broad of a spectrum', said Morgan. 'I don't think you can be all things to all readers. You've got to focus. And in our case, it's mainly literary culture.' But 'literary culture' wasn't to be interpreted narrowly. While literary fiction would be the main focus, they would also cover serious nonfiction and even certain kinds of genre fiction. They wouldn't cover commercial blockbusters – 'they get plenty of attention everywhere else' – but if Stephen King wanted to write a piece for the Literary Hub, 'we would welcome it.' Similarly, if a Harlequin romance writer wanted to write a piece comparing Harlequin romance to Jane Austen and Emily Brontë, that might work too. The aim was to be inclusive and open-minded: 'We're trying not to put any boundaries on it.' The only real criterion was quality – both because this is the kind of publishing that Morgan does and is interested in and because he genuinely believes that, at the end of the day, this is what will draw readers and keep them coming back. In the age of the internet, with the explosion of content of all kinds available online, it's a refreshingly old-fashioned view. 'You know what I believe? I believe that if you do something that's good enough, people will come. That's the theory by which I've run my business for however many years, and the great thing about this business, particularly in our corner of it, is that quality wins. It may not win right away, but it does win in the end.'

The Literary Hub launched in April 2015 and, within a year, they were seeing 450,000 unique visitors per month, with 250,000 returning regularly to the site, and 30,000 had signed up for the newsletter. The site is refreshed every day with five or six feature stories, the majority of which are original material written for the Literary Hub. It also has a new excerpt from a book every day. They subsequently added a new vertical on crime to broaden the range of books they cover and created LitHub Radio, a platform for podcasts about books. The newsletter, Lit Hub Daily, goes out six days a week and contains a brief mention of the new features on the site and a round-up of other literary stories gleaned from around the web. They'd also sold enough sponsorship packages to cover 60 or 70 per cent of the budget. The sponsorship packages are sold to publishers and entitle them to a certain amount of ad space on the site in return for an annual fee. Since all the ads are for books, they're in keeping with the ethos of the site – not dissimilar to the *New York Review of Books*. Morgan was confident that they'd be self-funding in a few years, but that, ultimately, is not really the point. Creating the site was never about making money: it was about trying to create new ways of making books visible, and enabling readers to discover books, in a world where the traditional mechanisms of visibility and discoverability are in decline. 'The traditional literary media are diminishing, not only in our country but all over the world, and the Literary Hub is an attempt to address that', explained Morgan. This is not to say that a feature in the Literary Hub will have the same effect as a review in the *New York Times* or an author appearance on NPR: 'I would prefer the front page of the *New York Times* to anything on the Literary Hub, trust me.' But it's not an either/or matter. The issue is what publishers can do, practically and concretely, to use the online world as a space to support and strengthen literature – or, as Morgan put it, 'to capture, for the literary discourse, that digital world.' If every publisher tries to go it alone and create their own proprietary sites, their efforts will be Balkanized and ineffective. But by co-operating and working together on a single platform, they increase the likelihood that they will be able to create a site of sufficient breadth and quality, featuring books and authors from many different publishers and a continuous stream of high-quality content, to draw readers to it and keep them coming back.

Building customer databases and websites and using targeted emails and newsletters to reach out directly to readers and inform them of new and forthcoming books provide publishers, on their own or in collaboration, with means to increase the visibility of their books and to take more control of the ways in which their books are made visible to consumers in a world where the traditional mechanisms of visibility are in decline and the new mechanisms of visibility are largely in the hands of others. It's too early to say whether these initiatives – and there are many, each with its own distinctive configuration and goals – will flourish, or even survive; too early also to say whether initiatives of this kind will enable publishers to wrest back some power from Amazon and chip away at the near-monopoly of information capital, in the form of user data, that Amazon now has in the world of the book. Amazon has a huge advantage in the struggle for control of information capital – with more than 300 million active users, they are far ahead of where any publisher, or even consortium of publishers, could ever hope to be. But publishers are not without cards to play in this game. After all, the relationship that most readers have with Amazon is a practical and functional one: Amazon provides an excellent service at a good price. Most readers don't want to have a relationship with Amazon beyond this practical and functional one. But there are many readers who do want to have some kind of connection or relationship with the authors they like to read, with ideas and stories – a relationship that is more than a purely functional one, that is richer, more engaged and more interactive, and publishers are much better placed than Amazon to facilitate these connections. Publishers who have seen this potential and used the digital resources at their disposal to reach out to readers have begun, in their own small way, to build and facilitate relationships of this kind. They have begun to learn something about their readers that publishers in the past never knew, and they have begun to think about how to use this knowledge to reach out directly to individuals who might be interested in buying and reading their books. The information capital they will be able to build up in this way will never match the vast quantity of information capital amassed by Amazon, but quantity is not the only virtue. Small databases of readers who are actively interested in the kinds of books and authors being published by a particular publisher or group of publishers may be just as valuable – perhaps even more valuable – than large databases of customers with diverse interests, and building databases of this kind may turn out to be one of the ways in which publishers can make some small shift in the balance of power in a game where the giant retailer holds most of the cards.

But it is not the only way. The rise of ebooks has also created new marketing opportunities that are specific to ebooks, opportunities with which many publishers, among others, have begun to experiment. One feature of ebooks that is of particular significance here is the fact that ebooks allow you to do price promotions with no marginal costs. This was the feature that underpinned Amazon's Kindle Daily Deal programme, launched in 2011, which offered readers the opportunity to buy a specific ebook at a price that was heavily discounted for one day. But Amazon was not the only player who saw that heavy discounting could be a particularly effective tool of discoverability in the digital age.

Visibility through discounting

Having majored in economics at Harvard and got an MBA at MIT Sloan, Josh Schanker was an internet entrepreneur looking for something to do when, in 2011, a friend from his undergraduate years got in touch and asked if he could help her solve a problem. His friend was a writer, and she and some of her writer friends were trying to figure out how to market the books they were writing and planning to publish. Josh didn't know much about publishing but he had some experience in email marketing, having founded an email marketing company called Sombasa Media in Boston, and he quickly saw that some of the techniques he had learned in email marketing could be applied to books. His friend was going to self-publish her book as an ebook, so many of the traditional practices used by mainstream publishers to get their books noticed, like front-of-store displays in bookstores, were not going to be relevant for her. Moreover, Josh, having done a little research on publishing, was aware that big changes were taking place in the industry – ebooks were becoming more important, Amazon was growing fast, bricks-and-mortar bookstores were declining, and book discovery was shifting into online spaces. 'The trick', he reckoned, 'was no longer creating discovery within the bookstore, the trick was how do you get consumers to want your book regardless of where they are.' Having started and sold a social networking company after he left business school, Josh had some capital, so he and his co-founder, Nicholas Ciarelli, decided to start a company that would address the problem that his writer friend had helped him to see. That was the beginning of BookBub, which was launched in 2012.

The original idea was to create a daily email that would offer readers deep discounts on ebooks, and they could put their friends' books in there too. Josh had used discounting at Sombasa Media, so he was familiar with the techniques. But he saw that, with book publishing, ebooks offered a special opportunity because, unlike print books, the marginal costs for ebooks were zero. So deep discounting of prices, even giving away ebooks for free, would be possible, and it could be an effective way of getting people to discover new books and new authors. They decided to experiment with the idea. They could also see that, if they got it right, they might be able to create a viable business by generating revenue from two sources: on the one hand, they could charge authors and publishers to include their books in their email, and, on the other hand, they could charge the retailer a commission on sales. But to make this work, they had to do two things first: they had to build a list of subscribers that was large enough to make the daily email an attractive proposition for authors and publishers, and they had to find a way of selecting the right titles to send to their subscribers in a daily email.

They spent some of their own money on online advertising to begin the process of building a list of subscribers. It was free to join and the subscriber list grew quickly: within two years, they had 2 million subscribers. They raised $4 million in VC funding in 2014 and another $7 million in 2015, and a good part of this was spent on growing the member base, which had risen to over 10 million subscribers by 2017. When individuals subscribed, they were invited to select the categories that interested them – 'Bestsellers', 'Thrillers', 'Romance', etc. As the subscriber base grew, the task of selecting titles for the daily email became ever more challenging. Every day, BookBub would receive around 200–300 books that authors or publishers were offering to them as potential discount titles, and they could only accept around 30–40 a day – that is, only 10–20 per cent of the books that were submitted. They had to be very selective because part of the appeal of their daily email was that it would offer only a small number of titles to each subscriber – usually around 6 or 7, but for heavy readers it could be up to 10. So how could they choose? They decided that they would have to look at each book submitted and make a decision on a book-by-book basis. 'Our editorial team looks through all the books, looks at how good the discount is, what the platform of the author is, how good a fit it is for the particular list that it would be going into and they decide which are the best ones', explained Josh. The author or publisher only pays if their book has been chosen for inclusion. The selection process is crucial here because you don't want to overwhelm readers with too many titles, and you want to align the titles selected with their interests so far as possible. 'One of the values we provide to readers is that we provide a curated experience and if we fail to do that, then our audience doesn't trust us and we're not an effective marketing vehicle for the publishing industry, so the model doesn't work.'

To increase the number of titles they can select and improve the alignment of selected titles with users' interests, they elaborated their model by creating more categories and asked users to refine their choices. So instead of one broad romance category, for example, readers are now invited to select one or more sub-categories like 'Contemporary Romance', 'Historical Romance', 'Paranormal Romance', 'Time Travel Romance', etc. Each email is customized to each member based on the categories they selected. 'It's a highly customized email', explained Josh. 'It's personalized but it's not uber-personalized, we're not looking through thousands of books and picking the three that are perfect for you.'

One of the remarkable features of BookBub is that editorial processes lie at the heart of its day-to-day activities. This is not an operation in which everything has been automated by algorithms and machine learning – far from it. The editorial selection process is done by an editorial team who go through all the books submitted: title selection is not done by using an algorithm-based recommendation engine. Once titles have been selected, BookBub's staff – either in-house editors or freelancers – write the blurbs for the books that go out on the daily emails; they don't just take the publisher's or author's blurb and use it as it is. This is important, said Josh, because they want blurbs that will resonate with their members: 'We read reviews, we read a lot about the book, we understand what the audience likes and we understand what are the things to emphasize about the book that the audience will like – why this particular book will resonate with this particular audience at this particular time.' In a world of tech start-ups where a great deal of faith is placed in technological solutions, this firm belief in the value of human creativity is refreshing. Of course, automation and the use of data play an important role at BookBub and they're experimenting with the use of algorithms for some features, but the core activities of title selection and blurb writing remain resolutely human. In part, this is because they realize that much of the value of BookBub lies in the extent to which users trust the brand, and the careful curation and thoughtful presentation of titles is an essential part of this. The key is to get the right balance between the human and the machine, between editorial judgement and the use of algorithms.

While BookBub began from the world of self-publishing (Josh's college friend who needed help was planning to publish her new book on Kindle Direct, and some of her friends were doing the same), it wasn't long before traditional publishers began to realize that BookBub had created a very effective way of increasing the visibility of some of their books for well-targeted readers. In the early days, BookBub's lists were made up mainly of self-published books, but gradually the balance shifted towards books from traditional publishers; now the mix is roughly half and half, though books from traditional publishers tend to be over-represented in the larger categories, like bestsellers. BookBub runs both free and discounted books, and self-published authors are more likely to make their books available for free as a way of building up their platform. A typical scenario is that a publisher or author will have a book that they want to promote – it could be a backlist book that isn't selling, or a backlist book by an author who has just published a new book and where they want to build awareness for the author and the new release. They'll submit the book they want to promote to BookBub as a discounted title. If BookBub decides to select it and feature it in their daily email to the appropriate categories of readers, then the publisher or author will often see a sudden spike of sales, 'somewhere from hundreds to thousands, in some cases more than 10,000 copies in that one day.' Three-day sales are the most common, though some publishers will run a sale for longer. In many cases, publishers and authors will then see a halo effect: higher sales may continue for some days after the sale has finished, even though the book is no longer discounted, and then the new steady state may be at a higher level than it was before, so if they were selling five books a day before the promotion, now they may be selling ten a day. The publisher or author may also find that their ranking goes up on Amazon's bestseller list, which increases the visibility of the book in key online spaces – 'It's on the bestseller list, other people see it, people who've read the book are now talking about it, so that gives it another life.' While most publishers and authors began by using this for backlist books, many are now experimenting with other kinds of books, like recent books that sold very well to begin with but where sales are now slowing down – 'Giving it this little boost actually helps perpetuate it as a bestseller for longer.'

Promoting a book on BookBub is not cheap. The fees charged to publishers and authors vary by category, book price and sales region (you can choose US only, international (which includes the UK, Canada, India and Australia but excludes the US) or all of these): in 2019, for a large category like Crime Fiction, it would cost a publisher or author $1,138 to have a book priced under $1 featured in a deal offered in all sales regions; $1,970 if it were priced $1–$2; $2,845 if priced $2–$3; and $3,983 if priced $3 or more.[16] You need to sell a lot of ebooks to recoup these costs.[17] But in categories with lower subscription numbers, the fees are significantly lower – in Time Travel Romance, for example, the fee for a

---

[16] See www.bookbub.com/partners/pricing.

[17] One analyst looking at 2018 data suggests that an average-performing campaign for an ebook discounted to 99¢ would yield a positive return on investment in 69 per cent (29 out of 42) of BookBub categories, but the average rate of return was down from 35.9 per cent in 2015 to 14.4 per cent in 2018. See http://dankoboldt.com/bookbub-analysis-update-2018.

book priced under $1 is $248, and for African American Interest it's $164; limit your promotion to the US only and the fee for a Time Travel Romance priced under $1 comes down to $198. These prices are geared not just to the number of subscribers in the category but also to the performance of each category: some categories have lower conversion rates than others, and the fees charged are therefore adjusted downwards.

While most of BookBub's revenue comes from the fees charged to publishers and authors for featuring their books and from the sales commission charged to retailers, they also introduced a display ad at the bottom of the daily email. This allows space for only one ad, and the book that appears in this space is determined by a real-time auction. Whenever a reader opens the email, there is a real-time auction around the anonymized profile of that reader. So if they know that this reader likes these categories of books, has clicked on these authors, uses these retailers and lives in this region, then there will be a real-time auction among all the publishers and authors who are bidding for that particular space to display an ad to that person using the second-price auction method (the highest bidder gets the space but pays the price bid by the second-highest bidder) – the same method used by Google and Facebook.

The combination of fees charged to publishers and authors, sales commissions charged to retailers and ad revenue has enabled BookBub to build a profitable business focused on the use of discounting to increase the visibility of books. Their large subscriber base and their carefully curated daily emails have made this a particularly attractive marketing tool for both self-published authors and traditional publishers, though getting your books selected by BookBub for inclusion in their promotions is not easy. Many publishers have launched their own daily-deal promotions, as have retailers like Amazon, but BookBub is able to cater for a wide variety of publishers and authors, including the self-publishing community. Of course, this method of heavily discounting books for a limited time period works well for ebooks where the marginal costs and delivery costs are negligible, and works well for those categories of books that sell strongly as ebooks, especially romance and other categories of genre fiction; it is less effective for print and for those categories of books that remain overwhelmingly print-based, including children's books and heavily illustrated books. But for those categories of books that have migrated strongly to ebooks and for self-published authors who have limited marketing tools at their disposal, the methods developed by BookBub have provided a powerful new mechanism for reaching out to readers and achieving visibility in the online space.

Visibility in a digital age

Books exist within a broader information and communication environment of which they are part, and by transforming this environment the digital revolution has also transformed the ways in which books circulate in our lives, how they appear to us, how we find them and choose them, as well as how we buy them and integrate them into our everyday lives. When all books were printed and most were bought and sold in bookstores, the bookstores, together with traditional media like newspapers, radio and TV, were the key spaces of visibility where books were seen and discovered by readers; publishers knew how to work these spaces, they knew the rules of the game, and they could calculate the costs and measure the effects of visibility in terms of increased sales. But with the decline of bookstores, the rise of Amazon and the growing importance of online media, the traditional rules and practices have been thrown into disarray. It's not that the old methods don't work anymore – they do. A glowing review in the *New York Times* can still drive book sales like nothing else. But with the decline of traditional media and the increase in the number of new books being published, it's harder than ever to get those reviews, and in any case the attention of many readers has migrated elsewhere. In the heyday of the book superstores, the front-of-store tables in Borders and Barnes & Noble were the main battlefields for eyeballs; increasingly, these battlefields have been eclipsed by the struggle for attention online.

Publishers were slow to wake up to the fact that readers were migrating to new pastures where others were busily tending the flocks. They struggled to understand the lay of the land and they found themselves having to experiment with new and untested methods. By the time they realized what was happening, Amazon had built up an unassailable position as an online retailer and had gathered an enormous amount of data on the individuals who browsed and bought books. Stuck in the old publishing world, most publishers still thought of retailers as their customers and paid little attention to readers. They had failed to see that the information environment of which the old publishing world was part had crumbled around them and was being replaced by a new information environment in which communication flows were more fluid and data was becoming a new source of power. It was not too late for them to do something about it, but they were starting from a weak position and they lacked both the resources and the advantages that were now held in abundance by the organization that had become the dominant player in their field.

— Chapter 7 —

THE SELF-PUBLISHING EXPLOSION

Throughout its 500-year-plus history, the publishing business has always been based on selectivity. No publisher ever published everything that came their way: they sifted through the range of possibilities and chose a selection of texts to publish. The criteria of selectivity varied from sector to sector and publisher to publisher – estimates of likely costs and likely sales, judgements of quality and importance, and considerations of appropriateness or suitability for the list are among the many factors that have played, and continue to play, a role in shaping the decision-making processes of publishing organizations. Publishers vary enormously in how selective they are: some are relatively indiscriminate and will place the bar fairly low (the 'throw the spaghetti against the wall and see what sticks' philosophy of publishing), while others are much more selective and will take on only a very small number of titles – an extreme example of the latter being Twelve Books, an imprint of Hachette that was launched in 2007 with the aim of publishing just twelve books a year, one a month, in order to maximize the potential of each book. But while the criteria and extent of selectivity vary from one sector and one publisher to another, the function of selectivity does not: all publishers exercise some degree of selectivity, deciding which books to invest their time, expertise and resources in and which to pass over. Publishers are gatekeepers, to use a well-known metaphor,[1] deciding

---

[1] The concept of gatekeeping dates back to the 1940s and was first used in relation to the media by White in his study of newspaper editors: David Manning White, 'The Gatekeeper: A Case Study in the Selection of News', *Journalism Quarterly*, 27, 4 (1950), 283–9. The concept was applied to publishers by Coser, Kadushin and Powell in their classic study of the publishing industry: Lewis A. Coser, Charles Kadushin and Walter W. Powell, *Books: The Culture and Commerce of Publishing* (New York:

which projects will be turned into books and made available to the public and which will not. And in the world of trade publishing, it is not just publishers who act as gatekeepers: agents do too, and in practice it is the agents who are the first to decide which projects should be taken seriously as potential books and which should not – the outer ring, as it were, of the circles of gatekeepers in publishing. Publishers and agents have always dealt in and perpetuated relative scarcity: by selecting out and publishing only a small sub-set of the range of possible books, they created a market that was populated by a small fraction of the number of books that might have existed if different processes had been in place. Even if the number of books being published was increasing significantly year on year, it would still be a small proportion of the total number of books that would be published if no mechanisms of selectivity had existed.

All that would change with the digital revolution. The very fact that publishers and their content suppliers are selective means that there has long been a large number of would-be books that never made it through the gates. What happened to all those would-be books that fell at one of the many hurdles that lie in the path of aspiring authors? No doubt many were consigned to the dustbin or languished in a drawer somewhere, covered with other papers and eventually forgotten. But the very existence of a large pool of would-be books and aspiring authors meant that there was a demand to be published that outstripped the willingness or ability of established publishing organizations to meet it (and possibly outstripped the demand to be read too). And it was this pent-up demand that provided the driving force behind the self-publishing explosion.

Self-publishing has become a world unto itself – a parallel universe of publishing, a sprawling, uncharted territory that has expanded enormously in recent years and whose dramatic growth shows no signs of slowing down. It is part and parcel of a burgeoning domain of what could be called 'non-traditional publishing' – the many forms of publishing books and other content that do not fit within the traditional model of book publishing, whereby a publisher acquires content from an author or agent, pays a royalty and/or advance, invests in the production and marketing of the book and

---

Basic Books, 1982). While the concept has its limitations when applied to publishing (see chapter 12, pp. 451–2; see also John B. Thompson, *Books in the Digital Age: The Transformation of Academic and Higher Education Publishing in Britain and the United States* (Cambridge: Polity, 2005), p. 4), it does nevertheless correctly highlight the fact that publishers have traditionally exercised a degree of selectivity in deciding which books to publish.

takes the key decisions about what and how to publish. There are many different forms of non-traditional publishing.[2] In terms of sheer quantity of output, some of the largest of the non-traditional publishing operations today are companies like Bibliobazaar, General Books and Kessinger Publishing – sometimes referred to as 'publishers of royalty-free content' – that specialize in scanning public-domain works and making them available through print-on-demand,[3] but these operations are very different from self-publishing. What is called 'self-publishing' is a particular form of non-traditional publishing – or rather a variety of forms, depending on how you understand the term and how widely you cast the net. And just as the world of non-traditional publishing is complex and varied, so too is the world of self-publishing – not so much one world but many worlds, from so-called vanity publishers to self-publishing service providers to self-publishing platforms, each internally differentiated and populated by many players working in different ways, as well as by a plethora of freelancers who have found a space to subsist in an emerging shadow economy of self-publishing services. This world, or these worlds, have evolved over time, as old players decline or go out of business and new players appear, often taking advantage of new technologies which enable books to be produced and distributed in new ways. No one has mapped these worlds in their entirety and traced their evolution over time – a proper history of the rise of self-publishing has yet to be written.[4] But, in broad terms, this history could be

---

[2] For a useful overview of the different forms of non-traditional publishing, see Jana Bradley, Bruce Fulton, Marlene Helm and Katherine A. Pittner, 'Non-traditional Book Publishing', *First Monday*, 16, 8 (1 August 2001), at http://firstmonday.org/ojs/index.php/fm/article/view/3353/3030.

[3] Bibliobazaar alone accounted for 1,461,918 ISBNs in 2010 – more than half the total of the non-traditional output at that time; and Bibliobazaar, General Books and Kessinger together accounted for 2,668,774 ISBNs, or 96 per cent of the total ('Print Isn't Dead, Says Bowker's Annual Book Production Report', at www.bowker.com/index.php/press-releases/633-print-isnt-dead-says-bowkers-annual-book-production-report). Of course, these titles are not being 'published' in a traditional sense: these organizations are simply scanning public-domain works, generating text and cover files, obtaining ISBNs and creating metadata to enable the titles to be sold and printed on demand. Moreover, these calculations are also based on ISBNs and don't take account of the many books that are published without ISBNs, including many self-published books – more on this later.

[4] There are many guides to self-publishing for would-be authors but no comprehensive account of the rise of self-publishing as a distinct sector of the publishing world. For some helpful accounts of aspects of self-publishing, see Laura J. Miller, 'Whither the Professional Book Publisher in an Era of Distribution on Demand?' in Angharad N. Valdivia and Vicki Mayer (eds.), *The International Encyclopedia of*

characterized in terms of three main phases or waves: the rise of the vanity presses; the emergence of print-on-demand self-publishers; and the growth of indie publishing. Let us look briefly at each.

From vanity to indie publishing

Self-publishing can be understood as a form of publishing in which the author of the work is also the principal agent involved in publishing the work. To say that the author is the principal agent involved is not to say that he or she is the only agent – on the contrary, as in all forms of cultural production, there are many intermediaries and third parties involved in the process of self-publishing. But these interme-diaries and third parties are seen, and see themselves, primarily as facilitators, enablers and service providers whose *raison d'être* is to enable authors to publish their own work. They are not so much publishers as facilitators and/or distributors of the author's work: the publisher is the author. The organizations that facilitate self-publishing aim to establish a framework or platform that enables authors to publish their own work more or less as they wish, freeing authors from the kind of selectivity that characterizes traditional publishing houses and allowing them, the authors, to take the key decisions about what to publish and how to publish it. At the same time, the facilitating organizations seek to turn this activity into a viable business for themselves by charging a fee or commission for the services they provide.

In self-publishing, many of the roles and responsibilities of publishing are reversed. In the traditional model of publishing, the publisher decides whether to publish a work, acquires the right to publish (often exclusively, and typically for the legal term of copyright), pays the author a royalty (and sometimes also an advance) for the right to publish, invests in the production and marketing of the work and takes all the key publishing decisions. In self-publishing, the author makes the decision about what to publish and how to publish it, retains the copyright and pays the publishing intermediaries – either directly, as an up-front fee, or indirectly, as

Media Studies, vol. II (Chichester, UK: Wiley-Blackwell, 2013), pp. 171–91; Sarah Glazer, 'How to Be Your Own Publisher', *New York Times Book Review*, 24 April 2005, pp. 10–11; Juris Dilevko and Keren Dali, 'The Self-Publishing Phenomenon and Libraries', *Library and Information Science Research*, 28 (2006), 208–34; and Timothy Laquintano, *Mass Authorship and the Rise of Self-Publishing* (University of Iowa Press, 2016).

a commission on sales – for the services he or she needs in order to publish the work. In self-publishing, the author retains the rights and control but also bears the costs and the risks. If the book does well, the author reaps the rewards, but if the book doesn't sell, the author absorbs any losses. The author is the decision-maker, the investor and the risk-taker: unlike traditional publishing, there is no third party who is taking the key decisions about what and how to publish, investing in the publication of the book and acting as the creditor of last resort.

The rise of self-publishing can be traced back to the so-called vanity presses that emerged in the early and mid twentieth century (sometimes described, less pejoratively, as 'subsidy presses'). Dorrance Publishing, founded by Gordon Dorrance in Pittsburgh in 1920, and Vantage Press, founded in New York in 1949, are commonly regarded as the first major vanity presses. They used offset printing and charged authors a substantial up-front fee to print a limited number of copies of their book, some of which would be owned by the author and the rest warehoused by the publisher. Offset printing was expensive and, given the high set-up costs, you had to print a significant quantity of books to get a reasonable unit cost. The fees that the vanity presses charged authors to publish their books were therefore considerable: they could be anything between $5,000 and $25,000 or more, depending on the quantity printed and the services provided – hence the label, 'vanity press'. This was a form of self-publishing that enabled authors to publish works that were not accepted by traditional publishing houses, but the financial burden placed on the author was substantial: you could get your manuscript published but you had to pay a lot for the privilege, and you might well find that most of the stock remained unsold in your garage, if you had one. Not surprisingly, this kind of self-publishing acquired a poor reputation in the eyes of many authors and critics, and the stigma associated with the term 'vanity press' proved hard to shake off. Vantage Press was sold to an investment banker in 2009 and ceased business in 2012, having published more than 20,000 titles over its sixty-year history. Dorrance Publishing continues to operate out of Pittsburgh and has evolved in the direction of a provider of self-publishing services, though it still charges authors up-front fees and is still seen by many as a continuation of the old-style vanity press.

The development of print-on-demand technology in the 1990s opened the space for a new set of players to enter the field of self-publishing. Print-on-demand was an early product of the digital revolution in the field of printing; it emerged out of the business of producing and supplying manuals and documents for the software industry. By the early 1990s, the quality of digital printing was reaching levels at which it could compete with offset printing – for straight text, the difference in quality between offset printing and digital printing was increasingly difficult to discern. Moreover, digital printing had the advantage that you could print in small quantities: rather than printing 500 or 1,000 copies or more in order to get a reasonable unit cost, as in offset printing, you could print 10 or 20 copies, or even print 1 copy at a time in response to a specific order – true print-on-demand (PoD). This enabled a new generation of self-publishing companies to emerge, offering authors a very different proposition at much lower cost. AuthorHouse (originally called 1stBooks), iUniverse, Xlibris, PublishAmerica and many other companies appeared in the late 1990s and early 2000s, all using digital printing and PoD technology to enable authors to publish their books at much lower costs – this was the second phase in the rise of self-publishing. Many of these PoD self-publishing companies continued to charge authors an up-front fee, and in this respect they were similar to the old-style vanity presses; but the fees charged by PoD self-publishing companies were typically much less than the vanity presses had charged – with a PoD self-publishing company, an author could turn a manuscript into a paperback book for as little as $299. Authors could purchase a range of additional services on an à la carte basis, which would commonly bump up the price, but this was still far below the kinds of fees that were charged by the earlier generation of vanity presses. Nevertheless, many of these PoD self-publishing firms found it difficult to escape entirely the stigma associated with the 'vanity press' label. The mere fact that they were charging authors up-front fees to provide them with publishing services left them open to the suspicion that they were preying on authors' dreams, and there was a mounting chorus of complaints from authors about services that were perceived as being over-priced and poorly executed. Tens of thousands of new books were being produced by these self-publishing firms – AuthorHouse, iUniverse and Xlibris together produced a total of 11,906 new titles in 2004 alone[5] – but there was a growing demand for something else. The self-publishing firms that built their businesses on PoD did not stand still – they evolved as technologies changed, and the companies themselves changed their organization, and sometimes their names,

---

[5] Glazer, 'How to Be Your Own Publisher'.

221

as they were bought and sold.[6] But in the early 2000s, a new kind of self-publishing was beginning to emerge that was quite distinct from the companies that had been built on PoD technology.

The third wave of self-publishing was also made possible by digital technologies but it was based on a very different conception of the relation between authors and the organizations that enabled authors to self-publish their work. The key idea that differentiated the third phase of self-publishing from the earlier phases was this: it was the idea that authors who want to publish their own work should not have to pay for the privilege, and the organizations that facilitated self-publishing should not be making money by charging authors. On the contrary, the whole payment structure should be turned on its head: rather than the author paying the publishing facilitator in order to publish their work, the publishing facilitator should pay the author if and when their work sells, taking a commission on sales to cover their costs. In this new model, no sales, no commission, no fee. This was the idea – simple but radical – that revolutionized self-publishing, separating the vanity presses and PoD self-publishers of the 1990s and before from the new wave of self-publishing organizations that emerged in the early 2000s. Now, at last, self-publishing could free itself from the idea that had tainted self-publishing since the days of the vanity presses – the idea that authors were paying for the privilege of publishing their work.

The new wave of self-publishing that emerged in the early 2000s was also associated with a new culture and ethos of self-publishing. This was a culture of do-it-yourself publishing in which authors were encouraged to take control of the publishing process and to be proactive. Don't outsource self-publishing to third-party intermediaries who are going to charge you an arm and a leg to publish your book: do it yourself. You can figure it out – and here's how. Take charge, be entrepreneurial, self-publish because it's a smart way to publish, not because it's the option of last resort. These are the ideas

---

[6] AuthorHouse was purchased in 2007 by the California-based investment group Bertram Capital, which also acquired iUniverse; AuthorHouse and iUniverse became imprints of a new company called Author Solutions. In 2009, Author Solutions acquired two more major players – Xlibris and the Canadian self-publisher Trafford Publishing. In 2012, Author Solutions was purchased by Pearson, the parent company of Penguin, for $116 million – a controversial acquisition that was seen by many as an ill-judged move on Penguin's part, given the tarnished reputation that these companies had in the eyes of many authors. Following the merger of Penguin and Random House, Author Solutions was sold in December 2015 to a private equity firm for an undisclosed sum.

that define what is now commonly referred to as the 'indie author': the author who actively *chooses* self-publishing as his or her preferred option, who makes the effort to understand what is involved in self-publishing and who wears this label as a badge of honour rather than a sign of desperation or of failure. By embracing the term 'indie author', these authors are signalling their view that their decision to self-publish in this way is a positive choice: I'm an indie author and I'm proud of it. They are also signalling that, in taking this decision, they are not alone, for this is not an isolated act but a decision taken in the knowledge that many others have taken it too: in deciding to be an indie author and embracing the term, they are becoming part of a movement – a progressive, supportive, forward-looking movement that is in tune with the spirit of the times. The long shadow cast by the stigma associated with the vanity presses may not have faded entirely but, with the third wave of self-publishing and the rise of the indie author movement, a new culture of self-publishing has emerged in which self-publishing has morphed into 'indie publishing' and in which many authors feel much more confident and assertive about the value of self-publishing, and feel that the decision to self-publish is a decision they can take without the slightest misgiving or regret.

This new phase of self-publishing was ushered in by a new set of intermediaries who came up with the idea that underpinned this phase, pioneered the infrastructures that enabled it to happen and were in tune with the new culture of the indie author that emerged with it. One intermediary that played an important early role in the transition to the third phase was Lulu. Founded in 2002 by the Canadian entrepreneur Bob Young, who had previously founded the open source software company Red Hat, Lulu was set up with the aim of offering editing tools and printing services to authors and other creators who wanted to publish their own work. Bob had written a book, *Under the Radar*, about the open source business model and his experience at Red Hat, and he had published it with Coriolis Books, an imprint of International Thomson; he was both surprised and disappointed by how little he had earned from it, even though it had sold some 25,000 copies in hardback. 'What that taught me was that the publishing world is broken and there's an opportunity to fix it', said Bob. 'With all of these books that sell 25,000 copies or less, the vast majority of the value of the sales was going to the publisher, not the person who actually created the story or the content or the knowledge. And I'm thinking to myself, hold on, we're the age of the internet. Why can't the author sell this book directly to his audience?' Bob had the commercial background, having built a successful open source software company, and he had the cash, having made a lot of money out of Red Hat's IPO. So he decided to start Lulu as an open publishing platform.

In setting up Lulu, Bob's aim was simple: 'It was to empower all the authors that all the publishers were turning away.' He knew that there were other self-publishing companies around – Author Solutions, iUniverse, Trafford Publishing, etc. – that were offering their services to authors, but the model he had in mind was completely different. 'In their model, the publisher made most of his money off of the author's desire to be published, whereas our model was empowering the author to publish himself.' An author choosing to self-publish on Lulu's platform wouldn't pay anything up front – it would be free to publish. Once a book was created using Lulu's self-publishing tools, a price would be determined based on factors such as page count, type of binding and the user's choice of margin; from the margin set on each copy, 80 per cent would go to the author and 20 per cent to Lulu ('which is the opposite of the royalty deal I had with *Under the Radar*'). When an order was placed by a customer, a copy of the book was printed on demand by a third-party printer or PoD vendor such as Lightning Source; the author received her share of the margin and Lulu got its 20 per cent. If no copies were sold, Lulu got nothing. This model, using PoD technology, enabled any author to get into print without paying an up-front fee.

Lulu was launched in 2004. While the self-publishing platform was the core of the business, Lulu also made available to authors a range of additional services for a fee, including editing, cover design, ISBN assignment, marketing and making the publication available through Amazon and other online retailers. In its first four years, Lulu grew rapidly: by 2008, about a million authors had published something with Lulu. Many of the books self-published through Lulu sold very few copies, but selling large quantities was never the point. 'A publishing house dreams of having 10 authors selling a million books each', said Bob; 'Lulu wants a million authors selling 100 books each.'[7] Lulu had pioneered a new kind of self-publishing where the self-publishing organization – Lulu in this case – was the facilitator providing a suite of tools and services to authors and where there was no up-front fee, only a revenue share on copies sold (if and when they were sold) and a fee for any additional services that authors might choose to purchase. While Lulu and its entrepreneurial founder had

---

[7] 'Lulu Founder Bob Young talks to ABCtales' (14 March 2007), at www.abctales.com/blog/tcook/lulu-founder-bob-young-talks-abctales.

helped to usher in a new form of self-publishing, they were soon joined, and in some respects overshadowed, by many others developing similar ideas – some focusing on printed books, some focusing on ebooks and some offering both. The field of self-publishing would quickly become populated by a plethora of new players, each figuring out in its own way how to use the new opportunities afforded by digital technologies to enable authors to self-publish their books, while at the same time trying to build a business as a self-publishing organization or intermediary that, like Lulu, didn't rely on charging authors up-front fees. Let's retrace the pathways of a few.

Self-publishing in the ebook age

Mark Coker was a frustrated author. He used to run a PR firm in Silicon Valley representing venture capital-backed companies. At a time when the firm needed some help to write copy, he hired a woman who worked as a reporter for a soap-opera magazine; he soon found himself fascinated by her stories of soap-opera celebrities. When the dot.com bubble burst in 2000, he took a break from the PR agency and decided to write a novel set in the soap-opera industry with his erstwhile employee. They went down to Burbank, California, interviewed dozens of people in the business, fictionalized the stories and produced a draft manuscript of some 900 pages. They knew nothing about the world of publishing but they were convinced that their book was a gem. They shopped it around to agents, found that several were interested and eventually chose to go with one. The agent was excited about the book – he was sure it would fly. But, as it turned out, no publisher wanted to buy it. He tried for two years but got nowhere. Apparently books with soap-opera themes hadn't performed well in the market and were seen as money losers. Publishers were unwilling to take a risk on a new book on this theme by two unknown authors with no track record.

It was the agent who suggested that they consider self-publishing. Mark had read Dan Poynter's self-publishing manual[8] – long

---

[8] Dan Poynter, *The Self-Publishing Manual: How to Write, Print and Sell Your Own Book* (Santa Barbara, Calif.: Para Publishing, 1979). Dan Poynter stumbled into publishing. With a background as a parachute designer in the aviation industry, he decided to write a technical book on the parachute and assumed that no publisher would be interested in it, so he printed it himself. He subsequently became interested in the new sport of hand gliding but couldn't find a book on the subject, so he wrote one and published it himself. Drawing on his own experience, he then wrote and

regarded as the bible of self-publishing – but he realized that, without distribution to book stores, he wasn't going to sell many copies, and they weren't interested in filling up their garage with lots of unsold books. Rather than reaching out to one of the many self-publishing firms who were offering their services, Mark decided to put the book on the back burner and focus on the problem of how authors get published – or don't, as in their case. 'I realized that publishers were unwilling, unable and uninterested in taking a risk on every author', explained Mark. 'It doesn't work for their business model to say yes to everyone. They are practising a culture of no. Publishers view the vast majority of writers as unworthy. And I thought this is just wrong in this day and age. This is wrong when anyone can be a blogger or a journalist. Anyone should be able to be an author too.' As someone who had spent most of his professional life working in Silicon Valley, Mark was naturally inclined to think that at least part of the solution could be found in technology. 'Technology forces whatever it touches to become more responsive to consumer desires. It forces faster, smaller, cheaper – that's the evolution that gets launched when technology bites into something.' When he applied this thinking to the publishing industry, he thought, 'Ok, print books are expensive, it's not economically feasible to publish every print book or distribute every print book to every corner of the globe, but with ebooks we could do that because ebooks are just ones and zeros, digital bits and bytes.' So, in 2005, he began thinking about how to create a new kind of publishing business that would be ebook only – this was the beginning of Smashwords. Here's Mark's own account of the thinking behind it:

> What if I could create a free online publishing platform that would allow me to take a risk on every author, that would allow me to say yes? I imagined these hundreds of thousands of writers around the world who would never be given a chance to publish simply because a publisher didn't see commercial potential in their work. It also rubbed me up the wrong way that publishing is really forced to view books through this myopic prism of commercial potential. I don't blame publishers for this, they're running a business and they need to bring

---

published *The Self-Publishing Manual*, a book that went through many editions and established itself as a key how-to guide for aspiring authors. While Poynter began self-publishing well before the ebook era, he is seen by many as the father of modern self-publishing and as an unappointed leader of the indie author movement, long before this movement had a name.

in money to keep the lights on. But it's a very restrictive business model and they're saying no to many books that, if only they had been given a chance, could have gone on to become bestsellers or cultural classics. Think about all the cultural classics that we've lost to humanity for all time simply because that manuscript died with the author.

So I imagined this free online publishing platform. It was important to me that Smashwords be free because I wanted to emulate some of the best practices of the very best publishers. Publishers invest in authors, take a chance on authors, the money flows from the readers and the publishers back to the author and not the other way around. And I knew that there were firms out there called vanity presses that were in the business of taking money from authors and not in the business of selling books. So I wanted to make sure that our business model was aligned with the interests of our authors and that means: we only make money if we sell a book, we don't sell any services and we don't sell any publishing packages. I also wanted to turn the compensation model upside-down. I knew from my research that publishers were typically paying authors between 4 and maybe 15, 17 per cent of the list price as their royalty for their print books and their e-books. And I thought, what if we could turn that model upside-down? So we decided that 85 per cent of net would go to the authors and we would take 15 per cent of net. So that was a pretty radical idea.

I also decided that I didn't want to be an editorial gatekeeper. I don't want to take on the responsibility to decide what's worth reading and what's not. I don't think that's a role that I should play, it's not really a role anyone should play; that's a role that readers can play. Give writers the freedom to publish what they want and give readers the freedom to read what they want, because in my utopian view that yields greater diversity, greater quality and greater freedom of choice.

Mark's plan involved two important departures from what was happening elsewhere in the world of self-publishing at this time. Unlike Lulu and other self-publishing organizations using digital printing and PoD technology, Mark decided to focus exclusively on ebooks and avoid print entirely, partly in order to avoid the costs associated with producing and distributing printed books. But, like Lulu, Mark wanted to turn the old revenue model of self-publishing on its head. Rather than charging authors a fee to publish their work, the service Mark offered would be entirely free to authors. If Mark was going to earn money, it would have to be by selling books to readers, not selling services to authors. He would take a commission on sales and the commission would be small: the author would get the lion's share of any revenue earned. The author would get 85 per cent of net and Mark would take only 15 per cent – the inverse, more or less, of the distribution of rewards in the traditional publishing model. By focusing exclusively on ebooks, Mark was convinced he could create a platform that would scale and allow him to say yes to every author without charging them a dime. It was a bold vision that combined the inversion of the traditional revenue model of self-publishing with a prescient focus on ebooks as the medium of choice for self-published books, a kind of creative destruction that was disruptive and exciting at the same time, just like the process of writing itself – 'Smashwords', with its forceful, angsty feel, seemed an apt name for this new venture.

Mark borrowed money against his house and hired a programmer to build the platform. They created a system that was very easy for authors to use. All you have to do is create an account, download a style guide that tells you how to format your book for Smashwords using a standard word-processing programme like Microsoft Word or Apple Pages. When the manuscript is ready, you upload it together with a cover image on the Smashwords site. You're asked for a title and a short description, you're asked to choose two categories by which your book could be classified and you're asked a few other questions and then the two files and the metadata go into the conversion engine, the 'Meatgrinder' as Mark calls it, which automatically converts your book into multiple ebook formats – PDF, ePub, Mobi, etc. 'So one upload and it would spit out seven different formats, and it was literally instantaneous – like five minutes or less, you watch the little thing spin as it spits out each format of the book, and then your book goes for sale instantly on the Smashwords homepage.'

Smashwords was launched in May 2008 and, by the end of that year, 90 authors had self-published 140 books on the site. The new venture was under way but it was a slow start. 'On a good day we were selling maybe $10 worth of books a day. We were only selling books on the Smashwords website, so our commission on $10 was $1.20 after credit card expenses. The business was not looking very viable but the feedback we were getting from authors was great!' Mark soon discovered that, for many authors, making money wasn't important – that isn't why they were writing: 'What I quickly learned is that for the vast majority of authors, there's a joy and pleasure that comes in self-publishing that can't be measured in dollars and cents. To me this illustrated the disconnect between the traditional publishing mind-set and the writer mind-set. I realized that writers often write for different reasons than publishers publish. Publishers are forced by their business model to value books through the myopic prism of commercial potential, whereas writers just want the freedom of expression that comes with writing.' Many authors were happy to give away their books for free, and from day one of Smashwords, authors were allowed to set the price of their books at free – they're the authors, it's up to them. But Mark knew perfectly well that he could never make the business work unless he could find a way to raise the revenue levels significantly – and fast.

The breakthrough came six months later, in the middle of 2009. At the outset, Mark had thought of Smashwords both as a means of enabling authors to publish their work and as a means of selling books: the books would be published on Smashwords' platform and sold on Smashwords' site. There was no need to distribute the books to retailers like Barnes & Noble – indeed, he saw them as competitors and he was dead set against working with them. But in the course of 2009, he began to have second thoughts. He realized that he hadn't really thought through the distribution issue ('distribution was a hole in my business plan') and, prompted by one of his authors who asked why his book wasn't available at Barnes & Noble, he started having discussions with them; to his surprise, he found that Barnes & Noble were keen to have Smashwords' books – and not just some of them, but all of them. Discussions with Sony followed soon after – Sony too wanted all Smashwords' books. By late 2009, Mark had also done a distribution deal with Amazon. Then, in early 2010, he heard that Apple was coming out with a tablet and were planning to include an ebook store, so he called Apple and managed to get through to the guy who was responsible for the iBookstore, who just happened to drive past Smashwords' office in Los Gatos every day on his way to Cupertino, so they arranged to meet. Mark was told that, if he could meet certain conditions, he could get Smashwords' books into the iBookstore when it launched. So he put the integration with Amazon on hold and focused on Apple. He did a deal with Bowker and acquired several thousand ISBNs so that their books could be assigned ISBNs (Smashwords hadn't bothered with ISBNs up till then but Apple required them). And when the iBookstore launched with the iPad on 2 April 2010, they had 2,200 Smashwords' books in the store.

Once he'd refocused the business on distribution, Mark found that sales began to grow. They were still losing money but the losses were declining. Nevertheless, Mark could see that he was going to run out of cash before the business was in the black – 'I estimated that we were maybe a year, year and a half, away from profitability, and so if we could just get enough runway to survive that long, then we would be self-sustaining.' He knew he needed help. 'So I went to my mom, like all self-respecting people do', and she lent him $200,000. This was enough to tide him over. Sales continued to grow and by September 2011 they were profitable.

Now Mark was in a position to hire someone other than a programmer. Up till then, he'd been doing everything else himself – business development, marketing, customer service and vetting. Vetting was the most time-consuming but it was crucial for the distribution deals that Smashwords needed in order to grow. When an author uploads a manuscript, it is instantly published at Smashwords, but not every book published at Smashwords is sent to retailers and libraries: only the books that are put in the 'premium catalogue' are sent to their retailer and library partners. So Mark and his team have to look at every book once it's been uploaded and decide whether or not it can be put in the premium catalogue. To a large extent, this is about formatting – 'You know, does it have first-line indents, are the paragraphs properly separated, are the fonts consistent throughout?' So not all uploaded books are like that? 'Oh god no! You'll have authors who have like 50-point font or they'll do all kinds of horrible things inside the book by accident.' The Smashwords style guide explains to authors what a well-formatted book should look like, but if you don't follow it carefully, or if you don't know how to use Word properly, you can end up with a mess.

It's not just about formatting, however. 'We're also looking for illegal content – so, like pornography with images or erotica with underage characters or, you know, over-the-top overt rape erotica, some of the taboo stuff we just don't allow.' They're also looking for content that infringes copyright. 'Some things are obvious. If someone uploads J. K. Rowling's book, we know it's not authorized, and so our vetting team catches those things and removes the content that's not allowed.' They're on the lookout for spam and generic content too, including private label rights content. 'There are services out there where you can pay about $30 a month and you'll be granted access to a massive database of thousands of articles. These are all generic, like 101 household cleaning tips, 101 weight loss tips – you know, generic topics. These services allow you to put your name on this content and try to sell it. We don't want these generic undifferentiated books.' All of this has to be detected and weeded out by the vetting team before titles can be moved into the premium catalogue and made available to retailers. This is a mammoth task – there are between 250 and 300 books going live every day on Smashwords' site. They can't read all of these books so they skim, looking for signs, 'signatures' as Mark calls them – 'You're looking for the sight or smell of something that you know is bad.' They look at the cover: 'Is it professionally designed or not?' They look at the English and at the book description: 'If they can't write a book description then they didn't write the book.' They look at the tags: 'If they use words like "under age" or "barely legal", that's a warning sign for us.' They also use automated systems to alert their vetting team to books that need greater scrutiny. 'And so we're good at this, and it takes a human to do this, to just spot what looks suspicious and then we can drill down and do text stream searches and identify stuff that doesn't belong.' Vetting all of this new content is a big job, even if you simplify the process by looking for signs and using automated systems – Smashwords has seven vetters on a staff of around twenty-five full-time employees, more than a quarter of its total staff.

So does this mean that Smashwords is functioning as a gatekeeper after all? A much less restrictive gatekeeper than a traditional publisher, to be sure, but a gatekeeper nonetheless? It's a touchy subject. 'We're agnostic, we don't want to be the editorial gatekeepers that judge the quality or the commercial viability of a book', explained Mark. 'But there are some standards that we are very strict about. If we view the content as illegal, then we want it off – those books have no right to be on our site, and no right to be anywhere, in our opinion.' But what about the borderline cases? Are there cases where the content is not strictly illegal, but where you judge it to be unacceptable in some sense? Yes, that happens, said Mark. 'There are multiple lines and some of the lines are fuzzy.' Barely legal erotica is a case in point:

> There's a lot of mainstream erotica that doesn't push any of these boundaries of acceptability. We love those authors and publishers, we love those books, we're happy to be associated with them. But it's when the authors and publishers try to push the limits of accept-ability. So, barely legal is one example of pushing the limits – they're right at the edge of acceptability. If we suspect that this publisher is really trying to target those people who are receiving titillation from a fantasy of sexual situations with a minor, even if they claim that all the characters are over 18 but it's not completely obvious, if we just feel like it's over the line, we're going to make a decision that we don't want to be associated with these publishers.

Books that are focused on rape and extreme violence can also cross the line. But it's not just extreme sexual content – it can be politically oriented material too. For example, they could be texts that are anti-Muslim or anti-Semitic: 'A lot of that stuff is more appropriate for a blog than a book because it's just someone's opinions and they're pulling stuff that they see online that matches the viewpoint that they want to get across', explained one of Mark's colleagues who joined the conversation at this point. If it's a real borderline case and the person who's vetting it is not sure, he or she may send it around to other members of the vetting team to get other people's opinions. On the rare occasions when the vetting team can't come to a consensus, the final decision is left to Mark. If they feel the work could be saved by changing the text, they'll put this to the author. 'Other times we'll just say we don't feel comfortable with this content – you know, this might be more appropriate for a blog. Or, please unpublish it, we're not a good partner for you.' Do these authors ever object? 'Yes, all the time. Sometimes we'll get quite angry responses and then they claim that we're censoring them.' But Mark and his colleagues are sanguine about this: 'We're looking to form professional relationships with professional writers. And if someone is going to deliberately try to subvert the rules or we feel is putting us or our retailers in jeopardy, especially if the author is being sneaky about it, we just don't want to work with them. Luckily these cases come up rarely, but we're always vigilant for them because there are a lot of unethical people out there.'

So the world of self-publishing is not without its gates. Platforms become gatekeepers even if they would prefer not to be because, at the end of the day, they care about their image and about the way they are seen by others: image matters, it is part of the symbolic capital that these organizations, like any organization in a competitive field, are engaged in creating, accumulating and protecting. But it is certainly true that the gates in self-publishing are far less restrictive than they are in the world of traditional publishing – there really is no comparison in terms of the strictness and selectivity of the gatekeeping. Self-publishing platforms like Smashwords are about as close as you can get to laissez-faire publishing. They are going out of their way to enable as many authors as possible to publish what they want, regardless of what those who run the platform might think of it. 'As the world's largest enabler of this tsunami of dreck (aside from Amazon), I'm very proud of that', said Mark, without the slightest compunction. 'There's the negative side of us enabling poor-quality books, but the other side of the coin is that we're enabling a greater diversity and a higher quality of books than ever before. We're giving every writer a chance and we're giving readers the chance and the freedom to decide what they want to read. Because I might think that a book is total dreck, that it is horribly written by any reasonable sense, but if that book brings satisfaction to a single person then that book is worthy.' On the relatively rare occasions when self-publishing gatekeepers shut the gates, they don't do so for commercial reasons – self-publishing organizations are not selecting titles they think will sell and turning down those they think won't, in the way that traditional publishers do. Rather, when self-publishing gatekeepers close the gates, they tend to do so for reasons that are technical (e.g., incorrect formatting), legal (the book could be in breach of the law) or normative (the content is regarded by the gatekeepers as offensive or unacceptable in some way, and/or as contrary to the ethos that they as an organization would like to cultivate and project).

Smashwords has remained profitable nearly every year since 2011, and by 2015 they were doing around $20 million in business – Mark had succeeded in turning an ebook-based self-publishing venture into a going concern. The growth in title output was staggering. In its first year of business, 2008, Smashwords released 140 titles; six years later, in 2014, 112,838 books were listed on Smashwords. By the end of 2019, it was listing 526,800 books published and live on its website, up 4 per cent from 507,500 the previous year,[9] and it was publishing 146,400 authors. From its small, unassuming office on the second floor of a two-storey wood-shingled building on a nondescript boulevard in Los Gatos, on the southern edge of Silicon Valley, Smashwords had quickly become one of the largest self-publishing platforms in the world. Mark had also earned a reputation as an outspoken and articulate proponent of self-publishing with a lively, informative and well-visited blog, and a strong advocate of the indie author movement, even going so far as to pen 'The Indie Author Manifesto'.[10] But all was not well on Los Gatos Boulevard. There were competitive forces emerging in the field of self-publishing that were casting a dark shadow over the future. Before we turn to these, let's go to the other side of Silicon Valley and retrace the emergence of another important player in the new wave of self-publishing.

---

[9] https://blog.smashwords.com/2019/12/2020.html. The net increase of 19,300 is less than the total number of new books released because it takes account of the churn in the catalogue as new books are released, some books are unpublished and some previously unpublished books are reactivated.
[10] https://blog.smashwords.com/2014/04/indie-author-manifesto.html.

A beautiful book of your own

Eileen Gittins was a keen photographer who happened to work in the technology industry. She'd been running web-based software businesses in San Francisco for twenty-five years and, as a personal project, she decided to photograph the fellow entrepreneurs with whom she'd built these businesses. There were about forty people in total and she wanted to give each of them a full set of all the photos. But it would take her a day to make a single set of prints – 'These were great friends and colleagues but I wasn't looking to spend the next year of my life making custom prints.' So she thought, 'I'll just make a book, I'll make it once and I'll get copies, right?' This was 2004–5. She started to investigate, and it turned out it wasn't so easy. With a market of only forty copies, no publisher was interested. They were only interested if they thought they could sell the book in sufficient volume to get a return on their investment. Eileen had stumbled upon a problem and, as a technology entrepreneur, she set about trying to figure out if she could use technology to find a solution. Instead of being guided by the traditional publishing question of how many copies of a book you need to sell to get a satisfactory return on your investment, she began to wonder if there was a different question. 'What if the question was: could we make money as a business on a book of one? And this became the whole basis of the company.' If she could develop a way of making money from a book if only a single copy was ever purchased, whether by the author or someone else, and if the price of that copy was not exorbitant, then this might open up a whole new way of thinking about publishing.

Eileen began pitching her idea to venture capitalists. As a former CEO of two other VC-backed companies, she was well connected in the technology world of San Francisco. Even so, it wasn't easy: 'This was 2005 and everything was going online, and here I am saying, "I've got this great idea, you guys. You know how everybody's using their digital cameras and camera phones to take photos? Well I'm going to take these mountains of digital content and I'm going to take them back into analogue and print them as books. Isn't that fantastic?" They thought I was a lunatic.' Despite the scepticism, she managed to raise $2 million and, in 2005, she founded Blurb. She hired a small team of software engineers and they set out to build the product platform that would enable them to build a business on a book of one.

234

Although Eileen was a technology entrepreneur and this was San Francisco in the early 2000s, heart of the high-tech start-up culture, Blurb was built on print. 'We started out in print because that was the hard thing for people to do. People could do a website, you could post your images on Flickr – screen-based sharing wasn't hard. The really hard thing was for mere mortals to make a book.' She had started the company from a personal problem she faced: she had her photos of her forty entrepreneur friends, high-quality digital photos, but she didn't want to send them digital files or a link to a website. She wanted to give them a book. 'That original book I was doing was really a gift and it's very hard to gift a link. I wanted to physically give somebody something, wrap it up with a bow and say, "hey, thank you, that was lovely".' Her intuition is that she was not alone: there were probably many people out there who would be keen to make their own books if only they could – if only there were some way to do it that wasn't too expensive and wasn't too complicated. And there would also be people out there who would like to make books in order to sell them – she wanted to help them too, why not? The challenge was to figure out how to enable people who are not designers and who know nothing about publishing to create a book – and not any book, but a truly beautiful book. Print and digital were just two different ways of creating books and sharing content – one wasn't necessarily better than the other, they were just different and they served different purposes. Print is like slow food, explained Eileen. Sometimes you're happy to grab a burger at Carl's Jr. – there are times when that is exactly what you want. But there are other times when you want to make a proper meal with the best ingredients, plan it carefully and eat it slowly, savouring the food. Digital is great for some purposes, but sometimes you want to turn the pages of a beautifully produced print book, linger on the page and gaze at the image (if it is an image) and return to it again and again. That doesn't mean that Blurb wouldn't do digital books too – they would. But they would have to wait until the devices were of sufficiently high quality to reproduce images to a high standard, a development that would eventually come with the iPad. In the meantime, given the kind of book she wanted to do, print seemed like the right place to start.

Like Mark, Eileen knew nothing about publishing before she realized that she had a need that was not being met, but, once she realized it, she did her homework. She quickly discovered that there were plenty of self-publishing firms out there already, the so-called vanity presses, but they didn't appeal at all. 'My reaction was to run away screaming, as fast as I could, and let me tell you why: because they were so horrible. They preyed on the aspirations of people who dreamed they had a bestselling book in them, and these people, of course, all want to believe that.' Like other start-ups in the new wave of self-publishing, Blurb was built on the explicit rejection of this older model: 'So when we came along, we said, OK, we don't want any of that. There will be no fee to use Blurb. All of our tools will be free, period. You may use any tool that we have on offer and the only time you will ever pay us a dime is if you decide to purchase a copy of your book. And, oh, by the way, the minimum units required for purchase is one. No stacks of books in your garage. None of that. One copy.'

There was something else that struck Eileen: both traditional publishers and vanity presses were very wordy. They all produced word-driven books. But for Eileen, with her background in photography, this seemed at odds with a world in which images were becoming ever more pervasive. In her eyes, the new lingua franca is images. Everyone is taking photos and communicating with images, whether by their smartphones or by Facebook, Flickr or Instagram. 'So I thought, why is it that books have so few images in them and why aren't they better designed and why don't they have color? Books today look like 1950s television. In what other part of our lives would we accept that?' It's not that people don't want images – they do. But the traditional models used by the publishing industry have made it difficult to include lots of images in books and to do it in a way that is both beautiful and affordable. But as a new start-up that was experimenting with new models, Blurb set out to do this differently. It would aim to create tools that would enable authors to produce beautifully illustrated books in colour. It would build its brand around photography and seek to establish a reputation for quality: 'We knew that if we could hit the quality mark – color management, bindery, all of that – for the population of people for whom the photograph was not a picture of the thing but the thing itself, the very work itself, then Tiffany would come calling someday. And, by the way, they did.'

Eileen and her colleagues built a suite of tools to enable people to create and design their books. They designed three tools for making a photo book. One tool, called Bookify, is an online bookmaking tool that enables someone to make a simple, straightforward book – 'say they have twenty images for an exhibition, one per page, caption on the left, hour and a half, we're good to go: hit the upload button, we're done. That's it. It's very simple bookmaking, no matter who you are.' A second tool, called BookSmart, is for books that are a little more complicated than one-image-per-page. It has templates and layouts into which you can drag and drop images and text – more complex than Bookify but still very straightforward. The third tool, BookWright, is designed for the person who has text and image and wants to do an ebook as well as print. It has templates and layouts but everything can be modified and customized, so it's very flexible. They also designed a tool for books that are straight text – a PDF-uploader that enables the author to write a book using, say, Word, output it as a PDF and upload it into a trade book. Finally, they developed a tool for Adobe InDesign users – that is, for use by graphic designers who already use Adobe InDesign ('the last thing we wanted to do was to force them to not use the tool they live with every single day'). They built a plug-in that enables them to work in Adobe InDesign and then upload directly from this application, and output to both print and ebook.

All the tools can be used for free. Blurb makes money by quoting the user a price for however many print copies they wish to order – whether it's 1 copy or 20 copies or 2,000 copies – and embedded in the print cost is a margin for Blurb, an internal mark-up on the actual cost of print manufacturing. 'Every time you buy a book, there's some profit margin that's built into that unit so that we make money on a book of one, going back to the very beginning of the business. Because if we couldn't make money on each and every copy, then we'd be just like a publisher who's dependent on volume and we'd be thinking, well, we better find titles that will sell through 10,000.' But if you're printing very small quantities – maybe only 1 copy – of a heavily illustrated book, isn't the cost of that 1 copy going to be exorbitant? 'It depends on what your intention is', explained Eileen. If you're a personal bookmaker and want to create a book that captures the birth of your first child and give it to your parents and in-laws, these books aren't going to be overly sensitive to price – 'They're somewhat price-sensitive, but if the book is $50 a copy, that is the best gift ever.' That's why they focused initially on the personal bookmaker: they could see the potential demand for a service that would enable people to create a high-quality, well-illustrated book that would be affordable but not cheap. On the other hand, if your intentions are more commercial, it gets trickier. In this case, the price per copy is going to be a very important consideration for the creator of the book. But if they're going to buy 300 or 500 or 1,000 copies or more, then the price per copy would come down quite a lot because they'd be printing a larger volume and using offset rather than digital printing.

Blurb launched at the end of March 2006 and by the end of the year they'd done around a million dollars in business. At roughly $30 a book, they'd sold over 30,000 units in the first nine months. Within eighteen months they were profitable, and they've remained profitable ever since. The volume of new titles that was coming through their system very quickly reached high numbers, especially at peak times like the run-up to Christmas when lots of people were making gift books: 'at peak volumes, we would see a new title come across our server every 1.5 seconds', recalled Eileen. By the end of 2010, just four or five years after they'd launched, they'd already published around 350,000 titles. When you consider that a small to medium-sized publisher might publish 200–300 new titles a year, and perhaps 1,000 or so new titles in four years, the volume of new-title output from this small self-publishing start-up was quite staggering. But most of this output remained invisible to the publishing world because most people who were using Blurb to publish their books didn't need or want an ISBN, since they were using their own distribution channels (or simply giving the book to family and friends).

Books that are self-published through Blurb can be purchased from the bookstore on the Blurb site: once Blurb receives the order, it prints the book and ships it directly to the consumer. But some authors wanted their books to be available on Amazon and at Barnes & Noble and other bookstores too, so Blurb set up relationships with Amazon and with Ingram, the Tennessee-based wholesaler and distribution group, which enabled them to put books self-published through Blurb into wider distribution networks. In the case of Amazon, Blurb simply registered as a third-party seller on Amazon, which enabled it to list Blurb books on Amazon's site, in return for which Amazon takes a percentage of sales. Authors can also choose to have broader distribution and to make their books available to other bookstores, both online and offline, in which case Blurb arranges for their books to be listed in Ingram's catalogues; bookstores can then order Blurb books through Ingram in the normal way, the order is forwarded to Blurb who prints and ships the copies to the bookstore and Ingram takes a fee as the distributor. In effect, Blurb operates as a print-on-demand supplier, fulfilling orders on demand and avoiding the need to hold physical stock.

Did Eileen worry about the content of what authors might self-publish on Blurb's site, especially given the emphasis on visual content and photography for which they were quickly becoming well known? 'When we first started the company, we were very concerned about this', said Eileen. 'We thought, oh my God, what

238

if there's all kinds of, you know, hate material, or offensive pornography or whatever?' But in practice this turned out to be much less of a problem than Eileen had feared. They didn't want to police the content and to get involved in trying to draw a line between nudity and pornography. They also didn't actually see the books that were flowing through their system: hundreds of books were coming in all the time and they didn't monitor and check them. What they did in practice was to work out an arrangement with their print partners whereby if they see anything that comes across their transom that they think is questionable, then they give Blurb a call. Then they both look at the file and make a decision. 'And I can comfortably say that in more than a decade there have been less than twenty such times in total when we went back to that customer and said, "I'm sorry, you'll need to get that printed somewhere else, we're not going to print that book." It's shockingly small.' Occasionally, someone will also contact Blurb and say that there's something on their website that seems inappropriate and they'll look at it and take it down if they agree. 'We'll contact the end user and we'll just say, "Look, we've had some concerns raised about this and with regret we're going to take it down."' But again, this happens rarely: 'In terms of what we feared, this has just not materialized.'

Although Blurb began life as a technology company and its main achievement was to build a user-friendly platform that enables authors and creators to self-publish their work, and although all the books that were self-published on Blurb's platform existed as digital files, the books themselves were, for the first few years of Blurb's life, published as printed books. This was understandable in 2006 and 2007, when the technology of ebook readers was just not good enough to command wide use, especially for the kind of visually rich illustrated book that was Blurb's stock-in-trade. But as the technology of reading devices improved and the iPad and other tablets appeared on the market, Blurb adapted their platform so that, from around 2010 on, they could output ebooks as well as print books. They also experimented with enhanced ebooks – 'we thought at the time that enhanced ebooks were going to be a bigger deal than they were, and we thought that that was the place where Blurb could add the most value in ebook land – a rich-media ebook. But people didn't want that, or at least not yet. They wanted the experience of a book without the distractions of all that other media.' Blurb offered authors and creators the option of enabling their books to be published as both ebooks and print books, but most people continued to buy print, which remains Blurb's core business.

But the business changed in other ways. In the early days, a lot of the people who were using Blurb were doing so for personal reasons: they were making books to commemorate an event, like a graduation or the birth of a child, or they were enthusiasts, like the amateur photographer or artist who was creating a book of the work they were doing. But with the rise of social media like Facebook, Instagram and Pinterest, there are many other options now for sharing images and photos with friends and family. This has raised the bar in terms of the level of motivation required to create a well-crafted book. Increasingly, the kind of person who uses Blurb is the creative professional and what Eileen calls the 'prosumer', the professional customer. 'A prosumer for us is somebody who's really an enthusiast', explained Eileen. 'They may be a cooking enthusiast or they may be writing a children's book for their children and maybe some other friends and family, but they're serious about it. Maybe it's a book for their business and obviously they're serious about that. So our growth now is all in the prosumer and creative professional categories – our business has shifted increasingly into those categories.' In fact, there are different kinds of individuals here. Some are people who are starting or running businesses and who are using books to try to grow their business – e.g., the photographer for whom the book is a kind of portfolio that can be given to prospective clients, or the person who is starting a cupcake business and wants to create a book of their favourite cupcakes to draw in more customers. Others are knowledgeable individuals with a particular skill or expertise who want to create a beautiful book and sell it in a serious way, in the hope that it will become successful and generate some revenue for them – and sometimes it does, as it did, for example, with Alder Yarrow.

Alder Yarrow is a professional designer in San Francisco who has a passion for wine. For some years, he had been blogging about wine on vinography.com, a wine blog that he started in 2004. Publishers had often approached him about writing a book but he hadn't taken up their invitations. But then he came up with the idea of doing a richly illustrated book that would explore, in words and images, the different individual flavours and aromas found in wine. Although Alder was himself a trained photographer, he knew that he couldn't take the kind of photographs that he would need for this book – his speciality was black and white landscape photography, not beautiful food photos in full colour. So he hooked up with a food photographer in San Francisco, Leigh Beisch, put together a book proposal and sent it to the publishers who had been keen to try to persuade him to write a wine book. But none of them were interested.

They thought it was going to be too big and too costly to produce, and they didn't see how they could sell enough copies to make it work. The gates to the traditional world of publishing were firmly shut. By sheer coincidence, Alder knew Eileen from another context and decided to discuss the idea with her: she was enthusiastic about the project and explained that the platform they had created at Blurb was particularly well suited to the kind of highly illustrated photography book Alder had in mind. The only problem was that it wasn't going to be cheap. Given the number of pages and format of the book he wanted to do, it would have cost Alder $197 per book using Blurb's standard one-off printing. Alder needed to get the price down to a much lower unit cost, something closer to $25, so that he could afford to sell the book at a reasonable price, and, to do that, he would need to get the print run up to 1,000 copies or more. But that would require an outlay of $25,000 and he couldn't afford to do that on his own. So he decided to launch a Kickstarter campaign, mainly because he knew some people who had run successful Kickstarter campaigns and they were able to give him some guidance and advice.[11] He set a goal of raising $18,000, with the aim of using the funds to pay for a professional copyeditor and designer and to produce a high-quality, beautifully illustrated 150-page hardcover book. Potential backers were invited to pre-order the book for $70 (or get a signed copy and an ebook for $150). As a well-known wine blogger, Alder was able to promote the project effectively through his own networks and social media, which is crucial for the success of a crowdfunding campaign. In the end, he raised $24,240 from 183 backers – more than enough to get the project off the ground. He wrote the book, Leigh did the photos, and they worked with a professional designer to lay out the internal design. Alder put in an order for 750 copies, sold them all and reprinted another 1,000, nearly all of which were sold. The book also won the Chairman's Prize at the Louis Roederer International Wine Writers' Awards in 2015. *The Essence of Wine* was a self-publishing success story that demonstrated not only how self-publishing platforms like Blurb could enable authors who had been rejected by traditional publishers to find alternative pathways to publication, but also how self-publishing could be harnessed to crowdfunding to overcome the financial obstacles that might be faced by authors who lack the backing of a traditional publisher.

By 2016, Blurb had become a major player in the world of self-publishing, with over 110 employees and turnover of around $85

---

[11] Kickstarter is discussed in more detail in chapter 8.

million. With a technology background and the instincts of an entrepreneur, Eileen had turned a local problem-solving task – how to make forty copies of a set of her photographs to give away to colleagues – into a multi-million-dollar business in under a decade. As with most success stories of this kind, there was an element of luck and the timing was good – Eileen saw the potential for a self-publishing platform of this kind early and she moved quickly to fill the gap. But she also made a number of strategic decisions that were crucial and that stood her and her company in good stead – four, in particular. First, she recognized early that the professional customer was going to be their main client and they focused on how to serve this customer well. Second, because they were serving primarily a professional customer, they knew that quality was going to be crucial. 'So we had to up our game in terms of quality, and when you do that, when you offer something of quality, people respond, they just do.' Third, given the kinds of books on which they were focusing, illustrated books with a lot of high-quality visual content, they made a wise but counter-intuitive decision to focus on print. It was counter-intuitive because they were essentially a technology start-up in Silicon Valley, and in that world at that time, the early 2000s, setting yourself up as a technology company that would enable people to produce beautiful printed books was about as far from the Valley zeitgeist as you could get. But Eileen sensed – rightly, as it turned out – that illustrated books had a longevity in print that was likely to be greater than books that were mainly text because, as she put it, 'the object itself has value. Not just the content in the book, the book itself as an object has value. It's beautiful, it's lovely to hold and to review. So when people have said, "Why are you focusing on illustrated books versus wordy books?" my answer has been: "Because in print, which is our hallmark, those books are going to be around for a very long time, they're not going to go away."' She bet on print and she won.

The fourth key decision that Eileen made was to get profitable as quickly as she could. Eileen was business savvy – Blurb wasn't the first company she'd started, and she knew very well how the world of venture capital worked. She raised VC money at the outset but she knew that markets could change quickly and she didn't want to find herself in a situation where she had to go back for more money and couldn't raise it – she knew that was a risk if the company remained unprofitable and dependent on subsequent rounds of VC fundraising:

So what we said was, we know it's kind of novel but we're going to build a business where people are going to open their wallets and give us money. It's not about eyeballs that we're going to convert and monetize later through some advertising scheme – no, we're going to create a very profitable business from a cash-flow point of view because we had no inventory to buy and no machinery to buy, we had a guaranteed revenue by taking a mark-up on printed books and the payment cycle back to our print partners was 30 or 45 days, so from a cash-flow point of view, it was a brilliant model. We didn't have to buy goods and manufacture anything because it was all on-demand. Our customers were bearing the costs of the book-making because they were paying for the book they just made.

The model worked: Blurb achieved profitability quickly and has remained profitable ever since. Of course, as a venture-backed company, the exit door is always open and the VCs may seek at any point to get a return on their investment, either by selling to a larger company or by going public through an IPO. But by developing a sound business model that ensured their profitability and gave them a strongly positive cash flow, they minimized the risk of running out of cash and finding themselves left out in the cold by a VC market that had moved on to other things.

As one of the larger players in the self-publishing space with a reputation for high-quality illustrated books, Eileen didn't worry overly about the competition. Many of the other self-publishing firms that had emerged in recent years were doing fiction with a particular emphasis on genre fiction – 'wordy books', as Eileen called them. In many cases, they were also focusing largely or even exclusively on ebooks. This was not the domain in which Blurb was operating, nor the kind of publishing for which it was known. This doesn't mean that Blurb had the field to itself – far from it. There are others, but in reality there's only one that matters. 'There's only one competitor', observed Eileen, 'and that's Amazon. They are the kahuna. But they're not in illustrated books. Amazon is really looking to enable the wordy book business, and when they go to print at all, it's soft cover, it's not hard cover and it's not color.' Not now, at any rate. 'But we're always watching what they're doing. They may change their mind at any time – I mean, they're Amazon.'

Amazon enters the self-publishing field

When Mark and Eileen were dreaming up their new ventures, the world of self-publishing was still largely associated with the vanity presses. Some new initiatives like Lulu had appeared, pioneering new models that were very different from the vanity presses, but there was no major player who had a dominant position in the field. Until, that is, Amazon decided to enter the self-publishing field.

In 2005, Amazon acquired two companies, BookSurge and CustomFlix Labs. BookSurge had been founded in 2000 by a group of writers as a self-publishing company using print-on-demand technology and offering authors a range of customized publishing packages. CustomFlix was launched in 2002 by four colleagues who wanted to make distribution easier for independent filmmakers by creating a DVD on-demand company. In 2007, Amazon changed the name of CustomFlix to CreateSpace, and in October 2009 Amazon merged BookSurge and CreateSpace under the CreateSpace name to form an integrated on-demand service that allowed authors, filmmakers and musicians to create and offer their works, including paperback books printed on demand, for sale on Amazon with no inventory, setup fees or minimum orders.[12] Parallel to and separate from these developments, Amazon also launched a self-publishing ebook platform as part of the roll-out of the Kindle in November 2007. The Kindle Digital Text Platform, as the Kindle self-publishing tool was initially called, enabled authors and publishers to self-publish ebooks by uploading their texts directly to Amazon and selling them in the Kindle Store with a minimum of fuss – all you needed was a title, an author's name, a text and a cover. The author/publisher selected a price – anything between 99¢ and $200 – and the book appeared, in a few hours, in the Kindle Store. Amazon kept 65 per cent of the receipts from any sales and passed 35 per cent to the author or publisher – a split that was later changed, in January 2010, to 30:70, where 30 per cent was kept by Amazon and 70 per cent was passed on to the author/publisher for sales in the US and the UK, provided certain conditions were met.[13] From January 2011, Kindle Digital Text Platform was renamed Kindle Direct Publishing (KDP) and the 70 per cent royalty option was extended to sales in Canada.

As Amazon quickly commandeered the lion's share of the ebook market, KDP became a very attractive option for authors seeking to self-publish their work. The Kindle Direct self-publishing tool was relatively straightforward to use, and once the text had been

---

[12] 'CreateSpace, an Amazon Business, Launches Books on Demand Self-Publishing Service for Authors', 8 August 2007, at www.createspace.com/Special/AboutUs/PR/20070808_Books.jsp. See also www.createspace.com/AboutUs.jsp.
[13] See chapter 5, p. 156.

uploaded, converted and made available in the Kindle Store, it could be sold internationally in what had become the overwhelmingly dominant ebook platform and distribution system. Moreover, if you were willing to go through the upload process with CreateSpace as well, then your book could be made available, more or less instantaneously and with excellent royalty rates, in both ebook and print formats through Amazon – a pretty compelling proposition from what was quickly becoming the largest retailer for both print books and ebooks in the English-speaking world. The only significant downside of KDP is that an ebook published through this platform would be available on Amazon's Kindle only, so if you wanted your book available on other devices, like the iPad, the Nook or Kobo, then you would have to self-publish with another platform and distributor as well. Savvy authors did just that: they self-published on KDP and also uploaded their book on Smashwords or Nook or the iBooks Store or another self-publishing platform and distributor. There was no reason not to self-publish on as many platforms as possible: if you were sufficiently motivated to do so and didn't mind the hassle, the more the better.

But then the configuration of options available to authors began to change. In December 2011, Amazon launched KDP Select, a new option that enabled KDP authors to earn a share of a new Lending Library fund and to gain access to various promotional tools and merchandising advantages, provided they made their books exclusive to the Kindle Store for at least ninety days.[14] Amazon would determine the size of the fund on a monthly basis – for December 2011, it was set at $500,000 – and the monthly payment for each KDP Select book would be based on that book's share of the total number of borrows of all participating KDP books in the Kindle Owners' Lending Library.[15] Authors who opted for KDP Select would be granted five free promotional days when they could give away their ebook for free. Their books would also be actively merchandised by Amazon – for example, appearing in Shopping Cart recommendations, 'More items to consider', 'Customers who bought

---

[14] 'Introducing "KDP Select" – A $6 Million Fund for Kindle Direct Publishing Authors and Publishers' (8 December 2011), at http://phx.corporate-ir.net/phoenix. zhtml?c=176060&p=irol-newsArticle&ID=1637803.
[15] The Kindle Owner's Lending Library is available to Kindle owners who are members of Amazon Prime. Prime members could select one free ebook per month from the Lending Library. When KDP Select was launched in 2011, Amazon Prime membership cost $79 a year and included reduced shipping rates and some free video streaming.

this item also bought x', etc. Authors could opt out after ninety days, but if they didn't opt out, their enrolment would renew automatically. The hitch was that a book that was enrolled in KDP Select had to be sold exclusively through the Kindle Store and could not be sold or distributed through any other retailer during this period. So, if a book were available through other retailers and distributors, such as the iBookstore, Barnes & Noble or Kobo, then the author/publisher would have to remove it from all those other retailers and distributors during the period when it was enrolled in KDP Select.

For many self-published authors, Kindle Select was an attractive option: it opened a new potential revenue stream, giving them access to a share of the fund set aside by Amazon for the Kindle Owner's Lending Library; it enabled them to use free promotions for a limited time period to stimulate sales; and it gave their books greater visibility on Amazon's site and in Amazon's promotional material. Moreover, given the huge market penetration of the Kindle and Amazon's overwhelming dominance in the ebook marketplace, it was a reasonable assumption on the part of many self-published authors that the increased revenue and visibility they would gain through KDP Select would compensate for any loss of sales they might suffer by removing their book from other retailers and distributors. The more dominant Amazon became in the ebook market, the more sense it made, in the eyes of many authors, to do everything you could to increase the visibility of your book on Amazon's site and maximize your sales on the Kindle, since the lion's share of your sales would come from the Kindle anyway.

For other self-publishing platforms, retailers and distributors, however, exclusivity on Amazon appeared less benign. In the eyes of some, this was a very aggressive move by the dominant player in the field that would make it much harder for other self-publishing platforms to retain their authors. Mark at Smashwords was particularly alarmed by what he perceived as a dangerous ploy by Amazon to destroy its competitors:

It was December of 2011, I remember it very clearly. I was on vacation at the time and the moment I saw that, I hated it and I blogged about it. I thought it was just really, really bad in terms of what it meant about the future. Because, in my view of the world, self-publishing is the future of publishing. Although self-publishing didn't really matter much to the overall publishing world in terms of sales, I had confidence that, in the long term, the power in publishing is going to transfer from publishers to authors – in my view of the

246

world, self-published indie authors are the future of publishing. And if Amazon creates this exclusive program that manages to attract a lot of authors, that eventually will starve all of Amazon's competitors of the most important authors – not only starve them of authors but also starve them of readers, because if readers want to read your book and it's only available on Amazon, eventually they're going to go shift all their book-buying habits to Amazon. So they're going to be leaving Barnes & Noble and Kobo and every other small or large retailer and moving their buying to Amazon. So they're going to starve out these other retailers and eventually put the other retailers out of business. That's the logical progression of how this will go if Amazon are successful with exclusivity.

Mark may be overstating the threat here – whether a pool, even a large pool, of self-published books is going to change consumers' buying habits as radically as he suggests may be doubtful. But Kindle Select probably did tip the balance of probability in favour of Amazon when it came to authors making decisions about where and how to self-publish their books and whether to take them down from sites other than Amazon's. 'When Amazon launched KDP Select in December of 2011, it was a shock to us because for the first time ever we saw thousands of books disappear from Smashwords overnight', said Mark. 'And we've seen that continue. So every single month thousands of books are removed from Smashwords to be enrolled in KDP Select. Thousands of books also come back to Smashwords – they cycle in and cycle out. But Amazon claims to have a renewal rate of about 95 per cent every three-month term. So what's happening is that authors are putting their books into KDP Select and leaving them there. It's like quicksand – once the authors get into it they never leave.' Or, as the founder of another self-publishing platform put it, using a different metaphor, 'Amazon is creating the world's biggest lobster trap: you go into Amazon and you never come out.'

Amazon strengthened its position further in July 2014 when it introduced Kindle Unlimited, the ebook subscription service that gives readers access to a large volume of ebooks and audio books for a monthly fee of $9.99.[16] Users who subscribe to Kindle Unlimited can read as many books as they like and keep them as long as they want, and they don't need to be members of Amazon Prime. For self-published authors, Kindle Unlimited feeds off KDP Select. Self-published authors can get their books into Kindle Unlimited only

---

[16] Kindle Unlimited is discussed in more detail in chapter 9.

by enrolling in KDP Select, and if their book is in KDP Select, then it will automatically be included in Kindle Unlimited. This means that they can't get their book into Kindle Unlimited unless they concur with the exclusivity requirements of KDP Select; it also means that if they don't want their book to be in Kindle Unlimited, then they have to remove it from KDP Select at the end of the enrolment period. In Mark's eyes, this only confirmed his worst fears. With KDP Select and Kindle Unlimited, Amazon were creating a funnel that would draw self-published authors into their proprietary Kindle environment, ring-fenced by the exclusivity conditions, where they would be entirely dependent on Amazon – enjoying its benefits, of which there were many, but also dependent on its good graces. Mark doesn't mince his words: 'My view of Amazon is that they're looking to turn all writers into tenant farmers tilling Amazon's soil. If Amazon owns the soil, the land, the access to the customers and if they own you, if 100 per cent of your income is dependent on Amazon's good graces, you have lost your independence and control: you're a tenant farmer.'

Mark's outspoken criticism of Amazon and the exclusivity of its KDP Select and Kindle Unlimited programmes sparked off a lively debate among self-published authors, some agreeing with Mark and some disagreeing – and, in some cases, strongly so. As many authors pointed out, the tenant farmer analogy breaks down as soon as you take account of the fact that KDP Select is optional – self-published authors don't have to join, and even if they do decide to give it a try, they can opt out at any point, once the ninety-day enrolment period is over. So if they're tenant farmers on Amazon's land, then they do have an exceptional degree of freedom for a tenant farmer: they're free to pack up and till the land elsewhere if it looks more attractive, or indeed to till both plots at the same time if they so wish, and if they choose to remain exclusively on Amazon's land, it may well be because they feel that Amazon's land is pretty fertile and it serves them well for the time being, whatever dangers may be lurking in the future.[17]

---

[17] This point was well made by one author who responded to Mark's blog post on KDP Select: 'While I understand your points, Mark, I have to disagree with your assessment that Amazon is forcing authors into this. The entire thing is optional. You can put none, one, some, or all of your books in this program. Yes, they become exclusive, but it is for a 90 day period. Two weeks before the renewal of enrollment, Amazon will send an email saying it will be renewed if you don't opt-out. It's not like this is a once-and-done decision, but you are painting it that way. I think this could be a great way for authors to promote their works. Personally, I've put three of my works in KDP Select, and yes, I removed them from Smashwords. Unfortunately, the

Whatever the merits and dangers of Amazon's exclusivity conditions, this acrimonious dispute underscores the fact that the world of self-publishing, just like the world of traditional publishing, has become a highly contested domain, with a large number of providers offering services of various kinds and different players vying for position, using whatever power they have at their disposal to attempt to strengthen or defend their position in the field. And this is a field in which, despite the proliferation of providers, one player has emerged as the overwhelmingly dominant force, capable of shaping and re-shaping the field to its advantage, often at the expense of smaller players who are seeking to carve out niches where they can flourish, or at least survive. For many authors aspiring to self-publish their work, this is bound to appear confusing – no less confusing than the world of traditional publishing, and perhaps even more confusing since you are unlikely to have an agent to whom you can outsource the job of trying to make sense of it all.

A spectrum of publishing services

Mark has a helpful way of seeing this: 'I view the publishing services marketplace as a spectrum', he says, grabbing a marker and drawing a line on a board (figure 7.1). 'At one end of the spectrum you've got full-service and at the other end is self-service', he explained. Traditional publishers are 'full-service' in the sense that they provide a full range of services to authors, from copyediting, typesetting, text and cover design, production and printing to marketing, sales and distribution, subsidiary rights and financial accounting – the full service. Once the book has been written, the author doesn't need to do very much (though in practice many may find themselves doing quite a lot). Traditional publishers may not think of themselves as service providers but that, in essence, is what they are (at least in part: Mark's model only captures part of what traditional publishers do, as they are also investors and risk-takers – more on this in chapter 12). 'At the other end of the spectrum you've got do-it-yourself', said Mark – those forms of self-publishing where authors

sales I get through Smashwords and who it distributes to are very, very, very low in comparison to Amazon, so I'm not during [*sic*] much harm to myself over the next 90 days. This is just my opinion, and I know other authors would completely disagree' – Smashwords (8 December 2011), at http://blog.smashwords.com/2011/12/amazon-shows-predatory-spots-with-kdp.html.

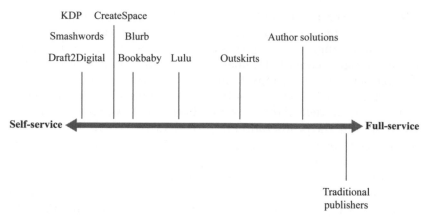

Figure 7.1　The spectrum of publishing services (1)

are self-publishers and the platform is self-service, where authors are expected to follow a series of steps to prepare their manuscripts for publication, design a cover and upload both manuscript and cover to the platform, then provide the metadata needed in order to publish the book. Smashwords and KDP are both at the self-service end of the spectrum. Between these two extremes are a plethora of other service providers who offer differing facilities and packages to authors – figure 7.1 mentions only a very small selection of these service providers to illustrate the differences, but there are many more. These providers also differ in terms of whether they are ebook-only, print-only or a combination of ebook and print – Smashwords and KDP are ebook-only, as is Draft2Digital, an Oklahoma-based self-publishing platform that was founded in 2012; CreateSpace is (or rather was[18]) a print-only provider, and Blurb is primarily print-based though it offers a variety of ebook options too, as we've seen; and companies like Lulu, Bookbaby, Outskirts and Author Solutions offer both ebook and print services. Whereas Smashwords, KDP, CreateSpace, Draft2Digital, Blurb, Bookbaby and Lulu tend to be near the self-service end of the spectrum, Author Solutions and its many imprints and divisions (AuthorHouse, iUniverse, Trafford

---

[18] CreateSpace and KDP were both set up as Amazon self-publishing services, one for print (CreateSpace) and the other for ebooks (KDP); they were run as parallel but separate services for a decade. In 2018, however, CreateSpace was merged into KDP. All CreateSpace books and account details were moved over to KDP, and KDP became a single, integrated Amazon platform for self-publishing print and digital books.

Publishing, Xlibris, etc.) and Outskirts tend to be closer to the full-service end, charging authors fees for the services they provide.

If we look at the publishing services spectrum in terms of the cost of these services to the author, then the spectrum begins to look more like a graph, explains Mark as he draws another figure on the board, with 'Service' on the x axis and 'Cost' on the y axis (figure 7.2).

In the lower left-hand corner of the graph, you have a set of providers that are low-service, low-cost – this is do-it-yourself self-publishing, like KDP, Smashwords, Draft2Digital, etc. As you move farther to the right, with self-publishers providing more services, the costs to the author tend to go up, with Author Solutions being among the most costly of the self-publishing service providers – and again, this is just a small selection of the many self-publishing service providers now available. Traditional publishers could be located in this graph in the lower right-hand corner: high service, low cost to the author (although the return to the author in terms of the author's royalty share tends to be significantly lower with traditional publishers than with self-publishing platforms). Indie authors who pride themselves on their independence and feel confident in

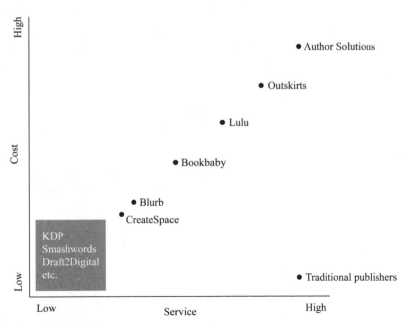

Figure 7.2   The spectrum of publishing services (2)

their ability to do it themselves tend to gravitate towards the lower left-hand corner of this graph, to that set of free, self-service platforms that provide authors with the tools to self-publish their work with no up-front charges and with relatively small commission fees on sales – these platforms are in the shaded box in the lower left-hand corner of the graph. Authors who prefer to let others do the work of publishing for them, or who lack the knowledge and/or the confidence to do it themselves, tend to gravitate towards the full-service end, either with a traditional publisher or with a self-publishing organization that offers various service and publishing packages to authors at a price – though in the eyes of indie authors who are proudly independent, self-publishing service providers like Author Solutions are anathema ('no self-respecting indie author uses them', said one well-informed commentator on the world of self-publishing).

If this picture wasn't complicated enough already, the boom in self-publishing has spawned a substantial secondary industry of support services that exist as a shadow economy alongside the self-publishing platforms. In practice, the various publishing services that are provided by full-service publishers, whether traditional publishers or the full-service self-publishing organizations like Author Solutions, have been unbundled and turned into discrete services that are offered to authors on an à la carte basis by freelancers and small companies. Essentially, these unbundled author services fall into three categories: editorial services, design services (including text design, jacket design and manuscript preparation) and marketing services (including publicity). Authors may find themselves directed to these support services by a self-publishing platform, many of which provide a list of recommended support services, or they may turn to services that have been recommended by friends or colleagues. Some freelancers work on their own as self-employed editors or designers – in some cases, doing this in their evenings and weekends while they hold down a full-time job at a traditional publishing house; in other cases, using it as a way to earn a living while they pursue their ambition to be a writer. Many freelancers also rely on publishing service agencies, such as New York Book Editors or London-based Reedsy, to provide them with a steady flow of work. Agencies like these operate as hubs that connect authors to freelancers; authors contact the agency, the agency assesses their needs and then outsources the work to suitably qualified and vetted freelancers, and the author's payment is then split between the agency and the freelancer.

New York Book Editors was set up in 2013 by Natasa Lekic. Having previously worked as an editor at a small nonfiction publisher called Atlas & Co., Natasa appreciated the importance of good editing, and when she left Atlas & Co. she decided to set up her own company offering editorial services to authors who were planning to self-publish. There was a lot of talk about self-publishing at the time, and Natasa thought there might be some demand from authors for the kind of editorial services she could provide. But she didn't want to do the editing herself – she'd edited a couple of books at Atlas & Co. and she didn't feel that she had the skill set and talent to do this well. So she wanted to bring on board some of the other editors with whom she'd worked. 'The idea was that we were going to work with self-publishing authors who wanted to follow a very similar editorial process to that of traditional publishing.' Authors were offered different packages, depending on the type of editing they needed and wanted. The 'structural edit' option would deal with big questions concerning the structure of the text, the plot, character development, etc.; the author would get an editorial letter or memo that commented on structural issues and offered suggestions about how to remedy the weaknesses and improve the text (and, for an extra fee, this could be followed up with a one-hour phone call). The 'line edit' option would involve going through the text line by line, paying attention to the clarity and flow of language from sentence to sentence and paragraph to paragraph. A more straightforward 'copyedit' would involve correcting the grammar, spelling, punctuation, etc. The different options were priced differently and varied by word count. Authors looking to get their text edited would complete a form and submit a synopsis and some sample material, and Natasa would decide which projects to take on for editing and, given the state of the manuscript, which package would be appropriate. Natasa then outsourced the work to a freelance editor and divided the fee with the freelancer. Most of her freelancers were trained in traditional publishing houses and were looking for some extra work to do on the side, or were thinking of leaving the company and freelancing full-time – and, in some cases, they had actually made that move and had fully become part of a flourishing shadow economy of publishing services.

While Natasa set up New York Book Editors thinking that she would be providing editing services primarily to authors who were planning to self-publish, in practice it didn't work out quite like that. She did get submissions from plenty of authors who were planning to self-publish, but the largest proportion of submissions came from authors who wanted to publish traditionally – roughly speaking, 50 per cent wanted to publish traditionally, 25 per cent wanted to self-publish, and the remaining 25 per cent were not sure which way to go and were keeping an open mind. Many of the authors who wanted to publish traditionally were hoping to get an agent and a book contract but had been advised, or had realized themselves, that their manuscript needed more work, and their chances of getting an agent and securing a good deal would be improved significantly if their manuscript were in better shape. Hence, it made sense to them to get in touch with New York Book Editors and invest in an editing package, even if it was unclear whether this would enable them to secure the kind of publishing deal they were dreaming of.

Reedsy was launched in London in 2014 by Emmanuel Nataf, Ricardo Fayet, Matthew Cobb and Vincent Durand. Unlike Natasa, the co-founders of Reedsy had not themselves worked in the publishing industry: Emmanuel and Ricardo had graduated from business school in Paris and they were looking for an opportunity to start a business. They knew that Amazon had made self-publishing very easy with KDP but they also saw that many of the books that were being self-published were not well edited or well designed. So they came up with the idea of creating an online marketplace to connect authors intending to self-publish their books with editors, designers and marketers who could help them create and produce their books to a higher standard. They raised some funding through Seedcamp, a European seed fund based in London, and they built and launched a platform that functioned as an open marketplace that would enable indie authors to access freelance publishing talent. While other marketplaces of this kind existed online, like Upwork and PeoplePerHour, Emmanuel and his colleagues wanted to create a marketplace that was tailored to publishing and would attract good editors. They didn't want to create a marketplace where everyone would get into a bidding war and only the cheapest people would win, as that would not attract the best editors. So they devised a system where the author could select up to five people they would like to reach out to – say, for editorial work – and invite them to bid; if two of those decline to bid for whatever reason – perhaps they're too busy – then the author can reach out to two more. Once the editors have submitted their bids, the author can chat with each of them before deciding which one to choose. This creates a space of limited competition that avoids a generalized auction in which the cheapest price would tend to prevail, while also giving authors the chance to interact with a selected number of freelancers before making a decision.

For an online marketplace like this to work, the clients (in this case, the authors) have to have confidence that the services they will be purchasing will be the real thing and will be good value for money – in other words, that it's not a scam. So vetting the freelancers is a key part of what Reedsy does. They invite anyone wishing to offer their services on Reedsy to fill in a profile that covers their qualifications, genres and languages they specialize in, work experience, portfolio, etc., and they then check all of this. Every time they list a genre, like fantasy or romance, they have to have at least one book in the portfolio that matches that genre. They make sure that what they say about their work experience correlates with the books in their portfolio. And if they have any doubts, they look at the acknowledgements in the books to see if they're mentioned there. It's a pretty thorough process and only 3 per cent of the people offering their services end up being listed on Reedsy. 'There are a lot of self-proclaimed editors, designers and people offering services to authors out there that aren't up to our standards, which are pretty high', explained Ricardo, one of the co-founders. They would expect an editor to have at least five years of experience and to have edited at least half a dozen books – not necessarily books published by traditional publishers, though that helps, but if they haven't worked for a traditional publisher, then they would expect some of their books to have been bestselling titles and to have had really good reviews, and lots of them, on Amazon.

An author who wants to find a freelancer through Reedsy fills in a form where they specify what they're looking for, uploads a chapter or two or the complete manuscript, checks out the freelancers who meet their specifications and selects up to five, inviting them to submit a bid. The author considers the bids and interacts with the bidders and then decides which one to accept. They agree a timeframe and a payment plan and the work begins. Reedsy takes a commission of 10 per cent from each party in the transaction – 10 per cent is deducted from what the author pays and 10 per cent is deducted from what the freelancer receives, so Reedsy takes 20 per cent of the total payment as its share. So if the editor is charging a fee of, say, $1,000, the author will pay $1100, $100 of which will be kept by Reedsy, and the editor will receive $900, with Reedsy deducting $100 from the editor's fee. Reedsy has its own messaging interface where the interaction between author and freelancer takes place so that all communication takes place on their platform and in their system; this ensures that Reedsy has a full record of the interactions between authors and freelancers in the event that a dispute arises, which does happen from time to time. Keeping everything in their system also reduces the risk that authors and freelancers might drift away from Reedsy and form direct collaborations on future projects.

While Reedsy began with the aim of creating a marketplace to help indie authors access freelance publishing services, their platform has attracted other clients too – both authors hoping to find a traditional publisher for their book, and traditional publishers themselves. By early 2020, Reedsy were overseeing around 1,000 new collaborations every month. About 70 per cent of the collaborations were for editorial services, 15 per cent for design and the rest divided between marketing, publicity and ghost-writing. Around half of the authors were intending to self-publish their books and around 30 per cent were looking to find a traditional publisher, while the remaining 20 per cent were keeping their options open. Some traditional publishers were also coming to Reedsy to find freelancers, and Reedsy was developing partnerships with some self-publishing platforms like Blurb whereby Blurb would recommend Reedsy to authors, and Reedsy would make it easy for authors to export their finished book to Blurb – a collaboration of self-publishing intermediaries. Although they had no background in publishing, Reedsy's co-founders had seen how the explosion of self-publishing was creating a need among an expanding population of indie authors for professional publishing services that would no longer be provided by traditional publishing houses and they created an effective online marketplace where these services could be bought and sold, a marketplace which helped authors to find suitable and well-qualified freelancers and helped freelancers find a steady stream of work.

For those who work in this shadow economy, freelance work can provide a viable livelihood and can be professionally rewarding too. Caroline had been working as an editorial assistant for two and a half years at one of the large New York publishing houses but found it frustrating and unfulfilling. She was mainly managing projects for a more senior editor and she rarely got the opportunity to edit manuscripts herself – and even when she did, she didn't feel that this was regarded as an important part of the job ('editing was no-one's priority, it was something you did at home, you absolutely had no time for it in the office'). She'd done some freelance editing in her spare time and enjoyed it, so she knew this was an option. After two and a half years, Caroline decided to quit her job at one of the Big Five publishers and go it alone. Some authors were finding her through the Editorial Freelancers Association – a not-for-profit organization based in New York that offers a job-listing service where authors can submit a job for posting. But Caroline had also heard about New York Book Editors and Reedsy and she signed up as a freelancer with both. They provided her with a steady flow of work, and within eighteen months she was in a position where she could afford to be more selective and turn work away. She was earning more than twice as much as she'd been earning as an editorial assistant and she was making plans to incorporate so that she could take on more private clients and subcontract some work to other freelancers, turning herself into an editorial services agency of her own. This would enable her to build a business while at the same time continuing to work with authors on their manuscripts, which is what she enjoys. 'I edit more now than I think I ever would have otherwise, and I love that. At the end of the day, that's what I enjoy doing', said Caroline.

> Even as my business grows and I end up becoming more business-oriented, I still get to edit however much I want to edit. And there's something about working directly with authors and working directly with the text and making it the best it can be without having to worry so much about commercial things. I take into consideration things like marketing and audience and all of that, but there was a difference in the publishing house when you have sales breathing down your neck where they don't care really about the story, they're just like, how many copies are you going to sell. I understand that business mentality but there's something about caring first about the manuscript, and then crafting that to be something that will sell or get picked up or anything like that.

Caroline is just one of thousands of people who are now working in the shadow economy of publishing services – some, like Caroline, earning a good living as a full-time freelancer; some supplementing their income from another job by doing some freelancing in their spare time; others earning just enough to get by while they pursue their ambition to be a writer or some other goal. Of course, traditional publishers have long relied on a shadow economy of freelancers, especially when it comes to tasks such as copyediting, proofreading, indexing and cover design – there is nothing new about this. Moreover, a substantial proportion of the authors who turn to services like New York Book Editors and Reedsy and who hire freelance editors are hoping to publish with traditional publishers, as we've seen. But there can be no doubt that the rise of self-publishing platforms and the enormous expansion of the range of opportunities available to authors to self-publish their work has fuelled the growth of the shadow economy of publishing services, greatly increasing the pool of authors who are looking for (and willing to pay for) help to revise and improve their texts and to format, design and market their books.

The rise of self-publishing platforms and the proliferation of publishing services associated with this has undoubtedly altered the landscape of publishing in the early twenty-first century – self-publishing is not new, but these developments are qualitatively different from anything that came before. Together, they have created an entirely new ecology of self-publishing that exists alongside the world of traditional publishing, distinct from it but overlapping with it in multiple and complex ways. In this new ecology, the author who decides to self-publish her work must now decide how to self-publish it, which platform to use, whether to avail herself of the various publishing services available and, if so, whether to do this by reaching out directly to freelance editors, designers and marketers/publicists or to go through a publishing services intermediary (or PSI) like New York Editors or Reedsy (figure 7.3). An author who wants to take the low-cost, do-it-yourself route can decide how much assistance he wants or needs and make his own arrangements with editors, designers and marketers/publicists – or make no arrangements at all, dispensing with these services and simply uploading his manuscript as it is to a self-publishing platform like Smashwords or

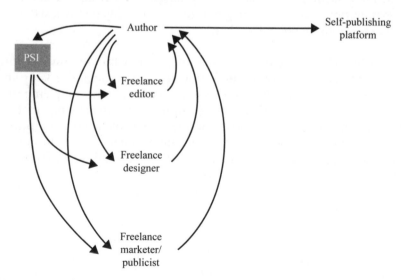

Figure 7.3   The new ecology of publishing services

258

KDP, with minimal professional input from others. Alternatively, an author who wants some professional input but doesn't know who to ask for help can use a publishing services intermediary to give her some vetted options and help her make an informed decision. The author who wants to self-publish and wants some professional input but doesn't want the hassle of trying to arrange it himself can choose a self-publishing platform that offers publishing services packages to authors, and he can buy the package that will provide the kind of input he thinks he needs.

While the explosion of self-publishing has created an expanding shadow economy of publishing services that exist alongside the self-publishing platforms and is largely independent of the world of traditional publishing – even if these worlds overlap and interact in complex ways – we still have no real sense of how big the world of self-publishing is. What scale are we talking about here? Do we have any way of gauging the size of this new world of self-publishing that has emerged in the wake of the digital revolution?

The hidden continent

In fact, it is surprisingly difficult to get an accurate measure of the size of the new world of self-publishing: self-publishing is the hidden continent of the publishing world. Beginning in 2012, the bibliographic service Bowker produced a series of reports that tried to estimate the output of self-publishers in the US from 2007 to 2018.[19] The reports show a steep and sustained growth in self-published books over this time period, with the overall total number of both print and ebooks increasing from 152,978 in 2010 to 1,677,781 in 2018 – an increase of elevenfold in eight years. However, while these reports are a useful indicator of the rapid growth in this sector, they are seriously limited as an account of the world of self-publishing, for two important reasons. First, Bowker's figures do not show the number of 'new books' or 'new titles' published in these years: they show the number of ISBNs registered in the Bowker Books in Print database, and published or distributed in the US. However, as noted

---

[19] For recent reports, see 'Self-Publishing in the United States, 2010–2015, Print vs. Ebooks' (Bowker, 2016); 'Self-Publishing in the United States, 2011–2016, Print and Ebook' (Bowker, 2017); 'Self-Publishing in the United States, 2012–2017, Print vs. Ebooks' (Bowker, 2018); 'Self-Publishing in the United States, 2013–2018, Print and Ebooks' (Bowker, 2019) – all at www.bowker.com.

earlier, authors and publishers may register several ISBNs for a single 'book' or 'title', one for each format – there is not necessarily a one-to-one correspondence between 'a book' and 'an ISBN'. For example, a publisher will commonly assign one ISBN for the print hardback edition, another ISBN for the print paperback edition, and separate ISBNs for each ebook file format (ePub, Mobi, PDF, etc.) – hence, one new title may have multiple ISBNs linked to it. While this is common practice among publishers, the extent to which self-publishing authors might use more than one ISBN for a book they are publishing is not clear, and some indie authors don't bother acquiring an ISBN at all: why bother acquiring an ISBN if you're self-publishing a book so that you can give copies to family and friends?[20] What the Bowker figures show are the number of new ISBNs registered by self-publishers and service providers, not the number of new books or new titles that were self-published in these years.[21]

The second important reason why the Bowker report is limited is that these figures exclude one of the largest self-publishing platforms of them all – Amazon's KDP. This is because KDP doesn't require ISBN registration – Amazon assigns its own unique ten-digit identifier, which they call an ASIN (Amazon Standard Identification Number), which is unique to the ebook and serves as the identification number for the ebook on Amazon. Hence, a large volume of self-publishing activity is not captured by Bowker's figures – and not just the books self-published on KDP, but any books self-published without an ISBN.

These important qualifications notwithstanding, let us look briefly at some of Bowker's figures. Tables 7.1, 7.2 and 7.3 summarize

---

[20] Bowker charges to supply ISBNs to indie authors – it can be as high as $125 for a single ISBN, or $250 for a pack of 10. Publishing houses routinely buy 1,000 ISBNs or more at greatly reduced rates of $1 or less per ISBN, so indie authors can often acquire an ISBN for $1 or for free from the self-publishing platform. But, even then, some indie authors don't bother, as you don't actually need an ISBN to self-publish your work on many platforms.

[21] Porter Anderson took up the issue of the discrepancy between ISBNs registered and titles published with Beat Barblan at Bowker. He asked him how many actual books, i.e. individual titles, were represented by the 727,125 ISBNs accounted for by self-publishers in 2015. Barblan said that the 727,125 ISBNs represented 625,327 individual titles. If this is an accurate calculation, then it would mean that most self-published authors register only 1 ISBN for their work. For a more detailed discussion of these issues, see Porter Anderson, 'Bowker Now Cites at Least 625,327 US Indie Books Published in 2015', *Publishing Perspectives* (October 4, 2016), at http://publishingperspectives.com/2016/10/bowker-indie-titles-2015-isbn/#.WGaOf_krKUk.

Table 7.1 ISBN output for US self-publishing platforms, 2010–2018: print books

Name	2010	2011	2012	2013	2014	2015	2016	2017	2018	% increase 2010–2018
CreateSpace/ Independently Published[1]	35,686	58,857	131,456	187,846	293,436	425,752	517,705	929,290	1,416,384	3689.02
Lulu	11,681	25,461	27,470	40,895	45,761	46,972	41,907	36,651	37,456	220.66
Blurb	0	0	0	752	15,943	31,661	21,365	19,223	17,682	n/a
Author Solutions[2]	11,915	18,847	18,354	28,290	25,529	20,580	19,270	15,667	16,019	33.44
Independent Publisher Services[3]	3,689	3,272	2,566	2,115	2,037	2,289	2,150	2,126	2,245	–39.14
Outskirts	1,576	1,489	1,824	1,931	1,802	1,968	1,523	1,157	1,186	–24.75
Small Publishers[4]	19,081	24,366	29,755	33,948	36,131	39,698	43,755	45,649	44,426	132.83
Totals[5]	114,215	158,972	235,639	305,160	429,240	577,213	657,062	1,060,821	1,547,341	1254.76

[1] Includes CreateSpace and KDP Print, both part of Amazon; Amazon merged CreateSpace into KDP in 2018.
[2] Includes the many different divisions and imprints of Author Solutions (Xlibris, AuthorHouse, iUniverse, etc.).
[3] Independent Publisher Services is a division of Bar Code Graphics that provides services and products to self-publishers. Among other things it facilitates single ISBN assignments with a publisher's name listed as the registrant.
[4] Small Publishers are those who have produced 10 or fewer ISBNs in total.
[5] Totals include ISBNs for many other self-publishers not listed in this table.
Source: Bowker, 'Self-Publishing in the United States, 2010–2015' and 'Self-Publishing in the United States, 2013–2018'.

Table 7.2 ISBN output for US self-publishing platforms, 2010–2018: ebooks

Name	2010	2011	2012	2013	2014	2015	2016	2017	2018	% increase 2010–2018
Smashwords	11,787	40,614	90,252	85,500	112,483	97,198	89,041	74,290	71,969	510.58
Lulu	8,597	12,544	30,061	33,892	37,126	38,465	33,336	30,747	30,021	249.20
Blurb	51	264	2,091	2,090	1,531	1,527	1,592	1,433	1,416	2676.47
Author Solutions[2]	11,915	18,847	18,354	16,627	8,635	4,007	11,018	10,304	10,565	–11.33
Independent Publisher Services[3]	132	285	306	380	344	603	389	335	387	193.18
Small Publishers[4]	5,328	12,528	13,458	12,706	11,161	10,645	10,451	10,749	14,476	171.70
Totals[5]	38,763	88,238	158,493	156,278	173,156	154,236	148,769	131,524	130,440	236.51

Table 7.3 ISBN output for US self-publishing platforms, 2010–2018: ebooks and print books

Name	2010	2011	2012	2013	2014	2015	2016	2017	2018	% increase 2010–2018
CreateSpace/ Independently Published[1]	35,686	58,857	131,456	187,846	293,442	425,752	517,707	929,295	1,416,384	3869.02
Smashwords	11,787	40,614	90,252	85,500	112,483	97,198	89,041	74,290	71,969	510.58
Lulu	20,278	38,005	57,531	74,787	82,887	85,437	75,243	67,398	67,477	232.76
Blurb	51	264	2,091	2,842	17,474	33,181	22,957	20,656	19,098	37347.01
Author Solutions[2]	41,304	52,548	49,885	44,917	34,164	24,587	30,288	25,971	26,584	–35.64
Independent Publisher Services[3]	3,821	3,557	2,872	2,495	2,381	2,892	2,539	2,461	2,632	–31.12
Outskirts	1,576	1,489	1,824	1,931	1,802	1,968	1,523	1,157	1,186	–24.75
Small Publishers[4]	24,409	36,894	43,213	46,654	47,292	50,343	54,206	56,398	58,902	141.31
Totals[5]	152,978	247,210	394,132	461,438	602,369	731,449	805,831	1,192,345	1,677,781	996.75

the ISBN output for a small selection of the leading self-publishing platforms for print books (table 7.1), ebooks (table 7.2) and print and ebooks combined (table 7.3) for the years 2010–18; the figures also give the total output for print books and ebooks, where the totals include the output of many other self-publishing platforms (some of which may be very small) that are not listed in these tables.[22] Table 7.1 shows that Amazon's CreateSpace / KDP Print is far and away the leading self-publishing platform for print: in 2018, more than 90 per cent of the ISBNs issued for self-published books in print were accounted for by Amazon's self-publishing platform, whereas in 2010 Amazon's share was just over 30 per cent. Lulu, Blurb and the combined imprints of Author Solutions account for significant numbers of ISBNs but they are dwarfed by Amazon's platform. Table 7.2 shows that Smashwords is the leading self-publishing platform for ebooks in terms of numbers of ISBNs – but here, Amazon's share of the self-published ebook market doesn't appear because KDP doesn't require ISBN registration. The number of ebooks self-published on Amazon's KDP platform is undoubtedly much greater than the number self-published through Smashwords, although exactly how much larger is known only to Amazon.[23] The combined figures for print books and ebooks show a similar pattern: CreateSpace well out ahead at the top of the table (and no doubt KDP would be there too, well out ahead, if we had the numbers), followed by Smashwords, Lulu, Blurb and the combined imprints of Author Solutions. Although there are many self-publishing platforms and companies, more than 95 per cent of ISBNs are accounted for by just five organizations – and if KDP were included, the concentration would be even greater. CreateSpace, Smashwords, Lulu and Blurb all display substantial growth over this time period in terms of ISBNs,

---

[22] For the full listings, see 'Self-Publishing in the United States, 2010–2015' and 'Self-Publishing in the United States, 2013–2018'. Where there are discrepancies in the two reports for the overlapping years of 2013, 2014 and 2015, I've used the numbers in the later report. The most recent Bowker report lists a total of forty-five self-publishers, plus fifteen separate imprints and divisions of Author Solutions, but many smaller self-publishers and some important self-publishing platforms like Draft2Digital are missing.

[23] One analyst of the US book market who has spent a lot of time trying to ascertain Amazon's numbers, using the surprisingly rich data available on their site, estimated in 2017 that about a million new ebooks were going into KDP every year. There is no way of knowing how accurate this estimate is, but with more than 1.4 million ISBNs allocated to Amazon's self-publishing platform for print in 2018, the figure of a million new ebooks being self-published on KDP every year is not implausible – indeed, the actual number could be significantly higher.

though Author Solutions and Outskirts show declining numbers of ISBNs. In the case of CreateSpace, however, the growth is continuous, it rises year on year, whereas with Smashwords, Lulu and Blurb, the numbers peak around 2014–15 and decline somewhat after that. The category of 'Small Publishers', by which Bowker means those self-publishers who have produced ten ISBNs or fewer during this period (these may be authors who self-publish their own books and register the ISBN in their name or the name of their company), also account cumulatively for a substantial number of ISBNs (58,902 in 2018) and display significant growth (up 141 per cent since 2010). The overall upward trend is clear, with the total number of ISBNs issued to self-publishers rising more than tenfold between 2010 and 2018, mostly to the benefit of Amazon and the more do-it-yourself self-publishing platforms like Smashwords, Lulu and Blurb, and at the expense of the older self-publishing imprints associated with author charges and vanity press publishing.

In terms of the sheer volume of output, the numbers and the growth are staggering – especially when you bear in mind that these numbers are only capturing part of the self-publishing activity taking place. But these are generic numbers: can we say anything about the *kinds* of books that are being published and sold? Mark at Smashwords analysed their retail sales over a twelve-month period from March 2015 through February 2016, breaking down their sales by category of book, and made the results available on his blog;[24] and although we can't generalize on the basis of one platform (the kinds of books self-published could well vary from platform to platform), Mark's breakdown is an illuminating indicator. Smashwords' sales are dominated by fiction – 89.5% of its sales are works of fiction – and the dominant category by a considerable margin is Romance: Romance (including Young Adult Romance) accounts for around 50% of all its sales. Erotica is also a significant category – it accounts for around 10%. Nonfiction – and this includes all categories of nonfiction – accounts for only 11% of sales. In terms of the bestselling titles, Romance is overwhelmingly dominant. Figure 7.4 gives the breakdown by category of Smashwords' top 200 bestsellers. Romance accounts for 77% of the sales of the top 200 bestsellers, while Young Adult accounts for another 11% – together, Romance and Young Adult account for 88% of the sales of the top 200 bestsellers. Nine of the top 10 bestsellers are Romance titles, as are

---

[24] https://blog.smashwords.com/2016/04/2016survey-how-to-publish-and-sell-ebooks.html.

**200 Bestselling Titles, percentage of sales from each category
(YA Romance in Romance)**

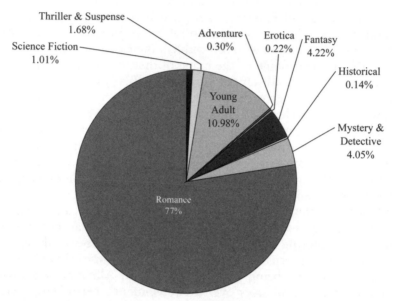

Figure 7.4   Breakdown by category of top 200 bestsellers at Smashwords

78% of the top 50 bestsellers. This is a fiction-heavy, Romance-heavy publishing platform.

Many outside observers might suspect that self-publishing is a world where there is a huge volume of output in terms of new titles being published but highly skewed outcomes in terms of sales, with a very small number of titles doing well and the vast majority selling in very small numbers – they would not be altogether wrong. This is a world where the power law prevails and where the long tail of slow-selling titles is very long indeed. Some of the data provided by Mark at Smashwords show this very clearly.[25] Half of all the revenue generated by the sales of Smashwords' books in 2013 was earned by the top 1,000 titles, which accounted for 0.36% of their published titles; the other half of the revenue was distributed among the remaining 274,000 titles. Figure 7.5 shows the sales distribution

---

[25] Mark Coker, 'Smashwords Survey Helps Authors Sell More eBooks' (September 2013), at https://blog.smashwords.com/2013/05/new-smashwords-survey-helps-authors.html.

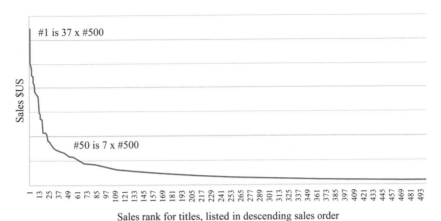

Figure 7.5   Sales distribution curve for top 500 bestsellers at Smashwords, 1 May 2012–31 March 2013

curve for the top 500 bestselling titles at Smashwords between 1 May 2012 and 31 March 2013. This displays the classic power law curve, where a small number of titles on the left account for a large volume of sales and the curve falls off very quickly as you move down the ranking of titles. The number one bestselling title earned 37 times the revenue earned by the title ranked number 500, and the title ranked number 50 earned 7 times the revenue earned by the title ranked 500. With 275,000 titles on the list at this time, the long tail extended 550 times further to the right – a very long tail indeed. A similar analysis for 2016 showed that the highest-earning author at Smashwords earned 73 times more than the author ranked number 500, and the author ranked number 50 earned 9.5 times more than the author ranked 500. Mark declined to provide values for the vertical axis, so we don't know how much any of these titles or authors are earning. But even without actual values, the power law curve demonstrates that, for this particular self-publishing platform (and it is unlikely that other platforms behave very differently), a small number of titles and authors account for a large proportion of sales, and the vast majority of self-published books sell in very small quantities (if at all).

The data from Smashwords give us an illuminating insight into the hard realities behind the mystique of self-publishing. The rise of self-publishing is a truly transformational change, opening up the opportunity to publish to anyone who can write a text and follow a few relatively straightforward steps to format and upload their text to a suitable platform, but this remains a world of highly skewed outcomes, where a very small number of authors and books can become very successful but where the vast majority will become part of an extremely long tail. Of course, for many authors, this may not matter: their reasons for writing and publishing their work may have nothing to do with commercial success. For them, all that matters is that the work is out there in the public domain, available to be read by others if they wish to read it, and they may be happy to give it away for free. But this might also be interpreted to mean that, in terms of the broader impact of self-publishing, it remains a marginal presence – an interesting and important development, to be sure, but one that remains on the margins of the publishing world. Many people might well suppose that the books that do really well are, in the vast majority of cases, books that are published by traditional publishers, and that self-published books are a rare exception among the pantheon of bestsellers. Would they be right?

It's not easy to answer this question convincingly. The most successful self-published books are very likely to be self-published ebooks, in part because ebooks allow self-published authors to use lower prices than traditional publishers, and in part because self-published authors don't have access to the distributional power of the traditional publishers and their ability to get physical books into the high-profile retail spaces where they need to be in order to sell in large numbers. But the problem with self-published ebooks is that the largest platform is KDP and the largest retailer is the Kindle Store, and Amazon don't disclose sales figures. So there is no way we can ascertain directly how well self-published ebooks are doing on Amazon and whether they are completely overshadowed by the ebooks published by traditional publishers. Can we ascertain it indirectly?

Estimating the indies

It's 10 a.m. and I'm on my way to a café in SoMa, a San Francisco neighbourhood ('South of Market') full of disused warehouses that are now home to many high-tech start-ups and some more established technology firms that have migrated from Silicon Valley into the city. I'm meeting a software engineer and self-published author who prefers the cloak of anonymity – he writes novels under a pseudonym and he communicates with me, and with anyone else who shows an interest in what he's doing, as Data Guy. Fortunately

266

for me, he's agreed temporarily to suspend anonymity and meet me for a coffee.

Data Guy rose to prominence in the middle of the 2010s because he developed an innovative technique to calculate sales on Amazon without Amazon's help. Using this technique, he was able to show that self-published ebooks have a much more significant share of Amazon's ebook sales than most people outside of Amazon had thought. Of course, we don't know if Data Guy's calculations are accurate – they are estimates, worked out by using a technique he devised. But, in the absence of direct access to Amazon's sales data, they are probably the best approximation we have.

The sales data he generated using this technique were published in a series of reports that were made available on the Author Earnings website.[26] The first report, published in February 2014, was startling: it appeared to show that self-published books were strongly repre- sented on Amazon's ebook bestseller lists in genre fiction, accounting for around 35% of titles on these bestseller lists, and around 24% of Amazon's daily gross sales of ebook genre bestsellers.[27] This was all the more striking when you see that titles published by the Big Five trade houses appeared to account for only 28% of the titles on Amazon's ebook genre bestseller lists – significantly less than self- published books. Titles published by the Big Five appeared to be earning a significantly higher proportion of the revenue generated by ebook genre bestsellers (52%, compared to 24% earned by indie authors). But when you take account of the fact that indie authors were earning a much higher percentage on the sales of their ebooks (typically 70% of the purchase price, compared to royalties of 25% of net receipts for most authors publishing with traditional publishers), indie authors appeared to be earning a substantially higher proportion of authors' earnings from ebook genre bestseller sales than authors publishing with the Big Five (47% of author earnings from ebook genre bestsellers appeared to be going to indie authors, compared to 32% to authors published by the Big Five). So if this report was to be believed, then a good number of self-published ebooks, far from

---

[26] http://authorearnings.com/reports. This website was closed down in 2017 and replaced by Bookstat.com, a new subscription-based data service started by Data Guy that some publishers now use to track sales in those sectors of the online book market that Bookscan is unable to cover.

[27] Hugh Howey, 'The 7k Report' (12 February 2014). Genre fiction includes Mystery & Thriller, Science Fiction & Fantasy, and Romance. According to Data Guy, these three genres accounted for 70% of the top 100 bestsellers on Amazon, and well over half of the top 1,000 bestsellers.

languishing on Amazon's long tail, were doing rather well, and a good number of indie authors were reaping the rewards. The fact that this report was written by Hugh Howey, and that subsequent reports using similar methods were either written by or co-authored with him, has led some people to view these reports with suspicion – it is well known that Hugh Howey is a very successful self-published author, a fervent advocate of indie publishing and no friend of traditional publishers. The reader might well wonder whether the data were being selectively marshalled, or perhaps even tailored, to champion the indie cause. It's not an unreasonable concern – we all know about lies, damned lies and statistics. So it seemed like a good idea to meet Data Guy in person and see what he had to say.

Data Guy is a software engineer in the games industry; in his day job, he did data analytics for a company that builds a game engine, the software that developers use to create games. He's also an indie author who has self-published a couple of books that have been pretty successful and he strongly identifies with the indie cause. That's how he met Hugh Howey and how their collaboration began: they were both successful indie authors, with books vying for top position on one of Amazon's bestseller lists, and this led them to start a conversation about a phenomenon that they were experiencing but that no one was really discussing – namely, the emergence of a set of writers who were earning a living, or at least part of a living, by self-publishing and bypassing the traditional middlemen of the publishing industry: 'the emergence of an entire writing middle class that never existed before', as Data Guy put it. For his own personal reasons, Data Guy had developed a piece of software that would enable him to scrape data from Amazon's bestseller rankings in order to see how well books by different publishers were doing, in the genres that interested him. He was already doing this kind of competitive analysis in the game industry, scraping data from the app store, so he just applied the same technique to the Amazon site: he wrote a spider that crawls the Amazon site, goes down every bestseller list, sub-bestseller list and sub-sub-bestseller list, and collects metadata on books including title, author, publisher, price, ISBN or lack of ISBN, etc. Amazon has thousands of bestseller lists, each subdividing into others – Romance, Historical Romance, Medieval, etc. – and each listing the top 100 titles in rank order. You can go down all of these lists and find details of the top 100 books on each list – the data is all there, you just have to gather it, but you can only gather it by using computerized techniques because there's just too much of it to gather by any other means. You can pull half a million books every time you run the spider, and about 200,000 of these are ebooks (another 250,000 are print books and 50,000 are audiobooks). Data Guy reckons that when he scrapes the data for 200,000 ebooks, he gets 65 per cent of Amazon's ebook sales on that day. This raw data forms the database of the numbers he crunches.

He starts by categorizing the publishers. The Big Five are easy to identify – the Big Five trade houses and all their imprints. The small and medium-size publishers aren't too difficult either – these are every publisher apart from the Big Five, Amazon's own imprints and the self-publishers. But the self-published titles can be tricky. When there's no listed publisher, it's clear – that's a straight KDP. But many indie authors choose to create a publisher's name for their book – it could be Sunnyside Press, whatever. Sunnyside Press might only publish the books of this author – maybe one book, maybe two, maybe more. But perhaps a friend or a neighbour or a husband has been writing a book too, and he wants to publish it under the name of Sunnyside Press: this is still self-publishing, but now the imprint may be a vehicle for more than one author. So if you come across Sunnyside Press, how do you know if it is a self-publisher or a small publisher? You have to do some research. Data Guy googled these, checked out websites and tried to figure out if they really were self-published books by indie authors – and when it's clear that they were, he called these 'Indie Published'. In the small number of cases where he couldn't track down any details and couldn't be sure that they were self-published books by indie authors, he put them in a residual category called 'Uncategorized Single-Author Publisher'; in all likelihood, these too were self-published titles, but to be on the safe side he left them uncategorized.

Having scraped the data for 200,000 ebooks on Amazon's bestseller lists and categorized the publishers so that he could distinguish between self-published books and books published by traditional publishers, Data Guy then needed to try to figure out what it means in real terms – that is, in terms of copies sold and revenue earned – to be ranked at any particular point on Amazon's bestseller lists. Having a book that appears on one of Amazon's bestseller lists is one thing, knowing what this means in terms of actual sales and revenue is quite another. But how can he do this if he doesn't know how Amazon is assigning books to ranks in its bestseller lists? Amazon's ranking is done by an algorithm which takes account of numerous factors and assigns titles to ranks continuously in time – ranks are updated every hour. Data Guy doesn't know what this algorithm is – nobody outside of Amazon does. So how can he convert rankings to sales and sales to revenue? To do this, he had to figure out a way to 'reverse engineer' Amazon's ranking algorithm. This is how he did it: he took data on actual sales, using precise daily sales figures for hundreds of individual books from many different authors who shared their sales figures with him, and he then mapped this data onto the rankings at particular points in time. This enabled him to create a rank-to-sales conversion curve which he could then test using a fresh set of data that were not used to create the curve, comparing the sales predicted by the equation with the actual sales – 'I'm typically within 2 to 4 per cent', he said. 'The most I've ever been off is 6 per cent.' The more data he uses, the more accurate the results are likely to be.

Data Guy refined the equation over time, using more data spanning a wider range of titles. He then ran the spider from time to time, crunched the data and produced a new report. He ran the spider on 10 January 2016 and the pie charts in figures 7.6–7.9 show some of the results.[28] Figure 7.6 shows that on the day that Data Guy ran the spider (10 January 2016), 27% of the positions on Amazon's ebook bestseller lists were held by self-published, or indie-published, ebooks. Another 12% were held by titles published by uncategorized single-author publishers – these too were probably self-published books. The largest category here is ebooks published by small or medium-sized publishers: they accounted for 47% of the slots on Amazon's ebook bestseller lists. By contrast, ebooks published by the Big Five publishers accounted for only 13% of the slots – significantly less than the self-published ebooks. The results also showed that 4 of Amazon's overall top 10 bestselling ebooks were self-published titles, as were 10 of Amazon's overall top 20 bestselling ebooks, and 56 of Amazon's overall top 100 bestselling ebooks.

Figures 7.7 and 7.8 were produced by applying the rank-to-sales curve to estimate sales on the basis of a title's rank on Amazon's bestseller lists. Figure 7.7 shows that indie-published ebooks account for 42% of unit sales of ebook bestsellers, Big Five titles account for 23% and ebooks from small or medium-sized publishers account for 19%. If this is right, then indie-published ebooks account for the same proportion of the unit sales of ebook bestsellers on Amazon as ebooks published by all traditional publishers. Some of the indie sales are accounted for by Kindle Unlimited borrows – Amazon's ranking algorithm treats KU borrows as sales, and, in 2015, KU payouts amounted to around $140 million, all or most of which went to indie authors. But there are also many self-published titles

[28] 'February 2016 Author Earnings Report: Amazon's Ebook, Print and Audio Sales'.

270

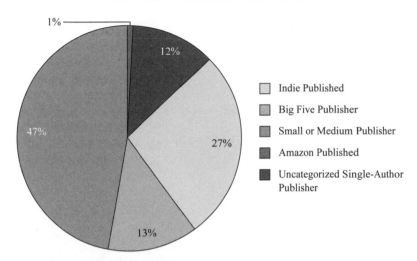

Figure 7.6   Number of titles in Amazon's ebook besteller lists*
* January 2016, fiction and nonfiction, 195,000 books comprising *c.*58 per cent of Amazon's ebook sales

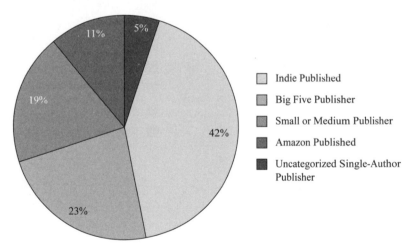

Figure 7.7   Daily unit sales of ebook bestsellers

in Amazon's bestseller lists that are not enrolled in KU. When unit sales are converted into dollars, the ebooks published by traditional publishers take a higher share of the daily sales of ebook bestsellers on Amazon: 40% is accounted for by Big Five titles, and 24% by titles published by small or medium-sized publishers; 23% of

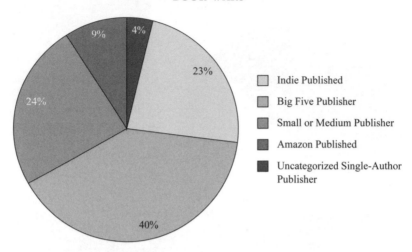

Figure 7.8   Daily gross Amazon $ sales of ebook bestsellers

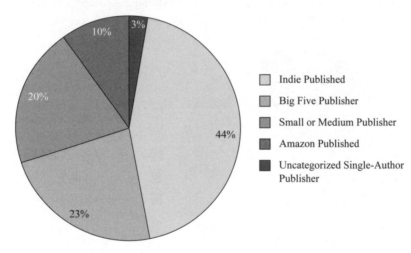

Figure 7.9   Daily $ revenue to authors from ebook bestsellers

the dollar sales are accounted for by indie-published titles (figure 7.8). This reversal of the percentages is explained by the fact that the ebooks published by traditional publishers are generally much more expensive than indie-published ebooks – self-published ebooks are commonly priced between 99¢ and $4.99, whereas ebooks published by traditional publishers are often priced between $9.99 and $14.99.

The final pie chart, figure 7.9, shows what happens when you take account of the fact that authors who are self-publishing on Kindle are taking home a higher slice of the sales revenue than authors who are publishing with traditional publishers: indie-published titles appear to account for 44% of the revenue going to authors from the sales of ebook bestsellers, whereas titles published by the Big Five account for 23%, and titles published by small or medium-sized publishers account for 20%. This suggests that indie authors, taken as a whole, might be earning about the same amount of revenue from the sales of ebook bestsellers as authors published by traditional publishers – a remarkable result if it's true.

By combining the data generated in January 2016 with similar exercises carried out regularly since the first report in February 2014, Data Guy could also show how the pattern has changed, or may have changed, over time – the graphs in figures 7.10–7.12 display the trends. Figure 7.10 appears to show that the market shares of ebook unit sales changed significantly between February 2014 and January 2016: in essence, the market share of indie-published ebooks appears to have increased while the market share of Big Five-published

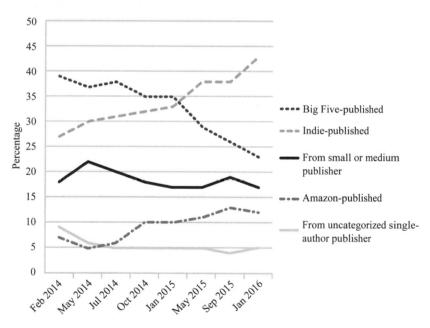

Figure 7.10   Market share of ebook unit sales by publisher type, 2014–2016
Source: Author Earnings

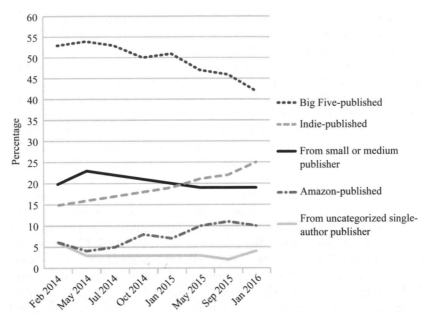

Figure 7.11   Market share of ebook gross $ sales by publisher type, 2014–2016

ebooks appears to have declined. The two lines crossed around January 2015, and by January 2016, indie-published ebooks were accounting for nearly 45% of unit ebook sales on Amazon, whereas ebooks published by the Big Five accounted for less than 25%. In terms of dollar sales (figure 7.11), Big Five-published ebooks continued to take the lion's share of revenue, though this share appeared to be declining with time. In terms of the share of author earnings (figure 7.12), the trend once again appears to be in favour of indie-published books, with the two key lines – Big Five-published and indie-published – once again crossing around January 2015, and with indie-published ebooks accounting for over 45% of ebook author earnings by January 2016, compared to less than 25% for ebooks published by the Big Five.

Data Guy's calculations were not based on Amazon's actual sales but rather on estimates of Amazon's sales, worked out using the methods described above, and there were various ways in which they could be skewing the figures in favour of indie-published, and specifically KDP-published, books. Since borrows in Kindle Unlimited count as sales for the purposes of Amazon's sales rank

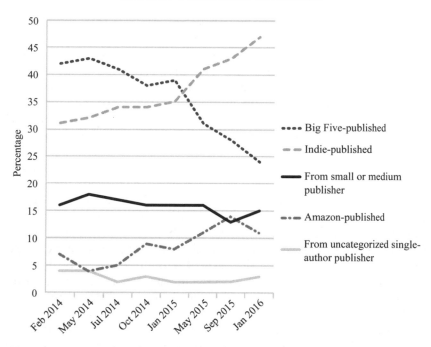

Figure 7.12   Market share of ebook $ author earnings by publisher type, 2014–2016

algorithm, and since books self-published on KDP are dispropor-tionately represented in Kindle Unlimited, it seems likely that a rank-to-sales curve that tried to reverse-engineer Amazon's sales rank algorithm would reflect this pro-KDP bias. Moreover, the pie charts, by focusing on Amazon's bestseller lists, are silent on the long tail, and on the question of whether your chances of ending up in the remoter regions of the long tail are related to the type of publisher – it could be, for example, that a much higher percentage of indie-published books end up in the remoter regions of the long tail, selling very few copies and generating very little revenue, than books published by traditional publishers. Perhaps most signifi-cantly, the calculations of authors' earnings, and the distribution of these earnings between indie-published and traditionally published books, is based entirely on estimated royalty earnings and takes no account of the advances paid by traditional publishers – and, since advances are a large part of the earnings of the most successful authors published by traditional houses and a substantial proportion of advances are never earned out, this is a major oversight. But while

Data Guy's methods and calculations are questionable on various grounds, his figures demonstrate pretty clearly that indie-published ebooks feature much more prominently in Amazon's bestseller lists than many people thought, and that they represent a substantial proportion of both the unit sales and the dollar sales of ebooks on Amazon. Whether this is really as much as 40–45% of the unit sales, and 25% of the dollar sales, we cannot know for sure; but even if these estimates were off by as much as 5–10%, these would still be sizeable proportions.

Moreover, since the shares of indie-published ebooks on Amazon appear to be both substantial and increasing relative to the shares of the ebooks published by traditional publishers (which appear to be either static or declining), this raises important questions about the extent to which we can generalize about what is happening in the ebook marketplace, and about the changing relation between print books and ebooks, on the basis of data drawn from traditional publishing houses alone. As we saw in chapter 1, the data from mainstream industry sources, like the AAP and BISG, and from traditional trade houses show ebooks as a percentage of total book sales growing steeply from 2008 to 2012 but then levelling off from 2012 on. The percentages vary greatly from one type of book to another, but in all categories the growth of ebooks as a percentage of total sales appears to have halted from 2012 on, and in some cases appears to have declined. But suppose what really happened is not that ebooks plateaued or even declined as a percentage of total sales, but rather that the ebook market share of traditional publishers was eroded by the growing market share of indie-published ebooks – might that be possible? The growing market share of indie-published ebooks – at least in terms of units sold, as distinct from revenue – might have been spurred on by the shift to agency pricing for ebooks by the Big Five in 2014, following the expiry of the 'Agency Lite' agreement imposed by the Department of Justice in 2012: this allowed publishers to fix the prices of their ebooks and to prevent retailers like Amazon from discounting these prices, thus increasing the gap between the prices of ebooks published by the Big Five and the prices of indie-published ebooks. And when you take account of the fact that over a million books self-published through KDP can be accessed for no charge by joining Kindle Unlimited for $9.99 per month, the cost per unit read of books self-published on Kindle becomes a small fraction of the cost per read of ebooks published by traditional publishers. The fact that the price differential is now so significant may have the effect of driving down ebook sales from traditional publishers, while self-published ebooks take a larger and larger share of the ebook cake.

So what exactly are we seeing when we see the apparent levelling off of ebook sales of trade books from 2012 on? Are we seeing an overall levelling off of both ebook unit sales and ebook dollar sales relative to print book sales in the total marketplace of trade books? Or are we seeing a levelling off of ebook unit sales and ebook dollar sales relative to print book sales among the traditional publishers who are publishing trade books, while in the total marketplace of trade books the sales of ebooks continue to grow, at least in terms of units, as consumers shift their ebook buying to cheaper indie-published ebooks, or access them through a subscription service like Kindle Unlimited? And if it's the latter, might ebook unit sales still be growing as a percentage of total sales of trade books, and might the apparent levelling off of ebook sales reflect not an overall levelling off of ebook sales in the total marketplace of trade books, but rather a declining market share of ebook sales captured by the traditional publishers?

These questions cannot be answered conclusively – we simply don't have enough data on actual sales of ebooks through Amazon and other retailers and distributors to give clear-cut answers. But it does seem likely that data drawn from traditional publishers is giving us, at best, a partial view of what is happening in the ebook market-place. Someone well placed to know what is happening at Amazon insisted that there has been no levelling off in terms of Amazon's ebook business: 'Our ebook business has grown every year that the publishers have said theirs has shrunk', he said. 'If you define the world of books as those published by traditional publishers, then you can reach a different conclusion than if you look at the actual world of books as it exists today.'[29] The world of self-publishing is to a large extent a hidden continent that is invisible to the mainstream industry sources that rely on the traditional publishing houses for the sales data they gather, or that rely on EPOS (Electronic Point of Sale) data. Exactly how big this hidden continent is, and what it looks like in terms of the kinds of books that make it up, no one knows. Given the importance of Kindle, KDP and CreateSpace / KDP Print, Amazon would have the fullest picture of what this hidden continent might look like, though even their picture would be partial and incomplete.

---

[29] While Amazon's ebook business may have continued to grow, we don't know by how much, and in all likelihood it was much less from 2012 on than it was during the intensive growth phase from 2008 to 2012.

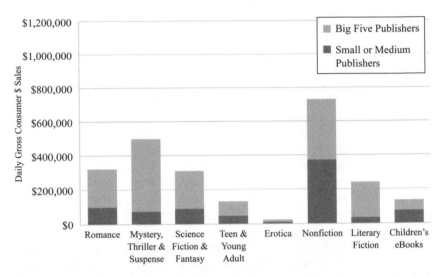

Figure 7.13   Daily gross Amazon $ sales of ebook bestsellers by category, January 2016 (1)

We know from other sources, such as Smashwords, that fiction, and especially Romance and other genre fiction categories, account for a large part of the sales of self-published books, so it seems probable that the hidden continent of self-publishing is particularly large in these areas. Data Guy's analysis of Amazon's bestseller lists provides further support for this view: figure 7.13 shows his analysis of the dollar sales of ebook bestsellers by broad category, broken down between his two types of traditional publishers – the Big Five and the small and medium-sized publishers.[30] The Big Five publishers clearly dominate in nearly all the categories, with the exception of nonfiction, where the split is pretty even. However, when you factor in indie publishers (figure 7.14), the picture changes quite dramatically: the hidden continent of self-publishing surges up from below. This is true in all categories, but especially in genre fiction: in Romance, for instance, ebooks published by self-published indie authors and by Amazon's imprints appear to account for more than half the dollar sales of ebooks on Amazon's bestseller lists, and they account for a substantial proportion in other categories of genre fiction – Mystery, Thriller & Suspense, Science Fiction & Fantasy, Teen & Young Adult, and Erotica. Figures such as these lend support to the view that, if we did have an accurate account of the hidden

---

[30] Data Guy, '2016 Digital Book World Keynote Presentation' (11 March 2016).

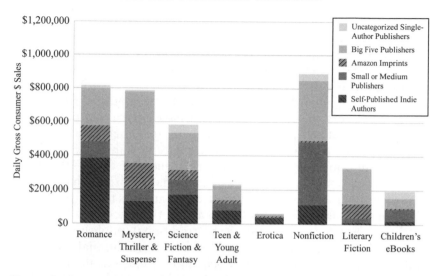

Figure 7.14 Daily gross Amazon $ sales of ebook bestsellers by category, January 2016 (2)

continent of self-publishing, then our picture of the actual trends of ebook sales, and of the changing relations between ebooks and print books, might look rather different from the picture we are able to produce on the basis of data drawn from the traditional publishers alone.[31]

Parallel universes, multiple pathways

The dramatic growth of self-publishing since the early 2000s has changed Anglo-American trade publishing in ways that are at once profound, poorly understood and still evolving, creating a new kind of publishing environment in which traditional publishers exist alongside a vibrant but largely invisible new world of self-publishing. From time to time, this growth has fuelled a debate about the possible 'disintermediation' of traditional publishers, giving rise to the suggestion that authors – and especially successful authors with an established fan base – would weigh up the higher share of the

---

[31] Data Guy believes that the ebook market is continuing to grow, albeit much more slowly than during the great expansion of 2008–12, but large publishers represent a declining share of overall ebook sales: he estimates that Big Five publishers accounted for 24 per cent of ebook unit sales and 39 per cent of ebook dollar sales in 2019.

revenue they could earn if they self-published their books and decide to jump ship, leave their traditional publishers behind and go it alone. Why accept a royalty of 25 per cent on ebooks when you could be earning 70–80 per cent by self-publishing on Amazon or another self-publishing platform? In practice, however, it's not worked out like that. There are, indeed, some authors who have migrated from traditional publishers to self-publishing and have been vocal proponents of the virtues of self-publishing, but there are others who migrated the other way and were happy to be accepted into the world of mainstream publishing when the doors opened for them – the traffic has not been one-way, and just as traditional publishers have feared that they may lose some of their bestselling authors to self-publishing platforms, the latter have also been aware that they may lose some of their most successful authors to traditional publishers. What's happened in practice is that these two worlds, traditional publishing and self-publishing, have developed and co-existed alongside one another, like two parallel universes that seldom overlap directly, and some authors have occasionally moved between them for specific books or at different stages of their career.

From the perspective of authors, the growth of self-publishing, and the proliferation of new platforms that arose during the third wave, have massively increased the range of options available to them: it's now easier than it has ever been to publish, and anyone who wants to publish a book, and who has access to a computer and a basic level of technical expertise, can do so with no or little expense and a minimum of fuss. This is a true 'democratization of publishing', as one figure active in the self-publishing movement put it. But this new publishing environment, in which traditional publishing and self-publishing co-exist alongside one another, is a structured space in which books that are published have very different chances of success depending on how they are published, by whom, with what kinds of resources behind them and what kinds of effort and expertise invested in support of them. Authors know that earning a higher royalty on ebook sales may be a gain not worth having if you end up selling very few books, as it's the overall revenue, not the revenue share, that matters in the end. In the world of self-publishing, there are very few truly successful authors, and the vast majority of self-published authors earn small amounts of money.[32] But the situation is

---

[32] A survey of self-published authors in 2011 found that only 7 per cent were earning $20,000 or more in royalties from all their self-published books, while over half were earning less than $500, and a quarter of all self-published books were unlikely

changing; self-published authors have become more entrepreneurial and better informed about all aspects of publishing, including how to market and sell their books more effectively – areas where they face particular challenges[33] – and more and more indie authors are managing to earn significant amounts of money from their writing, even if the commercially successful indie authors are still a very small fraction of the total. Moreover, individuals publish books for different reasons and with different aims – it's not all about making money. While earning money may be an important reason for some individuals, it may be unimportant for others – they may want to publish a book simply to be able to give a few copies to friends and family members, or just because it's something they always wanted to do. The personal satisfaction that comes from creating a work and seeing that it's available as a published book – either as an ebook or a print book or both – may be sufficient recompense for some.

It is therefore not surprising that this new publishing environment has become a fluid space in which authors move back and forth from traditional publishing to self-publishing and vice versa, depending on what they want to achieve and the options available to them at different points in time. There are some authors who see themselves as an author who will always publish with a traditional house, provided that option is open to them. The traditional publisher is their publisher of choice and, for many of these authors, the idea of self-publishing their work would never appeal – that's just not a path that they would ever want to go down. On the other hand, there are some authors who strongly self-identify as indie authors:

---

to generate sufficient revenue for their authors to cover the amount they spent to produce them (Dave Cornford and Steven Lewis, *Not a Gold Rush: The Taleist Self-Publishing Survey* (Taleist, 2012)). This survey was based on 1,007 self-published authors who responded to an invitation to take part in the survey. The respondents were self-selecting and may not be representative of the self-publishing population as a whole – it could be, for example, that indie authors who were more committed and more successful were more willing to respond to the survey.

[33] A plethora of websites, podcasts and courses offer advice to self-published authors on how to market and promote their books more effectively and how to increase their sales – see, for example, https://6figureauthors.com and http://selfpublishstrong.com. But none of this is easy and much of it is costly, and many authors who self-publish their work may find that the book into which they've poured their heart and soul remains largely invisible when it is finally launched into the world – 'you have to be tough to overcome the disappointment it brings', said one author who had worked for years on a series of sci-fi books that she self-published, having failed to find a traditional publisher willing to take them on. 'The author-publisher is for people who have money', she reflected; 'you have to spend a lot to be visible, and I don't have the money.'

the world of self-publishing has become their world, they are proud to self-publish and they wouldn't seriously consider publishing – or publishing again – with a traditional house. Some indie authors have principled objections to traditional publishers, seeing them as parasites that live off the creative work of authors and preferring to have nothing to do with them, but many indie authors are happy to live and let live: self-publishing works for them, and if others want to publish their books with traditional publishers, that's their business. And then there is a large and expanding pool of authors who are situated somewhere between these two poles, hybrid authors who are willing to avail themselves of different options at different points in time, depending on what the options are and the kind(s) of book(s) they want to write. An author who is a successful academic and has published several nonfiction books with academic presses may decide that she wants to write romance fiction on the side and may come to the view that the best way to do this is to self-publish her romance novels under a pseudonym – she becomes a hybrid author by choice, continuing to publish her nonfiction books with traditional academic publishers while at the same time availing herself of the opportunities opened up by self-publishing to pursue a shadow career as a romance writer. Another author who has published several thrillers with major trade houses may find that none of these houses want to publish his new book, doors that were previously open to him have now closed, and he may decide that the best route to take at this stage of his career is to self-publish – he becomes an indie author not by choice but by necessity. And then there are others who, like Andy Weir, start off their writing career as a blogger and a self-published author and are spotted by editors or agents who have come to see the world of self-publishing as R&D for traditional publishing houses: these authors may be delighted to be published by a traditional house and, as traditionally published authors, they may be earning far more than they ever would've earned if they had remained in the world of self-publishing. But the doors to the world of traditional publishing might never have opened for them had they not first availed themselves of the new opportunities opened up by self-publishing.

— Chapter 8 —

CROWDFUNDING BOOKS

Self-publishing is about using new technologies to bypass the traditional gatekeepers in the publishing world who control access to the channels of publication – the agents, the editors and the traditional publishing houses, among others; crowdfunding is about using new technologies to bypass the gatekeepers who control access to the financial resources you need – the capital – in order to develop and realize projects that require some financial investment, whatever the nature of the project might be. Just as there are gatekeepers in the world of publishing, so too there are capital gatekeepers: bank managers, angel investors, venture capitalists, grant-giving foundations, etc. If you have an idea and want to launch a new venture, create a new product or start a new business, you may need money to do it – where do you get the money? Maybe you have some savings, maybe your parents or siblings can lend or give you some money, but if you can't fall back on personal or family resources, you may have to knock on the doors of the capital gatekeepers. Maybe they'll like your idea and lend you money or invest in your project, but maybe they won't. Maybe they'll think it's too risky, too marginal, too daft, too ill-thought-through, or maybe it's just not the kind of thing they want to support. What do you do then? You can give up. Or you can look for other sources of funding. Crowdfunding gives you a way to try to gain access to capital without having to rely on the traditional capital gatekeepers. It relies on other people – the crowd.

Crowdfunding is as much about other people – the crowd – as it is about funding: the first word, 'crowd', is really the key. You have to engage with other people and persuade them to support you. Of course, raising money from traditional capital gatekeepers also requires you to persuade other people to support you, but there is a crucial difference here. What distinguishes crowdfunding from traditional forms of raising capital is this: with crowdfunding you're seeking to raise small amounts of money from large numbers of people who are personally interested in what you're proposing to do, whereas with traditional forms of raising capital you're trying to get large amounts of money from a small number of people who don't necessarily have a personal interest in your project but who want to get a return on their investment. The difference is in the numbers but also in the aims: with crowdfunding, you're seeking to persuade lots of people to invest small amounts of money to enable you to do what you want to do, not because they're hoping to make a windfall from their investment but because they believe in you and what you're doing and they want to have or enjoy or simply help to bring about whatever it is that you're proposing to do or create. 'It's a very altruistic way of getting stuff done and made', as one crowdfunding insider put it.

But there's another crucial thing here about the crowd: the crowd is not just the source of capital, it's also the future market for whatever it is you're hoping to create. This is another reason why crowdfunding is so different from borrowing money from a bank or raising funds from a venture capitalist: the bank manager or VC isn't going to buy your product (or whatever it is that you're hoping to make or do), but the individuals who make up the crowd are doing exactly that: they are, in effect, pre-committing to buying your product. Pledging money is pre-ordering: the pledge is a pre-order. Hence, the crowdfunding model, by its very nature, is a risk reduction device: it reduces the risk involved in creating something new. The model typically requires you to reach a certain threshold of pledges or pre-orders before you are able to go ahead, and hence it enables you to know before you begin whether there is enough interest in what you're proposing to do, and enough cash committed by a multitude of supporters, to make the project viable.

It's easy enough to see why crowdfunding might be useful as a way of funding ambitious projects that require a substantial amount of investment – making a short film could cost $10,000, for example, and a feature-length film could cost $100,000 or more. But it's not so expensive to publish a book, especially if you decide to self-publish using one of the many self-publishing platforms now available. So what's the point of crowdfunding in the world of books? Even with writing and publishing a book, there are plenty of things that could and do cost quite a lot of money: you might want to make a trip abroad to do research for the book; you might want to have the book professionally edited, designed and typeset; you might want to include lots of high-quality illustrations; you might want to pay an artist to do some original artwork; you might want it to be printed on a high-quality offset press rather than a digital printer; you might want to print some extra copies that could be sold in bookstores without being pre-ordered; you might want to have a serious marketing and publicity campaign and employ a professional marketer or publicist; and so on – any number of things that could add up to quite a lot of expense. If you're planning or hoping to publish with a traditional publisher, then some or perhaps all of these expenses may be picked up by the publisher – that, after all, is partly what publishers do: they are the bankers in the publishing chain who make financial resources available to pay advances and cover the costs of production, marketing, etc. But that means that publishers are not just gatekeepers to the world of publishing: they are capital gatekeepers too. In deciding whether to take on your project and give you a contract, they are deciding whether to back your project with the financial resources you may need to make it happen. Suppose they're not interested. Suppose they're not willing to take a chance with your project, place a bet on your book – what do you do then? You could, of course, pursue the low-cost route and self-publish in a way that involved minimal expense. But suppose you wanted to do something that would involve more – where would you get the resources to do this if you didn't have the money already? That's where crowdfunding comes in.

Not all crowdfunded books will be self-published – some will, but some will also be published by traditional publishers (indeed, some traditional publishers actively look for authors who have crowd-funded their books and offer to publish them – more on this below). And some will be published by one of the new publishing organiza-tions that are based on crowdfunding principles, where crowdfunding is built into the publishing model. But, while crowdfunding is not the same as self-publishing and there is no necessary connection between the two, there is, nonetheless, a deep affinity between crowdfunding and self-publishing: they are both part of the do-it-yourself culture enabled by the digital revolution, part of the democratization of culture that the digital revolution has helped to produce. You don't need to go through the gatekeepers of culture, rely on their benefi-cence, you can do it yourself: go directly to your potential readers and appeal to them. Forget the gatekeepers. Let the readers decide.

To understand the role of crowdfunding in the book publishing industry, we have to look at two different aspects. First is the rise of crowdfunding more generally and the emergence of large crowd-funding organizations that have come to play a significant role in the creative industries, especially Indiegogo and Kickstarter. These crowdfunding organizations are not specifically focused on books – they do fund book projects, but this is a small part of what they do. Moreover, they are 'pure' crowdfunding organizations in the sense that they are just about raising money: a platform for raising capital from the crowd. They don't actually publish your book once the capital is raised – you have to make separate arrangements for that, whether this is with a traditional publisher or by self-publishing. So crowdfunding is not, in and by itself, a form of publishing (or self-publishing): it is a form of fundraising *tout court*. Crowdfunding organizations like Indiegogo and Kickstarter can help you raise money to write and publish a book but they won't publish the book for you: it is your responsibility to arrange the publication as best you can.

However, there are some crowdfunding organizations that are specifically tailored to books and publishing, and where crowdfunding principles are built into the publishing model. There are two crowd-funding publishers of this kind that have assumed some significance in the world of publishing – Unbound in London, and Inkshares in Oakland, California. Unlike Indiegogo and Kickstarter, Unbound and Inkshares *are* publishers, and the crowdfunding mechanism is used as a way of raising funds for the book project before deciding whether to go ahead with it: if the threshold is reached, the project goes ahead, and if it isn't reached, it doesn't. So in these cases, crowdfunding is an integral part of the publishing process. And as a publishing model, this has some real advantages: not only does it remove a large part of the risk involved in publishing, since the capital needed to publish the book is being supplied by the crowd rather than by the publishing firm, but also it gives you a very effective mechanism for gauging the interest of readers. It's about as close as the publishing industry has ever got to an effective form of market research.

The rise of crowdfunding

The principle behind crowdfunding is not new: many commentators have pointed out that the Statue of Liberty was partially funded by the public when the American Committee of the Statue of Liberty failed to raise sufficient funds and Joseph Pulitzer launched a fundraising campaign in his newspaper, the *New York World*: in five months, he raised $101,091 from more than 160,000 donors, which was enough to cover the final $100,000 needed to complete the statue. But there is no doubt that the rise of the internet in the 1990s and early 2000s provided a powerful new medium for the development of crowdfunding: now it was possible to reach out to large numbers of potential backers and interact with them easily, cheaply and quickly. The early uses of the internet for crowdfunding were in the worlds of music and film. In 1997, the British rock band Marillion raised $60,000 through a fan-based email campaign to fund their US tour. Emboldened by their success, they then sacked their manager and emailed the 6,000 fans on their database to ask them if they would buy their next album in advance. They took over 12,000 pre-orders and used the money to fund the writing and recording of the album[1] – internet crowdfunding had begun, even if it wasn't called 'crowdfunding' at the time.

The use of web-based platforms to raise money from many people gained traction in the early 2000s. In 2003, Brian Camelio, a Boston musician and computer programmer, launched ArtistShare, a website where musicians could seek donations from their fans to produce digital recordings.[2] Their first project, Marian Schneider's jazz album *Concert in a Garden*, used a tiered system of rewards to encourage fans to contribute more. This so-called rewards-based system has since become standard practice in the world of crowdfunding. While web-based crowdfunding now existed in practice, the coining of the term 'crowdfunding' is usually attributed to Michael Sullivan, who used this term to describe the funding scheme involved in a site he launched in August 2006 called Fundavlog, an attempt (which subsequently failed) to create an incubator for videoblog-related projects and events.[3] Various other crowdfunding platforms were launched in the early 2000s, the most prominent of which were Indiegogo and Kickstarter.

Indiegogo was founded in 2008 by Danae Ringelmann, Slava Rubin and Eric Schell. All three had experienced or witnessed difficulties in raising funds for various purposes – Danae had worked with filmmakers, Eric was on the board of a theatre company and Slava had started a charity after his father died of cancer; Eric and

---

[1] 'How Marillion Pioneered Crowdfunding in Music', at www.virgin.com/music/how-marillion-pioneered-crowdfunding-music.
[2] David M. Freeman and Matthew R. Nutting, 'A Brief History of Crowdfunding' (2014–15), at www.freedman-chicago.com/ec4i/History-of-Crowdfunding.pdf.
[3] Daniela Castrataro, 'A Social History of Crowdfunding' (12 December 2011), at https://socialmediaweek.org/blog/2011/12/a-social-history-of-crowdfunding.

Slava were old friends, and they met Danae when Eric and Danae were doing MBAs at the Haas School of Business in Berkeley. In 2007, they hatched the idea of creating a new set of digital tools for raising money. They focused initially on film, partly because Danae and Slava were passionate about movies and partly because they felt film was under-served in terms of using digital tools to raise money, and they launched Indiegogo at the Sundance Film Festival in January 2008. While film was their starting point, their plan was always to move beyond film and provide a more general service to empower people to raise money for whatever creative project they wanted to undertake – 'anything cause, anything creative, anything entrepreneurial', as Slava put it[4] – and in December 2009 they opened up to everything.

Kickstarter's origins date back to 2002, when Perry Chen – a young New Yorker who was then living in New Orleans and was into the music scene there – wanted to put on a show for the New Orleans jazz festival and wondered how he could afford to do it. What if all the people who wanted to come to the show could have a say in it? And what if we could see how many people wanted to come to the show and then decide, on that basis, whether to put the show on? That show never happened but the idea stuck with him.[5] Three years later, Perry moved back to New York and teamed up with Yancey Strickler and Charles Adler. They raised some seed funding in 2006 and 2007, developed the website and launched Kickstarter in April 2009.

The model behind Indiegogo and Kickstarter is basically the same: anyone who wants to raise money for a project – a film, an album, a book, a tech product, a new business venture, a social cause, a personal cause, whatever it is – can create a page for their funding campaign, set funding goals (there can be several goals set at different levels) and a deadline (campaigns can vary from 1 to 60 days, though 30–40 days is typical), write a pitch for the project, make a short video that explains the aims and invites people to contribute, specify a list of perks or rewards for different levels of contribution, and launch a social media campaign. The site takes a 5 per cent fee for successful campaigns. One of the differences between Indiegogo and

---

[4] 'Wake Me Up Before You Indiegogo: Interview with Slava Rubin', *Film Threat* (5 October 2010), at http://filmthreat.com/uncategorized/wake-me-up-before-you-indiegogo-interview-with-slava-rubin.
[5] 'How I Built This with Guy Raz: Kickstarter: Perry Chen', NPR (31 July 2017), at www.npr.org/podcasts/510313/how-i-built-this.

Kickstarter is that Kickstarter is all or nothing: if the goal is not met by the deadline, no credit cards are charged, no funds are collected and no money changes hands. With Indiegogo, by contrast, users can decide at the outset whether to adopt a 'fixed funding' model, where they keep the contributions only if they meet their goal, or a 'flexible funding' model, where they keep what they raise regardless of whether they hit the goal (in the latter case, Indiegogo levies a 9 per cent fee). The flexible model works well for many projects in the arts because many creators know that, while it would be great to have $10,000, they could still do the project with less.

While anyone can sign up to Indiegogo or Kickstarter and launch a campaign, both of these organizations are also proactive about recruiting campaigners. They have dedicated members of staff in the different areas where they are active whose job it is to reach out to potential campaigners and encourage them to launch campaigns on their site. These recruiters, or 'outreach leads' as they are sometimes called, attend film festivals, writers' events, technology conferences and other occasions where potential campaigners gather and talk them through the practicalities of crowdfunding, hoping to attract new recruits. They are also experts at shaping campaigns to maximize their effectiveness. They know what works and what doesn't – many have run successful campaigns themselves and they are able to draw on personal experience. They also have access to lots of proprietary data on the campaigns that have worked and those that haven't which they can use to inform their advice. 'I help you run your campaign as best you can', said Tom, a staff member who had run several successful campaigns of his own before he began working for one of the crowdfunding organizations; 'as long as you do what I say you will be successful', he added, speaking with the kind of confidence that made you feel pretty sure he wasn't exaggerating much.

While both Indiegogo and Kickstarter are open platforms that allow pretty much anyone to launch campaigns in the areas where they are active, they are not totally laissez-faire. They each have their rules and their vetting procedures – they too are gatekeepers, though a very different kind of gatekeeper from the traditional guardians of capital. They are not deciding whether to back a project – that's a decision they leave to the wisdom of the crowd. But they are establishing the rules of the game and deciding whether particular projects abide by those rules and can legitimately launch a campaign on their site. Certain kinds of campaigns are explicitly ruled out (users cannot create campaigns to raise funds for illegal activities or to scam others, for example, and Kickstarter rules out projects that would seek to raise funds for a charity or a cause), certain kinds of language and imagery are not allowed (anything inciting hatred or abuse, anything explicitly sexual or pornographic, etc.) and certain perks are prohibited (e.g. financial incentives, drugs, alcohol, weapons, live animals, human remains, etc.). Kickstarter has a reputation for being more regulative in this regard. In the early days, every project that was launched on Kickstarter was reviewed by an actual human, though now the initial screening is done by an algorithm that determines whether a project is risky, and those that are judged to be risky are then reviewed by a member of the 'integrity team'. This is mostly a matter of ensuring that the project fits with the rules, and if it doesn't, someone reaches out to the creator and tells them what they have to do to rectify the problem. But it's also a matter of trying to detect fraud and scams and making sure that people really are who they say there are. For at the end of the day, the whole crowdfunding enterprise is based on trust: if there's a good chance that backers are going to get screwed, or that the campaigner will never deliver what he or she is proposing, then people are going to be reluctant to back projects where they don't know the campaigner personally. Backing a project that is being promoted by someone you don't know and have never met, simply because you like the look of their video and are intrigued by what they're doing, is a leap of faith, and people are much more likely to make that leap if they are confident that it isn't a scam and that campaigners are going to live up to their word. 'Trust is what makes crowdfunding work', explained Tom. 'If you lose that, you're done.'[6]

The key to running a successful crowdfunding campaign is knowing how to tap into the right community and give them a compelling reason to give you money – in other words, it's all about the crowd. 'That's the one constant in all crowdfunding, from products to books to movies to causes', continued Tom. 'Even causes, where it's more donation-based, you still have to tap into the right community and give them a compelling reason to give you that money.' So focusing

---

[6] In practice, non-delivery of promised outcomes appears to be relatively rare. One study of successfully funded Kickstarter projects in the categories of design and technology that had promised to deliver clear outcomes to funders by July 2012 found that only 14 out of 381 projects were outright failures – 3 had issued refunds and 11 had stopped responding to backers; that's a direct failure rate of only 3.6 per cent. However, the delayed delivery of promised outcomes is common: 75 per cent of projects were delayed and 33 per cent had yet to be delivered by June 2013. See Ethan Mollick, 'The Dynamics of Crowdfunding: An Exploratory Study', *Journal of Business Venturing*, 29 (2014), 11–12.

on the crowd and making the campaign about them, and what might be interesting for them, is key. To be more precise, you have to break the crowd into two crowds, explained Tom. First, there's the crowd that you as the campaigner bring to the platform: you have your own crowd, your family and friends, your readership, your movie fans, your Facebook friends, your Twitter followers, etc. When you plan your campaign, you're going to start with your crowd because you've got to bring them in first – for most campaigns, your family and friends and fans and followers are your first 30 per cent. 'When I first meet a campaigner', said Tom, 'I always ask, what's your network like? What's your email, your social media, what are your people like? Because I know that you have to bring those people in first.' They may not like your project all that much but they'll support you because they like you and want to help you out, or maybe because you supported them. 'If you can get that first 30 per cent in about three to five days, technically, your campaign is going to have a shit load of momentum to be able to sustain itself for the duration of the campaign.' But if you don't have the first 30 per cent, it's going to be an uphill struggle. 'We've done plenty of tests that show if you feature something and it's 10 per cent funded, psychologically nobody's going to contribute because they're going to think, oh, that's a losing campaign. I'm not going to give my money to that – it's not going to happen.'

The second crowd consists of all those people who might want to support your project because they're interested in it, even though they may not know you personally or be part of your network of friends, family and followers. You need to find those people online and start interacting with them. So, for example, if you're proposing to write a book or make a film about a particular artist, who are the people interested in that artist? You need to find them, reach out to them, start interacting with them, tell them about what you're planning to do and construct your campaign in a way that will be interesting to them, with perks that are the kinds of things they might actually value. And all of this is quite a lot of work: you can't just put projects up there and expect them magically to get funded. You've got to do the research, find out where the people are who might be interested in what you're doing and reach out to them, let them know who you are and what you're doing and why it might be interesting for them. 'The one thing that bugs me', said Tom, 'is that people still don't realize how much work is involved in running a successful campaign. People think, oh, I'll just crowdfund it. We'll put it up and it'll get funded. That never happened, not even in 2010. You have to do the work – it's a full-time job.'

While the promotion and outreach activity of the campaigner is crucial, the crowdfunding organizations can also make a big difference – both by providing campaigners with expert advice and by giving projects some visibility on the crowdfunding platform. While the crowdfunding platforms aim to minimize their gatekeeping role, they do actively curate projects on the site: 'we're not selective in that anyone can launch a project as long as it fits with our rules, but we do curate', explained Cindy, another crowdfunding staffer who specializes in publishing projects. 'We're trying to make sure that people who land on the site and go to the publishing category are seeing the best and the coolest and the most interesting of what the publishing category has to offer.' A large crowdfunding platform like Kickstarter will have 500–600 projects that are live at any one time in the publishing category alone – that's a huge number of projects and anyone browsing the site is unlikely to see more than a handful. So organizing these projects is important – this is what the curation team does. There is some input from category managers like Cindy – 'we're involved in the process', said Cindy, without going into details; she talks to the curation team and recommends the campaigns she likes. But the curation team also uses an algorithm that takes account of user engagement – views, pledges, etc. – to help them rank the projects on the site and within each category. 'The ones that we love and the ones that are very backed tend to sort to the top', explained Cindy. 'And as you scroll down, you'll see projects that have fewer backings, etc.' This tends to produce a self-reinforcing pattern: the more backing projects get, the higher they rise up in the rank order and the more visibility they get on the site, which tends in turn to result in more backing, increasing the likelihood of success. So getting the first crowd on board – the friends, family and followers that make up the first 30 per cent of most campaigns – is doubly crucial: not only does it get the project off the ground, it also gives it the kind of initial backing it needs in order to push it up in the rank order and give it some algorithm-generated visibility on the site. The platforms also have a large membership base – over a million members in each case – and they send out personalized newsletters to members recommending campaigns based on the campaigns they backed and looked at in the past.

With over 500 live projects in the publishing category at any one time, what proportion of these turn out to be successful? Calculating success is not a straightforward matter, especially when you bear in mind that the models used by Indiegogo and Kickstarter differ. In the case of Kickstarter, with its all-or-nothing model, success is a straightforward matter – either you reach your goal and the project goes ahead, or you don't. So what proportion reach their goal? 'Success rates vary by category', explained one Kickstarter insider. 'Overall I'd say our success rate in the publishing category is about 29 per cent.' So around 70 per cent of the publishing projects that are launched on Kickstarter will not reach their goal, and hence will not get funded.[7] That may seem like a dauntingly high failure rate, though it is perhaps a little less daunting if you bear in mind that the projects vary enormously in terms of their attractiveness, compellingness and design. 'Of the 500-odd projects that are live in the publishing category', she continued, 'probably 150 are half-assed attempts to just throw it against the wall and see what sticks. These aren't people who have done a lot of research and are trying very hard.' Take away those 150 half-assed attempts and the success rate would be more like 40 per cent, which sounds a lot better. But still, for anyone launching a crowdfunding project, the odds of reaching your target are against you. That's one reason why the flexible model used by Indiegogo might seem more appealing. Here, success is not an all-or-nothing matter – if you hit your goal, that's great, but the project can still move forward without that. Most of the creative campaigns at Indiegogo use the flexible model. So if success is defined in terms of whether a project moves forward regardless of whether it meets its goal, then Indiegogo's success rate is a lot higher.

Raising money for a book by crowdfunding is one thing, getting the book published is another: how do crowdfunding and publishing connect up in practice? What are the pathways from crowdfunding to publication? On the generic crowdfunding platforms like Indiegogo and Kickstarter, there are numerous pathways to publication – the follow-through to publication is a matter for the campaigner to sort out, it is not something that the crowdfunding platform does for them. Projects vary in terms of the care with which the publication plans have been thought through. There are some cases where an author already has a contract with a traditional publisher and is seeking to raise money to do research for the book or to cover the cost of illustrations or to pay for a special marketing and publicity campaign (or perhaps all of these). For example, Summer Brennan wanted to write a book about the life and work of the French painter and model Victorine Meurent, whose image was immortalized in

---

[7] The overall success rate across all categories may well be higher. Mollick's study of Kickstarter projects launched between its inception in 2009 and July 2012 put the overall success rate at 48.1 per cent (Mollick, 'The Dynamics of Crowdfunding', p. 4).

Manet's most famous paintings, including *Le Déjeuner sur l'herbe* and *Olympia*, but whose life and work have been largely forgotten. She had a contract with Houghton Mifflin Harcourt for a book that she was calling *The Parisian Sphinx*, but she wanted to travel to Paris and spend some time there to do archival research, so she launched an Indiegogo campaign. She set a goal of $25,000, with the aim of using half the funds to support her research and writing and using the other half for perk fulfilment. For $35, backers would get a signed hardcover copy of *The Parisian Sphinx*; for $60, they would get two signed books plus a personalized postcard from Paris; for $75, they would get a signed copy of the book and a lightweight travel bag that the author used 'to schlepp my research, computer, and groceries around Paris'; and so on. Pledge $1,000 and you'd get a person-alized walking tour of Paris with the author, visiting places where Victorine Meurent lived and worked (travel and accommodation not included). Summer reached her goal in two days and set two more 'stretch goals' at $40,000 and $60,000, eventually reaching a total of $53,130 which enabled her to unlock the first stretch goal and make a podcast telling Victorine Meurent's story. Since she already had a publishing contract, all she needed to do then was to do the research and finish writing the book (no small task, of course); from that point on, the route to publication would follow the traditional path.

The Parisian Sphynx is not the typical crowdfunded publishing project, however: in the vast majority of cases, authors do not already have a contract with a traditional publisher. Some might be hoping to attract the interest of a mainstream publishing house while others might be planning to self-publish through a self-publishing platform like Blurb or Lulu or CreateSpace. But even if they are hoping to attract the interest of a mainstream publisher, they are generally advised to play this down as it's not going to sound very convincing as part of a campaign pitch. 'I never advise anyone to say, I'm writing a book so that it will be picked up by a major publisher', said Cindy, the crowdfunding staffer who specializes in publishing. 'Because the backers who back projects want to be assured that they'll get the thing, so most of the time I would suggest that there is a plan to self-publish, with the hope that perhaps it will catch the attention of an agent or an editor who will bring it to a wider audience.' And, occasionally, a crowdfunding project will catch the attention of an agent or editor and get picked up by a traditional publishing house. An example would be Linda Liukas's project to write a children's book, *Hello Ruby*, that aimed to teach the fundamentals of computer programming to 4- to 7-year-olds through stories and kid-friendly activities. Linda set herself the goal of raising $10,000 to cover the cost of copyediting, design, purchase of fonts, production and shipping. Pledging $10 would get you the ebook, $20 would get you the ebook and the companion workbook, $40 would get you a hardcopy edition of the book plus the workbook, $60 would get you that plus a poster of Ruby and her friends, and so on. Linda's campaign was hugely successful: in thirty days, she raised $380,747 from 9,258 backers. This project caught the attention of publishers and Linda was offered a contract by Feiwel and Friends, a children's book imprint of Macmillan, who published the book in 2015.

Of course, *Hello Ruby* was exceptional – most book projects attract nowhere near this number of backers and generate nowhere near this level of funding, and most book projects that get funded will end up going down the self-publishing path, either because this is what the author wanted to do all along or because no traditional publisher picked it up. Alder Yarrow's *The Essence of Wine*, mentioned in the previous chapter, is a good example of a book that was successfully crowdfunded and self-published as part of the author's plan. Another example, equally successful but in a different way, is Margot Atwell's *Derby Life*. Margot is a dedicated roller derby skater: she'd skated with Gotham Girls for seven years, and skated with the WFTDA-champion Gotham All Stars for four seasons. She'd also co-founded a website, Derbylife.com, in 2011, and edited the site for several years. She decided to write a book about roller derby that would describe the history of the sport, explain the gear and the strategy of the game and offer advice to actual and aspiring players – a book for skaters and fans. Margot had also worked for a small independent publisher in New York, Beaufort Books, for seven years, so she knew a thing or two about publishing. She knew enough to know that she could print and publish *Derby Life* herself – she didn't need to go to a traditional publishing house. But she needed some resources for copyediting, typesetting, printing and shipping. She also wanted to be able to pay a small fee to other skaters who could send her brief stories about their experiences in the derby world which she could integrate into the book; and if she could raise a little more money, she would like to include some black-and-white photos. So she set herself the goal of raising $7,000; this included $2,600 for copyediting, typesetting and proofreading; $1,100 to pay other writers for their stories; $2,200 for printing and shipping; and $500 as a reserve. If she exceeded this and raised $8,000 – her stretch goal – then she would include 10–15 black-and-white roller derby photos in the book. For a pledge of $8, you'd get an ebook and a thank you in the book; for $25, you'd get a paperback, an ebook and a thank you in the book; for $40, two paperbacks, two ebooks and a thank you; for $50, a signed paperback, an ebook, a thank you and a limited-edition Derbylife moustache bottle-opener keychain; and so on. She launched her Kickstarter campaign in September 2014, ran it for four weeks and raised $9,183 from 254 backers. Drawing on her knowledge of publishing, she started her own company and self-published *Derby Life* under the imprint of Gutpunch Press. When she sent out the ebooks and paperbacks and other perks, her backers started tweeting and posting pictures on Facebook of them with the book and the moustache bottle opener; they also reviewed the book on Amazon and Goodreads and told their friends about it. So her 254 backers became the centre of an expanding network of potential readers, and because these potential readers were linked to the backers at the centre of the network, many of them were also interested in the subject matter of the book: this is the audience-building mechanism at the heart of the crowdfunding model. 'I ended up printing 1,200 copies and I'd sold pretty much through my first printing less than nine months after I came off press', said Margot.

The fact that Margot had worked in the publishing industry and knew quite a lot about the publishing process put her in a unique position and gave her the confidence to set up her own company to self-publish her book – indeed, her knowledge of the publishing industry is one of the reasons why she was taken on as a Publishing Outreach Lead by Kickstarter, where she now works. Most authors launching campaigns on a crowdfunding platform will not be quite so knowledgeable and autonomous, and they may, like Alder Yarrow, plan to publish through a self-publishing platform like Blurb or Lulu so that they can outsource some of the publishing and printing tasks to others. But, regardless of which pathway to publication an author may choose to follow, what makes the crowdfunding model so effective from a publishing point of view is that a successfully funded project is both pre-funded and pre-ordered. The money is important, to be sure, but just as important is the fact that the number of backers is an indication of the level of interest and potential demand. Indeed, this is one of the reasons why it is not just authors who launch publishing projects on crowdfunding platforms but publishers too, or authors and publishers working together. Sometimes, these crowdfunding collaborations between authors and publishers happen because the author wants to do something that is beyond what the publisher feels able to support financially, so the author launches a campaign, with the publisher's support, to raise extra funds – for example, the publisher has a budget for a three-city tour but the author really wants to travel across the country and do book events in a dozen cities. But the more fundamental reason why some publishers are willing, or even keen, to launch or actively support crowdfunding campaigns is because they recognize the value of the audience-building mechanism at the heart of crowdfunding. The publisher may not need the money – it's not particularly expensive to publish a book, especially these days when digital technologies have greatly reduced many of the costs. What publishers may need more than money is audiences – that is, readers who are sufficiently interested in the books they are publishing to fork out the money to buy them. Astute publishers see that crowdfunding does something other than raise money: it builds a network and an audience for a book. Crowdfunding is a pre-ordering and audience-building machine. Crowdfunding inverts the traditional way that publishers have always done business. In the traditional model, publishers sign up a book and then try to figure out how they can find an audience for it. With crowdfunding, you get the audience with the book – 'you've got an audience right there', explained Cindy, 'and then from that point you can build the audience further with this core of true believers behind it'.

It was this point – the audience-building mechanism that is the hidden genius of crowdfunding – that was grasped by the founders of two innovative publishing organizations that built crowdfunding into the structure of their publishing model. What distinguishes Unbound and Inkshares, on the one hand, from Indiegogo and Kickstarter, on the other, is that Indiegogo and Kickstarter are general crowdfunding platforms where creators can raise money for many different kinds of projects, from technology to the arts, and where, once the money is raised, it is up the creator to follow through with the project and produce what he or she promised to produce – in short, it is up to the creator to deliver. Unbound and Inkshares, by contrast, are crowdfunding organizations focused exclusively on book publishing, and if the crowdfunding goal is reached, these organizations act as publishers and follow through with the production and publication of the book. Whereas Indiegogo and Kickstarter are pure crowdfunding organizations that provide a platform for authors and publishers, among many others, to launch crowdfunding projects, Unbound and Inkshares are publishing organizations that use crowdfunding as a mechanism to raise money and build audiences. They are publishing organizations that depart from traditional publishers by making successful crowdfunding the condition of publication.

Crowdfunding as direct-to-consumer publishing

John Mitchinson, Dan Kieran and Justin Pollard had worked in or around the publishing industry for many years and were well aware of the limitations of traditional publishers. John had been a marketing director at Waterstones before becoming Managing Director of Harvill Press and then of Cassell & Co.; Orion acquired Cassell in 1998 and Hachette acquired Orion, so he had experienced first-hand the growing consolidation of the industry before he left publishing and became a writer. Dan and Justin were also writers – Dan wrote travel books and co-edited *The Idler*, from which he had spun out several successful books, while Justin wrote popular history books and worked as a screenwriter for TV and film. In the wake of the 2008 financial crash, Dan was finding it very hard to interest publishers in a new book; publishers were being extra-cautious and advances had collapsed. 'I was having my lunch break on the sea and I looked out at the ocean and thought I've sold over 400,000 copies of my books to people all over the world but I realized that I didn't have the name or address of a single person that had ever bought one of my books. I'd used all these intermediaries to get to these readers and I just thought, well, that's ridiculous.' He came up with the idea that he could make a video about his book, put it up on his website and try to get people to give him money through PayPal, and if enough people gave him money he would write the book. He discussed the idea with Justin and John, who at that stage were working together at *QI*, a BBC panel game and quiz show, and they thought it was a great idea, though they didn't see why it should be limited to Dan's book – they knew there were plenty of authors out there who were having the same problems as he was. John knew about Kickstarter, which had been around for about a year at that time, and he could see the similarities with some earlier kinds of publishing – 'It struck a chord with me, thinking this is very like the eighteenth-century subscription model only using the internet – it's efficient, you know, and it's moving more of the power towards the author and the reader.' That conversation, over a pint in a London pub in early 2010, was the beginning of Unbound.

From the outset, the co-founders wanted to create a business that would publish books, but one that would be very different from a traditional publisher. 'What had begun to oppress me in publishing', reflected John, 'is what I call the bad karma, which is that you spent your time saying no.' He elaborated:

And if you weren't saying no, you were sort of telling lies. You were saying to authors that their books were doing better than they were or they were going to do better next time. It was an industry that ran on bad karma. And it just felt frustrating because what I loved about being a bookseller was recommending a book to somebody and them coming back a week later and saying that was an incredible book. And that's what crystallized it for me when I came to do Unbound: I realized that traditional publishing's real conceptual problem is that there's no contact with the reader. You think you're doing it for the reader but you're really doing it for the retailers. You're the R&D department for Waterstones and Amazon; you're finding products for them to sell.

The challenge they set themselves was to try to come up with a new model that could bypass the intermediaries and connect directly with readers – 'what you needed to do was to try and have a model that covered the whole process, from the idea in the writer's head to the reader holding the book in their hand.'

They saw that the internet-based crowdfunding model developed by Kickstarter and Indiegogo could be very helpful here because it would enable them to raise money from readers and bypass the traditional publishing gatekeepers, but they also knew that raising money for a book was only the beginning: there was a whole range of publishing services that traditional publishers provided, from editorial and production to sales and marketing, that crowdfunding platforms like Kickstarter didn't provide. That left a gap: could they develop a crowdfunding platform aimed specifically at authors and readers that would fill in all the steps between an author writing a book and a reader getting a printed copy? The readers would decide which books went ahead by deciding which projects to back, just as in Kickstarter, but when the funding threshold had been reached, all the effort and expertise involved in producing and publishing the book would be handled by Unbound. They would be a full-service publisher, and they would also aim to produce high-quality books. This was not going to be a digital-only operation: John, Dan and Justin were too attached to the value of beautiful books that were well designed and well produced to want to give up on the physical object (though they did subsequently launch a digital-only list to allow them to set a lower funding target, intended primarily for writers of fiction seeking to publish their first book). 'We all had a vested interest in quality and we were never comfortable with the idea of an open platform and of just doing it digitally', explained John. 'We wanted to democratize it but it's still my theory that if you open the flood gates totally, you get silted up with crap very, very quickly.' So they would be curating a list and producing books in the traditional way. Authors would pitch the idea for a book to the Unbound editorial team; the editors would decide which projects would go forward for fundraising based on their assessment of the project, using essentially two criteria: the intrinsic interest of the project, and whether the author had the kind of network to get it funded (in short, 'quality of idea and quality of network – ideally both'); the crowd would decide which of these projects would actually get funded by pledging sums of money; and if a project passed the funding threshold, Unbound would then commit to publishing the book and would produce it as a beautifully designed, print-on-paper book. This was a curated crowdfunding model, and hence Unbound would be acting as a gatekeeper – this was never in doubt in the minds of the founders. Curation would reduce the number of projects that proceeded to the fundraising stage and improve the chances of success for the crowd-funding campaigns that went ahead. But by building crowdfunding into their model, they would give readers a voice in the decision-making process and thereby, they hoped, 'open the gate a lot wider'.

As a publishing venture founded by authors, it was important for the founders to come up with a publishing model that would give the author a good deal. So the Unbound publishing model was designed as a joint venture with the author – 'we can't make money unless our authors make money.' Unbound would work out the minimum number of copies they would need to print of the Unbound subscriber special edition (typically somewhere between 350 and 1,000 copies) and work out the amount of money they would need to raise to cover the costs of producing these books (typically in the range of £8,000 to £12,000 for a print edition, though for a digital-only edition the figure would be lower, typically around £4,000). Together with the author, they could then calculate how many people needed to pledge at what levels in order to raise the necessary funding. The campaign would be launched as a typical crowdfunding campaign – write a pitch, make a video and come up with a set of perks for those who were willing to pledge at different levels, with the added perk that all the pledgers would be listed at the back of the book. Once the funding level had been achieved, the 50:50 profit share kicks in. Unbound produces a P&L rather than a traditional royalty statement for each book. They factor in their production costs and an overhead charge, and everything beyond that is shared 50:50 with the author. In practice, most books that get funded will be funded above the target number, and it's this extra funding – 'what we call super-funding' – where Unbound and the authors make all their money. 'No book gets to 100 per cent and stays there', explained Dan, 'they get to 120 or 130 per cent. So if you're getting a £35 pledge for a book which is costing you £5 to print, once you're over-funded, the author is getting 15 quid a copy. The economics change *dramatically* once it's funded', he said, 'so that's why we have a team that helps them super-fund to push themselves up to 300 per cent. They're making really good money at that point.'

While the crowdfunding activity is focused on raising the money for the subscriber special edition that is sent directly to the individuals who pledge funds, the book, once published, can also be distributed and sold in the trade through the normal retail channels. Unbound did deals with other UK publishers to enable books published by Unbound to be distributed in this way, and subsequently worked out a joint venture with Penguin Random House to do this more systematically. In this case, Unbound provides PRH with a print-ready file so that PRH can print a trade edition, and the money received by Unbound from PRH for sales of the trade edition is split 50:50 with the author. But most authors make more money through crowd-funding, by reaching and then exceeding their funding targets, than they make through bookstore sales, and the same is true of Unbound – two-thirds of their revenue is from direct sales, and only a third from bookstore sales. 'The only bit of Unbound that has ever been painful and unpleasant has been trying to get books into bookshops and if we could wave a magic wand and not do that, we would. But it's still important for authors to have their books in bookshops', explained John. 'But we've always felt that the bigger we get, the less dependent we will become on that.'

The Unbound website went live on 29 May 2011 and they launched their first fundraising campaigns later that year. They were a small, London-based start-up – the three of them (only one of whom was working full-time for the start-up) plus one assistant. Growth was modest for the first few years – between 2012 and 2014, the total pledge money raised was between £250,000 and £320,000 per year. But from 2014 on, they began to grow more rapidly. Figure 8.1 shows the growth in money pledged from 2012 to 2017, together with Unbound's cumulative total revenue. Pledge money increased from £320,000 in 2014 to around £1.6 million in 2017, an increase of fourfold in three years. In total, Unbound had raised over £4 million in their first six years. By the middle of 2017, they had successfully funded 265 books and published around 110; they were

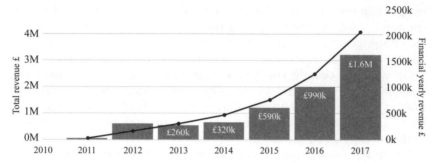

Figure 8.1   Unbound: growth in money pledged, 2011–2017 (black line is cumulative revenue)

launching 15–20 campaigns a month, and funding between 5 and 10 a month. Thanks in part to their curation model, the funding success rate was remarkably high: around 60 per cent were getting funding within twelve months of being put up on the list. In 2013, they also raised £1.2 million in start-up funding from Forward Investment Partners, DFJ Esprit and Cambridge Angels. They were also taking on more staff to support their growth, which made it hard to be profitable. 'We would love to be profitable', explained Dan, 'but the nature of publishing is that your backlist pays your costs and your frontlist gives you the profit and we don't have a backlist.' Buoyed by the start-up funding, they made a conscious decision to focus on growth rather than profitability at this stage – to increase their membership base and increase their title output and worry about profitability later. This was in line with the general zeitgeist of the investment community, but it also made sense because they had to scale up. By 2017, they had 130,000 users, and they reckoned that if they could increase this to a million, then they would be able to fund any book they wanted to fund and could begin to create what they were hoping, ambitiously, to create, which was an alternative ecosystem for books.

The key to this alternative ecosystem is building direct-to-customer relationships. The crowdfunding model means that every new author brings a few hundred new users into the system – their friends and family members and the people who have a particular interest in the book they're proposing to write. And many of these people are people who love and value books. They are similar in some ways to the people who will go to literary festivals just to be around books, to hear authors talk about their books and to talk with other readers about the books they've read and love. The crowdfunding model builds the energy of the literary festival into its structure. 'It was like finding an alternative energy source in the industry, rather than continually trying to beg the retailers to stock more of your books', said John. Through crowdfunding, Unbound could build an expanding network of engaged and committed readers – virtual literary festival goers, as it were – and enable authors to connect directly to them. It could thereby create a publishing model that is built on the one relationship that traditional publishing has always ignored: direct-to-consumer. The crowdfunding model not only enables Unbound to collect money up front and reduce the risk involved in publishing a book to zero (or nearly so), it also enables Unbound to sign up a new set of new users with every campaign that is launched and to gather data about their interests, preferences and pledging behaviour – 'that's where the real gold rush is.' They can then analyse this data, try to understand why people give what they do, how much they typically give and what kinds of projects they tend to support, and then develop appropriate ways of reaching out to the people who are part of this continuously expanding network. Pledging a sum of money to support a book project or an author (or both) is not the same as walking into a store and buying a book: buying a book is a transaction but pledging is a kind of patronage, it's supporting something in order to enable it to happen, to bring it into being. It is therefore a creative act in its own right, an act that makes the reader part of the creative process itself – without this act, or enough acts of a similar kind, the book would not come into being. So Unbound is creating a new kind of relationship between readers and authors, in which readers are not simply the buyers of books but, rather, their co-creators. It's not that readers want to tell authors what to write – for the most part they don't, they're happy to give authors the creative freedom to write the books they want to write. But many readers want to be part of a conversation around the idea of a book and they're willing to pay something – and sometimes pay quite a lot – to be part of that and to enable the book to be written. Unbound is building a constantly expanding database of these co-creators who have demonstrated their willingness to support book projects and who might be willing to support other projects too, in the same way that literary festival goers might find themselves attending events by authors they never heard of before but who sound interesting. They are giving readers a stake in the creative process, and at the same time building a direct-to-consumer relationship which, they believe, is where the future of publishing will be played out. 'When we started, authors brought

303

in 90 per cent of the money for their campaign, but it's gradually shifted. Now they bring in two-thirds of the money and the network brings in the other third.' The larger the network that Unbound is able to build and the more they know about the individuals who are part of it, the more they'll be able to connect authors to potential supporters who are not already part of the author's personal network of family and friends, and the more they'll be able to tap into the enthusiasm of readers.

And all of this happens independently of Amazon. Like most publishers, Unbound is happy to see copies of the trade edition of their books sell through retailers including Amazon, but this is not the focus of their activity and they are wary of building a publishing business that is reliant on Amazon – or on any other large retailer, for that matter. They acknowledge that Amazon is extremely good at what it does, but it reduces human purchasing activity to two factors: speed and cost. On these two factors, Amazon is unbeatable: it will get a book to you more quickly and cheaply than anyone else. But speed and cost are not all that matters here. By becoming increasingly reliant on Amazon as their principal retail channel, traditional publishers are slowly cutting off their own oxygen supply. The more dependent they are on this channel, the more power the channel has to negotiate terms that are more favourable to the retailer, thereby squeezing the publishers' margins and making it harder for them to keep control of the pricing of their most valuable asset – their content. At the same time, by selling their books through an intermediary, traditional publishers are cutting themselves off from the one asset upon which their future might well depend – their customers. 'The agonizing irony is that what we've really done is the two things that Amazon taught publishing', reflected Dan, 'which is that you have to go direct and own the customer, own the reader, and also you have to create an entirely new market, which they did with the Kindle and we've done through crowdfunding.' While traditional publishers become increasingly reliant on Amazon, which accounts for more and more of their business and captures all the customer data to which publishers have no access, Unbound is building a network that bypasses Amazon and enables authors to connect with readers directly via crowdfunding, while at the same time enabling Unbound to capture the customer data rather than leaving it for Amazon to hoover up.

By using crowdfunding not only to raise the funds needed to produce books and thereby reduce the risk involved in publishing them but also to build direct-to-customer relationships, Unbound shared something in common with another crowdfunding publishing venture that was founded a little later on the northern edges of Silicon Valley. But by building connections with Hollywood studios, this Silicon Valley start-up has given the emphasis on readers a new and distinctive twist.

Reader curation

I met two of the co-founders of Inkshares, Thad Woodman and Adam Gomolin, at their offices in an old industrial district in West Oakland, California; halfway through the conversation, we were joined by Alex, an executive at Legendary Entertainment, a Hollywood studio which was cultivating links with Inkshares. The offices are on the second floor of a nineteenth-century red-brick building in a small cul-de-sac that abuts the railway tracks running down to Oakland Point; it is just across the street from what used to be home to a Del Monte cannery that belonged to the California Packing Corporation. The small cluster of old industrial buildings had been renovated and rented out to a variety of small businesses and start-ups, attracted to the site because the rents were much lower than they would be across the Bay in San Francisco. The idea behind Inkshares emerged from a dinner party in Brooklyn, explained Thad, a softly spoken philosophy graduate from Reed College whose parents worked in publishing (they had founded a computer-book publishing company called Ventana Press in the 1990s). In late 2012, Thad was at a dinner party with some wealthy supporters of the arts who were bemoaning the demise of long-form journalism and how difficult it was to get into publishing. He was struck by how much they cared about the issue, and it occurred to him that they might actually be willing to fund the projects they care so much about and to have a direct relation with the author. That was the seed of the idea. The dinner party was a small microcosm of crowdfunding for publishing. But, of course, Indiegogo and Kickstarter already existed and Thad knew about them – why not leave the crowdfunding to them? Like those who created Unbound, Thad felt that the pure crowdfunding platforms, while great for raising money, didn't provide authors with the kind of infrastructure that many needed to get from having the funds, on the one hand, to publishing the book and getting it into the hands of readers, on the other. 'Some authors are very entrepreneurial and they're able to take a bunch of money and produce a great book, but it's very difficult for a lot of people. It's very difficult, almost impossible, to go from money to book to Barnes & Noble. There is a necessary infrastructure around publishing and it's not for nothing.' Thad's hunch was that the crowdfunding element would have to be conjoined with a more traditional publishing operation that would take the author's manuscript, turn it into a book and get it into the existing book distribution systems.

There was another way that Thad wanted to innovate here: he wanted to sell equity in book projects. So, going back to the dinner party, the idea was that the people who care about a book project would not just put in some money to fund it: they would buy equity in the project. 'So instead of just being a patron, you would be able to buy a share of the future revenue stream of a book', explained Thad. The royalties would be distributed and every supporter would have a financial stake in the future success of the book. Hence the name – Inkshares. The idea of equity crowdfunding was not new – it was a well-known model in the crowdfunding world, but it had never been used in relation to books. So that was the original vision: develop an equity-driven crowdfunding model for book publishing and conjoin it with an organizational infrastructure that can take a manuscript, turn it into a book and get it into the retail supply chain.

Thad moved out to San Francisco with another co-founder, Larry Levitsky, to start the company. Larry introduced Thad to Adam Gomolin, a corporate attorney who was doing securities, and the plan was that Adam would be able to work out the equity side of the crowdfunding model. The Jumpstart Our Business Startups Act – or JOBS Act – had just been signed into law in April 2012, and Title III of the Act created a way for companies to use crowdfunding to issue securities, something that had not previously been allowed. Thad, Larry and Adam were planning to use Title III to flesh out their equity crowdfunding model. But when the SEC (the US Securities and Exchange Commission) actually promulgated the rules to make this happen, they did so in a way that made it so complicated and impractical that Thad and his associates came to the conclusion that they would have to drop this idea. 'It was too big of an initial lift to do that. Because in order to do it properly, you've got to issue an LLC for each project, authors would have to incorporate and do all this auditing and it was just going to be too hard to get authors on board', explained Thad. 'And then the people who wanted to invest would also have to be audited. So it was just going to be way too much work.' Faced with these practical problems, they abandoned the equity model and replaced it with the idea of readers pre-ordering copies of books.

At the same time as they were grappling with the equity issue, Thad and his associates were trying to raise money for their new venture. This was turning out to be a lot harder than they thought. By this stage, Thad, Larry and Adam had been joined by a fourth – Jeremy Thomas, who had a background in software development and joined the team as CTO (though Jeremy subsequently left the company). They began pitching their idea to venture capitalists in Silicon Valley but it was hard going. 'We had 168 no's', recalled Jeremy. 'It was brutal. The notion of publishing books, and doing so with physical copies of books, was anathema to the Silicon Valley VC investment thesis.' Adam elaborated: 'Nobody in Silicon Valley believes in books. It just struck them as super-antiquated and, just ... unsexy. They said to us, like, "What if you did it without books?" And we were like, what would we be doing then? And they were like, "Just the front end." It was like being in a show. You'd sit there and you'd be thinking, what the fuck did they just say to us?' For Silicon Valley VCs who were looking to get back at least ten times their investment, book publishing was a turn-off. 'The industry is small. The industry is not exciting. There's no way that the industry is going to 10x in the next ten years', said Thad, summing up the VC's perspective. Book publishing was just not the kind of business that was going to quicken the pulse of a Silicon Valley VC. Despite this discouraging response, they did manage to raise $350,000 from friends and family, and they raised a seed round of $860,000, mostly from angel investors, though a couple of institutional investors also came in. So they raised just over a million dollars – enough to get started.

Inkshares was formally established in 2013 and it began operations in May 2014. The model they had settled on – the pre-order model – works like this: an aspiring author who has an idea for a book could start a book project by describing their idea in twenty words or less. Anyone can do it – there is no selectivity here, provided the author complies with the terms of service, which rule out any content that is defamatory, discriminatory, pornographic, obscene or that incites violence. The idea has a special page, its own URL, and people start to follow it and can write comments. As you gain followers, you can see how much interest there is in your idea; at some point, you may feel that there's enough interest to go to the next stage. So, you press a button that says 'create draft' and you upload part of the manuscript you're working on – maybe just the preface, or part of chapter 1. Pieces of it can be highlighted, commented on and shared on Twitter or Facebook, and that draws in more readers who can give more feedback. And maybe now you have 100 readers following you on Inkshares, and so you decide you're going to go all the way. You press another button that says 'sell pre-orders'. You still haven't written your book, but you've written enough to give readers a sense of what they're buying, and, more importantly, a sense that if they pre-order it now, they'll help the book to get written and published – that's the patronage psychology that is built into every crowdfunding platform. At the outset, the threshold was set at 1,000 pre-orders at $10 per pre-order, generating a fixed sum of $10,000 per title; but they soon realized that this was not enough and the threshold was changed to 750 pre-orders at $20 per pre-order, generating $15,000 per title. When an author reaches the stipulated number of pre-orders, Inkshares will greenlight the book. At this point, Inkshares says, in effect, 'There's sufficient evidence that there is demand for this book and so we are going to act as your publisher and publish your book.' From that point on, Inkshares operates in many ways like a traditional publisher. The book is assigned to a project manager who agrees a delivery date with the author and makes arrangements for editing, design, typesetting, proofreading, printing, etc. – all the stuff that a traditional publisher would do, except that Inkshares doesn't actually do all these things itself: it outsources most of them to others (to begin with, it outsourced them to an independent production company called Girl Friday Productions). When the book is finally printed, the pre-ordered copies are autographed by the author and other copies are distributed through the normal retail channels, thanks in part to an agreement with the distributor Ingram.

While Inkshares operates in some ways like a traditional publisher, there is one big difference: there are no commissioning editors. The pre-order crowdfunding model means that the readers are deciding which books go ahead by pre-ordering them – 'the readers are our acquisition editors', as Jeremy put it. 'Our idea is that readers can do as good a job selecting books as an acquisitions editor. We also believe that no one in publishing really knows which books are going to take off and sell.' He's right about that. He elaborates with an example. One of Inkshares's bestsellers was a book called *The Show*, a novel by an ex-Google employee that was inspired by his experiences at Google – 'it's essentially Wolf of Wall Street meets Silicon Valley.' No one at Inkshares would have bet on this one. The author didn't have a platform and the pre-orders were modest, but there were enough to greenlight the book. Then when it was published, it got picked up by *Business Insider* and a couple of other magazines, and all of a sudden there was interest from a European studio to buy the TV show option and interest from a major trade publisher to buy audiobook rights – they sold both for substantial sums of money. Here was a very successful book, with potential spin-offs into other media, that had been, in effect, commissioned by the readers: had it been up to the staff of Inkshares, they probably would've given this project a miss. But the readers made it happen. That's reader curation.

The funds raised by the first 750 pre-orders are used by Inkshares to cover their fixed costs and reduce the risks involved in publishing the book. From the 751st copy on, the revenue is split with the author. At the outset, this revenue share was very generous to the author. The Inkshares founders reckoned that their risks were low because their origination costs had been largely covered by the crowd through pre-orders; their capital outlay was much more modest than a traditional publisher's, so they could afford to be generous with their royalties. In the original model, the gross revenue – that is, the total revenue received – on all copies sold after the first 750 was split 50:50 on print sales and 70:30 in favour of the author on ebook sales. So if Inkshares received $10 from a retailer for a printed book, the author would get $5 and Inkshares would keep $5, and if they received $5 for the sale of an ebook, the author would get $3.50 and Inkshares would keep $1.50. On the print books, Inkshares would need to pay their printing costs and distribution costs out of the $5 they received. They soon realized, however, that this was leaving them with very little, especially since the funds raised through pre-orders were often less than their actual production costs, which meant that they were, in effect, subsidizing most books. Like many start-ups, they were experimenting: they had set out a financial model and they were seeing, through trial and error, if it worked. It didn't. They found themselves haemorrhaging capital ('we were taking on water, it was deeply unsustainable but we were still floating') and by 2016 they came to the conclusion, amid some internal disagreement, that the model had to change.

The new model, which was laid out by Adam in an article published in *Medium* in July 2016, was very different.[8] Author royalties would no longer be calculated on gross revenue but on net receipts – that is, the net revenue after certain costs had been deducted (for print books, they would deduct print costs, shipping and packaging fees and payment processing for direct orders, and they would deduct print costs, the distribution fee and payment

---

[8] Adam Gomolin, 'Restructuring Royalties', *Medium* (31 July 2016), at https:// medium.com/@adamgomolin/restructuring-royalties-38e7c566aa02.

processing for wholesale orders; for ebooks, there would be similar deductions but without the print costs). What's left over after these deductions would be split 65 per cent to Inkshares and 35 per cent to authors – in other words, authors would now get 35 per cent of net receipts. So on a book where the gross revenue was $10, the author would now receive about $2.20 (rather than the $5 in the original model). This was a big change and it didn't go down well with some authors, especially when they were in the midst of a fundraising campaign.[9] On the other hand, anyone who knows anything about the real costs of producing and distributing printed books can see that Inkshares's original model was unrealistic, so the fault – if one is going to attribute fault here – was almost certainly in the design of the original model, rather than in the belated decision to change it.

Changing the financial model was a moment of reckoning for the founders of Inkshares – they had to admit to themselves that they got it wrong and they had to take some draconian measures to put the company on a more sustainable basis ('not exactly a pivot, but it was like 45 degrees', conceded one). But it also helped them to focus on what was distinctive and innovative about Inkshares. What they had come up with, via the pre-order crowdfunding model, was a mechanism for doing market research for every book project in an industry that had always spurned market research. The pre-order system was a way of testing the water before any decision was taken about whether to go ahead with a book. 'The difference between something that's coming out of Simon & Schuster and something that's coming out of Inkshares is the fact that 750 people have already raised their hands, minimum', said Alex, the executive from Legendary Entertainment who had now joined our conversation. 'So there's something tangible about that. It's not just "We're in our echo chambers", and it's not just "Oh, this is a book for me." There's data to suggest that there is an audience for this.' Inkshares was creating a curated list, but the curation was done by readers, not by editors. Reader curation was the core.

The connection with Hollywood was not accidental. The movie industry faced a very similar problem to the book industry but on a much bigger scale. There were lots of movies they could make, but somehow they had to narrow the range down to a small number – and to a much smaller number than the book industry because the scale of the investment is much greater. How can you turn this

---

[9] See, for example, http://jdennehy.com/my-experience-with-inkshares-a-cautionary-tale.

decision-making process into something other than a crapshoot? If you had a way of gathering systematic evidence of what people wanted to see before they could actually see it, that might be very helpful. One way of doing this would be to see if there is an audience for a screenplay before you turn it into a movie. So you could novelize it, let Inkshares push it into the market and then use the data generated by Inkshares to help you decide whether to turn it into a movie. A studio could do this over and over again, using Inkshares's publishing system as a way to discover and vet intellectual property (IP) for the movie system. This is how Inkshares ended up forming partnerships with Legendary and other Hollywood studios – and why Alex was there and had now joined our conversation.

These partnerships have real advantages for Inkshares too. Among other things, they are a valuable source of new authors and new users, and they have been a crucial driver of growth for Inkshares. Legendary has acquired a number of media brands like Nerdist, Geek & Sundry and Smart Girls, and from time to time these brands will put out a call to their followers to come onto the Inkshares platform, submit their manuscripts and start collecting pre-orders, and Inkshares will publish the top three. On average, each new book that starts funding on Inkshares brings in another 142 new readers, simply because of the outreach that an author does on his or her behalf. So each competition of this kind results in a substantial influx of new readers who are brought into Inkshares's system. 'That's probably the best funnel we've had to date', explained Thad. By early 2017, they had around 100,000 users in their system, nearly double what it had been a year previously. About 5,000 projects had been started on the platform and around 60 books had been published since their first book, *The Cat's Pajamas*, appeared in November 2014; another hundred or so had been greenlighted and were in various stages of production. Given that anyone can start a project, the proportion that actually get greenlighted is quite small – only about 1 in 10. But whether they get greenlighted or not, they still add value because the authors reach out to their networks and bring new people in.

Increasing the number of readers who are in the system is crucial for Inkshares if it wants to create a reader curation system that has some degree of generalizability. If all the pre-orders for each book were made only by the individuals that the author of that book brought into the system, then this wouldn't tell you much about the appeal of that book to readers who had no personal connection to the author. So if the reader curation system is going to have a more general applicability and to be of interest to Hollywood studios and others, then it is essential to create what Adam calls 'liquidity', 'where there's a sufficient number of arm's-length disinterested readers with no social connection to the author, such that you'd have an actual manifestation of interest in the book, rather than a bunch of people who gathered around an author and wanted their buddy to get a book published.' If you can build an ecosystem where you have a large number of users and a high degree of liquidity, then you can begin to do some interesting things with the data. Thad elaborated: 'On the basis of each user's interactions on the platform, we're able to say, OK, here's the universe of content that you've not yet seen, and we're able to rank that and present you with the most relevant story. And you say, OK, that's good or that's not good, that then retrains the algorithm and it gets better and better at adapting to your taste and feeding you things that are going to be interesting.' But the important point here is not just that they can develop and refine a recommendation algorithm, it's that they're able to use readers' decisions to pre-order or not to pre-order – and in information terms, passing on something is just as meaningful as deciding to pre-order – to help solve the fundamental problem of sorting and filtering content, of deciding which content is to be selected out of the slush pile and turned into a product, a problem that is fundamental to every creative industry that deals with content. 'If the people within the industry whose job it is to sort and filter content are even 10 or 15 per cent more efficient, that's really valuable for them.'

There are moments when the founders of Inkshares express an even bolder vision. 'We wanted to create a portal where we could measure reader interest, decide to publish and greenlight books on the basis of measurement rather than guesswork, and then use that to move from the publishing industry to the global story industry, which is about ten times the size', explained Adam. Books are a good place to start if you're going to do this because books are pretty much the fulcrum of the global story economy. 'There's like 4,000 active projects in Hollywood, and 3,000, maybe 2,500, of them are based on some form of IP, and probably three-quarters are a book – the rest is video games, graphic novels, reboots of pre-existing movies, stuff like that', he continued. Alex, from Legendary, chipped in at this point: 'A big part of my job, as with a lot of creative executives in Hollywood, is just about panning for gold. We're all looking for the next big thing, the next big idea, and a lot of those things will come from publishing.' So if they could develop an effective system of reader curation that worked for books, it could feed in directly to the broader entertainment industry. The potential for synergies seemed considerable. They might even be able to roll out comparable user curation systems for other verticals – film, TV, games, etc.

The founders of Inkshares could not be accused of lack of ambition, and their vision of putting themselves at the heart of the global story industry may seem somewhat inflated. They remain a small, niche operation – by early 2017, they'd only published around sixty books and they were still struggling to achieve profitability. But the way they used crowdfunding to create a system of reader curation, building a publishing operation where it is the readers, not the publishers, who decide what gets published, was genuinely innovative and path-breaking. They used crowdfunding to turn the traditional model of publishing – where publishers, using a mixture of judgement, gut feeling, experience of other books and guesswork, decide which books to publish and then push them out into the market, hoping they will find readers – on its head. It was a radical move from which traditional publishers, and indeed those working in other sectors of the creative industries, could learn a thing or two.

The pull of the mainstream

From a publishing point of view, there is a lot to be said in favour of crowdfunding models – not only do they reduce the risk involved in producing a book but also, crucially, they create a market for a book before the book exists, even before a decision has been taken about whether to publish a book. It is a brilliant mechanism for testing the market – and, indeed, for creating a market – in an industry that, for 500 years, has operated largely without any effective form of market research, relying more on the judgements of editors and publishers than on the expressed preferences of readers. But what about the author's point of view – how appealing is the idea of crowdfunding a book if you're considering this as an author? Of course, the answer to this question will vary from author to author, and even from time to time in the course of an author's career – it may be attractive at one point in time, especially if other options don't seem to be available, and less attractive at a later point when other paths may open up. There is no single, simple answer to this question, but rather a plurality of answers depending on who you ask and when you ask them. There is no doubt that crowdfunding has proven to be an effective way for many authors to bypass the gatekeepers who regulate the flow of new content into the channels of the traditional publishing industry, enabling them to raise sufficient capital to get their book published when the gatekeepers have shown little or no interest or have declined to take it on. At the same time, it is also the case that, when authors go down the crowdfunding path, they are taking on an additional set of commitments that can be onerous. Tom, the staffer at one of the big crowdfunding organizations, was up front about this – 'You have to do the work – it's a full-time job.' And if you're crowdfunding with one of the generic organizations like Indiegogo or Kickstarter, you still have to make your own arrangements to publish your book, even if you've been successful at raising the cash. The crowdfunding organizations that have specialized in publishing, like Unbound and Inkshares, make it a lot easier for authors to publish their books once the funding has been raised: they act as traditional publishers once a project has passed the funding threshold, taking the book from the submission of the final manuscript through the different stages of production to the final printing and distribution of the book. But they might still offer less than a traditional publisher does. Or at least that's how it might seem in the eyes of some authors.

Sarah was an active user of Twitter, where she had built up a following of several thousand people who enjoyed reading her regular comments on current affairs, which were composed as witty aperçus with a humorous, tongue-in-cheek tone. The size of her Twitter following – 20,000 and growing – attracted the attention of one of the editors at Unbound, who reached out to Sarah and asked her whether she might consider turning her aperçus into a book and launching a campaign on Unbound. She was intrigued; she'd never thought about writing a book before and she'd never heard of Unbound, but she checked them out, did a bit of research and warmed to the idea: 'The more I looked into it, the more they seemed like a really good match for what I was doing. I'd never intended to write a book in the first place and the whole thing had come out of Twitter, and I'd be going back to those people on Twitter to say I've been sharing this free stuff with you, and now if you could do me a favour and buy it in the form of a book, I'd be really grateful. It just seemed like a nice fit, given its roots.' So she decided to give it a go. The people at Unbound guided her through the process, helped her put together a funding campaign with a set of goals and rewards and make a video, and before long she was ready to launch. She started tweeting her followers and gave them the details with a link to the crowdfunding page. It all happened very quickly and she hit her target after three days. The campaign ran for another few months, by which time she'd raised nearly three times the target figure. The book went into production, it was beautifully produced and it sold well – in addition to the thousand or so pledgers, the trade edition sold another thousand copies in hardcover and a few thousand copies in paperback. This was a crowdfunding success story: happy author, happy publishers, several thousand readers who were able to buy and read a book that would not have existed without this crowdfunding platform and the initiative of the staffers who worked for it.

Spurred on by the success of her first book and the generally positive experience of working with Unbound, Sarah was soon beginning to think about doing another book – 'a future of more of the same, doing another collection, probably with Unbound.' But now that her first book was out and doing rather well, agents began to get in touch with her. 'An agent, Lucy, wrote to me and suggested that we meet up and talk about my plans for the future, and so I met with her and I said, "Well, I don't really have any plans, other than what I'm currently doing." And she said, "Well, I think you should be more ambitious and think about writing something beyond what you're doing", and she gave me a few ideas and I mulled them over.' The more Sarah thought about it, the more she liked what Lucy was saying, so she decided to sign with her. Unbound were also in touch with Sarah about a sequel, but she was now moving in another direction. Lucy had her own ideas about what Sarah should be publishing and who she should be publishing with, and Unbound was low on her list of preferred publishers. 'Lucy had strong ideas from the start about who we might approach, and she was really keen on one publisher in particular – she'd worked with them in the past and she liked the team.' With Lucy's guidance and feedback, Sarah produced a new manuscript and they agreed to give Lucy's preferred publisher, 'Pacific', an option for a week. Pacific loved the text, made a good offer with a substantial, high five-figure advance and that was it – Sarah was now publishing with a mainstream trade house.

So what drew Sarah away from the innovative crowdfunding start-up that had been her gateway into the publishing world? Why not do another book with them – they wanted her to stay, and their 50:50 profit share seemed better, on the face of it, than the royalties she would be offered by any mainstream publisher. While she was grateful to Unbound for giving her the opportunity to publish her first book, the attractions of signing with an agent and moving to a mainstream publisher were hard to resist. In the first place, she liked having an agent who has views about what she should be doing, gives her helpful feedback on her work and wants to manage her writing and her career. Sarah didn't actually get much editorial feedback from Unbound – just a few minor suggestions, 'a few words here and there'. Lucy, by contrast, didn't shy away from giving her quite radical feedback. 'I was very resistant at first, and then I thought about it and thought, well, let's just try it and see what happens, and I realized she was exactly right. I would never have got there on my own.' She also liked the idea that she would be publishing with a trade house that had a serious commitment to marketing and publicity – that was the one real gripe she had about publishing with Unbound. 'Probably the one negative aspect was around marketing and publicity because it felt like I was the author, the marketer and the publicist, and there wasn't anybody else. And I think that's probably a case of resources because they were still a relatively small publisher, one that is reliant on authors having their own platforms rather than themselves really driving the sales. When the book finally came out, it didn't really stretch much beyond that Twitter circle. There were one or two reviews and that was kind of it.' With her new book, Sarah was hoping for something else. 'I don't really want to have to do my own marketing and publicity', explained Sarah, and she had no doubt that Pacific would have a bigger reach: 'The publicity director is really keen on the book and she's a pretty powerful publicity manager in the trade world.' And then, of course, there was the publisher's contract and the advance: the first few days of her crowdfunding campaign at Unbound had been exhilarating and she was thrilled that so many people responded so positively and were happy to support her book, but it would be hard to turn down a deal where the publisher was offering a big advance up front and investing all the funds needed to produce and publish the book, with no fundraising campaign required from the author.

That wasn't all. It wasn't just about editorial feedback, publicity and money – there was also a symbolic element, a sense that she would be gaining some recognition in the literary world by moving to a mainstream publisher. 'I think probably the other thing – and it pains me a little bit to say this – is a thing around legitimacy. Not that Unbound aren't a legitimate publisher – I'd overcome my qualms about that – but [Pacific] has the bigger name. You look at the other authors they've got on their list who regularly come back to them. And although I've always shied away from being associated with other writers and the writing scene, there's a bit of me that wants to be in there, to have my cake and eat it.' Although a little reluctant to admit it, Sarah valued the recognition, the symbolic capital, she would gain by publishing with Pacific and finding herself in the company of all the great writers they had on their list. It felt good, like she was being admitted into a select club, invited to sit at the table with other writers who were celebrated and respected, knowing that some of that respect would rub off on her simply by virtue of the fact that she was there, in the company of great writers. Unbound had published many excellent authors too, but their list was nothing compared to Pacific's. On this, there was no competition.

Looking back, Sarah was happy to have published her first book with Unbound, but happy to have moved on too. 'They were a kind of enabler – not that I knew I needed to be enabled – but because with their model the risks for them are low, they were happy to take a risk with someone like me.' It was also a great fit for the kind of thing she was doing at the time, when she was very active on Twitter and posting something almost every day – 'the marriage of the online community to the project worked perfectly.' But she was now at a different phase in her life. She wanted to build a career as a writer, and fostering a relationship with an agent and a bigger publisher felt like the right thing to do. This doesn't mean that she wouldn't publish again with Unbound at some point in the future – it was a positive experience overall, she had a lot of respect for the people there and she can imagine circumstances when it might make sense for her to do another book with them, maybe of things based around her life on Twitter. 'So I wouldn't say that I've ruled them out completely, but I can't see them as part of my immediate future.' As she sees things now, Unbound was a stepping stone rather than a final destination.

Of course, this is only one author, one story, one life: other authors will have different stories to tell, and not every author will be as successful as Sarah – indeed, her story is more the exception than the rule. But it does point to some important considerations. First, that, while crowdfunding may be an effective way for some authors to get a book published, it is not necessarily the pathway they would choose if they had other opportunities. It is quite a lot of work, and you need to be able to tap into networks of potential supporters in order to make it happen. Sarah, with her large Twitter following, was ideally positioned to do this, but even Sarah preferred to move to a mainstream publisher when she had the chance. Second, Sarah's story highlights the fact that the choices authors make will also depend on where they are in their life and their career, and a choice that might seem sensible at one stage is not necessarily the choice that they would make at a different stage. As the field of publishing becomes more varied and diversified, with many new players entering the field and offering a range of different options, authors will have more choices, and the trajectories they chart for themselves may involve different options chosen at different points in time, exactly as it was for Sarah. And, finally, as Sarah's story reminds us, an author's movement through this new and more diversified field may involve the movement from a new and innovative publishing organization – whether this is a crowdfunding publisher like Unbound or Inkshares, or a self-publishing platform like Smashwords or KDP – to a more traditional, mainstream publisher like Pacific, just as it may involve a movement the other way. Different organizations and platforms offer different things – each have their pros and cons, and authors who are in a position to make choices will weigh these up and chart a course that seems likely to deliver what matters most to them at that point in time.

— Chapter 9 —

BOOKFLIX

The digital revolution in the media industries has not only enabled individuals and organizations to produce and deliver content in new ways: it has also opened up new possibilities in terms of how content can be consumed. One of the most significant developments in this regard has been the emergence of internet-based on-demand streaming services in various media sectors. In film and television, Netflix has been one of the leading innovators. Founded in California in 1997 by Reed Hastings and Marc Randolph, Netflix began as a DVD sales and rental business, using the US postal service to send out and return DVDs and competing directly with Blockbuster.[1] It introduced a subscription service in 1999, and in 2007 it began streaming video on demand via the internet. The streaming video business quickly took off: by 2011, Netflix had more than 23 million subscribers in the US; by 2018, it had over 58 million US subscribers and over 137 million subscribers worldwide. Blockbuster, its main competitor in the early 2000s, went bankrupt in 2010, while other streaming video services emerged to compete with Netflix, such as Hulu and Amazon Video (available to all Amazon Prime subscribers). The streaming services provided customers with a new way of consuming movies, TV shows and, increasingly, original series produced by the streaming services themselves: by paying a monthly subscription fee, they could watch this content on demand, whenever they wanted and as much as they wanted, viewing it on their TV sets, computers or mobile devices. Consuming movies, TV shows and series had become much more flexible, allowing customers to choose what they wanted to view

---

[1] For a full account of the history of Netflix, see Gina Keating, *Netflixed: The Epic Battle for America's Eyeballs* (New York: Penguin, 2013).

from a large pool of audio-visual content that was available instantaneously and anywhere at the touch of a button.

A similar development occurred in the music industry. While Apple's iTunes pioneered the digital download business for music in the early 2000s, enabling consumers to purchase single songs for 99¢ as well as albums by downloading them directly to their devices, others took the lead in developing subscription-based streaming services for music. A key player here was Spotify, a music streaming platform founded in 2006 by two Swedes, Daniel Ek and Martin Lorentzon. Having grown up with Napster, Ek and Lorentzon were well aware of the benefits of being able to browse music collections online, but they wanted to embed this experience in a legal framework that would provide a legitimate alternative to piracy and would have the support of the artists and the record labels.[2] They built a service, launched in October 2008, that enabled users to access DRM[3]-protected content from record labels, media companies and independent artists. Users could listen to music streamed to their devices on a 'freemium' model, whereby basic services were free and supported by advertising, and premium services – which included ad-free listening and higher sound quality – were available by subscription. By March 2011, they had a million paid subscribers in Europe; by November 2018, they had 87 million paid subscribers and 191 million active users worldwide, making it the largest subscription-based streaming music service, though it now faces serious competition from Apple Music, which was launched in June 2015, Google, which now offers two streaming subscription services, and Amazon, as well as from other dedicated music streaming services which have been around for longer, such as Deezer. As with Netflix, these streaming music services enabled users to access music in new ways, browsing and selecting music from large databases and listening to it as and when they wish. Individuals' relationship to the music they listened to was changing: they were accessing or 'renting' music rather than owning it, and there was no longer any need for them to purchase the music outright. With a substantial proportion of users willing to pay a subscription fee to

---

[2] Sarah Lacey, 'How Daniel Became Goliath: An Interview with Spotify CEO Daniel Ek', Startups.co (12 March 2017), at www.startups.co/articles/how-daniel-became-goliath.
[3] Digital Rights Management (DRM) technologies are a set of tools that enable rights owners to specify and control the ways in which intellectual property can be used – for example, by allowing content to be accessed only by authenticated users, to be used only on a limited number of devices, not to be copied, etc.

access premium services that are free of ads, these services have also succeeded in generating strong revenue streams.

Streaming services are particularly attractive for content like movies and music because these are what economists call 'experience goods'.[4] An experience good is a product or service where the properties are difficult to know in advance: a consumer has to sample or experience the good or service in order to get the kind of information they need to guide their choices. Of course, consumers can and do use other sources of information as well, such as reputation, word of mouth from trusted others (such as family and friends) and product reviews, but the most reliable source of information is actually to experience the good or service oneself. The types of goods and services that are commonly described as experience goods are restaurants, bars, hairdressers, holidays, etc., but many media products could also be described as experience goods: it is difficult for a consumer to know whether they want to watch a movie or buy a new LP unless they are able to experience or sample the movie or music in some way – for example, by watching a trailer or listening to a few tracks. Given this characteristic of media products, it makes a lot of sense to be able to access them via a streaming service, which allows the consumer to sample lots of products and choose to watch or listen to at length (or repeatedly) only those which they really enjoy.

Since streaming services don't own the content they are making available to consumers, the attractiveness and sustainability of the service depend on their ability to acquire a large range of desirable content on viable terms. Two business models are commonly used to acquire content. One model is the up-front flat-fee licensing model: the streaming service pays an up-front licensing fee to the content owners, in return for which the service can make the content available to its subscribers on an unlimited basis for a defined time period; the fee is significantly higher if the rights are exclusive. This is the model used by Netflix and other streaming video services. In the early days of streaming video, Netflix was able to acquire licences for high-quality content for relatively low prices. But as the competition increased, the studios and media companies could hold out for higher prices and add more restrictive conditions; acquiring content using the up-front licensing fee model became increasingly expensive, creating a strong incentive for Netflix and other streaming

---

[4] Phillip Nelson, 'Information and Consumer Behavior', *Journal of Political Economy*, 78, 2 (1970), 311–29.

services to create their own original content in order to exercise greater control over the content acquisition costs. A second model is the fixed royalty-pool model: rather than paying an up-front licensing fee, the streaming service channels a proportion of its revenue into a royalty pool which it pays out to content owners according to a certain formula. This is the model used by Spotify and other music streaming services: the subscription service decides what proportion of its revenue will be channelled into a royalty pool (in the case of Spotify, the figure is around 70 per cent), they calculate the proportion of plays or streams represented by each artist and they then pay out to the record label that proportion of the revenue that has been channelled into the pool. How much the artist receives will depend on their agreement with the record label. Because the payouts from the royalty pool are proportional to the total number of plays and the total number of plays can be very large (effectively limitless), the amount paid per play can be very small – Spotify claims to pay an average of $0.006 to $0.0084 per stream to rights holders, though others estimate that the rate is generally between $0.004 and $0.005 per stream. Moreover, a proportional payment model of this kind tends to favour the major labels and the most popular artists; niche artists who are competing against very popular artists will find themselves earning a very tiny share of the royalty pool. The skewing of payouts in favour of the major labels and most popular artists, coupled with the fact that the value of each payout is very small, has elicited a growing chorus of criticism from artists and others in recent years, highlighted in 2014 by Taylor Swift's decision to remove all her music from Spotify amid a blaze of bad publicity for the company.[5]

If streaming services were proving to be popular with consumers of movies and music, why not with readers? The streaming services were taking off at the same time as ebook sales were growing exponentially, so it was entirely plausible to think that books could be accessed electronically via a subscription service in the same way as movies and music – why not? Like movies and music, books were experience goods: you don't really know whether you're going to enjoy reading a particular book until you start reading it, though of course there are many ways of reducing the risk (e.g., if you like

---

[5] Hannah Ellis-Petersen, 'Taylor Swift Takes a Stand over Spotify Music Royalties', *The Guardian*, 5 November 2014, at www.theguardian.com/music/2014/nov/04/taylor-swift-spotify-streaming-album-sales-snub. For an overview of the controversy between artists and Spotify, see L. K. R. Marshall, '"Let's Keep Music Special. F--- Spotify": On-Demand Streaming and the Controversy over Artist Royalties', *Creative Industries Journal*, 8 (2015), 177–89.

books by Stephen King or Lee Child, then you can be pretty sure that you're going to enjoy his next book). Moreover, the opportunity to read as much as you like for a modest monthly subscription fee might be a financial proposition that was difficult to resist for some heavy readers. These were among the considerations that led to the emergence of a number of subscription-based services for digital book content from 2010 on.

Scribd's wager

Trip Adler and Jared Friedman met as students at Harvard in the early 2000s. Jared was studying computer science, and Trip was majoring in physics and art. They wanted to start a company together but they weren't sure what the company would be. They worked on a bunch of different ideas, trying to get a feel for the start-up landscape and the current state of the internet, and eventually they came up with the idea that would turn into Scribd. Trip's father was a professor at Stanford and he was complaining that there wasn't a simpler way to publish a medical paper that he'd just finished. 'So we had the idea that we would just create a service that would let him take his paper and easily publish it and share it on the web', explained Trip. 'And then we quickly expanded that beyond medical papers to include all kinds of written content. So we basically became what we called the YouTube for documents – you can take any kind of document and just publish it on the web.' They moved out to the Bay area, raised $12,000 from the incubator Y Combinator, another $40,000 from an angel investor and then, shortly after that, $3.5 million from venture capitalists, and they launched Scribd on 6 March 2007. Like many start-ups at this time, the mantra was to build the user base and grow as fast as you can and worry about how to monetize it later – 'that's how Google started and Facebook started, so we had the same mindset.' The key was to focus on a metric that reflected the specificities of the company and just keep optimizing that metric. 'So for us it was the number of documents uploaded and traffic to those documents. So we got this viral loop going where we got people to upload documents and the documents would bring traffic, and then some of the traffic would upload their own documents, and the viral loop just began in that way.'

In those early days, Scribd was free: users could upload documents and access documents free of charge. Trip and Jared didn't start thinking seriously about revenue until a year or two in. As with many tech start-ups, much of this was experimental: you try something, see if it works – if it does you develop it, and if it doesn't you ditch it and try something else. In 2008, they put some ads on the site and generated a modest revenue stream. Then they tried selling content, especially books. 'We noticed from early on that book publishers were sharing book excerpts on our service to promote their books, so we figured we might as well let them sell their books.' They launched the Scribd Store and they got all the Big Five on board pretty quickly. They were acting as an ebook retailer, selling ebooks on the agency model. But this didn't work very well. Their users didn't want to pay for content, and, if they did, they were more likely to go to Amazon. So this experiment stalled – 'it just never really went anywhere.' They started experimenting next with a premium model, which was the other model that was popular at the time. The plan was to charge $8.99 a month as a subscription fee for a few premium features, like an ad-free experience, unlimited access, unlimited downloading, unlimited printing of content, etc. They began to experiment with the model in 2010 – by that time, they had around 80 million monthly visitors. Some users reacted badly: they got some irate emails, and some users expressed their anger on internet forums. Many users left and never returned. But a great many stayed too, and many decided to opt in to the premium service. Trip put this down to a combination of good content and a good user experience: 'It was really those two things: we had a library of content that no one else had, and we built a unique experience for browsing and looking at content.' As a revenue-generating mechanism, the premium subscription model was working much better than ads and much better than trying to sell content on the site. By 2012, they were profitable as a business.

But, while they were profitable, they weren't growing very fast; they needed to fuel the subscription model by putting more quality content in the premium service. They were aware that Netflix and Spotify were doing well and that they had succeeded in taking media industries where content had been sold on an à la carte basis and transforming them into subscription-based services. Scribd had lots of ebooks in their store that weren't selling and they realized that they were making much more money off content by driving the premium features than by trying to sell content. So they thought that, if they could partner with book publishers and put their books in the subscription service so that they would be available to premium users, then they might be able to make a lot more money – both for themselves and for publishers. They could do for books what Netflix had done for movies and TV, and Spotify had done for music: offer an ebook subscription service where users, in return for their monthly subscription fee, would have unlimited access to the books available in the service. They already had many of the elements in place: they had the reading platform, they had a large number of visitors to the site, they had a subscription service with lots of subscribers who were already paying money, they had a lot of demand for ebooks, and they had existing relationships with many publishers, including the Big Five.

The challenge now was to figure out how to persuade publishers to license their ebooks to a subscription service. No one had ever done a subscription service for ebooks, so it wasn't clear how it would work, whether any publishers would give them the rights to do it and whether they could acquire the rights on terms that would make the enterprise financially worthwhile for publishers and financially viable for them. So they went out and talked to publishers. The fact that Netflix and Spotify already existed made it easier: they could use these examples to show that the model had worked in other media sectors. But it still wasn't easy. Most of the publishers they talked to said 'No way, absolutely not, subscription services for ebooks will never work.' They had lots of reasons for thinking this – people don't read as many books as they listen to songs, so the consumer-value proposition is not as strong for books; the rights issues were insurmountable and it would be impossible to structure a deal in a way that would be fair for authors; subscription reading would cannibalize the sales of ebooks and publishers would come out worse; and so on. In short, they were not given a warm reception. 'We talked to many people in the publishing industry', recalled Jared; 'I would say that probably nine out of ten of them told us that the idea would never work and we were crazy and should give up.' But they persevered. They had some success when two small publishers in the Bay area, Berrett-Koehler and Inner Traditions, decided to give it a go, but they knew that they would have to find a way to get some of the big mainstream trade publishers on board in order to make this work. Much would depend on the financial model they used to pay the publishers. They knew about the up-front licensing fee model used by Netflix and the royalty pool model used by Spotify, but it seemed clear that neither of these models was going to work for ebooks: even if publishers could be persuaded to use an up-front licensing fee model (which is unlikely), the fees they would have to pay to license content in this way would be far too high; and mainstream publishers were strongly opposed to a royalty pool model, which shifts all the risk on to the content owners. One of their advisors in the publishing industry – someone who had worked as a senior executive for one of the Big Five and had a good feel for their concerns – suggested a different model, what could be called a 'threshold' or 'pay-per-use' model: Scribd would pay the publisher as if the book had been bought outright once the user had passed a certain threshold. So the proposal they came up with was this: Scribd would pay the publisher 80% of the price of the book whenever 20% of the book was read. The threshold itself was variable – it could vary from publisher to publisher, but 20% was the target.

The threshold or pay-per-use model had obvious attractions for publishers: it shifted the risk from the publisher to the service provider, ensuring that publishers were paid as if the book had been sold once a user had read 20% of the book. It didn't matter whether the user finished the book or even read another sentence: the 20% threshold had been reached and this triggered the payment. There was still a risk of cannibalization in this model, as readers could start to read lots of books and never reach the 20% threshold, and hence the publishers would be paid nothing for this below-the-threshold reading activity. But the risk was much lower than it was in the pool model, and, more importantly, the amount paid to the publishers when readers reached the 20% threshold was likely to be much higher and within the control of the publishers, since the publishers set the prices. But the threshold model carried big risks for the service provider – in this case, Scribd – because it assumed that subscribers to the service would, on average, read very few books. If all or most of the subscribers read several books every month, or even read more than 20% of several books every month, then the payouts to publishers would greatly exceed the revenues they earned through the monthly $8.99 subscription fee. So the viability of this model from Scribd's point of view depended on the assumption that relatively few subscribers would be heavy book readers, and that the heavy book readers would be compensated for by lots of light readers who read very few books and/or rarely got past the 20% threshold. In other words, this was the gym model for books: there are a few heavy users who go to the gym every day, but a substantial proportion of the people who take out a gym membership go to the gym very rarely or not at all. The general rule of thumb in the subscription business is that you need two-thirds of light users to subsidize one-third of heavy users – if everyone's usage pattern is at the heavy end, it doesn't work, whether you're running a gym or a subscription service for books.

Scribd went into this knowing full well the risks: they knew this would work for them financially only if the gym model worked for books and most subscribers turned out to be like those well-intentioned people who sign up for the gym and rarely, if ever, go. But they also knew they had little choice: if they wanted to get the mainstream trade publishers on board, then it seemed clear that this was the only model that would work. It was a gamble, a wager, a calculated bet. They had no idea whether it would work in the end, but they knew they would only find out if they tried. 'So we decided to go for it', said Trip, 'we figured there was room to optimize down the road.' First, they signed up a number of small and medium-sized publishers; they also added lots of self-published books, especially from Smashwords. Then one of the Big Five, HarperCollins, came on board, making available their entire ebook backlist: everything one year old and older. With HarperCollins on board, they felt they had enough content and credibility to launch the ebook subscription service, which they did on 1 October 2013. In May 2014, Simon & Schuster decided to make its ebook backlist available on Scribd, and in January 2015 Macmillan followed suit. So now they had three of the Big Five on board. In some of these cases, they were making sizeable up-front advance payments to encourage key publishers to participate. In November 2014, they added 30,000 audiobooks, to which subscribers would have unlimited access for the same $8.99 subscription fee. This was rapidly scaling up to a formidable offering.

It wasn't long, however, before the problems began to appear. The problems stemmed from the paradox that lies at the heart of the threshold model: your best and most loyal users are also your most unprofitable users. The more they consume, the more they cost you, so the heaviest users become your biggest liabilities. This creates a 'reverse incentive structure' where the provider begins to look for ways to limit or discourage use by the heaviest users. Following the launch of the ebook and audiobook subscription service, Scribd's financial position deteriorated quickly and it went from being a profitable business to a very unprofitable one. They had to find some way to stem the losses. When they examined the usage patterns, they found that there were two areas where the heavy-user paradox was particularly pronounced: romance fiction and audiobooks. 'It turns out that romance readers read a lot more than most types of readers, they'll read 100 books a month', explained Trip. 'They were going to cause the entire business to collapse, so we had to make some adjustments.' They took the radical decision to remove 90 per cent of the romance fiction books from June 2015. 'We pulled out all the expensive ones. What happened is that we signed Harlequin and we had almost the full catalogue for Harlequin, and that just started the payouts to go up exponentially.' The problem with audiobooks was similar: 'The listening activity was so high that a few months later we were losing like a million dollars a month just on audiobooks.' So they changed that too: in August, they limited usage to one audiobook per month.

These two changes made a difference and put a stop to the haemorrhaging of cash, but the service still wasn't profitable. So they had to make a decision at that point about whether to try to raise venture capital to fund the unlimited use model or to change the model in order to make the service profitable. They opted for the latter and, in spring 2016, they switched to a three books per month system. 'What we found', explained Trip, 'was that, outside of romance, there was only about 3 per cent of subscribers who were reading more than three books a month.' So rather than cut back even further on the catalogue and continue to offer unlimited access to a smaller catalogue, they decided to cap usage at three books a month and offer a larger catalogue to everyone, at the risk of disappointing the 3 per cent who were typically reading more.

The social media and the press didn't respond well to these changes in the terms of service. 'I am extremely disappointed in their "bait and switch" tactics', complained one user. 'I am not an avid fiction reader, usually 1–3 books a month, but enjoy utilizing nonfiction books for reference purposes. I will no longer use their "service" and will warn others about my experience, which will likely cost them a loss in revenue.'[6] 'As an avid reader, I had finally subscribed, only to get this notice a month later. I was really upset', complained another.[7] Trip admits it was tough: 'You do kind of upset everybody because, given what's happened in video and music, there's this expectation of unlimited use. Longer term, I'd love to get a truly unlimited model going, but we really need the publishers to be on board to make that work.' In other words, in Trip's view, unlimited access would work only if publishers were willing to accept a pool model, which would enable Scribd to exercise greater control over its outgoings. In the absence of that, and if Scribd is obliged to use a threshold model of payment, then limiting usage seemed like the only feasible way of making the service work. And, in practice, despite the complaints from some users, the number of cancellations was relatively small. 'If

---

[6] Comment from Jay on article by Glinda Harrison, 'Scribd Adds New Content Limits', eBook Evangelist, at https://ebookevangelist.com/2016/02/16/scribd-adds-new-content-limits.
[7] Comment from Michelyn Coffer, ibid.

you look at the actual data, it did slow growth, we saw cancellations, we saw fewer sign-ups. But it wasn't a huge slowdown in growth.'

Having made these significant adjustments to the terms of service, Scribd returned to profitability and continued with the task of adding content, improving the user experience and growing the subscriber base. In addition to documents, books and audiobooks, they added magazines in November 2016, giving users unlimited access to a variety of magazines including *Time, Fortune, People, Bloomberg Businessweek, Foreign Policy* and *New York Magazine*, and others were added later. Then, in May 2017, they added a selection of articles from some major newspapers and a few popular news sites, including the *New York Times*, the *Wall Street Journal*, the *Guardian*, the *Financial Times*, NPR and ProPublica. The aim was to provide users with access to many different types of content, documents, books, audiobooks, magazines and newspaper articles, all for the price of one subscription fee and all linked together to increase discoverability and enable users to move seamlessly from one content form to another.

By spring 2017, Scribd had over 500,000 paying subscribers and they were growing their subscriber base by about 50 per cent a year; two years later, in January 2019, they had more than a million subscribers. Unlike many subscription services which had to use advertising and other methods to recruit new subscribers, the vast majority of Scribd's new subscribers were being converted from the 150 million monthly visitors to their site. Once a subscriber had joined or started the free trial, the key was to retain them, and, to do that, you have to add more content and personalize the user experience. 'You have to get the right content in front of the right user in that first session of using the service in order for them to decide to stick around', explained Trip. 'We find that the leading indicator of a subscriber being retained is them using the service and reading books, so we're basically trying to optimize the number of subscribers who will read on the service in any given month, but particularly in their first month or their first week or even their first day. We're continuously trying to optimize that, both on the front end, which is the user experience for how they discover things and read things, and on the back end, which is what content we surface to them in our recommendations.' As with all subscription services, the algorithm used in the recommendation engine is a crucial part of this personalization. 'We use a number of different ways to do recommendations', Trip continued. 'We'll look at, if someone reads a particular book, what other books do readers of that book typically read; we'll look at text similarities – you know, if this book talks a lot about renewable energies, we'll see that another book talks about renewable energies and we'll match it that way. There are a number of different systems and we're just constantly optimizing it.' One feature that plays a big role at Scribd is cross-content recommendations – that is, if you're reading a document, Scribd will recommend relevant books; if you're reading a book, it will recommend relevant articles, and so on. 'It's that cross-content recommendation where we are uniquely positioned.'

Scribd succeeded in building a subscription service for ebooks and audiobooks that was both profitable and growing nicely, if still modest in size compared to subscription services like Netflix and Spotify. They had persuaded a good number of publishers to make available their backlist ebooks, including three of the Big Five, and they had found a way to make the threshold model work – more by trial and error and continuous iteration than by virtue of some fully formed plan that guided them from the outset. 'It might seem like there's some big plan but it's just a lot of iteration that leads to the vision', explained Trip. With a start-up like this, you have to be willing to take the plunge and then tweak things continuously in order to try to make it work. Thanks to a mixture of good timing, some prudent decisions at critical junctures and a dose of good luck, Scribd made it work, so far at least. But they were not alone, and others were not so lucky.

The rise and fall of Oyster

At pretty much the same time as Trip and Jared were trying to figure out how to expand their nascent subscription service for documents by adding ebooks, a young 23-year-old, not long out of college, was thinking along similar lines in New York. Eric Stromberg had majored in history and economics at Duke and joined a tech start-up in New York called Hunch which was developing recommendation-engine technology. When the company was sold to eBay in 2011, Eric decided to start his own company. This was a time when ebooks were beginning to take off and Eric was inspired by what he saw on Spotify ('it changed how I listened to music'), so he began to put the two together and think about how he could develop a subscription service for ebooks. What he particularly liked about Spotify was the way that it integrated the recommendation engine with the listening experience: this was much more interesting, in his view, than the fact that it was a subscription service. 'Subscription is not what's interesting', he reflected. 'What's really interesting is what subscription enables, and that is finding something, getting a recommendation and, in one click, trying it, all in one place. Having it all in one place is what really inspired me about the subscription model.' It was this all-in-one experience that he wanted to emulate in the emerging world of ebooks.

In February 2012, he started talking with people in the publishing industry – publishers, agents, authors and others – to try to figure out how the industry worked and whether they would be open to the idea of a subscription service for ebooks. Like Trip and Jared, Eric didn't find much enthusiasm for the idea among publishers: 'In 2012 a lot of people were still trying to figure out digital. Adding subscription into the mix was making an already complex two-dimensional chess board an extremely complex three-dimensional chess board. People weren't looking for more complexity.' Unswayed by this initial lack of enthusiasm, Eric persevered. He was joined by two co-founders, Andrew Brown and Willem van Lancker; they put together a business plan and went out to Silicon Valley to pitch the idea to investors. 'We had to prove that we were for real', explained Eric, 'and I think getting investment behind us, so publishers knew we'd be around for a few years at least, was key to that.' In October 2012, they raised $3 million in seed funding from Peter Thiel's San Francisco-based Founders Fund and others. With this initial funding behind them, they began to build the app and started to sign up publishers.

Persuading publishers to give them their ebooks wasn't easy. Eric brought in Matt Shatz, who had worked in the publishing industry for many years and was known and trusted by many in the industry, to reach out to publishers and help win them over. They had two main arguments in their pitch to publishers. The first was an attractive business model. Like Scribd, Oyster decided to use the threshold or pay-per-use model in order to persuade publishers to hand over their content. They didn't have the resources to pay an upfront fee to license content (à la Netflix) and they knew that the big publishers would not have signed up if they'd proposed a royalty pool model (à la Spotify), so the pay-per-use model was the only realistic option if they wanted to get the big houses on board. The precise figure that would constitute the threshold and trigger the payment was negotiated with each publisher – it was not a fixed percentage, but it was generally between 10 and 20 per cent. Once a reader had read more than the agreed percentage of any particular title, then Oyster would pay the publisher the digital price of that ebook less a discount that was agreed on a publisher-by-publisher basis.

The second argument they used was that participating in a subscription model would be a great way to address the discovery problem. They knew that publishers were concerned about this: with the demise of Borders and the continued pressure on bricks-and-mortar booksellers and with the decline of book supplements and other media spaces where books were discussed and reviewed, there were fewer and fewer places where readers could discover books that they didn't already know about. How were readers going to find out about a publisher's books if these spaces of discovery were declining? Part of Oyster's pitch was that, in these circumstances, a subscription service for ebooks would benefit publishers by making it easier for readers to discover new books. 'The core statistic that excites me', explained Eric, 'is that on Netflix, about 80 per cent of the content is older content that is found through discovery as opposed to search. On Spotify, about 80 per cent of what's listened to is non-new-release stuff. Whereas on retail platforms, whether it's Apple or Amazon, only 20 per cent is found through discovery and 80 per cent is found through search. So subscription is actually really good at helping people discover stuff.' Customers can find new stuff either by knowing exactly what they want and using a search engine to find it (and Amazon does an excellent job of enabling you to find something if you know what it is you want) or by knowing that they want something 'of a certain kind', even though they don't know exactly what they want. In the latter case, there is a gap between 'wanting something of a certain kind' and 'wanting a specific thing', and that's where a well-designed recommendation engine can be of real value. Moreover, if the recommendation engine is tied to a subscription model, it has the potential to be particularly effective, for the simple reason that the subscription model removes the purchase barrier: the reader (or listener) can dip into a book (or an album) and read as much (or listen to as much) as she likes before deciding whether to continue, and if she decides not to continue, she can try something else – there is no need to buy the book (or the album) in order to decide whether you like it enough to read (or listen to) the whole thing. The purchase barrier creates a certain amount of friction that discourages people from trying new things, and if you remove that barrier, people will be more likely to experiment. 'The subscription model is creating the best browsing experience in the world', averred Eric. It's particularly good at helping customers discover older content, like backlist titles, and books that are not bestsellers, because the recommendation engine can be geared in ways that drive users deeper and deeper into the backlist and to books that don't feature on bestseller lists. This was music to the ears of many publishers who were worried about the decline of bookstores and book review media and keen to experiment with new ways both to enhance the discoverability of their books and to extract more value from their backlists.

The first publishers to come on board were small presses and some of the more specialized trade houses. Persuading the Big Five to join in was much harder, but crucial for the scale and credibility of the service. It was only when HarperCollins agreed to give them 10 per cent of their backlist catalogue that they felt they had enough content to launch. 'We knew the first question everyone would ask was, "Are you working with any of the Big Five?" And there's such a big difference between saying No and saying Yes.' With HarperCollins on board, Oyster launched their subscription service on 5 September 2013, just a few weeks before Scribd launched its ebook subscription service on the West Coast. Heralded as the Netflix for books,[8] Oyster gave subscribers access to 100,000 ebooks for $9.95 a month – not only to HarperCollins's 10 per cent but also to titles from Houghton Mifflin Harcourt, Workman, Rodale and other smaller publishers, plus a large volume of self-published books from Smashwords.

Oyster continued to expand their service through late 2013 and into 2014, developing the user interface and extending it to other platforms, growing the number of subscribers and adding more content. At the end of 2013, they raised another $14 million from venture capital firms led by Highland Capital Partners. In May 2014, the HarperCollins deal was expanded to include 100 per cent of their backlist titles, and in the same month Simon & Schuster made available the whole of its backlist. In January 2015, Macmillan announced that it was putting 1,000 backlist titles into Oyster, and later that month Oyster announced that it had done a deal with Pottermore to make all 10 Harry Potter-related titles available on its subscription service. When I met with Eric in Oyster's headquarters in a converted loft in midtown Manhattan in March 2015, there was a palpable sense of excitement: they now had a million books available, three of the Big Five and eight of the top ten publishers were on board, bringing in Harry Potter was a coup ('just an unbelievable sensation for us – even I underestimated how big a deal that was for

---

[8] Steven Bertoni, 'Oyster Launches Netflix for Books', *Forbes* (5 September 2013), at www.forbes.com/sites/stevenbertoni/2013/09/05/oyster-launches-netflix-for-books/#35c703f14ce1.

people'), they'd built a product that was well received, the business was growing and they were hiring more people. The start-up seemed to be taking off, the subscription model for ebooks seemed to be working and the sky was the limit. Or so it seemed.

Then, on 21 September 2015, just six months after our conversation and two years after it had launched, Oyster announced that the service was closing. It was reported that Eric and some other members of the Oyster team would be joining Google, and that Google would be paying investors in the region of $15–20 million for the right to hire some of its staff – in other words, the service would be shut down and Google would 'acqhire' some of its staff.[9] Google wasn't buying a business, it was buying a product and a tech and editorial team that it could bring in-house to improve its own businesses. So what went wrong? Why did a start-up that seemed to be on the cusp of taking off suddenly turn belly up?

To the outside observer, it might seem obvious that the problem was the business model: the threshold or pay-per-use model was surely the hole that sunk the ship. By agreeing to pay the publisher the full digital price of the book once the reader had read 10 or 20 per cent, Oyster was surely locking itself into a business model that would oblige it to pay out to publishers more than it would be raising through subscription fees, draining its cash reserves and dashing any hope of becoming profitable. Likely though that may seem, this wasn't the main reason why Oyster failed. Oyster was profitable to some extent. The main problem was that Oyster wasn't increasing its subscription base fast enough and it was costing it too much to acquire new customers.

Like all subscription businesses, the viability of Oyster depended on the ratio between the so-called cost per acquisition (CPA) and the lifetime value (LTV) of a customer. Cost per acquisition is calculated by looking at how much you spend per month to acquire new customers (by advertising and other methods) and dividing that amount by the net number of new subscribers (that is, those who sign up less those who cancel). Lifetime value is determined by calculating how much you're making each month on each user and multiplying that by the number of months the average user sticks around (based on the actual churn rate). Investors in a subscription business like Oyster are generally looking for a ratio of 1:3 or 1:4, which means

---

[9] Mark Bergen and Peter Kafka, 'Oyster, a Netflix for Books, Is Shutting Down. But Most of Its Team Is Heading to Google', Recode (21 September 2015), at www.recode.net/2015/9/21/11618788/oyster-books-shuts-down-team-heads-to-google.

that for every dollar you spend on acquiring a new subscriber, you should be generating $3 or $4 of lifetime value.

Oyster was actually making a small gross profit on each user – for every $10 they were being paid in subscription fees, around $8 was being paid out to publishers, leaving them with a small surplus of around $2. They were using their recommendation engine pretty effectively to steer users towards books that would cost them less – would cost them $3 rather than $9, for example – while seemingly being equally satisfying for readers. So they were gross-margin positive, but the margin was small. On the other hand, Oyster was spending a lot of money trying to build its subscription base and acquire new subscribers. They were advertising online, primarily on Facebook and Google, and that was expensive. They were being careful to spend wisely – trying different messages, advertising at different times, spending more money in the months when it was cheaper, etc. – but it was still costing them a lot to acquire each new user: as much as $40 to $50 per user. The result was that the ratio of CPA to LTV was nowhere near 1:3 or 1:4 – in fact, it was slightly negative. 'That doesn't mean that subscribers were unprofitable – they were profitable', explained one former insider. 'But the amount of money we were spending to get them to sign up was still in excess.' Oyster's mistake, in his view, was that they relied too much on advertising and they ignored 'organic acquisition' – that is, word of mouth, 'getting people to share the story on their own instead of just buying each customer'. They focused on trying to grow their subscriber base as fast as they could and using advertising to do this, rather than making sure that they were getting the kind of CPA-to-LTV ratio that would satisfy potential investors. This ratio was a key metric for investors. Had Oyster been able to show that they were growing their subscription base at a good rate and with a CPA-to-LTV ratio in line with industry expectations, they might have found investors willing to come in on a Series B funding round. As it turned out, they weren't able to raise the Series B, and they weren't in a position financially to continue without another round of investment. So the next step was to look for what's euphemistically called 'strategic money', which means companies that might have an interest in buying your business in order to integrate it, or parts of it, into their own operations. Hence the Google deal.

This also explains why Scribd survived and Oyster failed. Because Scribd was a document business before it developed an ebook subscription service, it already had a very large existing user base of around 150 million monthly visitors and an existing subscription service and it could market its new ebook subscription service to its existing user base. It cost Scribd practically nothing to acquire each new subscriber because they could focus their effort on converting some of their existing users and visitors into paying subscribers. Oyster, by contrast, was using paid advertising to reach out to and acquire new subscribers, and it was costing them $40–$50 for each new subscriber. Most subscription services that succeed have something that gives them a leg up at the outset – Netflix did deals with electronics manufacturers to place free trial membership coupons in DVD players, and did a deal with Walmart that directed Walmart customers to Netflix; Spotify did a deal with Facebook which enabled it to reach millions of potential users; and Scribd had its existing document business. Oyster was starting from scratch. In a nutshell, it was Oyster's high cost per acquisition and Scribd's low cost per acquisition that sank Oyster and enabled Scribd to survive.

While Oyster's high cost per acquisition was the main reason for its downfall, its prospects certainly weren't helped by the arrival of another major player in the ebook subscription space.

Kindle Unlimited enters the scene

Scribd and Oyster had been around for 9–10 months when Amazon announced, in July 2014, that it was launching its own ebook subscription service, Kindle Unlimited (KU). This would be a standalone subscription service, different from the Kindle Owners' Lending Library (KOLL) that had been set up in 2011 (see chapter 5) to allow Amazon Prime members with Kindles to borrow one ebook per month from the Kindle Store, as a perk of Amazon Prime membership. Subscribers to KU would pay a monthly subscription fee of $9.99 and would have unlimited access to around 600,000 ebooks and 2,000 audiobooks. The ebooks could be read on a Kindle, or on other devices via the Kindle app. Given Amazon's scale and given that many readers were already using Kindles to read ebooks, this new offering from Amazon looked like it could be a serious threat to the two young subscription-service start-ups. On the face of it, Kindle Unlimited seemed very similar to Scribd and Oyster – same under-$10 subscription fee, same all-you-can-eat menu, etc. – but in fact there were fundamental differences. Two were particularly significant.

In the first place, KU was using a very different business model. In fact, Amazon was using a mixed model: it did a number of special deals with some publishers to acquire some high-profile content for KOLL – and, by extension, for KU – like *Lord of the Rings*, *The Hunger Games*, the Harry Potter series, etc.; for these exceptional titles published by mainstream publishers, Amazon was using a version of the threshold or pay-per-use model. But for the vast majority of content in KU, most of which was self-published books that were published through Kindle Direct (books that were enrolled in KDP Select were automatically enrolled in KU) and books published by Amazon's own imprints, the model used by Amazon was a version of the fixed royalty-pool model: Amazon created a KU pool or fund, and if someone read 10 per cent or more of a book, then the author would receive a proportional payout from the KU pool (Amazon had already set up an arrangement of this kind for KOLL). The amount in the pool would change every month; when KU was launched in July 2014, the pool was set at $2.5 million. The royalty-pool model enabled Amazon to keep down the costs of content in a way that Scribd and Oyster had not been able to do, but it also meant that the overall payments to content owners were much lower.

A year after it had launched, in July 2015, Amazon changed the payment model. Now, Amazon would pay authors a royalty based on pages read, rather than paying a royalty every time a reader read 10 per cent of a book. Some commentators suggested that Amazon made this change partly as a response to the flooding of KU with very short books of 20–30 pages which, under the 10 per cent rule, would reward the authors after a reader had read only 2–3 pages, whereas the author of a 300-page book would be rewarded only if the reader made it past page 30. The original KU model provided a strong incentive for authors to self-publish lots of short novellas and add them to the pool. As the self-published author C. E. Kilgore remarked, 'The longer page-count authors are leaving, while more and more authors are adding novellas to the pool, compounding the problem. It was only a matter of time before KU began to drown in the overcrowded, shallow pool in which readers who paid $10 a month were reading 30 25-page books, costing KU close to 80$/month in borrow fees.'[10] But the change in the terms of payment meant that authors were being paid a very small fee per page, generally less

---

[10] C. E. Kilgore, quoted in Kirsten Reach, 'You Don't Get Paid Unless People Actually Read Your Book: The New Kindle Unlimited Royalties', *MobyLives* (16 June 2015), at www.mhpbooks.com/you-dont-get-paid-unless-people-actually-read-your-book-the-new-kindle-unlimited-royalties.

than 0.5¢ per page. Hence an author who self-published a 250-page book would be paid around $1.25 if someone read the whole book, and would be paid less if the reader didn't finish it (if they stopped after 50 pages, they would get only 25¢); by contrast, if the reader had bought the ebook at $3.99, the author would have received a royalty of $2.79 regardless of whether the reader actually read it. The change in the terms of payment, together with the fact that Amazon required authors enrolling books in KDP Select to grant exclusivity to Kindle, was enough to persuade some authors to pull their books out of KU and KDP Select. But for many other self-published authors, KU became just another revenue stream in Amazon's expanding and increasingly diversified ecosystem and they were content, at least for the time being, to let their books be enrolled in KU and see what happens.

The second big difference was that very few mainstream publishers, and none of the Big Five, were willing to put their books into KU. The main reason for this was that Amazon's royalty-pool business model gave publishers no control over how much they and their authors would be paid when their books were borrowed and read. Amazon alone decided how large the royalty pool would be each month, and if a publisher was receiving $1.25 each time a 250-page book was read from beginning to end (less if it wasn't finished), that sum would have to be split with the author, leaving both the publisher and the author with a fraction of what they would have earned from a straight sale. From the publisher's point of view, and from the viewpoint of many authors too, this model was much less attractive than the threshold or pay-per-use model that was being used by Scribd and Oyster, and most publishers, including all of the Big Five, were not willing to participate on Amazon's terms. Some publishers may well have had, and continue to have, other reasons for not wishing to participate in KU – some because they were wary of Amazon's growing power and wanted to encourage competition in the marketplace, others because they were wary of subscription *tout court*. But the royalty-pool model favoured by Amazon was a strong disincentive for any mainstream publisher to participate.

As a result, the vast majority of books in KU ended up being books that were self-published through KDP and books published by Amazon's own publishing imprints – in other words, in terms of content, KU was heavily skewed towards books published and self-published through Amazon. So in terms of content, KU was a very different proposition from Scribd and Oyster: the latter prided themselves on being able to provide access to the backlist titles of many of the mainstream publishers, including several of the Big Five, whereas KU was restricted largely to books published or self-published through Amazon. Of the more than 1.4 million books available on KU in 2018, almost 1.3 million, or 92 per cent, were Amazon exclusives, which means they were self-published through Amazon or published by one of Amazon's own imprints. That left barely 100,000 non-exclusive books and a large portion of these were also self-published; only a very small proportion of the 1.4 million books in KU were from other publishers, and these were mostly from small publishing houses.[11]

Despite the preponderance of content published through Amazon and the absence of titles from mainstream publishers, KU appeared to be gaining some traction as a subscription service. It had the great advantage of being the only subscription service that worked on the Kindle, which was (and remains) the most popular e-reading device. As always, Amazon guards its numbers closely, but we can get some sense of the growth of KU by looking at the changing size of the royalty pool. Figure 9.1 shows the KU Global Fund, from which royalties are paid, from July 2014 when KU was started to the end of 2019.

The graph shows that the royalty pool expanded rapidly in the first eighteen months, from $2.5 million in July 2014 to $15 million in January 2016, an increase of six-fold in eighteen months. The pattern after that was more erratic and the growth was slower: over the next four years, the fund increased by 75 per cent, from $15 million in January 2016 to $26.2 million in December 2019. This suggests a certain levelling off in terms of the growth of the subscription base from early 2016 on. Although Amazon has never made public the number of subscribers, some commentators have used data on the size of the royalty pool, the average payout per page and the average number of books typically read by subscribers to estimate the total number of subscribers, putting this number at around 2.5 million in 2017.[12] This is a rough estimate at best, but a subscription base of somewhere between 2 and 3 million in 2017 would probably be a safe guess. There's some evidence to suggest that KU subscribers tend to read more books than non-KU readers, and that a significant

---

[11] Dan Price, '5 Reasons Why Kindle Unlimited Isn't Worth Your Money', makeuseof.com (updated 7 January 2019), at www.makeuseof.com/tag/kindle-unlimited-worth-money-why.

[12] 'How Do Kindle Unlimited Subscribers Behave (and How Does it Impact Authors)?' Written Word Media (13 April 2017), at www.writtenwordmedia.com/2017/04/13/kindle-unlimited-subscribers/#.

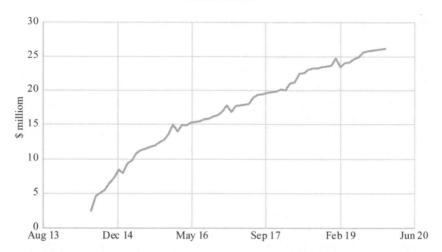

Figure 9.1   KU Global Fund
Source: Written Word Media

proportion are heavy readers who read more than twenty books a month.[13] There's also some evidence to suggest that KU subscribers are more likely to regard romance as their primary genre.[14]

While KU is Amazon's main ebook subscription service, they also extended their flagship membership programme, Amazon Prime, to include an ebook offering. In October 2016, Amazon launched Prime Reading, which gives anyone with Amazon Prime membership free and unlimited access to over 1,000 ebooks, comics and magazines. The selection of titles is constantly changed and updated. With yet another ebook offering from Amazon, readers could be excused for being confused: what's the difference between Prime Reading, KU and KOLL? Prime Reading is part of Amazon Prime's multi-benefit subscription service: if you become a member of Amazon Prime, you automatically get free access to the 1,000 ebooks, comics and magazines that are made available in Prime Reading (you also get

---

[13] Ibid. This is based on a survey of around 1,000 readers, some of whom were KU subscribers and some of whom were not. The survey found that over 71 per cent of KU subscribers said they read five or more books per month, compared with 57 per cent of non-KU readers, and 20 per cent of KU subscribers said they read more than twenty books per month. But these were self-reported results from Written Word's reader base. This is unlikely to be a representative sample, and it may not be an accurate picture of the reading practices of KU subscribers.
[14] Ibid. The survey found that 35 per cent of KU subscribers said romance was their primary genre, compared to 25 per cent of non-KU readers.

access to some movies, TV shows and music). KU is a completely separate, standalone subscription service dedicated to ebooks and audiobooks, for which you have to pay a separate subscription fee (in 2019, KU was $9.99/£7.99 a month; Amazon Prime was $12.99/£7.99, or $119/£79 a year); in KU, you have a much larger catalogue of ebooks – more than 1.4 million, as opposed to the 1,000 titles available on Prime Reading. Like Amazon Prime, KOLL is also freely available to Amazon Prime members. KOLL gives readers access to a much larger catalogue of more than 800,000 titles – the KOLL catalogue is similar in many ways to the KU catalogue. But in KOLL, the reader can borrow only 1 book per month, whereas in KU the reader has unlimited access to the library of 1.4 million titles.

Subscription in the ecosystem of books

Amazon's entry into the ebook subscription business changed the nature of the game. Up to that point, it had essentially been a battle between two start-ups, both running on venture capital and competing with one another for subscribers on the basis of very similar strategies and offerings. 'Kindle Unlimited changed everything', observed a senior manager at one of these start-ups. 'We always expected that Amazon would enter the market once Scribd and Oyster began to make a lot of noise. We always figured that they would feel the need to combat this new threat to their business. I think all of us were surprised at how quickly they were able to respond – for a large company, nine months is really quite a short time – and how aggressively they responded, and how willing they were to cannibalize their own business in order to defray the potential threat from Scribd and Oyster.' These start-ups were now faced with a competitor of a very different order of magnitude, one that had the scale and the resources to change the nature of the game, at least in principle.

Amazon had many advantages in what might look like a very uneven struggle. In the first place, Amazon was the dominant player in the ebook marketplace and they therefore had a very powerful platform on which to market their new ebook subscription service. They aggressively promoted KU on all their main websites; it was on their homepage for a long time, and it returned to the homepage several times after the original launch. And the mere fact that the Kindle edition of every book in KU appeared on the Amazon site as available for free in Kindle Unlimited was, in itself, a powerful and highly visible form of promotion for KU. A second big advantage was that only KU was available on Kindle reading devices – neither Scribd nor Oyster could offer their subscribers the option of reading their books on a Kindle. Since the Kindle was the dominant ebook reading device, the closed loop between KU and the Kindle gave KU a crucial edge over its rivals. Amazon exploited this by bundling KU with Kindle devices and doing special promotions with Kindles at key times like Christmas. A third advantage was that, since a great deal of content in KU was coming from Amazon's own self-publishing and publishing programmes, they could control the costs of acquiring this content by using a royalty-pool model, and this enabled them to keep down the average cost of acquiring content in a way that neither Scribd nor Oyster could do – in short, they could make KU more profitable than Scribd or Oyster by lowering the cost of content acquisition.

But this latter advantage was also KU's main weakness. KU was great if you wanted to read lots of books that were self-published through KDP or published by one of Amazon's own imprints, but if you wanted to read books that were published by mainstream publishers, KU was of very little use. Amazon had done some special deals with a few publishers to enable it to make some high-profile titles, like the Harry Potter books, available in KU, but most mainstream publishers, including all of the Big Five, declined to participate in KU. 'Kindle Unlimited has a lot of self-published content', observed Jared, one of Scribd's founders, 'but if you look at the demand-weighted completeness of the catalogue, Scribd has a much higher percentage of the world's books weighted by demand in its service than Kindle Unlimited does.' By virtue of being able to offer readers access to ebooks published by many mainstream publishers, including backlist titles from three of the Big Five, Scribd and Oyster were able to offer readers a very different selection of titles from those available on KU, even if they had to pay a high price for the privilege. Another advantage that Scribd and Oyster had was in the area of product design. True, KU had the closed loop with the Kindle, but neither the Kindle nor KU were built as a streaming service. 'If you look at streaming services, the way the products were designed is very different from ecommerce experiences', explained Jared. 'If you compare iTunes to Spotify, there's not just a difference in the way the users are billed: the products look very different. And Kindle Unlimited is structured as just a way to buy a book in the Kindle Store without paying for it, whereas Scribd and Oyster are really built as first-class streaming experiences.'

342

With the demise of Oyster, the subscription service space for ebooks has now polarized into two main offerings: Scribd, on the one hand, and Kindle Unlimited (together with the other Amazon offerings, KOLL and Prime Reading), on the other. The content differentiation between the two services means that consumers are faced with contrasting choices: if you want a subscription service that will give you access to the backlist books published by mainstream publishers, you have to go to Scribd, whereas if you want a subscription service that will give you access to romance fiction and to the hundreds of thousands of books self-published through Amazon or published by Amazon's own imprints, then you have to go to KU. Given mainstream publishers' unwillingness to participate in KU and given KDP Select's exclusivity condition, there is very little overlap between the content available on the two main subscription services. KU almost certainly has many more subscribers than Scribd, probably two to three times the number, but Scribd is holding its own and continues to grow. In February 2018, Scribd also resumed the practice of offering unlimited access to most subscribers, while limiting access to the most expensive titles for a small percentage of high-volume readers. Between these two services, there may be as many as 3–4 million users paying a monthly fee of $8.99 or $9.99 for access to an ebook and audiobook subscription service.

Given recent trends, it seems likely that ebook subscription services will remain a growing but relatively minor part of the retail environment for books for the foreseeable future. Assuming these two services together had 3–4 million users paying approximately $10 per subscription per month, this would represent total revenue of between $360 million and $480 million a year, in an industry that, in the US alone, generated revenue of over $26 billion in 2017 and around $16 billion for trade books (i.e. excluding educational, professional and scholarly books). These are not insignificant figures, but they still represent a very small percentage of the book market – only 3 per cent of US trade sales, and less than 2 per cent of US book-publishing revenue overall (and bearing in mind that not all subscribers are US-based, the real proportions are likely to be even smaller). Compared to the increasing centrality of subscription services in the music and audio-visual industries, the role of subscription services in the book industry is marginal (streaming services generated nearly two-thirds of all US music industry revenue in 2017,[15] and, by 2018,

---

[15] Joshua P. Friedlander, 'News and Notes on 2017 RIAA Revenue Statistics', at www. riaa.com/wp-content/uploads/2018/03/RIAA-Year-End-2017-News-and-Notes.pdf.

69 per cent of all US households had a video on-demand subscription service from Netflix, Amazon Prime and/or Hulu[16]). Of course, books don't have the kind of widespread popular appeal of music, films and TV, so the market penetration of a dedicated subscription service for books is unlikely to be as high as it is for subscription services focused on music and audio-visual entertainment. But the significant consideration here is not the overall market penetration of the subscription service, but rather the fact that, within the book industry itself, the revenue generated by subscription services remains a small fraction of overall book industry revenue. That's not to say that it will always be like this – it could change in the future. Whether it does so will depend on a number of factors, the most important of which are probably the following four.

The first and most obvious factor is that the appeal of ebook subscription services will depend on the extent to which readers wish to read books in a digital format, on screen, rather than as a physical book. In this respect, subscription services in the book industry are not directly comparable to subscription services for music, films and TV series, simply because the physical print-on-paper book remains the preferred format for many readers in a way that has no parallel in the music, film and TV industries. Today, the vast majority of consumers listen to music in some digital format (even with the renewed popularity of vinyl, which, despite its remarkable comeback, still accounted for less than 5 per cent of US music industry revenue in 2017), and films and TV series are always watched on a screen. So subscription services in music, films and TV are tapping into markets where content is typically and overwhelmingly delivered digitally and, in the case of films and TV, consumed on screens – there is simply no other way to consume it. With books, however, print remains the dominant medium, and for those readers who prefer the medium of print, a subscription service for ebooks will have no real attraction. It is in those areas and genres where ebook reading is particularly prevalent – e.g., romance, fantasy and thriller – that subscription services have gained traction and are likely to flourish in the future, both because these are genres where the e/p ratios are skewed in favour of ebooks and because heavy readers in these genres are likely to appreciate the financial benefits of accessing content through a subscription model. But if ebook sales are not increasing

---

[16] '69% of U.S. Households Have an SVOD Service', Leichtman Research Group, at www.leichtmanresearch.com/wp-content/uploads/2018/08/LRG-Press-Release-08-27-18.pdf.

relative to print, if they are plateauing or even declining, then the prospects for substantially increasing the numbers of subscribers may be limited – they may reach a point at which the ability to recruit new subscribers runs up against the enduring preference of many readers to read the printed page.

A second factor that has played an important role in the development of subscription services in the book industry is that the content owners – the publishers – have for the most part been willing to make their content available only on the basis of a business model that shifts most of the risk onto the subscription service. The business models that were used by subscription services in the music and audio-visual industries were simply not available to subscription services that wanted to acquire content from mainstream publishers, either because these services would not have the kind of resources they would need to pay large up-front licensing fees, or because the publishers would not accept a fixed royalty-pool model. Scribd and Oyster found themselves obliged to use a threshold or pay-per-use model to acquire books from mainstream publishers, a model that squeezed their margins and left them very little room to manoeuvre in financial terms. Amazon did special deals to acquire some high-profile content but the vast majority of content in KU is self-published or Amazon-branded content paid for by a royalty-pool model, which allows Amazon to determine how much it pays for this content. This bifurcation of business models underlies the polarization of the sector and limits the extent to which either of the two main players can grow.

The third factor that has inhibited the growth of this sector is the reluctance of some mainstream publishers to participate at all, regardless of the business model. While some publishers, including three of the Big Five, have made their backlists available on Scribd (and Oyster when it existed), other publishers have so far refrained from doing so, and most mainstream publishers, including all of the Big Five, have declined to participate in KU. The reluctance of publishers to participate in KU is understandable given Amazon's preferred royalty-pool model and given its dominance in the marketplace. But why would they refuse to participate in a subscription scheme like Scribd where they would be paid the full digital price of a sale whenever 10 or 20 per cent of the book was read? A senior manager at one of the large non-participating publishers expressed his concerns like this: 'We're not participating because we think the risks of that model right now are greater than the benefits offered by it.' In any subscription model, he explained, it is the heavy users who have the most to gain by joining a subscription service, but the more that heavy readers shift to subscription services, the greater the risk that publishers will see their overall revenue decline. 'In books, what we're afraid of is that heavy readers, which make up 70–80 per cent of the revenue of the industry, will be disproportionately attracted to a subscription model compared to light users, because, if I'm buying one book a year, why would I need to join a book subscription service? So given that dynamic, we think that the risk of the overall revenue pool declining is greater in the subscription model than it is in today's model.' If a heavy reader is buying 4–5 books a month, he might be spending $700–$800 a year on books; if instead he does all his reading in a subscription service, his annual spend on books would fall to $120. Of course, these two ways of consuming books are not necessarily mutually exclusive: a reader could read some books through a subscription service and also buy some books that were not available in that service. But there is still a risk here that the heavy readers' overall spend on books would decline. There is also an opportunity here: if many readers who are spending a lot less than $120 a year on books could be persuaded to join a subscription service, then this would compensate for the decline of the heavy readers' overall spend. But, at the moment, it's hard to see why lots of light readers would do this. 'So we just think that the risk is greater than the opportunity because we don't see much opportunity there.' And even if Amazon were to pay them some amount that is greater than the payouts from the royalty pool, that amount would still be a fraction of what they pay them for straight sales. 'So from both perspectives, from the perspective of the industry overall and from the perspective of the split between us and the platform, we just see this model as extremely risky.'

Not everyone in the large publishing houses shares this cautious view. A senior manager in another house explained that, in her company, subscription was seen more as an opportunity than a risk. When you look at consumers in other media industries like music, and especially young consumers, you see that many want access rather than ownership, so it's important to play in that space and try to learn what works and what doesn't – 'If you don't play, you won't learn and you'll have no say, and the models will be established without you.' For example, you might find that subscription models bring more readers to backlist titles which, with the decline of physical stores, have become increasingly invisible. So, provided the subscription service is using a threshold or pay-per-use model, then, in her view, it's worth experimenting with subscription to see

346

what works and what doesn't. She's well aware that there are risks – especially the risk of revenue loss associated with turning heavy readers into subscribers. But she reckons that the potential gains outweigh the risks, at least at this early stage in the evolution of subscription models. The publishing industry is divided on this issue and it remains to be seen whether other publishers will decide to adopt this 'experiment-and-see-what-happens' approach and, if they do, whether their experience will be sufficiently positive to incline them to continue with the experiment.

The fourth factor that will play a big role in shaping the future of subscription services is what Amazon decides to do. However impressive Scribd's achievement is (and it is impressive: they have performed the feat, rather unusual among tech start-ups, of growing their subscription base at a significant rate while at the same time running a profitable business), it remains a niche operation; Amazon's role is likely to be much greater than Scribd's simply because Amazon has a much greater reach – it has far more customers than Scribd, even if KU itself is relatively small. Hitherto, the growth of KU has been limited by the fact that its content is made up largely of books self-published through KDP or published by one of Amazon's own imprints – up till now, KU has been more a part of the Amazon ecosystem than of the book ecosystem more broadly. But that could change. It could change if Amazon decided, for whatever reason, to prioritize KU, and used the leverage they have in the marketplace to put pressure on publishers to participate. Then the ebook offering of KU would become much richer and more appealing to readers, and that could change the game. But couldn't publishers just refuse? They could, but this is a game of power, and a retailer that controls half of your sales is holding a lot of cards in its hands. 'They can say, "Well, if you choose that, then maybe we won't sell your books. The book won't be available on the platform at all." That's their leverage', reflected a senior executive in one of the large publishing houses; he'd been in this business for a long time and these were comments based on a sober assessment of market realities, not paranoia. 'That would only happen if they think it's a big enough priority for them, and we don't know if it's that high a priority for them.' But the mere fact that he raised the possibility is a testimony to the anxiety that many publishers feel about Amazon's retail power and the way they could use it to shape the evolution of the industry.

Another option open to Amazon would be to ramp up Prime Reading as a way of making Amazon Prime membership more attractive, expanding Amazon Prime as a multi-benefit subscription service in which ebooks are an integral and growing part. 'Let's suppose Amazon figures out that people who read a lot in Prime Reading are much more likely to renew their Prime Membership than people who don't read in Prime Reading', the publishing executive continued. 'Then they want to make this offering attractive because they will monetize people through other means on the Amazon platform, and then they could use their leverage to force publishers to put more quality books into something like this' – again, a hypothetical scenario but not beyond the realms of possibility. Any move in this direction would be viewed with alarm by many publishers, including this one, because in this environment, books would be used as an enticement to attract customers to the Amazon platform, where they would spend money on other things. And if consumers are able to get books for free, as a side benefit of Prime membership, then they may be less willing to pay for books, especially when their time for reading is limited.

Given publishers' suspicions of Amazon's intentions, coupled with the fact that the main alternative to Amazon in the subscription space remains a niche player, it seems likely that subscription will continue to play a relatively minor role in the evolution of the ecosystem of books in the Anglo-American world. Despite the many announcements of the arrival of the Netflix for books, subscription services in the book industry have not acquired anything like the significance they have in the music, film and television industries. But this could change – the retail environment for books has been transformed since the turn of the millennium, and it's quite possible that further significant changes in the ways that individuals buy and consume books could occur in the years and decades to come.

— Chapter 10 —

THE NEW ORALITY

In the 1970s, the literary critic Walter Ong, a disciple of Marshall McLuhan, observed that radio, television and other forms of electronic technology were ushering in a new age of what he called 'secondary orality', by which he meant an age in which the spoken word takes on a new lease of life by being processed electronically and made available to audiences that are much larger and more dispersed than the audiences that existed in primary oral culture.[1] Although many features of our culture have been deeply shaped by writing and print, as McLuhan had argued,[2] the electronic media were creating spaces in which the spoken word was being rehabilitated as a central feature of modern life. The kinds of spaces that Ong had in mind here were above all those created by radio and television, where a new kind of oratory is brought into being that differs from the oratory of the past, in the way that a televised debate between presidential candidates differs from the Lincoln–Douglas debates of 1858. In the old debates, the combatants had to project their voices before large assembled audiences which, in turn, made their presence felt by shouting, heckling and applauding, whereas presidential debates on television today are more controlled and managed: most of the audience is absent and the candidates tend to keep to script – 'Despite their cultivated air of spontaneity, these media are totally dominated by a

---

[1] Walter J. Ong, *Rhetoric, Romance, and Technology* (Ithaca: Cornell University Press, 1971); *Interfaces of the Word* (Ithaca: Cornell University Press, 1977); *Orality and Literacy: The Technologizing of the Word* (London: Routledge, 1982), pp. 135–40.
[2] Marshall McLuhan, *The Gutenberg Galaxy: The Making of Typographic Man* (University of Toronto Press, 1962).

349

sense of closure which is the heritage of print',[3] as Ong put it. While Ong's observations were focused primarily on the new kind of orality that emerged in the electronic media of radio and television, his argument about the emergence of a secondary orality helps to shed some light on one of the most surprising and unexpected features of the digital revolution in the publishing industry: the remarkable rise of the audiobook.

Of course, there is nothing new about the connection between the written and the spoken word. In the Ancient world, in the Middle Ages and as late as the eighteenth and nineteenth centuries, written and printed texts were often read aloud: literacy was a rare skill possessed by a select few, and a text read aloud could be listened to and enjoyed by others who couldn't read.[4] In early religious and monastic circles, texts were often read in a more solitary and meditative fashion; but even then, reading commonly had a semi-oral character – a murmured reading, like the buzzing of bees. The practice of reading silently – using the eyes only, without moving the lips – is a particular form of reading that became increasingly prevalent from the late Middle Ages on, and it existed side by side with other forms of reading throughout the early modern period. Today, we tend to assume that the printed text is one thing, the spoken word another, but for most of the history of written and printed texts, there was a much closer connection between the words written or printed on the page and the articulation of those words in speech.

Nevertheless, the audiobook creates a different kind of relation between the printed and spoken word. With audiobooks, words printed on the page are turned into speech that is recorded in a durable medium so that it can be listened to by others at different times and places. This is a special kind of secondary orality, to use Walter Ong's term, one that involves three key characteristics. First, the oral is derived in this case from the culture of print and dependent on it – in this respect, it is a literate or text-based orality. This is not simply the re-emergence of the spoken word in an electronically mediated space, like a televised debate: rather, it is a specific transformation of words from one medium to another, from words printed on a page into spoken words that are recorded electronically. In other

---

[3] Ong, *Orality and Literacy*, p. 137.
[4] Guglielmo Cavallo and Roger Chartier (eds.), *A History of Reading in the West* (Cambridge: Polity, 1999); Alberto Manguel, *A History of Reading* (London: HarperCollins, 1996); Paul Saenger, *Space Between Words: The Origins of Silent Reading* (Stanford University Press, 1997).

words, it is a specific kind of remediation – a controlled transformation from printed text to recorded speech. Of course, the specific relation between printed text and recorded speech is not fixed and it allows for a great deal of variability: every act of reading is itself an interpretation, and the history of audiobooks is replete with guidelines and debates about how exactly a text should be read, whether texts can be abbreviated or adapted, how different voices should be rendered in speech, how punctuation and other textual features should be handled, and so on – we'll return to some of these issues below. Moreover, once audiobooks had been invented and the genre had developed into a quasi-industry of its own, the audiobook would gain some recognition as an art form in its own right, with its own specialists and its own system of honours and awards (the 'Audies'); the audiobook would thus gain a degree of independence from the printed book that was its original foundation.

The second characteristic of audiobook orality is that, by being recorded in a durable medium, the spoken words acquire a permanence that words uttered in a face-to-face setting don't have, and the recorded speech can be reproduced and made available to many others who were not there to hear the words spoken. Recorded speech takes on a life of its own, freed from the context in which the words were originally uttered – 'distanciated', to use Ricoeur's apt term[5] – and made durable in a way that eclipses the ephemerality of the spoken word. The nature of the medium in which the spoken words are recorded plays an important role in shaping what can and cannot be done with audiobooks, and much of the history of audiobooks is the story of the march through the different formats, from vinyl records to MP3 – with each new format, new possibilities were opened up that were simply not possible before.

The third characteristic is that this transformation from text to recorded speech has a purpose. The purpose can vary – and it has varied over time. Initially, this purpose was to make books available to a particular segment of the population that was unable to read – namely, the blind and visually impaired. But once the technology had been developed, organizations began to use it for a different purpose: to repackage the content of books and sell it in another form. By producing an audiobook, a book originally published in print could be recommodified in another medium – in the medium of recorded

[5] Paul Ricoeur, 'The Hermeneutical Function of Distanciation', in his *Hermeneutics and the Human Sciences*, tr. John B. Thompson (Cambridge University Press, 1981), pp. 131–44.

sound. That is the essential point that underpins the development of the audiobook industry.

The development of audiobooks

The idea of recording the reading of books has a long history which can be traced back to the very origins of sound-recording technology.[6] Ever since Thomas Edison recorded 'Mary Had a Little Lamb' on the phonograph in 1877, people began speculating about the possibility of recording entire books so that they could be listened to rather than read. Edison himself imagined reaching new audiences through 'Phonographic Books', each consisting of around 40,000 words recorded on a 10-inch-square metal plate.[7] He even founded a publishing house in New York with the aim of recording novels, but the aim remain unfulfilled: the texts were simply too long, and the technology of the recording devices too limited, to make this feasible at the time. The dream of the recorded book would have to wait another fifty years before it could be realized.

The main impetus for the development of audiobooks came from the concern to make books available to the blind and the visually impaired. In the early 1930s, the American Foundation for the Blind and other advocacy groups pressed Congress to take a lead in exploring ways to make books available to the visually impaired in a form other than braille, and Congress responded by awarding annual funding of $100,000 to the Library of Congress's Books for the Adult Blind Project.[8] By this time, the technology for producing vinyl records had developed sufficiently to enable a typical novel to be recorded on around twenty records. The records were played on a special 'talking book machine' that was similar to a record player, with controls to adjust the speed, tone and volume. In 1934, the Library of Congress established the first talking book library to provide reading material to the visually impaired. By June 1935, the talking book library had twenty-seven titles – a selection of both classic and contemporary literature – and it expanded steadily from that point on.[9] A parallel development occurred in the UK with the

---

[6] For an excellent account of the history of the audiobook, see Matthew Rubery, *The Untold Story of the Talking Book* (Cambridge, Mass.: Harvard University Press, 2016). The next few paragraphs are indebted to Rubery's account.
[7] Ibid., p. 31.
[8] Ibid., p. 62.
[9] Ibid., pp. 84, 109.

founding of the Talking Book Library in 1935 at the initiative of the National Institute for the Blind and Blind Veterans UK (formerly St Dunstan's).[10]

While the development of the talking book was pioneered by organizations dedicated to the welfare of the blind and the visually impaired, it was not long before the opportunities opened up by recording technologies were seized upon by individuals with commercial ambitions. These included Barbara Holdridge and Marianne Mantell, two young graduates from Hunter College who, dissatisfied with their entry-level jobs in publishing and record companies, pooled $1,500 to start Caedmon Records in 1952. Impressed by the large audiences who turned up to hear Dylan Thomas read his poems at the 92nd Street Y in New York, they saw and seized a commercial opportunity: they arranged to meet the poet for lunch at the Chelsea Hotel and offered him $500 up front, plus a royalty of 10 per cent on sales after the first 1,000 albums, for the rights to one hour of him reading his verse. The album was released on 2 April 1952 and was a tremendous success, selling over 400,000 copies by 1960. Caedmon went on to record many other writers and books, including William Faulkner, W. B. Yeats and T. S. Eliot, and by 1959 their company had annual revenues of $500,000.[11] Caedmon's success, and that of competing labels which began around the same time, such as the Audio Book Company in the US and Argo Records in the UK, was due in part to the development of the long-playing vinyl record, or LP, which was introduced by Columbia in 1948 and which had both a longer playing time and better sound quality than the old 78 rpm record.[12]

While the vinyl LP created the conditions for the emergence of the audiobook industry, it was the development of the compact audio cassette that enabled audiobooks to take off. The compact cassette is a magnetic tape recording format that was invented by Philips in 1962. It was originally developed for dictation but, as the fidelity improved, cassettes were soon used for music as well: they were small and easy to use, and they could be played in a compact device.

---

[10] Ibid., pp. 129–57.

[11] Ibid., p. 186; Shannon Maughan, 'A Golden Audio Anniversary', *Publishers Weekly*, 249, 9 (4 March 2002), at www.publishersweekly.com/pw/print/20020304/38379-a-golden-audio-anniversary.html; Ben Cheever, 'Audio's Original Voices', *Publishers Weekly*, 252, 42 (21 October 2005), at www.publishersweekly.com/pw/print/20051024/33210-audio-s-original-voices.html.

[12] Andre Millard, *America on Record: A History of Recorded Sound*, Second Edition (Cambridge University Press, 2005), pp. 202–7.

The idea of using cassettes for audiobooks was pioneered by a former Olympic rower who was working at a brokerage firm in Los Angeles. Duvall Hecht travelled from his home in Newport Beach to his office in LA every day, and he found the two-hour commute very tedious. The radio wasn't much help – he was tired of music and news. He wanted something more stimulating. It occurred to him that listening to books would be an ideal way to pass the time. The only problem was that, in the early 1970s, very few full-length books were available on cassette. So he started Books on Tape in 1974 to fill the gap.[13] The business was initially run by Hecht and his wife, Sigrid, out of their home. They targeted commuters and rented cassettes to them for a fixed time period; commuters would then return the cassettes in a pre-stamped box. As commuting became more common and more cassette decks were installed in cars, the Hechts found themselves with a rapidly expanding market. While commuters were their main clientele, the introduction of the Sony Walkman in 1980 expanded the market still further. Audiobooks had now become truly mobile – now they could be listened to in the car, in the gym, or while jogging or strolling in the park. Cassettes provided a great way to listen to audiobooks whenever you were busy doing something but were not being engaged intellectually – when your eyes and hands were occupied but your mind was not. Books on Tape grew to meet rising demand and many other audiobook publishers joined the fray. In September 1985, *Publishers Weekly* identified twenty-one audiobook publishers.[14] By the late 1980s, many of the large publishing houses had opened their own audiobook divisions – Random House and Bantam were the first, and others soon followed. 'It was an exciting time', recalled a publisher who had set up one of these early audiobook divisions. 'All of a sudden we realized that there was a different way of rendering the words of an author and a whole new way of reaching readers.' Audiobooks had become a distinct sub-sector of the publishing business. Audiobooks were being sold in bookstores and made available in library collections, and audiobook rights were bought and sold alongside other subsidiary rights.

While audiobooks were well established by the end of the 1980s, the nascent audiobook industry was subsequently transformed by the

---

[13] Rubery, *The Untold Story of the Talking Book*, pp. 217–21.
[14] Virgil L. P. Blake, 'Something New Has Been Added: Aural Literacy and Libraries', *Information Literacies for the Twenty-First Century* (G. K. Hall & Co., 1990), p. 206, at https://archive.org/details/SomethingNewHasBeenAdded.

digital revolution. Digital recording brought significant improvements in sound quality and made it possible to store and transmit recordings in much more concise formats. The commercial introduction of the compact disc (CD) by Philips and Sony in 1982 was the first major step in this direction: compared to vinyl LPs and compact cassettes, the CD allowed for a very clean, almost clinical, recording, with no extraneous noise – no surface scratching of a needle in a grove, no hiss of a tape as it passes through the player head.[15] Just as importantly, CDs were more robust than LPs or cassettes – they didn't damage so easily, and a digital recording stored on a CD didn't degrade over time. As CD players became more common, audiobooks followed music and migrated from compact cassettes to CDs. However, with the growth of the internet in the 1990s and early 2000s and with the development of the MP3 file format, which used data compression to produce a large reduction in file sizes, a pathway was opened up for audiobook publishers and distributors to make audiobooks available as digital downloads – that is, as digital files that could be either purchased and downloaded onto a listening device or streamed over the internet. As increasingly compact and sophisticated devices with high-quality audio functionality were introduced into the consumer market – from the first iPod in 2001 to the proliferation of smartphones that followed Apple's introduction of the first iPhone in 2007 – the technical conditions were created for a radical shift in the way that audiobooks were stored, distributed and consumed. Now it was no longer necessary for audiobooks to be stored in a material carrier and purchased as a physical object, whether it was an LP, a cassette or a CD: like recorded music, an audiobook could now be stored as an MP3 file and downloaded or streamed directly to a consumer's listening device, which could be something as omnipresent and multifunctional as the smartphone that is always on, always connected and always in a consumer's pocket or bag. Thanks to the digital revolution, audiobooks had at last found a relatively frictionless path to listeners' ears.

These were the technical conditions that underpinned the striking growth of audiobooks since the early 2000s. In 2004, just over 3,000 audiobooks were published in the US; by 2017, this had risen to over 46,000 – an increase of around thirteen-fold in thirteen years. Output remained fairly static between 2004 and 2011, but from 2011 on, the number of new audiobooks published increased significantly year on year, rising from 7,237 in 2011 to 46,089 in 2017 – a six-fold

---

[15] Millard, *America on Record*, pp. 251–5.

Table 10.1   Audiobook title output

	Titles published
2004	3,430
2005	2,667
2006	3,098
2007	3,073
2008	4,685
2009	4,602
2010	6,200
2011	7,237
2012	16,309
2013	24,755
2014	25,787
2015	35,944
2016	42,960
2017	46,089

increase in six years (see table 10.1 and figure 10.1). Revenues also grew. Between 2003 and 2012, total consumer spending on audiobooks in the US was estimated to be between $800 million and $1 billion per year (see table 10.2 and figure 10.2[16]). In 2013, consumer

---

[16] The numbers in this table and figure are estimates of total consumer spending based on publisher receipts, taking into account average discounts and estimating the piece of the market that was encompassed by non-reporting publishers. The estimates are probably on the high side. In 2018, the Audio Publishers Association (APA) changed its method of reporting market size from estimated consumer dollars to responding publisher receipts in order to align more closely with other book industry statistical reports; twenty publishers provided data, including Audible Inc., Hachette Audio, HarperCollins, Macmillan, Penguin Random House and Simon & Schuster. As a result of this change of method, estimates of total sales and title output were revised downward significantly. Whereas total consumer spending on audiobooks in 2017 was estimated to be $2.5 billion using the old method, audiobook sales in 2018 were given as $940 million using the new method based on reporting publishers' receipts. This figure of $940 million was reported as an increase of 24.5 per cent on the previous year, which means that audiobook sales in 2017 would have been $755 million using the new method (not $2.5 billion). Similarly, whereas in 2017 the APA reported that a total of 46,089 audiobook titles were produced, in 2018 they reported that 44,685 audiobook titles were produced; this was reported as a 5.8 per cent increase on the previous year, which means that the title output for 2017 would have been 42,235 titles using the new method (not 46,089 titles). From 2018 on, the APA will no longer produce estimates of total consumer spending, so the APA data from 2018 on will not be directly comparable to the APA data for 2016 and previous years.

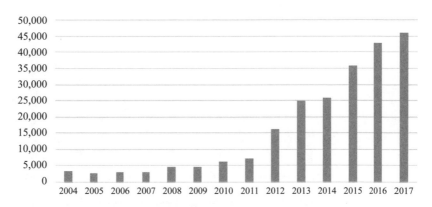

Figure 10.1 Audiobook titles published in US, 2004–2017
Source: Audio Publishers Association

Table 10.2 Estimated consumer spending on audiobooks in US, 2003–2017 ($ millions)

	Total spend $ millions
2003	800
2004	832
2005	871
2006	923
2007	1,033
2008	1,000
2009	900
2010	900
2011	1,000
2012	1,100
2013	1,300
2014	1,470
2015	1,770
2016	2,100
2017	2,500

spending on audiobooks began to increase sharply, rising from an estimated $1.1 billion in 2012 to an estimated $2.5 billion in 2017 – more than doubling in five years. Consumer spending on audiobooks in 2017 alone was up nearly 20 per cent on the previous year. At a time when overall revenue in the US book publishing industry was broadly static and ebook revenue for most major publishers was

357

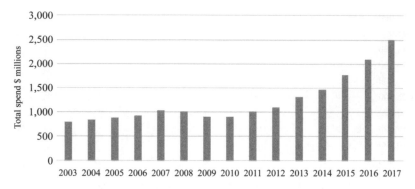

Figure 10.2   Estimated consumer spending on audiobooks in US, 2003–2017

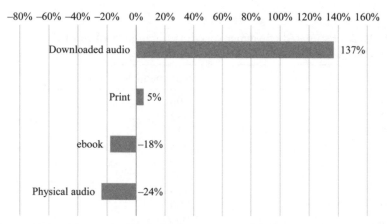

Figure 10.3   Change in US publisher revenues by format, 2012 to 2016
Source: Association of American Publishers and *Bloomsberg Businessweek*

declining, this strong growth in consumer spending on audiobooks was a strikingly positive trend in an otherwise sluggish market. For many of the large publishers, the only growth they were now seeing in the digital category was accounted for by audiobooks (see figure 10.3).

The growth of audiobook output and sales was accompanied by a clear shift in formats. Compact cassettes were the dominant format for audiobooks in the 1990s, but CDs were rapidly gaining ground. In 2003, cassettes and CDs were roughly equal in terms of the proportion of audiobooks sold in these formats, but, from that point on, CDs overtook cassettes and cassettes quickly declined (see table 10.3 and figure 10.4). From 2003 to 2010, CDs were the dominant medium for audiobooks, but downloads were taking a growing market share at CDs' expense. In 2007, CDs accounted for nearly 80 per cent of audiobook sales, and downloads accounted for less than 20 per cent; by 2016, these figures had been reversed and downloads were accounting for over 80 per cent of audiobook sales, with CDs accounting for less than 20 per cent. By 2017, downloads accounted for nearly 90 per cent of audiobook sales. This was a decisive format shift: one physical format (cassettes) was eclipsed by another physical format (CDs), and then the latter was largely replaced by digital downloads. For the vast majority of consumers, audiobooks are now being accessed as digital files, either downloaded or streamed, and the audiobooks that were still being sold in a physical format, as CDs, are being sold primarily into libraries.

While there has been a clear shift in the format of audiobooks, the types of books that are published as audiobooks have remained fairly constant since the early 2000s. Between 2013 and 2018, 70–80 per cent of the audiobooks sold were fiction, and 20–30 per cent were nonfiction. The most popular genres purchased in 2017 were mysteries/thrillers/suspense, science fiction and romance; this hadn't

Table 10.3   Audiobook formats as percentage of total sales, 2003–2017

	Cassette	CD	Download	Other
2002	58	35		
2003	49	45		
2004	30	63	6	2
2005	16.1	73.7	9.1	1
2006	7	77	14	1.4
2007	3	78	17	2
2008	3	73	21	4
2009	0.8	65.3	28.6	5.4
2010	0.6	58.4	36	4.6
2011	1	54	42	3.4
2012	0	43	54.4	2.6
2013	0	35.5	61.7	2.8
2014	0	29	69.1	2.1
2015	0	21.8	76.8	1.4
2016	0	16.2	82.4	1.4
2017	0	11.3	87.5	1.2

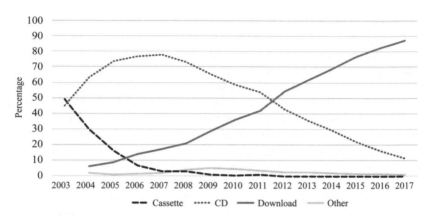

Figure 10.4   Audiobook formats, 2003–2017

changed much since 2008, when the five favourite audiobook genres were reported to be mystery/thriller/suspense, general fiction, science fiction/fantasy, biography/memoir and classic fiction.[17] Listening to audiobooks while driving has consistently been a popular activity – in a survey carried out in 2008, 58 per cent of audiobook listeners said they listened while commuting or on a long drive, as did 65 per cent in 2018. However, in recent years, listening to audiobooks in the home has become increasingly popular: in 2018, 45 per cent of listeners said that they listened to audiobooks while doing housework and chores in the home, and 52 per cent said they listened while relaxing before going to sleep. There has also been a strong shift towards listening on a smartphone: in 2018, 73 per cent of listeners were using smartphones, and 47 per cent were using this device most often, compared to 29 per cent in 2017 and 22 per cent in 2015.[18] Since many people have their phones with them all the time, they can listen while doing different things – commuting, exercising in the gym, relaxing at home, etc., picking up the story where they left off. With the smartphone, listening to audiobooks no longer required a dedicated audio device, like a cassette player, a CD player or an MP3 player: listening to audiobooks became just one more feature afforded by the multi-functionality of the phone that is with you all the time anyway. Thanks to the smartphone and it's always-on, always-with-you character, listening to audiobooks has become seamlessly

---

[17] Audio Publishers Association, Consumer Survey Results for 2008 and 2018, at www.audiopub.org.
[18] Ibid.

integrated into the practical flows of everyday life. Reading becomes listening, and print culture is absorbed through the ear rather than the eye – not because the listener is illiterate, as was often the case in the Middle Ages and the early modern period, but because the eyes are busy doing other things.

The ability to compress and download audio files and play them on compact and portable devices were crucial conditions for the structural shift in the audiobook industry that took place in the early 2000s, moving the industry away from the manufacture and distribution of physical objects, whether cassettes or CDs, and towards an industry focused primarily on platforms and digital downloads. But individuals and organizations had to perceive and grasp the opportunities opened up by these developments, and there was one individual who played a particularly important role in bringing about this shift – Don Katz, founder of Audible.

The rise of Audible

Don Katz was a writer and journalist who had studied literature at New York University in the 1970s. He was working on a book in the early 1990s about emergent technologies that would change the media world when he decided to take a break from writing to start an audiobook company – he had been taught by the writer Ralph Ellison at college, and Ellison's emphasis on the power of the American oral tradition had stayed with him ever since.[19] Katz's idea was simple but radical: might it be possible to create a business that allowed almost universal access to a catalogue of audiobooks, in a way that was open 24/7, that was not constrained by what was on the shelf in a bookstore, and that took out all the costs and dysfunctional features of the physical marketplace? This was the idea that inspired Audible, which Katz founded in 1995. He raised $3 million in funding and set about building a technological mechanism for delivering audiobooks directly to the end user as secure files. He wanted to get away from relying on desktop computers as the end point because he knew that many people listened to audiobooks while commuting and he saw that this was the key market – he needed to be in a mobile environment. But this was long before smartphones and even before

---

[19] Taylor Smith, 'The Spoken Word with Audible Founder & CEO Donald Katz', *Urban Agenda Magazine* (February 2017), at www.urbanagendamagazine.com/audible-founder-ceo-donald-katz.

the iPod, so he set out to build a dedicated audiobook device, the Audible Mobile Player, which was launched in November 1997: it cost $215 and it could hold two hours of audio at very low quality. The Player didn't last long – it was soon eclipsed by the iPod, which was released in 2001. But the proliferation of iPods did what Audible on its own never could have achieved: it created a mass market for downloading audio files and listening to them on mobile devices that could be easily carried with you in your pocket or bag. Paradoxically, the short life and early death of the Audible Mobile Player was not the end of Audible but its real beginning: it enabled Audible to find its true niche. It could leave the device business to others who were much larger and better equipped to develop it and focus its energies on acquiring audio rights, building a catalogue of audio content and creating a user experience that would be attractive to and valued by listeners.

In the early days, Audible was acquiring audio content of different kinds – audiobooks, to be sure, but also comedy sketches, lectures, speeches and performances – and re-purposing this content as digital files that were optimized for listening to the spoken word. Individuals could download audiobooks from Audible for around $8 – considerably less than the $20 typically charged for an audiobook on CD. But Katz was aware that, from the individual's point of view, the collection value of audiobooks was pretty limited – it was not like a physical book, which someone might want to keep as part of a collection, display on a book shelf in their home as a sign of their values and tastes, and even read again at some later point; nor was it like music that you want to play over and over again: once you've listened to an audiobook, you probably won't want to listen to it again. So, in 2000, Audible moved to a credit-based subscription model: while continuing to sell audiobooks as individual downloads, it also introduced memberships where, for a monthly subscription fee, individuals would be entitled to a certain number of credits that would enable them to download one or two audiobooks a month (depending on the plan), and they could purchase additional credits if they ran out. Not only did this produce a more reliable revenue stream, it also enabled Audible to develop a long-term relationship with its customers, who were now tied into Audible through a monthly subscription payment. The publishers who supplied audiobooks to Audible were remunerated when their audiobooks were downloaded, on terms that varied from publisher to publisher and depended on the nature of their agreement with Audible.

In 2003, Audible struck a deal with Apple that made Audible the exclusive supplier of the audiobooks that would be sold through the iTunes store. This was a major breakthrough for Audible because it gave them exclusive access to the iPod, the mobile device that would revolutionize the way that individuals listened to music. Now individuals could purchase and download audiobooks in the same way and in the same online environment where they were purchasing and downloading music, and they could carry those audiobooks with them in the small portable devices that they kept in their pocket or bag. Audible now had access to a true mass market.

With a platform optimized for audiobook listening and a subscription model that turned listeners into long-term paying customers, with an exclusive deal to supply audiobooks to iTunes and with the growing popularity of the iPod and other MP3 players, Audible was well positioned to grow, and grow it did. Revenues increased from $4.5 million in 2000 to $63 million in 2004, an increase of fourteen-fold in five years.[20] The company was on a steep upward trajectory in terms of revenue growth, but it had lost money in every year but one (in 2004 it posted its first profit of $2 million, but lost money again the following year). In 2006, Katz began talking to Jeff Bezos about selling to Amazon, which had already taken a small stake in the company, and in 2008 Audible was sold to Amazon for $300 million. The acquisition of Audible further consolidated Amazon's position as the leading player in the expanding audiobook market (Amazon had already acquired Brilliance Audio, the largest independent audiobook publisher in the US, in 2007). It gave Amazon access to Audible's subscribers, publisher contracts and more than 80,000 spoken-word recordings; it gave Audible access to much larger cash reserves, to Amazon's huge customer base and to the synergies and growth opportunities that would come from being integrated into the Amazon ecosystem.

While Audible was initially re-purposing audio content produced by others and making it available in a file format optimized for listening, it began to do its own recordings in 2007. This was driven in part by the need to increase the availability of audiobooks in the market: there simply wasn't enough new audiobook content being produced to keep people interested. Audible reckoned that if there were more potential choices in terms of content, they would have more potential listeners and more potential subscribers, so

---

[20] www.referenceforbusiness.com/history2/20/Audible-Inc.html.

they started buying up audiobook rights and becoming a publisher themselves. Initially, they outsourced production to studios, but they also built some studios in their offices in Newark, New Jersey, so that they could produce recordings themselves. Then, in 2011, Audible launched the Audiobook Creation Exchange (ACX), an online platform that enables audiobook rights holders – authors, agents and publishers – to connect with narrators and producers in order to create new audiobooks. Any author or other rights holder can register on ACX, choose a narrator and producer who are offering their services on the site (or choose to narrate and produce the audiobook themselves), and either pay up front for narration and production or opt for a 50:50 royalty share. When the audiobook is finished, you can distribute it through Audible, earning a royalty of 40 per cent of retail for sales on Audible, Amazon and iTunes if you do an exclusive deal with Audible, or 25 per cent if you want to retain the right to distribute your audiobook elsewhere. ACX was originally aimed at any rights holder, whether they were the publisher or the author, but in practice it became a platform to enable authors to produce their own audiobooks – in essence, a platform for audiobook self-publishing. The connection with self-publishing was strengthened by being linked up with KDP – Amazon's self-publishing platform – in the Amazon ecosystem. ACX was developed in order to increase the flow of audiobooks into the market and it certainly achieved its aim: more than 10,000 ACX titles were produced in 2013 alone.[21]

Audiobooks become routine

As the market for audiobooks expanded, the large publishers became increasingly reluctant to sell audiobook rights and began to treat the creation of audiobooks as a routine part of their own production process. In the early 2000s, large publishers were still very selective about which titles they would produce as audiobooks. Cathy, the head of the audiobook division of 'Everest', a large publishing house in New York, explained that the traditional rule of thumb in audiobook publishing in the early 2000s (we were speaking in 2007) was that audio sales would never be more than 10 per cent of the print number. So if a title sold 100,000 in hardcover, you

---

[21] Shannon Maughan, 'Audible's DIY Audiobook Platform Turns Three', *Publishers Weekly* (11 April 2014), at www.publishersweekly.com/pw/by-topic/industry-news/audio-books/article/61830-audible-s-diy-audiobook-platform-turns-three.html.

could expect to sell around 10,000 audiobooks. Given the 10 per cent rule and the cost of producing audiobooks, a large trade house like Everest would select a title for audiobook production only if they thought they were going to sell at least 50,000 copies of the hardcover – anything less than that and it probably wasn't going to be worth their while to do an audiobook. Of course, there were always exceptions. 'There will certainly be cases where we think that a book may only be going out at 25,000 copies but there's a certain level of buzz out there and we think that it's going to end up breaking higher than that', explained Cathy. 'So there are certainly books on every list that we will be doing in the hope that they'll end up performing better than forecasted.' But the general rule of thumb was that, if you were going to sell less than 50,000 copies in hardcover, then it wasn't worth doing the audiobook. So they would start with the number – how big was the book going to be? Then they would take account of other considerations, like whether it was the kind of book that would work well in audio. Rule out cookbooks and diet books except in rare cases; rule out heavily illustrated books and reference books. Commercial, plot-driven fiction works particularly well in audio, as do memoirs and some narrative nonfiction – general interest history, general interest biography, big ideas books, etc. Once you'd taken account of all those factors, you would end up with a small selection of new titles to be produced as audiobooks. In Cathy's case, she ended up with about 100 titles a season, or 300 titles a year – and that included titles where the audiobook rights were being bought from other publishers. Everest itself was publishing nearly 5,000 titles a year in print, so this was a small fraction of the total title output – less than 5 per cent of the total when you take account of the fact that some of the audiobooks were being bought in. That was not unusual for large publishing houses in the early 2000s – if anything, it was on the high side.

A decade later, the situation was very different. Sarah is Cathy's successor as head of audiobooks at Everest, where the audiobook programme is now much larger. She explained that now (we were speaking in 2018, ten years later), she would do between 1,000 and 1,100 titles a year – that is, between three and four times what her predecessor was doing. 'I'm publishing three audiobooks a day', she said, 'it's everything that [Everest] publishes that's appropriate for the format.' Part of the reason for this major expansion of their audiobook programme is that the market has changed and, with the proliferation of smartphones, the demand for audiobooks has grown: audiobooks were now a much more significant and

365

growing revenue stream. But there were other reasons too. Like other publishers, Everest wanted the audio rights included when they bought a book – they rarely buy a book these days without the audio rights. 'It would be akin to buying a book and not picking up paperback or ebook rights. It's just not going to happen', said Sarah. But if they're going to insist on having the audio rights, then they have to produce the audiobook: 'The audio right became a very valuable right and agents and authors rightfully said that if we're going to sell you the rights, you have to do it.' Moreover, the old 10 per cent rule of thumb was just too unreliable: it was fine as a rough guide, but trade publishing is a business of serendipity and books can surprise you – they can do much better than you think, or much worse than you think. And that's true of audiobooks too. Sarah recounted the story of a book they had published in print a few years earlier: it did well, but, in this case, the agent held the audio rights. They thought about acquiring the audio rights, did their calculations dutifully and came to the conclusion that it wasn't worth paying what they would have to pay to acquire the audio rights, so they passed on it. The audio rights were picked up by another publisher and the audiobook went on to become the number one bestselling audiobook in its category. The lesson was painful and clear: just do everything. 'If you don't pass and you do everything, sure, some may only be 1 per cent, but I have titles now where 50 per cent of the sales can be in audio.' In this new environment, the old 10 per cent rule is just too unreliable as a guide.

Just as ebooks had become a standard output of the production process, simply one more output alongside the print-ready file, so too audiobooks were now another standard output for the large trade houses – at least for the kinds of books that work in audio. Of course, producing audiobooks was not as simple and straightforward as producing ebook files: audiobook production needed an entirely different production track that was both costly and time-consuming. But for the large trade houses, the creation of audiobooks was now a routine part of the production process.

There was another significant shift that took place at the same time. In the early 2000s and before, most audio publishers produced two different versions of an audiobook: an abridged version for individual customers, and an unabridged version for the library market. The audiobook market was bifurcated into abridged and unabridged versions. Librarians had a clear preference for unabridged audiobooks, and the extra cost of the unabridged version wasn't an obstacle for libraries with an acquisitions budget. But for the retail market, where individual customers were buying audiobooks as boxed sets of CDs in bookstores, price was a more sensitive consideration – individual customers might be willing to pay $29.95 for an abridged audiobook but would balk at paying $80–$90 for an unabridged version. So, many audiobook publishers, including Everest, produced two different recordings, an unabridged version for the library market and an abridged version for the retail market. This also meant two different production processes that ran parallel to one another; the abridged and unabridged versions were often produced by different studios with different narrators, etc. But with the shift to digital downloads as the preferred mode of accessing audiobooks, the case for producing an abridged version became less and less compelling. Audiobook publishers gradually phased out the production of abridged versions, or reduced the number to a handful. 'Abridgements are pretty much gone', explained Sarah. 'We still do a few abridgements, maybe less than a dozen a year out of a thousand books. It changed with digital, because once it was a digital file, it doesn't matter. And consumers really wanted to hear the whole story – they didn't want the abridgements.' The handful of cases where they still do abridgements tends to be for particular customers who want the abridged version on CDs and need the lower price point. It's usually books by commercial authors who have always had their audiobooks available in an abridged format – authors like John Grisham, Lee Child, Stephen King, etc. And the customer, whether it's Walmart or Costco or another mass merchandiser, needs the lower price point in order to move the stock. But these are now the rare exceptions. For the vast majority of audiobooks today, the unabridged version is the only version produced.

In the early 2000s, some large publishers built or acquired studios to produce audiobooks, often producing a portion of their audio-books in their own studios and outsourcing the rest to independent studios. Most of the US studios were in New York or LA because this is where the largest concentrations of actors were – and most studios preferred, and still prefer, to use actors for the recording process. As audiobook sales increased and publishers began to ramp up their audiobook production, they expanded their production capacity by building or acquiring more studios, while still outsourcing a proportion of their audiobook production to others. At the same time, the audiobook supply chains became more ramified and complex, as a plethora of new players entered the field to compete with Audible, providing audiobook publishers with more channels to market and providing consumers with more ways to access audio-books. What had been a small cottage industry dominated by one retail player – Audible – was rapidly becoming a sub-field of labyrinthine complexity.

The audiobook supply chain

Today, there are many different players operating in the audiobook space, and many of these perform a variety of different roles. The space is constantly evolving as new players enter the field and older players expand their services and take on new roles. The easiest way to understand this space is to distinguish the key roles in the audiobook supply chain and then to position different players within this supply chain, while acknowledging that many players now occupy more than one position. Figure 10.5 provides a concise summary of the audiobook supply chain. We can distinguish five key roles in the audiobook supply chain: rights holders, publishers, producers, distributors, and retailers/subscription services/aggregators.

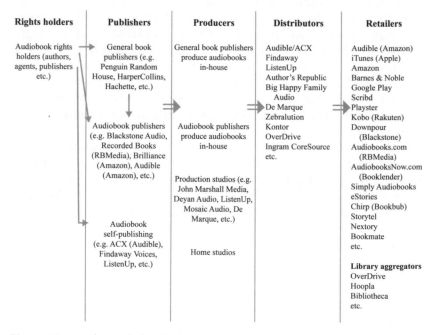

Rights holders	Publishers	Producers	Distributors	Retailers
Audiobook rights holders (authors, agents, publishers etc.)	General book publishers (e.g. Penguin Random House, HarperCollins, Hachette, etc.)	General book publishers produce audiobooks in-house	Audible/ACX Findaway ListenUp Author's Republic Big Happy Family Audio De Marque Zebralution Kontor OverDrive Ingram CoreSource etc.	Audible (Amazon) iTunes (Apple) Amazon Barnes & Noble Google Play Scribd Playster Kobo (Rakuten) Downpour (Blackstone) Audiobooks.com (RBMedia) AudiobooksNow.com (Booklender) Simply Audiobooks eStories Chirp (Bookbub) Storytel Nextory Bookmate etc.
	Audiobook publishers (e.g. Blackstone Audio, Recorded Books (RBMedia), Brilliance (Amazon), Audible (Amazon), etc.)	Audiobook publishers produce audiobooks in-house		
		Production studios (e.g. John Marshall Media, Deyan Audio, ListenUp, Mosaic Audio, De Marque, etc.)		**Library aggregators** OverDrive Hoopla Bibliotheca etc.
	Audiobook self-publishing (e.g. ACX (Audible), Findaway Voices, ListenUp, etc.)	Home studios		

Figure 10.5   The audiobook supply chain

The audiobook rights holders are the authors, agents or publishers who hold the audiobook rights. When an author signs a contract with a publisher, he or she generally assigns all subsidiary rights to the publisher, and these subsidiary rights typically include audiobook rights (though on older contracts, audiobook rights may not be explicitly mentioned, which may leave the status of these rights unclear, as was the case with ebook rights before publishers changed their contracts). Some agents may try to withhold audiobook rights in some cases so that they can sell them separately, but, as noted earlier, most major publishers with audiobook divisions will not acquire a book these days without also acquiring the audiobook rights. A publisher who acquires audiobook rights as part of their contract with the author may not necessarily exercise those rights – in many cases, they don't. They may hold the audiobook rights passively, without making any arrangements to produce an audiobook. But if an audiobook publisher were interested in producing the audiobook, they would have to license the audiobook rights from the publisher who holds them.

The second key role in the audiobook supply chain is the audiobook publisher. There are, in essence, three types of audiobook publishers. First, many mainstream book publishers are also audiobook publishers. If they are large publishers, they may have a dedicated audiobook division with their own studios, as is the case with Big Five publishers like Penguin Random House, HarperCollins and Hachette. In some cases, these publishers may have acquired audiobook publishers and integrated them into their publishing operations, as happened when Harper & Row (now HarperCollins) acquired Caedmon in 1987, and Random House acquired Books on Tape in 2001. Large publishers with audiobook divisions produce the audiobook versions of many of the books they publish in print, but these divisions also typically operate as semi-autonomous publishing operations that acquire audiobook rights for books that are published in print by other publishers – in other words, they are active players in the audiobook rights marketplace. Some smaller publishers also publish their own audiobooks. They don't have their own in-house studios, but they work with independent production studios or with freelance producers and narrators to produce audiobook versions of some of the books they publish.

The second type of audiobook publisher consists of those publishing organizations that were set up with the aim of publishing audiobooks; they are not general publishers who have added audiobooks to their publishing repertoire but, rather, specialized audiobook publishers whose main goal is to publish audiobooks. They generally acquire audiobook rights from publishers or other rights holders for a specified time period and then produce and publish audiobooks under their own imprint. They also produce and publish audiobook versions of classic books that are now in the public domain. Caedmon Records and Books on Tape began as audiobook publishers in this way, as did Recorded Books, Blackstone Publishing, Brilliance Audio and other dedicated audiobook publishing companies.

Recorded Books was founded in Charlotte Hall, Maryland, in 1978 by Henry Trentman, a travelling salesman who spent a lot of time on the road and saw audiobooks as an alternative to the radio. He envisaged producing unabridged recordings on cassettes that could be rented out by mail order – a model similar to that pioneered a few years earlier by Duvall Hecht at Books on Tape. Recorded Books expanded in the 1980s and 1990s, and was acquired by Haights Cross Communications in 1999; it changed hands a couple of times after that, and in 2015 it was acquired by Shamrock Capital Advisors, a private equity firm. Recorded Books now operates as an imprint of RBMedia, alongside several other imprints, including HighBridge Audio, which had been founded by Minnesota Public Radio in the early 1980s to produce recordings of Garrison Keillor's *A Prairie Home Companion* and was acquired by Recorded Books in 2014; Tantor Media, also acquired in 2014, which had been founded in San Clemente, California, in 2000 by Kevin, Laura and Allen Colebank; ChristianAudio, founded in 2004 under the name Hovel Audio; and GraphicAudio, also founded in 2004. With an overall output of around 3,000 titles annually, RBMedia is now one of the world's largest audiobook publishers. In 2018, RBMedia was sold by Shamrock Capital Advisors to KKR, another private equity firm with substantial investments in the media and technology sector.

Blackstone Publishing was founded in Ashland, Oregon, in 1987 by Craig and Michelle Black, originally under the name of Classics on Tape. Like many audiobook publishers, Blackstone had emerged from the experience of commuting: in the 1980s, Craig had a daily commute of three hours a day, and when a friend gave him the audiobook of George Orwell's *1984* to pass the time, he immediately saw the potential. Ashland hosted an annual Shakespeare festival, and this provided Craig and Michelle Black with a pool of talent from which they could draw narrators to record audiobooks. They produced 30 audiobooks in their first year, 1988; thirty years later, in 2018, they were producing 1,200 books annually, making them one of the larger independent audiobook publishers in the US.

Brilliance Audio was founded in Grand Haven, Michigan, in 1984 by Michael Snodgrass. It had become one of the largest producers of CD-based audiobooks by the time that it was acquired by Amazon in 2007, shortly before Amazon's acquisition of Audible.

While audiobook publishers typically began as organizations that would acquire audiobook rights from traditional publishers and other rights holders and produce and publish audiobooks, many have diversified over the years. In some cases, this diversification stemmed from the need to increase the supply of high-quality content. As more and more traditional publishers began to produce their own audiobooks, the supply lines for audiobook publishers were beginning to dry up; audiobook publishers found themselves in the same position as paperback publishers had found themselves several decades earlier when the traditional hardcover houses began to develop their own paperback lines. So some of the larger audiobook publishers began to morph into general publishers, signing books with all the rights attached and publishing print books and ebooks as well as audiobooks – Tantor Media added a print line in 2012, and Blackstone launched a print imprint in 2015. Moreover, with the shift to digital downloads, some audiobook publishers developed their own platforms to supply their content to libraries or directly to consumers. In 2013, Blackstone launched Downpour.com, an online audiobook store that was positioned as a direct competitor to Audible, offering a subscription service that allows users to download audiobooks from Blackstone and other audiobook publishers for $12.99 a month. In 2018, Recorded Books launched RBdigital, an app for libraries that allowed library users to access audiobooks and video content via a streaming service. And, just as organizations that had started out as audiobook publishers were diversifying downstream, establishing retail and distribution operations that were creating new channels to market, so too Audible, which had started life as a retail and subscription service, was expanding its operations upstream as an audiobook publisher, acquiring audiobook rights from traditional publishers and creating original audio content of its own. The lines between audiobook publishers, producers, distributors and retailers were becoming increasingly blurred.

The third type of audiobook publisher is the audiobook self-publisher – the equivalent, in the audiobook space, of the many individuals who choose to self-publish their own books in the world of print and ebook publishing. Just as it is now possible to bypass traditional publishers and self-publish your own print book and ebook, so too you can bypass audiobook publishers and self-publish your own audiobook – no need to rely on the established audiobook publishers, you can do-it-yourself. In the case of audiobooks, if you hold the audiobook rights, you really can do the full DIY audiobook – get a microphone, find a quiet space, produce a digital recording and upload the audiobook to a suitable distribution system. The enterprising author who wants to narrate and produce her own audiobook can find lots of advice and guidance online and in print, both from authors who've done it themselves and from individuals and organizations involved in the audiobook industry.[22] But the apparent simplicity of recording the reading of a text belies the complexity involved in creating a high-quality audiobook. Narrating a text is an art in itself, and it's often better to find an experienced narrator to record the audiobook rather than to do it yourself; and even when an author is going to record her own audiobook, she can improve the quality by getting some professional help. Just as with print books and ebooks, there are numerous audiobook self-publishing platforms which an author can use to self-publish her own audiobook. The largest and most well known of these is ACX – the Audiobook Creation Exchange created by Audible in 2011 (see above). Once you've created an audiobook on this platform, ACX takes care of distribution via Audible, Amazon and iTunes – and, for a lower royalty rate, you can also choose to distribute through other retail channels. But ACX is not the only option.

The main competitor to ACX is Findaway Voices, which was launched in July 2017 by Findaway, one of the leading audiobook distributors, partly as a way of increasing the flow of audiobook content that they could offer to retailers. Like ACX, Findaway Voices is aimed primarily at indie authors and the self-publishing community, though it can be used by publishers too. It offers those seeking to create audiobooks a set of options that is broadly similar to those offered by ACX, but it differs from ACX in several respects. In the first place, ACX is restricted to residents of the US, the UK, Canada and Ireland, whereas Findaway Voices is open to authors throughout

---

[22] See, for example, Chandler Bolt, 'How to Make an Audiobook: What Every Author Should Know', at https://self-publishingschool.com/creating-audiobook-every-author-know; Ricci Wolman, 'How to Publish an Audiobook: Your Guide to Audiobook Production and Distribution', at www.writtenwordmedia.com/self-publish-audiobook-production-and-distribution; Michele Cobb, 'Creating an Audiobook as a Self-Published Author', at https://blog.bookbaby.com/2018/06/creating-an-audiobook-as-a-self-published-author; and so on. The best guide in print to producing audiobooks is Jessica Kaye, *The Guide to Publishing Audiobooks: How to Produce and Sell an Audiobook* (Cincinnati, Ohio: Writer's Digest Books, 2019).

the world. Second, ACX is an open marketplace where authors can search for any narrator that seems suitable for their book, whereas Findaway Voices curates the selection of narrators for an author, gathering information from the author and then presenting him with a selection of five to ten narrators that seem particularly well suited to the project. Third, Findaway Voices gives authors and publishers full control over the pricing of their audiobooks: with Findaway Voices, the author or publisher sets the price of their audiobook, whereas with ACX, the price is set by each retailer at their discretion (and on Audible, the price is generally set on the basis of length). A fourth important difference is that Findaway Voices distributes to many audiobook retailers and subscription services, whereas ACX distributes only to Audible, Amazon and iTunes – though you can, as noted above, choose to go non-exclusive with ACX and use another distributor, like Findaway or Author's Republic, to distribute to other retail channels. Findaway Voices has proven to be attractive to the self-publishing community, in part because it represents an independent alternative to the Amazon ecosystem to which ACX belongs, and a number of ebook self-publishing platforms, including Smashwords and Draft2Digital, have struck deals with Findaway Voices to give self-published authors integrated access to audiobook production and distribution services.

While ACX and Findaway Voices are the main audiobook self-publishing platforms, there are players in the audiobook space that have opened up other pathways for indie authors and publishers to produce their own audiobooks. ListenUp Audiobooks was launched in 2016 by ListenUp, an audio production company based in Atlanta, Georgia. They offer authors and publishers a full-service audiobook solution that includes a director, choice of narrator, professional studio recording, full edit and final mastering; they also offer a distribution option that distributes to a wide range of retail and library outlets, including Audible. Author's Republic is an audiobook distributor that was created by Audiobooks.com in 2015; while it doesn't offer an audiobook production service of its own, it provides authors with step-by-step guidance on how to create an audiobook and recommends a number of production companies that could handle the audiobook creation process.[23]

The third key role in the audiobook supply chain is the audiobook producer (or production company). Here it is helpful to distinguish four different types of audiobook producer. The first type is the

---

[23] See www.authorsrepublic.com/creation.

traditional book publisher who has developed an audiobook division and does all or some of their own audiobook production in-house, in customized audiobook production studios that they have built or acquired. Most of the large trade houses now have their own audiobook production facilities, as noted above, though they still outsource some of their audiobook production to independent studios. Second, many audiobook publishers also have their own production studios and produce all (or some) of their audiobooks in-house. However, there are also many audio production companies which are not publishers but which specialize in high-quality audio production; they provide recording studios and audio production services to a range of clients, from musicians to publishers – this is the third type of audiobook producer. Two of the best-known audio production companies that are active in the audiobook space are John Marshall Media and Deyan Audio. John Marshall Media was founded in 1995 by John Marshall Cheary, an audio engineer who graduated from Berklee College of Music. Based in New York, where they have access to a large pool of narrating talent, they have established themselves as one of the leading audiobook producers and offer a full range of services to publishers, from studio rental to full casting-to-final-delivery audiobook production. Deyan Audio was founded by Bob and Debra Deyan in 1990 with the aim of producing audiobooks, at a time when audiobooks were still a very niche product. They started by recording at their home in Van Nuys, California, later expanding into a suite of studios in Tarzana, California. Being based in LA, they were able to tap into a large pool of actors to provide narrating talent. While John Marshall Media and Deyan Audio are two of the best-known audio production companies that specialize in audiobook production, there are many other audio production companies that offer audiobook production services – Mosaic Audio, De Marque, Edge Studio, Verity Audio, Audio Factory and Listening Books, to mention just a few.

The fourth type of audiobook producer is the home studio. Home studios are domestic spaces – e.g., a bedroom or closet or corner of a living room in the home – that have been fitted out to serve as a recording studio. They were initially developed by people who were doing voice-over work and narration and who wanted to avoid long commutes to work; in some cases, audio production companies would help fit out home studios and supply equipment and software. With the growth of audiobooks and the rise of audiobook self-publishing platforms like ACX, home studios have become increasingly popular with freelance narrators, who set up their own recording studios and work from home. Improvised soundproofing can be done at minimal expense and they can fit out the studio with basic equipment – microphone, laptop, editing software, etc. – at a level that is geared to their budget. Plenty of resources exist online to advise prospective narrators on how to set up a home studio, and to walk them through the basics of narration and editing.[24]

The fourth role in the audiobook supply chain is the distributor. Distributors are intermediaries in the supply chain; they exist to make it easier for suppliers to get their content into a plurality of retail channels, and to make it easier for retailers to acquire content from a plurality of suppliers. If there were only one supplier and one retailer, there would be no need for distributors – the supplier could supply directly to the retailer; but the more suppliers and retailers there are, the more important distributors become as intermediaries in the supply chain, giving suppliers access to as many retailers as possible, and giving retailers a one-stop shop to acquire content. The audiobook supply chain is skewed by the fact that Audible is the overwhelmingly dominant retail outlet and is also a major audiobook publisher and producer which distributes directly to iTunes and Amazon; this means that it operates across the entire supply chain, from audiobook publisher and producer to distributor and retailer, and it accounts for a large proportion both of audiobook production and of audiobook sales. This creates a large pipeline in the audiobook supply chain that is controlled by one organization – Audible, itself owned by Amazon, with ACX as its audiobook self-publishing platform. The significance of this pipeline was increased by the fact that, from 2003 on, Audible was also the exclusive supplier of audiobooks to iTunes, which meant that any publisher seeking access to the iTunes store had to go through the Audible pipeline. Following complaints by the German Publishers and Booksellers Association, this arrangement came under scrutiny by the European Commission and the German antitrust regulator, the Bundeskartellamt, and in January 2017 Audible and Apple announced that their exclusive arrangement for the supply of audiobooks to iTunes would cease. From this point on, publishers could supply their audiobooks directly to iTunes, or supply their content to iTunes through another third-party distributor.

There are numerous audiobook distributors that have emerged in the space between audiobook publishers and producers, on the one

---

[24] See, for example, the five video lessons on home audiobook narration by ACX, at www.acx.com/help/setup/202008260.

hand, and audiobook retailers, on the other – Findaway, Author's Republic, Big Happy Family, De Marque, Kontor, Zebralution, etc. Some audiobook publishers and producers, like ListenUp, also offer distribution services for their clients. Each of these distributors has its own history and particular emphasis. Based in Solon, Ohio, Findaway made its name by developing Playaway pre-loaded digital audio players in the early 2000s and then expanded into digital distribution, becoming one of the world's largest audiobook distributors. Author's Republic was launched in 2015 by Audiobooks.com, an audiobook subscription service, to help self-published audiobook creators to distribute their work. Big Happy Family was founded in 2006 by Jessica Kaye, a former audiobook publisher, with the aim of helping small and medium-sized publishers reach audiobook retail outlets. And so on. The distributors vary in terms of the emphasis of their activities and the markets they serve, but in each case the goal is the same: to act as a go-between, taking digital content – in this case, audiobooks – from publishers large and small; aggregating it into an integrated list and making it available to as many retail outlets, subscription services, download sites and libraries as possible; and then transferring royalty payments and revenues back upstream to the publishers. In this way, retail outlets could deal with a single supplier rather than hundreds of different publishers and producers, and publishers – especially small publishers and self-publishers – would gain access to retail outlets that they wouldn't be able to reach on their own. The distributor would simplify life for both parties and take a cut of the revenue for their services.

The fifth and final role in the audiobook supply chain is the retail outlet. Recent years have witnessed a veritable explosion of retail outlets for audiobooks, from subscription services and online stores to library aggregators and suppliers. There can be no doubt that, since the early 2000s, Audible has been the overwhelmingly dominant retail player in the audiobook space; with its credit-based subscription service for digital downloads, its synergistic relation with Amazon and its exclusive distribution arrangement with iTunes, Audible was well positioned to take full advantage of the decline of CDs and the rise of digital downloads as the principal medium for consuming audiobooks. By the beginning of the 2010s, Audible was pretty much synonymous with audiobooks, at least for many consumers in the US. But new retail players were entering the field, and some retail outlets for ebooks and other digital content began to add audiobooks to their offerings. Scribd added audiobooks to its subscription service in 2015, as did the Toronto-based entertainment subscription service Playster. In 2014, Barnes & Noble launched a new audiobook app that enabled users to purchase and download audiobooks onto their Nook. In 2017, Kobo added audiobooks to its offerings and introduced a $10-per-month credit-based subscription service similar to Audible's; in 2018, Walmart partnered with Kobo to launch Walmart eBooks, which included an audiobook subscription service where customers get one audiobook a month for a subscription fee of $9.99; and in 2018, Google added audiobooks to its Google Play Store. Some audiobook publishers and distributors created their own consumer-facing retail outlets, and a variety of independent audiobook subscription services were also launched, including Audiobooks.com, a credit-based subscription service founded in 2012 to compete with Audible, and acquired in 2017 by RBMedia, owner of Recorded Books; AudiobooksNow.com, a download and streaming service founded in 2012 by Booksfree, an online book rental company that was established in 2000 and rebranded as Booklender in 2016; eStories, an audiobook subscription service launched in 2016 by eMusic, the online music subscription service that began in the late 1990s; Libro.fm, an audiobook service founded in 2013 that enables indie bookstores to get a share of the audiobook market by partnering with Libro.fm; Chirp, an audiobook service founded in 2019 by Bookbub that offers consumers a selection of limited-time audiobook deals every day, which can be purchased à la carte; and so on. Many of these audiobook subscription services operate predominantly – or even exclusively – in the US, but a number of services have opened in Europe and elsewhere. The leader in Europe has been the Swedish firm Storytel, which is the largest audiobook subscription service in Scandinavia and is active in twenty countries, but Nextory (also based in Sweden) and Bookmate (based in London and Moscow) are significant players in the non-North American market for audiobooks. There are also a number of services that specialize in aggregating and supplying audiobooks to libraries – OverDrive has been the dominant player here but there are others, such as Hoopla and Bibliotheca.

The plethora of consumer-facing and library-supplying audiobook services makes for a confusing picture: as audiobook sales grow, more and more players are entering the audiobook space or expanding their activities within this space, creating a constantly changing landscape. But while the number of retail outlets has increased significantly in recent years and continues to grow, many remain small players; the consumer retail market for audiobooks in the US remains dominated by Audible and its owner Amazon,

BOOK WARS

which also sells audiobooks on its main site. According to the Codex Group, Amazon's total share of audiobook unit sales in the US in May 2019 (including Audible) was 54%, up from 42% the previous year, in June 2018 – in other words, by this estimate, more than half of all audiobook unit sales are now channelled through Amazon/ Audible. Codex estimated the share of Audible alone to be 34% of the market in May 2019, up from 29% the previous year. During the same time period, Barnes & Nobles's share of the audiobook market declined from 18% to 11%, and all other digital audiobook retailers declined from 26% to 22% – the market share of Amazon/Audible appeared to be growing at the expense of their competitors.[25] Others put Amazon/Audible's share of the audiobook market much higher than this – one analyst puts it at more than 90%.[26] The cessation of the exclusivity arrangement between Audible and iTunes may have curtailed some of Audible's market privileges but Audible remains by far the single most important retail channel for audiobooks, and most of the large audio publishers continue to distribute to iTunes through Audible. Audible's centrality in the different phases of the audiobook supply chain, its integration with Amazon and its increasing investment in the creation of original content that is exclusive to Audible – so-called Audible Originals – are likely to ensure that it remains the dominant player in the audiobook space for the foreseeable future.

The kind of work that is done by any particular organization or individual depends on where it is situated in the audiobook supply chain – the work that is done by an audiobook publisher will differ from that of a narrator, and a distributor will work differently from a consumer-facing subscription site. We can get some sense of how audiobooks are produced by dipping into this supply chain at a couple of different points.

---

[25] *U.S. Audiobook Participation and Market Unit Share, May 2019* (New York: Codex Group, 2019). Codex's estimates of market share are based on a national online consumer survey, carried out from 25 April to 13 May 2019, of 4,151 past-month book buyers aged 18 and over, balanced by age and region, who purchased at least one audiobook in the past month and at least three in the past twelve months.
[26] Paul Abbassi (formerly known as Data Guy) at Bookstat estimates that 95 per cent of the 130 million audiobook unit sales in the US in 2019 were Audible-distributed sales through Audible.com, Amazon.com and Apple iTunes – a much higher percentage than the 54% estimated by the Codex Group based on their consumer survey. Abbassi's estimates are based on the tracking of rankings on bestseller lists using methods similar to those he developed as Data Guy (see chapter 7, pp. 266–79). This may be on the high side, however, as some audiobook outlets, such as Scribd and the audiobook library suppliers like OverDrive, are not included in his analysis.

378

Producing audiobooks

Richard runs the audiobook division of 'Horizon', a large publishing house in New York. He started working on audiobooks in the same company in the early 2000s, so he's lived through both the shift in format, from cassettes and CDs to digital downloads, and the growth of the audiobook business. 'When I started here in the early 2000s we were publishing maybe 50 to 65 books a year, it might have been 20 to 30 per cent of the total output, and they were mostly abridged', explained Richard. 'This year we'll be publishing 700 books, all unabridged, and that's nearly 80 per cent of all our hardcovers.' In terms of revenue, audiobooks accounted for somewhere between 5 and 10 per cent of Horizon's overall revenue in 2018 – between a third and half of the proportion accounted for by ebooks, but with ebook sales stagnating and audiobook revenue growing, the gap was narrowing. In terms of revenue from digital sales, audiobooks were the new beacon of hope.

Given the number of books that Richard's division is now handling, he has had to streamline the process for selecting and producing audiobooks. It is no longer a matter of just picking out the likely bestsellers and doing those – now, virtually everything has to be considered as a potential audiobook. Richard begins by looking at what is coming through the pipeline for the coming year and dividing it into three groups:

> The green lights are the automatics. The reds are too small, too niche, like cookbooks, something that doesn't translate. The oranges are the ones where we proceed with caution – on our schedule these are all highlighted in orange. With these you start digging very deep. You start looking at marketing campaigns, publicity, whether there are author tours. Sometimes I'll go granular, I'll speak with the editor, I'll ask for sample pages – can I see the layout? Can I read some? We look at the print budget and the ebook budget – it's not just looking at one format anymore. How many are they going to sell digitally? So there's a lot more that goes into the orange sector.

The oranges that are not selected for audiobook production are then passed on to the sub-rights department to see if they can sell the audiobook rights to another publisher – they paid for these rights, so they want to exploit them even if they're not going to do the audiobook themselves.

Once they've decided which audiobooks they're going to do, they set them up in their system and assign a producer to each project. The producer takes the book, or a draft of the book, reads it, talks to the author and has a conversation about what the casting should be. Should it be one narrator or several different narrators? Does it need to be a narrator with a particular voice or accent – English or Scottish, rather than American, for example? These conversations can take place before they have the final text – at this stage, they can be working with a draft text or what they call the 'prep script'. But they can't start recording until they have the final recordable script. Time is then tight because they want to have the audiobook ready to release at the same time as the print book and ebook are published. That's new. 'Back in the day when audio was less of a mast on the ship, it didn't matter', explained Richard. 'People would publish the audiobook six months after. Now, with big authors, you need to be day in day with the print, with the ebook, side by side digitally, or on a shelf in stores together.' So they work as far in advance as they can, using the prep script to do the casting, reaching out to narrators or their agents to line up the narrator(s), booking studio time, etc. While authors are consulted as part of this process, only rarely are authors involved in doing the actual narration; the only times when authors will narrate their own books are when they are public speakers or actors and their voice is so well known that you couldn't imagine anyone else reading the book, and this is especially the case when it's a personal story – you want Bill Clinton narrating his autobiography *My Life*, Barack Obama narrating *Dreams from My Father*, Michelle Obama narrating *Becoming* and so on. But for the vast majority of recordings, Richard and his team prefer to use professional actors as narrators, especially actors who have chosen to focus on audiobook narration as part of their portfolio of activities. Professional actors who have had theatrical training make particularly good narrators, explained Richard, because they have the kind of focus, attention, vocal training and dramatic training that make for good narration; it also helps if they're book readers and read books for pleasure. Not all professional actors make good narrators, however. Audiobook narration requires endurance – it can be gruelling. You have to be able to sit in a studio for long periods of time and read continuous text with few breaks and interruptions. 'You can be a great television actor, you can be a stand-up performer in front of a live studio audience, and reading in an isolated booth for five days might not be your cup of tea.'

While most of the narrators Richard and his team use are professional actors, they do occasionally use celebrities as narrators. Using a celebrity can have some advantages in terms of marketing and sales – you can sometimes get a press release and some pick-up in the trade by having a well-known celebrity as the narrator. But you pay over the odds for celebrity narrators and it's often not worth it, said Richard. Moreover, it can be a headache in terms of production. 'We've hired narrators and they thought they were going to be free and suddenly they're offered a movie deal in Shangri-La, so they're gone. It becomes very complicated. The casting's hard, the location's difficult, and the location can add to the expense.' Professional actors who have chosen to make audiobook narration part of their portfolio are a much more reliable bet.

Horizon uses its own in-house studios, but, given the volume of throughput, they have to hire studios too – they can't do everything in-house. Richard wants to have a director and engineer in the studio as well as the narrator, separated by glass when the recording is under way so that the narrator is isolated. The director is there to make sure that no mistakes are made in the recording process, no lines are skipped, no words are slurred, no stomach grumbling can be heard in the background, to make sure that a character's voice doesn't change perceptibly from one chapter to the next, etc. 'To make a really seamless audiobook, you need someone in there', explained Richard. It takes roughly 3 hours in the studio for 1 finished hour, and the general rule of thumb in the audiobook business is that about 9,300 words of text equates to 1 hour of finished audio. So a book of 90,000 words would be about 9.7 hours of finished audio, and that means this would require around 29 hours of studio time – in other words, a full week of 6 hours a day in the studio.

In terms of costs, narrators are paid per-finished-hour (PFH) of audio. Rates vary from narrator to narrator, but many professional actors are members of the actors' union, SAG–AFTRA (Screen Actors Guild – American Federation of Television and Radio Artists), and their rates are negotiated by the union with different audiobook publishers and producers; the SAG–AFTRA member minimum rate for most publishers is around $200–$250 PFH. So the cost of the narrator alone could be $2,000–$2,500 for a 90,000-word book. You also pay by the hour for editing and proofing – the quality control that involves listening to the final audio and making sure that all errors have been picked up and corrected. If you're using your own studios and if the producer, director and engineer are on your staff, you'll save some costs there, but if you need to hire a studio, that will add further costs – hiring a studio in New York can be $100–$150 an hour, so 30 hours of studio time would cost $3,000–$4,500. Costs quickly add up; producing audiobooks is not cheap.

When you're producing an audiobook in your own studios with your own staff (apart from the narrator), you can make it work financially if you're able to sell at least 500–600 copies, explained Richard; 'If you're going to sell 500 or less, it's very questionable.' But if you have to use an external studio and outsource some of the work, 'the likelihood of turning a profit on selling less than 1,000 copies becomes much harder.' Richard works all this out in his head when he's setting the list. 'I do quick mental P&Ls when I determine the list. I'll do the production cost and the sale side by side, so we'll know what to add, we'll know what not to add, and we'll know if it's worth going forward with it.'

Horizon offers a premium audiobook service: this is high-quality audiobook production, with purpose-built in-house studios (or hired studios), experienced staff and professional narrators. But audiobooks can be produced more cheaply. At the other end of the spectrum is the ACX do-it-yourself model, where narrators can be hired for as little as $50–$100 PFH (though more experienced narrators will cost more) or where up-front narrator costs can be avoided altogether by choosing a royalty share. In between these two extremes is a range of intermediate models, and different audiobook publishers and producers will have developed their own practices and systems. Of particular importance in this evolving ecosystem of audiobook production is the development of the home studio, which enables narrators to work as freelancers from their own home and enables publishers and producers to dispense with the need to provide or hire a professional studio. A great deal of narration work – whether for established publishers or for authors seeking to produce their own audiobook on ACX or Findaway Voices – now takes place in the hidden economy of the home.

Performing the page

Stuart trained as an actor and began his career touring with a Shakespeare company, working in theatre, and teaching acting part-time. But when he decided to settle in New York and start a family, he felt he needed another option that would utilize the same skill sets. He did some on-camera commercial work – this was well paid but unreliable, bookings were made from week-to-week and you never knew exactly how much you were going to make. He needed a more stable source of income. He enjoyed reading and he'd often listened to audiobooks, especially on the long drives between home and grad school and while touring with the Shakespeare company, so he decided to look into audiobook narration. He needed to learn more about what was involved and how to get started, so he did what a lot of people in his situation do, 'which is to find a friend from grad school who is a successful audiobook narrator, take her out to coffee and pick her brains.' His friend helped him to see that, while the world of audiobooks is organized along somewhat similar lines to the worlds of theatre or film and TV or commercial voice-over work, the networks were completely different – there was very little overlap between them. And since the world of audiobooks was so much smaller than these other industries, direct one-to-one relationships with the producers and publishers were particularly important. His friend gave him some good tips about how to start networking in this world, like going to the events and conventions organized by the Audio Publishers Association – the trade association representing the interests of audio publishers – where you can meet publishers and producers as well as other narrators in the bar and other venues ('it's literally like a mixer') and chat about this and that and give them your card and try to make a good impression ('the trick is to talk about everything but publishing and make a real human connection with these people'). You have to play the long game, said Stuart. 'I would meet and talk with publishers and producers even a couple of years before I would work for them in some capacity. But you develop those relationships and you keep in touch with them through email – though not too enthusiastically', cautioned Stuart, 'otherwise you become a bother.'

Stuart's friend also gave him some helpful suggestions about who to go to for coaching and which workshops to attend in order to learn some of the skill sets of narration. While many of the skill sets for audiobook narration are similar to those acquired in theatre training, such as dialect work and voice maintenance (being able to talk for a long time without damaging your voice), there are some skills that are specific to audiobook narration which can be learned in workshops and coaching sessions. And she gave him some practical advice about how to set up a home studio and get started from a technical point of view. At the time, Stuart was living in an apartment that had a small walk-in closet, so he fitted that out in a way that would enable him to work uninterruptedly in a quiet space for long periods of time every day. This was not so much a matter of soundproofing – 'there's never really any notion of soundproofing', he explained. 'In this kind of context, it's more about acoustical treatment.' Basically, you need a quiet space to start with and you need to fit it out in a way that will enable you to produce a flat, warm, even sound – 'no reflective surfaces, and that includes your monitor.' You need certain basic equipment – a laptop, recording software, a good-quality microphone, etc., all laid out in the appropriate manner. You also have to learn how to operate the computer in the optimal way so that you can produce an accurate, clean and consistent recording. Stuart already had a laptop and an iPad to read from, and he borrowed a microphone and other equipment from a friend. He had the basics and he was ready to go. But how do you get started as a freelance narrator in an industry in which you've never worked before?

ACX was the way in for Stuart, as it is for many other first-time narrators. He registered on ACX as a producer and created a profile. The workshop he did had included some recording, and these recordings became his initial demos that he put up on ACX. He auditioned for a few books and got started that way. He wasn't sure how much to charge for his first book, so he did it for $150 PFH, though for the second one he asked for $200 PFH, which was the industry standard at the time. After he'd done four books on ACX, he caught the attention of Audible Studios and got a lucky break. Audible were running a workshop on production at one of the audiobook conventions and Stuart went to the workshop and did an audition. The Audible producer liked what she heard ('I can tell obviously you don't have a lot of experience but I can tell you really know your voice') and she hired him as a nonfiction reader. He did his next ten books with Audible, working in their studios rather than from home. His career as an audiobook narrator seemed to be taking off, but then Audible Studios closed many of their in-house studios to start a long-term renovation and Stuart, along with a lot of other narrators, found himself without an employer. He went back to ACX and auditioned for narration jobs; he reached out to people he'd met at the APA mixer events in the hope that they might be interested in hiring him; he even started reading books and checking to see if there was an audiobook made of them and, if not, he tried to find out who held the audiobook rights and talked with them about whether they would be interested in doing an audiobook, either through a publisher or independently through ACX. To fill some space, he did some books in the public domain through a small publisher that specializes in public-domain works. By doing these different things, he was able to keep adding books to his portfolio and improving the quality of his work in the hope that he would be in the right place at the right time when a publisher was thinking of him and needed him. But 'it was a long, slow start', reflected Stuart.

Eventually Stuart started working for a few other audiobook publishers like Tantor, and began working again for Audible once their studios had re-opened, and things picked up. This coincided with a move of house, which was an opportunity to upgrade his home studio. Stuart decided to invest in a professional recording booth, a StudioBricks One, and he installed it in the corner of a small room in their new apartment in Brooklyn. This was a substantial investment – a professional recording booth like this costs around $10,000 – but it greatly improved his working environment: 'I'm in a ventilated, quiet, dedicated space. The sound I'm able to create is acoustically superior to what I was able to do before. It's something I can tell people too, "Oh, I have a StudioBrick." If I put that out to a publisher, they know that I'm serious and I'm a professional.' The decision to make this investment was a sign that audiobook narration had now moved into the centre of Stuart's career. Narration was no longer a sideline that he was developing to earn some supplemental income: it was the main focus of his working life. Stuart still thinks of himself as an actor and he is happy to take TV work when he can get it, but his priority now is to develop his career as a narrator. He can fit in TV work because it's typically half a day for an audition and a day or two for a shoot, but theatre is much harder because it's a longer-term commitment and he would have to break contracts with publishers in order to do it, something which he is now reluctant to do. While he thinks of himself as an actor, audiobook narration is the way he makes a living and supports his family and career. 'If someone asks me what I do, "I'm an actor, I narrate audiobooks" is what I would usually say. I did six TV appearances last year so I'm not neglecting that, and maybe someday I can do theatre again when our children are older, but for now I'm happy to pack my schedule as much as possible with audiobooks.'

As a full-time freelance narrator, Stuart has to plan his schedule carefully. Ideally, he wants his schedule to be fully booked for the next couple of months so that he has a two-month buffer. When he starts a new project, he needs to set aside at least a day, maybe two, to read and prep the book before he starts, and then he'd typically allot four to five days for the narration unless he knows that it's much shorter and he can do it in two or three days. The publisher will send him the prep script and he'll read it and mark it up using iAnnotate. The first time a character comes up, he'll highlight it in blue, and once he's decided what voice he wants to give to that character, he'll do a voice memo and drop it in a folder so that he can maintain a consistent voice every time that character comes up. He'll do the same with unusual words or phrases where he's not sure of the pronunciation, looking them up online and doing a voice memo for future reference. Sometimes, authors let you know how they want their characters to sound, but in most cases it's left up to the narrator to decide what a person's voice is, based on the character as described. The voice has to fit the character, but also, crucially, it has to be sufficiently distinct from other voices so that the listener can hear the difference – 'The baseline', Stuart explained, 'is that the listener is always clear about who is talking.' This can be tricky when there are half a dozen characters, and, say, three of them are teenage boys. But recording samples so that you can come back to them and remind yourself of the voice you gave to each character is a good way to maintain consistency and avoid confusion.

When the prep work is finished, Stuart is ready to start recording. Every narrator will have their own way of thinking about what they're trying to achieve in narrating a book: they are turning a printed text with its visual cues for the reader, like paragraphs and punctuation marks, into spoken words with oral cues for the listener, and making that transition requires innumerable decisions – some large, like deciding what voice to give a character, and some small but significant nevertheless, like deciding how to convey a comma or a colon or a parenthesis in the flow of spoken words. None of this is self-evident. A narrator cannot read a book in a monotone voice – that would be unbearably dull. The reading has to have a certain rhythm or cadence, the narrator has to inflect his or her voice at certain points to express mood or feeling or intention or suspense or doubt, and every inflection has to be measured carefully – too little and the narration will fail to engage the listener, too much and it may come across as overly dramatic and put them off. You have to try to find the perfect balance of just enough and not too much. Audiobook narration is a complex practice with its own codes and conventions, an art form in its own right, and the world of audiobook narration abounds with videos and conference panels by well-known and well-regarded narrators who offer tips and sage advice on how to handle some of the trickier aspects of the narrator's art – how to deal with men's voices if you're a woman and women's voices if you're a man, how to handle accents, dialogue, punctuation, etc.[27]

---

[27] See, for example, www.youtube.com/watch?v=eMnIwAaFx3o.

Audiobook narration is also a performance, and, like all performances, there is an element of creativity and interpretation in the act
of execution, just as there is when a play is turned into a theatrical
production or a musical composition is performed by an orchestra.
This is one reason why a trained actor like Stuart finds a deep affinity
between acting on stage and narrating an audiobook. 'The basic goal
of any actor with a given text is to make a human connection with
it, an emotional and intellectual connection, and then to interpret it,
make artistic choices about what's happening at any moment, and
engage with it in such a way that the audience also has a human
connection with it. You create a bridge between the paper text and
the audience.' And when you narrate an audiobook, you're essentially
doing the same thing. 'If I'm reading a book or playing a character,
I have to find a part of myself that resonates with that book or
character and be able to speak precisely but at the same time with the
freedom that comes from that emotional or intellectual perspective,
in a way that is clear and engaging for the listener.' And yet, while
the narrator must make countless choices, explicitly or implicitly, in
the course of narrating a book, they are not free to do as they please,
because they are reading a text that has been written by someone else;
they have to read the words that appear on the page and take their
cues from the written text. So the creativity of the narrator is always
constrained by the words and cues embedded in the text. Stuart put
it like this:

> Narration is part of an artistic collaboration between the author and
> myself. I am taking as many cues as I can from what they've written
> but I am also adding my own artistic choices and interpretations.
> There is always a story or intention or point of view that the author
> is trying to convey and my job is to understand that point of view,
> translate it through my own understanding of things and demonstrate
> that point of view as effectively, clearly and interestingly as possible so
> that I'm delivering to the listener the content of the book as best I can.
> I am trying to find the tone of narration that fits that book and that
> makes that book as unique as possible for the listener. I am taking the
> cue from the text but I'm the one who has to execute it in a believable
> way. And so I'm making choices, but I'm patterning my choices after
> the author's choices, sometimes elaborating upon them but never
> detracting from them, and the two put together is the audiobook.

In practice, the distinction between the author's choices as
embedded in the text and the narrator's choices is not always so

clear-cut, as some authors are directly involved in the decisions that a narrator makes as they prepare for and narrate a book. It varies from author to author; some authors are not involved at all, while others are happy or even keen to participate, to answer emails and even to talk on the phone. Some authors have clear ideas about what the voice of a character should sound like and they make their views known to the publisher and narrator at the outset. Sometimes a narrator will email an author if they're unsure about some aspect of the text. Often this is an issue about pronunciation – an unusual name, for example – but it can also be because the narrator has stumbled upon what appears to be an error or typo and wants to know if they can correct the text: '"Hey, I noticed this typo, is this a good correction?", fire it off to them and often I get a response back quickly saying "oh, that's fine, here's the change I would like" and we approve it and move forward that way.' But sometimes there's just not enough time for every choice to be vetted in that way, so the narrator has to make a decision and move on. 'So, as opposed to a mutual back-and-forth collaboration, it's just a different kind of collaboration', explained Stuart: 'It's a form of collaboration that happens in stages. There may be one contribution, then a secondary contribution that works in concert with the initial one, and then that process brings you to the end product. I'm working from the material and I want to honour the material, even if I'm not developing it side by side with the author in the final product.' The final product, the audiobook, is not the same as the printed book on which it is based even though it is closely tied to it, because the creation of the audiobook is a separate process that is shaped by its own codes and conventions and that requires countless decisions – often taken by the narrator alone, or by the director and narrator together – in order to turn a printed text with its visual cues into an extended sequence of spoken words.

In practical terms, Stuart divides his time between going out to publishers' studios to record and recording in his home studio. The big difference between recording at home and recording in the studio is that in the studio you are working with an engineer and a producer and/or director who are guiding you, giving you some direction and letting you know if you miss something and need to go back and record it again, whereas at home you are your own producer and director and you have to operate your own equipment yourself. As a trained actor, Stuart is accustomed to making choices – acting involves a lot of self-direction, constantly making choices rather than waiting to be told what to do, so Stuart didn't find it difficult to direct his own work as a narrator. But you do need to develop an autonomous working method that pays great attention to consistency and detail, because there is no one else in the studio who will be following the recording and telling you, 'Oh, let's do this again because it's such and such.' It's up to you to keep focused and committed, 'to keep making acting choices for all the characters, to make the dialogue believable even if it's an outlandish fantasy situation, or, if it's nonfiction, to be that person who believes passionately enough about a given topic to want to take the time to write a book about it. That's the character I'm stepping into. So I have to keep that up otherwise the listener's interest will flag.' But Stuart is also his own producer, which means that he sets his own hours, manages his own time and is responsible for ensuring that he can keep to the production targets that he's agreed with the publisher.

In terms of the pragmatics of recording, there are two main ways of doing it, explained Stuart. One is called 'open record', where you just let the tape roll, re-reading lines if you make a mistake or a poor choice, and then going back afterwards to edit out the errors. The main problem with this method is that it can be very time-consuming as you may have to do hundreds of edits when you've finished the recording. The other method, called 'punch and roll', speeds things up by allowing you to edit while you're recording. In this method, if you make a mistake while recording, you stop, drag the cursor back to before the mistake – you can see what you've been saying from the wave form on the screen – and the programme automatically backs up 3 seconds, it plays what you've just been saying so you can hear your pacing and tone of voice, and when it drops over the point into the new recording it automatically starts recording again and you just pick up and go – punch and roll. This produces a much better and more finished product, but it takes some practice to do it fluently and effortlessly. 'These are skills that you get better at over time, the muscle memory builds, I'm not thinking consciously about, "oh, I messed up so I have to do this and this and this." It's more like tap, tap, tap. It's a routinized physical gesture for me at this point and that keeps my flow better and my ratio down.'

While narrators are typically paid by the finished hour, it always takes more than an hour to produce an hour of finished audio, and the financial benefits of narration work for the narrator depend not just on the rate per finished hour but also, crucially, on the efficiency of the narrator – that is, on the ratio between the amount of time invested in the recording process relative to the finished hour for which you are being paid. As narrators get more efficient with time and experience, they are able to bring this ratio down. Stuart has become a lot more efficient over time and his normal ratio is now 2:1. 'Sometimes I'm on a roll and do a little better than that, sometimes it's not quite as sharp as that', but, on average, for every 2 hours of work, he ends up with 1 finished hour of recording. So if he's in the recording booth from 10 to 5 with an hour's break for lunch (though always a light lunch so that your stomach doesn't start growling when you go back into the booth), this 6 hours of work will result in 3 finished hours of recording; and if he produces 3 finished hours a day and it's a 10-hour book, 'That's your four days right there.' But some books are longer than that, maybe 12 or 14 hours, some are a little shorter – 'So on average I would say four to five days is what I allot.' That doesn't take account of prep time, however; if you add in the prep time, it's more like 3:1. So if Stuart takes a job where he's being paid $200 PFH, then that works out at around $100 per hour of studio time and $67 per hour of actual work on Stuart's part, including prep time. If he's getting paid a higher fee, say $250 PFH, then his earnings per actual hour rise proportionately to around $125 per hour of studio time and $83 per hour of actual work including prep time.

Audiobook narration doesn't pay as well as TV shoots and commercial voice-over work but it enables Stuart to make a good living – in fact, he's earning much more now than he was before, when he was cobbling together an income from a mixture of theatre, TV work and teaching. It's true that he can make more on one day of a TV shoot than he makes in four or five days narrating a book, and for much less effort – audiobook narration is time-consuming work ('we put in the hours'). But TV work is inherently unpredictable: you just don't know when the next gig will come your way. With narration, you can plan ahead in a way that you can't do when you're living day-to-day in the world of TV and commercial voice-over work. The main risk for Stuart now is that he might not have enough audiobook jobs coming in to keep his calendar full, so the constant challenge is to try to diversify the range of companies he's working for. That means he must continue to network at conventions, stay in touch with the producers he meets there and keep knocking on the doors of the companies that are producing audiobooks. The experience of being dropped by Audible when they closed their studios for renovation was a lesson not easily forgotten. 'I want to be sure to be working for as large a number of publishers as possible and not relying on any one publisher to be conveying a higher volume of work to me.' By diversifying his producer list, he can try to keep his calendar full and reduce his dependence on any one publisher.

Stuart is well aware of the fact that his timing was good – 'I feel like I lucked out because I got into the industry at the best possible moment in terms of its growth, the availability of books and the number of actors in it.' He often finds himself competing with other narrators for the same book, but there's enough to go around so he doesn't mind losing out from time to time. But he knows that it might not always be like this – 'We're always bracing ourselves for the winds to change.'

Books in the audio-visual mix

Stuart is not alone in wondering how long the audiobook surge can last: everyone in the industry is wondering this too. For the time being, they're enjoying the growth, and enjoying the attention that comes with being the only sector of the book publishing industry that is experiencing double-digit growth year on year. But they know it is unlikely to last. It is still early days in the audiobook surge – audiobooks only began to take off in 2013–14, and with many publishers ramping up production, the surge may continue for some while yet. But, at some point, the growth curve will undoubtedly begin to level off, just as it did with ebooks, though at the moment no one knows when and at what level. Trying to predict the future of audiobooks would be just as futile as the attempts in the early 2000s to predict the future of ebooks.

Regardless of what happens to audiobooks in terms of sales, they have already achieved something remarkable in terms of the broader culture of the book: they have provided a unique, flexible and inexpensive way of incorporating the book – the epitome of print culture – into the audio-visual culture of the digital age. There are, of course, other ways of doing this: the movie or TV adaptation of a book has a long pedigree. But turning books into movies or TV series is an expensive business requiring substantial investment and extended production schedules; turning books into audiobooks is relatively quick and cheap. The audiobook lacks the visual component of the movie or TV series, but what it lacks in the visual register it makes up for in terms of its audio richness and duration, and in terms of its fidelity to the printed text. Moreover, the absence of the visual register can be a virtue as well as a limitation, for the

391

reasons indicated earlier: the audiobook engages only the ear (and part of the mind), freeing up the eyes and the hands and every other aspect of the body (apart from the brain, partly) to do other things, whether it be driving or running or cooking or doing housework or just relaxing in the evening at home. Thanks to the smartphone and other digital devices (like smart speakers in the home – Amazon Echo, Google Home, etc.), books are becoming part of the audio-visual mix of digital culture in ways that are seamlessly integrated into the practical flows of everyday life.

But as soon as books become part of the audio-visual mix of digital culture, they also bump up against the biggest challenge that any cultural good faces in this space: the competition for consumer attention. And this competition is intensified by the fact that smart-phones have become the most commonly used device for listening to audiobooks and everyone now has many different things on their smartphone, which functions as a personal portable music player, gaming console, movie theatre, TV set, radio, newspaper, magazine, ebook reader and audiobook player, not to mention internet browser, social media hub, text messaging device, email device and, last but not least, telephone. 'That's the biggest challenge we face', reflected Sarah, the head of the audiobook division at Everest. 'With so much content on one single device where a consumer can go absolutely anywhere, how do you break out audiobooks, and a specific title and a specific author, and bring more people to use the two hours before they go to sleep at night to listen to a book instead of binge watching *Billions* on Showtime? How do you get those consumer hours on your product? That's the challenge for us, and that's the challenge for everyone in media today.' Even in the audio-only segment of this audio-visual mix, audiobooks are but one of many options available to consumers: they can listen to music, either from their personal music library on their smartphone or from a streaming service like Spotify, they can listen to any number of radio stations which are now streaming online and they have a huge and growing choice of podcasts and podcast services which are advertising-supported and freely available to listeners. The future of audiobooks will depend to a large extent on whether they can establish a durable presence in the audio-visual mix of digital culture for a significant number of people, and whether that presence is growing, shrinking or remaining static in the face of the competition created by the ever-increasing flood of audio-visual content clamouring for the attention of consumers.

— Chapter 11 —

STORYTELLING IN SOCIAL MEDIA

Storytelling was never the sole preserve of the book publishing industry. Telling stories is as old as human social life and, from time immemorial, human beings have found many ways to share their stories, apart from publishing them through the established institutions and channels of the book publishing industry. So there is nothing new about sharing stories in ways that bypass publishers: publishers have always been just one set of players – a relatively small set, appearing relatively recently – in the much larger universe of storytelling. But there is something new about the way that, with the digital revolution and the development of the internet, it has become much easier than ever before to write stories and share them with hundreds or thousands or even millions of others you don't know personally and don't interact with in your day-to-day life. The development of the internet has been accompanied by a proliferation of sites and online spaces where individuals can post stories, or instalments of stories, and make their writing available for others to read and comment on, from blogs and personal websites to a diverse range of websites and platforms that host stories and fiction of various kinds. Some of these sites would become nurseries for the creation of new content that would eventually feed into mainstream publishing, in much the same way that Andy Weir's blog entries about an astronaut stranded on Mars were to become a bestselling novel. The most well-known example of the migration from online fiction sites to bestsellerdom is, of course, *Fifty Shades of Grey*, which started out as a 'Twilight' fanfiction series on FanFiction.net before it was eventually picked up by Random House and turned into an international bestseller.[1]

---

[1] The actual story is a little more circuitous. Erika Leonard, aka E. L. James, a

Of course, successes of this kind are extremely rare, and many of the online sites are niche venues where small numbers of individuals share stories with handfuls of like-minded readers, indulging their preferences for particular subgenres of fiction. But not all are like that. Some are huge, drawing hundreds of thousands, even millions, of individuals into online storytelling spaces that have become worlds unto themselves, with their own codes and conventions and stars – worlds that are almost entirely disconnected from the world of mainstream publishing. These are worlds in which writers write and readers read and sometimes comment on what they read, and all of this activity takes place without the slightest contribution from traditional publishing houses.

Another distinctive feature of these worlds is that, with the development of social media, they typically involve a degree of interactivity and user-participation that was simply not possible in the early days of the internet, let alone in traditional media industries like book publishing. Readers are not just readers: they can comment on the text they're reading in such a way that their comments are available both to the writer and to other readers. And, more importantly, readers can become writers too: in these online worlds, the door that separates readers from writers is wide open, you don't need a key to unlock it or special permission to pass from one role to the other. You can just walk through the door and start posting your own story for others to read. It's as easy as writing a text and pressing 'publish'.

While many sites, platforms and repositories now exist for reading fiction online,[2] there is one platform that has been particularly

---

Londoner in her mid-forties, was an admirer of Stephanie Meyer's vampire novel series *Twilight* and, in 2009, she wrote a text inspired by the series. She called it *Master of the Universe* and she posted it on the fanfiction site FanFiction.net under the pen name Snowqueen's Icedragon. The text featured characters named after the characters in *Twilight*, Edward Cullen and Bella Swan. After receiving complaints about the sexual nature of the material, E. L. James removed the text from the fanfiction site and put it on her own website, 50Shades.com. Later, she rewrote the text, renaming the principal characters Christian Grey and Anastasia Steele, and published the first instalment of *Fifty Shades of Grey* through a small Australian publisher, The Writer's Coffee Shop Publishing House, in May 2011, with another two volumes appearing over the next eight months. As news of the books spread by social media and word of mouth, they attracted the attention of mainstream publishers. Random House acquired the rights and re-published the trilogy in 2012. By 2015, the books had been translated into fifty-two languages and had sold over 125 million copies worldwide. The trilogy was turned into a series of films which, while panned by the critics, earned more than $1 billion at the global box office.

[2] For a small selection of some general web fiction sites, see https://medium.com/@axp/the-best-6-web-novel-sites-to-read-fiction-online-d901fbb3eec8; for a larger

successful, especially among young people – Wattpad. In August 2019, Wattpad had over 80 million monthly users worldwide, and there were more than 565 million story uploads on the site. But the raw numbers, staggering though they are, don't tell you what this platform is all about. Wattpad is not just another repository of online fiction – though it is a repository and it is dealing with fiction. It doesn't share much in common with self-publishing either, because, for the most part, it is not dealing with completed works that authors want to publish themselves as books and sell to readers through the established channels of book distribution, digital and physical. Wattpad is something entirely different: it is a social media platform in which readers and writers interact around the shared activity of writing and reading stories. Wattpad is serialized storytelling in social media that is accessed largely via mobile devices, and it is these three features – serialized storytelling, social media, mobile devices – that are its defining features and the keys to its success.

Building YouTube for stories

Wattpad was the creation of two software engineers who were specialists in mobile communication, Allen Lau and Ivan Yuen. After graduating from university, Allen joined a tech incubator in Toronto and started his own company, Tira Wireless, which specialized in mobile gaming on the Nokia phone. He was more interested in reading than gaming, however, so in 2002 he prototyped a mobile reading app that ran on the Nokia phone. But the screen on a Nokia was tiny – you could only read five lines of text – and he decided to shelve the idea for the time being. A few years later, in 2006, Allen began working on the project again in his basement, and at around the same time his friend and collaborator, Ivan Yuen, who had worked for Tira Wireless and was now living in Vancouver, messaged Allen to say that he'd developed a new prototype that enabled people to share stories and read them on mobile phones – it was very similar to what Allen had been working on in his spare time. Allen flew

---

selection, see www.fictionontheweb.co.uk/p/resources.html; for fanfiction sites, see https://ebookfriendly.com/fan-fiction-websites; for sci-fi, fantasy and horror, see www.kirkusreviews.com/features/best-websites-read-free-and-good-science-fiction-f; for some more recent apps that specialize in serialized storytelling, see www.nytimes.com/2017/05/12/books/review/new-apps-provide-a-world-of-literature-one-chapter-at-a-time.html.

out to Vancouver, met Ivan in the airport and, two hours later, they started Wattpad together.

Their first product was a reading app for a Motorola Razr, a flip phone that was very popular in the early 2000s, before the advent of smartphones. The screen was small but large enough – just – to see half a dozen short lines of text at a time. But they needed content too – readers had to have something to read. Allen and Ivan didn't know anything about publishing and they didn't want to try to license content from publishers. So, in the beginning, they relied on public-domain works: Michael Hart, who founded Project Gutenberg, helped them to import around 20,000 public-domain works, like Charles Dickens's *A Christmas Carol* and Jane Austen's *Pride and Prejudice*. But they knew that public-domain works weren't going to be enough to attract lots of readers, so they began looking for other ways to add content. At that time – 2006 – YouTube was getting big and was being acquired by Google, so they thought, '"What else could we apply the YouTube methodology to?" It made perfect sense for us to build a YouTube-like model around the book and we were hoping for some interesting results.'[3] They reckoned that more and more people would access content through mobile devices, and more and more people would become content creators, and their aim was to bring the two together around the reading and writing of stories. So they built a website that enabled people to write stories which could then be downloaded and read on a mobile phone. They wanted to create a network that would connect readers and writers, enabling individuals to read user-generated content on mobile devices.

It was a great idea but the take-up in the first couple of years was painfully slow. 'The growth was there', recalled Allen, 'but when your starting point is 100 users, it's pretty depressing.' They stuck with it, however, and by the middle of 2009 they had almost half a million users – that was serious growth, albeit from a low starting point. The environment was changing – people were becoming more accustomed to using social media and, with the launch of the iPhone in 2007, the experience of reading text on a mobile device had greatly improved. In early 2010, they raised a small amount of funding, half a million dollars, rented a small office and hired a couple of developers to accelerate the process. By the middle of 2011, five years after

[3] Allen Lau, quoted in Sophie Rochester, 'Wattpad: Building the World's Biggest Reader and Writer Community', *The Literary Platform* (October 2012), at http://theliteraryplatform.com/magazine/2012/10/wattpad-building-the-worlds-biggest-reader-and-writer-community.

they started, they had around 3 million monthly users, and that was when they went out to raise their first round of venture capital. Their pitch to the VCs was both simple and startlingly ambitious:

> There are around 5 billion people in the world who can read and write, and over 3 billion people with access to the internet. And reading and writing are among the core human activities – there's watching video, listening to music, viewing pictures and images, and then there's the written word. So it's a big, big market, and there's no one building a network for this media type. People build networks for video, like YouTube, people build networks for pictures, like Instagram. But no one was working on the written word, no one was building a network that catered to storytelling – we were the only ones, and we're still the only ones. So we want to build the largest network in the world for reading and writing.

The VCs took them seriously. In 2011, they raised $3.5 million from Union Square Ventures, and in 2012 they raised a further $17 million from Khosla Ventures and Jerry Yang, co-founder of Yahoo!. With these resources, they were able to move to larger offices in Toronto, take on more staff and scale up the business.

By 2015, Wattpad had increased its user base from 3 million (where it had been in 2011) to 45 million – an increase of fifteen-fold in just four years. In 2015, Allen was expecting this rapid growth to continue and was predicting that they would be at half a billion users by 2020. As it turned out, this prediction was much too optimistic: by 2019, Wattpad had 80 million monthly active users. The rate of growth had slowed down significantly. The number of users had nearly doubled in the four years since 2015, but this growth rate was much less than the fifteen-fold increase in the previous four years, and the total was well short of half a billion. The number is astonishing nonetheless: that's 80 million people, spread across several continents, who had downloaded the Wattpad app and were reading stories on their mobile devices, mostly on their phones. The US was the biggest single market with over 14 million users – around 20 per cent of the total – but Wattpad was big in Asia too, with large user bases in the Philippines and Indonesia and growing markets in India, Turkey and elsewhere.

Most of Wattpad's users are young and female. 'And by young, I would define that as under 30', explained Sophie, one of Wattpad's employees who oversees content production. 'It's about 45 per cent 13–18, about another 45 per cent 18–30, and then the rest is above that.' The female–male split is about 60:40. 'We're very popular with teenage girls', said Sophie. As with other user-generated content platforms, most of the people who join Wattpad aren't joining to become writers: they're joining to read stories and to connect with their friends and others online. Participation tends to follow the 100-10-1 rule: of the 100% user base, around 10% will interact with content by writing comments, but only 1% – the 'super-users' – will actively contribute new content; the remaining 90% of users will only be reading. In Wattpad's case, the proportion of active writers tends to be higher than the usual 1% super-user rule: it's closer to 5% – around 4 million of their 80 million monthly users are active writers. Most of the active writers on Wattpad started out by reading stories. The stories on Wattpad are usually serialized: writers post chapters or updates, and readers can follow the story as it's being written, and comment on it if they wish, and other readers can read the comments as well as the story. 'And it's usually in that time between updates, where they may not be able to find something they want to read, that some users will choose to write something of their own', said Sophie. They can start small, post a few pages and see how it goes; it's much less daunting that trying to write a whole book, and that's part of its appeal. 'Writing is a very solitary exercise', continued Sophie. 'But to be able to put a chapter up and then to get feedback on that, that's very motivating to continue. When you see that someone is listening and someone is reading and reacting and enjoying it.'

For the most part, the people who write on Wattpad don't see themselves as forging a career as a writer. For the vast majority of them, writing is not a profession to which they aspire but rather a hobby they enjoy: they just want to tell their story and to be read, and Wattpad gives them an easy way to do it. They want to see that others are reading their work and reacting to it – the social media component is not an added extra but is integral to the writing process. They also want to be popular, and getting likes and comments on their stories is a way of garnering popularity online. 'They compare who's getting the most likes, who's liking whose works – it's a social currency, they're all signals of popularity.' For the very small fraction of Wattpad writers who achieve a significant following and find themselves contemplating the idea of publishing or self-publishing their story elsewhere, the very thought of removing their story from the Wattpad environment can be distressing because the comments and the likes are part of the story itself – they are the forms of validation that kept them writing and made them feel that it was all worthwhile. To strip away these forms of validation is to tear the story out of the community of readers and followers that gave it life.

Just as writers on Wattpad are not what many people might think of as 'writers', so too many of the readers on Wattpad are a little different from the kinds of readers who might read a printed text. Because most stories in Wattpad are serialized and many readers will comment on the stories as they develop, these readers are invested in the stories in a way that is not typically the case with printed texts. In however minor a way, readers on Wattpad can help to shape the characters and what happens in the story through their comments. They can also interact directly with the writer – they can send the writer a private message and have a conversation. You can't do that on a Kindle, let alone with a printed book. So just as the social media component is vital for those who choose to write on Wattpad, it's also vital for many of those who choose to read and follow stories on Wattpad too.

Given the profile of the user community, it's not surprising that the most popular stories are in the areas of teen fiction, fanfiction and romance. 'On Wattpad we see a lot of real person fanfiction, which is fiction about bands and celebrities', explained Sophie. 'We see things like alternate universe fanfiction, which is what *Fifty Shades of Grey* was – you know, what if we took these two characters but he wasn't a vampire, he was an executive and she was a student interviewing him and what would happen.' There is also a great deal of teen romance, as well as paranormal and horror genres including vampire, werewolf and 'creepypasta'.[4] Some might scoff at the amateurish quality of the writing, but Sophie has little time for normative judgements of this kind. She takes a firmly agnostic stand: 'We try to make no judgements, we let the crowd decide. If a lot of people want to read it, it's clearly good in some way. It might not be good technical writing, but when we look at a lot of the top stories, often they are compelling stories. They have an interesting plot or narrative arc.' But there's also something empowering about the fact that uploading imperfect writing is OK. People realize that they don't have to have

---

[4] Creepypasta is a genre of web-based horror fiction. The term is derived from 'copy and paste' since it originally involved copying and pasting online chunks of text that tell a horror story, though it's now used more generally to refer to web-based horror fiction that originates online and has a believable character. See Lucia Peters, 'What is Creepypasta? Here's Everything You Need to Know about the Internet's Spookiest Stories', Bustle (25 December 2015), at www.bustle.com/articles/130057-what-is-creepypasta-heres-everything-you-need-to-know-about-the-internets-spookiest-stories.

a degree in creative writing in order to write things that others might want to read. Here is a space where someone who never thought of herself as a writer and has had no formal training can start to write, experiment with writing and get comments and encouragement from others, and perhaps even improve her skills as a writer – and all of this happens without a publisher, without a gatekeeper and with no money changing hands.

While there is no gatekeeper, there are rules – not just anything can be uploaded. Wattpad has content guidelines that specify what can and cannot be posted on the site; prohibited content includes material that infringes copyright, pornography, non-consensual sexual content, and content that praises or glorifies violence, terrorism, hate groups or extremist organizations.[5] They use two main methods to enforce these guidelines. First, they use a filter that screens unwanted content – 'that filters out perhaps 90 per cent of the unwanted content', explained Allen. And then they rely on users to alert them to any content that doesn't seem right. They also have a strict code of conduct that is intended to encourage certain kinds of language and expression in communicating with others.[6] 'We try very hard to build a very positive community', continued Allen. 'We make a ton of effort to make sure that the community has a very positive and supportive vibe. If there are offensive comments, we remove them, and we will block certain users if their behaviour is offensive. If they are repeat offenders, we would remove their accounts.' Allen is well aware that, notwithstanding their agnostic view of content quality, these guidelines on content and conduct mean that Wattpad is a normatively regulated online community in which the limits of what is permitted are drawn a good deal more narrowly than the limits of what is legal. Certain kinds of content that would not be illegal are excluded as inappropriate in this community. 'Screaming and yelling is not illegal and everyone has the right to scream and yell. But if I'm a restaurant owner and if you come into my restaurant and scream and yell, I reserve the right to send you out', said Allen. 'It's all about setting the principle. Once you have the principle, we don't want this, we don't want that, and the foundation is set up properly, then the content guidelines and the culture are self-reinforcing.' In other words, there is no gatekeeping on Wattpad in the sense that anyone can upload their stories, but the stories have to comply with certain conditions, both legal and normative, and users have to comply with

---

[5] See https://support.wattpad.com/hc/en-us/articles/200774334-Content-Guidelines.
[6] https://support.wattpad.com/hc/en-us/articles/200774234-Code-of-Conduct.

certain codes of conduct; failure to comply with these conditions can result in content being removed, and violating codes of conduct can lead to exclusion from the site. These rules are rigorously enforced, and this can cause some distress in cases where accounts have been deleted, precisely because the deletion of an account is not just the removal of a writer's content but also the removal of all the comments of others with whom a writer has formed a certain bond – that is, it is expulsion from a community.[7] So this is the absence of gatekeeping with limits.

Sharing stories for free

A remarkable feature of Wattpad is that most of this storytelling activity – the constant uploading of instalments, reading of stories and posting of comments – takes place free of charge, with no money changing hands: joining Wattpad is free and, once you've joined, you can read as much or as little as you like for as long as you like. Most Wattpad readers are not getting paid, and most Wattpad readers are not paying to read stories. How is that possible? How can a company like this survive, employing 160 staff in its offices in Toronto, without charging the users a dime?

Like many tech start-ups, Wattpad has survived so far largely on venture capital. When Allen and Ivan started the company, they didn't worry too much about money because they assumed that if the product took off, then it wouldn't be too difficult to find ways of making money. 'We didn't really think about the business model because we believed that this would create new behaviour to some extent, and if this new behaviour is really taking off and if we can get millions of users, then there will be many interesting ways that we can make money. So let's make sure the product is working, let's get some users, and if people are using it, we can figure out a way to make money.' This way of thinking was very much in line with most VCs' way of thinking too. For an internet-based company like Wattpad, growth was the key: focus on growth, scale up, get as big as you can as quickly as you can, and then you can start worrying about how to make money. At some point, you will have to start thinking about revenue and profitability but it can be a mistake to do it too soon: it's much easier to start generating revenue if you

---

[7] For an illustration of how distressing this can be for an individual, see www.youtube.com/watch?v=HnbPxNLBsfQ&list=RDgRxxKVaR5u8&start_radio=1.

have several hundred million users than if you have only a million or two. So investing to improve the offering and build the user base without expecting an immediate financial return can be the wiser strategy in the long run. After raising $3.5 million in 2011 and $17 million in 2012, Wattpad raised another $46 million in April 2014 and a further $51 million in January 2018, in the latter case from the Chinese tech giant Tencent, among others, bringing the total amount raised to over $117 million since 2011.

Allen started thinking seriously about the business model around 2015, when they'd grown their user base to around 45 million users. Over the next few years, the business model would evolve into three main strands: generating revenue from free users through advertising; generating revenue from users who are willing to pay; and generating revenue from off-platform activities. Let's briefly look at each of these strands.

It was important, in Allen's view, to allow users to continue to share and read stories on the platform for free – that's how Wattpad was used by millions all over the world and he didn't want to change that. But as the user base grew, advertising on Wattpad would become more attractive for companies and would enable the site to generate some revenue while keeping the platform free for users. Wattpad introduced banner ads on the site and began inserting video ads in stories; video ads appear in between chapters and at regular intervals during a reading session. They also developed a distinctive type of 'native advertising' (the kind of advertising that matches or mimics the form and content of the platform on which it appears), which they called Wattpad Brand Partnerships. Here, native advertising took the form of reaching out to companies that produce movies or consumer packaged goods like Sour Patch Kids or pimple cream and inviting them to tell their brand story as a story on Wattpad, so that the story builds and promotes the brand image. They can commission writers on Wattpad to write the story, so in this way the writers get paid, Wattpad gets advertising revenue and the company builds its brand in a well-targeted milieu. 'It's a win, win, win for everyone', ventured Allen. 'The advertiser gets the promotion and builds the brand image they want, we get paid and our writers get compensated.' Does he worry that there might be a dubious ethical side to this kind of tacit commercialism? Not really. 'We're very transparent', he said, 'we tell everyone that it's brought to you by AT&T, brought to you by Sony Pictures and so on.' Moreover, this isn't like traditional advertising where you're taking away people's time and attention. 'We are actually giving you entertainment during the time as well, so it's a net additive, not a net negative.' And, of course, you don't have to read it – you can just ignore any story that is sponsored by a company.

As advertising became more present on the site, this also created the opportunity to develop a premium service that would enable users to avoid the ads if they were willing to pay for it. So, in October 2017, Wattpad introduced an optional subscription service: for a subscription fee of $5.99 per month or $50 a year, users could read in an ad-free environment and get access to some features that were restricted to subscribers only. Wattpad also introduced various schemes to enable writers to earn some money from their stories. In August 2016, it introduced the Wattpad Futures programme, which allowed a selection of writers to earn a share of the advertising revenue that was generated when the video ads inserted in their stories were viewed. Then, in October 2018, Wattpad introduced the Wattpad Next programme, which allowed some writers to place their stories behind a paywall so that readers would have to purchase the stories, by chapter or as a complete work, using Wattpad's virtual currency ('Wattcoins'). In March 2019, the Wattpad Next programme was replaced by a new programme called Paid Stories which followed similar principles, allowing a small selection of writers to place stories behind a paywall and charge readers by chapter or for the complete work. Part of the reason for introducing the Paid Stories programme was the realization that they needed more content to attract more readers and they needed to keep the most popular writers on the platform, and 'for us to have more content and retain our writers, we have to give them tools for monetization. So Paid Stories is not just for us', explained Allen. 'We share the majority of the revenue with the writers.'

But advertising, the Premium Service and Paid Stories were only the more 'local', platform-based strands of Wattpad's revenue-generating strategy. Perhaps more important in the long run were the off-platform strands. As Wattpad evolved, it became increasingly clear that the content that was being created on Wattpad had commercial potential outside the Wattpad ecosystem. The challenge for Wattpad was to figure out how to allow that potential to be developed, and to ensure that they had a stake in that development, without damaging Wattpad or allowing it to be weakened by the migration of content out of the Wattpad ecosystem. Since writers who create their stories on Wattpad own the copyright in their own stories, Wattpad is not in the position of a traditional publisher that, when they sign a contract with an author or agent, acquires the rights to exploit that content in a variety of forms and formats.

Staff at Wattpad first became aware of the risks here when a young teenager from South Wales, Beth Reekles, struck a three-book deal with Random House in 2013 while she was still doing her A-levels. Beth had started writing a story on Wattpad called 'The Kissing Booth' in 2011, at the age of 15; 'The Kissing Booth' won a 'Watty Award' in 2011 for Most Popular Teen Fiction and was read 19 million times on Wattpad. The book caught the attention of an editor at Random House who got in touch with Beth via a private message on Wattpad, set up a meeting in their offices in London and offered her a contract for three books. But when the writer did the deal with Random House, the publisher insisted that 'The Kissing Booth' was removed from the site and Wattpad lost one of its most popular stories. 'Everyone that's writing on Wattpad owns their own work and can do with it what they want at any point in time', explained Sophie. 'The problem we're being put in with the traditional publishing industry is that, to them, acquiring this work means that we have to remove it from here, and we were pointing out that this is a bit of an artificial restriction. It doesn't have to be an either/ or – there are other ways that writers can do both. You can build a new product out of what you've written, you can commission them to write something else, you can take novellas they have written and adapt them.' And it was partly in order to pre-empt this situation that Wattpad started to take a more proactive role.

Anna Todd was another young Wattpad writer who developed a big following. In April 2013, when she was looking after her son and doing odd jobs in Fort Hood, Texas, she began posting a story on Wattpad called 'After', which she was writing on her cell phone in her spare time.[8] 'After' was a fanfiction story in which an innocent 18-year-old college girl named Tessa meets a rude, tattooed boy named Harry, fashioned after the One Direction lead singer Harry Styles. In early 2014, staff at Wattpad noticed that Anna was attracting a big following and that her appeal was accelerating at a rapid rate – 'she was driving about 5 per cent of our total traffic', recalled Sophie, 'people just coming to read her story. It was very clear that she was an outlier from the beginning, and as an outlier, we thought that that made her more at risk to be approached by external publishers. So we wanted to create a relationship with her.' In other words, they didn't want to lose her. So they reached out to Anna,

---

[8] For more on the background to 'After', see Bianca Bosker, 'The One Direction Fan-Fiction Novel that Became a Literary Sensation', *The Atlantic* (December 2018), at www.theatlantic.com/magazine/archive/2018/12/crowdsourcing-the-novel/573907.

asked her what her goals and ambitions were and what she wanted to see from her writing. 'She was a fanfiction writer, so she hadn't really thought about publishing. For her it was just a hobby.' But staff at Wattpad could see the potential – and also the risk. So they decided to be proactive. They set up media interviews for her and they took her to New York to meet publishers. They wanted to see if they could broker a deal that would benefit the author, benefit a publisher and benefit Wattpad too – in part by allowing 'After' to remain on the Wattpad platform. They found a publisher, Simon & Schuster, who was keen to turn 'After' into a series of four books, and they were happy to allow the original story to remain on Wattpad. The first book was published in October 2014 and hit the *New York Times* bestseller list. The book was translated into thirty-five languages and reached number one in France and Spain. The author got a lucrative publishing deal, Wattpad earned a handsome commission and Simon & Schuster acquired a bestseller. And 'After' is still a story on Wattpad, where, by 2019, it had totted up 572 million reads, while the five stories in the 'After' series had accumulated 1.5 billion reads.

But turning Wattpad stories into bestselling books was just the beginning.

From stories to studios

If stories composed on Wattpad can be turned into bestselling books, why not turn them into television shows or movies too? Why not think of Wattpad as a content incubator where anyone who wants to write can create stories that could be enjoyed in lots of different media, not just by reading the story on an app on a mobile device? After all, not everyone wants to read, and stories can be shared in many ways other than the written word. That's the intuition that lies behind the array of new ventures that are now beginning to flow from Wattpad. 'The way to consume Wattpad content has expanded', explained Allen. 'We are not *only* a reading and writing community anymore', he said, with the emphasis on 'only'. 'We are a multi-platform company. We leverage the reading and writing community for us, as a factory, to generate the original content and then we figure out ways to monetize that content whether it's on-platform or off-platform in multiple different formats.'

The first major initiative in this direction was Wattpad Presents, a collaboration with the TV5 Network in the Philippines to create a weekly TV show adapted from a popular Wattpad story and aimed at teens. Wattpad is very popular in the Philippines – the Philippines, along with Indonesia, is one of Wattpad's two largest markets outside of the US. Wattpad Presents started as an experiment in 2014 but it proved very successful, attracting weekly audiences of 2–3 million. Wattpad agreed a revenue-sharing arrangement with TV5 so that they get a cut of the TV advertising revenue and of merchandising. And if Wattpad could do deals with TV studios in the Philippines, why not replicate this idea elsewhere?

Early indications that this might be a realistic possibility were afforded by the movie adaptations of two of Wattpad's success stories, 'The Kissing Booth' and 'After'. With 'The Kissing Booth', a small movie studio bought the movie rights from the author in 2011, the year that it won the 'Watty Award' for Most Popular Teen Fiction. They sat on the rights for five years and did nothing, but then Netflix discovered the book in 2016, acquired the rights and greenlighted the movie. The movie was released on Netflix in May 2018 and it quickly became one of Netflix's most successful movies, topping the list of the most re-watched films of 2018.[9] The movie was panned by critics, gaining a positive review from only 17 per cent of the critics on Rotten Tomatoes, but it was a huge commercial success for Netflix, which announced in January 2019 that a sequel would be made.

The movie rights for 'After' were initially sold to Paramount Pictures, but Paramount ran into difficulties and reverted the rights to Wattpad, who found independent investors to finance the movie. In this case, Wattpad was directly involved in the production of the movie, along with CalMaple Media, Offspring Entertainment and others – Wattpad was involved in the adaptation and was on the set when it was being filmed. The movie was released on 12 April 2019 and was an immediate commercial success: by the third week of May, it had grossed more than $50 million at the international box office and more than $12 million in the US, after opening number one in seventeen countries, and it was soon announced that a sequel would be made.[10] Again, the movie was not popular with the critics, with an approval rating of only 15 per cent on Rotten Tomatoes, but clearly it had found a market.

---

[9] Elizabeth MacLeod, 'The Kissing Booth Tops Netflix's Most Re-Watched Films of 2018', *The Telegraph* (12 December 2018), at www.telegraph.co.uk/on-demand/2018/12/12/kissing-booth-tops-netflixs-re-watched-films-2018.

[10] Leo Barraclough, 'Sequel to Independent Movie Hit "After" Launches in Cannes', *Variety* (20 May 2019), at https://variety.com/2019/film/news/sequel-after-cannes-1203220820.

The movie adaptation of 'After' provided Wattpad with a template of how they could expand their content creation activities beyond the writing and reading of stories on the Wattpad platform. In April 2016, they started Wattpad Studios, which was charged with the task of forging partnerships with companies in the entertainment industries to co-produce Wattpad stories for film, television and other media. But why would film and TV studios be interested in partnering with Wattpad? What might Wattpad be able to offer them that they couldn't find elsewhere? Three things.

In the first place, Wattpad can offer original content, original IP, but not just any old content: this is pre-tested content. The stories have been composed in Wattpad and, since all the reading and commenting takes place on the Wattpad platform, Wattpad knows a great deal about how these stories have been received by readers – not only how many times they've been read, but how many people followed the story and read the chapters as they were posted, how many people commented on them, which bits they liked and which bits they didn't like and so on – in other words, Wattpad has a great deal of knowledge about the ways that these stories have been received by readers. Wattpad can select those stories that have a big following, knowing that they have been 'validated' or 'pre-tested' in the Wattpad ecosystem, and propose these stories to the studios with the assurance, 'They're all proven. They have a built-in audience.' Wattpad also typically reviews the selected stories to make sure that they would work well in an audio-visual format like TV shows and movies – that is, that they would lend themselves to visual adaptation and work well on the screen. 'So we will make sure that the story is great but is also visually appealing', explained Allen.

The second thing Wattpad can offer is informed, data-based input on the adaptation of stories for the screen. Wattpad's preferred approach is not simply to sell the movie or TV rights and then leave it to the studio to adapt the story for the screen, because they feel that they have knowledge about the ways that these stories were received by readers that would be of real value in the adaptation process. Allen put it like this:

How many times do you watch a movie that is based on a book and you say, 'oh, the adaptation is so crappy, the book is so much better'? One of the reasons is, a typical book is about 400 or 500 pages, a screenplay is only 90 pages, so you have to cut out 80 per cent of the content. But how would you know what to cut? The screenwriters, historically, have no data to back them up. There's no insight, it's based on their imagination. And you have to say it's most likely they're wrong because they may not be the target audience. But with Wattpad, they have all the numbers and all the insights to back them up. We can tell the screenwriter 'keep chapter one, chapter five, chapter seven, and with chapter seven keep only the first two paragraphs because these two paragraphs are the most emotional paragraphs in the entire story based on the 200,000 comments that we received. And by the way, based on the comments on the entire story, we know that you can cut out the second main character. No one likes him. Save the budget.'

Wattpad can use the data they've gathered in the Wattpad ecosystem – all the readers' comments, the likes and dislikes, etc. – to inform and guide the scriptwriting process. Here, using machine learning becomes vital. Since some stories have hundreds of thousands of comments, it would simply not be feasible for a member of staff, or even several members of staff, to read through all the comments and digest them – 'asking a human to manually read 400,000 comments is Mission Impossible', said Allen. 'But machines can do this in a second.' Moreover, machines can analyse the language of the comments. You can use natural language processing to dissect the comments, and the machine can then be tasked with analysing the emotional arc of the story. 'So, graphically, visually, we can see how this story is being developed, how the story plots from an emotional standpoint. And all this information wasn't humanly possible before. So that's our secret sauce.'

The third thing Wattpad can offer is an inside track for marketing. The Wattpad stories that are being turned into movies or TV series already have an established fan base – there are hundreds of thousands of people, in some cases millions of people, who are already fans of the stories and who will be keen to see the movie or TV series when it appears. Moreover, Wattpad can work with the studios to develop targeted marketing campaigns, including native advertising in the form of sponsored stories, aimed at individuals in the Wattpad community – which, at 80 million users worldwide, is a formidably large potential audience. Wattpad can point to some successful examples of marketing campaigns of this kind. When Sony Pictures released the movie *Pride and Prejudice and Zombies* in 2016, an adaptation of Seth Grahame-Smith's 2009 novel that was a parody of Jane Austen's book, Sony worked with Wattpad to commission a writer to write a zombified fanfiction of 'After'. The idea was that fans of 'After' would be drawn to this story in Wattpad and, while reading the story, they would see trailers of the movie *Pride and Prejudice and Zombies*. Wattpad could leverage the fan base of 'After' to help create a market for the movie – and in this way, Wattpad gets advertising revenue, the fanfiction writer gets paid and Sony gets the eyeballs of potential viewers.

By providing all three elements – original pre-tested IP, data-based input into the adaptation process, and marketing – Wattpad Studios can provide a much more active collaboration with studios than would be the case if they were simply selling movie or TV rights. 'It's a full, complete cycle', as Allen put it. 'And we are commercially involved in every single step along the way.' Of course, it's still early days – Wattpad Studios was only launched in April 2016. But the fact that sequels of both *The Kissing Booth* and *After* have been released provides some evidence to suggest that Wattpad may be onto something here. So too does the fact that they have numerous initiatives under way with studios in the Philippines, Indonesia, Singapore, Korea, Italy, Germany, France and elsewhere ('we're doing twenty-six movies in Indonesia', mentioned Allen in passing, without skipping a beat). Also encouraging is the fact that Hulu picked up 'Light as a Feather, Stiff as a Board' – a teen supernatural thriller by Zoe Aarsen with 4.1 million reads on Wattpad – and turned it into a ten-part TV series, *Light as a Feather*, which was produced by Viacom's AwesomenessTV and premiered on Hulu in October 2018. In February 2019, they announced that the series has been renewed for a second series of sixteen episodes. In this case, Wattpad plucked 'Light as a Feather, Stiff as a Board' from its platform when it noticed that it had gained a million reads in under six months; they presented it to the studios and Hulu picked it up – the model worked exactly as they had hoped. There was just one thing that partially slipped away from them: Wattpad did a deal with Simon & Schuster to bring out a book version of 'Light as a Feather' to coincide with the TV series. But why let Simon & Schuster bring out the book when, with a little more organizational innovation, Wattpad could do it themselves?

From stories to books

This was the line of thinking that led Allen to launch Wattpad Books in 2019, a book publishing imprint within Wattpad Studios. It is perhaps a little ironic that an organization that was founded on the writing and reading of stories should have migrated into movies and TV shows before it moved into books, but the move into books was a natural development for Wattpad given its primary subject matter, even if it came late in the innovation cycle. By this time, Wattpad had been collaborating with publishers, including most of the Big Five trade houses, for five years and had brokered many deals, acting as an agent in some cases and as a co-publisher in others. Two things had become clear in this process. First, traditional publishers are very slow and very cautious. 'They don't fuss about data as much as we do', said Allen. 'Many times, they put a lot of emphasis on the creative side. Very subjective. Making decisions based on hunches. So we had to convince them that this story is going to sell.' Despite the evidence Wattpad had at its disposal to show that some of their stories were very popular with their users, they got lots of rejections from mainstream publishers. The second thing they noticed was that Wattpad writers were much more likely to earn out their advances than non-Wattpad writers: their data was showing that 90 per cent of Wattpad writers were earning out their advances, whereas the industry average is much lower than that.[11] 'So we know that our batting average is much higher than the industry average', and this suggested that Wattpad authors might perform better than others if they could get more of them into print.

Setting up its own book publishing division would therefore enable Wattpad to achieve several things at once. First, they could move a lot faster because they would be making the publishing decisions themselves, and they wouldn't have to invest a lot of time and energy trying to convince traditional publishers to take a risk with their content. Second, they could get more of their stories into book form because they wouldn't have to partner with another publisher for each book project. And third, they could capture more value because they would be the publisher rather than the agent or a partner. It made perfect sense.

But it also meant that Wattpad – which had always existed as a virtual community where writers and readers shared stories and comments in an online environment, usually via the app on their mobile phone, and had never produced a physical product and never had any interest in producing a physical product – would now have to re-invent the publishing wheel and set up the infrastructure of a traditional publisher. Neither Allen nor his co-founder Ivan had any experience of book publishing, though there were some staff at Wattpad who had worked in the publishing industry and knew

---

[11] Estimates of the industry average vary, ranging from 10–20 per cent to 30 per cent to 'less than half'.

something about it. Acquiring the content was not going to be too difficult – Wattpad had no shortage of content, precisely because they had thousands of writers already producing content on their platform. So the challenge for them was going to be one of selection: how to use the data they were able to gather on the popularity of stories to inform their decision-making processes. Then there was the editing and the content development side, and here again Wattpad could bring something new to the publishing process: they could use the data they have on how readers reacted to the story on Wattpad to inform and guide the editing process. Many of the most popular stories on Wattpad are much longer than a typical book – since the stories exist in Wattpad only as digital texts, there's no need to limit the length or the number of chapters. To turn a long Wattpad story into a book of 300–400 pages or less, you have to cut out a lot of content, but how do you know what to cut? Here they can use their data on readers' responses to help them decide what to keep and what to cut. 'That's why the output of what we are doing may look the same as a piece of traditional content – it may look the same as a traditional movie in the theatre, it may look the same as a traditional book on paper. But there's a lot of data science behind it, it's all machine learning', explained Allen. The rest of the publishing elements are pretty standard: they have an in-house production manager and they outsource the printing to printers and outsource the sales and distribution to a third party, like many small publishers. Marketing they handle in-house, using the marketing skills and know-how they've developed in their advertising campaigns on Wattpad and in their collaboration with studios. So, apart from the specifics of the book publishing business, the strategy of Wattpad Books is basically the same as the strategy of the movie and TV collaborations: start with pre-tested content that has a built-in audience, use data and machine learning to guide the adaptation of the content for the medium concerned, and then market it – 'the complete circle'.

The first six titles in Wattpad Books were published in autumn 2019, all teen fiction (or Young Adult, to use the publishing industry term). They included *The QB Bad Boy and Me* by Tay Marley, the story of a romance between a bad-boy quarterback and a cheerleader, which, with 26.2 million reads, was Wattpad's most popular book of 2018; *Saving Everest* by Sky Chase, the story of a relationship between a popular but unhappy guy named Everest and a shy girl named Beverly, which had totted up more than 17 million reads on Wattpad; and *Cupid's Match*, a supernatural teen romance by Lauren Palphreyman that had accumulated more than 46 million reads on

Wattpad. Time will tell how successful these stories are as books, but there is something remarkable – revolutionary even – about the publishing model created by Wattpad. It turns upside-down the model on which most book publishing has been based for the last 500 years.

Book publishing in general, and trade publishing in particular, has always been a business of serendipity: publishers and editors have a hunch about what might sell, they may use some weak forms of evidence to help guide their judgements (such as the track record of the author or the sales of similar books) but more often than not their hunch is just a hunch, and then they take a punt – they decide to go ahead with some book projects and they pass on others, hoping that they called it right but never being entirely sure until they see what actually happens when the book is published. Book publishing, especially trade publishing, has always been a top-down business: publishers decide what they think might work in the marketplace, they invest in it, produce it, put it out there and see what happens. Of course, there are lots of exceptions to this general rule. Brand-name authors, for example, have an established base of fans who can be relied on to buy their next novel, which is precisely why these authors are so valuable for publishers and why they can command such high advances in the market for content: in a business of serendipity, brand-name authors are as close as you'll ever get to a dead cert. But for most books, and for almost all first-time authors, publishing is a crapshoot: no one really knows just how well a book will do.

What is so clever and original about Wattpad Books is that it has replaced the top-down model of decision-making with a bottom-up model: here, decisions about which books to publish are being taken on the basis of the actual popularity of stories on the Wattpad platform. Because Wattpad can track who is reading what on the platform and they record any comments made, they can produce a fine-grained picture of which stories are popular with which kinds of readers; they know if they are becoming more popular and, if so, how quickly, or if, on the contrary, lots of readers are tiring of the story and giving up; and they can use the comments to help identify those chapters or characters or twists in a story that work for lots of readers, and those that don't. Given the number of people who are reading and commenting on the most popular stories, they have to rely on computerized methods of machine learning to process all this information, but it gives them a unique and valuable basis of fairly hard data – a lot harder, at any rate, than the data most publishers have – which they can use to inform their decisions about

412

which stories to publish as books, and how to abridge and adapt those stories to make them work most effectively in the book format. Wattpad are not alone in seeking to develop this kind of bottom-up publishing – as we saw in chapter 8, crowdfunding publishers like Unbound and Inkshare have developed somewhat similar ways of thinking. But the big difference between Wattpad and the crowd-funding publishers is scale: Inkshare may have 100,000+ users in their system, but Wattpad has 80 million+, roughly 800 times the number. And when you're using data in this way to assess popularity and analyse patterns, size matters.

Wattpad's bottom-up publishing model has emerged organically from its network-based approach to building a reading-and-writing community online. Allen and Ivan didn't start from book publishing – they didn't know anything at all about book publishing when they set out to build the app and the website that would become Wattpad. They began from something more basic: from the human desire to tell stories – to create them, share them and consume them. It just so happens that, by making it very easy for people to create, share and comment on stories in an online environment, and especially on the mobile devices that people now carry around with them all the time, they built a platform that might call into question some of the assumptions and practices of those institutions which, for the last 500 years, have played a central role in determining which stories get shared, and how they get shared, in our culture. 'One thing most disrupters have in common', reflected Allen, 'is that disrupters are bottom-up, they are not top-down. Their starting point will not be the traditional industry. Their starting point will be a blank sheet of paper. If you look at us, if you look at YouTube, if you look at Netflix, it's the same – Netflix didn't start with the studios.'

Of course, Wattpad's publishing model, and its off-platform devel-opment strategy more generally, while radical in design, is quite restricted in terms of its range, simply because the content drawn from Wattpad will reflect the demographic profile of the Wattpad community – young, mostly teen, predominantly female. If you're publishing young adult fiction, then Wattpad Books is an imprint to watch: they might well become a formidable competitor, and their ability to develop synergies across the media industries – from books to movies to TV series – might go well beyond anything you'll ever be able to do. But for the rest of the publishing industry, the question is whether anything can be learned from the bottom-up model developed so brilliantly by Wattpad – and if so, what, exactly. That is a question to which we shall return.

— Chapter 12 —

OLD MEDIA, NEW MEDIA

For established companies that have been doing what they do for a long time, a technological revolution is a scary thing. Suddenly, they are faced with the prospect that their traditional practices may be eclipsed by new ways of doing things, or, even more alarmingly, that their products or services may no longer be needed in the new economies and supply chains that are ushered in by new technologies. They may need to adapt quickly to survive – try to reposition themselves in a new emerging economy while still servicing the old, since much of their revenue may continue to come from the old economy even if the future seems to lie elsewhere. This is true of all industries, but particularly true of the media or creative industries facing the digital revolution, precisely because, as I noted earlier, these industries deal with a kind of content – symbolic content – that can, to a large extent, be digitized, converted into sequences of 0s and 1s that can be processed by computers, stored in devices and transmitted electronically. The physical medium in which symbolic content was traditionally embedded in order to be bought and sold in the market – whether that medium took the form of the printed newspaper or magazine, the vinyl LP or the print-on-paper book – could be sidelined by new devices and new channels that allow symbolic content to be exchanged without embedding it in a physical object. Such, at any rate, was the perfectly reasonable fear shared by many people working in the media and creative industries as the digital hurricane struck their shores.

But if there is one lesson we've learned – or should have learned – from living through the first few decades of the digital revolution, it is that this revolution does not have the same impact everywhere. And if there's a second lesson, it is that the seemingly beneficent fruits of the digital revolution may harbour elements that are less benign than the champions of this revolution would like us to believe. Nothing is quite as good as it seems.

Digital disruption in the creative industries

It is tempting to think that the digital revolution will have similar consequences in many, or even all, sectors of the media and creative industries, but this is far from the truth. The reason is simple: the impact that new technologies have on particular sectors of industry, or particular spheres of life, depends not just on the technologies themselves and what they can do (their 'affordances', to use Gibson's felicitous term[1]), but also, and crucially, on the contexts in which they are developed, implemented and used, contexts which include the agents and organizations that have an interest in promoting or obstructing these technologies, the relations between these organizations and their relative power in a particular market or field, and the many individuals with their varied interests, practices, preferences and tastes who may or may not wish to use these technologies and integrate them into their lives. Social contexts are complicated and messy places, and they vary enormously from one sector of the media and creative industries to another. Technologies that work very well in one context may not work at all well in another – and that may have less to do with the technology itself than with the characteristics of the contexts in which they are being developed, implemented and used (or not used, as the case may be). Similarly, the pattern of disruption brought about by the digital transformation in one sector of the media and creative industries may be very different from the pattern of disruption in another – and again, this may have less to do with the technologies themselves than with the characteristics of the sectors and with the different practices, preferences and tastes of the individuals who may or may not wish to use those technologies in the particular domains where they are being deployed.

Viewed in this way, the fact that the digital transformation in the book publishing industry has, at least so far, taken a course that is quite different from the course it has taken in other media and creative industries, such as the music industry or the newspaper industry, is less surprising than it might at first seem. As we saw in the

---

[1] James J. Gibson, 'The Theory of Affordances', in his *The Ecological Approach to Visual Perception* (Boston: Houghton Mifflin, 1979).

415

Introduction, revenues in the US recorded music industry collapsed in the first decade of the twenty-first century, a combined effect of the shift from the sale of LPs and CDs to digital downloads and rampant file sharing: by 2009, total revenues in the US recorded music industry were roughly half what they had been a decade earlier. The newspaper industry also experienced a sharp decline in fortunes during the first decade of the twenty-first century, with US daily newspaper circulation falling from over 60 million in the 1980s and early 1990s to 40 million by 2010, and advertising revenue falling from around $50 billion in 2004 to around $25 billion in 2012 – half of what it had been less than a decade before.[2] To many in the book publishing industry who were watching these developments with growing alarm, it seemed distinctly possible that their industry could be heading for a similar fate. Why not? Like the music industry, book publishers were in an industry based on the control and commodification of symbolic content, and, just as the music industry found that digitization made it much harder to retain control of symbolic content and, even when they could control it, to prevent the price from deflating, so too book publishers might well find that the symbolic content they controlled would be subjected to the same powerful pressures of piracy and price deflation – pressures that could undermine the whole model of value creation on which the industry was based, not to mention the livelihoods and careers of the many people who worked within it. The uncertainty was unsettling and the anxieties were deeply felt. Many in the publishing industry were waiting, with some trepidation, for their iPod moment.

When the Kindle was launched in November 2007 and ebook sales began at last to take off, it looked to many like their iPod moment had finally come. The Kindle would do for the book industry what the iPod had done for music: make it easy and legal for people to download books as digital files and read them on a compact, portable, modestly priced and user-friendly device that could hold a small library of books. As people within the industry watched ebook sales grow at a dramatic rate from 2008 to 2012, there were many who thought, quite understandably, that this was the beginning of the end for the old-fashioned print-on-paper book. It was only a matter of time, they thought, before ebooks would account for the majority

---

[2] Michael Barthel, 'Despite Subscription Surges for Largest U.S. Newspapers, Circulation and Revenue Fall for Industry Overall', Pew Research Center (1 June 2017), at www.pewresearch.org/fact-tank/2017/06/01/circulation-and-revenue-fall-for-newspaper-industry.

of book sales, and that in turn would have grave consequences for the traditional print-based supply chains, including the bricks-and-mortar retailers who would lose a substantial share of their traffic. Fears of an industry meltdown were widespread. But, as we've seen, the rise of ebooks came to a sudden halt in 2013 – much sooner and more abruptly than many had expected. The fear that ebooks would eclipse the traditional print-on-paper book, relegating it to a place alongside the vinyl LP in the museum of obsolete technologies, turned out to be unfounded – at least for the time being.

Not only did print-on-paper books turn out to be more resilient than many had expected, but also the book publishing industry has so far weathered the digital storm more successfully than the music industry did. In the Introduction, we looked at a graph that shows the collapse of revenues in the US recorded music industry between 1998 and 2010 (figure 0.1, p. 18); compare this with figure 12.1 which shows the overall revenue in US trade publishing between 2008 and 2015, and with figure 12.2 which shows the overall revenue in the US book publishing industry more generally. What these figures show is that revenues in the US book publishing industry as a whole remained largely flat over this period, while US trade publishing revenues continued to grow, albeit modestly; ebooks represented a growing proportion of this revenue until 2014, though print continued to account for the bulk of the revenue. During this period, US trade publishing revenue increased by around $2.6 billion overall, from $13.2 billion in 2008 to $15.8 billion in 2015, an increase of around 20 per cent in eight years, while US book publishing revenue

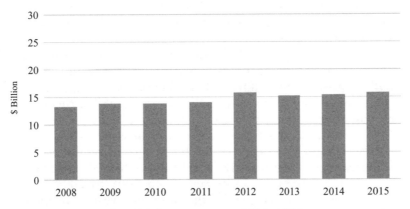

Figure 12.1   US trade publishing revenues, 2008–2015
Source: Association of American Publishers

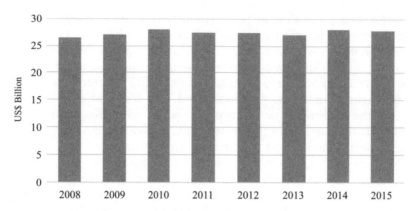

Figure 12.2   US publishing industry revenues, 2008–2015
Source: Association of American Publishers

more generally increased by $1.3 billion overall, from $26.5 billion to $27.8 billion, an increase of around 5 per cent in the same time period. Compare this with the experience of the US recorded music industry, where overall revenues fell from $13.8 billion to $5.6 billion between 2000 and 2010 – that is, to only 40 per cent of what they had been a decade earlier. Unlike the case of music, where the growth of digital download revenue did not fully compensate for the steep decline of revenue from CD sales, in the case of trade publishing, the decline in revenue from print sales was much more modest, and the loss of revenue from print sales was more than compensated for by the revenue from ebook and audiobook sales. The continued robustness of print sales, which still accounted for around 80 per cent of total trade publishing revenue in 2015, provided a bulwark for the industry that prevented revenues from collapsing.

Moreover, most book publishers also found that, while their overall revenues were remaining pretty constant, their bottom lines were actually improving. Even if the bulk of their sales were still accounted for by printed books, the shift to digital was enabling them to take some costs out of the supply chain, thereby improving their profitability. Table 12.1 and figure 12.3 show the total sales, operating profit and margin for one of the Big Five US trade publishers, Simon & Schuster, from 2008 to 2018. Total sales remained static over this time period, dropping by 7 per cent from 2008 to 2009 but then remaining largely unchanged for the next nine years. On the other hand, operating profits and margins grew over the same time period. Profits and margins dipped from 2008 to 2009, but from 2009 to

Table 12.1 Total sales, operating profit and margin for Simon & Schuster, 2008–2018

	Total sales ($ millions)	Profit ($ millions)	Margin (%)
2008	857	88	10.2
2009	795	50	6.2
2010	791	72	9.1
2011	787	85	10.8
2012	790	80	10.1
2013	809	106	13.1
2014	778	100	12.8
2015	780	114	14.6
2016	767	119	15.5
2017	830	136	16.4
2018	825	144	17.4

Source: *Publishers Weekly*

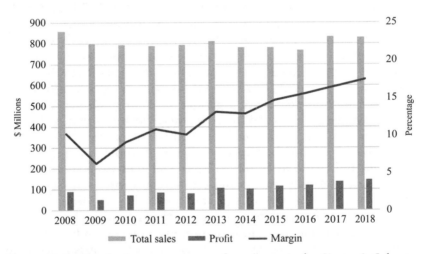

Figure 12.3 Total sales, operating profit and margin for Simon & Schuster, 2008–2018
Source: *Publishers Weekly*

2018 they grew significantly: profits increased by almost three-fold from 2009 to 2018, and the margin increased from 6.2 per cent in 2009 to 17.4 per cent in 2018. Partly this was due to improved efficiencies and higher backlist sales, but the fact that digital products – mainly ebooks, but increasingly audiobooks too – were accounting for 25 per cent of Simon & Schuster's sales by 2015 also played an important role in improving profitability, as ebooks have lower production and distribution costs and there are no returns.

The experience of other large trade houses was similar to that of Simon & Schuster: what we see in the period from 2008 to 2018 is a flatlining of overall revenue and a growth in profitability. Since ebook sales were largely substitutional rather than incremental (that is, they were largely replacing print sales rather than adding to them) and since ebooks were typically priced somewhat lower than printed books, the growth and levelling off of ebooks in the period from 2008 on meant that a significant proportion of publishers' sales were generating less value per unit of sale, which tended to have a levelling or depressing effect on overall revenue from one year to the next. On the other hand, since ebook sales are more profitable than print sales because the cost of sales is much lower and there are no returns, profitability has grown while overall sales have remained fairly static. That is the new business profile of a large trade publisher in the digital age – quite different from the 1980s, 1990s and early 2000s, when the preoccupation in the large houses, under pressure from their corporate masters, was to achieve significant year-on-year growth, typically aiming at 10 per cent per annum, along with steady improvements in profitability.[3] It is also a development that has fuelled fresh calls, from authors, authors' associations and agents, for authors to receive a greater share of publishers' profits, now unexpectedly enhanced by a 'digital dividend' – that is, by the efficiencies and cost reductions generated by the digital revolution.[4]

The mystery is why the impact of digital technologies in the book publishing industry turned out to be so different from their impact in the music and other media and creative industries – how can we explain this? The answer to this question will vary depending on which industry you compare it to, because the factors that have shaped the course of the digital transformation in the media industries vary from industry to industry. Here, I'll focus on the comparison with the music industry. No doubt there are many factors that are relevant to

---

[3] See Thompson, *Merchants of Culture*, ch. 6.
[4] See, for example, Nicola Solomon, 'The Profits from Publishing: Authors' Perspective', *The Bookseller* (2 March 2018), at www.thebookseller.com/blogs/profits-publishing-authors-perspective-743226; Alison Flood, 'Philip Pullman Calls for Authors to Get Fairer Share of Publisher Profits', *The Guardian* (5 March 2018), at www.theguardian.com/books/2018/mar/05/philip-pullman-calls-for-authors-to-get-fairer-share-of-publisher-profits. Some agents have been calling for authors to receive a higher royalty on ebooks for many years, and some publishers acknowledge (in private, if not in public) that there is a case for this.

explaining why the experience of the book publishing industry has been so different from that of the music industry (so far, at least), but the following six seem to me to be of particular importance.

In the first place, the digital revolution began to have a serious impact on the music industry some years before the ebook surge. Napster, the peer-to-peer file-sharing service that allowed users to share MP3 files, started operating in June 1999 and continued until it was shut down by court order in July 2001, by which time it had over 26 million users worldwide. Apple released the first version of iTunes in January 2001 and it opened the iTunes Store in April 2003, which created a legal marketplace for digitized music and enabled users legally to download, organize and listen to digital music files; five years later, in April 2008, the iTunes Store had surpassed Walmart to become the largest music retailer in the US, with over 50 million customers and a music catalogue of over 6 million songs.[5] By the time ebooks began to take off in 2008 and 2009, the transition to digital downloads in the music industry was already well under way. And because the impact of the digital revolution was experienced 5–10 years earlier in the music industry, it meant that executives and senior managers in the book publishing industry could learn from what happened in the music industry and try to avoid repeating the same mistakes as the digital revolution began to take hold in their own industry – a kind of second-mover advantage.

There were two areas where this second-mover advantage proved to be particularly significant – and these are the second and third factors. One was the area of illicit file-sharing. Senior managers in the book publishing industry were well aware that the reluctance of many in the music industry to embrace the digital revolution and make their music available as downloadable files had helped to create a pent-up demand that was exploited so effectively by Napster. Like Prohibition, the non-availability of desirable content through legitimate channels served to stimulate the illegal trade in contraband goods. Managers in the book publishing industry learned the lesson and invested a great deal of time and money in ensuring: (a) that they had digital rights for their content; and (b) that they were converting it into suitable digital formats so that they would be in a position to supply the market if and when the demand for digital content arose. As one senior manager at a large trade house explained in 2007, before a truly successful reading device had been introduced,

---

[5] 'iTunes Store Top Music Retailer in the US' (3 April 2008), at www.apple.com/newsroom/2008/04/03iTunes-Store-Top-Music-Retailer-in-the-US.

'We just want to make sure, when that happens, that the industry is there to support the right kind of sell-through to that device so that we don't end up with a piracy-dominated industry, as opposed to a legitimately sold industry.' Thanks in part to the experience of the music industry, he knew that reluctance on the part of the publishing houses to make their content available in suitable digital formats would only work against them in the long run. Better to go with the flow than try to swim against the tide.

The second area where managers in the book publishing industry learned from the experience of their counterparts in the music industry was in relation to the fraught issue of price. As a general rule, the digitization of content tends to produce a downward pressure on prices. This is a consequence of two features of the information economy. The first feature is that, while it may be costly to produce information in the first place, the marginal cost of reproduction is close to zero: once you've produced the information and converted it into a suitable digital format, it is very easy and very cheap to reproduce. The second feature is that the key players who are distributing content online are generally not producing it, and hence they are not bearing the cost of production; their interests are to maximize distribution to as many users as possible and to strengthen their position as the dominant channel of distribution, and these interests are often best served by pushing prices as low as possible. When Apple launched the iTunes Store, most songs were priced at 99¢ – an eye-catching price that was set just below the $1 threshold in order to maximize sales. But the more that music was being sold at lower prices, the more likely it was that the overall revenue flowing into the industry would decline over time – unless, of course, unit sales were increasing at a sufficient rate to offset the decline of revenue per unit (the proponents of lower prices often claim that this will happen, though in practice many markets are less elastic than they think). In other words, price deflation would, in all likelihood, lead to a haemorrhaging of value out of the industry. As the digital revolution took hold in the music industry during the first decade of the twenty-first century, this appeared to be exactly what was happening. It is therefore not surprising that senior managers in the book publishing industry reacted so strongly to the news – which came as a complete surprise to them – that *New York Times* bestsellers and many new releases would be priced at $9.99 on the Kindle when it was launched in November 2007: like Apple, Amazon was setting the price of some of the most highly valued content at just below a symbolic threshold, in this case $10, and well below the price at which these books would be selling in their print editions. It is also not surprising that the major trade publishers were keen to move to the agency model for ebook sales (even though this would cost some of them dear in terms of litigation, as we saw in chapter 5). The major trade publishers wanted to move to the agency model for one simple reason: as they saw it, this was the only way that they could retain control of the price of their content and stop it from being discounted, and therefore ensure that there was a floor to the price deflation that would occur as more and more of their books were sold in digital formats. They might earn less per unit sale under the agency model, but in the long run they would retain control of price and be in a stronger position to try to prevent – or at least to limit – the kind of haemorrhaging of value that had occurred in the music industry. And, in this respect, setting aside whatever missteps they may have taken along the way, the trade publishers were probably right.

Apart from these strategic considerations, it is also true that the music industry and the book publishing industry were dealing with very different kinds of symbolic goods – this is the fourth factor. In the music industry, the album was always a rather artificial product. It was typically a collection of different songs, bundled together and sold as a single album, but, from the listener's point of view, not all of these songs were of equal value. For consumers, it was not an uncommon experience to buy an album for one or two songs you really liked and then find that the rest of the album was filled with another ten or twelve songs that did nothing for you. One of the great innovations of the iTunes Store is that it unbundled the album and sold individual songs for 99¢: now you were no longer obliged to acquire the other ten or twelve songs that you never wanted to listen to anyway. This was enormously attractive for consumers, who could now build their own playlists without having to listen to a swathe of unwanted songs. But in the book publishing industry, unbundling was never going to have the same kind of appeal, simply because most books are not arbitrary collections of chapters but, rather, integrated texts in which one chapter follows another in a structured sequence as the narrative or plot or argument unfolds. There would be no point in buying one chapter of an Agatha Christie novel and ditching the rest. Of course, there were real advantages in being able to separate out chapters or parts of the text and make them available to readers as samples, a practice that became common in the book publishing industry; but sampling was not the same as unbundling the book and selling individual chapters à la carte. The digital unbundling of content simply didn't have the same kind of potential in the book publishing industry as it had in the music industry.

Perhaps more importantly, there were more downsides for book consumers in moving from print to digital than there were for music listeners in moving from analogue to digital consumption. Listening to vinyl LPs required a dedicated player and gave the listener very little flexibility; LPs scratched easily, they couldn't be listened to on the move and you couldn't easily skip over the tracks you didn't want to hear. CDs gave the listener high fidelity and greater flexibility and mobility, and digital downloads gave the listener even more flexibility and mobility, while also allowing the album to be unbundled so that songs could be purchased à la carte or listened to via a streaming service – in short, the transition to digital music brought many advantages for the consumer with very few drawbacks. With books, however, the situation was much less clear-cut. Reading long-form texts on a screen undoubtedly brought some advantages – books could be purchased easily and downloaded quickly, the price was generally lower, the size of the typeface could be adjusted to suit the user, many books could be carried on a single device, etc. – but it also brought some real disadvantages, the most significant of which was that, for many readers, the experience of reading long-form texts on a screen was just not as good as the experience of reading them on the printed page. This disadvantage may have been less pronounced for readers of romance and commercial fiction, but for many readers of literary fiction and of nonfiction – and especially of books that required a lot of concentration, books that were illustrated and books that were used as reference works – there were clear advantages to reading on the printed page, rather than a screen: it's easier on the eyes, it's easier to move back and forth in the text or to dip in at a particular place for a particular reason, and there is a pleasure, both tactile and aesthetic, in holding a printed book, turning the pages and reading a printed book that is well designed and well produced. Of course, some of these perceived and felt advantages may be rooted in custom and habit: individuals accustomed to reading books in a certain way may find it difficult to change, and new generations may be less bound by the customs and practices of those who grew up with the printed book. But it is also likely that the remarkable resilience of the printed book stems in part from the very real advantages and benefits that derive from reading books on the printed page. The printed book is both an excellent reading device that allows for a high-quality reading experience – better, in the eyes of many, than the experience of reading long-form text on a screen – and an aesthetically pleasing cultural object that is valued in and for itself, as something to be handled, admired and enjoyed. Whatever value the vinyl LP had (and undoubtedly it had some aesthetic value too, with cover design becoming an art form in itself), the balance of advantages and disadvantages in the case of music weighed heavily in favour of the transition to digital, whereas in the case of books, the pros and cons were much more evenly balanced, and for some kinds of books, they weighed in favour of print.

There is a further factor that is relevant here – what, in chapter 1, I called the possession value of books. What I mean by this is that some books are objects that an individual wants not just to read but also to own, put on their shelf, return to at a later point in time, share with others, maybe give to others, perhaps display in their living room as a signifier, a symbolic token of who they are and the kinds of books they like and value (or would like others to think they like and value). All of this is much easier to do with a printed book than an ebook. When we buy a printed book, we own it and can do with it as we please (read it, display it, share it, give it as a gift, even resell it) whereas when we buy an ebook, we license it and the licensing conditions typically restrict what we can do with the content (for example, they may limit the number of devices on which we can read it, may not allow it to be shared, etc.). So owning a book as a physical object has real benefits and advantages. Music has possession value too, but in a different way. Individuals have their musical collections, whether in the form of their iTunes library or their collections of CDs or vinyl LPs, but CDs and LPs are not displayed in the same way that books are, and music can be easily shared or given as gifts in digital formats (for example, as CDs). Moreover, as music streaming services like Spotify and Apple Music become more popular, it may well be that access is becoming more important than possession for many listeners: owning music may matter less than having continuous on-demand access to it. The fact that printed books are cultural objects that many people want to own, keep, display, share and give to others – that is, they have a high possession value – has, in all likelihood, contributed to the resilience of the printed book.

These six factors go some way to explaining why things have turned out so differently in the book publishing industry compared to the music industry, despite the fears of those in the publishing industry who thought that the fate of the music industry would be their fate too; and they also underline why it's so dangerous and potentially misleading to assume that what happens in one sector of the media and creative industries is likely to be a good guide to what

425

will happen in others: there are just too many factors specific to each field, and to the forms of cultural production and consumption that take place in that field, to generalize in this way.

These factors, together with the trends of the last few years, also suggest that how things evolve in the book publishing industry in the coming years may be rather different from the way that things have gone in the music industry and in other sectors of the media and creative industries. Of course, predicting the future is a mug's game – we only have to consider how wildly off-mark many commentators have been when speculating on the future of books to realize that anyone would be ill advised to follow in their tracks. But we can reflect on the patterns of the last few years and extrapolate from them, though even then we must acknowledge that any view about the future developed in this way can never be more than a hunch: the future is unknowable and we simply don't know whether the patterns that have emerged in recent years will continue into the future or whether some new developments, not yet apparent, will intervene and alter the course of events. On the basis of recent patterns, my view is that the future of book publishing, at least for the next few years, will not be a one-way shift from print to digital, but rather a mixed economy of print and digital. What we're likely to see in the book publishing sphere is *co-existent cultures of print and digital*: books in the digital age will thrive in a hybrid culture where print and digital co-exist side by side, rather than one eclipsing the other, and the proportions of sales accounted for by print and digital will vary by category of book. As I argued in chapter 1, ebooks are best regarded as just another format in which the content of books can be fixed and delivered to readers – it is no different, in this respect, from the paperback, which was also a radical innovation when it was first introduced, even if today that seems hard to imagine. Like the paperback, ebooks will find their place in the panoply of formats available to publishers and others who are creating books and making them available to others to purchase, borrow or otherwise acquire in order to read. But, for the foreseeable future, they are unlikely to eclipse the printed book, which will hold its own as the delivery mechanism of choice for many readers. Yet, while this seems the most likely scenario from where we stand today, I'd be the first to admit that I could be wrong. By their very nature, these are unpredictable trends, dependent on a host of incalculable factors, from as yet unknown innovations in technology to the habits and tastes of readers, and there is no way that anyone can know for sure how these trends will pan out in the years to come.

Data power

It is understandable that much of the debate about the impact of the digital revolution on the book publishing industry has been focused on the question of ebooks and the extent to which they will displace printed books, but to focus all one's attention on ebooks would be to lose sight of other developments that are much bigger and more fundamental in character. We have considered many of these other developments in previous chapters, but I now want to stand back from the detail and put these developments in a broader context. Technological change doesn't happen in a vacuum. It is inextricably interwoven with broader social and economic processes which new technologies may resonate with and amplify, but which they can also erode and undermine. I want to focus now on some of these broader social and economic processes.

The digital revolution and the rise of the internet were interwoven with two broader processes that are characteristic of modern Western societies: on the one hand, the growing emphasis on the individual and the capacity of the individual to shape his or her own destiny, which Ulrich Beck and others have called 'individualization';[6] and, on the other, the expansion and metamorphosis of capitalism, as it was freed from some of the political and legal structures that had constrained it in the 1950s and 1960s and was invigorated by the new opportunities opened up by the conjunction of globalization and the digital revolution. As the digital revolution gathered pace from the 1970s on, its imbrication with these two broader processes was unmistakable. Digital technologies and the internet were commonly championed as tools that would empower individuals and expand their opportunities: they would enable individuals to do things for themselves or in collaboration with others, bypassing traditional institutions and their top-down structures of power. Digital technologies and the internet would become key drivers of the do-it-yourself culture which was part and parcel of the growing emphasis on the individual in modern societies, where the self becomes a reflexive and open-ended project of self-creation, a do-it-yourself biography

---

[6] Ulrich Beck, *Risk Society: Towards a New Modernity*, tr. Mark Ritter (London: Sage, 1992); Ulrich Beck and Elisabeth Beck-Gernsheim, *Individualization: Institutionalized Individualism and its Social and Political Consequences* (London: Sage, 2002); Anthony Giddens, *Modernity and Self-Identity: Self and Society in the Late Modern Age* (Cambridge: Polity, 1991); Zygmunt Bauman, *Liquid Modernity* (Cambridge: Polity, 2000).

427

in which individual initiative, taking responsibility for your own life projects, is both encouraged and celebrated. The emphasis on individual freedom and the personal power to shape one's own life and future was a common theme in the countercultural and libertarian ideas that shaped the early development of the internet and influenced many of the early entrepreneurs of Silicon Valley, who often presented what they were doing as a way of empowering the individual in the face of large corporations and an overbearing state.[7] On the other hand, digital technologies and the internet were also seized upon and developed by organizations – both commercial organizations, or entrepreneurs and venture capitalists seeking to build commercial organizations, and states – in order to expand their existing activities and open up new opportunities. For commercial organizations, entrepreneurs and venture capitalists, digital technologies and the internet represented a new, vast and uncharted territory for experimentation and investment, one where many of the old rules and regulations no longer applied, where new forms of revenue could be generated and where, if you got it right, enormous wealth could be created. But huge amounts of capital would be squandered too, and the uncharted territory of the internet would become a graveyard for most of the new ventures that were launched in its domain.

Much of the course of the digital revolution as it unfolded from the 1970s to the present, as well as the public perception of its key players, can be understood in terms of the interplay between these two broader social processes, and the complex ways in which they interacted with the development of the internet-based economy. As the scale of the wealth and power that was being created by the large tech companies became increasingly clear and the abuses of power began to surface (whether in the form of abuses by the state, as disclosed by Edward Snowden and others, or in the form of abuses or blunders by the tech giants themselves, as revealed by the Cambridge Analytica scandal, among other things), the earlier and more optimistic views of the digital revolution and the internet – which tended to emphasize its emancipatory and countercultural character, its encouragement of horizontal as opposed to vertical relations of power, and so on – began to morph into a darker and altogether more pessimistic view which underlined the more insidious aspects of the digital revolution. Behind the fine-sounding words of Silicon Valley's company slogans

---

[7] See Fred Turner, *From Counterculture to Cyberculture* (University of Chicago Press, 2008).

(Google's 'Don't be evil', Facebook's 'Making the world more open and connected', etc.), there was a powerful corporate machine that was pursuing its interests ruthlessly and creating unprecedented wealth for its founders and shareholders. As this realization dawned with increasing clarity, the techno-optimism of the early internet years began to morph into techno-pessimism and the critical voices speaking out against the largely unbridled power of Silicon Valley grew louder – the techlash had begun. The cultural and political climate was changing but the underlying dynamics remained pretty much the same. The broader social processes with which the digital revolution had been interwoven from the outset were still in play and still shaping the development of the internet-based economy, although the sheer scale of the corporate monoliths spawned by the digital revolution, and the glimpses into their largely hidden operations afforded by recent scandals, have altered our cultural and political perception of their virtues and vices.

As the digital revolution took hold in the book publishing industry, its imbrication with these two broader processes was equally clear. While many publishers were initially wary of the digital revolution and fearful of the changes it could bring about, it was not long before most publishers recognized that they would need to re-structure their organizations and re-engineer some aspects of what they do in order to adapt to the changing environment and take advantage of the new opportunities that were opening up. At the same time, there was a proliferation of entrepreneurial activity in the publishing field as individuals and organizations sought to use new technologies and the internet to create or facilitate new kinds of activity in a space that had been dominated by a particular constellation of players. Not unlike other sectors, most of this entrepreneurial activity would end in failure. There would be some striking successes, to be sure, but the history of technological innovation tends to view the past through distorted lenses that accentuate the successes and obscure or obliterate the failures, which are typically much more numerous.[8]

---

[8] The conventional wisdom is that 90 per cent of internet start-ups end in failure, though the real situation is likely to be much more complex than this simple statistic would suggest, depending in part on how you understand 'failure'. Research by Shikhar Ghosh at the Harvard Business School suggests that about three-quarters of venture-backed firms in the US don't return investors' capital, and 30–40 per cent end up liquidating all assets, with investors losing all their money. These figures are based on 2,000 companies that received venture funding between 2004 and 2010 (Deborah Gage, 'The Venture Capital Secret: 3 Out of 4 Start-Ups Fail', *The Wall Street Journal*, 20 September 2012, at www.wsj.com/articles/SB10000872396390443720204578

Some of this entrepreneurial activity would also resonate well with the do-it-yourself culture that was linked to the growing emphasis on the individual in modern societies: the explosion of self-publishing is the perfect illustration of this do-it-yourself culture in the field of book publishing, though many other developments resonate with this emphasis as well, such as the crowdfunding of books and the creation of social media platforms for writers and readers to interact with one another. With the development of self-publishing platforms, individuals are given the tools to publish their own books themselves, without having to rely on established publishing institutions, and the culture of indie publishing that has grown up around these platforms celebrates this activity as a positive choice, as a path that individuals can actively choose in order to take control of their own publishing decisions and their own destiny as an author.

While some entrepreneurial activity in the field of book publishing resonated with the individualization of modern societies, there were other aspects that were more in tune with the way that digital technologies and the internet both facilitated and were interwoven with the emergence of new forms of capital accumulation and power. The single most important consequence of the digital revolution in the field of Anglo-American trade publishing to date has not been the explosion of self-publishing (significant though that is), nor has it been the rise of ebooks and the proliferation of digital content in other forms (again, significant though that is): rather, it has been its transformative impact on the retail sector, exemplified above all by the rise of a powerful new player in the publishing field which is entirely a product of the digital revolution – Amazon. It is hard to over-state the significance of the rise of Amazon for the world of Anglo-American publishing. Today, Amazon accounts for around 45 per cent of all print book unit sales in the US[9] and more than 75

004980476429190). Aggregate data from the VC firm Horsley Bridge Partners, based on just over 7,000 investments made by funds in which it invested from 1985 to 2014, showed that around half of all investments returned less than the original sum invested; a very small percentage – 6 per cent based on this data – resulted in a major success of at least 10x return (Benedict Evans, 'In Praise of Failure' (10 August 2017), at www.ben-evans.com/benedictevans/2016/4/28/winning-and-losing). Venture capitalists 'bury their dead very quietly', says Ghosh. 'They emphasize the successes but they don't talk about the failures at all.'

[9] According to Paul Abbassi of Bookstat, 339 million, or 49%, of the 690 million US hardcover and paperback unit sales reported by NPD Bookscan (formerly Nielsen Bookscan) in 2019 were sold through Amazon.com. This total figure of 690 million units doesn't include library sales, publisher-direct and author-direct sales, and sales through the smallest distribution channels, but it does include Amazon.com, Barnes

per cent of all ebook unit sales,[10] and for many publishers, around half – in some cases, more – of their sales are accounted for by a single customer, Amazon. Never before in the 500-year history of book publishing has there been a retailer with this kind of market share. And with market share comes power – including the power to negotiate terms with suppliers and the power to command the attention of readers. Moreover, Amazon has a dominant position not just in book retail, but also in other emerging sectors of the publishing industry – it is the dominant player in self-publishing with Kindle Direct, it is the dominant player in audiobooks with the acquisition of Audible,[11] and so on. Amazon's power is likely to grow as the position of traditional bricks-and-mortar booksellers like Barnes & Noble weakens. It is not surprising that the CEO of one large publishing house averred that 'The power of Amazon is the single biggest issue in publishing today.' He was right.

But what exactly is the basis of Amazon's power, and how has it managed to establish such a seemingly unassailable position in the field of book publishing? Of course, the retail book business was Jeff Bezos's starting point, and books were an ideal product for the kind of internet-based retail business that he wanted to build when he founded Amazon in the 1990s, as we saw in chapter 5. By offering a huge range of titles that greatly exceeded anything that any bricks-and-mortar bookseller could offer, by discounting aggressively and providing outstanding customer service that was second to none, by developing the most successful ebook reading device in the market and creating a closed loop with the ebooks sold in the Kindle Store, by establishing a strong foothold in audiobooks through the acquisition

---

& Noble, Books-A-Million, Hudson News, the mass merchandisers (Walmart, Target, etc.) and 700+ ABA-reporting independent bookstores and it is widely considered to represent around 85 per cent of all US print sales. Taking account of this additional 15% of sales not covered by NPD Bookscan, Abbassi estimates Amazon's actual US print market share to be around 43–45%. This is the dominant market share by far, and more than double that of the next-largest retailer (Barnes & Noble, which accounts for around 21% of US print sales). Amazon's market share of NPD Bookscan-reported US print unit sales has also grown significantly in recent years, up from 38% in 2015 to 49% in 2019 (personal communication). It is likely that this trend will be strengthened by the lockdowns imposed during the coronavirus pandemic in 2020, which could see Amazon's share of US print sales increase by an additional 5–10% in 2020. If the lockdowns result in some permanent bookstore closures, then some of this 2020 increase could become a permanent gain in market share for Amazon.

[10] See chapter 5, pp. 154–5.
[11] On Audible's share of the audiobook market, see chapter 10, p. 378.

of Audible and Brilliance, and by integrating these and many other product lines and services into a platform where books were part of a much larger ecosystem that bestowed real benefits on users and members, Amazon was able to overrun its main competitors in the form of the book superstore chains, which were, for the most part, stuck in a pre-internet age of high-street retail where large cavernous bookstores were seen as temples of commerce that would draw in the crowds. But these temples quickly turned into graveyards when book buyers realized that they could find many more books at better prices online. Amazon became the destination of choice for more and more book buyers, who preferred the simplicity of ordering online, often at discounted prices, and having books delivered to their door free of charge to the hassle of going to a bookstore to buy a book, knowing that, if it were an older backlist title or a more specialist book, it probably wouldn't be there anyway.

But while Amazon's appeal to customers was crucial to its rapid growth and success, this was not the real source of its power. Like many other tech companies that were building internet-based businesses in the late 1990s and early 2000s, Amazon soon realized that the internet enabled it not only to grow its business very fast, but also to gather information about the users of its services – in this case, individuals who were browsing and buying books and other goods on its platform and who were using its various services – and to build a large store of proprietary data that was exceptionally rich in terms of the detail that it captured on the tastes, preferences and behaviour of its users, as well as personal details such as addresses, post codes and credit card details. The behaviour of individuals online – every click, every search, every page view, every purchase – became so much raw data in a giant data-extraction operation that was being pioneered by the big tech companies. The sheer volume of data gathered in this way meant that the data was not particularly useful on its own – there was simply too much of it, and each data record was too specific. But, by using algorithms, machine learning and high-power computing, this data could be turned into forms of knowledge about individuals' preferences, wants and likely behaviour, present and future, that was immensely valuable. The transformation of large volumes of raw data into behavioural knowledge of this kind can be, and was, used for different purposes, including marketing and selling more goods more effectively to the existing customer base. But the tech companies soon realized that this knowledge was a valuable commodity in itself which could be traded in a new kind of marketplace where firms would be willing to pay for access to this knowledge in order to develop highly targeted advertising for their goods and services.

These 'behavioural futures markets' are the basis of what Shoshana Zuboff aptly calls 'surveillance capitalism' – a new form of capitalism, or rather a new form of capital accumulation, that is based not on the production and sale of goods but, rather, on the manipulation and sale of data extracted from human experience.[12] Gaining access to this data, suitably transformed into behavioural knowledge, would enable organizations to target their products and services in a much more granular and effective way than traditional forms of advertising were ever able to achieve, and would also thereby enable them to influence and shape individuals' behaviour, or at least to seek to do so, whether that behaviour is a decision to buy or otherwise consume a product or service or a decision to act in some other way (e.g., to vote for a particular candidate). As Zuboff has shown, the extraction, manipulation and sale of personal data is the hidden economic logic that underlies the staggering wealth of tech giants like Google and Facebook, which have become some of the world's most highly valued corporations on the basis of transforming vast quantities of personal data into behavioural knowledge and then trading this knowledge in behavioural futures markets where third parties are willing to pay significant sums of money to advertise their products and services. Google was the pioneer of this process but Facebook, Twitter and other tech companies quickly followed suit, for one simple reason: this was a very effective way to generate large revenues without charging users directly for the privilege of using your services. Users could use your services free of charge, on one condition – that they gave you access to their personal data (and, in practice, very few users bothered to read the conditions, or seemed to care much about them). Their personal data, relinquished without much hesitation, could be transformed into behavioural knowledge and then sold in behavioural futures markets, where the price would depend on the volume and granularity of the data and the size of the network, among other things. The companies that accumulated the most data could sell targeted advertising at the highest price. Hence, expanding your network and user base as aggressively as possible so that you could gather more data than your competitors was the best way to maximize your position in behavioural futures markets. In the

---

[12] Shoshana Zuboff, *The Age of Surveillance Capitalism: The Fight for a Human Future at the New Frontier of Power* (New York: Public Affairs, 2019).

internet economy, 'data is the new oil', to use a phrase that has now become commonplace.[13]

For many of the large tech companies, user data is not just one asset among others: it is the most valuable asset they have, and it is the principal source of their power. Without this asset, and without the ability to turn this asset into behavioural knowledge that can be used for their own sales and marketing operations and sold for advertising in behavioural futures markets, they would have much less revenue-generating capacity and much less power – it's as simple as that. Given the importance of user data in the internet economy, it is helpful to give it a name: I'm calling it 'information capital', and I'll use the term 'data power' to refer to the specific form of power that is based on information capital. As I explained earlier,[14] information capital is a particular kind of resource that consists of bits of information that can be gathered, stored, processed and used to pursue particular aims; it doesn't have to assume a digital form, and for many centuries it didn't, but digital technologies make it possible to accumulate and use information capital in new ways that greatly enhance its value. Information capital is not the same as economic capital (that is, money and other financial resources), human capital (trained and talented staff), social capital (established social relationships and connections) or symbolic capital (accumulated prestige, recognition and respect), and data power is not the same as economic power, political power or symbolic power. But information capital can be converted into economic capital by being used to sell goods and services and by being traded in behavioural futures markets, and the ownership of information capital gives you a special kind of power vis-à-vis those who don't have this capital but would like access to it, and vis-à-vis the multitude of individuals whose personal data were the raw material for the information capital you now

---

[13] The phrase is usually traced back to a statement by the Sheffield mathematician Clive Humby. It was picked up by *The Economist* in 2017 ('The World's Most Valuable Resource Is No Longer Oil, but Data', *The Economist* (6 May 2017), at www.economist.com/leaders/2017/05/06/the-worlds-most-valuable-resource-is-no-longer-oil-but-data) and used by Jonathan Taplin in his important book, *Move Fast and Break Things: How Facebook, Google and Amazon Have Cornered Culture and What It Means for All of Us* (New York: Little, Brown, 2017). Of course, data is a very different kind of resource from oil: for one thing, data, unlike oil, is not necessarily depleted through use; for another, data requires a lot of manipulation before it can be turned into a valuable resource that can be traded in behavioural futures markets. But the general point is that data is as important to surveillance capitalism as oil is to industrial capitalism.

[14] See chapter 6, p. 172.

own.[15] By accumulating large quantities of information capital, tech companies can commoditize it in various ways and thereby convert it into economic capital, strengthening their financial position and increasing their own value as a company. This helps to explain why most tech start-ups are often sanguine about their profitability (or lack of it): they know – and are told in no uncertain terms by their VC funders – that growth and scale are the primary goals in the internet economy, because the more users you have, the more user data you will be able to generate, and more user data strengthens your position in behavioural futures markets. Moreover, because of network effects, the value of a network increases with each additional user, so larger networks tend to crowd out smaller ones, leading to a winner-takes-most economy. Even if tech companies are unprofitable in the short term, they may become hugely valuable and profitable in the medium to long term if they have accumulated large quantities of information capital in a winner-takes-most economy.

While Google and Facebook were pioneers in developing powerful corporations based on the extraction of data and the accumulation of information capital, Amazon has proceeded in a similar way. Harvesting data on its customers was an integral part of Amazon's original business plan – not data collection for its own sake, but in order to sell more effectively to each customer, to monetize customers and maximize their lifetime value.[16] It has now built a large store of proprietary user data on the hundreds of millions of people worldwide who use Amazon to purchase goods and services online,[17] whether those goods are supplied by Amazon or by the hundreds of thousands of third-party sellers who are hosted by Amazon Marketplace, the e-commerce platform owned and operated by Amazon. As an online retailer, as well as a hardware manufacturer and provider of various

---

[15] This is not the place to elaborate my account of the different forms of power and the resources on which they are based, but the basic elements of this account can be found in John B. Thompson, *The Media and Modernity: A Social Theory of the Media* (Cambridge: Polity, 1995), pp. 12–18, and Thompson, *Merchants of Culture*, pp. 3–10.

[16] Amazon's emphasis on data collection was there from the beginning. James Marcus, who worked at Amazon in the early days, recalled how this point was highlighted during a company retreat at the Sleeping Lady Resort in 1997: 'It was made clear from the beginning that data collection was also one of Amazon's businesses. It was made clear to us that all customer behaviour that flowed through the site was recorded and tracked, and that itself was a commodity' (James Marcus, in 'Amazon: What They Know About Us', *BBC Panorama*, aired 17 February 2020, at www.bbc.co.uk/programmes/m000fjdz).

[17] On the user numbers, see chapter 6, note 1.

services both to companies and to consumers, Amazon has a highly diversified portfolio – it is by no means reliant exclusively on trading information capital in behavioural futures markets. But Amazon uses the personal data it gathers in order to sell advertising on its website, competing directly with Google and Facebook for advertising revenue, and it also uses this data to develop marketing tools to increase the sales of its own goods and services and to strengthen its position as the go-to online retailer for everything from books and music to technology, toys, clothes, beauty products, household appliances, garden tools, pet supplies and groceries. Moreover, with the launch of its smart speaker system Echo, and its virtual assistant Alexa, Amazon has joined Google and Apple in developing a home automation hub that is able to harvest personal data from users' homes. What makes these home-based voice-controlled devices so significant is that they are able to tap into new data streams from the everyday lives of users, such as data on what we listen to, on our daily movements and interactions within the home, and data drawn from connected domestic devices – the so-called internet of things. With these smart speaker systems, tech companies no longer need to compete for our attention in order to gather data: they can simply tap into the live stream of everyday life and draw a continuous flow of data from it.[18] Nothing is now off-limits: without really thinking about it (what could be more harmless than buying an Echo?), our home becomes a glasshouse and the most intimate spaces of our lives become another terrain for gathering data. This adds more raw data to the databases of Amazon and other tech companies supplying smart speaker systems, expanding the range of data in new ways and further augmenting their already large stocks of information capital.

While the rise of Amazon is thus an integral part of the metamorphosis of capitalism in the digital age and, like the other tech giants, it has built much of its power and wealth on the accumulation of information capital, at the same time Amazon also resonates with and celebrates the emphasis on the individual that is part and parcel of modern societies. The individual *qua* consumer has always been at the heart of Amazon's business philosophy – 'We want to be earth's most customer-centric company', said Bezos. 'We want our brand to be known for this abstract notion of starting with the customer and working backwards.'[19] Thanks to the sheer range of products

---

[18] See Siva Vaidhyanathan, *Anti-Social Media: How Facebook Disconnects Us and Undermines Democracy* (New York: Oxford University Press, 2018), pp. 98–105.
[19] Jeff Bezos, in 'Amazon: What They Know About Us'.

available, constantly expanding to ever new territories of consumer goods, Amazon can enable individuals to find whatever they might want, to indulge their desires and discover whole worlds of new things that they never before realized they wanted.[20] But the ethic of individual freedom and the do-it-yourself culture runs through other aspects of Amazon too. Amazon was one of the early players in the self-publishing explosion ushered in by the digital revolution, and the people within Amazon who drove forward the expansion of KDP – Amazon's self-publishing platform – were genuinely committed to the idea of treating authors as customers too and giving them the tools to tell their own stories without having to go through the established gatekeepers of the publishing industry. When one Amazon employee described KDP as 'the democratization of the means of production', he really meant it: that's exactly what it was in his view. This emphasis on the do-it-yourself culture of individual empowerment and creativity is an integral part of Amazon, which is one reason why so many indie authors are enthusiastic champions of Amazon and KDP. But, as in many organizations spawned by the digital revolution, this emphasis goes hand-in-hand with a no-nonsense focus on the pursuit of growth and market power, using the means at its disposal – which include the accumulation and exploitation of information capital – to build a huge new corporation with global reach. Of course, these two complementary emphases don't always sit so easily together, but in the day-to-day reality of developing a business with many different subsidiaries and strands, the potential tension between the emphasis on individual empowerment and the hard-nosed focus on corporate growth is easily dissipated in the cacophony of corporate culture.[21]

Given Amazon's dominant position as a retailer of both print books and ebooks and its large stock of information capital, publishers increasingly find themselves locked in a Faustian pact with their largest customer. On the one hand, as Amazon has grown to become the single most important retail channel for most publishers, in some cases accounting for 50 per cent or more of a publisher's total sales, publishers cannot afford not to deal with Amazon: if you

---

[20] According to Marcus, 'The whole mission was to make the customer happy, to bring the customer ecstasy – that was the spiritual state that Jeff was aiming for' (James Marcus, in 'Amazon: What They Know About Us').

[21] This point was often emphasized by one of my sources who had been a senior manager at Amazon for many years: 'Many people have the impression of Amazon as this remarkable strategic juggernaut with a finely tuned sense of direction and mission but it wasn't like that at all. It was a lot of shit thrown at the wall.'

didn't supply your books to Amazon, your sales would collapse and your credibility in the eyes of both authors and readers would take a serious hammering. For Amazon is not just a retail channel: in the eyes of many authors and readers, it has also become the de facto public record of the availability of a book, and, for many authors and readers, if a book is not listed on Amazon, it doesn't exist. On the other hand, every sale through Amazon only increases Amazon's stock of information capital and increases their market share, and hence increases still further their power in a relationship that is already highly asymmetrical. Amazon is a drug on which publishers have become hooked and, once hooked, it's very hard to let go. But the more that a publisher's sales go through Amazon, the more information capital Amazon accumulates on the tastes, preferences, browsing and purchasing behaviour of book buyers and customers, and the more they are able to strengthen their position in the market by using this capital to market and sell more books and other goods to their customers and to sell advertising to publishers and others. Amazon's market share grows and it becomes increasingly indispensable to the publishers whose books it is selling. By supplying their books to Amazon, publishers are also handing over the ultimate customers and readers of their books to a retailer and tech company which knows much more about these readers – and, with every sale, knows a little bit more – than the publishers will ever know. The relation of power between publishers and Amazon is heavily skewed in Amazon's favour, and the asymmetry in terms of information capital is pretty much total.

The fact that Amazon's power is based in part on its control of information capital enables us to see why Amazon's power is both different from, and so much greater than, the power of large book retailers in the past. In the 1980s and 1990s, there was much concern among publishers about the power of the large book superstore chains – Barnes & Noble and Borders in the US and Waterstones and Dillons in the UK – and it is often said or assumed that Amazon's dominance as a book retailer is no different from the dominance of Barnes & Noble and Borders in an earlier era. But to think this would be to misunderstand the nature of Amazon's power. Even with the merging of Waterstones and Dillons in the late 1990s and with the bankruptcy of Borders in 2011, which left Barnes & Noble as the sole remaining book superstore chain of any scale in the US, none of the book superstore chains ever achieved a market share in print books that was comparable or even close to the market share that Amazon now enjoys; and the only one of these retailers that tried seriously to compete in the market for ebook reading devices – Barnes & Noble with its Nook – failed to mount a sustained challenge to Amazon's dominance in this market. But that is not all. At a more fundamental level, what distinguishes Amazon from all previous book retailers, including the book superstore chains, is that Amazon has amassed information capital on a scale that was never possible before. Since all book retailers in the past, including the book superstore chains, were primarily bricks-and-mortar stores selling to customers in-store, they were never able to accumulate the kind of information capital on which Amazon, as an internet-based retailer, has built its business. This gave Amazon a huge competitive advantage: not only did they know much more about customers and readers than publishers did, they also knew much more than any other retailer did, including the book superstore chains. They could sell advertising and target marketing much more effectively than the superstore chains, which continued to rely on traditional in-store displays funded in part through co-op. But in-store displays only work if people are coming into your store, and if readers are migrating to online purchase – in part because they are being effectively targeted through online marketing and advertising – then in-store displays will be increasingly ineffective. In the competitive space of the book retail business, Amazon has a key resource, and a way of accumulating and using that resource, that the bricks-and-mortar bookstores will never be able to match. They can compete with Amazon in other ways, but the unequal distribution of information capital will always give Amazon a competitive advantage.

If there is an asymmetry of information capital in the relation between Amazon and publishers and in the relation between Amazon and other book retailers, so too there is an asymmetry in the relation between Amazon and its customers – this is a Faustian pact of its own. Every book buyer knows very well the attractions of buying books from Amazon, just as every customer knows the attractions of buying other things from the everything store: unrivalled range, good prices that are often discounted, excellent customer service, fast and free delivery to your home – what's not to like? And yet every purchase on Amazon is both more revenue and more data for them, contributing in an infinitesimally small but cumulatively significant way to the growing market share and increasing information capital of the world's largest retailer and driving the nail a little deeper into the coffin of its competitors. The transaction is so simple, the purchase so convenient and commonplace, that we lose sight of what we've given away in this small ordinary act of everyday life:

our data. Information about ourselves and our tastes, preferences and practices, information that comes back to greet us in the form of a cheerful and nicely targeted email recommending other books or goods we might like to purchase or in the form of recommendations tailored to us that we see the next time we visit the Amazon site. Our choices are being subtly guided and shaped by processes and algorithms that are informed by our data but whose modus operandi are completely opaque to us. And, once again, the asymmetry here is pretty much total: Amazon knows all of our browsing and purchasing behaviour on their platform, and if we use Amazon services like Kindle Unlimited, Audible or Prime Video, they know our behaviour in these services too, but we, the users, know nothing at all about Amazon, and we know nothing about what Amazon knows about us either. From the user's point of view, Amazon is a black box, completely shrouded in mystery. Of course, this asymmetry is not unique to Amazon: it is a structural feature of surveillance capitalism and the existential condition of every organization that has built its power on the accumulation of information capital that is exploited for commercial ends.[22]

So what can be done? What should be done? These questions raise complex issues that go far beyond the scope of a study concerned with the impact of the digital revolution on the book publishing industry. They call for a much broader reflection on the new forms of power that have emerged in the wake of the digital revolution. The time has come to look again at how our social, economic, political and cultural lives are being reshaped by a transformation that is so pervasive and profound that it is practically invisible, and at how this transformation has given rise to a new set of players whose unprecedented wealth and power are based on a new kind of resource that is different from the kinds of resources that underpinned the great corporations of the industrial age – a resource that is intangible and easy to overlook, but enormously valuable nonetheless. Regulatory policies that were devised for an earlier era of capitalism need to be reconsidered in a new era in which the accumulation and control of information have come to form a crucial basis of corporate power, and in which network effects tend to produce a winner-takes-most economy where the largest players are able to establish virtual monopolies that crowd out smaller players and make it very difficult, if not impossible, for new competitors to enter the field. Moreover, when the largest players operate not just as buyers or sellers but as

---

[22] Zuboff, *The Age of Surveillance Capitalism*, p. 11.

platforms in a network economy, they acquire new forms of power that stem from their pivotal role and from their ability to capture data from all the transactions that take place on the platform. Dominant platforms will benefit from network effects and they can use their privileged access to customer data to make it very difficult for rival platforms to compete. And when dominant platforms become virtual monopolies, they can easily veer into monopsonies that have a great deal of market power over the suppliers of goods and services, who find themselves in a market situation where they have little choice but to deal with a retailer who now controls a large share of the market and who, because of that, now holds all or most of the cards. When a particular supplier needs a particular retailer much more than that retailer needs that supplier, then the negotiating power when it comes to specifying the terms of trade is firmly in the retailer's hands.

In the field of the book publishing industry, these general considerations translate into a number of practical measures. First, the time has come to examine seriously Amazon's market power in relation to antitrust law. Given the broad shift in US antitrust policy since the 1970s which we examined in chapter 5, it is not surprising that Amazon has so far escaped the scrutiny of the Department of Justice: if your primary concern is consumer welfare rather than concentration and the power of large corporations, then Amazon is not going to be high on your list of regulatory concerns. But there are other ways in which large corporations with excessive amounts of power can distort market processes and reduce competition, and using a de facto monopoly position to drive out retail competition and place excessive pressure on suppliers to alter terms of trade in your favour are two such ways. Moreover, there are legitimate questions to be asked about whether a single player should be allowed to have a dominant position in so many different retail sectors of a single industry – in this case, print books, ebooks and audiobooks. Amazon now has an overwhelmingly dominant market share in all of these sectors – no other player comes anywhere near Amazon in terms of market share. It is not just that this gives a single player an inordinate amount of power in controlling the channels that connect publishers with readers, important though that is; in the digital age, it also means that this one player is able to pool data from consumer activity in several key sectors of the book publishing industry and thereby augment its information capital in a way that makes its position unassailable. There is a strong case for subjecting the large tech companies – Google, Facebook, Amazon and others – to antitrust scrutiny from this perspective. A good case could be made to require these companies to divest themselves of some of the companies they have acquired in order to reduce imbalances of power, redress the distortion of market processes and nurture competition and diversity in the marketplace. But, apart from deconcentration, there are numerous other important issues concerning the anticompetitive effects of excessive market power in a network economy – such as predatory pricing, targeted discounting and exclusionary practices that harm competitors and suppliers – that should be reconsidered from an antitrust perspective.[23]

It is not just about antitrust legislation, however: it is also about the attitudes of the other players who find themselves locked in Faustian pacts with Amazon, and, more broadly, about the structures and implications of the new data regime in which we now find ourselves. Given Amazon's centrality in the retail channels of the book trade and their dominant market share, it is perfectly understandable that most publishers, with very few exceptions, have taken the view that they cannot not work with Amazon. But it's all too easy for publishers in this situation to become overly dependent on this one retail channel, like an addict who has become hooked on a drug and given up on the idea of living without it. As organizations that are responsible for their own fate, publishers have an obligation to seek out and cultivate alternative retail channels, to diversify their revenue streams and not to allow themselves to become overly dependent on one retailer which, with every further increment of market share, gains more power over the publishers who are increasingly dependent on it – indeed, it is in Amazon's interest too for publishers to do this, because Amazon has reached a point where further significant increases in its market share will increase the risk of antitrust scrutiny. There are other things that publishers can do to wrest more control over their fate (we'll return to this below) but actively cultivating alternative retail channels and working with other retailers to create a more diversified marketplace are undoubtedly important steps, whether these are independent bookstores, the large bookstore chains or other new retail initiatives that are opening up, like Bookshop.org.[24] Similarly, while it's perfectly understandable

---

[23] For a valuable overview of the antitrust issues raised by the activities of large tech companies, see Baker, *The Antitrust Paradigm*, esp. chs. 7–9.

[24] Bookshop.org is a new online bookstore that was launched in January 2020 by Andy Hunter, in collaboration with the American Booksellers Association and the wholesaler Ingram. Andy Hunter is a well-known figure in the world of independent and digital publishing; he had founded Electric Literature, co-founded Catapult and was a founding partner of the Literary Hub. Like many in the publishing industry,

that Amazon has become the default bookstore for many readers and book buyers, given its unmatchable range and excellent customer service, buying books exclusively from Amazon serves only to strengthen its market position and weaken its competitors, thereby contributing, in however small a way, to the creation of a marketplace that is increasingly dominated by one online giant and a high street that is increasingly deserted. And every act of commerce on Amazon's site is, at the same time, a small contribution to its personal data-extraction machine and a further tug on the rope that is strangling the high street. So every consumer decision to buy a book from a retailer other than Amazon is an act of market diversification that is just as important, even if smaller in scale, as the effort made by publishers to cultivate alternative retail channels.

However, the structural asymmetries involved in the harvesting and use of personal data and its conversion into information capital cannot be addressed by the decisions of individual users and suppliers alone: they raise fundamental issues about the ownership and use of personal data in the digital age that can only be addressed collectively, and ultimately by the concerted action of states. The tech companies have become much too large and powerful, and much too deeply embedded in our social and economic lives, for individuals – or even individual organizations on their own – to be able to alter their practices in any significant way. To lose one user, or even a few thousand users, is nothing to an organization that counts its users in the hundreds of millions or even billions. To lose one supplier in one industry, even an important supplier in that industry, won't make much difference to an organization that works with thousands of suppliers in dozens of industries. Ultimately, the questions at the heart of this new economy based on the extraction, manipulation and

---

he had become increasingly alarmed by the growing dominance of Amazon and the plight of many independent bookstores; Bookshop.org was designed as an alternative to Amazon that would at the same time support independent bookstores. The model is simple: anyone who wants to promote books can sign up to Bookshop.org as an affiliate – bookstores, publishers, authors, reviewers, review media, book clubs, etc. Affiliates receive 10 per cent on each sale they create. Another 10 per cent goes into a pool that is distributed equally among participating independent bookstores. For a small start-up like this to try to establish a foothold in a market dominated by a tech giant like Amazon might seem like Mission Impossible, but, by a cruel coincidence, Bookshop.org was given an unexpected leg-up by the lockdowns imposed during the coronavirus pandemic: having launched in January 2020, they met their first year's sales target in just eight weeks, and by June 2020 they announced that they had raised $4,438,970 for local bookstores. Whether they can maintain this momentum when the pandemic is over remains to be seen, but it is an encouraging start.

exploitation of personal data are questions that have to be addressed at a broader social and political level. We need to think again about the legal frameworks that allow both private organizations and states to harvest personal data, store it and use it for their own ends, with very little protection for individuals and a vast asymmetry in terms of knowledge, wealth and power between the organizations that own and control this data and the individuals who provide it. Privacy and data security laws in both the US and Europe have generally lagged far behind the transformations brought about by the digital revolution. The General Data Protection Regulation (GDPR), which came into force in the EU in May 2018, is a step in the right direction, and the threat of substantial fines – of up to €20 million or 4 per cent of global turnover, whichever is the higher – has undoubtedly focused corporate minds, but how much difference this will actually make to the economic logic that underpins the large tech companies, and to their market dominance, remains unclear.[25] What is clear, however, is that the large tech companies will not change significantly the ways that they gather, process and use the personal data of users unless they are forced to do so by states. They simply have too much to gain by continuing with the practices that have turned them into some of the most highly valued companies in the world, and too much to lose by surrendering control of the personal data which is the basis of their wealth, to undertake by themselves a fundamental reform of their practices. At the end of the day, these are issues for the collective deliberation of citizens and the concerted action of states. We need to think collectively about the price we are paying, in terms both of our privacy and autonomy as individuals and of the health of our democracies, for the gains that come from greater connectivity, and, where appropriate, we need to use the democratic means available to place appropriate limits on the activities of those organizations that have built, and continue to build, their power and wealth on this connectivity.

---

[25] There is some evidence to suggest that GDPR has been financially beneficial for the two largest platforms, Google and Facebook, both of which significantly increased their revenue from ads shown in Europe in the year following the introduction of GDPR, and their revenues from Europe increased more than Europe's digital advertising market as a whole (see Nick Kostov and Sam Schechner, 'GDPR Has Been a Boon for Google and Facebook', *The Wall Street Journal*, 17 June 2019, at www.wsj.com/articles/gdpr-has-been-a-boon-for-google-and-facebook-11560789219). In the short term, the GDPR appears to be pushing some firms to concentrate their digital advertising budgets with the biggest players in the expectation that they are less likely to run afoul of the law, though how this plays out in the long term remains to be seen.

Nurturing content, colonizing culture

The tension and conflict that have arisen between publishers and tech companies stems in part from the power that has accrued to Amazon on the basis of its market share and its stock of information capital, but there is another source of tension that is also linked to the different economic logics that govern old media industries like publishing and the new internet-based tech companies. In an old media industry like book publishing, the key organizational players (in this case, publishers) are essentially concerned with the creation and curation of symbolic content, and their primary revenue stems from the sale of that content, whether the sale comes in the form of a transaction or in the form of a licensing or subsidiary rights deal (for example, licensing rights for translation, audiobook publication, serialization, etc.) – that is, they are in the content creation business. Of course, this is not all that publishers do (we'll return to this below) and it is not only publishers who are concerned with the creation and curation of book content (most book content is actually created by authors, and other players, such as agents, are also involved in content creation); but for publishers, content matters, and therefore it also matters to them to ensure that there is a content supply line that is sustainable in the long term. For without the continuous supply of new content that is of a kind and quality that will enable publishers to produce and publish books that can be sold directly (through transactions) and indirectly (through licensing and subsidiary rights), publishers' revenue streams will dry up, as will the revenue streams of those who depend on payments from publishers, such as authors and agents. In other words, for key players in the book publishing industry, a sustainable culture of content creation is essential.

Most of the big tech companies that impinge on publishing are not themselves in the content creation business, however – or if they are, it is only a small part of what they do. They are making their money in other ways – e.g., from advertising, retail, the sale of hardware, the provision of services, or some combination of these; and, as tech companies operating in the internet economy, they need to be big because only with scale are they able to achieve network effects, and they need to become big fast because only by squeezing out their competitors will they become the winners in winner-takes-most markets. But to become big fast, they need content – and lots of it. They need users to be active and engaged on their platform, to be busy searching or commenting or liking or browsing or buying or whatever it is that users typically do on that platform, for it is only when they do something on the platform that the company is able to harvest more data and ingest it in its data-processing machine, thus augmenting its most valuable resource, its information capital. So for many of the big tech companies, content is not an end in itself, it is a means to another end, and the end is to build its user base and its stock of proprietary user data – its information capital. Hence, the economic logic of many big tech companies is to drive the price of content as low as possible in order to maximize activity on its platform. User-generated content is ideal because it is completely free: users generate it, other users read it, watch it, like it and share it and no one gets paid. All of that user-generated content draws in users and keeps them engaged on the platform while the platform itself harvests their data and uses it to generate revenue in behavioural futures markets. It is the perfect magician's trick: everyone's attention is focused on the content while the platform is making money elsewhere, in the place where no one is looking. If you are a search engine company striving to become the dominant player in the search engine field, then being able to dump a large amount of high-quality book content into your servers without paying anyone for it and using it to improve your search engine results is also an excellent strategy: it would quickly give you another important competitive advantage as you seek to outmanoeuvre your competitors in the search engine war, and once you had become the winner in a winner-takes-most market, then you would be able to charge a premium for your services in the behavioural futures markets where your money is made. If you are a retailer, it's not quite so simple, because your job as a retailer is to resell someone else's products, so the content can't be completely free. But you can apply the same logic, which in this case means exerting as much downward pressure on prices as you can: the cheaper the better, because your interest as an online retailer is to maximize sales activity on your platform, and lower prices (along with better service) are going to bring more customers to your platform and generate more activity on it. Of course, as a retailer, you want margin as well as low prices, so the downward pressure on prices goes hand-in-hand with applying as much pressure as you can on suppliers to improve the terms of trade: you can lower prices to consumers and protect or improve your margin as a retailer only by getting higher discounts and lower prices from suppliers. And here scale matters too: if you are the dominant retailer and have become so important for suppliers that they cannot afford not to do business with you, then you will have a great deal of leverage when it comes to negotiating advantageous terms of trade with your suppliers.

The different economic logics that underpin old media industries like publishing, on the one hand, and new media players like the internet-based tech companies, on the other, help to explain why publishers and tech companies became locked in long-running and bitter disputes, such as the dispute over the Google Library Project and the confrontation with Amazon over ebook pricing that ended up with the Department of Justice's suit against publishers and Apple for alleged price-fixing. A key part of what lies behind these disputes is a very different way of thinking about the value of content. In the case of the Google Library Project, Google's primary motivation – notwithstanding any dreams the founders may have had about creating a universal library – was to improve its search engine by allowing snippets from books to appear in search results. If content from books could turn up in Google search results along with content culled from the internet, which was often of much lower quality than the content you find in books, this would give Google a competitive edge over Yahoo! and Microsoft in the search engine war. From the old-media-industry perspective of the publishers, however, the Google Library Project looked like a straightforward case of copyright infringement: Google was digitizing the content of millions of books that were still in copyright and using it for its own commercial ends without paying the content creators – publishers or authors – anything, and without even asking their permission. In the end, the legal case turned on the interpretation of fair use doctrine under US copyright law, but the broader issue at stake was the very different perception of the value of content. For Google, book content was grist to the mill of their omnivorous search engine: the more content they had, the better their search engine would be, and if the content was high quality, better still: it would help them deliver better search results, gain more users, gain more market share, harvest more data, generate more information capital, make more money in the behavioural futures markets – a seamless logic. Book content was helpful for Google but it wasn't essential – it was nice to have it but they would still have a business without it. For old-media-industry publishers, on the other hand, book content was everything: they were in the content creation business, and if you take away their content (or make it freely available online), they have nothing left (or their only real asset is heavily compromised) because creating and selling content was their business. Of course, whether the Google Library Project would in any way compromise publishers' ability to control and sell the content they were creating is a moot point, since Google was proposing to show only snippets, not full texts, and a full text would still have value even if snippets from it were freely available online. But, as part of the project, Google was proposing to provide the participating libraries with fully digitized copies of their books, and with no limits on what the libraries could do with these digitized copies, there was a real danger, in the eyes of publishers, that their books – full books, not just snippets – could become freely available online. In the final analysis, it was this divergence – book content was grist to the mill for Google, but the lifeblood of publishers – that underpinned the long-running dispute over the Google Library Project.

A similar divergence of views about the value of content under-pinned the dispute between publishers and Amazon over ebook pricing. When Amazon launched the Kindle in November 2007, they were entering the field as a retailer and hardware manufacturer and their principal aim was to establish the Kindle as the dominant e-reading device; and, given that only Amazon could sell ebook content to the Kindle, it would be a closed loop: once a consumer had chosen the Kindle as their preferred e-reading device, they would be locked into Amazon for all their ebook content. Since Amazon was by no means the first manufacturer of e-reading devices and wouldn't be the last, they knew that they had to establish a dominant position quickly in order to ward off the threats that would inevitably come soon enough – from Jeff Bezos's old rival, Apple, among others. Taking a leaf out of Apple's book, Amazon adopted the same strategy on ebook pricing as Apple had adopted on songs: price them below a critical threshold in order to make them look mouth-wateringly cheap to consumers. For songs, the threshold was 99¢; for ebooks, it was $9.99. The fact that Amazon might be losing money on many of the *New York Times* bestsellers and new releases they were selling at this price was neither here nor there: they could absorb these small losses if they achieved their bigger goal, which was to establish the Kindle as the dominant e-reading device and Amazon as the dominant ebook retailer, outmanoeuvring the competition and creating a position that was unassailable in the longer term. But the strategy would only work if they were able to price the content as they wished, even if it meant selling some ebooks at a loss. This is why the decision by some publishers to change the terms of trade for ebooks from the wholesale model to the agency model was so threatening for Amazon: the agency model meant that the publisher fixed the price of ebooks, not the retailer, and hence it meant that Amazon could no longer price ebooks at $9.99 if the publishers chose to price them higher. For Amazon, the $9.99 price was determined by a strategic decision to undercut competitors in order to establish their dominant position in the ebook market. There were undoubtedly many at Amazon (and elsewhere) who genuinely thought (and still think) that publishers were (and are) pricing ebooks too high, given that the marginal cost of reproduction of digital content is close to zero, and who genuinely thought (and still think) that by pricing ebooks much lower, they could sell many more copies; but the main factor that shaped the $9.99 decision was the view that, by pricing highly sought-after ebooks below the critical $10 threshold, Amazon would increase its chances of establishing the Kindle as the dominant device in the field and establish Amazon as the dominant ebook retailer. From the viewpoint of many publishers, however, Amazon was using publishers' content for its own strategic ends, and selling its content at a price that didn't reflect its real value; and, moreover, in doing so, they were devaluing that content in the eyes of consumers, creating the impression that the content was only worth $9.99, and under-cutting the sales of the hardback editions on which publishers relied in order to recover their costs, especially the advances paid to authors. By fixing the price of ebooks at an artificially low level in order to sell devices and gain market share, Amazon was sucking value out of the content creation business – that, at any rate, is how it was perceived by publishers. The only way they could arrest this process was to assert control over the pricing of ebooks, and the only way they could do this was to change the model – hence, the move to agency. The fact that five of the large trade publishers, along with Apple, found themselves in the dock for conspiracy to fix ebook prices suggests that publishers didn't make this move in the most adept manner, but it doesn't impugn the logic of their position. From publishers' point of view, creating high-quality content is a difficult and expensive business, and it didn't make sense to let a retailer and tech company, with its own interests to pursue and its own battles to fight, decide what that content was worth. It is therefore not surprising that, once the temporary agreements imposed by the settlement decree had run their course, all of the Big Five trade publishers moved over to the agency model. For publishers, what mattered most was to protect the value of their content so that they had a sustainable model of content creation in the long term, rather than allowing that content to become cannon fodder in a large retailer's battle for market share.

It is this fundamental divergence in the way of valuing content that lies at the heart of so many of the conflicts that have characterized the often fraught relations between old-media-industries like publishing and the new tech companies, and, for the most part, the growing wealth and power of the tech companies has been at the expense of old-media industries that were focused on content creation. The rise of the tech giants has gone hand-in-hand with the haemorrhaging of value out of the content creation businesses: the two processes are inextricably linked, as Jonathan Taplin rightly observes, in part because the tech companies have driven down the value of content as a means of driving up the value of their own businesses.[26] The book publishing industry may have suffered less from this value see-saw than some other creative industries, such as the music industry and the newspaper industry (so far, at least), but the dynamic is just as strongly present in book publishing as it is in other old-media industries, as the struggles with Google and Amazon show.

This is why it made perfect sense for publishers to take a stand against the Google Library Project and to move to agency pricing, even if they found themselves caught up in costly legal battles. It made sense because, as with many other media and creative industries, the fundamental business of book publishing is the creation and curation of content. It is in the interests of publishers to ensure that there is a supply line for high-quality content that is sustainable in the long term, and the best way to do this is to try to ensure that the reverse flow of revenue into the industry doesn't collapse. As key players in the supply line of book content, publishers have both an interest and an obligation to nurture and support the content creation process, and creating high-quality content is not cheap: quite apart from the cost of writing, which publishers support (however inadequately) through royalties and advances, there are the costs of editorial work, design, production, marketing and distribution, among other things – all costs that have to be paid by publishers and that don't go away when content is distributed digitally, even if some of these costs are reduced or eliminated by digital distribution (such as the warehousing and distribution of physical copies and the handling of returns). But if that content is appropriated without payment by third parties for their own ends, or made available for free by individuals or organizations who believe that 'information wants to be free' whatever the costs involved in creating it, or sold by retailers at prices that bear little or no relation to the actual costs incurred in its production, then the content creation process is threatened and culture is being colonized for other ends. Maintaining a sustainable

---

[26] Taplin, *Move Fast and Break Things*, pp. 6–8.

culture of creativity that is capable of producing high-quality content over time, providing a supporting environment for writers and other content creators and the resources necessary to develop, produce and market content effectively, requires a consistent and substantial revenue flow, no less than a flourishing garden requires water, and if the revenue sources dry up or shrink substantially with no compensating forms of revenue being created, then everyone – consumers as well as creators – will be worse off in the end.

Publishing in the digital age

I said that publishers are in the business of creating and curating content (among other things), but in an age of content abundance, why should publishers continue to exist? When it is easier than ever to make content freely available online, whether that content is a written text, a song, a video or some other form of content, who needs publishers? What do they bring to the content creation process that can't be done without them? That's the question that has often lurked in the background of debates about the impact of the digital revolution on the publishing industry and on other media industries – what is commonly referred to as 'disintermediation'.

To address this question properly, we need to step back from the practical day-to-day activities of publishers and separate out the key functions or roles that they typically perform. While there are different ways of conceptualizing these functions or roles, they essentially boil down to four[27] – figure 12.4. Let me deal briefly with each.

First and foremost, publishers are concerned with the creation and curation of content. They are a mechanism for selecting and filtering content, but also an organizational apparatus for creating and developing content. They do select and filter: publishers typically receive many more proposals and manuscripts than they can publish and they will use various methods to select some and reject others – in this respect, they are cultural gatekeepers, to use the concept that is often invoked to describe cultural intermediaries of this kind. But the term 'gatekeepers' doesn't do justice to the active role that many publishers play in the creation and development of content: in many cases, they actively come up with ideas for books and seek out

---

[27] Some of these functions or roles could be divided up into two or more separate roles and labelled differently, which would produce a more elaborate schema, but here I've opted for simplicity in order to focus on the essentials.

451

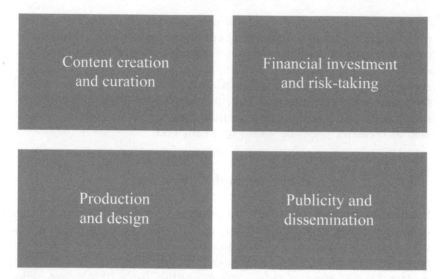

Figure 12.4   Key functions of the publisher

authors to write them, or they see the potential of an idea and help an author bring it to fruition. While the actual writing of a book is done by authors, the creation of a book is often a much more collaborative process that involves editors, readers and, in some cases, agents. Through this collaborative process, the quality of a work is often improved – characters are developed, language and style are honed, the plot or argument is refined, and so on. In addition to creating content, publishers are curating it – that is, selecting it, organizing it and putting it in a determinate relation to other content. The curation of a list or collection is a way of making things intelligible by organizing them, creating a context for them and connecting them to other things, in the same way that a curator puts together an exhibition of works of art.[28]

But what exactly is 'content'? Are not publishers concerned with producing books? Why speak about 'content' when, in fact, the content being produced is the book? It is helpful to speak about 'content' here because it shifts the discussion to a higher level of abstraction. The problem with the word 'book' is that it is ambiguous. On the one hand, it refers to a particular kind of material object, the print-on-paper book; on the other hand, it refers to a particular form

---

[28] See Michael Bhaskar, *Curation: The Power of Selection in a World of Excess* (London: Piatkus, 2016).

452

of symbolic content, a particular way of structuring symbolic content as a sequence of chapters, extended in length, etc. So, to be more precise, we need to separate out five different elements here: content, form, genre, medium, format. 'Content' is symbolic content – that is, content that expresses and conveys meaning. Content, understood in this broad way, can assume many different forms: meaning can be expressed and conveyed in words, images, sounds, etc. 'Form' is the way that content is organized and framed.[29] The book is a form for organizing textual content, just as the movie is a form for organizing audio-visual content and the song is a form for organizing musical content – that is, a way of structuring content in accordance with certain shared conventions and cultural norms. While the book is a form in this sense, there are numerous sub-variants of this form that have their own specific conventions – the novel, the thriller, the biography, the scholarly monograph, etc. These sub-variants are what we could call genres, and every genre has its own conventions. Authors write, publishers publish and readers read knowing what these conventions are: they all work with more or less the same set of conventions and background assumptions about what a book is and how it is organized, and they know (or have some inkling of) how these conventions and assumptions vary from one genre to another. The form and its sub-variants, the genres, are what enable creators to create in ways that will be readily understood by others. As recipients of the symbolic content, we know what we're getting: it's a book, it's a movie, it's a song. And we know the sub-variants too: it's a thriller, it's a romance, it's a biography. Forms and genres are the structures on which symbolic content is hung.

Symbolic content is structured by forms and genres but it still has to be stored and conveyed from A to B, and that's where the medium comes in: the medium is the mode of storage and conveyance or transmission. The medium can be a physical object. The print-on-paper book is a medium in this sense: it is a physical container for the particular form of symbolic content that we call a book. But the book can be conveyed by other media too. That was the first great lesson of the digital revolution in publishing: the print-on-paper book is just one medium in which the symbolic content of the book can

---

[29] See Michael Bhaskar, *The Content Machine: Towards a Theory of Publishing from the Printing Press to the Digital Network* (London: Anthem Press, 2013). Bhaskar helpfully conceptualizes publishing as the filtering, framing and amplifying of content. But his notion of frame is too broad in my view and mixes together elements that are very different, elements that I separate out by distinguishing between form, genre, medium and format.

be embedded and transmitted, but it can be conveyed by other media too. If the content of the book is codified digitally, as a sequence of 0s and 1s, then it can be conveyed as a digital file rather than as a physical book. The digital medium is not just the file, of course: a file has to be transmitted, which requires networks, and a file has to be decoded and displayed on a screen, which requires both hardware and software. The digital medium is no less complicated than the medium of print, and in some ways it is more complex. It presupposes and requires a complex technical and organizational infrastructure that enables digital files to be created, stored, transmitted, decoded and displayed in an appropriate form for end users.

The format is separate from the medium but dependent on it. The format is best understood as a way of packaging or presenting content. Take the medium of print: a book can be published and conveyed as a print-on-paper book in a multiplicity of different formats: as a trade hardback, as a trade paperback, as a mass-market paperback – all are different formats of a book published in the medium of print, that is, different ways of packaging or presenting the printed book. In all of these formats, the content is essentially the same; what changes is the mode of presentation and the packaging, and also the way in which that content is commoditized by the publisher. Similarly, in the digital medium, a book could be conveyed in different formats – as an ebook, an enhanced ebook, an app, etc. Moreover, by using different file formats (PDF, ePub, etc.), an ebook published in the digital medium can be given different properties (such as static pages or reflowable text) and priced differently.

The creation and curation of content is at the heart of publishing, but content is shaped by the form: book publishers, and the authors whose work they publish, are creating and curating content that is in the form of the book, which means that it is shaped by certain conventions and assumptions about what a book is, and about what this particular kind of book is – a novel, a thriller, a biography, a work of history, etc. But the content is also shaped by the medium: a book that is published as a print-on-paper book has to comply with certain conditions and constraints, although these conditions are malleable and they change over time. The most obvious constraint is length: length adds cost in the medium of print, so there is a strong incentive to keep books to an optimal length of around 300 pages. That works well with the various formats of the printed book. But, of course, this is flexible and printed books come in many shapes and sizes. In the digital medium, length is no longer a constraint – books could be much shorter or much longer. A book could go on for thousands of pages and millions of words, and it need not have any pages at all. Indeed, in the digital medium, the very form of the book itself could be changed, radically re-invented for the digital age, at least in principle. But, as we saw in chapter 2, this possibility, despite much clever and creative experimentation, has not – or, at least, not yet – come to pass. In the terminology I'm using here, the ebook is best understood as another format of the book, comparable to the trade paperback or the mass-market paperback in the medium of print. Publishing in the digital medium has not yet altered the form of the book in any significant way.

The creation and curation of content in the form of the book is the core function of publishers, but it is not their only function. Publishers are also financial investors and risk-takers: the publisher is the banker who makes available the financial resources to create and publish a book.[30] This economic dimension is essential because creating, producing and disseminating content is not costless, it takes time and uses up materials, and someone at some point has to foot the bill. Of course, in the medium of print, the costs are typically higher because printers have to be paid and physical copies have to be manufactured, stored and physically transported. But even in the digital medium, there are costs – the costs of creating the first copy, which include the time and creative work of the author, the cost of editorial work and the cost of design, as well as the costs of distribution and marketing. In the traditional publishing model, the publisher is the investor and risk-taker who makes available the money to make this process happen. If the book does well, then the publisher will reap the rewards, but if the book fails, then it is the publisher who will be out of pocket. In the book publishing chain, the publisher is the creditor of last resort.

The third key function of the publisher is production and design. This is often overlooked or treated as inessential because so many aspects of book production and design are outsourced by publishers: copyediting, typesetting, cover design and printing are all commonly outsourced to freelancers and printers. But managing and coordinating all of this takes time and requires specialist knowledge. Even if this work is outsourced, freelancers need to be given instructions, their terms of work have to be agreed and they must be paid, and all

---

[30] In my view, this function is underplayed in Bhaskar's otherwise excellent account of the nature of publishing. It is not absent from his account, but it features only in the form of the 'models' that shape the filtering, framing and amplifying process, rather than as a key function of publishing in its own right.

of this requires management time and expertise. Similarly, decisions must be taken about prices and print runs, which are critical to the financial viability of a publisher, and stock must be managed throughout the life-cycle of the book. Even if a book exists only as a digital file, that file needs to be produced in a certain way and inserted into appropriate distribution channels in appropriate formats, which again requires a degree of specialist knowledge and expertise. Some of these processes can be automated to some extent, but creating and maintaining the systems to make this possible require time, cost and expertise.

The fourth key function is what I've loosely called publicity and dissemination. In this function I am bundling together a range of activities that bear on the most basic sense of the verb 'to publish': to publish is to make public, to make known to others. It is not enough to create and curate content, invest in it and produce a book: a book is not published if no one other than the creator knows about it. A book can be written without being published: it can remain on a writer's desk or computer hard drive, an unpublished manuscript that never sees the light of day. A book can also be produced without being published: if it remains as a file on a publisher's hard drive or a stack of books in a warehouse, it is not published. It becomes published only when it is *made available* to the public – that is, to a broader collectivity of people – and *made known* to others. That is why the range of activities relating to publicity, marketing, dissemination and sales are not added extras but essential to the process of publishing: publishing does not exist without them. But they are also among the most difficult and challenging tasks that publishers face, especially in the age of the internet when the subtle but crucial distinction between 'making available to the public' and 'making known to the public' becomes more important than ever. To publish in the sense of making a book available to the public is easier today than it ever was: when you make available a text online, posting it on a website or self-publishing it as an ebook, you are publishing it in the sense that you are making it *available to the public*. But to publish in the sense of making a book *known to the public*, visible to them and attracting a sufficient quantum of their attention to encourage them to buy the book and perhaps even to read it, is an altogether different matter – it is extremely difficult to do, and never more so than today, when the sheer volume of content available to consumers and readers is enough to drown out the most determined and well-resourced marketing campaign. Good publishers are market-makers in a world where attention, not content, is scarce.

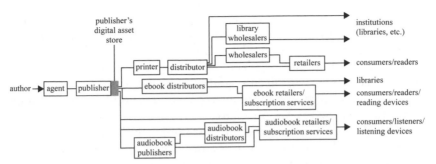

Figure 12.5   Book supply chain for mainstream publishers

In carrying out these various functions, the publisher is only one player, albeit an important player, in a book supply chain that has been rendered increasingly ramified and complex by the digital revolution. In the 1980s and before, this supply chain was relatively straightforward because there was only one basic output: the print-on-paper book, albeit in several different formats. But, with the digital revolution, the rise of the digital workflow and the freeing of content from the medium of print, the print-on-paper book is now only one of numerous different outputs in different media that emerge from the digital workflows of most publishing houses. Figure 12.5 provides a simple visual representation of the book supply chain as it exists today for many mainstream trade publishers. The author creates the content and supplies it to the publisher; in trade publishing, this process is often mediated by the agent, who acts as a filter that selects material and directs it to appropriate publishers. The publisher buys a bundle of rights from the author or agent and then carries out a range of functions – editorial development, copyediting, design, etc. – to generate a set of files in appropriate formats that can be lodged in the publisher's digital asset store or archive. The print-ready file is then delivered to the printer, who prints and binds the books and delivers them to the distributor, which may be owned by the publisher or may be a third party. The distributor warehouses the stock and fulfils orders from both retailers and wholesalers, who in turn sell books to or fulfil orders from others – individual consumers in the case of retailers, and retailers and other institutions (such as libraries) in the case of wholesalers. In the traditional book supply chain, the publisher's customers are not individual consumers or readers but, rather, intermediary institutions in the supply chain – namely, the wholesalers and retailers; it is the retailers (or libraries) who deal directly with readers, and these organizations are, for most readers, their only point of contact with the book supply chain. Parallel to this process, and usually simultaneous with it, the publisher will supply ebook files in appropriate ebook file formats to ebook distributors and retailers. They may also produce their own audiobook edition, or license audiobook rights to an audiobook publisher, and supply audiobooks to consumers and listeners through a separate audiobook supply chain.

While this remains the predominant book supply chain and would be recognized by mainstream trade publishers as an accurate representation of their world, the digital revolution has spawned many developments which have given rise to new supply chains that differ from this in significant ways. The self-publishing book supply chain is quite different from this because, in the self-publishing model, authors are no longer dealing with traditional publishers (or agents) but are self-publishing their own books by uploading them directly to a self-publishing platform – figure 12.6. The gatekeeping role of the traditional publisher is largely bypassed: self-publishing platforms are much less selective than traditional publishers and most have an open-door policy, though there are limits on what is permissible here too. A degree of selectivity continues to operate, but it is much less restrictive than the selectivity characteristic of traditional publishers. Many of the other functions of the publisher, such as editing, design and publicity/marketing, have not disappeared in this model, but they have been re-assigned: now it is the responsibility of the author to carry out these functions and, as we've seen, a hidden economy of services has emerged to meet the growing demand, now paid for by the author rather than the publisher. The author can carry out some or all of these functions herself or can contract with freelancers to carry out these functions, and, in the latter case, she can track down freelancers and contract with them directly or use a publishing services intermediary (PSI) to facilitate this process. The alternative is for the author to re-assign these activities, or some subset of these

Figure 12.6   Self-publishing book supply chain

functions, to the self-publishing platform for a fee – again, paid for by the author. In the self-publishing model, the role of financial investment and risk-taking has not disappeared but it has been taken on by the author, in return for which she gains much more control over the publishing process – starting, crucially, with the decision to publish – and stands to earn a much higher share of the revenue from any sales. Unlike the old vanity presses, however, the author is not expected to pay the self-publishing platform for the privilege of being published: with some platforms they can choose to purchase discrete services but this is optional, not a condition of access to the platform. In the self-publishing model, the traditional publisher has been disintermediated, but the functions carried out by publishers have not disappeared: for the most part they have been re-assigned, taken over by the author as self-publisher or outsourced to freelancers, bespoke services or self-publishing platforms (or, in some cases, they have largely been done without).

In the case of crowdfunded publishing, the supply chain is different again, and in an important way. The real innovation of crowd-funded publishing is that consumers/readers play a crucial role in the selection process and they also provide the financial capital to fund the production of the book – this is represented by the feedback loop in figure 12.7. In this model, the selection function of the publisher is based directly on the expressed preferences of consumers and readers, who decide whether to back a project by pledging money to it, and only when a project reaches a critical threshold of funding does the book go ahead. How the book is then produced depends on which version of crowdfunding is being used. If it is the Kickstarter or Indiegogo version, then the author will need to find a publisher who is willing to publish the book with the funding and readership

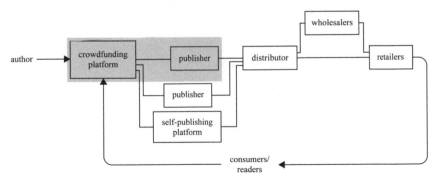

Figure 12.7   Book supply chain for crowdfunded publishing

provided by the crowdfunding campaign, or use the funds to self-publish the book through a self-publishing platform. If, however, the author is using a crowdfunding organization that is dedicated to book publishing, like Inkshare or Unbound, then the book project, once it has reached its funding threshold, simply passes from the crowdfunding operation to the publishing wing of the same organization. But the critical innovation in this model is that the consumers or readers are actively involved in the selection and funding process: it is their willingness – or otherwise – to support the project with firm pledges of cash that determines whether a project goes ahead and a book is produced. Pledging money is a creative act in its own right: without it, the book would not come into being. In this respect, those who pledge money are more than influencers: they are co-producers whose acts of pledging help to create the book. This doesn't mean that the crowdfunding platform and publisher have no role in the selection process – they do. A crowdfunding platform will have its own rules and guidelines about the kinds of projects it will allow on its site, and it may actively seek out certain kinds of projects, including certain kinds of book projects, and work with creators to help them shape their project and plan and execute their fundraising campaign. A platform like Unbound plays a particularly pronounced curatorial role, actively selecting the projects that are allowed to proceed to the crowdfunding stage and working closely with authors to increase the chances of success. Moreover, if an author who has raised funding on Kickstarter or Indiegogo wants to publish the book with a mainstream publisher, then he will have to submit to the publisher's selection process – though in this case the acceptance threshold may be lower, given that the author is bringing crowd-funded resources to the table. With the financial resources provided by crowdfunding, the publisher's risk is much lower than it would otherwise be, since a certain number of readers, who are also firm buyers, are guaranteed.

A somewhat similar feedback loop is an integral part of the supply chain developed by Wattpad. In this case, a book publishing operation has been spun out of a social media platform designed for the writing and reading of stories – here, there is not just one feedback loop but two (figure 12.8). On the one hand, authors and readers are directly linked by the social media characteristics of the Wattpad platform: readers are following authors and reading and commenting on their stories as they are being written, and authors can take account of these comments as they work on the next chapter (feedback loop 1). On the other hand, the popularity of stories on

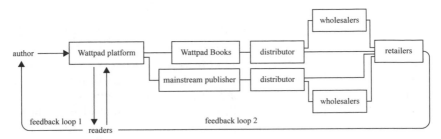

Figure 12.8   Book supply for Wattpad Books

the Wattpad platform is used as a guide to decide which stories could be turned into books – or, indeed, into other cultural products, such as movies and TV shows. Moreover, the ways that readers respond to stories on the Wattpad platform – which aspects they like and don't like, the comments they make, etc. – are fed into the content development process, so that the creative and editorial aspects of book production (or movie/TV production) are shaped by input from readers. As with the crowdfunding model, this reduces the publisher's risk (or the movie/TV studio's risk) because they have firm evidence that the content is positively valued by a large number of readers/consumers who would be a potential market for the book (or movie/TV show). Unlike the crowdfunding model, the publisher still has to make available financial resources and invest in the production, but the risk of failure is significantly reduced and the existence of a large pre-established following on Wattpad gives the publisher a serious head start when it comes to market-making. Some of the books emerging from the Wattpad platform are published by Wattpad's own publishing division, Wattpad Books, while others are routed through mainstream publishers like Simon & Schuster, in some cases as a straight licensing agreement and in other cases as a co-production. The original readers of the stories on the Wattpad platform provide a substantial pre-existing market for the books emerging from this development process (feedback loop 2), though the books are also marketed and sold to a much wider readership.

With the new opportunities opened up by the digital revolution, we see a proliferation of new book supply chains – or 'circuits of communication' to use Robert Darnton's apt term.[31] The book

[31] Robert Darnton, 'What Is the History of Books?' *Daedalus* (summer 1982), reprinted in his *The Case for Books: Past, Present, and Future* (New York: PublicAffairs, 2009), pp. 175–206.

publishing ecosystem is now more complex than ever and no single model of communication flows could adequately capture the multiplicity of systems that are now in play – and here I have highlighted only a few. But one thing that the new models bring out very clearly is that the digital revolution has made possible something that was never really part of the traditional book supply chain – namely, a closer and more direct relationship between authors and publishers, on the one hand, and readers and consumers, on the other.[32] For the digital revolution has not simply spawned new initiatives within particular fields like publishing: rather, it has changed the very nature of the information environment within which publishing, along with all the other media and creative industries, exists. Not only does this present traditional publishers with a plethora of new challenges and competitors, it presents them with some new opportunities too.

Taking readers seriously

Throughout the 500-year history of book publishing, publishers have, for the most part, regarded intermediaries like retailers as their main customers: publishers sold their books to retailers or wholesalers, and they left it to retailers to sell the books to readers. They relied on booksellers to display their books to the ultimate consumers, the readers, and to drive demand. This meant that publishers had little or no direct contact with readers: they were primarily B2B rather than B2C businesses, to use the jargon of business studies. It also meant that they knew very little about readers and their purchasing and reading practices: what they knew was gained indirectly, anecdotally or second-hand, by talking with the buyers who worked for retailers, monitoring their sales figures, reading reviews, talking with readers

---

[32] In Darnton's original model of the traditional book supply chain, there is a loose feedback loop between readers and authors, indicated by a dotted line in his original figure (p. 182 of *The Case for Books*), on the grounds that the reader 'influences the author both before and after the act of composition', and 'Authors are readers themselves. By reading and associating with other readers and writers, they form notions of genre and style and a general sense of the literary enterprise, which affects their texts' (p. 180). But this is a very weak and diffuse feedback loop, best understood in terms of the notions of form and genre that I developed above – that is, the set of conventions and background assumptions that are shared by writers and readers in particular social and historical contexts, coupled with the fact that some authors may have some concept of the audience for which they are writing, though even when they do, this is usually a very diffuse and quite general concept and it may bear little relation to the preferences and practices of actual readers.

they might encounter fortuitously and extrapolating from their own experience as readers – all very indirect and haphazard. Not that retailers knew that much either: sure, they had more opportunities to encounter book buyers and readers in the course of their working day as customers came into the bookstore, but for the most part this was pretty random and dependent on customer inquiries. Of course, it was the bookseller's job to try to anticipate which books their customers would be interested in and to purchase accordingly, and they were in a position to see – literally – which books were selling and which were languishing on the tables and shelves. Some retailers also maintained accounts with some of their customers and held some information about them – their address, maybe their credit card information, etc. Some put together lists of titles and other forms of marketing and sent them directly to their customers. So retailers were in a position to know more about readers and their buying practices than publishers were, and some retailers did gather and hold some information about some of their customers and market directly to them. But, in reality, none of the players in the traditional book supply chain knew that much about readers and their browsing, buying and reading practices. In a pre-digital world, it wasn't easy to know these kinds of things, wasn't easy to gather this information systematically, and wasn't easy to communicate with your customers. With the digital revolution, all of this would change.

Once customers began browsing and buying books and other goods online, their activities left digital traces that could be gathered systematically, potentially providing the retailer with a comprehensive record of their browsing and purchasing activities. Every click on the retailer's platform, whether it was an actual purchase or simply a page view, could be tracked, recorded and preserved, giving the retailer a comprehensive picture, stretching back in time, of the online behaviour of every customer. Moreover, since the retailer also has personal details of all of its customers, such as names, email addresses, postal addresses, post codes and credit card numbers, they know a great deal about their customers and are able to communicate directly and easily with them. And this communication could be personalized. No need now to send out a standardized catalogue of titles to all their customers by post: each email could be customized to align with the track record of each individual customer. By using algorithms and machine learning, all of this could be automated, so that each customer could receive customized recommendations based on her previous browsing and buying activity, targeted to reflect the retailer's prediction of what that customer might be interested in

463

buying. The retailer can also customize each customer's home page so that when the customer comes to the site, he sees a personalized display of books and other goods that reflect the retailer's prediction of his interests. And the retailer can also use the same knowledge and mechanisms to sell advertising to publishers and other suppliers. This is how the behavioural futures market in books works. And in the late 1990s and early 2000s, there was one retailer, Amazon, that cornered the market. Now, thanks to the digital revolution, there really was a retailer who knew more – immeasurably more – about the browsing and purchasing behaviour of readers than any publisher knew, or would ever know. The publishing game had changed and most of the cards were now in the hands of one retailer who, thanks to its virtual monopoly of information capital concerning readers, was in a dominant position in the field.

As the 2000s gave way to the 2010s, it became increasingly clear to many publishers that the field was evolving in a way that could make life increasingly difficult for them. The bankruptcy of Borders in 2011 brought into sharp relief the precarious position of bricks-and-mortar booksellers: publishers were becoming increasingly dependent on an online retailer, Amazon, which was rapidly gaining market share and who knew much more about the readers of their books than publishers could ever possibly know. Readers, knowledge of whom could be transformed into information capital, were the chips in a new publishing game, and the chips were stacking up overwhelmingly on Amazon's side. But was that necessarily so? That's the question that began to preoccupy some senior managers in mainstream publishing houses from around 2010 on. Maybe the time had come for publishers to think again about their traditional self-understanding as a B2B business and see if they could do something that publishers had never done before: build direct channels of communication with readers.

Thanks to the digital revolution, this was now possible in a way that it had never been before. Not only had the digital revolution digitized publishers' content, digitized their workflow and created new digital channels for content delivery: it was also transforming the broader information environment within which publishing, like other media and creative industries, was operating. More and more people were migrating to the online environment, which meant that new opportunities for interaction and communication were emerging that didn't require physical co-presence in a bookstore, and if Amazon could tap into these new forms of interaction and communication, why couldn't publishers do this too? They could open up new channels of communication directly with the individuals who read and were interested in their books, build up their own databases of knowledge about them, get to know what their interests are and what kinds of books might appeal to them, and reach out to them directly to inform them about the new books they were publishing. Publishers didn't have to rely on Amazon to do this for them, often paying for the privilege in the form of advertising fees: publishers could communicate with their readers directly. They didn't have to sell books to their readers; they could direct readers to an existing retail channel, to Amazon or Barnes & Noble or Waterstones or independent booksellers, and let the retailer complete the sale – though if they were able to sell direct, they could eliminate the retailer's discount, make themselves less dependent on third-party intermediaries and possibly improve their margin as well (depending on their fulfilment arrangements). But selling direct and bypassing the retailer was not the essential point. The essential point was that publishers could now be in direct communication with the readers of their books in ways and on a scale that was simply not possible before.

In the past, when publishers looked beyond themselves, they tended to focus their attention on authors and retailers, on creators and clients. Publishers were service providers who were linking the creators of content (authors) with the consumers of content (readers) via the intermediaries of the book supply chain (retailers and whole-salers). They focused on authors (and agents) because they needed to discover and nurture creative talent and hold on to it, as this was the source of the content they needed in order to have a business at all; and they focused on retailers (and wholesalers) because these were their immediate customers, to whom they outsourced the task of making books available to the public and selling them to individual consumers. Readers, the ultimate customers, were further down the book supply chain and beyond publishers' reach (and, for the most part, beyond their range of interest too). This model worked well provided that there was a multiplicity of retailers and a large number of bookstores that offered a diverse array of physical spaces for the display and discovery of books. But with the decline of physical retail space and the migration of more and more sales to the platform of one online retailer that is amassing customer data on an unprec-edented scale, the old model that had prevailed in the publishing world for so long seems increasingly out of step with the new world in which we are now living. Of course, publishers still need to focus on authors and still need to maintain good relations with their clients in the book supply chain, the retailers and wholesalers, but now they need to reach beyond the retailers and build direct relationships with the ultimate consumers of their books, the readers. An organization facing in two directions, towards authors and retailers, now needs to face in a third direction – towards readers too. In short, publishers need to take readers seriously. And, thanks to the digital revolution, it is now possible for them to do this in a way that was simply not feasible before. Now it is possible for publishers to become reader-centric, not just author-centric and bookseller-centric – to enter into communication with readers and learn about them as well as market to them, and to do this at scale. This, in the eyes of some publishers, was the true significance of the digital revolution. The CEO of one of the large trade houses put it like this:

> The essence of the digital transformation is that we have to become much more reader-centric. We have to become much more consumer focused as publishers because we've always been very B2B oriented, we've always served our booksellers and tried to display our books in the most prominent way in bookstores, and the bookseller had the task to drive demand. And then early on in the digital transformation, we lost 800 stores overnight when Borders went bust, and we all knew at that point that we have to become more reader-centric, that there had to be a mind-set shift in publishing houses from being mainly B2B, bookseller-oriented, to become more B2C, reader-centric – that's the essence of the digital transformation.

This was a radical shift of focus, both demanded and enabled by the digital revolution, and it could be pursued in a variety of ways.

At the most basic level, publishers could seek to build a database of email addresses of readers and potential readers, together with information about their interests, tastes and preferences, and use this as a resource to market directly to consumers. The great advantage of doing this is that now, thanks to email and the internet, publishers can develop a cost-effective way of reaching out directly to readers who may be interested in the books they're publishing. They don't have to rely on generic, costly and poorly targeted ads in traditional media like newspapers and magazines, they don't have to rely on Amazon to decide whether it was going to recommend their books to its customers, and they don't have to rely on internet advertising bought from Amazon, Google, Facebook and other platforms; they can do all or some of these things, of course, but they can also take more control of their own digital marketing by opening up a direct channel of communication with readers. They can do for themselves what Amazon has done so effectively before them: gather data on their ultimate customers, the readers, and use this data to market directly to them, without having to rely on a powerful intermediary whose interests and aims may not align fully with their own. In other words, they can amass a little information capital of their own. But, unlike the tech companies, publishers are not – or should not be – in the business of trading this data in behavioural futures markets: they are not building databases of customer information in order to sell advertising to third parties, they are building databases of information on their readers in order to be able to interact with them, learn about them and inform them about new books they are publishing which might be of interest to them. This can be highly targeted marketing because it can be based on what a publisher knows about a set of readers who have expressed an interest in the kinds of books that are being published by them. The readers have demonstrated their interest and openness to communication from the publisher by virtue of the fact that they have subscribed to the publisher's newsletter or provided their email address, and they are free to unsubscribe at any time.

While the building of an email database can be an effective marketing tool for publishers, it's not easy to do. Readers have to be induced to sign up to a newsletter or give their email address and other details to a publisher so that the publisher can communicate directly with them. Publishers don't have the great advantage that Amazon has, which is that readers and other consumers have an incentive to provide personal details to Amazon in order to purchase books and other things from the enormous range of goods available on the Amazon platform. So publishers have to resort to other means to try to persuade readers to join their lists. Offering incentives of various kinds – for example, entering them in a sweepstakes, or offering free books or a substantial discount on their next order if the publisher is set up to sell direct – is one way to encourage readers to sign up. But, even with incentives, it is a long and arduous process, especially in territories (like the EU) where companies have to comply with strict legal conditions concerning personal data held in databases. It may seem hardly worth the effort if you end up with only a few thousand email addresses. But what if you're able to gather 100,000 email addresses of individuals who are interested in the kinds of books you publish and willing to hear from you? What if you gather a million, or even 10 million, and are able to communicate directly with them about your new and forthcoming books, as well as relevant backlist titles? Then you have what is potentially a very powerful way of reaching out in a highly targeted fashion, and at virtually no cost, to a large number of individuals who are active book readers and whose tastes, interests and preferences are known to you.

While building a database of readers is an important step, it is only one way of shifting the focus to readers. The real challenge for publishers is to figure out whether becoming more reader-centric can mean something more than building a database of customers' email addresses and becoming better at direct marketing to them – and, if so, what exactly it does mean. For example, it could mean building readers' interests and preferences more directly into your own commissioning and publishing processes. Some of the start-ups on the margins of the publishing field have been particularly creative and forward-thinking in developing novel ways of taking account of readers' feedback. The crowdfunding models systematically build readers' responses into the decision-making process, as a decision to go ahead with a book depends on the extent to which individuals are willing to back the project with firm commitments of financial support. This turns the traditional publishing model on its head: it is no longer 'publish the book and then try to find a market for it' but, rather, 'try to find a market for the book and then decide whether to publish it.' It's a terrific model that takes account of readers' preferences and greatly reduces publishers' risk, though it's time-consuming and administratively complex and it would be difficult to scale up to a large publishing operation releasing thousands of new books a year. Wattpad's social media model incorporates readers' feedback in other ways, both by enabling writers to take account of readers' comments as they are writing a story and by using data on the number of readers and the nature of their comments to inform decisions about which stories should be turned into books and/or movies and to guide the development process. Given that Wattpad is already operating at scale as a social media platform with more than 80 million users worldwide and more than 565 million story uploads, the potential for scaling up its publishing operation is considerable. The question here is whether this model would be generalizable beyond the specific genres – predominantly teen fiction – in which Wattpad has developed a particularly strong following. This feedback model presupposes a pre-existing community of users who have chosen to join Wattpad's social media platform and whose actions on that platform – the stories they are following, the comments they are making, etc. – form the raw data for the feedback processes. The kinds of stories that feature prominently on Wattpad – teen fiction, teen romance, fanfiction, etc. – are the kinds of stories that have attracted a large international following of young people, especially teenage girls, and it's not clear that other types of fiction, let alone nonfiction, would attract a following of sufficient scale to generate the kind of user data that Wattpad are harvesting on their platform.

While the kinds of feedback processes developed by crowdfunding models and by Wattpad's social media platform may be hard for mainstream publishers to replicate directly, there are other things they can do to open up channels of communication with readers. If publishers have begun to build an email database, they can use this not simply to inform readers about new books that might be of interest to them but also to open up a conversation with them that treats readers not just as consumers of books but as partners in dialogue. For online communication is potentially interactive, two-way, multi-way communication: readers are potential participants in a dialogical interaction, not just the potential recipients of a targeted marketing message. To treat readers as potential participants in an interaction means that publishers need to learn how to listen to them, actively solicit their views and develop new ways of responding to them. Publishers need to ask themselves not simply how they can market more effectively to readers, but how they can listen to them too, learn more about what readers would like to see from publishers and what would be of interest to them. And they need to think through the ways in which they can use the new communication channels opened up by digital technologies – email, social media and more – to facilitate interaction between the authors they publish and the readers who want to read these authors' work. For publishers were only ever intermediaries in a process of cultural exchange, creating pathways between writers and readers that enabled books to become part of a broader cultural dialogue. Readers are interested in what authors have to say – in their stories of worlds actual and imagined, in their accounts of how things have come to be and how they could be different and so on; they are not really interested in publishers *per se* (or retailers for that matter). So the fundamental question facing publishers today is: how can publishers facilitate and participate effectively in a cultural dialogue that is now taking place in multiple milieux – both online and offline, but increasingly online – and how can they ensure that books continue to have some place in the changing information environment of the twenty-first century?

Books in the digital age

There are some who may feel that this is a lost cause. They may feel that the book as a cultural form is fundamentally out of sync with our increasingly online, screen-based digital culture and the bright, noisy, constantly changing world of the internet, a world that tends to draw people out of the depths of immersive reading and into the shallows of distraction, to use Nicolas Carr's evocative phrase.[33] Maybe we are becoming increasingly incapable of the kind of sustained concentration required for long-form reading and less drawn to it – might that be so?

Perhaps. It's true that today, many people spend much more time consuming audio-visual content on screens of various kinds – from TV to computer screens to mobile devices – than they spend reading books. A recent survey in the US found that Americans spent on average 2.8 hours a day watching TV and 47 minutes a day playing computer games and using the computer for leisure, compared to only 26 minutes a day reading – in other words, they spend on average more than 8 times the amount of time watching TV and using the computer than they spend reading.[34] On the other hand, the proportion of Americans who say that they've read at least one book in the last year has remained largely unchanged in recent years, and print books remain substantially more popular than either ebooks or audiobooks.[35] Books, and especially print books, seem to have a more entrenched presence in our increasingly screen-based digital world than many people thought, even if the average time spent reading books is much less than the time spent watching TV and engaging in other screen-based activities. How can we explain the stubborn persistence of the book?

No doubt there are many answers to this question, as people read and value books for many different reasons. But might it be that books, especially print books, are valued today by many people in part precisely because they are different from a screen-based digital culture? The more that people's lives become bound up with a screen-based culture, the more value they might ascribe to those

---

[33] Nicholas Carr, *The Shallows: How the Internet Is Changing the Way We Think, Read and Remember* (New York: W. W. Norton, 2010).
[34] See 'American Time Use Survey – 2018 Results', released 19 June 2019, Bureau of Labor Statistics, at www.bls.gov/news.release/atus.nr0.htm.
[35] Andrew Perrin, 'Book Reading 2016', Pew Research Center (1 September 2016), at www.pewinternet.org/2016/09/01/book-reading-2016.

forms of activity that are not fully absorbed within it. A recent study carried out in Germany found that one of the main reasons why people enjoyed reading books was that they feel overwhelmed by the constant pressures of everyday life and the constant demand to multi-task with digital devices: reading books provides them with the opportunity to withdraw from these pressures and demands and to immerse themselves in another world for a while. 'I feel that the world is becoming more and more hectic', said one reader, 'and you just need an island where you can take it easy.'[36] For some people, reading books provides them with an opportunity to step back from screen life and extricate themselves temporarily from a world which has come to absorb more and more of their daily lives, a world in which their attention is constantly being pulled in different directions, with the ceaseless ping of emails and messages all clamouring for a quick response. It allows them to step away from the shallows and immerse themselves in another world that has more depth.

This may be about more than the desire to disconnect and to take a break from the pressures of everyday life: it may also be about seeking to reassert some control over time. The feeling that we are living in a world that is constantly speeding up, an 'acceleration society' as Hartmut Rosa has called it,[37] is a widespread sentiment in contemporary Western societies: many people feel rushed, harried, pressed for time more than ever before.[38] This is not due solely to the development of new technologies: other factors are important here, such as changing patterns of work, and new technologies by themselves do not necessarily lead to a speeding up of daily life. But when the deployment of new technologies is accompanied by significant increases in what is expected (in terms of goods produced, activities to be completed, number of communications to be sent, etc.), then individuals tend to experience a heightening of the pace of life and a growing scarcity of time.[39] Rather than freeing up time for leisure and other activities (the great unfulfilled promise of technological

[36] 'Buchkäufer – quo vadis?', Börsenverein des Deutschen Buchhandels (June 2018), p. 66.
[37] See Hartmut Rosa, *Social Acceleration: A New Theory of Modernity*, tr. Jonathan Trejo-Mathys (New York: Columbia University Press, 2013).
[38] See Judy Wajcman, *Pressed for Time: The Acceleration of Life in Digital Capitalism* (University of Chicago Press, 2015). According to one study, the proportion of Americans saying that they always feel rushed rose from 25 per cent in 1965 to 35 per cent forty years later, and just under half now say that they almost never have time on their hands (Wajcman, p. 64).
[39] Rosa, *Social Acceleration*, pp. 65–70.

innovation), the deployment of new technologies can lead instead to an intensification of work and higher levels of stress as individuals find themselves trying to do more things in the same – or less – time. Time-saving technologies morph into time-consuming technologies, absorbing more rather than less time and leaving people with the feeling that they have less and less time for themselves. This is part of what is fuelling the growing calls and movements for a slowing down of life, from slow food to slow fashion, slow travel to slow media.[40]

Viewed in this context, books and the activity of reading might take on a new significance. In a world where many people feel that their lives are speeding up, that they have less and less time for themselves, reading books can become a way of breaking out of the cycle of acceleration and reasserting some control over time. For most people, reading a book is not a fast activity; you have to set aside time to immerse yourself in a text and stick with it for many hours – in all likelihood, many days. To choose to read a book is to make a substantial time commitment; it is deciding to invest a significant amount of time in a particular activity that will require sustained concentration and attention. It is to choose to engage in an activity that by its very nature is time-consuming, and that cannot be speeded up in any significant way. Reading books has a different tempo from many of the activities that absorb people's time and attention in their everyday lives and, rather than being a drawback, that may be part of its appeal: it is a way of clawing back some time for oneself in a world where time seems increasingly scarce, a mundane circuit-breaker in an accelerating world. Reading books is not so much a matter of slowing down, but rather of readjusting, of finding a different kind of balance in the flow of everyday life – one that is less rushed, less harried, less tied to the demands of a world experienced as constantly speeding up. It is not withdrawing or escaping from the world into an 'oasis of deceleration' where time stands still, but rather a matter of establishing a different way of being in the world, of recalibrating one's relationship to the world so that it feels less fraught, less strained – the kind of relationship that could perhaps be characterized by what Rosa calls 'resonance': a way of being in the world in which the individual feels in tune with the world rather

---

[40] See Carlo Petrini, *Slow Food Nation: Why Our Food Should Be Good, Clean, Fair* (New York: Rizzoli, 2007); Carl Honoré, *In Praise of Slow: How a Worldwide Movement is Challenging the Cult of Speed* (New York: Harper Books, 2005); Wendy Perkins and Geoffrey Craig, *Slow Living* (Oxford: Berg, 2006); Jennifer Rauch, *Slow Media: Why 'Slow' Is Satisfying, Sustainable, and Smart* (New York: Oxford University Press, 2018).

than harassed, propelled or overwhelmed by it.[41] Of course, reading books is not the only way in which individuals look for and find a more satisfying way of being in the world – there are many other ways, from listening to music or walking in the countryside to just relaxing at home with family and friends. But by enabling individuals to recalibrate their way of being in the world, reading books may turn out to have a place in the cultural mix of contemporary societies that is more enduring than was assumed by those who predicted (or feared) that screen culture would sweep away all before it.

To say this is not to claim that we are entering a 'post-digital age' in which digital culture will be eclipsed by the return of the analogue – far from it. Ours is thoroughly and irreversibly a digital age, and there is no sector of the media and creative industries, including publishing, that has not been and will not be profoundly transformed by the digital revolution. But that is not to say that all cultural goods will be turned into digital products, nor is it to say that individuals will choose to consume all cultural goods as digital artefacts or to engage only in cultural activities that are screen-based – that was never likely to be so, and only an impoverished imagination in hock to the charms of the digital would have projected that unlikely scenario upon us. Technologies don't necessarily succeed one another sequentially but sometimes co-exist, in the way that radio continues to occupy a place in many peoples' lives despite the greater audio-visual richness of TV. And so, too, print-on-paper books may well continue to co-exist with ebooks and audiobooks and whatever new medium may emerge for books in the future – not despite the fact that we live in an increasingly digital age, but because of it.

---

[41] Hartmut Rosa, *Resonance: A Sociology of Our Relationship to the World,* tr. James C. Wagner (Cambridge: Polity, 2019).

CONCLUSION

Worlds in flux

The first two decades of the twenty-first century have been an enormously challenging time for all of the media and creative industries, including book publishing. These industries were uniquely exposed to the transformative impact of the digital revolution precisely because they were dealing with a particular kind of content – symbolic content – that could be digitized, turned into sequences of 0s and 1s, with all of the far-reaching possibilities that this digitization of content opened up. At the dawn of the twenty-first century, there was no shortage of visionaries who saw in this technological shift the beginning of the end of those media and creative industries that had built their businesses on the production and distribution of things, the material artefacts in which symbolic content had been embedded, whether these were vinyl LPs, paper newspapers or print-on-paper books: a new era would be born, one in which symbolic content would be created, disseminated and consumed electronically, via the internet, without the friction and the cost of producing, storing and transmitting physical objects. The cultural goods with which earlier generations were so familiar would become artefacts of a bygone age, collectors' items of largely antiquarian interest, and new generations would look back with bemused curiosity at a world that seemed increasingly far removed from their own world, one where vast quantities of content were available easily, quickly and cheaply, often at the touch of a screen or the click of a mouse, and often for free. Goodbye Gutenberg – it was nice while it lasted, but your time is up.

Like so many stories that are based on the idea that technologies have a transformative power of their own, this vision of the impact of the digital revolution on the media and creative industries was a gross over-simplification of what would be an enormously complex and multi-faceted process. Not only would this process vary greatly from one sector of the media and creative industries to another, it would also turn out to be much more complicated within each particular industry, including the book publishing industry. This is in part because technologies never act on their own: they are always developed, deployed, taken up or ignored in specific social and historical contexts in which there are existing institutions and practices that shape the way they are created and used and real human beings with their interests, aims, desires and tastes who choose to use them or not. Technologies are not some *deus ex machina* that has the power to transform the world in and by itself: they are resources that are developed and deployed by actors seeking to pursue their interests and aims in particular social contexts, actors who are using technologies and seizing the opportunities opened up by them to pursue or develop something that they value or deem worthwhile. Not all such courses of action will succeed – many, indeed most, will fail. Some courses of action will also hurl actors into conflict with others as they pursue opportunities that impinge on others' interests or are perceived by others as threatening. The social reality of technological change in any industry – and especially an old media industry like book publishing – is a messy affair that is inseparably bound up with power and conflict, as the pursuit of new opportunities by some is often at someone else's expense.

While the dramatic surge of ebooks in the first few years following the introduction of the Kindle in 2007 looked to many at the time like this might be the technological innovation that would usher in the post-Gutenberg era, much as MP3 and the iPod had altered the course of the music industry, this too turned out to be an over-simplification of a complex reality and, more importantly, a misunderstanding of what the digital revolution was all about. To be sure, the rise of ebooks in those first few years was as striking as anything the book publishing industry had seen in its long 500-year history: for those who were living through it or observing it at close quarters, there was every reason to think that this could be a turning point. Only it wasn't. For just as quickly as ebooks had taken off, their precipitous rise came to a sudden halt and the many pages of ink that had been written about the end of the book as we've known it were laid bare as the gross over-simplification that they always were. But, beneath the headline figures, a more complex reality was taking shape. The ebook was turning out to be a format that was well attuned to certain kinds of books, especially certain kinds of genre fiction like romance, erotica, sci-fi, fantasy and thrillers. But for many other categories of books, including many types of nonfiction, print was proving to be remarkably resilient – ebooks were selling in these categories too, but in much smaller quantities. There was, in short, a great variation in the extent to which books were migrating from print to digital formats. For publishers who were publishing genre fiction, the strong shift to digital, coupled with the explosion of self-publishing, were major developments that were having a significant impact on these particular areas of publishing. But for publishers who were focused on other areas, especially specialized areas like children's books but also mainstream areas like literary fiction and nonfiction, the rise of ebooks was turning out to be much less consequential. In short, the ebook was not the radical disrupter that many had thought or feared, nor was it a medium in which the very form of the book would be re-invented, as some commentators and entrepreneurs had imagined. In practice, the ebook was turning out to be just another format in which publishers could package books and deliver them to consumers, not dissimilar to the way in which the paperback became another format available to publishers from the 1930s on.

But the impact of the digital revolution on the book publishing industry was never just about ebooks anyway – this was only ever part of the story, and those who thought that ebooks would be the game-changer were mistaken. There was something much more fundamental going on: the digital revolution was rapidly and irrevocably transforming the broader information and communication environment of our societies, changing the ways in which information flowed through the social and political world and the ways in which individuals communicated with one another and consumed symbolic content, and the book publishing industry – like all media and creative industries – would have no alternative but to adapt to this changing environment. Like all great technological revolutions, the digital revolution was much more about the way that social relationships were changing than it was about technologies *per se*. Book publishers found themselves sailing into a brave new world without a compass and without a map, unsure what they would encounter and unable to turn around and return to the familiar world of the past: they had to find their way, experimenting where they could, learning from other industries that had been obliged to go before them, opening themselves up to the new opportunities that arose while at the same time keeping their wits about them, remembering that at any moment things could go disastrously wrong and everything they had built up over decades, or even centuries, could be very quickly lost. For however big a publisher might be in the world of book publishing, they soon discovered that in the brave new world into which they were now unavoidably sailing, they were very small players. This was a world in which the movers and shakers were large tech companies, mainly based on the West coast and capitalized on a scale that made even the largest of the large publishers look Lilliputian. As some of these tech companies began to take a serious interest in what publishers were producing, or to establish a serious presence in the field in which publishers had lived reasonably comfortably for centuries, the possibility of conflict was always present. Not that conflict was the intended outcome – most often it was not. Intentions were often good, even admirable, and publishers benefited in countless ways from the new forms of information processing and e-commerce developed by the tech companies. Amazon had greatly expanded the marketplace for books, making books readily available to readers who had no easy access to bookstores and making the supply chain much more efficient than it had been in the past, and the Kindle was a gift that created a secure environment in which ebooks could be bought and sold legally and consumed on a reader-friendly device. But the interests of publishers and the interests of tech companies were not always aligned with one another, and it was on those occasions when these interests diverged most sharply that the book wars broke out.

What was at stake in these conflicts were different ways of thinking about content and different ways of generating power. For old media industries like book publishing, content was everything: publishers were in the content creation business, they needed a continuous supply of new content, and their viability as businesses depended on their ability to commoditize and exploit that content in a sustainable way. For the tech companies, by contrast, content was the means to another end. They were not (or not primarily) in the content creation business. Their main businesses were elsewhere – they were in the search engine business or the retail business or some other business, and, for them, content was a way of driving or amplifying or improving these other businesses, not an end in itself. Moreover, the tech companies had discovered an important trait of the network economy that they could use to their advantage: they discovered that proprietary user data could be turned into a particular kind of resource, information capital, which, given the right conditions, was extremely valuable and which they could sell to advertisers in behavioural futures markets. The more users you had, the more user data you could generate and the stronger your position would be in the competition for advertising revenue, which was flowing in ever greater volume through the internet. The tech companies wanted content because the more content they had, the more users they could attract and the more user data they could generate. But the value of the content was not important to them – they were not commoditizing content, they were commoditizing user data. They had no interest in keeping the value of the content high. For the tech companies, the cheaper the content, the better, because content was a way of attracting users and the real asset of the tech companies – their most valuable asset and the principal source of their power – was their user data. It was these different economic logics underlying the old media industries like book publishing and the new tech companies like Google and Amazon that played themselves out in the long-running disputes around the Google Library Project and the confrontation with Amazon over ebook pricing: at stake in these disputes were different ways of thinking about the value of content, and different ways of generating the financial resources on which the power of these companies was based.

On the face of it, the publishers appeared to lose their battles with the tech giants. In the case of the Google Library Project, the US courts eventually ruled in favour of Google, affirming that Google's use of copyrighted works was fair use under US copyright law. But by the time this ruling was announced, Google's interest in book content had faded: in the early 2000s, it had seemed to Google like a good idea to add book content to its servers in order to improve its search results and strengthen its position in the search engine wars, but by the time the courts ruled in its favour, the search engine wars were over and Google had already won, without the help of books. Moreover, the publishers had reached a private settlement with Google that established limits on what Google and the libraries could do with the copyrighted material and they had demonstrated that they were prepared to take legal action against parties they judged to be infringing copyright: given the legal imbroglio in which the Google Library Project had become ensnared, it seemed unlikely that any other party would choose to venture down a similar path anytime soon. In the case of the ebook pricing controversy, the Department of Justice had come to the view that Apple and the five trade publishers had conspired to raise ebook prices and limit competition in violation of US antitrust law, and, rather than face the prospect of lengthy and costly litigation – potentially ruinous if they lost – the publishers opted to settle with the DoJ and accept the punitive terms of the settlement decree, while Amazon, who had the most to lose from the publishers' decision to move to agency pricing and who had urged the DoJ to investigate the publishers' deals with Apple, emerged from this episode unscathed and in a position that was stronger than ever. But once the temporary agreements imposed by the settlement decree had run their course, all the Big Five trade houses moved to agency agreements, thus reasserting their control over ebook pricing, which is what the ebook pricing controversy had been about in the first place. They got their way in the end, even if they paid a hefty price by being dragged through an antitrust investigation that they could and should have avoided.

While the Google Library Project and the ebook pricing controversy were the most visible and bitter confrontations in the book wars, they were just two of the many flashpoints in the complicated new world into which publishers now found themselves moving, a world where many of the old rules no longer applied and where the long-term direction of travel was hard to discern. Where there were new dangers and risks, there were new opportunities too, and the challenge for publishers was to seize new opportunities where they could while doing their best to minimize the risks. But publishers were not alone in this process, for the digital revolution was breaking down the boundaries of a field that had been relatively closed to outsiders and that had developed largely according to its own internal logic. It was lowering the entry barriers and creating the conditions where new players could enter the field and challenge incumbents. Just as importantly, it was blurring the boundaries of the field itself, so that new spheres of activity could emerge on the boundaries of the field and develop into new ecosystems with their own players, practices and shadow economies, in some cases overlapping with the old field and in other cases developing largely independently of it.

The new entrant that was to have by far the biggest impact on the publishing industry was, of course, Amazon. It is hard to overstate the significance of this child of the digital revolution: from its humble beginnings in a Seattle garage in 1997, Amazon would revolutionize the retail sector of the book business in a way that was much more far-reaching and profound than the retail revolution that had been carried out by the book superstore chains in the 1980s and 1990s. It's not just that Amazon would gain a market share in physical book sales that greatly exceeded the market share that the largest of the superstore chains had managed to achieve in their heyday, and not just that Amazon would develop the most successful ebook reading device and establish an overwhelmingly dominant position in the ebook market: it was also that Amazon would see, early on, the importance of user data and would develop methods to gather and use it in the book publishing industry in ways and on a scale that had never been attempted, or even imagined, before. Amazon was the pioneer of information capital in the world of the book and this was the source of the unprecedented power that it would eventually come to wield in the publishing industry. Its dominant market share as a retailer of both print books and ebooks coupled with its large stock of proprietary user data on book customers – its information capital – put it in a commanding position in the field and gave it a great deal of leverage when it came to negotiating terms of trade with suppliers: no publisher would wish to invoke the wrath of a retailer who controlled half or more of their sales. Amazon's dominance in the field stemmed not just from its role as a retailer: it was also prepared to develop its own publishing operations and to acquire innovative start-ups in order to secure dominant positions in emerging sectors on the margins of the field – including self-publishing, subscription services and audiobooks. Amazon was much more than a book retailer: it was (among many other things) an entire ecosystem for the production, dissemination and consumption of books in multiple formats, from print to ebooks to audiobooks, an ecosystem which could co-exist harmoniously with publishers but which could also work against them. Publishers now had to reckon with the fact that the digital revolution had given rise to a tech behemoth in its midst – to a new kind of retail organization that had far more power, and a different kind of power, than anything they had ever known.

But the digital revolution was also blurring the boundaries of the field and giving rise to new spheres of activity that would take on a life of their own. The rapidly expanding world of self-publishing is undoubtedly the most significant of these – nothing less than a parallel universe that has evolved on the outskirts of the publishing field, a universe that is immensely complicated in its own right, offering would-be authors a great variety of pathways to publication that bypass the traditional gatekeepers of the publishing world. But there are many other new spheres of activity too: the new crowdfunding publishing ventures, like Unbound and Inkshares; the new ebook subscription services, like Scribd; the new social media platforms for writing and reading, like Wattpad; and the expanding world of audiobooks, which has evolved into a quasi-industry of its own, with its own specialized institutions, practices and conventions

480

and its own system of honours and awards. Thanks to the digital revolution, the world of book publishing had become a much more complicated place with many more players and start-ups, some of which would become viable businesses with an ongoing presence in the field while others would fall by the wayside, unable to forge a sustainable pathway to the future.

While the digital revolution was lowering barriers to entry and blurring the boundaries of the field, it was also transforming the broader information and communication environment within which publishing as an industry existed, and thereby creating both the necessity and the opportunity for publishers to change and adapt to a new world of information and communication flows. For centuries, publishers had existed within a book supply chain that was populated with intermediary organizations. Publishers served to bring books into existence and to connect content creators (authors) with content consumers (readers), but they relied on a variety of intermediaries, including booksellers and wholesalers, to transmit books to the end users in a book supply chain that had remained largely unchanged for centuries. It was left to the booksellers to make books visible to consumers and to provide the physical spaces in which readers could browse and discover new books. This was a unilinear model of communication in which publishers acted as gatekeepers, using their editorial judgement to decide which books to publish and then launching them into the market via the publishing chain intermediaries; their de facto customers were not the readers but rather the intermediaries, the booksellers and wholesalers with whom they cultivated close business relationships and on whom they relied to make their books available to readers. Publishers never paid much attention to their ultimate customers – the readers – so long as they were selling enough copies to run a viable business. But this model, which has structured the publishing industry for centuries, was being radically disrupted by the digital revolution.

It was being disrupted because the intermediaries in the book supply chain were being increasingly displaced by a powerful new tech company that operates in a very different way from the old bricks-and-mortar bookstores. As bookstores began to close and book superstore chains began to scale back or go under, publishers increasingly began to realize that they could no longer count on physical bookstores to do what the intermediaries in the traditional book supply chain had always done: make books visible and available to readers. It became increasingly clear that readers were finding books in new and different ways – less by walking into a bookstore and browsing the tables at the front of the store, more by browsing online or receiving an email with a list of recommended titles or in some other way. But since publishers had never paid much attention to the readers of their books and knew very little about them, they were hardly in a position to influence the ways in which readers might discover – or fail to discover – their books in the new information and communication environment that was being brought into being by the digital revolution. Worse, they were now at the mercy of the one player who had seen the significance of this early on and had busily amassed for itself a large amount of data on the browsing and purchasing behaviour of readers.

With varying degrees of understanding and commitment, publishers have come to realize that their best chance of securing their own future in this brave new world is to jettison the old model of the publisher as a bookseller-focused business and rethink their role as a service provider whose job it is to connect content creators (authors) with content consumers (readers) through the particular form of the book. That this should require them to remain agnostic about the medium in which readers might prefer to read, and indeed to be proactive about making content available in new media which might appeal to readers, is only the most obvious first step – one that was recognized long ago by publishers. Much more challenging for publishers is to re-orient their businesses in such a way that readers are not an afterthought, but rather a central focus of their concern – to become organizations that are both author-centric and reader-centric, and to build into their DNA the idea that they will flourish as an organization only to the extent that they are providing an excellent service to both. This does not mean that booksellers are no longer important for publishers – they are. Indeed, they are more important than ever, precisely because so many other places where books were made visible in the past (the book review pages of newspapers, the TV shows dedicated to books, etc.) have declined or disappeared. But the focus on booksellers has for too long served as a proxy for the relationship that ultimately matters much more and that publishers have long neglected: the relationship with readers.

Fortunately, just as the digital revolution has forced publishers to recognize the importance of the relationship with readers, so too it gave them the tools to develop this relationship at scale. With commitment and creative thinking, publishers could take advantage of the new forms of communication and information flow brought into being by the digital revolution and build direct relationships with readers, not simply in order to market directly to them but, more importantly, to interact with them and listen to them, to learn about what interests them, and to use the resources at their disposal to facilitate dialogue between writers and readers. While the traditional model of publishing was rooted in a unilinear model of communication, publishers now have the opportunity to restructure their businesses in a way that is more in keeping with the new dialogical forms of information and communication flow that have been created by the digital revolution, reconceiving themselves as service providers who are able to use their accumulated skills, resources and expertise to help bring books into existence and to connect writers and readers who wish to communicate through and around the form of the book.

Despite the disruptive potential of the digital revolution and the turbulence that has characterized the book publishing industry since the dawn of the third millennium, this industry has fared remarkably well – and much better than many other sectors of the media and creative industries. Book revenues have not collapsed, print books have not disappeared and even brick-and-mortar bookstores have begun to make a modest comeback: counter to the predictions of many prophets of doom, the book publishing apocalypse has not come to pass (or, at least, not yet). Books, including old-fashioned print-on-paper books, appear to have a place in our lives that is not easily dislodged, even by a technological revolution as radical and far-reaching as the digital revolution. But there are no grounds for complacency. The digital revolution has brought into being an organization that now wields unprecedented power in the publishing field, while many other organizations survive on revenues so small and margins so thin that a small downtown in the economy, let alone a major lockdown or prolonged recession, could push them into insolvency. Ebook sales may have levelled off but ebooks were never the essence of the digital revolution in the publishing industry: they were just one manifestation of a much deeper and more profound transformation that was taking place in our societies. Thanks to the digital revolution, the information and communication structures of our world are in flux. People are communicating differently and spending their time differently, old practices that worked well in an earlier era may no longer be so effective in this new world of digitized information and communication flows. In contrast to those who fear that screen culture is destroying our capacity to concentrate, I suspect that long-form reading will continue to play a vital role in our social, political and cultural life for many years and decades to come: we will not easily give up the rich exploration of imaginary worlds, and the sustained analysis of actual worlds, that long-form reading both encourages and makes possible. But whether publishers will continue to be part of the communication chain through which long-form reading takes place, what kind of publishers they will be and what role they will play, will ultimately depend on how effectively and imaginatively they are able to adapt themselves to the new information and communication environment that is being forged by the great technological revolution of our time.

— Appendix 1 —

SALES DATA FROM A LARGE US TRADE PUBLISHER

'Olympic' is a pseudonym for a large US trade publisher that generously provided me with proprietary data on ebook sales for the years from 2006 to 2016. The data analyst at Olympic was able to break the data down into both broad categories (Adult Fiction, Adult Nonfiction, Juvenile) and subject categories, using a selected number of standard BISAC subject headings. The data were expressed not in terms of actual sales in units and dollars, but in terms of percentages: that is, ebooks as a percentage of total sales in these categories by net units and net revenue. The occasional titles that performed exceptionally well were stripped out of the data to minimize the distorting effect of outliers. The data for the broad categories are given in chapter 1. The data for the subject categories are given in tables A.1 and A.2 below. Figures 1.8 and 1.9 in chapter 1 are based on these tables.

Table A.1 Ebooks as a percentage of total sales by subject at Olympic, net dollars

	Biography & Autobiography	Business & Economics	Cooking	Family & Relationships	Fiction – General	Health & Fitness	History	Juvenile Fiction	Juvenile Nonfiction	Mystery	Religion	Romance	Science Fiction & Fantasy	Self-help	Travel
2006	0	0.1	0	0	0.1	0	0	0	0	0.1	0	0.3	0.5	0.1	0
2007	0.1	0.1	0	0.1	0.1	0.1	0.1	0	0	0.2	0.1	0.5	0.5	0.1	0
2008	0.6	0.6	0.2	0.2	0.6	0.5	0.9	0.1	0	1.1	0.3	1.6	1.7	0.3	0.1
2009	2.9	3.2	0.5	1.3	3.9	1.7	2.9	0.4	0	4.9	1.4	6.7	5.8	2	0.5
2010	7.7	8.9	2.7	4.7	12.2	4.9	7.4	1.4	0.2	16.6	4.1	15.5	16	5.3	1.8
2011	25.8	13.9	3.5	12.4	24.9	17.1	17.3	5.5	0.7	33.5	10	44.2	30.8	11.3	4.7
2012	25.6	19.3	4.8	19.2	32.9	20.1	20.8	9	1.2	42.6	12.9	39.7	40.3	13.3	6.6
2013	24.7	18.9	4.8	19.4	33	17.2	21.7	9.7	1.5	40.7	16.7	55.7	39.7	16.6	6.8
2014	20.4	20.4	5.1	18.6	38.7	21.7	25.7	12.7	1.8	44.9	16.9	55.9	43.1	16.2	8.1
2015	27.2	15.7	5.1	15.3	35.1	24.3	27.7	7.6	2	38.1	16.3	45.4	29.6	16	11.2
2016	20.8	16.6	4	14.8	28.6	17.5	19.4	6	2.6	37.8	11.8	52.8	34.6	16.7	22.4

Table A.2 Ebooks as a percentage of total sales by subject at Olympic, net units

	Biography & Autobiography	Business & Economics	Cooking	Family & Relationships	Fiction – General	Health & Fitness	History	Juvenile Fiction	Juvenile Nonfiction	Mystery	Religion	Romance	Science Fiction & Fantasy	Self-help	Travel
2006	0	0.1	0	0	0.1	0	0.1	0	0	0.1	0	0.3	0.6	0.1	0
2007	0.1	0.1	0	0.1	0.1	0.1	0.2	0	0	0.2	0.1	0.4	0.7	0.1	0
2008	0.6	0.6	0	0.2	0.6	0.4	0.9	0.1	0	0.9	0.3	1.4	1.7	0.2	0.1
2009	2.5	2.5	0.3	1.1	3.2	1.4	2.5	0.3	0	3.8	0.9	5.6	5.2	1.7	0.5
2010	7.2	7.2	0.7	3.8	10.4	4.5	7.3	1	0.1	13.6	2.9	14.8	15.8	4.5	1.9
2011	24.7	13.1	2.9	10.9	24	15	19.1	4	0.5	31.1	7.4	40.6	27.7	10.1	5.5
2012	27.5	19	4.7	16.7	31.1	20.3	23	5.9	1	39.5	10.2	40.1	33.8	11.8	7.6
2013	25	19.3	5.7	17.7	31.3	18.2	23.6	6.7	1.8	41.1	13.3	55.7	36.6	14.7	8.1
2014	22.4	18.9	6.7	16.4	36.8	21.9	26.8	8.3	2.1	40.7	14	57.1	38.6	14.2	9.4
2015	31.7	16.1	7.8	13.6	36.6	27.7	30.6	4.1	2.3	42.9	12.2	51.2	27.8	15.9	12.6
2016	26.4	18.9	10.5	14.2	31.8	23.3	21.9	3.5	1.8	42.1	12.7	56.2	36.7	18	24.6

— Appendix 2 —

NOTE ON RESEARCH METHODS

This book is based on research that was carried out in the US and the UK over a six-year period between 2013 and 2019. A generous grant from the Andrew W. Mellon Foundation enabled me to spend extended periods of time in New York and San Francisco, and to make trips to other parts of the US where some of the companies I wanted to study were based. Having previously examined the evolution of Anglo-American trade publishing from the 1960s to the early 2000s, I wanted to focus this new research on one specific question: what was the impact of the digital revolution on Anglo-American trade publishing? This would require me not only to look carefully at what was happening inside established publishing houses and in the field of trade publishing more broadly, but also to look at developments that were taking place outside of this field and that were having, or could have, an impact on the publishing industry. I needed to cast my net widely and to take account of the many players, large and small, who were working with or experimenting with digital technologies in ways that could affect the creation, production, distribution and consumption of books and long-form reading. Understanding the experience of traditional publishers was important – too many commentators on the publishing industry had not bothered to find out what was actually going on inside publishing houses, and I was determined to avoid that mistake. But I also knew that I couldn't restrict my attention to traditional publishers because some of the new developments that could be of real significance for books and long-form reading were likely to be happening elsewhere.

While most of the research for this book was done between 2013 and 2019, I also drew on research that I had done previously on the book publishing industry – research that stretches back to

2000. I was therefore able to draw on first-hand fieldwork on the publishing industry that extended over two decades – and, crucially, two decades when the issue of the digital transition in the publishing industry was uppermost in the minds of many people who worked in the industry. This extended period was important because it enabled me to place recent developments in a broader context and view them with the aid of a deeper understanding of how organizations change – or don't change – over time. With any work on new technologies, short-termism is always a risk. We tend to focus on the short term and we're inclined to see flashy new gadgets as harbingers of a new age when, in fact, they might just be small episodes in the long history of gadgets that come and go. I wanted to get beyond the preoccupation with gadgets and to focus instead on agents and organizations – on the social actors who were seizing the opportunities opened up by technological change, coming up with new ideas and seeking to develop new products, new practices, new ways of creating, manipulating, disseminating and consuming content, and trying to figure out how to turn these new ways of doing things into activities that are sustainable over time. I wanted to be able to see how these activities of innovation panned out, which worked and which didn't, and, in those cases where innovation didn't work, I wanted to see if this could tell us something about the conditions of successful innovation in this particular sector of the media and creative industries. I wanted to view this process from the perspective of the innovators who were often proceeding by trial and error, not knowing for sure whether the ideas that seemed good to them would work out in practice and whether their efforts would succeed or fail. And if you want to view this process from the perspective of the innovators, then you have to leave the possibility of failure on the horizon – anyone involved in technological innovation knows that success is not guaranteed. To minimize the risks of short-termism, I needed time – and the more time, the better. For only time would tell which innovations would gain the kind of traction in the marketplace that would enable them to become sustainable features of our world and which would fall by the wayside, becoming yet another entry in the large catalogue of great ideas that fail.

The main research method I used was the semi-structured in-depth interview. The great advantage of this method for the kind of research I was doing is that it enables you to get inside organizations and get a feel for how they work, and it enables you to see the world from the viewpoint of the individuals who are players in it – whether they are the CEOs or senior managers of traditional publishing houses, the entrepreneurs who have launched start-ups and are trying to steer them to success, or the many other individuals who are situated at some point in the field and pursuing their own interests and aims. I always assured my interviewees that they and their organizations would remain anonymous unless we agreed otherwise, and that anything they said that was confidential would remain so; I wanted interviewees to feel free to discuss issues openly, without having to worry about whether the views they expressed in the interview situation would subsequently be attributed to them in print. However, I also told them that, if I did want to identify them by name and attribute quotes to them in the text, then I would come back to them at a later stage and show them the text. I knew that I would need to keep this option open because in some cases I would be discussing particular organizations that were unique, so it would simply not be possible to anonymize them and still give a rich, grounded account of what they were doing. In every case where I did go back to interviewees and show them the text that dealt with their organization, they were happy for me to use the text (in some cases, with minor corrections and changes). As I noted in the Preface, when I wrote the book I used the following conventions to distinguish between those individuals and organizations that remain anonymous and those where the real names are used: when I use a pseudonym for an individual, I use a first name only – Tom, Sarah, etc.; when I use a real name for an individual, the full name – Christian name plus surname – is given on the first occasion of use (though, after the first occasion, the Christian name only is used); when I use a pseudonym for an organization, I put the pseudonym in inverted commas on the first occasion of use; and when I use a real name for an organization, the name appears as it is, without inverted commas, on the first and subsequent occasions. These conventions enable me to maintain anonymity where it is important to do so and, at the same time, to describe the trajectories of particular organizations with precision and in detail, doing justice to their specific characteristics.

For the most part, gaining access to organizations and arranging interviews with key people were not difficult. In part, this was because I had done research in the field of trade publishing before and I already had many contacts in the publishing houses who were happy to see me again or put me in touch with others. But working on tech start-ups was new for me and I had very few contacts in this world. To begin with, I simply had to map out the field or sub-field, try to identify the players in it, and try to figure out what they did and who was behind them. I was fortunate that one of the individuals whom I had interviewed for my previous research was very well connected in the world of publishing-related tech start-ups in the US – it seemed like he knew everyone, and if he didn't know someone in some particular start-up, then in all likelihood he knew someone else who did. He became a key source. Whenever I needed to reach out to a senior figure in a start-up, I got in touch with my key source and he was usually able to help. Nothing was ever too much trouble. Thanks to his generous assistance and his warm personal introductions, doors invariably opened.

While access to publishing-related tech start-ups was relatively easy, access to tech giants was not – doing research on large tech companies is notoriously difficult and my experience was no exception. The paradox is as ironic as it is disconcerting: these are organizations that know a great deal about us and yet we know virtually nothing about them. They are black boxes full of data about us. For these organizations, privacy doesn't matter much, so long as the privacy at stake is not theirs. They are very secretive organizations, sequestrated spaces that are closed off to the outside world, and elaborate procedures are put in place to prevent outsiders from learning much about them. In some respects, this is perfectly understandable: the world of high tech is intensely competitive, and sharing information with outsiders could weaken – or at any rate, would not strengthen – an organization's position in this highly competitive field. Moreover, given the scale of these organizations and their dominant, if not monopolistic, position in the domains where they are active, the risk of legal action or antitrust investigation is never far from their concerns; controlling the messages conveyed to outsiders becomes an institutionalized mechanism of self-defence. But there may be something deeper here too. These are organizations that have built their businesses on the basis of systematically harvesting large quantities of personal data, and this data is the principal source of their power – without it, and without their exclusive control of it, they would not be able to do what they do. Their businesses are built on information capital, on the private ownership and control of personal data – for them, data is power, and walls are erected to ensure that there can be no leakage of this vital resource.

The two tech giants that mattered most for my research were Google and Amazon. With Google, I was lucky: I'd known a senior manager at Google since the early 2000s, and he was both very well informed and always willing to talk. We met regularly at Google's expansive New York headquarters – the former Port Authority building on Eighth Avenue – and talked through every aspect of

Google's long and troubled entanglement with the book publishing industry, often over lunch in Google's well-stocked and famously free cafeteria. Amazon was more challenging. I knew who the key people at Amazon were, but all my attempts to reach out to them were channelled through a public relations manager who was tasked with the job of organizing any interaction with the individuals to whom I wished to speak. Interviews were granted, but under strictly controlled conditions: by telephone only, strictly limited to one hour, no site visits, and the PR manager monitored the interview, listening in and occasionally interjecting to steer the discussion away from any topic she judged to be sensitive. My interviewees were happy to speak with me and were reasonably forthcoming, but there was a limit to how much I could learn about Amazon on the basis of a carefully managed interaction of this kind. Fortunately, these interviews with company personnel were not my only source. I had been introduced to someone who had previously worked at Amazon – thanks, again, to my key source – and who was happy to meet up with me informally, usually in a bar in the late afternoon, and talk me through the practical realities of corporate life in a large tech company. While there were limits in terms of what he would or could say (numbers were strictly off limits, and any question that touched on Amazon's power and its troubled relations with publishers made him visibly nervous), this was an invaluable source who greatly helped me to see the world from Amazon's point of view.

Altogether, I did around 180 interviews for this book. Most were done during the period 2013–18, though I returned to the field in 2019 to update some of my earlier work and to take account of some more recent developments, such as the growing importance of audiobooks. These were in addition to the 280 interviews I had conducted for the previous book, and which I drew on here when it was helpful to do so. Most of the 180 new interviews took place in New York and Silicon Valley, though some took place in London, Boston, Philadelphia, Toronto and other cities in the UK and the US – unlike the traditional Anglo-American publishing industry, which is heavily concentrated in New York and London, publishing-related tech start-ups are geographically dispersed. Some interviews were conducted by phone or Skype, especially if they were follow-up interviews, though where possible I always preferred to interview face-to-face, both because this enabled me to get a feel for the organization and its physical premises and because it is easier to build a relationship of trust with someone when you meet them face-to-face. In some companies, I was also able to sit in on meetings and, when

I did so, I put the recorder on and recorded the conversations that took place around the table. I kept detailed field notes that filled half a dozen wirebound notebooks where I registered the circumstances of interviews and commented on things that would not have been captured in the audio recordings. Most interviews lasted between an hour and an hour and a half, though a few were shorter and many were longer, often two hours or more – people were extraordinarily generous with their time. Once the interviews had been transcribed, I read them, noted common themes, filed them away and returned to them later when I began working on the text. When I quoted from interviews, I stuck pretty closely to the language used in the interview, though I took the liberty of tidying up the grammar and removing some of the idiosyncrasies of the spoken word when I felt they would hinder, rather than help, the reader.

When I was working with particular organizations, I tried to return on several occasions and interview key people more than once. This enabled me to go into much greater depth, picking up points that had been touched on in a previous interview and exploring them in more detail. It also enabled me to track the development of an organization over time, see whether the projections that had been made earlier – e.g. concerning the growth of sales or the number of subscribers – had been met or had turned out to be wishful thinking. In some cases, it also enabled me to track the pathways of success and failure and, in those cases where innovation ended in failure, to explore the reasons for failure with those who had once passionately believed in their product or service and now found themselves going down with the ship. It was not always a happy story, but it was a salutary reminder that, in the field of technological innovation, failure is far more common than success.

To interview well is an under-appreciated art. Superficially, it seems easy: what could be difficult about asking questions and letting people talk? But a great deal depends on the quality and precision of your questions, on how quickly you respond to what is being said and follow up with pertinent and well-timed supplementary questions, and on the kind of rapport that you establish with the person you are interviewing. You need to be well prepared but you also need to be flexible and alert, always willing to deviate from your prepared plan if things emerge that you had not expected. Some of the best interviews I've done, the ones that proved to be most valuable in helping me to understand how an organization worked or what was at stake in a field, were interviews that didn't follow any script: early on in the conversation, my interviewee said something that caught my attention and when I asked him or her to elaborate, a whole world opened up, one that I had not foreseen at all despite my diligent preparation. That's the beauty of interviews: when they're conducted well in a context of mutual trust, you may find that your interlocutor will walk you into their world.

While interviews were my primary source of data, I also gathered statistics and sales data where I could. Some of this was material in the public domain, such as the data produced by the AAP (Association of American Publishers), BISG (Book Industry Study Group), the PA (Publishers Association) and the APA (Audio Publishers Association). All of these organizations were very helpful in providing additional material and in answering my queries when data (or the methods used to gather it) were unclear: in an industry as sprawling as the book publishing industry, getting reliable data and understanding what exactly it means are less straightforward than they might seem, especially when so much activity in this field takes place under the radar screens of the industry's professional bodies. I was also very fortunate to be granted access to the proprietary data of one of the large US trade publishers and to be able to work with their statistician to analyse this data, which enabled me to document rigorously and in detail the sales of ebooks and print books over the crucial ten-year period from 2006 to 2016. I was thus able to show exactly what happened in terms of ebook sales over this decade in the experience of a large US trade publisher.

Gathering data is one thing, making sense of it all is quite another. The more I worked on this topic, the more I was struck by the sheer diversity of new activity and new developments that were concerned, in one way or another, with the book publishing industry, all triggered off (or reinvigorated and redirected) by the digital revolution. This was not like a nicely orchestrated concert but more like a wild and noisy cacophony, with countless musicians playing their own tunes in their own way on a great variety of new and bizarre instruments. Trying to discern some order in this diversity, some melody in the noise, was neither easy nor straightforward, but my thinking was guided by one overarching idea – namely, that technological innovation and change are always deeply contextual. They always happen in specific social and historical contexts that are structured in certain ways and within which particular actors are seeking to achieve certain things, using the resources at their disposal to pursue and achieve certain ends.[1] In this work, and in

---

[1] Science and technology studies have long emphasized that technologies are shaped

my previous work on the publishing industry, I conceptualize social contexts in terms of the concept of field, a concept I borrow from the French sociologist Pierre Bourdieu.[2] This concept enables us to break down the components of social contexts and analyse their constituent features – the different kinds of resources, or forms of capital, that individuals and organizations accumulate and deploy in pursuit of their interests and aims; the asymmetrical distribution of resources and relations of power that constitute the field; the way that actors are positioned (and position themselves) in relation to other players in the field; the forms of cooperation, competition and conflict to which the activities of these situated actors give rise; and so on. When we study technological innovation from this perspective, we see it for what it is: a set of activities carried out by individuals and organizations situated in particular fields, using the materials, forms of knowledge and resources at their disposal (economic, technical and social) to pursue certain ends – in other words, we see technologies as inescapably wrapped up with the realities of human motivation and social relations, with interests, resources and power. Technological innovation never happens in a vacuum: it is always part of the messy reality of social life.

While I've always found the theory of fields a helpful way to think about the ways in which social contexts are structured (especially those contexts in which cultural goods are being produced, which has been my particular area of interest), I was also conscious of the fact that I needed to move beyond this theory as developed by Bourdieu in order to address the issues that concerned me. To begin with, technology never featured very prominently in Bourdieu's work. While he wrote perceptively about literature, journalism and television, he never paid much attention to the specific media in which these cultural forms were articulated and transmitted. I needed to put the question of technology into field theory and look in detail at

---

by social factors, not only in their usage but in their design and production too (see, for example, Donald MacKenzie and Judy Wajcman (eds.), *The Social Shaping of Technology*, Second Edition (Maidenhead: Open University Press, 1999)). I share this broad orientation; where I differ from some of this work is in the way that I conceptualize the social.

[2] See Pierre Bourdieu, *The Field of Cultural Production: Essays on Art and Literature*, ed. Randal Johnson (Cambridge: Polity, 1993); Pierre Bourdieu, 'Some Properties of Fields', in his *Sociology in Question*, tr. Richard Nice (London: Sage, 1993), pp. 72–7; and Pierre Bourdieu, *The Rules of Art: Genesis and Structure of the Literary Field*, tr. Susan Emanuel (Cambridge: Polity, 1996). For an explanation of how I use Bourdieu's theory of fields to analyse the publishing world, see Thompson, *Merchants of Culture*, pp. 3–14.

what technological innovation amounts to in practice – how it makes possible different forms of practice within particular fields, how it feeds into the practices of both incumbent players and new entrants and how it changes the very nature and boundaries of the field, in some cases lowering entry barriers and enabling newcomers to enter a field that had been largely closed to outsiders. I also needed to keep open the possibility that technological innovation could facilitate the emergence of new fields or sub-fields which would develop their own codes and conventions and their own cultural economies – in some cases, overlapping with long-established fields and, in other cases, spinning off from them to form their own semi-autonomous space.

But it was not just technologies that needed to be integrated into field theory: I also wanted to put organizations back into the heart of field theory and to analyse their trajectory over time – that is, to develop a longitudinal analysis of organizations and technologically based organizational change, so that I could paint a dynamic portrait of a field in motion, a field in which organizations were constantly evolving to try to cope with the disruption and uncertainty caused by technological innovation. This was crucial, because technological innovation never happens in an instant: it is often a long, drawn-out affair, a process of experimentation, of trial and error, as individuals, most commonly working in teams or in collaboration with others, try to figure out what is going to 'work' and what isn't. They may have a great idea, but making it work in practice most commonly depends on developing an organization, like a company, that can carry it forward – that can raise money, employ staff and get things done. And, just as technologies evolve, so too do the organizations that carry them forward, and the extent to which these technologies become stable and ongoing features of our lives often depends on whether these organizations survive and flourish. So, understanding the fate of technological innovation is inseparable from under-standing the trajectory of the organizations that underpin it.

Finally, I wanted to make sure that the account I offered was not only focused on fields, technologies and organizations, but also populated by real, flesh-and-blood human beings – that is, I needed to put people back in, or, rather, ensure that people and their ideas were there at the outset and an essential part of the story. In some academic work on technologies, there's a tendency to focus on processes and artefacts, as if these alone were sufficient to drive innovation and change. But technological innovation is intrinsically bound up with people and their ideas, motivations, ambitions and desires: they can neither be extracted from the story nor dropped into it later as if they were an incidental ancillary. Their aims and ambitions needed to be there from the start. Of course, individuals don't act in a void: they are always situated in certain contexts in which some things are possible and others are not, their perceptions and ambitions are shaped by their particular trajectories through social space, and even the most determined individuals will fail if all the cards are stacked against them. But, like all history, the history of technological innovation is made by people as well as processes, individuals as well as the organizations, technologies and contexts in which they are embedded, and to leave people out of the story would be as partial and one-sided as it would be to write the political history of a nation without mentioning the people – leaders as well as citizens – who made it.

Fields, technologies, organizations, individuals: I have tried to weave all together, giving each their due and privileging none, in my account of what happens when an old and well-established media industry collides with the great technological revolution of our time. Whether I have done so successfully is for the reader to judge.

INDEX

Numbers in italics refer to a figure.

Aarsen, Zoe: 'Light as a Feather, Stiff as a Board' 409
academic and professional publishing 14
'acceleration society' 471–2
actors as audiobook narrators 380, 382–91
Adler, Trip 323–4, 327–30
Adobe In-Design 237
advances 7, 105, 410
  vs 'assignment fee' 74
  vs crowdfunding 316
  vs partnership 110
advertising *see* marketing and advertising
agency model 149–50, 167–71
  Apple: ebook pricing lawsuit 151–7, 161–7, 441–2, 448–9, 478–9
agents 6–7
  audio rights holders 369
  authors and estates: ebook rights 105–7, 108, 109, 110–11, 116
  crowdfunded and mainstream publishing 315–16
Alexa 436
algorithms 184–94

Amazon ranking 269–70
Google PageRank 123, 124
Kickstarter 290, 292
recommendation 173, 185–6, 189–90, 329–31, 332–3, 335
Allen Lane 50–1
Amazon 479–80
  agency model 150, 167–71
  and Apple *see* Apple, ebook pricing lawsuit
  and Audible audiobooks 363
  bookstores 191–4
  crowdfunded publishing 304
  Daily Deals promotions 115, 117, 208
  data collection and information capital 172–3, 207–8, 435–40, 443–4
  digital shorts/e-singles, price limits on 74–5
  ebook reader / ebooks *see* Kindle
  –Hachette dispute 157–9, 160–1
  market power 139, 149, 159–67
  origin and rise of 6, 143–50
  readers' role 464–5
  retail sector transformation 141–3, 430–2, 437–8
  self-publishing 243–9

bestseller ranking and
  estimated sales 269–79
Blurb 238, 243
Smashwords 229
website personalization and
  recommendation algorithm
  184–6, 187–8, 189–91
Amazon Prime 193, 194, 336
Prime Reading 340–1, 347–8
Amazon Publishing 157
Amazon Whispernet 148
AmazonCrossing 157
AmazonEncore 157
American Society of Media
  Photographers (ASMP) 134
Amphio 100
Anderson, Chris 14
Andreesen, Marc 144
anti-trust law 151–7, 161–7, 441–2,
  448–9, 478–9
App Store 84, 85, 93, 95, 97
App of the Year award 95–6
Apple
  and Audible audiobooks 363
  ebook pricing lawsuit 151–7,
    161–7, 441–2, 448–9, 478–9
  iBooks 155
  iBookstores 149–50, 229, 245,
    246
  iPhone, release of 355, 396
  iPod 355, 362, 363, 416
  music distribution channels 16–17
  see also iPad
apps
  Amazon 193
  Atavist 80, 83
  ebooks as 83–7
  Touch Press 87–100, 101
ArtistShare 287
'assignment fee' vs advance 74
Association of American Publishers
  (AAP) 58, 127, 128, 130–1,
  417, 418
Association of American University
  Presses 127

Atavist Books 77–83
Atwell, Margot: *Derby Life* 295–6
Audible 361–4, 367–8, 371, 373,
  377–8, 384, 385
Audible Creation Exchange (ACX)
  364, 372–3, 384
Audible Mobile Player 361–2
Audio Publishers Association 383
audiobook producers / production
  companies 373–5
audiobook publishers 369–71
audiobook rights / rights holders
  363–4, 366, 369, 370, 371
audiobooks
  audio-visual mix and future of
    391–2
  characteristics of 350–3
  development of 352–61
  downloads 367, 371
  narrators 372, 373, 380–1,
    382–91
  production of 379–82
  rise of 361–4
  as routine 364–8
  Scribd subscription service 327–8
  supply chain 368–78
Author Solutions 250–1, 252, 263
AuthorHouse 221–2
authors
  agents and estates: backlists and
    ebook rights 105–7, 108,
    109, 110–11, 116
  app 91
  and audiobook narrators 387–8
  crowdfunding 300–1, 302–4,
    313–18
  digital shorts/e-singles 72, 73
  Hachette–Amazon dispute 158
  manuscripts 11–12, 13
  publishing contract 23, 104, 369
  reader loyalty / emotional
    connection 175, 198, 208
  self-publishing ('indie authors')
    219, 222–3
  Amazon KDP 244–6

fees 220, 221
motivation and revenue 227–9, 233, 266, 279–82
publishing services 251–2
role in supply-chain 458–9
video (Open Road) 113–14
see also royalties; social media; Wattpad
Authors Guild 127, 128, 131, 137–8
HathiTrust Digital Library 132–4
Author's Republic 373, 376
automated bots/spiders 124, 268–9, 270

B. Dalton Booksellers 5, 142, 188
backlist 13–15, 44
backlist and ebook rights 103–5
limits of 115–21
Open Road Integrated Media 108–18, 119–20
RosettaBooks 105–7, 115–17, 118–19, 120
Baer, Jr., Harold (judge) 133–4
Barnes & Noble 5, 57, 188, 189*n*
and Amazon 142, 145, 194–5, 438–9
audiobooks 377, 378
ebook reader *see* Nook
ebooks
backlist and ebook rights 105–6
self-published 229
Beck, U. 427
behavioural futures markets 433–6, 446
Beisch, Leigh 240–1
Bezos, Jeff 143–4, 145, 146–7, 184–5, 363, 431, 436
Bibliobazaar 218
Big Happy Family 376
Birch Tree 83–4
BISAC genre categories 36–41, 46–7

Black, Craig and Michelle 370
Blackstone Publishing 370, 371
blindness and audiobooks 352–3
Blurb 234–43, 250, 262–3
Bodleian Library, Oxford 122, 126
BookBub 116, 117, 208–14, 377
Bookify 236–7
Bookish 190–1, 206
Bookmatch 185
Books on Tape 354, 369, 370
Books Rights Registry (BRR) 129
Bookshop.org 442–3
bookshops 5–6, 57, 142–3, 438–9
Amazon 191–4
visibility struggles 176–8, 184, 186–90, 194–5
BookSmart 236–7
BookSurge 244
BookWright 237
Borders 5, 57, 142, 145, 188
Bork, Robert 164–5
Bowker 174–5*n*, 229, 259–63
Brennan, Summer: *The Parisian Sphinx* 293–4
Brilliance Audio 371
Brin, Sergey 123–4, 126, 140
Buchwald, Naomi Reice (judge) 111–12
business and economics ebooks 47–8
business re-orientation 99
business-to-business (B2B) model 462–3, 464, 466
businesses and disruptive technologies 146
buyers: monopsony 160, 162–4
Byliner 72, 73–7, 78, 81–2

Caedmon Records 353, 369, 370
Camelio, Brian 287
capital gatekeepers 283–4, 285
capitalism
globalization and 'individualization' 427–8
'surveillance capitalism' 433, 440

Carr, Nicolas 470
cassettes, audiobook 353–4, 358–9, 370
CDs 424, 425
    audiobook 355, 358–9, 371
Chase, Sky: *Saving Everest* 411–12
Children's BAFTA 96
Chin, Denny (judge) 130–5, 138
China: ebook sales and reading devices 65–6
Christensen, Clayton: *The Innovator's Dilemma* 146
Ciarelli, Nicholas 209
'circuits of communication' 461–2
co-op / co-operative advertising 159, 176–7, 187
Coady, Francis 77–9, 80–1
Cobb, Matthew 254
Coker, Mark 224–33, 246–7, 248, 249–50, 251, 263, 265
Committee on Institutional Cooperation, US 133
content
    creation and curation of 451–2, 454–5
    and culture 445–51
    defining 452–3
    guidelines 400–1
    symbolic 10–11, 170–1, 414, 416, 452–4
    unbundling 423–4
Copyright Act, US 131–2
copyright infringement *see* backlist and ebook rights; Google Library Project
cost per acquisition (CPA) and lifetime value (LTV) of customers 334–5
Cote, Denise (judge) 152, 154, 166–7
Covey, Stephen: *The 7 Habits of Highly Effective People* and *Principle-Centered Leadership* 107
CreateSpace 244, 245, 250, 262–3

creation and curation of content 451–2, 454–5
Crombie, John 90
crowdfunding 283–6
    development, platforms, models and campaigns 286–97
    direct-to-consumer publishing 298–305
    Literary Hub 205–6
    and mainstream publishing 313–18
    reader curation 300, 305–13, 468
    and self-publishing 285, 295–6
    supply chain 459–60
    and Wattpad 413
'crowdsource by invitation' model 205
curation
    and creation of content 451–2, 454–5
    reader 300, 305–13, 468
    see also gatekeeping/selection
customer/email databases 196–204, 207–8, 466–8
CustomFlix Labs *see* CreateSpace

Daily Deals promotions, Amazon 115, 117, 208
Darnton, Robert 48–9, 461–2
data
    machine learning 407–8, 411, 412–13
    and symbolic content 10–11, 170–1
    see also algorithms
data power 434
    and tech companies 427–44
Department of Justice (DOJ), US
    'Agency Lite' pricing model 35*n*, 58–9, 151–2, 159, 276–7
    Google Library Project, objections to settlement 129–30
design and production role of traditional publishers 455–6

desktop publishing 15
Deyan, Bob and Debra 374
Deyan Audio 374
Digital Book Awards 96
digital files 12, 13
Digital Rights Management (DRM) 320
digital shorts / e-singles 69, 71–7, 81, 119
Diller, Barry 77–8
Dillons 6, 142
direct-to-consumer publishing 298–305
discounting
    'Agency Lite' model 35n, 58–9, 151–2, 159, 276–7
    BookBub 208–14
    Kindle Daily Deal 115, 117, 208
'disintermediation' 451
Disney Animation Studios / Disney Animated 94–7, 98
'distanciated' speech 351
distribution/distributors
    audiobooks 373, 375–6
    crowdfunding 301, 308
    music channels 16–17
    self-publishing 229, 230, 238, 373, 375
do-it-yourself culture 430
Dorrance Publishing 220
Durand, Vincent 254

e-ink technology 24, 25, 147–8
e-readers 23–4
    see also iPad; Kindle; mobile phones; Nook; smartphones
e-singles see digital shorts / e-singles
ebook uptake model 44–8
ebooks 475–6
    as apps 83–7
    digital shorts / e-singles 69, 71–7, 81, 119
    downloads 19
    enhanced 69, 77–83, 239

experimental forms 68–71, 101–2
    form vs format 48–59
    origins and early models 25–7
    see also backlist and ebook rights; price; sales/revenues; self-publishing; subscription services/models; and specific companies
Echo 436
Edison, Thomas 352
editing 13
    and printing tools: Lulu 223–4
    self-publishing services 252–8
    Wattpad 411
editorial autonomy: backlists and ebooks 118
editorial feedback: crowdfunded vs mainstream publishing 316
Elements, The 88–9, 97
Eliot, T. S. 353
    The Waste Land 91–3, 94
email marketing 209–11, 212
email/customer databases 196–204, 207–8, 466–8
enhanced ebooks 69, 77–83, 239
Entrekin, Morgan 204, 205–6, 207
entrepreneurial activity 429–31
equity model of crowdfunding 306–7
EU General Data Protection Regulation (GDPR) 444
Europe (including UK): ebook sales/ revenues 59–65
Evans, Charles 50–1
Everest 364–6, 367, 392

Faber and Touch Press 91–4
Facebook 444n
    and Twitter 183, 197–8, 199–200, 201–2, 291, 296, 307–8, 433
fair use doctrine 131–2, 133–4, 135, 137–8
fanfiction see Wattpad

FanFiction.net 393
Fayet, Ricardo 254, 255
Federal Trade Commission 151, 162
feedback model 468–9
file-sharing (P2P) 16
film rights 3–4, 406
film/television
    crowdfunded books 310–13
    streaming services 319–20, 321–2
    Wattpad 405–9
financial investment role of traditional publishers 455
Findaway Voices 372–3, 376
fixed royalty-pool subscription model see royalty-pool subscription model
form factor: ebook reader experience 42–3
forms and formats 49–51, 453–5
    ebooks 48–59
    windowing 51, 53–6
forms and genres 453–4
Frankfurt Book Fair 125
Frauenfelder, Mark 182–3
free apps 97, 98
free user-generated content 446
freelancers
    audiobook narrator 382–91
    publicist and online media specialist 182–3
    self-publishing editorial services 252–8
Friedman, Jane 108–10, 111, 112, 113, 114–15, 117, 119
Friedman, Jared 323–4, 325, 342
front-of-store displays 176–8
Fundavlog 287
funding see crowdfunding; venture capital (VC)

gatekeeping/selection
    audiobooks 365, 379
    capital gatekeepers 283–4, 285

crowdfunding organizations 289–90, 300, 459–60
    self-published ebooks 230–3
    traditional and non-traditional publishing 216–19
    Wattpad 400–1, 411
General Data Protection Regulation (GDPR), EU 444
General Publishing 218
genres
    audiobooks 359–60
    ebook sales 32–41, 46–7
    forms and 453–4
George, Jean Craighead: Julie and the Wolves 111
Gittins, Eileen 234–7, 238–9, 240, 241, 242–3
Global eBook Reports 64–6
Gomolin, Adam 305, 306, 307, 309–10, 312
GoodFood.com 201–2
Goodreads 192–3
Google
    acquisition of YouTube 396
    data, power and wealth 433, 444n
    and Oyster 334–5
Google Books 125–6, 138–40
Google Library Project 122–3, 126–8, 447, 450, 478, 479
    negotiations and settlements 128–35, 136
    and Partner Program 125–6
    search engine wars 123–8
    snippets issue 127, 128, 135–8
Google PageRank 123, 124
Google Play 139, 154, 155
Google Playstore 377
Google Print 125, 127
Grahame-Smith, Seth: Pride and Prejudice and Zombies 408–9
Graphic Artists Guild (GAG) 134
Gray, Theo 88, 91, 98–100
Grove Atlantic 204, 205–6
Gutpunch Press 296

Hachette, Simon & Schuster and
Penguin 190–1
Hachette–Amazon dispute 157–9,
160–1
HarperCollins
audiobooks 369
and ebook subscription services
327, 333
Epic Reads site 204
and Open Road: copyright
infringement 111–12
Hart, Michael 21–2, 122–3, 396
Harvard University 122, 126
HathiTrust Digital Library 132–4
Hecht, Duvall 354
Holdridge, Barbara 353
home studios: audiobook
production 374–5, 385
Horizon 379–82
Howey, Hugh 268
'hub-and-spoke' conspiracy 151
Hulu 409
Hunter, Andy 442–3n
hybrid authors 282
hybrid culture 426
hybrid media and visibility 181–3
hybrid publishing 86
ebooks as apps 83–7

IAC/InterActiveCorp 77, 78, 81
iBooks 155
iBookstores 149–50, 229, 245, 246
illegal file sharing 421–2
In-App Advertising 97
In-App Purchase 97
independent bookstores 6
independent publishing houses:
mergers and acquisitions
7–8
indie authors see authors,
self-publishing;
self-publishing
Indiegogo 287–8, 288–9, 293, 297,
460
'individualization' 427–8

information
and communication environment
11, 481, 483–4
see also data
information capital 172–3, 207–8,
434–5, 443–4, 446
Ingram 238
Inkshares 286, 297, 305–13, 413,
460
intermediaries
self-publishing 223–4
traditional publishing 6, 15–16,
175
internet 15–16
and Amazon 143–4
music industry 16–17, 18
see also crowdfunding; specific
sites
Internet Archive 123
internet-based economy/businesses
see tech companies
internet of things 436
iPad 25, 43, 60, 73, 149–50
app commission 84, 85, 91
Disney Animated app 95–6
see also Touch Press
iPhone 355, 396
iPod 355, 362, 363, 396, 416
ISBNs 174–5, 229, 259–63
iTunes 319, 363, 373, 378, 421
iTunes store 145, 363, 421, 422,
423

Jacobs, Dennis (judge) 153, 154
James, E. L.: Fifty Shades of Grey
393, 399
John Marshall Media 374
Jumpstart Our Business Startups
(JOBS) Act, US 306

Kahle, Brewster 122–3
Karkauer, Jon: Three Cups of
Deceit 73, 74
Katz, Don 361, 362, 363
Kaye, Jessica 376

Keller, Michael 126
Kessinger Publishing 218
Kickstarter 241, 288–90, 292–3, 296, 297, 299, 460
Kieran, Dan 298, 301, 302, 304
Kilgore, C. E. 337
Kindle 142
  and Amazon ecosystem 168
  competitors 24–5
  ebook price 146–7, 448–9
  ebook sales 26–7, 31, 107, 416–17
  linear vs non-linear text 42–3
  The Martian (Weir) 2, 4
  origins, development and success 145–9
  UK release 60, 73
  US release 24, 107
Kindle Direct Publishing / Digital Text Platform (KDP/DTP) 156, 244–5, 250, 251
  ASIN (Amazon Standard Identification Number) 260
  KDP Select 245–8
Kindle Owners' Lending Library 245, 246, 336
Kindle Store 24, 148, 156, 244–5
Kindle Unlimited (KU)
  self-published books 59, 169, 247–8, 270–1, 274–5, 347
  subscription model 155, 247–8, 336–41, 341–2, 343
King, Stephen: *Riding the Bullet* 19
Kirshbaum, Larry 157
Klebanoff, Arthur 105–6, 107, 118
Krugman, Paul 160–1
Kunzru, Hari: *Twice Upon a Time* 79–80

large publishing corporations *see* traditional publishers/ publishing
large tech companies *see* tech companies

Lau, Allen 395–7, 400, 401–3, 405, 407–8, 409, 410–11, 413
LCD touchscreen 25
Legendary 311, 312
Lekic, Natasa 252–4
Leval, Pierre 131–2
Levitsky, Larry 306
librarians: Google Library Project 126
libraries and retail market: audiobooks 366–7
Librié 1000-EP, Sony 24
lifetime value (LTV) and cost per acquisition (CPA) of customers 334–5
Lightning Source 14, 224
linear vs non-linear texts 42–3, 45–7
ListenUp Audiobooks 373
literary agents *see* agents
Literary Hub 204–8
LitHub Daily 206
LitHub Radio 206
Liukas, Linda: *Hello Ruby* 294–5
Livingstone, Debra Ann (judge) 153–4
London Book Fair Digital Conference 87
Lulu 223–5, 262–3

machine learning 408, 411, 412–13
McKinsey: email marketing study 197–8
McLuhan, Marshall 349
MacMillan 150, 152, 327
  Tor.com 204
magazines subscription service 329
mainstream publishers *see* traditional publishers/ publishing
Mansion House 71–2, 82, 83, 84
Mantell, Marianne 353
manuscripts 11–12, 13

marketing and advertising
backlists and ebooks 109–10,
112–14, 116–17, 119–20
co-op / co-operative advertising
159, 176–7, 187
data uses 436, 439
Google Books 125–6
subscription services 335, 336
traditional publishers 180–2, 456
vs crowdfunding 316
Wattpad 402–3, 408–9, 411
see also visibility
Marley, Tay: *The QB Bad Boy and
Me* 411–12
Marshall Cheary, John 374
Martian, The (Weir) 1–5, 182–3,
282, 393
'mass media', visibility of 178–80
Mathematica 88–9
media and creative industries
415–26, 474–5
mediated visibility 178–83
mergers and acquisitions 7–8
Michigan University 122, 126, 133,
137
Microsoft (MSN) 123–4, 125, 135
miniaturization of devices 11
Mitchinson, John 298–300, 303
mobile phones 395–7
see also smartphones
monopoly 130, 131, 147, 153–4,
160, 441
monopsony 160, 162–4
Moondog (Louis Hardin) 79–80
Mortenson, Greg: *Three Cups of
Tea* 73
Most Favoured Nation (MFN)
price-matching clause
149–50, 151–2
MP3 files
audiobooks 355, 363
Napster 16, 421
multimedia *see* enhanced ebooks;
hybrid media and visibility;
hybrid publishing

music apps, Touch Press 92–4
music industry 16–17, *18*, 416, 417
and traditional publishing 421–5
music/musicians
crowdfunding 287
Moondog (Louis Hardin) 79–80
streaming services 319–20, 322

Napster 16, 421
narrative linear text vs non-linear
texts 42–3, 45–7
narrators, audiobooks 372, 373,
380–1, 382–91
Nataf, Emmanuel 254
National Public Radio (NPR)
182–3
native advertising 402–3
Netflix 319–20, 321–2, 336, 406,
413
network effects / network economy
167, 435, 440–2, 445–6,
477–8
'new books' 174–5
New York Book Editors 252–4, 257
New York Public Library 126
New York Times 79, 110–11, 112,
158, 179, 207, 214
bestsellers 4, 24, 146, 148, 182,
405, 422, 448
newspapers 416
book reviews 179, 183
Nielsen 60
non-linear texts, linear text vs 42–3,
45–7
'non-traditional publishing' *see*
self-publishing
Nook
audiobooks 377
and online bookstore 24–5, 149,
154, 155
self-publishers 245

Ong, Walter 349–50
Open Road Integrated Media
108–18, 119–20

Oprah's Book Club 179–80
OR Books 195
Orchestra, The 92–4
orphan works 129–30
outsourcing
    design and production 455–6
    see also freelancers
Owen, Laura 74
Oxford University: Bodleian Library
    122, 126
Oyster 330–6, 342

Pacific 315–17
Page, Larry 123–4, 125, 126, 127,
    140
PageRank 123, 124
Palphreyman, Lauren: Cupid's
    Match 411–12
paperback books 50–1, 53–6
pay-per-click (PPC), Amazon 187
pay-per-use see threshold/
    pay-per-use model
Penguin 50–1, 152, 190–1
    Random House (PRH) 204, 301
Periodic Table (The Elements) 88–9,
    97
personal data 433–6
personalized virtual visibility 184–5,
    188, 194
Phantom 84–5
Philippines: Wattpad 405–6
Phillips, Angus 68
photographers and graphic artists:
    class action lawsuit against
    Google 134
photographs: Blurb 234–43, 250,
    262–3
'Plain Vanilla ASCII' 22
Pollard, Justin 298
Posner, Richard 164
possession value 43–4, 425
Poynter, Dan: The Self-Publishing
    Manual 225–6
pre-ordering 284, 297, 307–8, 309,
    310

pledge money 301–2, 303, 460
Preston, David 158
price
    agency model 170–1
    ebooks 146–7
        'Agency Lite' model 35n, 58–9,
            151–2, 159, 276–7
        anti-trust law 151–7, 161–7,
            441–2, 448–9, 478–9
        digital shorts / e-singles 74–5
    historical perspective 50–2
    music industry and traditional
        publishing 422–3
    tech companies and traditional
        publishing 446–51
    see also discounting
price-matching (MFN) clause
    149–50, 151–2
PricewaterhouseCoopers 19
print-on-demand (PoD) 14–15,
    220–2, 224, 238
printed books
    Amazon sales 144–5
    Blurb 234–43, 250, 262–3
    and digital media
        length 454–5
        reading experience 424–5,
            470–3
    and ebooks 20–1, 68, 426
        app 84–5, 86–7
        Atavist Books 78–9, 80, 81
        sales data 29–32, 53–6
        see also backlist
    limitations and definition of 20–1
    persistence of 470–3
    possession value 43–4, 425
    see also forms and formats;
        Google Library Project;
        traditional publishers/
        publishing
printing 13–15
production and design role of
    traditional publishers 455–6
production process 12–13
    ebooks 44

professional actors as audiobook narrators 380, 382–91
Professional Photographers of America (PPA) 134
Project Gutenberg 122–3, 396
origins of 21–2
prosumers 240
publicity
and dissemination role of traditional publishers 456
see also marketing and advertising
Publishers Association (PA) 60, *61*, 62–4
publishing contracts 22–3, 104–5, 369
Pulitzer, Joseph 286–7
pyramid model of scholarly books 48–9

radio 349, 350
LitHub Radio 206
National Public Radio (NPR) 182–3
Random House
audiobooks 354, 369
Penguin (PRH) 204, 301
publishing contract 23
and RosettaBooks: copyright infringement 106–7
social media authors 3, 4, 393, 404
RBMedia 370, 377
reader curation: crowdfunding model 300, 305–13, 461, 468
readers' role 462–9, 482–3
reading experience 424–5, 470–3
recommendation algorithms 173, 185–6, 189–90, 329–31, 332–3, 335
Recorded Books 370
Recording Industry Association of America (RIAA) 16
Red Hat 223–4

Reedsy 254–6, 257
Reekles, Beth: 'The Kissing Booth' 404, 406, 409
'resonance' 472–3
Restless Books 82–3*n*
retail sector
audiobooks 376–7
bricks-and-mortar see bookshops
importance of readers 462–9
see also Amazon
Richard & Judy Book Club 180
Ricoeur, Paul 351
Riggio, Steve 105
Ringelmann, Danae 287–8
risk-taking role of traditional publishers 455
Rosa, Hartmut 471, 472–3
RosettaBooks 105–7, 115–17, 118–19, 120
royalties
audiobooks 364
crowdfunded publishing 309–10
ebooks 107, 109, 118, 156
royalty-free content publishers 218
royalty-pool subscription model 325–6, 337–8, 342, 345
streaming services 322
Rubin, Slava 287–8
Rudin, Scott 77–8
Russell, Karen: *Sleep Donation* 79, 80

S-curve pattern of technology adoption 30–1, 32, 36–9
sales/revenues
Amazon 144–5, 154–5, 267–79, 339–40
audiobooks 355–60, 363
ebooks
beyond US 59–67
early prediction of 18–19
and future of printed books 416–18, 426, 427
US 25–48, 53–6
US 417–20

Salonen, Esa-Pekka 93
Sargent, John 150, 152
Schanker, Josh 208–9, 210–11
Schell, Eric 287–8
Schnittman, Evan 87
screen technology 24
  vs printed books 424–5, 470–3
Scribd 323–30, 335–6, 342, 343
Scribd Store 324
search engines
  automated bots/spiders 124,
      268–9, 270
  companies 446, 447–8
  marketing (SEM) 199–200
  see also algorithms; Google
      Library Project
'secondary orality' 349–50
selection see gatekeeping/selection
self-publishing 15, 480–1
  Amazon see Amazon; Kindle
      Direct Publishing / Digital
      Text Platform (KDP/DTP);
      Kindle Unlimited (KU)
  audiobooks 364, 371–3
  and crowdfunding 285
  do-it-yourself culture 430
  ebooks 58–9, 225–33
  growth of 279–82
  hidden continent of printed
      books and ebooks 259–66
  origins and development 219–25
  selection 230–3
  spectrum of publishing services
      249–59
  supply chain 458–9
Shatz, Matt 331–2
Shaw, Fiona 92
Sherman Antitrust Act 151, 154,
    161–2
Silicon Valley
  Amazon 144, 146
  crowdfunding 305, 307
  e-readers and ebooks 23, 75, 77
  self-publishing 225, 226, 233,
      242

Similarities 185
Simon & Schuster 107, 190–1, 405,
    409
  Hachette and Penguin 190–1
  total sales 418–20
smart speaker systems 436
smartphones
  audiobooks 355, 360–1, 365–6,
      392
  iPod 355, 362, 363, 396, 416
  see also mobile phones
Smashwords
  audiobooks 373
  ebooks 226–33, 245, 246–7, 250,
      251, 262–6, 333
snippets: copyright issue 127, 128,
    135–8
Snodgrass, Michael 371
social media
  authors and Random House 3, 4,
      393, 404
  book promotion/marketing
      179–80, 181–3, 199–200
  Goodreads 192–3
  storytelling 393–5
  see also Facebook; Twitter;
      Wattpad
Sombasa Media 209
Sony 24, 229
Sony Pictures: Pride and Prejudice
    and Zombies 408–9
Sony Reader 24, 26, 60
spiders / automated bots 124,
    268–9, 270
Spotify 320, 322, 336
standardized spatial visibility 184,
    187–8, 194
Stanford University 122, 126
state sovereignty immunity 137
Stein, Sidney (judge) 106
streaming services 319–23, 425
Stromberg, Eric 330–1, 332,
    333–4
Styron, William: Sophie's Choice
    and other titles 110–11

subscription services/models
  audiobooks 362, 363, 376, 376–7
  ebooks
    backlist titles 116
    digital shorts / e-singles 75
    discounts 209–10
    Kindle Unlimited 155
  ecosystem of books 341–8
  film and music streaming services 319–23, 343–4
  Kindle Unlimited (KU) 336–41
  Oyster 330–6, 342
  Scribd 323–30
  Wattpad premium service 403
Sullivan, Michael 287
supply-chains 481–2
  audiobooks 368–78
  'circuits of communication' 461–2
  crowdfunded publishing 459–60
  self-publishing 458–9
  traditional publishers 9, 457–8
surveillance capitalism 433, 440
Swed, Mark 93
symbolic content 10–11, 414, 416, 452–4
  and packaging see forms and formats

talking books 352–3
Tayman, John 72–5, 76
tech companies 11, 439, 477–8
  content and culture 445–51
  data power 427–44
  information capital 172–3, 207–8, 434–5, 443–4, 446
  network effects 167, 435, 440–2, 445–6, 477–8
  see also specific companies
techno-optimism and techlash 429
teen fiction see Wattpad
television
  book reviews 179–80
  secondary orality 349–50
  see also film/television

Thomas, Dylan 353
Thomas, Jeremy 307, 308
threshold/pay-per-use model 326–8, 330, 331–2, 337, 345, 346–7
  and limited use model 328–9
Titan 196–203
Todd, Anna: 'After' series 404–5, 406–7, 408–9
top-down and bottom-up publishing models 412–13
Touch Press 87–100, 101
touchscreen, LCD 25
traditional publishers/publishing
  and Amazon ebook pricing strategy 146–7
  audiobooks 369, 371
  contracts 22–3, 104–5, 369
  and crowdfunding 294–5, 296–7, 298–9
  gatekeeper role 216–17
  impact of digital revolution 5–19, 476–84
  key functions 451–7
  Literary Hub 204–8
  marketing 180–2, 456
  mergers and acquisitions 7–8
  and music industry 421–5
  readers' role 465–9, 482–3
  and self-publishing model 219–20
  and social media authors 393–4, 403–5, 410
  and subscription model 324–6, 327–8, 330, 331–4, 345–7
  and tech companies see tech companies
  and Wattpad authors 403–5
  and Wattpad Books model 412–13
  see also backlist; Google Library Project; specific publishers
transformative copyrighted material see fair use doctrine
Trentman, Henry 370

Twitter 314, 317
 see also Facebook, and Twitter
typesetting 12–13, 15

Unbound 286, 297, 298–305,
 314–17, 460
unbundling of content 423–4
UNESCO: definition of book 20–1
university libraries see Google
 Library Project
University of Illinois: Materials
 Research Lab 21–2
up-front licensing fee 321–2
user-generated content 446

van Dam, Andries 21
'vanilla ebook' 68
vanity presses 220, 235–6
Vantage Press 220
venture capital (VC) 123, 144,
 242–3, 307
 ebook publishing 74, 75–6, 77,
 108, 110
 failure of start-ups 429–30n
vetting see gatekeeping/selection
video
 author 113–14
 see also streaming services
vinyl LPs 353, 417, 424, 425
visibility 172–5, 214–15
 algorithms 184–94
 discounting 208–14
 Literary Hub 204–8
 mediated 178–83
 reaching out to readers 194–204
 see also marketing and
 advertising

visual impairment and audiobooks
 352–3

Waldenbooks 5, 142, 188
Waterstones 6, 57, 142
Wattpad 395–401
 book publishing 409–13
 business model 401–5
 feedback model 468–9
 origins and users 395–401
 supply chain 460–1
 television and film 405–9
Wattpad Paid Stories 403
Wattpad Premium Service 403
Wattpad Presents 405–6
Wattpad Studios 407–9
Weir, Andrew: The Martian 1–5,
 182–3, 282, 393
WH Smith 6, 180
Whitby, Max 87–8, 91, 96–7,
 98–100
windowing 51, 53–6
wireless 3G connectivity 24, 25
Wischenbart, R., et al. 64–6
Woodham, Thad 305–7, 311, 312
Word 237

Xlibris 221–2

Yahoo! 123, 125, 135
Yang, Jerry 397
Yarrow, Alder: The Essence of Wine
 240–1, 295
Young, Bob 223–5
Yuen, Ivan 395–6, 401, 413

Zuboff, Shoshana 433